W9-CJE-909

Arguing in Communities

Gary Layne Hatch

Brigham Young University

Mayfield Publishing Company
Mountain View, California
London · Toronto

Copyright © 1996 by Mayfield Publishing Company

All rights reserved. No portion of this book may be reproduced in any form or by any means without written permission of the publisher.

Library of Congress Cataloging-in-Publication Data

Hatch, Gary.
    Arguing in communities / Gary Hatch.
       p.   cm.
    Includes index.
    ISBN 1-55934-382-6
    1. Persuasion (Rhetoric) 2. Reasoning. 3. Communication—Social aspects. 4. Rhetoric—Research—Methodology. I. Title.
P301.5.P47H38   1996
808—dc20   95-45175
                                           CIP

Manufactured in the United States of America
10 9 8 7 6 5 4 3

Mayfield Publishing Company
1280 Villa Street
Mountain View, CA 94041

Sponsoring editor, James Bull; production editor, Julianna Scott Fein; manuscript editor, Mark Gallaher; art director, Jeanne M. Schreiber; text and cover designer, Claire Seng-Niemoeller; art manager, Robin Mouat; illustrator, Joan Carol; manufacturing manager, Amy Folden. The text was set in 10/12 Galliard by G & S Typesetters, Inc. and printed on 50# acid-free Text White Opaque by The Maple-Vail Book Publishing Group.

Acknowledgments and copyrights continue at the back of the book on pages 484–486, which constitute an extension of the copyright page.

Preface

O UR CULTURE HAS TAUGHT US to view arguing as something negative, the equivalent of quarreling or fighting, a view which—unfortunately—closely reflects the quality of arguing we are most familiar with. Despite the efforts of those who teach argumentation and critical thinking, much of the arguing in our communities is simply contentious bickering. Often, people think they are arguing productively when they are really just contradicting one another or expressing their opinions forcefully without supporting those opinions with thoughtful reasons. Even many so-called experts have never advanced beyond the strategies we learn as small children to get what we want.

Arguing productively, however, should be an important part of living in any community. Without effective arguing, a community has difficulty making decisions, coming to consensus, living with and negotiating difference, and simply getting things done. And when arguing breaks down, people must usually resort to some sort of force to accomplish their goals, whether it's physical violence or the force of law. Rather than using the power of language to live with one another, it seems as though many people would rather fight out their differences, either in the streets or in the courts.

I'm not certain that a class in argumentative writing can actually make communities more productive at resolving their differences, but this book is my attempt. I found, as a teacher, that many of my students saw no connection between the kind of arguing I was teaching in class and the arguing they practiced every day outside of class. Of course, some students would begin to identify a few logical fallacies or go around tormenting their classmates and families by forcing them to define their terms, state their assumptions, and back up their beliefs. Still, for most students, arguing was still an academic game rather than a way of living. I realized that I was partly to blame for my students' inability to make connections between my class and their lives. I had often displayed arguments as though they were zoological specimens: neatly dissected, arranged, and analyzed, but so removed from their native habitats that they no longer had any connection to the real world.

This book, then, is an attempt to take students where arguments live, to their habitats, so to speak, the communities where we live and argue every day. My central premise is that arguing is an essential part of living with others; my central goal is to improve arguing and, with luck, to improve communities in the process.

I have divided the book into two parts. The first emphasizes arguing as a means of rational persuasion within communities. I describe the means of persuasion from Aristotle's *Rhetoric* and the structure of arguments based on a model adapted from Frans van Eemeren's social theories of argumentation, a model that is essentially a simplified form of Stephen Toulmin's model for reasoning as it is usually taught in writing courses. Although I have not relied on Toulmin's terms exclusively in this text, I have included them at appropriate points for those instructors and students who may be familiar with them. In this first part, I also teach students to identify the communities in which they live and to record, analyze, and evaluate the conversations that take place in their communities so that they can begin to make useful contributions to these conversations.

The second part of the book focuses on arguing different kinds of claims: claims about existence, causality, language, values, and actions. This second part is an adaptation of classical stasis theory. Stasis theory involves asking a set of standard questions in order to identify what is at issue in a particular debate or disagreement, what kind of claims are being made, and how one can evaluate and respond to these claims. In addition to the examples and readings I have provided, I encourage students, throughout the book, to identify and evaluate examples from the conversations that surround them so that they can productively join these conversations and make a difference in the life of their communities.

▪ ▪ IMPORTANT FEATURES

This text includes the following features to help your students understand how arguing works in communities:

- *An easily understood model of the structure of arguments,* based on theories of social argumentation. Similar to Toulmin's, this model derives from Franz van Eemeren's critique of the way Toulmin is often used in the teaching of writing. Eemeren's model is more closely related to the classical enthymeme and emphasizes the social nature of arguing, identifying arguing as a kind of conversation that takes place within communities. I include models for identifying, recording, and evaluating these conversations, as well as a list of common fallacies.
- *An emphasis on studying arguments where they live.* I introduce the idea of "sites of communication" or "conversation," the "places" where people

gather to argue and converse, and I show how to identify and analyze these "sites."

- *A description of how ethos and pathos are integrated with logical appeals* with particular advice on how to use these appeals effectively and ethically. As a social theory, arguing cannot be reduced to "logic." To move people to action, arguing must include appropriate ethical and emotional appeals, but students must also be aware of how these appeals may be misused.
- *Advice on how to adapt arguments to the needs of different audiences.* I describe how to analyze an audience and provide several models for organizing arguments in addition to the "classical" form most frequently used in academic writing. These other models include delayed thesis, conciliatory arguments, Rogerian arguments, "option three," and Monroe's motivated sequence.
- *An overview of research both in the library and beyond.* While much research is the process of recording conversations in academic communities, the academic community is only one among the many communities students belong to, and academic writing is only one form of arguing that students participate in (and certainly not the most common form). I expand the notion of what counts as "research" and present library research as an example of how to identify and record conversations.
- *A sample student essay* based on library research and using MLA documentation.
- *Examples of MLA and APA documentation* for various sources, including on-line material.
- *An exercise using folklore* to encourage students to "do research" in the stories told in their own families and groups of friends.
- *Readings related to on-line and virtual communities,* along with a list of interesting e-mail discussion lists.
- *Other professional readings* that not only present models of argumentative writing or topics for student discussion but also relate to the issues discussed in each chapter. For example, in the first chapter I have paired an essay by Walter Lippmann with an essay by Christopher Lasch responding to Lippmann. Both essays discuss the function of arguing in American communities. In the chapter on communities and conversation, I have included readings on how language works within three particular communities: schools, businesses, and on-line communities. The readings in Part Two provide examples of arguing the particular claims being discussed in each of the chapters there.
- *A glossary* of key terms.

ACKNOWLEDGMENTS

I thank Jim Bull and Tom Broadbent of Mayfield Publishing who first recognized the potential for this book—particularly Jim, who saw the book through development and patiently encouraged me throughout the entire process. I am grateful to April Wells-Hayes and Julianna Scott Fein, who guided this book through production. I owe a particular debt to Mark Gallaher for his careful reading of earlier drafts of the text and insightful comments and suggestions. I am also grateful for the help of Pamela Trainer and Uyen Phan in securing permissions.

For my first introduction to many of the ideas in this book, I thank my former teachers at Arizona State University: Frank D'Angelo, David Schwalm, Keith Miller, and John Ramage. I owe special thanks to two of my fellow graduate students there, Jackie Wheeler and Elizabeth Vanderlei, who helped me develop my first course in argumentative writing.

Thanks are also due to the following individuals for their helpful reviews of the manuscript: Scott Cawelti, University of Northern Iowa; Doug Hesse, Illinois State University; Nancy L. Joseph, York College of Pennsylvania; Hephzibah Roskelly, University of North Carolina, Greensboro; and Carol Severino, University of Iowa.

Finally, my most humble apologies and sincere thanks to AnneMarie, who endured with me the many trials and few joys of producing a textbook, and to Aubrey and Carson, who always knew when Daddy needed a break from his computer.

Contents

3   Communities and Conversation   65

4   Identifying and Recording a Conversation   119

5 Evaluating Arguments

PART ONE

Arguing and
Living in Communities

Chapter 1

Arguing as Rational Persuasion: Logos

What Is Arguing?

"Don't argue." That's what my mother always told me and my brothers. Our arguments usually went something like this:

"Did not."

"Did too."

"Did not."

"Did too."

"You're a big [insert nasty name here]."

"Mom! Gary called me a [nasty name.]"

When my mom said, "Don't argue," she meant, "Don't stand there and contradict each other and call each other names." This certainly is one definition of arguing: quarreling, bickering, contending, trying to get the upper hand.

Little kids argue in this way all the time. They don't need anyone to teach them how. But adults often argue this way too. Just turn on any day-time talk show, or listen to talk radio. The names and issues may be different, but the arguments often follow a format similar to the arguments I used to have with my brothers:

"Liberal!"

"Conservative!"

"Baby killer!"

"Fanatic!"

(Did not. Did so. And so on.) There are plenty of models of this kind of arguing around you, and you don't really need much formal instruction to argue in this way. Sure, there are books that will tell you how to "win every argument" or "sell anything" through intimidation, name-calling, distortion, and deception.

But these strategies only offer a more sophisticated version of the quarrels we used to have as kids.

In this book I hope to help you learn how to argue more effectively, but not the kind of arguing I've been describing. I define arguing as follows: Arguing is rational persuasion. Let me elaborate a bit. To persuade is to urge or influence or entice through language. The word *persuasion* comes originally from a Latin word that means "sweet" and is related to the ancient Greek word for "pleasure" or "sweetness." Speaking of the Greeks, it may be useful to demonstrate persuasion with a fable attributed to the ancient Greek storyteller Aesop. This is how I remember it:

> *The Fable of the Sun and the Wind*
>
> The sun and the wind were boasting about which one of them was stronger. They decided to have a contest. The wind noticed a man walking down the road wearing a coat. The wind said, "Whichever of us can get this man to remove his coat is the stronger." The wind blew and blew, but the harder he blew, the tighter the man pulled his coat around him. Finally, the wind gave up. Then the sun came out and shined down on the man. The man was grateful for the sun's warmth and removed his coat, laying it over his arm.

One moral for this fable is "persuasion is stronger than physical force." Zeno, another Greek, defined persuasion in a similar way. He called persuasion an open hand rather than a closed fist. Persuasion, then, is inviting, not constraining or threatening.

Arguing, as I've noted, is rational persuasion. It is a kind of persuasion that appeals to the human ability to think and to reason. In fact, the word *rational* comes from a Latin word meaning not only "the ability to think and reason" but also "reasons as justification." Thus, arguing involves supporting beliefs and opinions with reasons. The word *argument* itself comes from the Latin word for "silver" and literally means to make an idea clear, just as you can see your reflection clearly in polished silver. Obviously, the arguments I had with my brothers and the arguments you hear on day-time talk shows are really not arguments in the sense that I use the term in this book: They are not based on reasons.

Rational Persuasion

Persuading and arguing come as naturally to humans as language. Children learn early on how to use language to get what they want from their parents, older siblings, and friends. They learn the power of trust and of emotion, as well as the effectiveness of plain stubborn repetition in getting their way. The practice of persuasion is no doubt as old as human civilization, but the Greeks were really the first, in the European cultural tradition, to try to understand how persuasion works. They called the art of persuasion "rhetoric." The Greek philosopher

Aristotle, in his *Art of Rhetoric*, defined three types of persuasive strategies, identified by the Greek words *ethos, logos,* and *pathos.* The Greek word *logos* is related to the English word *logic,* but it has a much broader meaning. Logos can mean "word," "thought," or "law." It represents something like "the expression of thought in language," the appeal to reason and to the intellect. Logos is the predominant persuasive appeal in argumentation. It is the basis of rational persuasion. In this chapter we'll look at logos in greater depth; Chapter 2 will focus on the other forms of persuasion.

According to Frans Van Eemeren, a philosopher of language and persuasion, arguing is a social activity.[1] When we argue, we argue *with* others. When we persuade, we are persuading *someone.* Unfortunately, students often study arguments apart from any social context. Students taking a course in argumentative writing are often presented with an anthology of written arguments lined up like zoo animals removed from their native habitat, and many fail to realize that arguments are all around them. Whenever we are engaged with ideas and reasons, we are arguing. And although arguing is mainly a verbal activity, there may also be nonverbal elements, such as gestures and facial expressions (when we are speaking to each other) and various aspects of document design and visual presentation (when we are writing to each other). We are all involved in arguing all the time: It is part of using language and part of being human.

Throughout this book, I will try as much as possible to return arguments to their native habitats, and in Chapter 3 I'll explain in detail how I think arguing works within communities. But for now, to make this discussion easier to follow, I'm going to consider arguments apart from their contexts.

■ ■ THE STRUCTURE OF AN ARGUMENT: CLAIMS

An argument consists of three parts: claims, reasons, and assumptions. The claim is the statement under dispute. It is the focus of the argument, a statement that is controversial, a proposition about which at least some people disagree. For many people the first three statements that follow would be claims or "opinions" because they are under dispute; the fourth statement would be a "fact," a statement that is commonly accepted as true.

> The wealthy should pay a greater percentage of their income in taxes than the poor.
>
> Second-hand smoke causes lung cancer.
>
> The U.S. government should guarantee basic health care.
>
> Paris is the capital of France.

Of course, what is a fact for some people may be an opinion for others; what some accept as true, others may dispute. For instance, many people accept as fact

[1] F. H. van Eemeren, *The Study of Argumentation* (New York: Irvington, 1984), 2–4.

the statement that second-hand smoke causes cancer. Others dispute or qualify this statement. The Tobacco Institute argues that second-hand smoke from tobacco *may* cause lung cancer, citing as evidence examples of people who lived with smokers and did not develop lung cancer and studies that question the link between second-hand smoke and lung cancer. Scientists, who try to be careful in how they describe causes and effects, might claim that second-hand smoke may cause lung cancer *in some cases* and *under certain conditions* (when, for instance, there is repeated exposure to the smoke).

The level of disagreement really depends on the people involved. Some people dispute the existence of a supreme being, while others take this existence for granted. Some accept a religious text such as the Bible or the Koran as authoritative, as a reliable index of truth; others dispute such a claim. Some take as a given that capital punishment is always wrong, while others hold the opposite view.

If a group of people all agree on a particular belief, then its status as a claim might not be noticed. Such a belief becomes part of the "common sense" or "self-evident truths" shared by that community. In fact, our opinions and biases often go unnoticed until someone calls them into question by raising an alternative opinion. At that point, we may find ourselves arguing, explaining, or justifying our opinions with reasons. Through this process of arguing, we may realize — perhaps for the first time — why we hold the opinions we do. We may also realize that some long-held opinions have no rational basis. The process of arguing, then, is part of the process of gaining an education. Through informed and responsible arguing, we recognize truths that would otherwise have gone unnoticed.

The process of testing claims through arguing is a particularly important part of a college education. According to the philosopher Richard Rorty, a college serves two functions: providing students with "cultural literacy" and with "critical literacy." Cultural literacy is an awareness of the common knowledge of the community, what members of the community are expected to know. A degree in law or medicine, for example, certifies that the student who receives it has adequately learned the body of knowledge the legal community or medical community assumes its members to have. In this function a university passes on what is believed to be true by scholars. But, as noted above, a university serves the additional function of teaching critical literacy. Critical literacy is the ability to question or explore what is believed to be true, to challenge or dispute the claims and opinions of others in an attempt to clarify and understand. Ideally, a university is a place where members of the community or members of different communities come together to ask questions, debate, and discuss ideas in a responsible fashion. This process of questioning and responding can be called *critical thinking*. It takes place through language, through reading, writing, and speaking. It can create tension, but it also represents the ideal for education.

Identifying Claims   In order to question or discuss a claim, you first have to identify it. To do so, begin by asking "What is the topic or issue?" Then ask "What positions can people take on this issue?" Here is an example:

What is the issue? Second-hand smoke.

What position can people take on this issue? Second-hand smoke causes cancer.

In academic writing, the claim of an argument is often the thesis, and this thesis usually comes near the beginning of the essay, following some kind of introduction. But this need not always be the pattern. The claim may come at the end of an argument and, in some cases, even in the middle. A claim may not be explicitly stated anywhere in the argument itself, and sometimes it may begin as a question. When the purpose of arguing is to discover for yourself what you believe, the claim you state may be only an initial attempt to take a position. Note that claims are *not* examples, definitions, background information, evidence, or data.

Types of Claims   Some claims are absolute. They are either always true, or they are true for all cases:

All humans are mortal.

Copenhagen is the capital of Denmark.

No one has ever visited Mars.

Some claims are modified. They either may be true, or they are true only in some cases. Modified claims refer to what is generally the case or what is probable or possible rather than to what must always, absolutely be:

Most mass murderers are men.

It might snow tomorrow.

Eating broccoli may prevent cancer in some patients.

To identify an absolute claim look for words such as *every, all, each, everyone, anyone, always, must, never, none, no one*. To identify a modified claim, look for words such as: *some, many, most, sometimes, someone, may, might, could, possibly, probably*. The philosopher Stephen Toulmin uses the term *qualifier* to describe words or phrases, such as these, that modify the scope of a claim.

The different types of claims will be described in detail in later chapters, but here I will introduce each of them briefly.

ARGUING ABOUT EXISTENCE   Some claims relate to our experience of reality. One type of claim about reality is the claim about existence. A claim about existence responds to abstract questions such as these: What is really there? What is happening? What happened in the past? What will happen in the future? Here are some examples of claims about existence:

There is a hole in the ozone.

There is a tenth planet in the solar system.

Three million people live in Phoenix, Arizona.

The accused was at the scene of the crime between 11:00 and 11:30 p.m.

The Cleveland Indians will win the World Series.

Other claims about existence involve measuring or describing our experience of reality, responding to questions such as these: How large? How long? How much? How far? How many? How fast? Here are some examples:

That horse is brown with white spots.

The recent earthquake was the largest in over a decade.

It is sixty-five miles to the next gas station.

Claims that describe or characterize experience may require elaborate models and maps. For instance, no one has experienced a black hole directly. The claim that black holes exist relies upon mathematical models about the structure of the universe. And when the earth is viewed from space, no national boundaries are visible; these boundaries can only be shown on a map.

ARGUING ABOUT CAUSALITY   Our experience of the world may lead us to make claims about causes and effects, responding to abstract questions such as these: What will happen if we do that? What brought this about? Why are we doing this? What will this lead to? What caused that? What will that do? What is the purpose or motive? Can it be changed? Here are some example claims about causality:

Smoking causes lung disease.

Violence on television contributes to the high rate of violent crime in America.

He is only saying that because he wants your money. (Motivation is a type of cause.)

Raising interest rates further will put the economy into recession.

The economic differences between the North and the South made the Civil War inevitable.

Like existence, claims about causes and effects can refer to past and future experience as well as to present experience.

ARGUING ABOUT SYMBOLS   A symbol is representation of our experience, our thinking about experience, or our thinking about symbols themselves. The word *tree* is not a concrete tree that we experience outside. It is a symbol that refers to our experience of trees, our concept of "a tree." Other symbols could be used to refer to the same concept. Danes use the symbol "træ." Germans use the symbol "baum." One could just as easily represent the concept of tree through some sort of picture or visual image.

Since all arguing takes place through symbols — usually written and spoken language — all arguing is to some extent "about symbols." But claims about symbols express arguments about the nature of symbols themselves, about what they mean or represent. Some claims relate to the definitions of terms:

Anyone who tells ethnic jokes is racist.

Most great artists are insane.

You have to be able to read a job application to be considered literate.

Acceptance of these claims depends upon how one defines "racist," "insane," or "literate." Some claims about symbols may relate to the interpretation of a text, particularly an authoritative text such as the Constitution, the Bible, the Koran, or the rules for major league baseball.

The First Amendment does not protect pornographic or obscene speech.

The Bible does not forbid homosexual relations.

The Koran requires death for those who blaspheme.

The rules of baseball indicate that a ball going under a fence should be considered a double.

Some claims about symbols relate to how we use symbols and answer questions such as these: How should we read or understand symbols? Are there symbols that cannot be used? Who should be allowed to use language? Under what circumstances and in what manner should one use particular symbols?

ARGUING ABOUT VALUES   A value is something that an individual or community holds to be of worth or esteem. Our values are related to our desires. To say that we desire to be free means that we value "freedom." If we desire to have the esteem and regard of others, we hold "fame" or "success" as a value. Sometimes, values are stated explicitly in an argument, but often they are implied or understood. Whenever an argument contains claims about what is "good" or "bad," or about what we "should" or "ought" to do, then it is an argument about values. The claim may not actually use the words *good/bad* or *should/should not,* but the force of these words will be there. Value claims always pass judgment or "evaluate":

That painting is beautiful.

The proposed landfill will be an eyesore.

Plagiarism is wrong.

Euthanasia is ethical.

This diamond is priceless.

What a great film!

I didn't care for the plot.

Values come into conflict with each other when we have to choose between two things we desire (or dislike) or when we disagree with one another about what we desire. In such cases, we may have to choose between the better of two good things or the lesser of two evils. Some claims about values refer to the order or hierarchy of values, to what desires we should prefer above others:

> Mexican food is better than Italian food.
>
> It is best to find a parking space close to the store.
>
> He is the "most preferred man" on campus.
>
> Camping in the mountains is more fun than camping in the desert.
>
> A woman's right to privacy takes precedence over any government interest in the life of the fetus during the first trimester of pregnancy.
>
> A fetus's right to life is more important than any right of the mother.

ARGUING ABOUT ACTIONS   Claims about actions are closely related to claims about values; they usually imply an evaluation of an action and recommend some different action. Any judgment about good/bad, right/wrong, beautiful/ugly, or moral/immoral usually implies a "should" or "ought," and "should" and "ought" refer to actions. We first observe how others act, then we argue about how they should or ought to act. Or we recognize a state of inaction — no one is doing anything — and recommend some type of action. Claims about actions typically propose a change in the way things are now.

Action implies some degree of choice on the part of the performer or performers of the action. To explain how action implies choice, the philosopher Kenneth Burke distinguishes between action and motion. A lot of things move but don't act. Golf balls and baseballs move, for example, but humans act by swinging clubs and bats. Action, then, implies movement with a purpose and a direction. Humans choose to act, but note that they may "move" without choosing. If I trip and fall down a flight of stairs, I am definitely moving, but unless I tripped myself intentionally, I'm not acting. Actions always require some agent, some person or group of people performing the action. The agent may be stated in the claim or may be implied:

> The federal government should impose national standards for education.
>
> Students ought to graduate from college in four years.
>
> Students should be taught foreign languages in elementary school.
>
> This river needs to be cleaned up.
>
> Let's eat out.
>
> Practice your piano lesson!

The last three claims in this example show instances where the agent, the one performing the action, is implied or understood. (For the action of cleaning up the river, the agent is an unspecified "someone.")

■ ■ THE STRUCTURE OF AN ARGUMENT: REASONS

Just because people have a disagreement about something does not mean that they are arguing, at least not in the way that I am describing arguing in this book. And merely setting forth an opinion or making a claim is not arguing or reasoning either. Arguing is rational persuasion. It is based on reasons. So to be an argument, a claim must be supported by one or more reasons. Stephen Toulmin calls reasons "data," the Latin root for which literally means "that which is given." Reasons, or data, are the evidence given for a claim. If you believe the reason or reasons, then you also believe the claim.

Identifying the Reasons   Like claims, reasons are statements. After you have identified the claim, you should then look for the reason or reasons given to support that claim. A word such as *because* may be used to show that a "reason" is about to follow. Here is an example: You should wear a heavy coat today because it will probably snow. In this example, the claim is "you should wear a heavy coat today" (a claim about actions). The word *because* indicates that the reason for the claim is that "it will probably snow." (The reason, in this case, is a statement about existence, a statement about what will happen in the future.) Note that sometimes the reason precedes the claim, particularly when the claim is signaled by a word such as *so* or *therefore:*

It will probably snow (reason), so you should wear a heavy coat today (claim).

It will probably snow (reason); therefore, you should wear a heavy coat (claim).

Once you have identified the claim, the reason is often close by, particularly in academic writing, where reasons often follow the claim as part of a thesis statement. In some cases, however, the reason may be implied rather than stated. In such a case, you need to ask a further question: What do I need to believe in order to accept the claim the author is making?

Chains of Reasons   In a simple argument, the claim is the only statement under dispute because the reason is something that others accept as true. In a more complex argument, however, the statement offered as a reason may itself require support before others will accept its truth. In a complex argument, the statements offered as reasons may actually be "claims" requiring further reasons. In the example I have been using, what if the person being addressed is not convinced that "it will probably snow"? The reason is then under dispute and needs to be justified. So the statement functioning as the reason itself becomes a claim:

You should wear a heavy coat today because it will probably snow. I watched the weather report this morning, and the meteorologist reported a 90 percent chance of snow today and tomorrow.

The simple argument now becomes a complex argument with a chain of claims and reasons. If you accept the statement about existence (the meteorologist reported a 90 percent chance of snow), then you will accept the statement that it will probably snow. Of course, it is possible that these additional supporting statements may also be disputed. You might not accept the authority of the meteorologist, for example, or believe that she really predicted snow. If supporting statements are disputable, then they in turn need to be justified or explained through further reasons, extending the chain.

Non Sequiturs   Some of the reasons in a chain of reasons may be implied rather than stated. If so, you will need to reconstruct these links in the chain based on what you can infer from the argument. Sometimes, so much of the chain is left unstated that it is difficult to make the connections. A reason or chain of reasons that cannot be connected to the claim in some logical way is called a "non sequitur." This Latin phrase means "does not follow" and refers to an argument in which the claim does not clearly follow from the reasons. Here are some examples:

> You should buy our product because we are showing you a picture of a beach.

> Our pizza is the best because we give away free soft drinks.

Some arguments appear to be non sequiturs but make sense with a little more background information. Consider the following instance:

> You should wear your coat today because I'm going shopping.

Without having more information about this argument, it is difficult to make any connection between the claim and the reason. With a little more information about context, however, this non sequitur makes more sense:

> You should wear your coat today because I'm going shopping. I won't be able to pick you up after school, so you will have to walk home.

Actually, we make statements all the time, particularly among those we know quite well, that others may take to be non sequiturs because they don't understand the context or background implied in the statement. When my wife calls me at work and says, "Pick up something to eat on the way home because I couldn't get a babysitter," I can fill in the context enough to know that the reason she gives is not a non sequitur. Here is the reconstructed chain of reasons:

> (You should) Pick up something (for us) to eat on the way home. (claim)

> We don't have anything for the two of us to eat for dinner. (implied reason)

> We were planning on going out for dinner. (implied reason)

> Now we are eating at home. (implied reason)

> I couldn't get a baby sitter. (stated reason)

▩ ▩ THE STRUCTURE OF AN ARGUMENT: ASSUMPTIONS

In discussing reasons, I suggested that arguments usually don't make much sense without some information in addition to the claim and the reason. Even if you accept the reason, there may be gaps you have to fill in before accepting the claim. The statements that fill in these gaps are called "assumptions." They are sometimes stated, but more often they are implied, even in academic writing. Found in the movement from reasons to claims, assumptions fill in the gaps in a chain of reasons. In his system for describing the structure of arguments, Stephen Toulmin refers to assumptions as "warrants."

Identifying Assumptions   In order to identify an assumption, first identify the claim and reason, then ask the following question: If the reason is true, what else must be true for the claim to be true? An assumption can usually be identified from the actual language of the claim and reason. Here is an example:

Claim: Richard Nixon was a good president.

Reason: He was skilled at foreign policy.

Assumption: Any president who is skilled at foreign policy is a good president.

To identify the assumption in this case, look for the term that is common to both the claim and the reason (Richard Nixon) and replace it with a more general term (any president). Here is another example:

Claim: You should visit Paris.

Reason: Paris has the world's best art museums.

Assumption: You should visit a place that has the best art museums.

In this argument, "Paris" is the common element between the claim and reason. Replace it with a more general term, "place," and combine the remaining elements of the claim and reason.

Let's go back to the example I used in discussing reasons:

You should wear a heavy coat today because it will probably snow.

The assumption here is that, in general, one should wear a coat when it snows: Snow justifies the wearing of a coat. A related assumption is that what is true of the general is true of the particular. In other words, if you should generally wear a coat on a snowy day, then you should wear a coat on this particular snowy day. This second assumption may seem like a statement of the obvious, and it is obvious in an argument this simple. Most arguments are not laid out this simply, however, and in more complex arguments, it can be challenging to identify all the assumptions.

Assumptions can often be the most crucial part of an argument. Identifying assumptions may lead to qualification of the claim, reservations about the claim, or possible objections to it. When you find yourself agreeing with the reason or reasons but still having difficulty accepting the claim, stop to take a careful look at any implied assumptions. Consider the following dialogue:

Student Y: What a dumb movie. There was no action in it.
Student X: I really liked it. It made me think.
Student Y: But nothing happened!
Student X: You just don't appreciate a good movie.

This appears to be an argument: Both students are making claims and putting forth reasons. But their arguing is not very productive because they have not examined the assumptions implied in each of their arguments. Take the first argument: The movie was dumb because it had no action. First, identify the claim: The movie was dumb (a statement about value). Then, identify the reason: It had no action (a statement about existence). Obviously, the two students disagree about the claim; yet they agree about the reason, that the movie had no action. So why do they disagree? Because they have different assumptions about what makes a movie a good movie (an issue of value). In the first student's argument, the implied assumption is that a good movie must have action. The second student's argument implies that a movie must make a viewer think. After recognizing these assumptions, the argument might be extended as follows:

Student Y: What a dumb movie. There was no action in it.
Student X: That's true, but does a movie need action to be a good movie? I think that a good movie is one that makes you think.
Student Y: This movie does make you think. I just prefer an action movie.
Student X: Perhaps we should find a movie that does both.

Student X's final statement is probably overly optimistic, but at least the discussion now focuses on the crucial point of disagreement between the two: What makes a movie good? Before they resolve this point, they will never agree on a good movie.

Assumptions in a Chain of Reasoning   As the previous example shows, an assumption, like a reason, can be disputed and become a "claim" in a new chain of reasoning. Identifying assumptions takes an argument in a new direction. In the example, the focus of the argument shifts from whether a particular movie is good to the larger question of what a good movie should have or do. As with any chain of reasons, the chain can continue until the two sides agree to disagree or until they together identify some common ground that can help resolve the issue. Perhaps our two student moviegoers could appeal to an authority they both accept, such as a movie critic. Or perhaps, they could agree on a higher value than "action" or "thought" that determines the value of a movie.

Identifying assumptions in a chain of reasoning can be particularly difficult when some elements of the chain are implied rather than stated. In such a case, you must first identify or reconstruct the claims and reasons before identifying the assumptions. I recently saw the following statement on a bumper sticker:

Abortion stops a heart from beating.

Although only a single statement, this is an argument. But it only makes sense as an argument if we know something about the context. Only one part of the argument is stated; the others are implied or understood. But what element is stated here? Claim, reason, or assumption? The people who produced this bumper sticker took for granted that their audience would know what an abortion is and be aware of the controversy over legalized abortions. So the statement on this bumper sticker is probably not intended as a claim: Anyone who knows what an abortion is understands that, if a fetus has developed a heart, then an abortion will stop that heart from beating. (Those who disagree that abortion *always* stops a heart from beating might see this as a claim, however. They could point out that abortions may take place at any point during a pregnancy, even before the fetus's heart is formed. There are, they would argue, some abortions that do not stop a heart from beating.)

In fact, this statement is probably intended as a reason for a claim that is understood, the claim that abortion is wrong or that it should be made illegal. Interpreted this way, the argument can be reconstructed as follows:

Claim: Abortion is wrong.

Reason: Abortion stops a heart from beating.

Assumption: Any act that stops a heart from beating is wrong.

As an argument, the statement on the bumper sticker is a bit deceptive because it *appears* to be a claim rather than a reason. And taken as a claim, the statement is much less controversial and more factual than the actual claim "Abortion is wrong." Reconstructing this argument is crucial for understanding and responding to it.

In order to reconstruct the argument on the bumper sticker, I had to conjecture about the people who made the bumper sticker and their intended audience. In order to do this, I relied upon my interpretation of contemporary American culture and politics. Someone else might reconstruct the argument differently, and the two of us might even disagree about how the argument should be reconstructed. The point is that reconstructing arguments and identifying assumptions can never be an exact process. Arguing in everyday life is not, like quantitative logic or mathematics, governed by strict rules. Understanding an argument requires some understanding of its context and its history. You have to understand the definitions of key terms used in the argument, and you have to understand, as much as possible, what people accept as true and what they still disagree about.

Consider the argument implied by the bumper sticker. The assumption is "Any act that stops a heart from beating is wrong." This statement is so broad that it is nearly impossible to defend, without qualification, against all objections.

Consider the exceptions, all the "things" that could stop a heart from beating but are not necessarily "wrong." Old age stops a heart from beating, but is it wrong? Again, relying on my knowledge of the context, I can suggest that the creators of this bumper sticker probably mean that any unnatural and intentional act that stops a heart from beating is wrong. But my restatement of the assumption is only a conjecture. To be sure, I would need more information about the conversation and context for this argument.

Applying the Principles

As I've noted, what usually passes for arguing is really just quarreling, bickering, and contending with words. Arguing as a form of rational persuasion, however, is based on reasons and attempts to clarify. In order to understand and respond to an argument, you must be able to identify its parts so that you can identify points of agreement and disagreement. Try asking the following questions:

What is the issue?

What claim is being made about the issue?

What kind of claim is it?

What reason or reasons are given to support the claim?

What assumption or assumptions are implied by these reasons?

What additional reasons or chains of reasons support the points made in the reasons and assumptions?

Where do I agree or disagree with this argument?

Let's use these questions in analyzing an essay by Christopher Lasch on the nature of political debate. Lasch (1933–1994) was a historian at the University of Rochester. Because of the broad knowledge of history he reveals in this essay, less well-informed readers may find the level of detail intimidating. To avoid this, remember that Lasch's main interest is in interpreting the present. He is best known for two books criticizing contemporary American culture, *The Culture of Narcissism* and *The Minimal Self*, in which he argues that American culture is decaying from the inside because of our concern with material wealth, youth, and physical beauty and our rejection of spiritual values. In politics, Lasch suggests here that Americans have become passive consumers of "expert" opinion as portrayed by the mass media, particularly television and that Americans need to become more actively involved in the political process, making their own voices heard. Lasch saw debate and arguing as important to living in the American community.

The Lost Art of Political Argument

CHRISTOPHER LASCH

L ET US BEGIN with a simple proposition: What democracy requires is public   1
debate, not information. Of course it needs information too, but the kind
of information it needs can be generated only by vigorous popular debate. We
do not know what we need to know until we ask the right questions, and we can
identify the right questions only by subjecting our own ideas about the world to
the test of public controversy. Information, usually seen as the precondition of
debate, is better understood as its by-product. When we get into arguments that
focus and fully engage our attention, we become avoid seekers of relevant information. Otherwise, we take in information passively — if we take it in at all.

From these considerations it follows that the job of the press is to encourage
debate, not to supply the public with information. But as things now stand the
press generates information in abundance, and nobody pays any attention. It is
no secret that the public knows less about public affairs than it used to know.
Millions of Americans cannot begin to tell you what is in the Bill of Rights, what
Congress does, what the Constitution says about the powers of the presidency,
how the party system emerged or how it operates. Ignorance of public affairs is
commonly attributed to the failure of the public schools, and only secondarily
to the failure of the press to inform. But since the public no longer participates
in debates on national issues, it has no reason to be better informed. When debate becomes a lost art, information makes no impression.

Let us ask why debate has become a lost art. The answer may surprise: Debate began to decline around the turn of the century, when the press became
more "responsible," more professional, more conscious of its civic obligations.
In the early nineteenth century the press was fiercely partisan. Until the middle
of the century papers were often financed by political parties. Even when they
became more independent of parties they did not embrace the ideal of objectivity
or neutrality. In 1841 Horace Greeley launched his *New York Tribune* with the
announcement that it would be a "journal removed alike from servile partisanship on the one hand and from gagged, mincing neutrality on the other."
Strong-minded editors like Greeley, James Gordon Bennett, E. L. Godkin, and
Samuel Bowles did not attempt to conceal their own views or to impose a strict
separation of news and editorial content. Their papers were journals of opinion
in which the reader expected to find a definite point of view, together with unrelenting criticism of opposing points of view.

It is no accident that journalism of this kind flourished during the period
from 1830 to 1900, when popular participation in politics was at its height.
Eighty percent of the eligible voters typically went to the polls in presidential
elections. (After 1900 the percentage began to decline sharply.) Torchlight parades, mass rallies, and gladiatorial contests of oratory made nineteenth-century
politics an object of consuming popular interest.

In the midst of such politics, nineteenth-century journalism served as an ex-   5
tension of the town meeting. It created a public forum in which the issues of the
day were hotly debated. Newspapers not only reported political controversies
but participated in them, drawing in their readers as well. And print culture
rested on the remnants of an oral tradition: Printed language was still shaped by
the rhythms and requirements of the spoken word, in particular by the conventions of verbal argumentation. Print served to create a larger forum for the spoken word, not yet to displace or reshape it.

The "best men," as they liked to think of themselves, were never altogether
happy with this state of affairs, and by the 1870s and 1880s their low opinion
of politics had come to be widely shared by the educated classes. The scandals
of the Gilded Age gave party politics a bad name.[1] Genteel reformers —
"mugwumps," to their enemies — demanded a professionalization of politics,
designed to free the civil service from party control and to replace political ap-
pointees with trained experts.

The drive to clean up politics gained momentum in the Progressive era. Under the leadership of Theodore Roosevelt, Woodrow Wilson, Robert La Follette,
and William Jennings Bryan, the Progressives preached efficiency, "good government," "bipartisanship," and the "scientific management" of public affairs, and
declared war on "bossism." These reformers had little use for public debate.
Most political questions were too complex, in their view, to be submitted to
popular judgment. They liked to contrast the scientific expert with the orator —
the latter a useless windbag whose rantings only confused the public mind.

Professionalism in politics meant professionalism in journalism. The connection between the two was spelled out by Walter Lippmann in the Twenties, in a
series of books that provided a founding charter for modern journalism — an
elaborate rationale for a journalism guided by the new idea of professional objectivity. Lippmann held up standards by which the press is still judged.

In Lippmann's view, democracy did not require that people literally govern
themselves. Questions of substance should be decided by knowledgeable admin-
istrators whose access to reliable information immunized them against the emotional "symbols" and "stereotypes" that dominated public debate. The public,
according to Lippmann, was incompetent to govern itself and did not even care
to do so.

At one time this may not have been the case, but now, in the "wide and   10
unpredictable environment" of the modern world, the old ideal of citizenship
was obsolete. A complex industrial society required a government carried on by
officials who would necessarily be guided — since any form of direct democracy
was now impossible — by either public opinion or expert knowledge. Public
opinion was unreliable because it could be united only by an appeal to slogans

[1] The Gilded Age refers to a time of economic excess, materialism, and blatant political corrup-
tion during the 1870s. Political party leaders, corrupt politicians, and greedy capitalists used
government for their own benefit. The Gilded Age led to an age of reform called the Progressive Era. [Ed.]

and "symbolic pictures." Lippmann's distrust of public opinion rested on the epistemological distinction between truth and mere opinion. Truth, as he conceived it, grew out of disinterested scientific inquiry; everything else was ideology. Public debate was at best a disagreeable necessity. Ideally, it would not take place at all; decisions would be based on scientific "standards of measurement" alone.

The role of the press, as Lippmann saw it, was to circulate information, not to encourage argument. The relationship between information and argument was antagonistic, not complementary. He did not take the position that argumentation was a necessary outcome of reliable information; on the contrary, his point was that information precluded argument, made argument unnecessary. Arguments were what took place in the absence of reliable information.

Lippmann had forgotten what he learned (or should have learned) from William James and John Dewey,[2] that our search for reliable information is itself guided by the questions that arise during arguments about a given course of action. It is only by subjecting our preferences and projects to the test of debate that we come to understand what we know and what we still need to learn. Until we have to defend our opinions in public, they remain opinions in Lippmann's pejorative sense — half-formed convictions based on random impressions and unexamined assumptions. It is the act of articulating and defending our views that lifts them out of the category of "opinions," gives them shape and definition, and makes it possible for others to recognize them as a description of their own experience as well. In short, we come to know our own minds only by explaining ourselves to others.

The attempt to bring others around to our own point of view carries the risk, of course, that we may adopt their point of view instead. We have to enter imaginatively into our opponents' arguments, if only for the purpose of refuting them, and we may end up being persuaded by those we sought to persuade. Argument is risky and unpredictable — and therefore educational. Most of us tend to think of it (as Lippmann thought of it) as a clash of rival dogmas, a shouting match in which neither side gives any ground. But arguments are not won by shouting down opponents. They are won by changing opponents' minds.

If we insist on argument as the essence of education, we will defend democracy not as the most efficient but as the most educational form of government — one that extends the circle of debate as widely as possible and thus forces all citizens to articulate their views, to put their views at risk, and to cultivate the virtues of eloquence, clarity of thought and expression, and sound judgment. From this point of view, the press has the potential to serve as the equivalent of the town meeting.

[2] The philosopher, writer, and psychologist William James (1842–1910) argued that the question being asked or the problem being considered determines the "truth" of a theory. If a theory is useful in answering a question, then it is "true" for that question. This philosophy, called "pragmatism," was adopted by John Dewey (1859–1952) in his attempts to reform American education. Dewey maintained that students learn best by doing. [Ed.]

This is what Dewey argued, in effect — though not, unfortunately, very   15
clearly — in *The Public and Its Problems* (1927), a book written in reply to
Lippmann's disparaging studies of public opinion. Lippmann's distinction between truth and information rested on a "spectator theory of knowledge," as
James W. Carey explains in his recently published book, *Communication as Culture*. As Lippmann understood these matters, knowledge is what we get when
an observer, preferably a scientifically trained observer, provides us with a copy
of reality that we can all recognize. Dewey, on the other hand, knew that even
scientists argue among themselves. He held that the knowledge needed by any
community — whether it is a community of scientific inquirers or a political
community — emerges only from "dialogue" and "direct give and take."

It is significant, as Carey points out, that Dewey's analysis of communication
stressed the ear rather than the eye. "Conversation," Dewey wrote, "has a vital
import lacking in the fixed and frozen words of written speech. . . . The connections of the ear with vital and outgoing thought and emotion are immensely
closer and more varied than those of the eye. Vision is spectator; hearing is a
participator."

The proper role of the press is to extend the scope of debate by supplement-
ing the spoken word with the written word. The written word is indeed a poor
substitute for the spoken word; nevertheless, it can serve as an acceptable substitute as long as written speech takes spoken speech (and not, say, mathematics)
as its model. According to Lippmann, the press was unreliable because it could
never give us accurate representations of reality, only "symbolic pictures" and
stereotypes. Dewey's analysis implied a more penetrating line of criticism. As
Carey puts it, "The press, by seeing its role as that of informing the public, aban-
dons its role as an agency for carrying on the conversation of our culture." Having embraced Lippmann's ideal of objectivity, the press no longer serves to
cultivate "certain vital habits" in the community — "the ability to follow an argument, grasp the point of view of another, expand the boundaries of understanding, debate the alternative purposes that might be pursued."

The rise of the advertising and public-relations industries, side by side, helps
to explain why the press abdicated its most important function — enlarging the
public forum — at the same time that it became more "responsible." A responsible press, as opposed to a partisan or opinionated one, attracted the kind of
readers advertisers were eager to reach: well-heeled readers, most of whom probably thought of themselves as independent voters. These readers wanted to be
assured that they were reading all the news that was fit to print, not an editor's
idiosyncratic and no doubt biased view of things. Responsibility came to be
equated with the avoidance of controversy because advertisers were willing to
pay for it. Some advertisers were also willing to pay for sensationalism, though
on the whole they preferred a respectable readership to sheer numbers. What
they clearly did not prefer was "opinion" — not because they were impressed
with Lippmann's philosophical arguments but because opinionated reporting
did not guarantee the right audience. No doubt they also hoped that an aura of

objectivity, the hallmark of responsible journalism, would rub off on the advertisements that surrounded increasingly slender columns of print.

In a curious historical twist, advertising, publicity, and other forms of commercial persuasion themselves came to be disguised as information and, eventually, to substitute for open debate. "Hidden persuaders" (as Vance Packard called them) replaced the old-time editors, essayists, and orators who made no secret of their partisanship. And information and publicity became increasingly indistinguishable. Today, most of the "news" in our newspapers consists of items churned out by press agencies and public-relations offices and then regurgitated intact by the "objective" organs of journalism.

The decline of the partisan press and the rise of a new type of journalism professing rigorous standards of objectivity do not assure a steady supply of usable information. Unless information is generated by sustained public debate, most of it will be irrelevant at best, misleading and manipulative at worst. Increasingly, information is generated by those who wish to promote something or someone — a product, a cause, a political candidate or officeholder — without either arguing their case on its merits or explicitly advertising it as self-interested material. Much of the press, in its eagerness to inform the public, has become a conduit for the equivalent of junk mail. When words are used merely as instruments of publicity or propaganda, they lose their power to persuade. Soon they cease to mean anything at all. People lose the capacity to use language precisely and expressively, or even to distinguish one word from another. The spoken word models itself on the written word instead of the other way around, and ordinary speech begins to sound like the clotted jargon we see in print. Ordinary speech begins to sound like "information" — a disaster from which the English language may never recover.

20

What is the issue? Based on the title, Lasch's essay seems to have something to do with political argument. In his first sentence, Lasch states his opinion that democracy requires "public debate" instead of "information." In the first sentence of the second paragraph, he states that "the job of the press is to encourage debate, not to supply the public with information." These sound like claims, the points that Lasch is trying to argue. Lasch appears to be addressing a couple of issues: How important is public debate? Who is responsible for encouraging public debate? As you read through the essay, did you identify any other issues that Lasch may be responding to?

What claim is being made about the issue? I would state Lasch's claim as follows: The press should encourage public debate rather than merely provide information. Everything in the essay seems to support this statement, and it is located near the beginning of the essay, one of the places where we expect to find a claim or thesis. However, analyzing an argument always involves some interpretation, and the claim I have identified may not be the only possible claim. How would you state Lasch's claim?

What kind of claim is it? The claim I have identified is a claim about actions. This claim involves an agent ("the press") and a proposed action ("should encourage public debate").

What reason or reasons are given to support the claim? Identifying the reason is a bit tricky. Lasch's main reason seems to be that public debate is essential to democracy. It is interesting that Lasch begins the essay with his reason and labels it as a "simple proposition," almost as a self-evident truth. Lasch's argument also implies that the lack of public debate threatens democracy.

What assumption or assumptions are implied by these reasons? This reason implies that democracy is something to be valued. In paragraph 14 Lasch elaborates on the value of democracy. He states that it is valuable because it is "the most educational form of government — one that extends the circle of debate as widely as possible and thus forces all citizens to articulate their views, to put their views at risk, and to cultivate the virtues of eloquence, clarity of thought and expression, and sound judgment." This statement describes what "virtues" or values Lasch associates with democracy: eloquence, clarity of thought and expression, and sound judgment. He seems to value the responsibility of each individual in a democracy to contribute to public decision-making. Lasch also values information, but he argues that public debate will provide better information than the public currently receives. Lasch's claim implies further that the press is able to encourage public debate in a way that will preserve democracy if it chooses to do so.

What additional reasons or chains of reasons support the statements made in the reasons and assumptions? Lasch makes certain assumptions about his audience, about what he thinks his readers will accept without further proof and what he thinks they will question. In order to support his claim that the press should encourage public debate, he needs to show that the press is not currently doing so, that the art of public argument is "lost." Lasch does this by relating the history of the press's becoming more "responsible," which takes up the bulk of the essay. Lasch assumes that his readers will accept his story as factual: He refers to particular events and individuals and cites particular sources. He also assumes that following its transformation into the "responsible" and "objective" press of the earth twentieth century, the American press has continued in that role to the present. It is interesting that Lasch does not really give any evidence that the current media do not encourage public debate. He seems to think that his readers will already accept this opinion based on his explanation of how the press used to be.

Where do I agree or disagree with this argument? I accept Lasch's values. I believe that democracy is important and that individual citizens should participate fully in the democratic process with "eloquence, clarity of thought and expression, and sound judgment." I am also willing to accept as fact Lasch's account of the development of the "professional" and "responsible" media. (I'm no expert on journalism history, so if I were really going to engage Lasch's arguments, I would probably read what some other historians have written and check some of Lasch's sources to see what version of history he is reporting.) I am willing to accept Lasch's "reason": Public debate is an essential part of a democratic society. I would qualify that statement somewhat, however, because I think there is more to preserving a democratic society than public debate. Public debate alone won't suffice. Finally, I'm not totally convinced that the press does not encourage public debate now. Every newspaper I know of has a "reader's forum" or accepts letters to the editor. Television news programs are beginning to include tele-conferences or call-in programs. Talk radio is the fastest growing format in the mass communications industry. And anyone who has "surfed" the Internet and participated in an electronic discussion group or Usenet group knows that there are thousands of debates taking place each day. I do believe that the public needs to be involved in more *meaningful* debate, debate that has a real effect on public decision-making, but I'm not sure that the press, by itself, can make this happen. Where do you agree or disagree with Lasch's argument? Where do you agree or disagree with my assessment of this argument?

Another Voice

In his essay on the decline of public debate, Christopher Lasch blames Walter Lippmann for removing the media from public debate. He responds directly to *Public Opinion* (1922), Lippmann's most famous book. If Lippmann's name is unfamiliar to you, your grandparents or great-grandparents would probably have heard of him. Lippmann witnessed the development of American society from World War I to the Vietnam War and wrote over four thousand magazine and newspaper columns and twenty books. His writings on politics after World War I influenced Woodrow Wilson's ideas on the League of Nations and international relations. As assistant Secretary of War, Lippmann helped to negotiate the Treaty of Versailles that brought an end to World War I. To write his columns, he traveled the world, observing political systems in many countries. He was a firm supporter of democracy and a believer in the need for public debate, even though he questioned the ability of most people to participate in political debate in a meaningful way. Some consider him one of the last true public intellectuals.

The following essay, "The Indispensable Opposition," was originally published in the August 1939 issue of the *Atlantic Monthly*. Lippmann wrote this article in response to the spirit of intolerance, oppression, and totalitarianism that accompanied the rise to power of European dictators such as Adolf Hitler and Benito Mussolini. In this essay, Lippmann argues for diversity, freedom of speech, and public debate. As you read, consider the following questions:

1. According to Lippmann, how do most Americans feel about freedom of speech? What reasons does Lippmann give for the necessity of free speech?
2. What is the "opposition"? Why do we need opposing or dissenting views?
3. What is the role of free speech and dissent in the search for truth?

4. How do free speech and dissent function in a dictatorship and in a democracy? How should free speech, dissent, and toleration function within a community?
5. Do you believe that the opposition is indispensable? Why or why not?
6. How do Lippmann's views compare with Lasch's views? After reading Lippmann's essay, do you still accept Lasch's characterization of him?

The Indispensable Opposition

WALTER LIPPMANN

I

WERE THEY PRESSED hard enough, most men would probably confess that   1 political freedom — that is to say, the right to speak freely and to act in opposition — is a noble ideal rather than a practical necessity. As the case for freedom is generally put to-day, the argument lends itself to this feeling. It is made to appear that, whereas each man claims his freedom as a matter of right, the freedom he accords to other men is a matter of toleration. Thus, the defense of freedom of opinion tends to rest not on its substantial, beneficial, and indispensable consequences, but on a somewhat eccentric, a rather vaguely benevolent, attachment to an abstraction.

It is all very well to say with Voltaire, "I wholly disapprove of what you say, but will defend to the death your right to say it," but as a matter of fact most men will not defend to the death the rights of other men: If they disapprove sufficiently what other men say, they will somehow suppress those men if they can.

So, if this is the best that can be said for liberty of opinion, that a man must tolerate his opponents because everyone has a "right" to say what he pleases, then we shall find that liberty of opinion is a luxury, safe only in pleasant times when men can be tolerant because they are not deeply and vitally concerned.

Yet actually, as a matter of historic fact, there is a much stronger foundation for the great constitutional right of freedom of speech, and as a matter of practical human experience there is a much more compelling reason for cultivating the habits of free men. We take, it seems to me, a naïvely self-righteous view when we argue as if the right of our opponents to speak were something that we protect because we are magnanimous, noble, and unselfish. The compelling reason why, if liberty of opinion did not exist, we should have to invent it, why it will eventually have to be restored in all civilized countries where it is now suppressed, is that we must protect the right of our opponents to speak because we must hear what they have to say.

We miss the whole point when we imagine that we tolerate the freedom of 5 our political opponents as we tolerate a howling baby next door, as we put up with the blasts from our neighbor's radio because we are too peaceable to heave a brick through the window. If this were all there is to freedom of opinion, that we are too good-natured or too timid to do anything about our opponents and our critics except to let them talk, it would be difficult to say whether we are tolerant because we are magnanimous or because we are lazy, because we have strong principles or because we lack serious convictions, whether we have the hospitality of an inquiring mind or the indifference of an empty mind. And so, if we truly wish to understand why freedom is necessary in a civilized society, we must begin by realizing that, because freedom of discussion improves our own opinions, the liberties of other men are our own vital necessity.

We are much closer to the essence of the matter, not when we quote Voltaire, but when we go to the doctor and pay him to ask us the most embarrassing questions and to prescribe the most disagreeable diet. When we pay the doctor to exercise complete freedom of speech about the cause and cure of our stomachache, we do not look upon ourselves as tolerant and magnanimous, and worthy to be admired by ourselves. We have enough common sense to know that if we threaten to put the doctor in jail because we do not like the diagnosis and the prescription it will be unpleasant for the doctor, to be sure, but equally unpleasant for our own stomachache. That is why even the most ferocious dictator would rather be treated by a doctor who was free to think and speak the truth than by his own Minister of Propaganda. For there is a point, the point at which things really matter, where the freedom of others is no longer a question of their right but of our own need.

The point at which we recognize this need is much higher in some men than in others. The totalitarian rulers think they do not need the freedom of an opposition: They exile, imprison, or shoot their opponents. We have concluded on the basis of practical experience, which goes back to Magna Carta and beyond, that we need the opposition. We pay the opposition salaries out of the public treasury.

In so far as the usual apology for freedom of speech ignores this experience, it becomes abstract and eccentric rather than concrete and human. The emphasis is generally put on the right to speak, as if all that mattered were that the doctor should be free to go out into the park and explain to the vacant air why I have a stomachache. Surely that is a miserable caricature of the great civic right which men have bled and died for. What really matters is that the doctor should tell *me* what ails me, that I should listen to him; that if I do not like what he says I should be free to call in another doctor; and that then the first doctor should have to listen to the second doctor; and that out of all the speaking and listening, the give-and-take of opinions, the truth should be arrived at.

This is the creative principle of freedom of speech, not that it is a system for the tolerating of error, but that it is a system for finding the truth. It may not produce the truth, or the whole truth all the time, or often, or in some cases ever. But if the truth can be found, there is no other system which will normally and habitually find so much truth. Until we have thoroughly understood this principle, we shall not know why we must value our liberty, or how we can protect and develop it.

II

Let us apply this principle to the system of public speech in a totalitarian   10
state. We may, without any serious falsification, picture a condition of affairs in which the mass of the people are being addressed through one broadcasting system by one man and his chosen subordinates. The orators speak. The audience listens but cannot and dare not speak back. It is a system of one-way communication; the opinions of the rulers are broadcast outwardly to the mass of the people. But nothing comes back to the rulers from the people except the cheers; nothing returns in the way of knowledge of forgotten facts, hidden feelings, neglected truths, and practical suggestions.

But even a dictator cannot govern by his own one-way inspiration alone. In practice, therefore, the totalitarian rulers get back the reports of the secret police and of their party henchmen down among the crowd. If these reports are competent, the rulers may manage to remain in touch with public sentiment. Yet that is not enough to know what the audience feels. The rulers have also to make great decisions that have enormous consequences, and here their system provides virtually no help from the give-and-take of opinion in the nation. So they must either rely on their own intuition, which cannot be permanently and continually inspired or, if they are intelligent despots, encourage their trusted advisers and their technicians to speak and debate freely in their presence.

On the walls of the houses of Italian peasants one may see inscribed in large letters the legend, "Mussolini is always right." But if that legend is taken seriously by Italian ambassadors, by the Italian General Staff, and by the Ministry of Finance, then all one can say is heaven help Mussolini, heaven help Italy, and the new Emperor of Ethiopia.[1]

For at some point, even in a totalitarian state, it is indispensable that there should exist the freedom of opinion which causes opposing opinions to be debated. As time goes on, that is less and less easy under a despotism; critical discussion disappears as the internal opposition is liquidated in favor of men who think and feel alike. That is why the early successes of despots, of Napoleon I and of Napoleon III, have usually been followed by an irreparable mistake. For in listening only to his yes men — the others being in exile or in concentration camps, or terrified — the despot shuts himself off from the truth that no man can dispense with.

We know all this well enough when we contemplate the dictatorships. But when we try to picture our own system, by way of contrast, what picture do we have in our minds? It is, is it not, that anyone may stand up on his own soapbox and say anything he pleases, like the individuals in Kipling's poem who sit each

---

[1] Dictator of Italy from the 1920s to 1945, Mussolini invaded Ethiopia in 1935. [Ed.]

in his separate star and draw the Thing as they see it for the God of Things as they are. Kipling, perhaps, could do this, since he was a poet. But the ordinary mortal isolated on his separate star will have an hallucination, and a citizenry declaiming from separate soapboxes will poison the air with hot and nonsensical confusion.

If the democratic alternative to the totalitarian one-way broadcasts is a row of separate soapboxes, then I submit that the alternative is unworkable, is unreasonable, and is humanly unattractive. It is above all a false alternative. It is not true that liberty has developed among civilized men when anyone is free to set up a soapbox, is free to hire a hall where he may expound his opinions to those who are willing to listen. On the contrary, freedom of speech is established to achieve its essential purpose only when different opinions are expounded in the same hall to the same audience.

For, while the right to talk may be the beginning of freedom, the necessity of listening is what makes the right important. Even in Russia and Germany a man may still stand in an open field and speak his mind. What matters is not the utterance of opinions. What matters is the confrontation of opinions in debate. No man can care profoundly that every fool should say what he likes. Nothing has been accomplished if the wisest man proclaims his wisdom in the middle of the Sahara Desert. This is the shadow. We have the substance of liberty when the fool is compelled to listen to the wise man and learn; when the wise man is compelled to take account of the fool, and to instruct him; when the wise man can increase his wisdom by hearing the judgment of his peers.

That is why civilized men must cherish liberty — as a means of promoting the discovery of truth. So we must not fix our whole attention on the right of anyone to hire his own hall, to rent his own broadcasting station, to distribute his own pamphlets. These rights are incidental; and though they must be preserved, they can be preserved only by regarding them as incidental, as auxiliary to the substance of liberty that must be cherished and cultivated.

Freedom of speech is best conceived, therefore, by having in mind the picture of a place like the American Congress, an assembly where opposing views are represented, where ideas are not merely uttered but debated, or the British Parliament, where men who are free to speak are also compelled to answer. We may picture the true condition of freedom as existing in a place like a court of law, where witnesses testify and are cross-examined, where the lawyer argues against the opposing lawyer before the same judge and in the presence of one jury. We may picture freedom as existing in a forum where the speaker must respond to questions; in a gathering of scientists where the data, the hypothesis, and the conclusion are submitted to men competent to judge them; in a reputable newspaper which not only will publish the opinions of those who disagree but will reexamine its own opinion in the light of what they say.

Thus the essence of freedom of opinion is not in mere toleration as such, but in the debate which toleration provides: it is not in the venting of opinion, but in the confrontation of opinion. That this is the practical substance can readily be understood when we remember how differently we feel and act about the censorship and regulation of opinion purveyed by different media of communication. We find then that, in so far as the medium makes difficult the confrontation of opinion in debate, we are driven towards censorship and regulation.

There is, for example, the whispering campaign, the circulation of anony- 20 mous rumors by men who cannot be compelled to prove what they say. They put the utmost strain on our tolerance, and there are few who do not rejoice when the anonymous slanderer is caught, exposed, and punished. At a higher level there is the moving picture, a most powerful medium for conveying ideas, but a medium which does not permit debate. A moving picture cannot be answered effectively by another moving picture; in all free countries there is some censorship of the movies, and there would be more if the producers did not recognize their limitations by avoiding political controversy. There is then the radio. Here debate is difficult: it is not easy to make sure that the speaker is being answered in the presence of the same audience. Inevitably, there is some regulation of the radio.

When we reach the newspaper press, the opportunity for debate is so considerable that discontent cannot grow to the point where under normal conditions there is any disposition to regulate the press. But when newspapers abuse their power by injuring people who have no means of replying, a disposition to regulate the press appears. When we arrive at Congress we find that, because the membership of the House is so large, full debate is impracticable. So there are restrictive rules. On the other hand, in the Senate, where the conditions of full debate exist, there is almost absolute freedom of speech.

This shows us that the preservation and development of freedom of opinion are not only a matter of adhering to abstract legal rights, but also, and very urgently, a matter of organizing and arranging sufficient debate. Once we have a firm hold on the central principle, there are many practical conclusions to be drawn. We then realize that the defense of freedom of opinion consists primarily in perfecting the opportunity for an adequate give-and-take of opinion; it consists also in regulating the freedom of those revolutionists who cannot or will not permit or maintain debate when it does not suit their purposes.

We must insist that free oratory is only the beginning of free speech; it is not the end, but a means to an end. The end is to find the truth. The practical justification of civil liberty is not that self-expression is one of the rights of man. It is that the examination of opinion is one of the necessities of man. For experience tells us that it is only when freedom of opinion becomes the compulsion to debate that the seed which our fathers planted has produced its fruit. When that is understood, freedom will be cherished not because it is a vent for our opinions but because it is the surest method of correcting them.

The unexamined life, said Socrates, is unfit to be lived by man. This is the virtue of liberty, and the ground on which we may best justify our belief in it, that it tolerates error in order to serve the truth. When men are brought face to face with their opponents, forced to listen and learn and mend their ideas, they cease to be children and savages and begin to live like civilized men. Then only is freedom a reality, when men may voice their opinions because they must examine their opinions.

III

The only reason for dwelling on all this is that if we are to preserve democracy we must understand its principles. And the principle which distinguishes it from all other forms of government is that in a democracy the opposition not only is tolerated as constitutional but must be maintained because it is in fact indispensable.

The democratic system cannot be operated without effective opposition. For, in making the great experiment of governing people by consent rather than by coercion, it is not sufficient that the party in power should have a majority. It is just as necessary that the party in power should never outrage the minority. That means that it must listen to the minority and be moved by the criticisms of the minority. That means that its measures must take account of the minority's objections, and that in administering measures it must remember that the minority may become the majority.

The opposition is indispensable. A good statesman, like any other sensible human being, always learns more from his opponents than from his fervent supporters. For his supporters will push him to disaster unless his opponents show him where the dangers are. So if he is wise he will often pray to be delivered from his friends, because they will ruin him. But, though it hurts, he ought also to pray never to be left without opponents; for they keep him on the path of reason and good sense.

The national unity of a free people depends upon a sufficiently even balance of political power to make it impracticable for the administration to be arbitrary and for the opposition to be revolutionary and irreconcilable. Where that balance no longer exists, democracy perishes. For unless all the citizens of a state are forced by circumstances to compromise, unless they feel that they can affect policy but that no one can wholly dominate it, unless by habit and necessity they have to give and take, freedom cannot be maintained.

Chapter 2
Ethos and Pathos

Ethos: Persuasion through Credibility

Although logos (the appeal to reason) is the primary persuasive strategy in arguing, arguments rely on other persuasive strategies as well. As mentioned in Chapter 1, the other two persuasive strategies that Aristotle describes in his *Art of Rhetoric* are *ethos* and *pathos*.

▓ ▓ WHAT IS ETHOS?

Ethos is related to the English word "ethics" and refers to the trustworthiness or credibility of a speaker or writer, based on how others perceive his or her character. Ethos is an effective persuasive strategy because whom we believe is often as important as what we believe. Some people can convey the "goodness" of their character through their speaking and writing, and others will respond positively because they trust the character that is presented. Can you think of a time when you have done something or accepted an opinion for no other reason than that you trusted the person giving the advice or offering the opinion? For example, when a trusted physician gives you advice, you may not understand all the medical reasons behind the advice, but you follow it anyway because you believe that the physician knows what he or she is talking about. Similarly, a religious leader may argue for the rightness of a particular way of living, and because you trust this leader's character, you choose to accept this way of life. In another instance you know that a fire fighter teaching the proper method for administering CPR has saved many lives using the method, so you accept its effectiveness and value. These are all examples of persuasion through ethos.

▒ ▒ CREATING ETHOS

Ethos is present in every act of communication. We are always giving some impression of ourselves, whether favorable or otherwise. The key in arguing is to be in control of one's ethos as much as possible.

Sharing Personal Information   Credibility can come from what we know about a speaker or writer: his or her prior behavior, position or role in the community, and knowledge or expertise. People believe doctors, religious leaders, and fire fighters in part because of the position they hold in the community, because of their reputation, and because of the training and experience they have accumulated. People who are not well known in a community may need to share much information about themselves in order to establish their credibility.

In analyzing the credibility of written arguments, the first step is to consider a writer's background. If you don't know anything about the writer, then consider the background information he or she reveals:

What is the writer's standing in the community?

What position does he or she hold?

What kind of authority and credibility come along with those positions?

What is his or her reputation?

What is his or her education, experience, or expertise?

According to Aristotle, we tend to believe those who hold positions of trust, those who have a lot of experience and education, and those who observe the ethical principles of the community and develop a reputation for fairness and goodwill.

Sounding Credible   Writers can also create credibility through the way they present themselves. For instance, it is important for a job applicant to make a good impression through a resume and in an interview. Even if an applicant has experience, education, and expertise, if these qualities do not come through on the resume and during the interview, then he or she may not be hired.

One way speakers and writers can sound credible is by adopting a voice of recognized authority. We trust doctors, scientists, and other experts because they sound like experts. They speak the language of "science" and "education," languages that our American society recognizes as authoritative. Studies, experts, and statistics are not only an important part of a logical argument; citing them can also establish credibility.

It is also possible to present an authoritative voice through a technique called "voice merging." Voice merging occurs when a speaker or writer quotes, paraphrases, or alludes to an authoritative voice or a voice that represents the values of the community, transferring some of that authority to the speaker or writer. A political speaker, for example, may quote Thomas Jefferson, James Madison, George Washington, or some other political hero to lend authority to the argument, while a religious leader might quote the Bible or some other sacred text. Some writers quote or allude to the works of literary figures considered great or important by the community: William Shakespeare, Charles Dickens, George Bernard Shaw, Virginia Woolf, W.E.B. Dubois, or others.

As you are probably aware, some people have mastered the art of sounding credible even though they have very little idea of what they are talking about. Of course, in most cases it is easier to sound credible and trustworthy if one really is, but there are people who can manipulate others by sounding credible when they really are not — con artists, for example, and people who falsify credentials in order to get into a prestigious school or obtain an important job. Like other forms of communication, persuasion through ethos can be abused.

Identifying with the Reader   In analyzing written arguments, consider how writers convey or create credibility by identifying with the values of the community. When politicians show themselves with their families, playing football with a group of marines, or visiting a homeless shelter, they are trying to establish that they identify with the values of the community. A writer does the same thing by using recognizable examples, sharing personal information, or appealing to reasons that support community values. Writing to an American audience, Christopher Lasch in his essay on the press in Chapter 1 supports the values associated with democracy.

Point of View   Point of view is another important element in creating ethos. How does a writer establish his or her relationship to readers? When writers adopt a first-person point of view, they use "I" or "we." Using "I" can create an intimate, personal, and friendly relationship between writer and readers, but "I" also draws direct attention to the writer as an individual. Doing so can be useful when a writer has particular expertise or relevant personal experience or when he or she can speak as a representative member of the community. Using "I" may not be as effective, however, on formal occasions or when the personal experience of the writer may appear limited and biased.

Using "we" emphasizes what a writer shares with readers, but "we" can also alienate people who feel that they share very little with the writer. Readers can also reject a writer who seems to sound overly intimate in order to draw them in. You've probably had a similar experience when someone you didn't know well put an arm around your shoulder or gave you a hug, pretending a more intimate relationship than you actually shared.

Using "you," a second-person point of view, immediately gains an audience's attention, as when someone calls your name out in a crowd or looks you directly in the eyes. The second-person is often used in instructions or warnings, and it lends itself very well to giving commands. Used too much, it can make a writer appear dictatorial, preachy, or condescending. It can also create a distance between the writer and reader or put readers on the defensive, particularly when they have some doubts about the writer's claims.

The third-person point of view gives the appearance of objectivity. The pronouns associated with this point of view are "he," "she," "it," "one," and "they." These pronouns create a certain distance between the writer, the reader and the subject, and they give the impression that the writer is a detached and unbiased observer. However, the third-person point of view can make an argument seem uninvolved and passionless. Scientists and scholars often use the third-person point of view to create this sense of objectivity. Recently, however, many academic writers have begun using "I" in their essays when sharing relevant personal information.

Word Choice   Ethos is also created through word choice. Those who "speak our language" or who speak with a voice of authority generally have greater credibility than those who do not. One who speaks the language of a community seems to identify with that community and demonstrate a strong commitment to its values. Martin Luther King, when addressing the African-American community, spoke the language of that community, drawing upon his experience and training as a folk preacher. But when he addressed liberal white audiences, a main source of support for his campaign for civil rights, he adapted his language, drawing upon his university training. In both instances, he strengthened his credibility by speaking the language of the community he was addressing.

▦ ETHOS AND STATUS

Long-standing or high-ranking members of a community can usually rely on their position in the community and need not worry much about constructing an ethos. For instance, within the Catholic community the Pope has a great deal of credibility by virtue of his position as Pope, and his credibility is enhanced by his acts of service, theological writings, and years of experience. In his writings the Pope must still rely on constructed ethos, but in doing so he also can rely heavily on his position and his reputation. A non-Catholic who wished to be regarded as an authority on Catholic teachings would have to work really hard to establish an ethos. Supreme Court justices also have established ethos by virtue of their position, education, and experience. Even though other members of the legal community may know as much or more about particular legal issues, a Supreme Court justice has considerable credibility simply by virtue of the position. But you don't have to be a world religious leader or Supreme Court justice to have credibility. Although my position as an English professor does not lend me much credibility to speak out on constitutional or religious matters, my position does give me credibility in some communities to speak out on matters related to English language and literature. As a teacher, my position gives me a lot of credibility in the classroom. Even students may have positions of authority and responsibility in areas of life that provide standing and credibility.

Members of a community who have little official status, however, must usually rely heavily on constructed ethos to be persuasive. Such is the case in the academic community. Because of their traditional role in the classroom, students often have very little credibility. Even though a student may be quite knowledgeable and experienced, the educational system defines the teacher as the expert and the student as the beginner, so that even when students know what they are talking about, they must construct a convincing ethos to convince the teacher. This is particularly true when the teacher knows very little about the student or judges the student based on stereotypes, believing, for instance, that women don't do well in math, that men are generally not creative, or that athletes are not as intelligent or well-prepared as other students.

Consider the traditional research paper, for example. Teachers expect students to include their own reflections and conclusions, but they also expect them to rely heavily on the voices of experts and authorities. Students quote, paraphrase, and summarize other writers, merging their voices with voices of authority in order to create a sense of credibility and show what they have learned about their topic. If a research paper came in with very few references, the teacher would probably be suspicious, wondering whether the student was guilty of plagiarism.

Teachers have different expectations for their fellow teachers and scholars. In an essay by an established scholar, a lot may be left unsaid, a body of common knowledge and assumptions about the topic that one has mastered as an expert. Established scholars rely much more upon their own authoritative voice and less upon the voices of others. Saying something that everyone knows can label one as a beginner. For instance, if there are three main scientific theories to explain a certain event and experts are all familiar with them, then an authoritative writer may refer to them in an article without citing the works in which the theories were originally explained. Students, however, would be expected to cite all such works. Experts can also make generalizations about their field that students can't. When a student opens an essay with a sweeping historical introduction, beginning with "Throughout the ages . . . ," for example, or "In today's society . . . ," teachers may fault them for overgeneralization and lack of support. But a famous historian can make sweeping claims about the course of history without a lot of specific detail and without quoting the opinions of other historians. Ethos makes a difference.

Pathos: Persuasion through Emotion

▨ ▨ WHAT IS PATHOS?

Pathos is related to the English words *pathetic, sympathy,* and *empathy.* It is the Greek word for "emotion" or "feeling," and it refers to the ability of language to evoke feelings in us. These don't have to be feelings of pity, as the word *pathetic* implies. They may be any emotion: love, fear, patriotism, guilt, joy. Whenever you act or accept an opinion based on your feelings, even without fulling understanding why, you are acting on pathos. As you examine the emotional aspects of arguments, consider the full range of emotions.

Advertisers, who have to present a convincing message in a thirty-second television spot or on a single magazine page, often try to evoke an emotional response in consumers. Ads may make you laugh so that you'll feel good about a product. Clothing ads may appeal to your sense of vanity, to your need to belong, to your fear of rejection, or to your desire to succeed. Tire ads appeal to your fear of being stranded on the road. Food ads appeal to your hunger and appetites. Many ads use the appeal of sex to sell their products.

Although the emotional appeal can be manipulative, it is also essential for moving people to action. People can be convinced logically that they ought to do something and still not follow through. But when people are made to feel strongly about something, they will often act on those feelings — even when they're not sure why. Human feelings are powerful, but the key to sustained work and commitment is acting even when the powerful emotions have waned. The emotional appeal can be a way of sustaining such emotions and, consequently, the commitment to act.

▪ ▪ CREATING PATHOS

Concrete Examples   One way that writers evoke an emotional response in their readers is through descriptive language. Instead of telling readers how they should feel, writers try to recreate the experience in such a way that readers do feel the associated emotion. Mark Twain once gave the following advice to fiction writers: "Don't say, 'The woman screamed.' Bring her on and let her scream!" Concrete examples and detailed descriptions give an argument "presence." They make the argument real and immediate for the readers. Journalists understand that running a photograph along with a news story makes the story more immediate. Showing a picture of a young child who has been kidnapped will create a much greater emotional response than merely reporting the child's kidnapping. Providing personal information about the child (showing her toys, talking about what she did the day she was kidnapped, showing pictures of the family, interviewing classmates) heightens the emotional response. Recall the 1995 bombing of the Alfred P. Murrah Federal Building in Oklahoma City. The horror and emotion of the moment were captured in news footage of a fire fighter carrying the body of a little girl, hurrying to see if there was any hope of reviving her. This picture, and others like it, touched an emotional chord in the American people, causing a public outpouring of grief and sympathy. A news story may contain statistics on how many families are without adequate food, shelter, or clothing, but no one responds. But if a reporter describes the plight of one particular family, then readers are likely to provide all kinds of help. The emotional response created by the second kind of story makes the difference between action and inaction.

Word Choice   Word choice is also important in creating an emotional response. Some words carry more emotional weight than others. Writers need to pay particular attention to the connotations of words, their suggested or implied meanings, in addition to their denotative or dictionary meanings. For instance, the words *cheap* and *inexpensive* both have similar denotative meanings. They both refer to something that can be bought at a lower price than expected. However, *cheap* can carry a negative connotation of "lower quality" as well as "lower price." To say that a person is "cheap" means that he or she is careful with money but with the negative connotation of "miserly" or "stingy." More positive words with roughly the same denotation are "frugal" or "thrifty." Chapter 9 provides more information about denotation and connotation.

Writers must also pay close attention to figurative language, such as metaphor, simile, hyperbole, understatement, personification, and irony. A metaphor is an implied comparison that is not meant to be taken literally. For instance, if you call someone a "snake," you are using a metaphor. You don't mean that the person is literally a snake, but "*snake*" suggests similarities between the person and the characteristics traditionally associated with snakes (such as sneakiness, quickness, or deception). A simile is a similar kind of comparison using *like* or *as:* "mean as a snake," for example. Well-chosen metaphors and similes give presence to an argument through concrete images that are vivid and memorable. Hyperbole is an extreme exaggeration or overstatement used for emphasis. If you plan a party and call it the "party of the century," then you are using hyperbole. Understatement is the opposite of hyperbole. To say that a devastating earthquake "did a bit of damage" would be an understatement and would actually draw attention to the extensive damage. Personification is assigning human characteristics to nonhuman objects. If you argue that a certain river should not be dammed because it is the "life blood" of a wilderness area, you are personifying the river and the wilderness in order to emphasize the importance of the river. Finally, irony is an incongruity or difference between what is said and what is meant or between what is expected and what actually happens. For instance, a writer might use irony to criticize an idea by seeming to praise it or to attack an idea by pretending to defend it. One of the most famous uses of irony is "A Modest Proposal" by Jonathan Swift, the seventeenth-century author of *Gulliver's Travels.* In this essay Swift suggests that the Irish economy could be improved if the children of the Irish were raised like cattle to provide food for the English. In seeming to promote this idea, he is really attacking the exploitation of the Irish by the English landowners.

Figures draw attention to themselves because they deviate from the expected. For instance, an environmental activist might refer to the clear cutting of forests as a "rape of the earth." *Rape* is a highly emotional term with seriously negative connotations. It suggests violence and domination. Readers would have difficulty responding positively to a word such as *rape*. At the same time, the word *rape* is used metaphorically, and the comparison of clear cutting with the act of rape is obviously meant to shock. The comparison also suggests personification because rape is an attack by one person on another. Presenting the earth as a woman in this way may gain the unconscious sympathy of readers who feel for other victims of sexual violence. On the other side, supporters of clear cutting might refer to this act as "harvesting," using a word that carries much more positive connotations. *Harvesting* suggests farming and gaining the benefits of one's own labors. It may also evoke the nostalgia and respect that many Americans have for the traditional farmer.

LOCATING THE EMOTIONAL APPEAL

Emotional language can be used throughout an essay, but the direct emotional appeal is often stated at the beginning or the end. An emotional appeal appearing at the beginning can catch readers' interest and predispose them to read the argument with a favorable attitude. An emotional appeal at the end of an essay can serve to move readers to action.

Note that in most academic writing, the appeal to emotions is considered less convincing than logos or ethos, particularly when the appeal is exaggerated or manipulative. The academic community expects that any appeal to the emotions be used to reinforce a logical argument.

Applying the Principles

ANALYZING ETHOS

One of the best ways to analyze how writers try to establish authority and credibility is by looking at short arguments by people who are not well known in their community. First, short arguments are excellent for this type of analysis because a writer must establish credibility rather quickly. And people who are not well known have to rely heavily on constructing credibility in developing their arguments.

Letters to the editor of a newspaper provide especially good examples for analysis. The writers of such letters have a range of abilities and show a surprising variety of approaches to establishing credibility.

THE UTAH WILDERNESS DEBATE: LETTERS TO THE *DESERET NEWS*

The following selection of letters all appeared in the "Readers' Forum" of the *Deseret News*, one of two major daily newspapers in the state of Utah. Because of its wide circulation, this newspaper is a forum for issues that concern the state as a whole. The writers of these letters are debating a controversial proposal by Utah's governor to substantially expand the amount of land in the state designated as wilderness. Many ranchers, miners, and developers oppose this expansion because they believe the federal government already has too much control in the state and because they rely on land resources for their businesses. Environmentalists and others favor the proposal because Utah's increasing population and expanding development in the state threaten some of the last and largest undeveloped tracts of land in the United States. Some people, particularly "off roaders" and family campers, feel that the proposal will limit their recreational opportunities. Others, particularly backpackers, feel that it will open additional opportunities. Those who live in rural communities feel threatened by those who live in the large population centers of the state, including Provo and Salt Lake City. They also feel threatened by the large number of people moving to rural Utah from California, a state seen by many Utahns as the source of everything bad in the country.

As you read these letters, consider the following questions:

1. How does the writer try to establish his or her status in the community? What personal information does each offer?
2. How does the writer try to create a voice of authority? What other people does the writer quote or refer to? What kind of authority do these other sources lend to the writer? Do some letters sound more "expert" than others?
3. How does the writer try to establish a relationship with readers? What is the point of view? How does the writer try to identify with readers? Do some sound more like "representative members of the community" than others?
4. Which writers sound more like they know what they are talking about? Which are you more ready to believe and why?

I have provided a sample analysis of the first two letters. I'll leave the rest up to you.

Wilds Designation Benefits Few

A. DERK BECKSTRAND (PROVO)

P UBLIC LANDS BELONG to the people. Any legislation concerning them   1
should therefore be to the good and benefit of the majority of the people.
Wilderness designation does not fit this criterion. Wilderness designation will benefit only a small minority of land users. The elimination of vehicular travel on wilderness lands effectively bars 95 percent of citizens from using them. Families with young children could not hope to enter. The handicapped and elderly are also barred. People wanting to make a livelihood through logging, mining or grazing are also exempted. Whom then does wilderness benefit? —

only a small group of wealthy and healthy individuals who have the time and inclination to enter these lands on foot or animal.

Recent studies indicate that once people were informed as to the true extent of wilderness restrictions, the overwhelming majority were against wilderness designation.

It is therefore recommended that we use the 3.5 million acres proposed by the BLM[1] for wilderness designation as a guide and reduce wilderness across the board by 90 percent. The remaining 10 percent could be considered for wilderness designation.

These areas should be areas where there are no existing roads. Adverse environmental impact to non-wilderness areas should be managed through conservative-use guidelines designed to minimize or eliminate adverse environmental impact.   5

This approach, if implemented correctly, should address the concerns of the wilderness movement while allowing the common citizen to use these lands for recreation and livelihood.

If we allow public lands to be designated as wilderness, we allow our best lands to be used only by a privileged few. This is totally unacceptable. Public lands cease to be public when their use is severely curtailed.

In the first letter in this set, A. Derk Beckstrand begins by making an appeal to popular sovereignty, to the "rule of the majority." This establishes a link with readers because he gives the impression of having everyone's interests in mind. In the second paragraph he names those that he is particularly concerned about: families with young children, the handicapped and elderly, loggers, miners, and ranchers. He distances himself from the "wealthy and healthy" elite who are able to use wilderness. Beckstrand presents himself as one who is concerned for the ordinary citizen, and he appeals to community values by showing a distrust of the selfishness of the elite.

Beckstrand speaks with a voice of authority, from an objective third-person point of view, in a formal bureaucratic tone. He chooses formal words such as "vehicular travel," "conservative-use guidelines," "adverse environmental impact," "implemented." He even uses a rather old-fashioned rhetorical question: "Whom then does wilderness benefit?" Beckstrand identifies himself with scientific objectivity by referring to "recent studies" and citing statistics.

In the final paragraph, he breaks from his objective stance to emphasize his relationship to the "common citizen." Here he uses the plural first-person "we" to include himself with his readers in opposition to the "privileged few."

---

[1] The U.S. Bureau of Land Management. [Ed.]

Don't Tag Too Much Land for Wilds

DAVID CARMAN (SALT LAKE CITY)

I APPLAUD THE county commissioners on their reduction of acreages proposed for wilderness. I agree some land must be kept as wilderness, but not 2 million to 6 million acres. I have read about all the polls which have been taken. I do not believe they are a valid statistical sample and therefore may not represent the majorities as stated in the polls.

For years my family and friends have enjoyed riding and racing motorcycles, camping, driving around to see the area, etc., in the desert. With this recreational activity, which is enjoyed by many, support is provided to camping equipment suppliers, motorcycle shops, riding gear suppliers, gas and oil companies, hotels and motels in various small towns, and a variety of other businesses throughout urban and rural Utah.

My son and many other children race motorcycles in the desert. This activity provides them with an outlet to channel their energies in a positive direction. In order to race they must maintain their bikes, and my child must earn the privilege of riding by keeping up his grades. This also does not allow them the time to sit in front of a TV for hours. This in itself, I believe, helps keep these children off the streets and out of trouble.

Campers, motorcycle riders and other ORV[1] enthusiasts pay for off-road permits, property taxes on vehicles and campers used for this recreation, all of which puts money into the state budget. If this privilege was removed, due to restrictions on the land, the money put into the state through permits, taxes on campers, trailers, etc., could also be reduced. How much money do the wilderness coalitions put into the state budget? Where do they propose the monies lost, if this happens, should come from? Higher taxes?

David Carmen tries to establish his credibility by using a first-person singular point of view and a very intimate and informal tone. He shares a lot of information about himself. He begins by stating his position against the expansion of wilderness areas. Then he tries to show that he is knowledgeable by stating that he has "read about all the polls." He further tries to show some knowledge of statistics by questioning the "validity" of the "statistical samples." Even though he is adopting the language of scientific authority here, Carman continues to use "I."

In the next two paragraphs, Carman talks about his personal experiences camping in the desert and driving motorcycles with his family. He praises family togetherness as a way of keeping kids away from television and "off the streets

---

[1] Off-road vehicle. [Ed.]

and out of trouble." Carman is appealing here to common values in the community he belongs to. He presents himself as a "good man," a "concerned citizen" who wants to preserve these values.

In the final paragraph, Carman associates those who favor wilderness with "tax and spend" politics and special interest groups that do nothing to support the community. He portrays himself and his supporters as hard-working taxpayers, who could benefit from tax relief (in reduced permit fees and vehicle taxes).

Support Wilds for Sake of Beauty

DAWN B. BRIMLEY (PROVO)

I RECENTLY RETURNED from a trip to one of my favorite places in the entire world: Utah's redrock country. What a world of beauty and contrast we live in if we are fortunate enough to live in Utah. 1

While in St. George, I noticed a discouraging trend all too often repeated in the name of development. The red hills east of the community are being seriously eroded and marred by a road that is literally a gash in the landscape and by the construction of homes on the very top of the mesa.

True, homes must be built and communities will continue to grow, especially in desirable places like St. George. However, there must be limits to the destruction of what distinguishes Utah — a fantastic natural landscape.

Thomas Jefferson advised each generation of Americans to ask of themselves the question, "What are we doing with the Earth?" Unfortunately, there are those (including Rep. Jim Hansen) who seem to be insensitive to the urgency many of us feel in regards to preservation of large areas of the earth in Utah. Again, it is vital that we preserve for ourselves and for those who come after us that wondrous and peaceful wilderness we now have.

I fully support the designation of 5.7 million acres of Utah's redrock country as protected wilderness. If we fail to do this we will see Congress, business and industry destroy what makes our state uniquely beautiful. Consider how you would feel if you and members of your family could no longer enjoy the wonder and serenity of your favorite places in Utah's wide wilderness. 5

Don't Lock Up the Lands as Wilds

GLENN C. ANDERSEN (VERNAL)

A S WE DROVE from St. George to Vernal last week, I never saw 1 square foot of those majestic mountains that needs to be designated as wilderness.

Oh, I saw a road or two snaking up and over some of the ridges, but that just made it possible to gain access to a certain area so it could be used if necessary but not destroyed in any way.

Wilderness advocates keep harping about the fact that the federal lands belong to all of us, but will it be if it is locked up as wilderness? I don't think so. It will be a travesty to designate any wilderness. It will be a lot more sensible to keep it as it is, because once it gets designated as wilderness, it will take an act of Congress to get it out if needs be.

Wilderness advocates claim that unless it is designated wilderness it will be destroyed. I have never seen a road, an oil well or a mine that has destroyed anything. They only affect a minute area that leaves adequate pristine area still available for generations to come.

When this wilderness fiasco started, all the meetings were packed with those in favor from urban areas. Now the meetings are getting to the people who know a lot more about how devastating wilderness would be to their livelihood and to the economy of the state.

When Ken Rait was cut off at one of the meetings, he said that the people there didn't understand wilderness. They understand it very well.

We have several national and state parks here in Utah that provide beautiful scenery and facilities for a lot of people to enjoy. That's enough.

Members of the Sierra Club and Southern Utah Wilderness Alliance are downright cruel people. It doesn't make any difference to them if they deprive people of making a living in the forest, mining or agricultural industry. They are costing the taxpayers millions of dollars in court battles and environmental studies.

Do the Right Thing: Protect Earth

TERRY BREWER (SALT LAKE CITY)

I HAVE BEEN HEARING much talk of the introduction of a BLM/Utah Wilderness Bill into Congress. The specifics have not as yet materialized. Our state and federal representatives are in the process of assessing how various demographic voting populations will react at the polls to the multiple "gross" acreage proposals being floated.

Being a recent transplant from California I would like to think these politicians covet my approval and vote. There are many thousands of like-minded refugees here who have fled the urbanization and overcrowding of the Golden State.

I do not consider myself a "tree hugger" or a wild-eyed fanatic. I enjoy fishing and backpacking. I think intelligent management of our resources can leave room for all types of recreation and enterprise. Economic stability does not rise from slash-and-burn capitalistic endeavors. Long-term planning and conservation are required to preserve what we have for future generations to flourish.

It is with little wonder that I see children carry guns and drugs to grade school when I see the callous disregard we adults have for the Earth we propose to leave them. The message we send is all too clear.

Generous allocation of wilderness areas and associated water protection at this point in state history will serve as a cultural beacon to the whole country. Ecosystems should be protected and not just "gross" acreage. Utah Wilderness Association's proposals may not seem fair to some development minded groups. Certainly jobs stand to be lost. But doing the right thing is never easy. Once wilderness is gone it can never be replaced. Leave something untouched for the future.

Wilderness Is for the Elite

F. T. GARDINER (PROVO)

A RECENT FORUM LETTER describes me as being "incredibly ignorant." I plead guilty as charged. As a matter of fact, I am having trouble deciding if the writer meant it as insult or a compliment. Perhaps he is trying to place me as a jury member on the next O.J. murder trial, make me a financial adviser to Congress or land me a lead role in the remake of "Forrest Gump."

This is the age of ignorance, and opportunities for those of us in that category seem to abound. According to the spokesman for the rich out-of-state wilderness clubs: Utah County commissioners are too dumb to "hold a pen." The study by Utah State University that describes the proposed Utah wilderness plan as having negative economic impact is described as "garbage." We are certainly lucky to have enlightened out-of-state guidance to direct Utah policy.

The thought I had intended to convey in my original letter was that the entire environmental extremist movement (including spotted owls in the Northwest, wilderness set-asides for the few, removal of cattle and ranchers from public lands) are all programs that forbid any wise use of natural resources by man. Wilderness also limits recreational access to those elite few of the backpacker world.

Wilderness by definition means no roads and no motorized vehicles. My critic's statement that "anyone can enter" wilderness is disingenuous in that he did not finish his sentence by saying that entry must be on foot; no families with kids in the station wagon.

As of 1993, the U.S. had already set aside 95.5 million acres as designated wilderness areas. Of that, 796,600 are in Utah. The BLM has an additional 26.6 million U.S. acres under study as proposed wilderness, according to a 1993 report. The Forest Service has an additional 6.7 million acres under study.

The above figures do not include the 7-million-acre Mojave Desert parcel in California (which is a subject in and of itself), nor do the figures reflect the huge parcel of valuable northwest forest land for spotted owl habitat.

At some point, several questions need to be answered for those of us who are ignorant. Just how much land do the backpackers need? How many acres of natural resources can be locked up before our descendants return to caves to recite nature poetry and compete with the bears for wild berries?

Wilderness More Than "Resource"

AMY S. MELLING (SALT LAKE CITY)

I AM A lifelong resident of Salt Lake City, and I consider all of Utah's public lands to be my homeland. I am outraged and appalled by the Utah delegation's BLM wilderness process, through and including the regional hearings.

The residents of Salt Lake County and the Wasatch Front have been summarily excluded from this process. Furthermore, public hearings which allow only a select few to speak, and then for only one or two minutes on just a small fraction of the statewide proposal, are an insult to the meaning of public process.

At the age of 25, I carry a great sadness in my heart to have been denied the privilege of knowing countless formerly wild, pristine and breathtaking places in Utah — canyons flooded by dams, plateaus decimated by oil wells, mountains crisscrossed by roads and mines, the drone of ATVs and snowmobiles engulfing the songs of the birds, the wind and the wildlife.

Wilderness — pristine, wild, ecologically intact land — is much more than simply a resource for human use. While I've backpacked extensively, there are nevertheless many wild areas in Utah that I haven't seen. And I don't need to. I do need to know that those areas exist, that they are protected, and that there is hope for our fellow beings' survival, whatever their form: tree, shrub, amphibian, snail, large mammal, native fish, bird . . . and that there is hope for future generations to appreciate what little is left of wild Utah.

As Utahns, we must protect large intact parcels of wilderness, and we must 5 include under that protection the lifeblood of those areas, the rivers. And finally, we must allow for the continued protection of those areas not designated as wilderness. I strongly support the Utah Wilderness Association's recommendation of critical areas as a very measured, yet viable solution to the wilderness debate. I challenge all Utahns to be visionary in our quest for a continued high quality of life and demand that the Utah Congressional delegation protect those wild lands that are so critical to our well-being and to the well-being of all critters. Let's have wilderness!

We Must Protect Our Wilds — Now

CARL CHINDREN (SALT LAKE CITY)

THE MERE MENTION of the word "wilderness" to many individuals con- 1 jures a strong emotion of anti-wilderness. The Earth was once virtually all wilderness, and, as a consequence of ever-increasing population growth, the demands on wilderness have exceeded the balance needed to maintain plant and animal life as well as human life. Protection of wilderness helps to restore the balance and prevent a further deterioration and loss of additional life forms.

There is no readily accessible region known that can compare with southern Utah's beautiful and diverse scenery. Within a day's driving time, the magnificence of the landscape is breathtaking to behold. The country is big, colorful and grander than one can imagine. The low population density and distant vistas enhance a great feeling and desire to protect this land from ever changing.

Mother Nature blessed Utah with this unique, masterfully crafted landscape. What a shame and tragedy if these and other remarkable Utah areas, now being considered for preservation as wilderness, are sacrificed for short-term mining, timber or other monetary business. What has taken nature millions of years to create, man can selfishly destroy in a few short generations. By maintaining these high-quality lands in their pristine state for Utahns and all people to marvel at and enjoy, there would be acknowledgment and praise for the good judgment for centuries to come.

National parks and monuments were originally the best of the outstanding wilderness areas. So that the parks could be enjoyed by everyone, roads were built to provide easy access. Exploding population growth and traffic congestion is now a confronting problem. In order to escape crowding and provide the opportunity for a true wilderness experience and protection for plant and animal life, the need for wilderness areas with walking and hiking trails, but no vehicular roads, is bound to increase.

Utahns should now be aware of a decrease in their quality of life because of 5 the uncontrolled population growth and resultant traffic congestion all along the Wasatch Front.[1] The wilderness areas of Utah now are needed more than ever to provide areas of escape from confining city life and tensions.

The following are op-ed pieces that also appeared in the *Deseret News*. Rainer Huck is president of the Utah Trail Machine Association. Wayne Owens is a former member of Congress and chair of the Southern Utah Wilderness Alliance.

Everyone Should Have Access to Wilds

RAINER HUCK

Now that the Utah BLM wilderness process appears to be reaching a 1 climax, the environmentalists have shifted their propaganda machine into overdrive. Each and every day we are bombarded with news reports and stories designed to frighten us into accepting huge wilderness set-asides so that our "fragile" environment might somehow be saved. Once wilderness is gone, they tell us, it is gone forever.

This is pretty heady stuff, and it no doubt goes a long way toward building up membership roles and draining dues from well-meaning folks who don't bother to question the motives of self-serving authoritarian edicts.

A little critical reflection reveals that the fundamental premise of the preservationist's environmental theory is completely false; far from being fragile and finite, wilderness is a renewable resource. It is so renewable and persistent that it requires man's full-time efforts just to keep it from reclaiming that small portion of the Earth's surface that has thus far been civilized. The natural environment results from an equilibrium of global forces that far exceeds man's ability to either manipulate or control. The instant human efforts cease, the ever-present natural forces will act to restore the system to its previous state.

Rather than an environmental issue, wilderness designation could be more

---

[1] Utah's main population center along the base of the Wasatch mountain range, which includes Salt Lake City, the capital, and more than 80 percent of the state's population. [Ed.]

accurately described as a zoning issue. It will define and enforce, through police action, who will be allowed to access certain tracts of public lands and, more importantly, who will not. The defining criteria for this decision will be muscle power. If you possess sufficient muscle power to propel yourself you may enter and enjoy. If you do not, you are a persona non grata, subject to fine and/or arrest for venturing upon what was once your public land.

All vehicles are prohibited from entering designated wilderness lands. That 5
means no cars, four-wheel drives, ATVs,[1] snowmobiles, motorcycles, hang gliders or bicycles. Existing roads and trails are rudely cut off at the boundary with barricades and offensive signs. If you suffer from a disability or infirmity that prevents the exertion required to hike to distant spots, then you are no longer welcome. If you are too old, have a bad back, weak knees or arthritis, that's your tough luck.

One recent writer, in an insulting rationalization, suggested that such people ought to be content to reminisce over photos and memories of past experiences. Wilderness designation blatantly discriminates against most of our people.

This queer situation exists possibly because the Wilderness Act of 1964 predated civil rights legislation and thereby reflected a more primitive, elitist mentality. It was born of a time when individuals who were not members of the "in" groups were of no significance and could be suppressed with impunity.

But we are, nowadays, supposedly more enlightened and recognize that our public resources must be made available to all. This realization lies at the core of the Americans with Disabilities Act. But somehow the elitist environmentalists have not gotten the message. They still feel that it is OK to reserve our most precious public lands for the young, strong and healthy and to direct the rest of us to the back of the bus.

There is indeed something that will be lost forever when public lands are designated wilderness. This is the ability of the majority of our people to access and experience these places. An individual has only one life, and when it's over he can never again visit the places he was denied. This is the price that the environmentalists demand in order to reserve exclusive use of these lands for themselves.

The environmentalists do not seem to understand that people who travel via 10
vehicle also love solitude and appreciate that elusive "wilderness experience." They scoff at the protests of local residents who have lived in and traveled these lands for generations. We all love the natural beauty of Utah and are offended to be branded as inferior beings unworthy of admission to these places. We resist being sacrificed for the benefit of the cult of the environment.

We do not have to acquiesce to their strident demands. We do not have to give them title to our most precious and priceless public lands. We can say no thanks: These lands are the heritage of all of the American people, and all of our people must be permitted to access them.

---

[1] All-terrain vehicles. [Ed.]

Wilderness Bill Offers No Protection

WAYNE OWENS

Y OUR JULY 3 editorial, "A neverending wilderness saga," urges that the
Utah congressional delegation's wilderness proposal be allowed to pass
into law because you consider it a "tiresome" subject that's been around too
long and you think this "worn-out saga" should come to an early end.

I hope it's not offensive to you to say that, on the surface, your editorial
appears to be somewhat shallow because it attempts no rational discussion of any
issues, using those empty, intolerant terms and finds it "maddening" that President Clinton is considering vetoing the wilderness proposal.

It is always a temptation in such cases to ask whether your editorial writer
studied the bill before writing his editorial. Did he know, for example, that the
delegation bill does not even protect the 1.8 million acres as wilderness, as it
claims, that theirs is, in fact, a wilderness development bill, not a wilderness preservation bill.

By allowing multipurpose uses in most all of the 1.8 million acres the bill
deceptively pretends to protect, it mocks the concept of wilderness as, in fact,
pretty much all of Utah's delegation have made a political living doing up and
down the state for so many years (which is why, perhaps, you are so tired of the
subject).

I hope this doesn't sound like sour grapes from the only Utah politician to
ever champion wilderness, and who was roundly defeated partly as a result of the
political capital found in such anti-wilderness haranguing. But I suggest to you
that it is a disservice to Utah's interests when one of its leading daily newspapers
editorially throws up its hands and yields to issue fatigue.

Please first consider that, under the bill, Utah's most uniquely beautiful and
best-known natural assets — its red-rock wilderness that scientists tell us took
God at least 300 million years to sculpture — would be opened to mining, oil
exploration, dam building, vehicle traffic and almost any destructive exploitation
scheme that the minds of future developers can concoct.

My mother taught me at an early age as I grew up in southern Utah that
our state was settled by inspired leaders who understood God's will. Brigham
Young,[1] in fact, set the tone for us when he admonished the early settlers of Utah
to protect our natural beauty, calling it God's handiwork. He was known particularly to love Utah's red rocks. It seems appropriate to me that, as we prepare
to rebuild his gravesite into a more natural park with a redirected City Creek

---

[1] Brigham Young, the second president of the Church of Jesus Christ of Latter-day Saints (the
Mormons), led a group of settlers in 1847 to the territory that later became the state of Utah.
Members of the Mormon church refer to themselves as "saints." Most of the population of the
state of Utah still belongs to the Mormon church and many are descended from these early
settlers.

traversing it, that we remember how much he loved private, unspoiled natural places.

Let us hope the site planners leave extra room so that our founder and first governor can turn over in his grave as he witnesses the attempted removal of protection and the principled battle to protect them so cavalierly dismissed by the newspaper he founded.

When Brother Brigham and the Saints arrived, Utah was nothing but wilderness. Even at the beginning of this century, there remained some 18 million acres of unchanged lands — about one-third of our state. Now there are fewer than 6 million acres that are still basically unspoiled by man's stewardship. How can anyone stand to see all of God's handiwork left to vagaries of man's interests? Unfortunately, the real argument here is not how much of our wilderness to protect — their bill would decree, in essence, that none of it will be so preserved.

Utah would have no genuine wilderness at all.   10

My argument when, as congressman in 1989, I originally introduced HR1500 to preserve over 5 million of wilderness, was that we should set aside 10 percent of Utah's lands as a natural tithe, and, as the principle requires, they should be our most beautiful. That is what my bill would have done. It is also what New York Rep. Maurice Hinchey's proposal would do.

And these lands are the most beautiful, and not just in Utah. There is nothing anywhere like this red-rock country in the entire world. No comparable vistas anyplace on the earth. What is maddening, it seems to me, is that Utah's political leadership should not want to protect some of it from man's appetites.

That is why our organization, and the entire Utah Wilderness Coalition, indeed tens of thousands of Utahns and nature lovers nationally — who share in its ownership with us — will try to defeat this abominable bill that would have such drastic and permanent impact on our few remaining wild places. And, should the Senate pass this bill (House passage looks quite probable) we will work to get President Clinton to do exactly what you find "maddening" — to veto it to protect the last vestiges of Utah's wild red sandstone lands.

As I grew up in these red rocks surrounding Panguitch, I learned a special love, even reverence for these extraordinary manifestations of what God decided would be most beautiful in our area. There is profound spiritual enrichment to be found in these solitary places that will be lost if we don't step forward to stop this wanton effort to open up all these lands to commercial use.

In this state where tourism is rapidly becoming our greatest revenue pro-   15
ducer, it is the red rocks that most people come to see, along with Temple Square, where we wouldn't dream of allowing any commerce. How foolish to put our red-rock wilderness up for economic development. They are our symbol, our icon, which we put forward in our brochures, our advertisements, on our license plates and, indeed, in our campaigns to attract businesses.

Yes, we should consider, lastly, how the delegation's bill would indirectly threaten our economic vitality. Surveys reiterate what is obvious. Utah's economic strength is tied to its quality of life, which is, in turn, tied to Utah's great outdoors and its unspoiled red-rock beauty. Not only tourists are attracted to

Utah by our wild lands, people come here to establish their businesses because outdoor life is so pleasant here. The red-rock wilderness is the magnet. Don't destroy it.

Please don't tire of political conflict and dismiss it as "tiresome" and "a worn-out saga," because there is great principle at stake here. The real nature of our state will be forever changed if this wilderness bill becomes law, because these wild red-rock lands are the last pure areas that remain exactly as God created them.

▦ ▦ ANALYZING PATHOS

It is often easier to recognize pathos when it is not working well. When a writer is effective in evoking an emotional response in his or her readers, then readers are probably so caught up in the emotion that they don't notice how the writer is working. Still, because persuasion through emotions can be so powerful, it is important to learn how to recognize when a writer is trying to make you feel something. It is particularly important to recognize when a writer is trying to play on your emotions as a reader, trying to create an emotional response in the audience that isn't warranted by the situation.

Letters to the editor and advertisements provide excellent examples for analysis because those who compose these arguments frequently use emotional appeals. People who write letters to the editor are usually trying to get readers to change their minds about something or to do something, and their letters often result from powerful emotions in the writers, who are upset enough or feel strongly enough about something that they need to express their feelings in public. It is difficult, however, to convey such strong emotion in a short space, usually fewer than 500 words. Advertisers face a similar problem. The average television ad is thirty to sixty seconds — not much time to make a pitch for a product. A print ad has to catch the immediate attention of readers as they thumb through a magazine or newspaper. Further, the nature of an advertisement does not allow for the detailed elaboration of a logical argument. So most ads try to make an immediate emotional impression. According to one old advertising adage, "Don't sell the steak; sell the sizzle." In other words, if you get people excited about your product, they will want to buy what you are selling.

The following set of readings provide different examples of persuasion through emotional appeals. The first few are short arguments, one an editorial addressing the issue of second-hand smoke, followed by three magazine ads. Each of these tries to leave a lasting emotional impression with the reader. The final selection is a short story by fantasy and science fiction writer Ursula Le Guin. In this story Le Guin is able to work out her emotional appeal in much more detail than an ad writer or journalist can. As you examine these selections, consider the following questions:

1. Identify words that seem to carry emotional weight. How do you respond to these words? How do you think the writer wants you to respond?

2. Identify instances where the writer provides concrete examples or detailed descriptions. What kind of emotional response do these examples evoke?

3. Find instances of figurative language: metaphor, simile, hyperbole, understatement, personification, or irony. In what way do these figures deviate from the meaning you would normally expect? What kind of emotional weight do these figures carry? What do these figures emphasize? How do they focus your attention?

I have provided a sample analysis of the first two selections.

Tiny Fighters Are Victims of Mothers' Smoke

GRETCHEN LETTERMAN

F EW SIGHTS make such an unforgettable impression on the mind and heart   1
as the neonatal intensive care unit at All Children's Hospital in St. Petersburg, Fla. Babies more tiny than seems imaginable are fighting, with the help of tubes and machines and hovering nurses, to get big enough and strong enough to go home to their families.

Depending on their sizes and conditions, some stay in this post-natal womb longer than others. Their Isolettes are adorned with sweet touches (a hand-lettered sign proclaiming "Robin's Nest," a cuddly teddy bear keeping watch from atop a monitor) in the hope that babies burdened with life-threatening complications will soak up the same love they would if they were snugly nestled in their own cribs at home.

Many newborns have to take such a detour before they can leave the hospital in their parents' arms because they are born too small, organs too immature to function properly.

There are many reasons for this cruel reality, but one that is completely preventable is highlighted by the recent work of two doctors from the University of Massachusetts.

Doctors Joseph DiFranza and Robert Lew analyzed 40 years of research to   5
determine that 53,000 babies a year are born with low birthweight and 22,000 need intensive care at birth because their mothers smoked while they were pregnant. Their analysis also found that pregnant women's smoking caused 1,900 babies to die each year from Sudden Infant Death Syndrome and that an additional 3,700 infants die within one month of birth due to complications from the smoke their mothers inhaled during pregnancy. The doctors also attribute 115,000 miscarriages annually to smoking.

It's not news that a woman's smoking can harm her fetus, but this is the first time the numbers have been calculated, and they are astonishing. Smoking women, addicted to a legal substance, are poisoning their children, some with fatal conclusion, by the thousands every year.

The sins of tobacco are being reported with increasing frequency. Just two weeks ago a thorough review of research damned secondhand smoke more soundly than ever before. The hearts of nonsmokers are more vulnerable to damage from passive smoking than are the hearts of smokers to the firsthand drag, researchers concluded, because their bodies haven't built up defenses to tobacco's toxins. That's especially bad news for children.

Yet the tobacco industry keeps winning, even in the face of unprecedented legal attack such as lawsuits by Florida, Mississippi and other states against tobacco companies to recoup the cost of state-financed medical care for sick smokers.

A bill that would have banned smoking in Florida restaurants is likely dead because, preposterously, lawmakers didn't want to take the time needed to debate it — "at least an hour and a half," according to Rep. Ben Graber, who chairs the health-care committee that would have had to spare the precious moments.

Children are still being hooked, despite efforts in schools to keep them smoke-free, by kid-appealing advertisements and promotional products. Despite all we know about what smoke in a woman's lungs can do to a fetus she carries, pregnant women continue to light up.

For some, stopping the smoking habit is as easy as making up their minds to do so, especially when the health or pleas of a loved one are influencing factors. For the majority of smokers, however, quitting is either an undesired goal or a seemingly impossible one. That's the power of addiction.

Anyone who spends a minute in a neonatal intensive care unit gazing at a premature baby, the translucent skin stretched tight over miniature ribs, shouldn't have any trouble feeling heartache for the little life struggling to survive, especially for the 22,000 babies a year whose struggle could have been avoided if their mothers hadn't smoked.

Who knows, the experience might even have an effect on tobacco industry executives and their lobbyists.

In this essay, Gretchen Letterman denounces what she calls the "sins of the tobacco industry." She focuses on the harmful effects that smoking during pregnancy can have on an unborn baby. Letterman's main emotional appeals are found at the beginning and end of her essay, common positions for emotional appeals.

Letterman begins her essay by describing a concrete example, a particular scene of suffering babies born prematurely. Letterman doesn't indicate exactly why these particular babies are premature but allows her readers to make the connection between their suffering and the suffering of babies whose mothers smoked. The scene is All Children's Hospital in St. Petersburg, Florida (where Gretchen Letterman lives). She describes seeing "babies more tiny than seems imaginable" hooked up to "tubes and machines." Hospitals are an uncomfortable place for most people anyway. If you are nervous about getting a shot or giving blood, then imagine having all kinds of strange tubes running in and out of your body. Then imagine this being done to a newborn. This is the powerful image that Letterman is trying to convey. In her second paragraph, Letterman elaborates on this disturbing image by describing the "sweet touches" that "adorn" their special care cribs: "a hand-lettered sign proclaiming 'Robin's Nest'" and "a cuddly teddy bear keeping watch from atop a monitor." In the next-to-last paragraph, Letterman focuses on one particular detail to capture the suffering of these infants: "the translucent skin stretched tight over miniature ribs." This detail calls to my mind the pictures of starving, diseased, and malnourished children so familiar from advertisements for children's aid programs. It also reminds me somewhat of pictures of Holocaust survivors. Whether Letterman intended these associations doesn't really matter. The image of a suffering child speaks to something instinctual in most human beings. By describing these details, Letterman changes these infants from statistics to real people.

Letterman also uses words that carry a lot of emotional weight: the "cuddly teddy bear," "cruel reality," "poisoning their children," "sins of tobacco," "tobacco's toxins." She uses words with a negative connotation when referring to the suffering of the children and the actions of the tobacco industry and legislators. She uses words with positive connotations to describe those who care for these infants.

Letterman's argument does not rely solely on emotion. She establishes her credibility as a writer by sharing her first-hand experience in a post-natal ward. She speaks with the authoritative voice of science by citing the "40 years of research" conducted by Joseph DiFranza and Robert Lew. She also refers to "a thorough review of research" that showed the harm of second-hand smoke. Letterman gives the impression that she is knowledgeable by reviewing the legislative history of anti-smoking legislation. And she demonstrates her goodwill by identifying with an important value in the community: the protection of innocent children.

Dakin Toy Advertisement

Is it any wonder the prisons are full?

In the mid 1950's, researchers at the University of Pennsylvania began conducting what has become a landmark study.

Its purpose: to determine the effect violent toys have on our children.

What they found was rather disturbing. The researchers stated that violent toys cause children to become more violent. That they actually may, in fact, teach children to become violent.

At Dakin, we've always tried to produce toys that teach children some other things.

Toys that, rather than teach a child how to maim, would teach a child how to love.

That, rather than teach a child how to hurt, would teach a child how to care for something.

Toys that, rather than being designed to be played with in only one way, would challenge the child's imagination to use them in a variety of ways. From playing house. To playing veterinarian. To playing Mr. Big Shot Hollywood movie director.

Naturally, researchers and child psychologists have had something to say about toys like the Dakin stuffed animal you see on the left. That they can play a very important role in helping children develop into secure, well-adjusted individuals.

You see, as parents ourselves, we at Dakin don't design toys solely on the basis of whether or not they'll make money.

We design them on the basis of whether we'd want our children playing with them.

DAKIN

Gifts you can feel good about.

Courtesy of Applause, Inc.

To be successful, a magazine ad must make an immediate and lasting impression. The writers of this ad use visual images to contrast Dakin toys with other toys. Featured in the center of the ad is a cute stuffed puppy, an image that calls to mind the dogs I had as pets when I was younger, as well as the stuffed animals I owned. This picture speaks "soft and cuddly." The phrase underneath the dog's foot contains an interesting double meaning: "Gifts you can feel good about." They are gifts that literally feel good because they are soft and cuddly, but parents can also rest assured that Dakin stuffed animals are not going to lead to violence. After reading this phrase, the reader's eye is led to the Dakin logo, a cuddly teddy bear.

The contrasting image in this ad is the collection of combat toys at the top of the page: the squirt gun in the shape of a real gun, the tank, the fighter plane, and the action figure. Most disturbing of all to me is the commando knife with dried blood along the blade. This knife is placed just above the dog, and the point of the knife leads your eye over and then down to the puppy. The large typeface at the top of the ad emphasizes the link between combat toys and violence in adults: "Is it any wonder the prisons are full?"

The elements of the ad are enough to send a message and associate an emotional image with that message: If you don't want your kids to be violent, then buy the kind of toys that Dakin sells. The ad does have a logical argument, however. The ad copy, which doesn't receive as much emphasis as the emotional imagery, cites studies linking violent toys to increased violence. The ad copy also contains an ethical appeal, an attempt to establish Dakin's credibility as a company that distances itself from toy makers who care only about profits and to appeal to the community value of teaching a child "how to love" rather than "how to maim."

American Red Cross Advertisement

When you give blood you give another birthday, another anniversary, another day at the beach, another night under the stars, another talk with a friend, another laugh, another hug, another chance.

American Red Cross

Please give blood.

Courtesy of the American Red Cross.

Humane Farming Association Advertisement

Q: Why can't this veal calf walk?

A: He has only two feet.

Actually, <u>less</u> than two feet. Twenty two inches to be exact. His entire life is spent chained in a wooden box measuring only 22 inches wide and 56 inches long. The box is so small that the calf can't walk or even turn around.

Most people think animal abuse is illegal. It isn't. In veal factories, it's business as usual. "Milk-fed" veal is obtained by making a calf anemic. The calf is *not* fed mother's milk. He's fed an antibiotic laced formula that causes severe diarrhea. He must lie in his own excrement —choking on the ammonia gases. He's chained in a darkened building with hundreds of other baby calves suffering the same fate. They are immobilized, sick, and anemic.

Toxic Veal

The reckless use of oxytetracycline, mold inhibiting chemicals, chloramphenicol, neomycin, penicillin, and other drugs is not just bad for calves. It is toxic to you.

But doesn't the USDA prevent tainted veal from being sold? Absolutely not. The USDA itself admits that most veal is never checked for toxic residue.

Antibiotics in veal and other factory farm products create virulent strains of bacteria that wreak havoc on human health. *Salmonella* poisoning is reaching epidemic proportions.

Veal factories maximize profits for agribusiness drug companies because they are a breeding ground for disease. To keep calves alive under such torturous conditions, they are *continually* given drugs which are passed on to consumers.

It doesn't have to be this way. And with your help, it won't be. Please, don't buy veal!

- -
Campaign Against Factory Farming

YES! Factory farms must be stopped from misusing drugs, abusing farm animals, and destroying America's family farms. Enclosed is my tax-deductible contribution of:

☐ $20   ☐ $50   ☐ $100   ☐ $500   ☐ Other_____

Name_____

Address_____

City/State/Zip_____

A free Consumer Alert pack is available upon request.

THE HUMANE FARMING ASSOCIATION
1550 California Street • Suite 4 • San Francisco, CA 94109
- -

Courtesy of the Humane Farming Association.

The Ones Who Walk Away from Omelas (Variations on a Theme by William James)

URSULA K. LE GUIN

W ITH A CLAMOR of bells that set the swallows soaring, the Festival of Summer came to the city Omelas, bright-towered by the sea. The rigging of the boats in harbor sparkled with flags. In the streets between houses with red roofs and painted walls, between old moss-grown gardens and under avenues of trees, past great parks and public buildings, processions moved. Some were decorous: old people in long stiff robes of mauve and grey, grave master workmen, quiet, merry women carrying their babies, and chattering as they walked. In other streets the music beat faster, a shimmering of gong and tambourine, and the people went dancing, the procession was a dance. Children dodged in and out, their high calls rising like the swallows' crossing flights over the music and the singing. All the processions wound towards the north side of the city, where on the great water-meadow called the Green Fields boys and girls, naked in the bright air, with mud-stained feet and ankles and long, lithe arms, exercised their restive horses before the race. The horses wore no gear at all but a halter without bit. Their manes were braided with streamers of silver, gold, and green. They flared their nostrils and pranced and boasted to one another; they were vastly excited, the horse being the only animal who had adopted our ceremonies as his own. Far off to the north and west the mountains stood up half encircling Omelas on her bay. The air of morning was so clear that the snow still crowning the Eighteen Peaks burned with white-gold fire across the miles of sunlit air, under the dark blue of the sky. There was just enough wind to make the banners that marked the racecourse snap and flutter now and then. In the silence of the broad green meadows one could hear the music winding through the city streets, farther and nearer and ever approaching, a cheerful faint sweetness of the air that from time to time trembled and gathered together and broke out into the great joyous clanging of the bells.

Joyous! How is one to tell about joy? How describe the citizens of Omelas?

They were not simple folk, you see, though they were happy. But we do not say the words of cheer much any more. All smiles have become archaic. Given a description such as this one tends to make certain assumptions. Given a description such as this one tends to look next for the King, mounted on a splendid stallion and surrounded by his noble knights, or perhaps in a golden litter borne by great-muscled slaves. But there was no king. They did not use swords, or keep slaves. They were not barbarians. I do not know the rules and laws of their society, but I suspect that they were singularly few. As they did without monarchy and slavery, so they also get on without the stock exchange, the advertisement, the secret police, and the bomb. Yet I repeat that these were not simple folk, not dulcet shepherds, noble savages, bland utopians. They were not less complex

1

than us. The trouble is that we have a bad habit, encouraged by pedants and sophisticates, of considering happiness as something rather stupid. Only pain is intellectual, only evil interesting. This is the treason of the artist: a refusal to admit the banality of evil and the terrible boredom of pain. If you can't lick 'em, join 'em. If it hurts, repeat it. But to praise despair is to condemn delight, to embrace violence is to lose hold of everything else. We have almost lost hold; we can no longer describe a happy man, nor make any celebration of joy. How can I tell you about the people of Omelas? They were not naïve and happy children — though their children were, in fact, happy. They were mature, intelligent, passionate adults whose lives were not wretched. O miracle! but I wish I could describe it better. I wish I could convince you. Omelas sounds in my words like a city in a fairy tale, long ago and far away, once upon a time. Perhaps it would be best if you imagined it as your own fancy bids, assuming it will rise to the occasion, for certainly I cannot suit you all. For instance, how about technology? I think that there would be no cars or helicopters in and above the streets; this follows from the fact that the people of Omelas are happy people. Happiness is based on a just discrimination of what is necessary, what is neither necessary nor destructive, and what is destructive. In the middle category, however — that of the unnecessary but undestructive, that of comfort, luxury, exuberance, etc. — they could perfectly well have central heating, subway trains, washing machines, and all kinds of marvelous devices not yet invented here, floating light-sources, fuelless power, a cure for the common cold. Or they could have none of that: it doesn't matter. As you like it. I incline to think that people from towns up and down the coast have been coming in to Omelas during the last days before the Festival on very fast little trains and double-decked trams, and that the train station of Omelas is actually the handsomest building in town, though plainer than the magnificent Farmers' Market. But even granted trains, I fear that Omelas so far strikes some of you as goody-goody. Smiles, bells, parades, horses, bleh. If so, please add an orgy. If an orgy would help, don't hesitate. Let us not, however, have temples from which issue beautiful nude priests and priestesses already half in ecstasy and ready to copulate with any man or woman, lover or stranger, who desires union with the deep godhead of the blood, although that was my first idea. But really it would be better not to have any temples in Omelas — at least, not manned temples. Religion yes, clergy no. Surely the beautiful nudes can just wander about, offering themselves like divine soufflés to the hunger of the needy and the rapture of the flesh. Let them join the processions. Let tambourines be struck above the copulations, and the glory of desire be proclaimed upon the gongs, and (a not unimportant point) let the offspring of these delightful rituals be beloved and looked after by all. One thing I know there is none of in Omelas is guilt. But what else should there be? I thought at first there were no drugs, but that is puritanical. For those who like it, the faint insistent sweetness of *drooz* may perfume the ways of the city, *drooz* which first brings a great lightness and brilliance to the mind and limbs, and then after some hours a dreamy languor, and wonderful visions at last of the very arcana and inmost secrets of the Universe, as well as exciting the pleasure of sex beyond all belief; and it is not habit-forming. For more modest tastes I think there ought to be beer. What else, what else belongs in the joyous city? The sense of victory, surely, the celebration of courage. But as we did without clergy, let us do without soldiers. The joy built upon successful slaughter is not the right kind of joy; it will not do; it is fearful and it is trivial. A boundless and generous contentment, a magnanimous triumph felt not against some outer enemy but in communion with the finest and fairest in the souls of all men everywhere and the splendor of the world's summer: this is what swells the hearts of the people of Omelas, and the victory they celebrate is that of life. I really don't think many of them need to take *drooz*.

Most of the processions have reached the Green Fields by now. A marvelous smell of cooking goes forth from the red and blue tents of the provisioners. The faces of small children are amiably sticky; in the benign grey beard of a man a couple of crumbs of rich pastry are entangled. The youths and girls have mounted their horses and are beginning to group around the starting line of the course. An old woman, small, fat, and laughing, is passing out flowers from a basket, and tall young men wear her flowers in their shining hair. A child of nine or ten sits at the edge of the crowd alone, playing on a wooden flute. People pause to listen, and they smile, but they do not speak to him, for he never ceases playing and never sees them, his dark eyes wholly rapt in the sweet, thin magic of the tune.

He finishes, and slowly lowers his hands holding the wooden flute.   5

As if that little private silence were the signal, all at once a trumpet sounds from the pavilion near the starting line: imperious, melancholy, piercing. The horses rear on their slender legs, and some of them neigh in answer. Soberfaced, the young riders stroke the horses' necks and soothe them, whispering, "Quiet, quiet, there my beauty, my hope. . . ." They begin to form in rank along the starting line. The crowds along the racecourse are like a field of grass and flowers in the wind. The Festival of Summer has begun.

Do you believe? Do you accept the festival, the city, the joy? No? Then let me describe one more thing.

In a basement under one of the beautiful public buildings of Omelas, or perhaps in the cellar of one of its spacious private homes, there is a room. It has one locked door, and no window. A little light seeps in dustily between cracks in the boards, secondhand from a cobwebbed window somewhere across the cellar. In one corner of the little room a couple of mops, with stiff, clotted, foul-smelling heads, stand near a rusty bucket. The floor is dirt, a little damp to the touch, as cellar dirt usually is. The room is about three paces long and two wide: a mere broom closet or disused tool room. In the room a child is sitting. It could be a boy or a girl. It looks about six, but actually is nearly ten. It is feeble-minded. Perhaps it was born defective, or perhaps it has become imbecile through fear, malnutrition, and neglect. It picks its nose and occasionally fumbles vaguely with its toes or genitals, as it sits hunched in the corner farthest from the bucket and the two mops. It is afraid of the mops. It finds them horrible. It shuts its eyes, but it knows the mops are still standing there; and the door is locked; and nobody will come. The door is always locked; and nobody ever comes, except that sometimes — the child has no understanding of time or interval — sometimes the door rattles terribly and opens, and a person, or several people, are there. One of them may come in and kick the child to make it stand up. The others never come close, but peer in at it with frightened, disgusted eyes. The food bowl and the water jug are hastily filled, the door is locked, the eyes disappear. The people at the door never say anything, but the child, who has not always lived in the tool room, and can remember sunlight and its mother's voice, sometimes speaks. "I will be good," it says. "Please let me out. I will be good!" They never answer. The child used to scream for help at night, and cry a good deal, but now it only makes a kind of whining, "eh-haa, eh-haa," and it speaks less and less often. It is so thin there are no calves to its legs; its belly protrudes; it lives on a half-bowl of corn meal and grease a day. It is naked. Its buttocks and thighs are a mass of festered sores, as it sits in its own excrement continually.

They all know it is there, all the people of Omelas. Some of them have come to see it, others are content merely to know it is there. They all know that it has to be there. Some of them understand why, and some do not, but they all understand that their happiness, the beauty of their city, the tenderness of their friendships, the health of their children, the wisdom of their scholars, the skill of their makers, even the abundance of their harvest and the kindly weathers of their skies, depends wholly on this child's abominable misery.

This is usually explained to children when they are between eight and twelve, whenever they seem capable of understanding; and most of those who come to see the child are young people, though often enough an adult comes, or comes back, to see the child. No mater how well the matter has been explained to them, these young spectators are always shocked and sickened at the sight. They feel disgust, which they had thought themselves superior to. They feel anger, outrage, impotence, despite all the explanations. They would like to do something for the child. But there is nothing they can do. If the child were brought up into the sunlight out of that vile place, if it were cleaned and fed and comforted, that would be a good thing, indeed; but if it were done, in that day and hour all the prosperity and beauty and delight of Omelas would wither and be destroyed. Those are the terms. To exchange all the goodness and grace of every life in Omelas for that single, small improvement: to throw away the happiness of thousands for the chance of the happiness of one: that would be to let guilt within the walls indeed.

The terms are strict and absolute; there may not even be a kind word spoken to the child.

Often the young people go home in tears, or in a tearless rage, when they have seen the child and faced this terrible paradox. They may brood over it for weeks or years. But as time goes on they begin to realize that even if the child could be released, it would not get much good of its freedom: a little vague pleasure of warmth and food, no doubt, but little more. It is too degraded and imbecile to know any real joy. It has been afraid too long even to be free of fear. Its habits are too uncouth for it to respond to humane treatment. Indeed, after so long it would probably be wretched without walls about it to protect it, and darkness for its eyes, and its own excrement to sit in. Their tears at the bitter injustice dry when they begin to perceive the terrible justice of reality, and to accept it. Yet it is their tears and anger, the trying of their generosity and the acceptance of their helplessness, which are perhaps the true source of the splendor of their lives. Theirs is no vapid, irresponsible happiness. They know that they, like the child, are not free. They know compassion. It is the existence of the child, and their knowledge of its existence, that makes possible the nobility of their architecture, and poignancy of their music, the profundity of their science. It is because of the child that they are so gentle with children. They know that if the wretched one were not there snivelling in the dark, the other one, the flute-player, could make no joyful music as the young riders line up in their beauty for the race in the sunlight of the first morning of summer.

Now do you believe in them? Are they not more credible? But there is one more thing to tell, and this is quite incredible.

At times one of the adolescent girls or boys who go to see the child does not go home to weep or rage, does not, in fact, go home at all. Sometimes also a man or woman much older falls silent for a day or two, and then leaves home. These people go out into the street, and walk down the street alone. They keep walking, and walk straight out of the city of Omelas, through the beautiful gates. They keep walking across the farmlands of Omelas. Each one goes alone, youth or girl, man or woman. Night falls; the traveler must pass down village streets, between the houses with yellow-lit windows, and on out into the darkness of the fields. Each alone, they go west or north, towards the mountains. They go on. They leave Omelas, they walk ahead into the darkness, and they do not come back. The place they go towards is a place even less imaginable to most of us than the city of happiness. I cannot describe it at all. It is possible that it does not exist. But they seem to know where they are going, the ones who walk away from Omelas.

Chapter 3

Communities and Conversation

Communities

■ ■ DEFINING "COMMUNITY"

According to the definition offered in Chapter 1, arguing is a social activity. It takes places within communities and contexts. Up until now we have looked at arguments out of context. Now I would like to focus on arguments in their native habitat: human communities.

The word *community* comes from a Latin word meaning "common" or "shared." In its broadest sense, *community* describes a group of people who have something in common. Even though every human is unique, we still have much in common. We were all born. We all eat. We will all die. And because human babies, unlike the young of some other animals, are unable to provide for themselves at first, those of us who survived infancy had someone to take care of us and provide for us. This relationship between child and parent (whether biological or adopted) is perhaps the most fundamental of all human communities.

We have other things in common besides our basic humanity. We are social by nature. Even though we might be able to get along by ourselves, most of us choose to be with other people. Communities may be formed by those who share the same social interests: a bridge club, a bowling team, a literary society, a group of friends, a couple out on a date. Or people may join together because of shared business interests: a professional partnership, the employees of a company, shareholders in a corporation, real estate agents, home buyers and other consumers. Communities may be defined by political views: Republicans, Democrats, legislatures, courts, school boards, political action groups, Rush Limbaugh's radio audience.

Communities may be defined by geographical location or may consist of people sharing a common history, language, and culture. The United States is a nation consisting of states, counties, cities, neighborhoods, and individual dwellings. These are communities, defined geographically. The United States also consists of many groups of people with different histories, languages, and cultures. Even those who speak English may not speak the same English as that spoken in other communities. Communities may consist of those who share common values and beliefs, possess common characteristics, or have a common mission or goal. Religious organizations, for instance, often transcend geographical boundaries, involving people from various backgrounds in a common form of worship. Disciplines within the university and scholarly organizations often define themselves according to a common body of knowledge, method of inquiry, or domain of study. Even though they are both part of the university or college community, the English department and the physics department define themselves quite differently as separate communities.

You may have noticed that many of these communities overlap. I, for instance, belong to one community defined geographically. I live in the city of American Fork, a small town in the state of Utah. I live in the United States. I belong in other communities because of my employment and economic status in society. I live in a new home in a suburban, middle-class neighborhood. Many of the people who live around me have also built new homes. Most have white-collar jobs, many of them in software design and development. (When I was in graduate school at Arizona State University, I rented an apartment in a working-class neighborhood where nearly everyone rented. Most made just enough money to live on.) I commute fifteen miles each way to Provo to teach English at Brigham Young University. Because I am an English professor, I belong to a department, in a college, at a university. I also belong to professional organizations made up of English professors and others who share my research and teaching interests. I am a member of other communities because of my political and religious beliefs.

▨ ▨ LANGUAGE AND COMMUNITY

Nearly all people who interact with one another in any community do so, to a certain extent, through a common language. In a way, this common language helps to define any community. Language initiates us into the world of the community and allows us to participate by giving us the power to communicate. The word *communicate* actually comes from the same Latin root as the word *community*. Communication is the process of sharing and making things common through language. We learn the common names for people, places, objects, emotions, and actions. We receive the values and beliefs of the community through language. Language creates a common bond among humans — a community — and this community then passes on its common knowledge to new members of the community through language.

This process begins in the most basic of human communities, the relationship between parent and child. As young children, we spend much of our time developing language skills at home, but the process does not stop there. We soon join other communities: school classes, church groups, groups of friends and acquaintances, clubs, work groups, states, and nations. Each time we attempt to enter a community, we do so through the process of acquiring the knowledge of that community through learning its language. When I was a child, my friends and I had a club with our own secret terms and code words. Those secret words identified us as a group and distinguished us from those who did not belong. Anyone who wanted to join our group had to learn the secret language. Much the same principle applies whenever an individual wants to join any new community. We acquire what is common by learning to communicate in the particular language of that community.

Fraternities, sororities, and other social organizations have certain rituals, creeds, and oaths by which new members are initiated into the group and learn its values. Golfers use special terms to describe their game, and you can often identify an experienced golfer by the way he or she talks. One joins the medical profession by learning the skills of a doctor and what doctors know. Students acquire this knowledge by learning the language of medicine, how doctors talk about their work. Doctors learn about the body by naming its parts and describing its functions. Surgeons can certainly be shown how to perform an operation, but in order to "see" the separate steps of the operation, they also learn to describe the process in language.

Of course, you may be able to learn the language of a community without becoming a full member. Talking like an experienced golfer does not make you one. You can't become an experienced golfer without learning the language of the sport, but you can learn the language of the sport without even being an actual golfer. No one could be a member of my childhood club without learning the code words, but someone could learn the code words and still not be a member. Learning the language is an essential part of joining a community, but it is usually not the only requirement.

▨ ▥ THE COLLEGE COMMUNITY

Sometimes, writing teachers refer to the common language that binds a community as "discourse" and a community defined by this common language as a "discourse community." A university or college is a discourse community. It is separated from the world around it not only by geographical boundaries and physical barriers but also by language. Terms from the language spoken at a university include "associate professor," "credit hour," "add/drop," "general education," "electives," "majors," "rush week," "study group," "quad," "student union," "syllabus." Some first-time college students struggle with this foreign language, and no one bothers to define these terms for them because experienced members of the community have forgotten that there was a time when the terms weren't familiar. The problem is compounded by the fact that the larger university is made up of many smaller discourse communities defined by separate disciplines, departments, majors, and fields of study. When students come to the university, they may plan on studying biology or history or economics, but a lot of what they end up studying is how scholars talk about these subjects. Even classes that focus on skills require students to learn the vocabulary for talking about these skills.

Applying the Principles

■ ■ IDENTIFYING COMMUNITIES

I described some of the communities I belong to. Now it's your turn. Use the following list to give you ideas. (You may be able to come up with some ways of defining community that I haven't thought of here.)

geographical location

values and beliefs

characteristics

economic, political, and professional interests

social and recreational interests

history, culture, and language

education and skills

family and race

gender

In what ways do these communities overlap? In what ways are they different? In what ways do they come into conflict with one another? Do you act differently when you are in one community rather than another? Do you act the same way with your friends as you do at home, at school, at work, or at church? How do you account for these differences?

Try to understand as much about the community as you can. Is it an intimate or private community, such as a family? Is it recreational or social community, such as a fraternity, club, or team? Is it an educational community, such as a class or study group? Is it a vocational or professional community, such as a workplace or a labor union? Is it a political or public community, such as a group supporting a particular candidate or a volunteer organization?

Consider the forces that have shaped the community. What are members of the community like as individuals? What is their personality and temperament? Are some members of the community more influential than others? What is the influence on the community's beliefs or other social institutions and groups, such as families, marriage partners, schools, churches, or peer groups? What influence do political and economic concerns have? What are the common beliefs of the community? Where is there agreement and disagreement? What is the spectrum of attitudes found in the community?

If you take some time to share your list with other members of the class, you will begin to understand the diversity of experiences that you and your classmates bring to the community formed by your common membership in the class.

▦ ▦ YOUR COLLEGE COMMUNITY AS A LANGUAGE COMMUNITY

Because you are a student, a lot of your life right now is associated with school. And a lot of the communities you belong to are school-related. You are going to be doing a lot of writing in that college community called the "classroom," so you need to think about how college communities are defined. In the following essay, David Russell, an associate professor of English at Iowa State University, describes college discourse communities and talks about some of the problems students have entering into these different communities. As you read through this essay, think about the following questions:

1. How is the contemporary college or university different from the college of the nineteenth century?
2. What "different worlds" can you identify within your own college or university? How are these "small worlds" different from communities you belong to outside the university?
3. What differences in language exist in these different worlds? Is what you write and the way you write different for classes in different departments and for professors in different disciplines? Is what you read or what you say different? Is the way you read or the way you talk different?
4. As a student, how do you identify these differences and adapt to them?

Writing in the Academic Disciplines

DAVID RUSSELL

BEFORE THE ADVENT of the modern university in the 1870s, academia was indeed a single discourse community. Institutions of higher learning built an intellectual and social community by selecting students primarily on the basis of social class (less than 1 percent of the population was admitted), which guaranteed linguistic homogeneity, and by initiating them intellectually through a series of highly language-dependent methods — the traditional recitation, disputation, debate, and oral examination of the old liberal curriculum. Equally important, most students shared common values (Christian, often sectarian) with their teachers (primarily ministers). They pursued a uniform course of study and were then duly welcomed as full members of the nation's governing elite.

The modern university changed all that. It provided the specialized knowledge that drove the new urban-industrial economy and a new class of specialized *professionals* (the term came into use during the period) who managed that economy, with its secular rationale and complex bureaucratic organization — what Burton J. Bledstein has aptly called "the culture of professionalism." Beginning with the land-grant colleges of the late nineteenth century and continuing with the rise of the modern university on the German model, the academic discourse community became fragmented. Numbers swelled, with enrollments tripling as a percentage of the population between 1900 and 1925 alone. Students from previously excluded social groups were admitted, destroying linguistic homogeneity. The new elective curriculum was introduced to prepare students for a host of emerging professional careers in the new industrial society. The elective curriculum compartmentalized knowledge and broke one relatively stable academic discourse community into many fluctuating ones. And the active, personal, language-dependent instructional methods of the old curriculum were replaced by passive, rather impersonal methods borrowed from Germany or, later, from scientific management: lecture, objective testing, and the like. Ultimately, the professional faculty who replaced the gentlemen scholars and divines of the old curriculum came to see secondary and undergraduate education as only one of several competing responsibilities (along with graduate teaching, research, and professional service). And the teaching of writing — initiating the neophytes into a discourse community — suffered accordingly.

Because it is tempting to recall academia's very different past and hope for a very different future, the term *academic community* has powerful spiritual and political connotations, but today academia is a *discourse* community only in a context so broad as to have little meaning in terms of shared linguistic forms, either for the advancement of knowledge (which now goes on in disciplinary communities and subcommunities) or for the initiation of new members (who are initiated into a specific community's discourse). Thus, to speak of the academic community as if its members shared a single set of linguistic conventions and traditions of inquiry is to make a categorical mistake. In the aggregate of all the tightly knit, turf-conscious disciplines and departments, each of its own discourse community, the modern university consists. Many have wished it otherwise.

Despite these profound changes, American educators have continued to think of the academic community as holding out a single compositional norm, which would speak intelligently about the multiform new knowledge to a "general reader." . . . Though academia held onto a generalized ideal of an academic community sharing a single advanced literacy, there was never any consensus in the modern university about the nature of that community or its language. Academic discourse, like academia itself, continued its drive toward increasing specialization. The university became an aggregate of competing discourse communities; it was not a single community. But the myth of a single academic discourse community — and a golden age of student writing — endured.

American academia today (and for the last hundred years or so) is a com- 5
munity primarily in a broad institutional sense, a collection of people going
about a vast enterprise, in much the same way that we speak of the "business
community" as a sector of national life. The academic disciplines are in one sense
united through their common missions: teaching, research, and service. But disciplines have been so diverse, so independent, and so bound up with professional
communities outside academia that they require no common language or even
shared values and methods within the university in order to pursue those missions. Those genres and conventions of writing that are shared by all academic
disciplines are also shared by professional communities outside academia. And
within academia, the conventions (and beyond them the assumptions and meth-
odologies) of the various disciplines are characterized more by their differences
than by their similarities. . . . Indeed, an academic is likely to have more linguistic
common ground with a fellow professional in the corporate sector than with
another academic in an unrelated field, except in regard to purely institutional
matters (governance, academic freedom, teaching loads, etc.). As a leading sociologist of higher education, Burton Clark, puts it, academia is made up of
"small worlds, different worlds."

The Organization of Communities

▓ ▓ UNDERSTANDING HOW COMMUNITIES ARE STRUCTURED

Every community has an organization, a structure of power, a "hierarchy"
of positions or roles taken by individuals within the community. I use the term
organization to refer to the relationships of power and influence among individuals in a community and the effect that these power relationships have on the life
of the community. An organization can be as complex as an international corporation or government body or as simple as a family or a tennis doubles team.
It can consist of two or three people or of many millions. Some organizations
have numerous subdivisions, smaller organizations with the larger organization.
Organizations usually involve some sort of work, mission, or set of goals, and
they are as varied as the communities they structure.

Within every organization is a distribution of power as well as processes for
exchanging information (communicating), making decisions, and enforcing decisions. The organization of a community may govern conditions for the use of
language: who speaks, when they speak, how, in what manner, for how long,
what they are allowed to say, why they speak. It may also determine how decisions are made, enacted, and enforced: Who makes decisions? How are they
made? When and where are they made? In what manner? To what end or purpose? The communication and decision-making processes of an organization
may be explicit and formal, as in the case of legislative bodies, committees, and

courts, or they may be implicit and essentially informal, as in the case in families and social groups. For example, a group of friends may make up a community within which a certain organization exists with its own communication and decision-making processes. When the group gets together for a night out, it is because someone made some decisions, influenced others through language, and brought about this group action.

Even communities that have an official organization may still have communication and decision-making processes that are implicit and informal. There may be an "unofficial" organization behind the explicit organization, and the people with the most important titles may not necessarily have the most power in the organization. Considerable power, for example, may be in the hands of staff or support people who work behind the scenes. Discovering such an unofficial organization may be more important than learning the official structure.

It is easy to recognize formal organizations, such as a court or a legislature. The U.S. Senate, for instance, is a community of one hundred political representatives from the fifty states. Within this community is a hierarchy of power, an organization. First of all, there is a formal organization. The vice president of the United States is the president of the Senate, but a member of the Senate is selected as the Senate's president *pro tempore,* or acting president. There is a Senate majority leader and minority leader. The Senate is divided into committees with representatives from the two major political parties. The floor of the Senate is divided according to party affiliation. Each senator has one vote. There are rules governing such matters as who can speak, how long each can speak, who can propose a bill or resolution, and how debate and voting are to be conducted. There are also informal structures of power. Some senators wield more influence than others. Some have been in the Senate longer. Some are more persuasive or more knowledgeable about the political process. Some come from larger states with valuable electoral votes. The organization of the Senate influences the life of the community in important ways, and anyone who wants to join the community and take a place within this organization needs to understand how it works.

Understanding the organization of the community — its distributions of power, its processes for communication and decision-making — is an essential part of living in any community. David Bleich defines the essence of persuasive power as knowing how to say something that matters to the people that matter. For instance, a group of first-year writing students debating the issue of national health care may influence one another's beliefs and may even have an effect on how some individuals vote. But these students can actually have very little influence on national health care policy — unless they can persuade a powerful member of our national community — such as a member of Congress, a lobbyist, or an influential member of the media — to represent their views. The influence a group of individuals can have on major policy issues may still seem quite small, but understanding something about arguing and the structure of organizations may allow individuals greater access to power than they realized was possible. Sometimes a few letters to a congressional representative can influence his or her vote on an issue, particularly when the issue is not a highly publicized one such as national health care.

■ ■ THE ORGANIZATION OF YOUR COLLEGE COMMUNITY

The university or college community that you belong to as a student is a complex organization. Beginning students are often frustrated because they don't understand who to go to for help with a problem, who has the power to make and enforce decisions, or who they can talk to when they have questions. Students often complain about the "impersonal" nature of the university bureaucracy, but such is the nature of any complex organization. When students leave the university and enter the world of work, they often have some of the same feelings of frustration and alienation. Understanding something about organizations may help ease these frustrations and perhaps encourage you to make the organizations you enter more responsive to the needs of individuals.

My University Community   Brigham Young University, where I teach, is a large and complex organization, serving over 28,000 students. It is a church-sponsored university, governed by a Board of Trustees made up from the leadership of the church. It has a president, who is responsible for all the affairs of the university and is accountable to the Board of Trustees. Working beneath the president is a provost, who oversees the daily functions of the university and coordinates the council of vice presidents. These vice presidents oversee the academic and nonacademic organizations of the university. Academic organizations include colleges, departments, libraries, and research centers, while nonacademic organizations include student housing and life, the physical plant, grounds and maintenance, the bookstore, and employee benefits.

I belong to the English department, which is part of the College of Humanities. The chair of the English department answers to the dean of the college, who is governed by the academic vice presidents. The chair has two associate chairs who help administer the department. The chair's decisions are guided by the Department Advisory Council, a council made up of professors of different ranks, some of whom are elected by department members and some of whom are appointed. Various other committees and subcommittees within the department also advise the chair and make decisions related to their sphere of influence.

I am the Associate Composition Coordinator. I work along with the Composition Coordinator, who is a member of the advisory council. Together we oversee all general education composition courses taught through the department. We plan course material, hire and train instructors, and handle student complaints. I also teach graduate and undergraduate courses in rhetoric and writing and in eighteenth-century English literature, and I am assigned to spend a quarter of my time doing research.

Your Community   What is your place within the university organization? How does the organization you find yourself in as a college student affect how you write? What role do you have in debating, deciding, and enforcing community beliefs and actions? What role do you have in deciding what is taught or how it is taught? What role do you have in deciding how students, faculty, and staff are treated, how funds are allocated, or how the university interacts with other communities?

Unfortunately, at most universities students usually have little power and responsibility, even though they provide the university with its existence. Most of the writing students do — exams, papers, lab reports, class notes — does not have much of an effect on the university organization, certainly not as much as the memos written by presidents, deans, department heads, professors, and regents.

Applying the Principles

As a class, describe the organization of your college or university in as much detail as you can. Pay particular attention to how your class is organized and how your class fits into the larger structure of the university. You may need to do some research in the university catalogue or handbook. As an individual, consider how you fit within the organization of the class. Make an outline of the organization for the department that houses your major. Who is the department chair? Are there any associate chairs? How are decisions made in the department? What role do students have in the decision-making process? How does the department fit within the larger structure of the university? It might help for you to talk to some of the professors in your major department, if you have decided on one.

"Sites" of Communication

■ ■ IDENTIFYING SITES

It is important to understand the channels, or "sites," of communication within an organization and how these relate to the structure of power and decision-making. Here are some important questions to ask:

How do individuals within the organization communicate with one another?

Where do they meet? When? Under what circumstances?

In what way do they communicate? Who is allowed to speak? For how long?

How is the communication process tied to the decision-making process?

How are the communication and decision-making processes tied to the mission or work of the organization?

The sites of communication are the "places" that members of the community meet to discuss, debate, and decide the affairs of the community. These can be quite diverse: legislatures, courts, churches, newspapers, call-in radio shows, television talk shows, electronic bulletin boards, libraries, and computer databases. By investigating the sites of communication yourself, you will become aware of the different rules and conventions that govern a community.

First of all, try to identify the common forms or genres that arguments take within the community: letters to the editor, letters to public figures, presentations at public forums, demonstrations and protests, fliers and newsletters, articles and essays, memos, detailed policy proposals, informal and formal debate.

Pay attention to the differences among communities and the differences within a single community. The same people who gather at a local church are not all the same people who gather at the town hall or the student union, and they don't talk about the same issues in the same way. Even within the same site, there can be significant differences in how individuals use language. Take a church congregation for example. A church is a place where people come together to worship and use language as part of the act of worship: praying, singing, preaching, instructing, conversing. It is a site of conversation for a religious community. Although the congregation is defined by the physical place in which they meet and by the registration of their names as members of that church, not all members of the congregation use language in the same way. The minister, for instance, has a different relationship to the rest of the congregation than the individual members have to one another. And ministers use language in a way different from the other members of the congregation.

Sites of communication can be actual locations: church buildings, courtrooms, the student union. Nearly every university has a place on campus where people gather to speak out on public issues. At Arizona State University, people gather near the fountain in front of the student union or on the lawn west of the library. They discuss religion and politics but also promote campus and club events. Universities also have more formal sites: classrooms, seminars, panel discussions. These have a different set of rules than, say, the fountain in front of the student union.

▦ ▦ MEDIA AS SITES

Sites of communication can be more abstract "places" as well. The telephone can create a place where a community of two can gather, and conference calling can open the electronic community to even more participants. You can use the telephone to participate in a conversation about political issues. For instance, you can call the White House:

To register your opinion: (202) 456-1111

To find out when a bill was signed or vetoed: (202) 456-2226

To reach the president: (202) 456-1414

To reach the vice president: (202) 456-2326

You can call the Sierra Club for the latest environmental news at (202) 547-5550 or get information on AIDS from the AIDS hotline (1-800-AIDS-411) or find out about cancer research by dialing 1-800-4-CANCER.

A newspaper or a magazine is a site where staff and readership "gather" to discuss public issues, although the discussion is written rather than spoken. A newspaper or magazine also consists of smaller sites of communication that differentiate the readership of the publication into smaller communities. A newspaper's opinion page, for example, provides a forum for the editors to express their views on public political issues and usually includes space for readers to express their views in the form of letters. This forum is very different from the food section or the sports section. One reader of a newspaper may belong to the community defined by the opinion page, while another may only look at the sports section.

Similarly, a television program is a site where producers, on-camera personnel, and viewers gather to use language in particular ways. Radio call-in shows create a community of listeners, some of whom use the combined media of the telephone and the radio to speak out on public issues.

Of course, like other communities, the communities created by the media reflect power relationships. Not everyone in the community is equal: Some have greater access to the media as a site of communication. Newspapers and magazines have editors and publishers who decide which voices are heard in their publications. Television and radio stations have station managers who decide what gets on the air. Even radio call-in programs, which seem rather democratic, have a producer who decides what callers get on the air, what they get to talk about, and how long they get to speak. In addition, not everyone has access to newspapers, radios, or televisions. Most people can only participate in these media in limited ways. But understanding how the media work as sites of communication may provide you with greater access.

▪ ▪ COMPUTER NETWORKS AS SITES

Computers have created new sites of communication. You may be familiar with electronic discussion groups or conferences. If your computer is equipped with a modem, it can establish links with other computers, and you can send messages back and forth through electronic mail (e-mail).

Many colleges now have e-mail accounts that can be created for students for a small fee. Many businesses now strive for "paperless" offices where all correspondence takes place electronically. If you have access to e-mail, you can even fire off a quick note to the White House at the following addresses:

president@whitehouse.gov

vice.president@whitehouse.gov

Of course, you can still send mail to the White House the old fashioned way by writing to the following address:

The White House
1600 Pennsylvania Avenue N.W.
Washington, D.C. 20500

You can also send e-mail to congress:

househlp@hr.house.gov (for information on Congressional e-mail services)

comments@hr.house.gov (to make comments about the service)

georgia6@hr.house.gov (Newt Gingrich, Speaker of the House)

slabmgnt@hr.house.gov (Subcommittee on Labor-Management Relations)

natres@hr.house.gov (Committee on Natural Resources)

housesst@hr.house.gov (Committee on Science, Space, and Technology)

Check with your local senator or representative to see whether he or she has e-mail access.

Electronic mail also makes electronic discussion groups possible. An electronic discussion group is made up of a list of subscribers who receive mail at a common computer address. A message sent to that address is distributed to all members of the group. The participants in this electronic conversation may never meet one another face to face; rather, they meet in an electronic space created by the computer, called "virtual space." Now, participants in electronic communities communicate through written text, but with the refinement of computer graphics and interactive video, participants may be able to meet in a virtual reality of their own creation.

Learning to communicate through virtual media is becoming an increasingly important part of a writer's education. If you have access to e-mail, you may want to experience one of these electronic communities first hand. Joining an electronic community is similar to joining the university community: You have to learn a new way of writing, you become familiar with authorities, and you even become a bit of a specialist yourself, advancing to the point where you may feel comfortable entering the conversation.

You can access all kinds of information and conversations through a network of computers called the "World Wide Web." Some colleges universities make "web" connections available to students through library terminals or computer classrooms and labs. You can navigate the web using software such as Netscape, Mosaic, or Lynx. (Check with your school's computer support office for more information.) The White House now has an on-line "Interactive Citizens' Handbook" that provides access to all electronic government information on the Internet, information about Cabinet-level and independent agencies, a virtual tour of the White House, and facts about the president, vice president, and their families. Citizens can access this handbook using Netscape, Mosaic, or Lynx at http://www.whitehouse.gov

See the appendix for more information on electronic discussion groups and World Wide Web sites.

▓ ▓ THE LIBRARY AS A SITE

Among the most abstract sites of communication are those housed in the library: academic journals, trade magazines, popular magazines, newspapers, government documents, books, and other library resources. Academic journals are publications written and edited by scholars and researchers for other scholars. They are usually published every three or four months, although some may only be published twice a year. Academic journals are typically bound in card stock (a kind of heavy paper) and printed on plain paper, with few advertisements or photographs. They meet the needs of very specialized academic communities and include titles such as *Protein Science, Harvard Law Review, Journal of Abnormal Psychology, Journal of Public Policy,* or *Shakespeare Quarterly.*

Trade magazines, which often have a format similar to popular magazines, are geared toward particular trades, professions, or interest groups. They are usually published once a month, often on slick paper and with many advertisements and photographs. Some trade magazines look more like newspapers or academic journals, particularly if the readership is somewhat limited. Trade magazines include titles like *WordPerfect Magazine* (for the software industry), *Waste Age* (for the sanitation industry), or *Photography* (for professional photographers as well as hobbyists).

Popular magazines are published at least once a month, and some are published weekly. Nearly all are published on slick paper, with high-quality, glossy photographs and professional page layout and design. Many popular magazines try to attract a large audience from across the nation. Others focus on specific interest groups. As popular magazines become more specialized, it becomes more difficult to distinguish them from trade magazines. Popular magazines include titles such as *People, Seventeen, Parenting, Newsweek, Time, Cosmopolitan, Woman's Day, Esquire,* and *Business Week.*

Government documents include the records and publications of local, county, and state governments, as well as publications of the U.S. government, some foreign governments, and international organizations such as the United Nations or the World Health Organization. They include the proceedings of the U.S. Congress, as well as the reports of specific committees and subcommittees. Government documents usually resemble academic journals, printed on plain paper and bound in card stock.

Journals, magazines, government documents, books, and other library resources are all "places" where people communicate with one another and are all part of a great conversation. Kenneth Burke describes this conversation in figurative terms:

Imagine that you enter a parlor. You come late. When you arrive, others have long preceded you, and they are engaged in a heated discussion, too heated for them to pause and tell you exactly what it is about. In fact, the discussion had already begun long before any of them got there, so that no one present is qualified to retrace for you all the steps that had gone before. You listen for a while until you decide that you have caught the tenor of the argument; then you put in your oar. Someone answers; you answer him; another comes to your defense; another aligns himself against you. . . . However, the discussion is interminable. The hour grows late, you must depart. And you do depart, with the discussion still in progress.[1]

Writers are separated from another by time and space, but they "speak" to each other from the shelves of the library. When you do library research, you follow some thread in this conversation. Research is the process of getting caught up on the conversation and preparing to join the conversation yourself. Of course, you can't ask a book questions the way you might ask friends questions to help you catch up on a conversation you were just entering. But still a book or academic journal can reveal a lot about the conversation of which it is a part and the communities that participate in that conversation.

Applying the Principles

▒ ▒ OBSERVING SITES OF COMMUNICATION

You can't understand what sites of communication are or how communities are organized by reading about them in a book. You have to get out and observe these sites and communities yourself. Go to the places on campus where people gather to talk. Pay attention to what goes on in your classes. Find out what people talk about and how. Figure out how these sites fit within the larger organization of the college community. Visit some sites of communication in your city or town: city council meetings, courts, and other political meetings. Observe the communities created by electronic media, including computer media.

▒ ▒ ANALYZING THE SITES IN THE LIBRARY

Library research is an important part of identifying and reviewing parts of the various academic conversations in progress. (Actually, any time you observe a site of conversation, you are "doing research"; you are finding out what people have said, what the important issues are, what claims have been made regarding

[1] Kenneth Burke, *The Philosophy of Literary Form: Studies in Symbolic Action* (Berkeley: U of California P, 1973) 110–11.

these issues, and how people go about debating and discussing these claims.) Before doing library research on a particular topic, it will help you to learn something about the kinds of conversations that take place in library resources, particularly in journals and books.

Journals   Academic journals are often associated with a formal scholarly organization. For instance, *PMLA* is a journal published by the Modern Language Association, an association of scholars devoted to the study of language, literature, and writing. It is the official site of conversation for members of this community. *The Quarterly Journal of Speech* is an official publication for the Speech Communication Association of America, while *The Journal of the American Medical Association* is sponsored by the national society for the medical profession. Although not every journal is affiliated with a particular scholarly organization, most are nonetheless associated with a community of scholars, organized by their common interest in a particular field of study.

Recent issues of academic journals are usually found in a "current periodicals" or "unbound serials" section of the library. Locate this part of the library and examine some journals that represent a field of study you are interested in. Learn what you can about the community that is represented by the journal and the conversations that take place there. Examine the outside cover, the inside cover, and title pages. Usually, an academic journal will have some sort of editorial statement, defining the kinds of articles it publishes and the required format for articles to be considered for publication. It usually lists the name and address of the editor, the place of publication, and an editorial board. The editorial board is generally made up of established members of the scholarly community associated with the journal. They review articles that are submitted to the journal and give the editor advice on which should be published and how they should be revised. A journal may identify its association with a professional organization.

You can learn about the community it represents by examining the contents of a journal. Find out what kind of writing is included: essays, reviews, reader comments, calls for papers, announcements, advertisements? Read a few of the essays. How are they organized? How do authors introduce and conclude the essays? What kind of documentation style is used? What counts as evidence? What issues are important? What kind of claims do authors make? Scan some of the past issues of the journal. (Usually, the library binds past issues of journals and shelves them among the library books or in a separate "bound periodicals" section of the library.) By reviewing past issues, you can see how the conversation has evolved over time. Pay particular attention to the first issue. It will usually contain a statement about why the journal came into existence and what community it is designed to serve.

You may find your first attempt to follow the conversation in an academic journal a bit frustrating. The authors use unfamiliar words and allude to ideas and other essays that you may know little about, leaving you disoriented. This is a normal feeling for anyone entering into a conversation for the first time. The longer you listen in, however, and the more you read, the more familiar you will become with the conversation. You are taking the first steps toward becoming an experienced member of the community. If you remain committed to the community, one day you may find yourself one of the experienced members of the community. Every member of the editorial board of an academic journal also began his or her life in the scholarly community ignorant and inexperienced.

To understand how journals and magazines represent different types of communities, you may also want to examine journals that are directed toward a profession or trade and compare these journals with other academic journals. Try *Journal of the American Medical Association,* the *Harvard Business Review, Waste Age, Psychology Today,* or *Personal Computing (PC).* As you briefly review the conversations in these journals, how do they differ from those in other journals you have surveyed? How do these academic and trade journals differ from some of the popular magazines you may be familiar with?

Books   You can examine a book in much the same way that you examine a journal. Check the cover and title page for as much information as you can find about the book and its author. Find out which company or press published the book and whether it is part of a series. Look up any information you can find about the publishers of the book. Do they have some statement of editorial policy and some sense of the community they serve? Look for biographical information about the author, often found at the end of the book or on the dust jacket. Read any forewords, prefaces, or acknowledgements, in which the author speaks to the reader about the book, often offering valuable information about how the book came into being. Read the table of contents and the opening section; scan the remaining sections to discover what context the author provides for his or her writing. Survey the bibliography or list of "works cited" to get a sense of the conversation of which this book is a part. Finally, read published reviews of the book to find out how other members relate the book to the larger conversation of the intellectual community. (Your library may have the *Book Review Index* or *Book Review Digest* to help you find reviews of books. For more recent reviews, check a newspaper index, such as the *New York Times Index* or the *Washington Post Index.* The *New York Times Book Review* is a particularly good place to find reviews of recent books.)

All of this may seem like a lot of work, but it is preparing you to enter into a conversation about ideas by identifying and observing places where that conversation takes place. Understanding the conventions of a site of conversation is an essential part of joining that conversation, not only for academic communities but for all communities. As you read and observe, you not only become aware of issues that you may want to know more about or respond to, you also learn how to make a response.

The activities I have been recommending are, in fact, library research. These may be unlike the kinds of library research you have done in the past, when you began with a topic or topic question and then went to the library to find information on the topic. For a traditional research paper assignment, your classroom is the site of academic conversation, and your teacher is the primary audience; your research goal is to find out what others are saying about your topic so that you can report this information to your teacher. In some classrooms, the conversation takes place only between teacher and student, but many teachers now try to expand the conversation to involve other students through group work, collaborative writing, or oral reports. These teaching techniques expand the community within which you write beyond the individual student and teacher. I'm asking you to expand that sense of community even further — beyond the classroom — by examining the sites where academic and other conversations take place. Find out what the issues are, and then prepare to join the conversation.

■ ■ OTHER COMMUNITIES AND OTHER VOICES

Academic communities are very important for students, but most students leave the academic community when they graduate. Because this book is designed, in part, to help you succeed in your academic writing, I have focused on the college community in this chapter. But you can apply the same techniques you used in analyzing your college community to analyzing other communities you belong to. The following readings describe other communities: a high school, a business, a virtual computer community, and political communities. They also analyze how each community is organized and how language works within the community. As you read these selections, consider the following questions about how the community described in each is organized:

1. Who makes decisions? How are they made? When and where are they made? In what manner? To what end or purpose?
2. What are the sites of communication? Who speaks? When do they speak? How long? In what manner? What are they allowed to say? What motivates people to participate in the discussion?
3. How does the description of each community fit with your own experience of the community?

What High School Is

THEODORE R. SIZER

MARK, SIXTEEN and a genial eleventh-grader, rides a bus to Franklin High School, arriving at 7:45. It is an Assembly Day, so the schedule is adapted to allow for a meeting of the entire school. He hangs out with his friends, first outside school and then inside, by his locker. He carries a pile of textbooks and notebooks; in all, it weighs eight and a half pounds.

From 7:30 to 8:19, with nineteen other students, he is in Room 304 for English class. The Shakespeare play being read this year by the eleventh grade is *Romeo and Juliet*. The teacher, Ms. Viola, has various students in turn take parts and read out loud. Periodically, she interrupts the (usually halting) recitations to ask whether the thread of the conversation in the play is clear. Mark is entertained by the stumbling readings of some of his classmates. He hopes he will not be asked to be Romeo, particularly if his current steady, Sally, is Juliet. There is a good deal of giggling in class, and much attention paid to who may be called on next. Ms. Viola reminds the class of a test on this part of the play to be given next week.

The bell rings at 8:19. Mark goes to the boys' room, where he sees a classmate who he thinks is a wimp but who constantly tries to be a buddy. Mark avoids the leech by rushing off. On the way, he notices two boys engaged in some sort of transaction, probably over marijuana. He pays them no attention. 8:24. Typing class. The rows of desks that embrace big office machines are almost filled before the bell. Mark is uncomfortable here: typing class is girl country. The teacher constantly threatens what to Mark is a humiliatingly female future: "Your employer won't like these erasures." The minutes during the period are spent copying a letter from a handbook onto business stationery. Mark struggles to keep from looking at his work; the teacher wants him to watch only the material from which he is copying. Mark is frustrated, uncomfortable, and scared that he will not complete his letter by the class's end, which would be embarrassing.

Nine tenths of the students present at school that day are assembled in the auditorium by the 9:18 bell. The dilatory tenth still stumble in, running down aisles. Annoyed class deans try to get the mob settled. The curtains part; the program is a concert by a student rock group. Their electronic gear flashes under the lights, and the five boys and one girl in the group work hard at being casual. Their movements on stage are studiously at three-quarter time, and they chat with one another as though the tumultuous screaming of their schoolmates were totally inaudible. The girl balances on a stool; the boys crank up the music. It is very soft rock, the sanitized lyrics surely cleared with the assistant principal. The girl sings, holding the mike close to her mouth, but can scarcely be heard. Her light voice is tentative, and the lyrics indecipherable. The guitars, amplified, are tuneful, however, and the drums are played with energy.

The students around Mark — all juniors, since they are seated by class — 5 alternately slouch in their upholstered, hinged seats, talking to one another, or sit forward, leaning on the chair backs in front of them, watching the band. A boy near Mark shouts noisily at the microphone-fondling singer, "Bite it . . . ohhh," and the area around Mark explodes in vulgar male laughter, but quickly subsides. A teacher walks down the aisle. Songs continue, to great applause. Assembly is over at 9:46, two minutes early.

9:53 and biology class. Mark was at a different high school last year and did not take this course there as a tenth-grader. He is in it now, and all but one of his classmates are a year younger than he. He sits on the side, not taking part in the chatter that goes on after the bell. At 9:57, the public address system goes on, with the announcements of the day. After a few words from the principal ("Here's today's cheers and jeers . . . " with a cheer for the winning basketball team and a jeer for the spectators who made a ruckus at the gymnasium), the task is taken over by officers of ASB (Associated Student Bodies). There is an appeal for "bat bunnies." Carnations are for sale by the Girls' League. Miss Indian American is coming. Students are auctioning off their services (background catcalls are heard) to earn money for the prom. Nominees are needed for the ballot for school bachelor and school bachelorette. The announcements end with a "thought for the day. When you throw a little mud, you lose a little ground."

At 10:04 the biology class finally turns to science. The teacher, Mr. Robbins, has placed one of several labeled laboratory specimens — some are pinned in frames, others swim in formaldehyde — on each of the classroom's eight laboratory tables. The three or so students whose chairs circle each of these benches are to study the specimen and make notes about it or drawings of it. After a few minutes each group of three will move to another table. The teacher points out that these specimens are of organisms already studied in previous classes. He says that the period-long test set for the following day will involve observing some of these specimens — then to be without labels — and writing an identifying paragraph on each. Mr. Robbins points out that some of the printed labels ascribe the specimens names different from those given in the textbook. He explains that biologists often give several names to the same organism.

The class now falls to peering, writing, and quiet talking. Mr. Robbins comes over to Mark, and in whispered words asks him to carry a requisition form for science department materials to the business office. Mark, because of his "older" status, is usually chosen by Robbins for this kind of errand. Robbins gives Mark the form and a green hall pass to show to any teacher who might challenge him, on his way to the office, for being out of a classroom. The errand takes Mark four minutes. Meanwhile Mark's group is hard at work but gets to only three of the specimens before the bell rings at 10:42. As the students surge out, Robbins shouts a reminder about a "double" laboratory period on Thursday.

Between classes one of the seniors asks Mark whether he plans to be a candidate for schoolwide office next year. Mark says no. He starts to explain. The 10:47 bell rings, meaning that he is late for French class.

There are fifteen students in Monsieur Bates's language class. He hands out tests taken the day before: "*C'est bien fait, Etienne . . . c'est mieux, Marie . . . Tch, tch, Robert . . .* " Mark notes his C+ and peeks at the A− in front of Susanna, next to him. The class has been assigned seats by M. Bates; Mark resents sitting next to prissy, brainy Susanna. Bates starts by asking a student to read a question and give the correct answer. "*James, question un.*" James haltingly reads the question and gives the answer that Bates, now speaking English, says is incomplete. In due course: "*Mark, question cinq.*" Mark does his bit, and the sequence goes on, the eight quiz questions and answers filling about twenty minutes of time.

"Turn to page forty-nine. *Maintenant, lisez après moi . . .* " and Bates reads a sentence and has the class echo it. Mark is embarrassed by this and mumbles with a barely audible sound. Others, like Susanna, keep the decibel count up, so

10

Mark can hide. This I-say-you-repeat drill in interrupted once by the public address system, with an announcement about a meeting for the cheerleaders. Bates finishes the class, almost precisely at the bell, with a homework assignment. The students are to review these sentences for a brief quiz the following day. Mark takes note of the assignment, because he knows that tomorrow will be a day of busy-work in French class. Much though he dislikes oral drills, they are better than the workbook stuff that Bates hands out. Write, write, write, for Bates to throw away, Mark thinks.

11:36. Down to the cafeteria, talking noisily, hanging, munching. Getting to room 104 by 12:17: U.S. history. The teacher is sitting cross-legged on his desk when Mark comes in, heatedly arguing with three students over the fracas that had followed the previous night's basketball game. The teacher, Mr. Suslovic, while agreeing that the spectators from their school certainly were provoked, argues that they should neither have been so obviously obscene in yelling at the opposing cheerleaders nor have allowed Coke cans to be rolled out on the floor. The three students keep saying that "it isn't fair." Apparently they and some others had been assigned "Saturday mornings" (detentions) by the principal for the ruckus.

At 12:34, the argument appears to subside. The uninvolved students, including Mark, are in their seats, chatting amiably. Mr. Suslovic climbs off his desk and starts talking: "We've almost finished this unit, chapters nine and ten . . . " The students stop chattering among themselves and turn toward Suslovic. Several slouch down in their chairs. Some open notebooks. Most have the five-pound textbook on their desks.

Suslovic lectures on the cattle drives, from north Texas to railroads west of St. Louis. He breaks up this narrative with questions ("Why were the railroad lines laid largely east to west?"), directed at nobody in particular and eventually answered by Suslovic himself. Some students take notes. Mark doesn't. A student walks in the open door, hands Mr. Suslovic a list, and starts whispering with him. Suslovic turns from the class and hears out this messenger. He then asks, "Does anyone know where Maggie Sharp is?" Someone answers, "Sick at home"; someone else says, "I thought I saw her at lunch." Genial consternation. Finally Suslovic tells the messenger, "Sorry, we can't help you," and returns to the class: "Now, where were we?" He goes on for some minutes. The bell rings. Suslovic forgets to give the homework assignment.

1:11 and Algebra II. There is a commotion in the hallway: someone's locker   15
is rumored to have been opened by the assistant principal and a narcotics agent. In the five-minute passing time, Mark hears the story three times and three ways. A locker had been broken into by another student. It was Mr. Gregory and a narc. It was the cops, and they did it without Gregory's knowing. Mrs. Ames, the mathematics teacher, has not heard anything about it. Several of the nineteen students try to tell her and start arguing among themselves. "O.K., that's enough." She hands out the day's problem, one sheet to each student. Mark sees with dismay that it is a single, complicated "word" problem about some train that, while traveling at 84 mph, due west, passes a car that was going due east at

55 mph. Mark struggles: Is it $d = rt$ or $t = rd$? The class becomes quiet, writing, while Mrs. Ames writes some additional, short problems on the blackboard. "Time's up." A sigh; most students still writing. A muffled "Shit." Mrs. Ames frowns. "Come on, now." She collects papers, but it takes four minutes for her to corral them all.

"Copy down the problems from the board." A minute passes. "William, try number one." William suggests an approach. Mrs. Ames corrects and cajoles, and William finally gets it right. Mark watches two kids to his right passing notes; he tries to read them, but the handwriting is illegible from his distance. He hopes he is not called on, and he isn't. Only three students are asked to puzzle out an answer. The bell rings at 2:00. Mrs. Ames shouts a homework assignment over the resulting hubbub.

Mark leaves his books in his locker. He remembers that he has homework, but figures that he can do it during English class the next day. He knows that there will be an in-class presentation of one of the *Romeo and Juliet* scenes and that he will not be in it. The teacher will not notice his homework writing, or won't do anything about it if she does.

Mark passes various friends heading toward the gym, members of the basketball teams. Like most students, Mark isn't an active school athlete. However, he is associated with the yearbook staff. Although he is not taking "Yearbook" for credit as an English course, he is contributing photographs. Mark takes twenty minutes checking into the yearbook staff's headquarters (the classroom of its faculty adviser) and getting some assignments of pictures from his boss, the senior who is the photography editor. Mark knows that if he pleases his boss and the faculty adviser, he'll take that editor's post for the next year. He'll get English credit for his work then.

After gossiping a bit with the yearbook staff, Mark will leave school by 2:35 and go home. His grocery market bagger's job is from 4:45 to 8:00, the rush hour for the store. He'll have a snack at 4:30, and his mother will save him some supper to eat at 8:30. She will ask whether he has any homework, and he'll tell her no. Tomorrow, and virtually every other tomorrow, will be the same for Mark, save for the lack of the assembly: each period then will be five minutes longer.

Most Americans have an uncomplicated vision of what secondary education   20
should be. Their conception of high school is remarkably uniform across the country, a striking fact, given the size and diversity of the United States and the politically decentralized character of the schools. This uniformity is of several generations' standing. It has, however, two appearances, each quite different from the other, one of words and the other of practice, a world of political rhetoric and Mark's world.

A California high school's general goals, set out in 1979, could serve equally well most of America's high schools, public and private. This school had as its ends:

- Fundamental scholastic achievement . . . to acquire knowledge and share in the traditionally academic fundamentals . . . to develop the ability to make decisions, to solve problems, to reason independently, and to accept responsibility for self-evaluation and continuing self-improvement.
- Career and economic competence . . .
- Citizenship and civil responsibility . . .
- Competence in human and social relations . . .
- Moral and ethical values . . .
- Self-realization and mental and physical health . . .
- Aesthetic awareness . . .
- Cultural diversity . . .[1]

In addition to its optimistic rhetoric, what distinguishes this list is its comprehensiveness. The high school is to touch most aspects of an adolescent's existence — mind, body, morals, values, career. No one of these areas is given especial prominence. School people arrogate to themselves an obligation to all.

An example of the wide acceptability of these goals is found in the courts. Forced to present a detailed definition of "thorough and efficient education," elementary as well as secondary, a West Virginia judge sampled the best of conventional wisdom and concluded that

> there are eight general elements of a thorough and efficient system of education:
> (a) Literacy, (b) The ability to add, subtract, multiply, and divide numbers,
> (c) Knowledge of government to the extent the child will be equipped as a citizen to make informed choices among persons and issues that affect his own governance, (d) Self-knowledge and knowledge of his or her total environment to allow the child to intelligently choose life work — to know his or her options,
> (e) Work-training and advanced academic training as the child may intelligently choose, (f) Recreational pursuits, (g) Interests in all creative arts such as music, theater, literature, and the visual arts, and (h) Social ethics, both behavioral and abstract, to facilitate compatibility with others in this society.[2]

That these eight — now powerfully part of the debate over the purpose and practice of education in West Virginia — are reminiscent of the influential list, "The Seven Cardinal Principles of Secondary Education," promulgated in 1918 by the National Education Association, is no surprise.[3] The rhetoric of high school pur-

---

[1] Shasta High School, Redding, California. An eloquent and analogous statement, "The Essentials of Education," one stressing explicitly the "interdependence of skills and content" that is implicit in the Shasta High School statement, was issued in 1980 by a coalition of educational associations. Organizations for the Essentials of Education (Urbana, Illinois).

[2] Judge Arthur M. Recht, in his order resulting from *Pauley v. Kelly,* 1979, as reprinted in *Education Week,* May 26, 1982, p. 10. See also, in *Education Week,* January 16, 1983, pp. 21, 24, Jonathan P. Sher, "The Struggle to Fulfill a Judicial Mandate: How Not to 'Reconstruct' Education in W. Va."

[3] Bureau of Education, Department of the Interior, "Cardinal Principles of Secondary Education: A Report of the Commission on the Reorganization of Secondary Education, appointed

pose has been uniform and consistent for decades. Americans agree on the goals for their high schools.

That agreement is convenient, but it masks the fact that virtually all the words in these goal statements beg definition. Some schools have labored long to identify specific criteria beyond them; the result has been lists of daunting pseudospecificity and numbing earnestness. However, most leave the words undefined and let the momentum of traditional practice speak for itself. That is why analyzing how Mark spends his time is important: from watching him one uncovers the important purposes of education, the ones that shape practice. Mark's day is similar to that of other high school students across the country, as similar as the rhetoric of one goal statement to others'. Of course, there are variations, but the extent of consistency in the shape of school routine for a large and diverse adolescent population is extraordinary, indicating more graphically than any rhetoric the measure of agreement in America about what one does in high school, and, by implication, what it is for.

The basic organizing structures in schools are familiar. Above all, students are grouped by age (that is, freshman, sophomore, junior, senior), and all are expected to take precisely the same time — around 720 school days over four years, to be precise — to meet the requirements for a diploma. When one is out of his grade level, he can feel odd, as Mark did in his biology class. The goals are the same for all, and the means to achieve them are also similar.

Young males and females are treated remarkably alike; the schools' goals are the same for each gender. In execution, there are differences, as those pressing sex discrimination suits have made educators intensely aware. The students in metalworking classes are mostly male; those in home economics, mostly female. But it is revealing how much less sex discrimination there is in high schools than in other American institutions. For many young women, the most liberated hours of their week are in school.   25

School is to be like a job: you start in the morning and end in the afternoon, five days a week. You don't get much of a lunch hour, so you go home early, unless you are an athlete or are involved in some special school or extracurricular activity. School is conceived of as the children's workplace, and it takes young people off parents' hands and out of the labor market during prime-time work hours. Not surprisingly, many students see going to school as little more than a dogged necessity. They perceive the day-to-day routine, a Minnesota study reports, as one of "boredom and lethargy." One of the students summarizes: School is "boring, restless, tiresome, put ya to sleep, tedious, monotonous, pain in the neck."[4]

The school schedule is a series of units of time: the clock is king. The base

---

by the National Education Association," *Bulletin* no. 35 (Washington: U.S. Government Printing Office, 1918).

[4] Diane Hedin, Paula Simon, and Michael Robin, *Minnesota Youth Poll: Youth's Views on School and School Discipline,* Minnesota Report 184 (1983), Agricultural Experiment Station, University of Minnesota, p. 13.

time block is about fifty minutes in length. Some schools, on what they call modular scheduling, split that fifty-minute block into two or even three pieces. Most schools have double periods for laboratory work, especially in the sciences, or four-hour units for the small numbers of students involved in intensive vocational or other work-study programs. The flow of all school activity arises from or is blocked by these time units. "How much time do I have with my kids" is the teacher's key question.

Because there are many claims for those fifty-minute blocks, there is little time set aside for rest between them, usually no more than three to ten minutes, depending on how big the school is and, consequently, how far students and teachers have to walk from class to class. As a result, there is a frenetic quality to the school day, a sense of sustained restlessness. For the adolescents, there are frequent changes of room and fellow students, each change giving tempting opportunities for distraction, which are stoutly resisted by teachers. Some schools play soft music during these "passing times," to quiet the multitude, one principal told me.

Many teachers have a chance for a coffee break. Few students do. In some city schools where security is a problem, students must be in class for seven consecutive periods, interrupted by a heavily monitored twenty-minute lunch period for small groups, starting as early as 10:30 A.M. and running to after 1:00 P.M. A high premium is placed on punctuality and on "being where you're supposed to be." Obviously, a low premium is placed on reflection and repose. The students rush from class to class to collect knowledge. Savoring it, it is implied, is not to be done much in school, nor is such meditation really much admired. The picture that these familiar patterns yield is that of an academic supermarket. The purpose of going to school is to pick things up, in an organized and predictable way, the faster the better.

What is supposed to be picked up is remarkably consistent among all sorts 30 of high schools. Most schools specifically mandate three out of every five courses a student selects. Nearly all of these mandates fall into five areas — English, social studies, mathematics, science, and physical education. On the average, English is required to be taken each year, social studies and physical education three out of the four high school years, and mathematics and science one or two years. Trends indicate that in the mid-eighties there is likely to be an increase in the time allocated to these last two subjects. Most students take classes in these four major academic areas beyond the minimum requirements, sometimes in such special areas as journalism and "yearbook," offshoots of English departments.[5]

Press most adults about what high school is for, and you hear these subjects listed. *High school? That's where you learn English and math and that sort of thing.* Ask students, and you get the same answer. High school is to "teach" these "subjects."

What is often absent is any definition of these subjects or any rationale for

---

[5] I am indebted to Harold F. Sizer and Lyde E. Sizer for a survey of the diploma requirements of fifty representative secondary schools, completed for *A Study of High Schools.*

them. They are just there, labels. Under those labels lie a multitude of things. A great deal of material is supposed to be "covered"; most of these courses are surveys, great sweeps of the stuff of their parent disciplines.

While there is often a sequence *within* subjects — algebra before trigonometry, "first-year" French before "second-year" French — there is rarely a coherent relationship or sequence *across* subjects. Even the most logically related matters — reading ability as a precondition for the reading of history books, and certain mathematical concepts or skills before the study of some of physics — are only loosely coordinated, if at all. There is little demand for a synthesis of it all; English, mathematics, and the rest are discrete items, to be picked up individually. The incentive for picking them up is largely through tests and, with success at these, in credits earned.

Coverage within subjects is the key priority. If some imaginative teacher makes a proposal to force the marriage of, say, mathematics and physics or to require some culminating challenges to students to use several objects in the solution of a complex problem, and if this proposal will take "time" away from other things, opposition is usually phrased in terms of what may be thus foregone. If we do that, we'll have to give up colonial history. We won't be able to get to programming. We'll not be able to read *Death of a Salesman*. There isn't time. The protesters usually win out.

The subjects come at a student like Mark in random order, a kaleidoscope of worlds: algebraic formulae to poetry to French verbs to Ping-Pong to the War of the Spanish Succession, all before lunch. Pupils are to pick up these things. Tests measure whether the picking up has been successful.

The lack of connection between stated goals, such as those of the California high school cited earlier, and the goals inherent in school practice is obvious and, curiously, tolerated. Most striking is the gap between statements about "self-realization and mental and physical growth" or "moral and ethical values" — common rhetoric in school documents — and practice. Most physical education programs have neither the time nor the focus really to ensure fitness. Mental health is rarely defined. Neither are ethical values, save at the negative extremes, such as opposition to assault or dishonesty. Nothing in the regimen of a day like Mark's signals direct or implicit teaching in this area. The "school boy code" (not ratting on a fellow student) protects the marijuana pusher, and a leechlike associate is shrugged off without concern. The issue of the locker search was pushed aside, as not appropriate for class time.

Most students, like Mark, go to class in groups of twenty to twenty-seven students. The expected attendance in some schools, particularly those in low-income areas, is usually higher, often thirty-five students per class, but high absentee rates push the actual numbers down. About twenty-five per class is an average figure for expected attendance, and the actual numbers are somewhat lower. There are remarkably few students who go to class in groups much larger or smaller than twenty-five.[6]

[6] Education Research Service, Inc., *Class Size: A Summary of Research* (Arlington, Virginia, 1978); and *Class Size Research: A Critique of Recent Meta-Analyses* (Arlington, Virginia, 1980).

A student such as Mark sees five or six teachers per day; their differing styles and expectations are part of his kaleidoscope. High school staffs are highly specialized: guidance counselors rarely teach mathematics, mathematics teachers rarely teach English, principals rarely do any classroom instruction. Mark, then, is known a little bit by a number of people, each of whom sees him in one specialized situation. No one may know him as a "whole person" — unless he becomes a special problem or has special needs.

Save in extracurricular or coaching situations, such as in athletics, drama, or shop classes, there is little opportunity for sustained conversation between student and teacher. The mode is a one-sentence or two-sentence exchange: *Mark, when was Grover Cleveland president?* Let's see, was 1890 . . . or something . . . wasn't he the one . . . he was elected twice, wasn't he . . . *Yes . . . Gloria, can you get the dates right?* Dialogue is strikingly absent, and as a result the opportunity of teachers to challenge students' ideas in a systematic and logical way is limited. Given the rushed, full quality of the school day, it can seldom happen. One must infer that careful probing of students' thinking is not a high priority. How one gains (to quote the California school's statement of goals again) "the ability to make decisions, to solve problems, to reason independently, and to accept responsibility for self-evaluation and continuing self-improvement" without being challenged is difficult to imagine. One certainly doesn't learn these things merely from lectures and textbooks.

Most schools are nice places. Mark and his friends enjoy being in theirs. The 40 adults who work in schools generally like adolescents. The academic pressures are limited, and the accommodations to students are substantial. For example, if many members of an English class have jobs after school, the English teacher's expectations for them are adjusted, downward. In a word, school is sensitively accommodating, as long as students are punctual, where they are supposed to be, and minimally dutiful about picking things up from the clutch of courses in which they enroll.

This characterization is not pretty, but it is accurate, and it serves to describe the vast majority of American secondary schools. "Taking subjects" in a systematized, conveyer-belt way is what one does in high school. That this process is, in substantial respects, not related to the rhetorical purposes of education is tolerated by most people, perhaps because they do not really either believe in those ill-defined goals or, in their heart of hearts, believe that schools can or should even try to achieve them. The students are happy taking subjects. The parents are happy, because that's what they did in high school. The rituals, the most important of which is graduation, remain intact. The adolescents are supervised safely and constructively most of the time, during the morning and afternoon hours, and they are off the labor market. That is what high school is all about.

What Is Management All About?

A. L. MINKES

W HAT IS management itself? What does it mean, and what are the tasks and   1
qualities which are required of managers?

There are three ways of looking at this topic. The first might be called the
conventional way of examining definitions of the kind which many books consider. The second is concerned with the reality of the manager's day, the fragmented life and varied pressures which are the regular experience. The third
approach is to analyze management as an idea — what it is that managers are
doing when they are engaged in management. This focuses not on the specific
functions they perform but on the inherent nature of management activity.

ON DEFINITIONS OF MANAGEMENT

Definitions can serve several purposes. They tell the reader what the subject
means, or at least what the author means by it. In this way, they mark out the
area of discussion, influence the method of approach to a subject, and simultaneously indicate what is *not* included within it. This can be extremely important;
think of the following examples drawn from economics.

In 1932 the late Lord Robbins published his famous book *An Essay on the
Nature and Significance of Economic Science,* in which he defined economics as a
science which studied the allocation between competing ends of scarce resources
which have alternative uses. This definition greatly influenced many economists
and the way the subject was studied, because it focused attention on relative
scarcity and on prices. That is quite different from studying economics as, say,
the history and structure of economic institutions. Jacob Viner said that "economics is what economists do": and Keynes, in his introduction to the *Cambridge Economic Handbook Series* (1922), characterized the theory of economics
as a method, "a technique of thinking." This way of looking at the subject in-
clines economists towards the construction of analytical models rather than the
empirical study of behavior in organizations.

Similarly with management: some definitions emphasize the element of co-   5
ordination of resources, others the task of managing people. For some writers,
the elements of leadership and direction hold the center of the stage; for others,
planning and control are the crucial features.

So what can be picked out as characteristics of management in the profusion
of definitions?

1. A first and striking feature of management is that it exists essentially because of the existence of organizations. Of course it is true that individuals are
said to manage their affairs, personal, financial, and career: an individual may
"manage" his investment portfolio or his estate, and a one-man business, which
can hardly be said to be an organization, can be said to require managing. But

this is a rather superficial use of the term "management," which means no more than to say that men and women have to look after their business matters and personal concerns. When they are members of organizations, as when they are employed in a firm, their arrangements are part of a network which involves other people, perhaps in very large numbers.

This may seem so obvious as to be hardly worth saying: managers must be very well aware of this. But it is worth emphasizing for a number of reasons. A manager is not a Robinson Crusoe: he does not carry on his activities or make his decisions on his own. Herbert Simon put it in this way, that when an executive makes a decision, he does so with one eye on the matter in hand and one eye on its organizational consequences. Managers know, in other words, that what they do affects other members of the organization and they in turn are affected by the actions of others. Thus management involves a relationship of interdependence, in all kinds of ways. Decisions about production involve requirements for the purchase of materials or components; the transfer of staff from one task to another creates the need to consider the vacancies it causes.

Just as managers are not isolated individuals, so their actions are not isolated incidents, and management requires, therefore, an awareness of a whole set of interrelationships. The study of management is partly the study of managerial action, but it is also the study of how that action is generated and processed in the framework of organization.

2. A second feature is that management is about the genesis and progress   10
of change. In a totally unchanging world, there would be no requirement for management at all. When people say that there is a problem of managing change, they are in a sense understating matters, because management *is about* change. One way of expressing it is to say that in an unchanging world there would only be the administrative task of keeping things going, of administering established routines and procedures. Suppose, for example, that a large retail organization has an established system allowing customers to return articles which they have purchased and which turn out not to be suitable. Marks and Spencer do this: clothing bought in any of their stores can be returned to any other of their stores throughout Britain. The rules which Marks and Spencer apply in this respect are well-known and long-established. A store manager may doubtless exercise discretion in borderline cases, but the procedure appears to be quite standard. This is fundamentally a matter of administration.

Consider another instance: a group of civil servants in a very closely regulated, partly legally-based department (overseas) were discussing with a visiting academic the possibility of running a series of management seminars for the staff. The academic visitor asked some of them what their work consisted of, and they replied "We administer the ordinances." Since they claimed that they had no discretion in interpreting the ordinances and when in doubt "We consult a senior officer," he concluded that they had explicit administrative tasks but they had not shown him that they exercised a managerial function. Once again, this was a matter of administration.

At what point could these examples be translated into a management situation? When a business is considering whether or not to *change* its procedures, or when, as in the case of the civil-servants, the discussion turned to possible *changes* in the organization of their department, management questions were bound to arise. These are quite modest examples of changes, which serve to show, nevertheless, that a transition from administration to management occurs as soon as questions are raised of the type: what procedures should we institute, what new rules are appropriate, what new methods are appropriate? These are management questions: it is only when they have been answered and decisions have been made about them that the task of administering the rules can begin.

Of course, the point has been exaggerated for the sake of exposition: the distinction between management and administration is not always perfectly clear and precise. But the principle is valid.

3. An important approach to definitions of management is that it involves working through other people. The work of managers requires them to organize others: they have to allocate tasks to subordinates and to supervise and control the results. One consequence is that managers are dependent on the skills and performance of other people, and, interestingly enough, this is more significant the higher up the management chain they are. The apex of the pyramid ultimately rests on its base. In a sense, therefore, to be at the top of the organization means both to be in a position of authority and to be in a position of dependence. The balance between authority, and the power conferred by it, and reliance on others will vary from one business to another, depending on their size, managerial style, cultural traditions, and so on. But companies do recognize this factor. For example, John Neville, who was chief executive of Manganese Bronze, spoke of the relationship between the group headquarters and the subsidiaries as one in which the center had to rely on the ability of the senior executives in the subsidiaries. It had to trust them; and the word *trust* was used explicitly by Sir Patrick Meaney, who was chief executive of Thomas Tilling, and Gordon Yardley, managing director of its subsidiary company Newey and Eyre, to describe the relationship between them. In turn, Yardley saw his relationship with his subordinates in the same light: he expressed it by saying that when he planned a visit to a branch of his company, he checked first with the branch manager that it was acceptable. This picture of dependence does not imply absence of authority and power. The same John Neville made it clear that the subsidiary had to deliver the goods: if not, the company could replace the senior executives with others who would do the job. What this means is that choosing people in whom reliance can be placed, who can be *depended on,* in other words, is a critical task in management. But this dependence which comes from working through other people has two other substantial consequences. One is that management has a waiting aspect; managers spend part of their time waiting for the results of tasks which they have delegated to others. The other, and more important, consequence is that management means taking responsibility for the activities of others. In a marvelous and courageous passage in his history of *The Second World War,* Winston Churchill comments as follows about his horrified discovery that Singapore, far from being a fortress, was acutely vulnerable to landbased

attack: "I ought to have known. My advisers ought to have known and I ought to have been told, and I ought to have asked."

Churchill was here emphasizing the doctrine of ultimate responsibility — where the buck stops — and it is a lesson which can be applied at all levels of management where managers are concerned with the work of others who report to them. How this responsibility can be honored and by what means of control, formal and informal, managers can reconcile the burden of responsibility with the delegation of tasks to others (who cannot be supervised every moment of the day) is one of the major management questions in the modern business corporation.

4. Since management is concerned with change, it can be seen to have an entrepreneurial as well as an administrative aspect. There is a good deal of debate about the meaning of the term "entrepreneur," but for the purposes of this chapter entrepreneurship is taken to be concerned with three things:

a. determination of the mission or basic direction of the enterprise;
b. choice of strategy for effecting the business purposes;
c. creation of the corporate structure, i.e. the organizational means for devising and implementing strategy.

Thus Sir Adrian Cadbury in defining the strategic characteristics of Cadbury Schweppes made this series of statements. At one time, before the merger with Schweppes, Cadburys' business could have been defined in terms of its basic raw material, the cocoa bean. Now it could be classified as the supply of snack foods of which it happens that many are covered with chocolate: since, furthermore, the company is essentially a marketing concern, it can be defined in the context of its distribution outlets, e.g. supermarkets.

Similarly, Robin Martin, who, at the head of Tarmac, presided over its development into a major construction company, categorized it within construction and civil engineering, a view which top direction of the company continued to hold. In going on to strategic choice, Martin spoke particularly of diversification, within that context, as a means of fostering growth.

Concern with "mission" and "strategic choice" must lie with managers; with whom else? With which managers and at which levels of the organization are other matters, which belong to later chapters. That they are part of management responsibility is crucial, since from this idea flows a whole set of commitments and tasks, and a picture of what constitutes an effective manager.

The third point mentioned above was the creation of the organization. Professor Ansoff has pointed out that in traditional economic theory the manager was perceived as what he calls "an operator of a fixed arm." By this he meant that the manager was regarded as somebody who took a set of inputs (labor, materials, equipment) and used them in the "best" combinations so as to produce output at minimum cost. In reality, however, a large part of management is concerned with the design and establishment of the structure of the organization. As will be seen later in this book, the formation of strategy is an abstract exercise without the organizational means of making it effective. Textbooks of management rightly concentrate attention on the importance of organization, and this is not a "given": it has to be designed and created. In a very large company with numerous departments and divisions this may seem obvious, but it is interesting that management has to face this task even when the business is of quite modest size. The British industrialist John Crabtree emphasized this point in an unpublished manuscript describing the growth of his firm, which made electrical products, from its inception with "a man and a boy" in 1921 to about 1,000 employees in 1935, when he died. He thought that organizations did not grow "naturally" and that at successive increments of two or three hundred employees, management needed to consider how to reconstruct the ways in which it handled its tasks.

On the Manager's Working Day

In a conversation with the author a number of years ago, Professor Bela Gold   20
remarked that at the University of Pittsburgh it had been his custom to take graduate students downtown to observe for themselves how executives actually spent their time. He thought it might disabuse them of the notion that executives sat back in order to brood on long-term strategic developments: It could be that in fact they were struggling to keep the in-tray from overflowing.

The daily life of the manager is filled with specific tasks and current pressures. The managing director of a large British company, when asked how he felt that industrial management differed from academic life, replied that he thought it much more *fragmented*. "I do not find it difficult," he said, "to find a spare hour to devote to one job, but I find it extremely difficult to find two successive hours."

Curzon give a very apt example of a manager's working day, illustrating an imaginary but realistic factory manager responsible to the company's managing director. His engagement diary records his anticipated arrangements:

0845	Deal with day's correspondence	1145	Work on preparation of preliminary estimates documents
0915	Meeting with R & D department head: discussion on delay in presentation of new design	1230	Working lunch with industrial editor of national newspaper
0930	Meeting with union representative: grievances concerning new shift system	1345	Further tour loading bays
1000	Tour of loading bays: observations of procedures	1415	Further preparation of estimates document
1030	Meeting with departmental heads: discussion of preliminary estimates for next financial year	1515	Meeting with . . . overseas marketing manager: discussion on developments in S E Asian markets.

Curzon goes on to comment:

> In the event, the 0930 meeting continues until 1030, and preparation of the estimates document, programmed for 1145, is abandoned in favor of an emergency meeting with factory shop stewards, designed to head off a conflict concerning the allocation of overtime. Throughout [his] day he is involved in the process of communication, e.g. listening, observing, ordering, persuading, writing.

These passages are used by Curzon to stress the manager's role in "the processes of communication," but they also serve to underline four critical aspects of management life. The first, as has already been suggested, is its *fragmentation* and the short time which can be given to individual important topics. The second is the *variety* of matters which come before the manager's attention: new design, union grievance, loading bay procedures, estimates, working lunch with journalist, overseas markets. Thirdly, there is the variety of *people* with whom he is involved: department heads, union representative, journalist, company marketing manager. Lastly, there is the problem of *delay and interruption* — the extended 0930 meeting, and the emergency meeting which leads him to defer the preparation of the estimates document, very important job though that must clearly be. And if the experience of being dean of a faculty in a university is any guideline, there are other interruptions: for example, the telephone, the indispensable deadly instrument, and the sheer amount of time it takes to get from one place to another.

It is not surprising, therefore, that writers like Handy should lay stress on the manager's problem of living "in two or more dimensions":

> The manager is, above all, responsible for the future. . . .
> But this management of the future has to go hand in hand with the responsibility for the present. . . . It is not easy to live in two or more time dimensions at once. It is hard to plan creatively for five years hence with a redundancy interview scheduled for one hour's time. Just as routine drives out non-routine, so the present can easily obliterate the future. By concentrating on the problems of the present the future becomes in its turn a series of present problems or crises, intervention by the manager in a power role becomes legitimate, even essential, there is still less time available for the future, the manager feels indispensable and legitimized by crisis. The cycle has become self-fulfilling. *Unless the manager is able to live successfully in two time dimensions he will make the present more difficult than it need be and will unsuccessfully manage the future.* [Italics added]

This passage has been quoted at length because it forms a whole and poses the well-known problem of reconciling attention to present pressures with the need to attend to future concerns. This is not something which is confined to middle managers. Sir Isaac Wolfson, asked at a University of Birmingham seminar if running so large a business as Great Universal Stores did not give him ulcers, replied — jestingly, it is true — "No: they are for middle managers." But even top managers face the problem of fragmentation and variety of specific problems.

It is not difficult to find examples, and those which follow, from the experience of the Midlands Postal Region in Britain, illustrate the point. Senior management could not spend all its time thinking about long term strategic plans. It had to consider a range of individual topics.

As the mechanization of letter sorting offices advanced, the prospect arose in 1978–9 that, except for early morning mail, the "Stratford-upon-Avon" postmark would disappear, to be replaced by "Coventry" or a generic title. A simple enough matter of efficiency, it might be thought, but in fact a complicated, quite time-consuming affair which engaged attention at senior level. The local MP, district councillors and many local bodies, headed by the Shakespeare Birthplace Trust, lobbied fiercely to retain the Stratford postmark. They argued that it was regarded by overseas tourists, on whom Stratford depends so much for its prosperity, as an important feature for which "Coventry" was no substitute at all. Hence, the simple matter of efficiency turned out to be sufficiently significant to engage attention at the highest Post Office level (with the additional complication that in a public corporation political pressure is more difficult to resist). Or again, a postal business will be seriously affected by the availability and punctuality of the railway service, and any deficiencies may cause short-run crises as well as long-term policy problems. Machinery breakdown or industrial disputes with engineers assume a significance in the context of mechanization which can result in an engagements diary very like the hypothetical one outlined by Curzon.

One more example from the postal business deserves to be cited because it illustrates so well the "localized," specific problems which can occupy the time of managers. The business is labor-intensive, i.e. it has a relatively high input of labor, by contrast with telecommunications. It also involves an important element of what are called unsocial hours, because postal employees who make early morning deliveries of letters have to arrive very early at the sorting offices in preparation for their delivery "walk." Scrupulous though the Post Office may be in explaining this to young recruits to the business, the experience sometimes comes as an unpalatable shock in the dark early hours of winter, and some of them leave within a fairly short time. This creates problems for the business, and hence occupies the attention of managers, both in respect of supply of labor and of the cost of the training which has been invested in personnel and which has to be repeated for the replacement intake. 25

This chapter has given much attention to specific examples: they are certainly particular, but they are also typical. They are not intended to prove that managers are rushed off their feet all the time, that the pressure is unrelenting, and that time is an inexorable enemy of even a single long-term thought. But they lend practical force to the view expressed in the passage from Handy cited above, and they oblige managers to consider how to secure that life in two dimensions which he regards as essential if they are to perform successfully. That is why companies quite often try to devise means by which their managers can be got away from day-to-day pressures. They may use special "think tank" gatherings away from the office, "brainstorming sessions," seminars, project groups:

they may provide for occasions and facilities to encourage informal exchange of ideas.

THE CONCEPT OF MANAGEMENT

So far in this chapter, the implications of some characteristic definitions of management have been considered and some picture of the managerial day has been given. In this penultimate section, the purpose is to analyze the *nature* of management as an idea. In any organization, be it business or otherwise, men and women play many parts; each individual may play more than one part. The finance director of a company will have regard to financial matters and will also contribute to wider policy discussions on the board of directors of the enterprise. A manager may be engaged in some specific function and also be managing a department. The question to be examined now is: what is it that is being done which can properly be called *management?*

Consider an example. Suppose that a young man or woman has graduated from a university with a degree in chemistry and has found a job in the research and development department of a business enterprise. And suppose that he or she is put to work on the chemical properties of the materials which the company utilizes. Clearly such a person cannot be said to be engaged in *management,* since, whatever the formal status in the company, the work is that of a chemist — much as it might be if the same person were working in, say, a university laboratory.

Now suppose that the chemist is promoted to be head of the R & D department. It appears to become immediately obvious that the kind of work — *or significant part of it* — can legitimately be classified as management. Why is this so?

1. In the first place, it is virtually certain that there will no longer be as much time for chemistry and, particularly, for keeping up to date with fresh developments in the subject. Of course this will partly depend on the size of the department: the bigger and more varied its activities, the stronger the argument. (Similar circumstances are experienced by academics who assume significant administrative responsibilities.)

2. The kinds of decision with which the new head of the department is now concerned are quite different. Imagine that the department has been allocated a fixed budget of £x thousand, that it has ten chemically feasible projects in hand, and that to persist with all of them would exceed the budget. The head must accordingly either persuade higher management to increase the budget allocation or pare down the ten projects to, say, the *best* eight. But the criteria for choosing and the language in which the case will be argued will be economical, commercial, market criteria. Interested though the company may be in the inherent intellectual quality of the ideas which are generated in its research laboratories, its budget allocations must be judged against the contribution those

ideas will ultimately make to the "bottom line," the profit account of the company.

Or consider again:

3. As head of department, the manager has to think about a variety of staff questions. Colleagues whose projects do not receive what they regard as adequate funding may feel aggrieved. Then there will be matters of recruitment and promotion of staff to consider and questions of how to balance individual talents with organizational harmony. This requires an understanding, once again, of factors other than the chemistry of research products; it requires, rather, the chemistry of organization and human relations, of personnel and social psychology.

This analysis suggests that the transition into management is a movement *from specialist to generalist.* Beginning as a specialist in chemistry, working strictly within that discipline, the chemist has now to be concerned with a range of activities and decisions. This means co-ordinating variables from a variety of disciplines in which it is virtually certain that this particular individual is *not* expert and in which the company does employ experts. Thus, all management can be regarded as *general* management: the phase "specialist management" is a contradiction in terms.

Is this an exaggerated picture of the idea of management? Is it an excessively academic view? Is it not at variance with the earlier sections of this chapter which show the manager as a busy, practical person? Do managers sit back and analyze problems in terms of economics, sociology, and social psychology? Not everybody goes into business with a specialist training in chemistry or accounting or anything else with immediate applicability to a particular aspect of a company's activity. Graduates in English, history, geography, and young men and women who are not graduates at all take jobs in industry and commerce: on the other hand, many entrants have degrees or diplomas in business studies, so that they are quite well-equipped in the relevant disciplines. And even if the analysis is valid, is it not applicable mainly to large and bureaucratic business corporations?

It is true that the story of the chemist is hypothetical and simplified, that it is chosen partly to make a point: but that does not mean that it fails to get at the essence of management. Suppose, for example, that the head of the R & D department is promoted further so that the career progress looks like Figure 1.

Thus, the further that managers advance, the less can they be seen in a specialist function; and the more departments which fall within their ultimate responsibility, the more evident it becomes that their decisions are generalist and interdisciplinary in character. Although it is perfectly true, therefore, that managers perform specific tasks within specific functional areas of a company, it is also true that the peculiar characteristic of management as an idea lies in its generalist nature. Sometimes, in fact, this is expressed in the title "general manager" given to managers responsible for an area or division in which they are concerned with a number of departmental functions.

35

R & D department

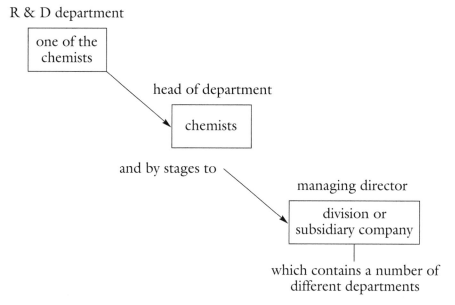

Figure 1
Career progress of the head of R & D.

SOME IMPLICATIONS AND CONCLUSIONS

The first implication which may be drawn from the foregoing analysis is by way of being a puzzle or a paradox. On the one hand, there has been a striking increase in the number of "expertises" and experts. Once upon a time, men spoke of the Renaissance man as the ideal, with a wide-ranging culture, and of the generalist, grounded perhaps in the classics, as the most appropriate man for top-level administration. But nowadays many subjects which once filled a single textbook have opened up into numbers of separate specialisms: there are accountants and tax accountants, lawyers and company lawyers, systems analysts and computer programmers. How is this compatible with the view that management is general management?

It means, first of all, that the task of management is more complex than in the past, because the number of special fields which are relevant to ultimate decisions is larger and the element of expertise is greater. This means, secondly, that the kind of general training which is suitable for development of managers had also changed, as was already pointed out in 1963 by the Franks Report on *British Business Schools*. This training, whether in formal education or through experience, is more likely to turn on business subjects, but not on any single discipline.

A second implication concerns the problem of promotion in management life. If management is general — so that the head of a police force need not have

40

been a policeman or the head of a postal business a postman — what are the advantages and disadvantages of bringing in managers from outside a company? This question is especially acute in organizations which have a high professional content: hospitals, social work departments, schools, colleges and universities. But they also exist in business. For example, if a company appoints a new sales director, what kind of background is essential or simply desirable? The late Sir Frederick Hooper, who was managing director of Schweppes (a considerable time before its merger with Cadbury), once described how, after looking at a number of candidates who had come up through the sales function, the company eventually chose as director a man from production. He had the qualities of understanding data and handling organization which outweighed his inexperience in the field of sales.

This anecdote is not a universal recommendation, and choices of this kind may raise very difficult problems within an organization. But it illustrates the point about general management and the practical difficulty that can arise in finding suitable general managers in a world where recruits enter on employment in a specific function.

There is a third aspect, which is concerned with what a business enterprise is required to do. In Professor Drucker's view, it exists essentially to supply products to consumers, who have to be willing to pay for them: This is the primary test of its performance and the measure of its success. He particularly, and other writers too, see business management, therefore, as an economic instrument, using economic resources to generate wealth and the power to create wealth. Management derives what Drucker calls its authority from its ability to meet customer demand at the relevant prices, and everything that managers do and all the decisions they make must be assessed against the test of economic performance. This means that the ability to identify where the market lies, to decide who the customer is, and to know how to satisfy wants, are inherent in the management task.

Even in a non-business, non-market situation, decisions have to be made about what are the right things to supply and how they can be most efficiently supplied. But the task of actually managing a complex organization, business or non-business, requires, as Drucker himself appreciates, a variety of skills and activities. The ultimate test may be economic performance but the management tasks cannot be defined solely in terms of economics. If there were a single "bottom line" for every management activity and decision, life would be immeasurably easier for managers: but there is not. Rosemary Stewart, who says that since "Managers' jobs vary so much" she doubted "the truth of the common statement 'a good manager can manage anything,'" adds:

> We quoted Sune Carlson's pioneering study of nine managing directors and subsequent studies, which show that typically the manager's day is a very fragmented one. This makes it harder to organize one's time effectively. Research has shown that *many managers require political skills* as well as the, more commonly emphasized, supervisory skills. [Italics added]

Two further implications may be drawn from the argument of this chapter. One is that a considerable part of the management task is concerned with the *internal environment* of the organization. Managers certainly have to be alert to the external environment, of customers, competitors, technology, government: without that they would be lost. But a great deal of this work centers round internal management: organizational design, committee or board meetings, discussions with other managers about personnel, and generally, in fact, maintaining the health of the organization and ensuring its innovative development.

The other implication is that management is an integrative activity. One of   45
the most forceful expressions of this view is made by Professor Kanter, who distinguishes organizations which are integrative and see problems as wholes from those which work by what she terms "walling off a piece of experience and preventing it from being touched or affected by any new experiences." She emphasizes a point which has been of basic importance in this chapter, that management requires the coordination of a variety of specialists, each with an approach to problems which reflects a specific background and training. The strength of an organization resides in its diversity, but, of course, the point is to bring together the diverse views so as to arrive at agreed courses of action. Within an organization, an integrative approach which avoids "walling off" means that ideas can move across internal, departmental frontiers, and that innovative practices can challenge the old and generate change.

Professor Kanter contrasts this approach with what she terms "segmentalism," which "assumes that problems can be solved when they are carved into pieces and the pieces are assigned to specialists who work in isolation." This is another issue: to the extent, however, that it emphasizes the significance of integrating specialisms, it underlines a central point of this chapter.

Life on the Net: We Hear America Modeming

PHIL PATTON

O NE NIGHT not long ago, Ed Krol, the venerable guru of the Internet,   1
alumnus of the National Center for Supercomputing Applications, and author of *The Whole Internet Catalog*, was "appearing" in one of America Online's "auditoriums." There, you could talk to him, or rather type to him, and he to you, albeit with the usual frustrating time hiccups called netlag.

Ed was carrying on, as is common these days, about bandwidth and the future of the information highway when all of a sudden, in front of a million potential audience members, a character with the on-line name PQ_4 Freak popped in and asked, "Wuzzup?" Ed went on about how fiber would bring the Internet to your home by the year 2000, and PQ_4 Freak typed, "HEL-

LOOOOOOOOOOOOOOO?" and was gone. Soon someone else wandered in to say, "Hello . . . I'm lost" as Ed continued typing about how you need a TCP/IP connection for raw Internet: "Oh, well, I'm outta here. Have fun."

Then a battery warning went off, and Ed himself ran off to plug in his PowerBook Duo Dock. "Back in about ten seconds," he typed.

It was just another evening in America's new living room, the world on-line, where the serious and the silly crossbreed surreally. Imagine if Letterman did his show on the sidewalk and people wandered in off Broadway.

All of a sudden, it seems that everyone is on-line. Rosie O'Donnell tests out   5
punch lines under dozens of names on America Online, and Madonna "reads bedtime stories" to promote her new single on the Underground Music Archive. ("You can interact with me," she begins, "but you can't touch me.") Rush Limbaugh and Billy Idol, NBC and *Scientific American* are on-line. There are downy-cheeked B-1 pilots and grizzled B-36 vets, gay square-dance clubs and bagpipe players. For all the high-minded, high-tech visions, a lot of the net is soft-core porn on ThrobNet, discussions of Spam and *Star Trek* on Prodigy, sadsack stories in "discussion rooms," and lounge-lizard come-ons on Teen Chat on AOL's People Connection. The net is the Lubavitchers and the Russians — Relcom and GlasNet helped turn back the coup of 1991. It is a report on the National Information Infrastructure from Al Gore's office and bits of gossip about Amy Fisher.

Once, the vision of cyberspace was a shimmering city in the sky. But what we've got on the screen so far is mostly words — words of SEC filings and NASA shuttle maintenance schedules, of conspiracy theories and alt.sex.stories. It's as if we had built the imaginary ultimate library Borges dreamed of, all the books in the world, linked together, but when we walked in, we found Bart Simpson at the checkout desk, playing Nintendo.

I. THE NET DEFINED

It's the Internet, of course, and the estimated ten to twenty million people around the world who use it, but it's much more. It's the commercial services — 1.3 million on Prodigy, 2 million on CompuServe, a million on AOL. It's Genie, Apple's eWorld, and thousands of small bulletin boards and access providers.

And the Internet itself? It's a network of innumerable computer networks representing thousands of hot, buzzing machines tended by dozing wireheads with cans of Jolt in their hands. For most of us, it is a vast thicket of services and files brought by an Internet access provider, who sells us the on-ramp, and in some cases the vehicle, to ride it — to chat, to download *Moby Dick* or twenty dissertations on *Moby Dick*.

But the real net is not located in hard disks or copper wires; it is a buzzing in our collective synapses — especially the synapses of dreamy, futuristic countercultural types. The net is the whole information infrastructure today and any number of dreams of what it can be tomorrow.

A decade ago, the vision of the net was introduced as "the matrix" in Wil-   10 liam Gibson's novel *Neuromancer*. Gibson made jacking into this cyberspace sound like a combination of Jack Daniel's and Disneyland. "Consensual hallucination," he called it, a place where "all the data in the world stacked up like one big neon city, so you could cruise around."

The reality is a dizzying landscape of domains and servers, nodes and browsers, where infobots scuttle through hyperlinks and trace threads, and whose ruling philosophy is complexity theory — the happy belief that this chaos will all sort itself out somehow, someday, and meanwhile, hey, go with the flow.

Getting on It: What You Need

What you need is a fast computer and a fast modem. Modems come in various speeds, from 2400 baud to the generally standard 9600 to 14.4K and higher. Don't buy anything less than 14.4 from now on. Don't worry about what the numbers mean: Big is faster and better.

You need a phone line and software. The software can be as simple as the terminal program supplied free with your Windows operating system. On-line services supply disks and free memberships — typically for a month or so — with many computers or shrink-wrap disks with computer magazines, modems, or other products. They know that giving away the razor will pay off in sales of blades.

Nothing but Net

Computers are connected directly to the Internet by something called TCP/IP, developed mostly by a man with a devilishly sharp beard named Vint Cerf. If you use a service such as the WELL or Echo, you in effect make use of the service's direct connection to the Internet. This is called a shell connection, and its indirectness limits the programs you can use to explore the net. Your bandwidth is frequently limited as well.

To get "raw net" — as close as a private citizen is likely to get to a direct Internet connection — you need a SLIP or PPP connection. SLIP stands for serial line Internet protocol, PPP for point-to-point protocol. Suffice it to say that both serve as diplomats to the empire of UNIX, translators of the vernacular of your computer into the lingua franca of the net. This kind of connection is available through such Internet service providers as PANIX, Netcom, Cerfnet, or PSI. But getting software to work happily with SLIP or PPP is not for the fainthearted.

You pay for two things: the local phone call to reach a service or access provider on the net, and a fee for the service itself — for most users, a number remarkably close to the amount of their cable-TV bill. After that, computers in Singapore or Sri Lanka linked to the net are as accessible as they'd be if they were close by. That is because the network of lines and phone services that connect all of these machines is effectively paid for by government agencies, universities, companies, and access providers. Each piece of E-mail provides a sketch of how the net works in the form of the "shirttail" that shows where your mail has arrived from: Like Michael Jordan's shot in the commercial, it travels here, there, up, around, over — nothing but net.

II. WHAT'S ON

The net is actually many nets, overlapping but only partially interlinked, from crude local bulletin boards to the "hypermedia" World Wide Web.

Bulletin Boards

The crudest unit of the net is a computer with a phone line linked to it, left on permanently for other computers to call. There are hundreds of thousands of such "bulletin-board systems" (BBSs), containing everything from the catalogs of local public libraries to photos of German girls romping with German shepherds.

The biggest BBS is probably FedWorld, an example of your tax dollars at work. On FedWorld, you can find such government documents as the complete text for NAFTA, or you can browse the reports of your favorite watchdog agencies — the General Accounting Office or, say, the Office of Technology Assessment. Access it independently by dialing 703-321-8020, or as a menu item through an Internet provider or on-line service.

A number of leading BBSs with prurient themes have joined together in   20
KinkNet, a kind of agricultural co-op that is to porn what Ore-Ida is to potatoes. That's free enterprise for you. "Welcome to KinkNet. How are you bent?"

Commercial On-Line Services

Cybersnobs look down on commercial services. Telling them you have an E-mail address at AOL, CompuServe, or, God forbid, Prodigy is like saying your computer is a Commodore 64. But these are the malls of cyberspace, and as David Byrne once said, you can keep up with what's going on in America by visiting a mall a week.

America Online: With the bright, upbeat air of *USA Today* or *Good Morning America,* AOL is probably the best-run and certainly the fastest-growing of the commercial services. It has NBC, MTV, *The New York Times, Time* (read it Sunday afternoon), and other periodicals on-line. It has created the best links to the Internet of any commercial service. AOL's biggest drawback is its slow pace in providing service at 9600 baud. At the more common 2400 baud, it can be teeth-grittingly slow.

CompuServe: Compares favorably with AOL, but with more emphasis on selling things, which few people have shown an inclination to buy. And CompuServe now offers connections to Internet news groups.

Prodigy: Founded by IBM and Sears, it is slow and ugly, with huge, spidery letters and a running band of ads. Its virtues include an interactive ESPN department and services for kids.

Delphi: "Explore the Internet for free," the ads run, and Delphi's introduc-   25
tory deal — five free hours — is appealing. Delphi is a service as well as an Internet shell connection. It gives you a command menu but no modern interface.
Rupert Murdoch believes in it, however, and improvements are due soon. In
keeping with the Murdoch style, Delphi also offers "R-rated celebrity" images
you can download.

eWorld: Apple's on-line service is still new; with a friendly interface based on
the metaphor of a town, with post office — click on the mail truck to get your
E-mail — library, arts center, and so on. The style is part Peter Max, part Saul
Steinberg. But short of E-mail, there is no means for access to the Internet. It's
still only for the Mac, with a Windows version due next year.

The Internet Itself

To grasp what the Internet really means, it is more useful to look at the
vehicles than the highway. On the Internet, those vehicles are a series of tools or
programs that bring words and images to your screen from files and programs in
distant computers — or close ones. (Distance or placement on the great reticu-
lated mystery of the net is irrelevant.) The tools are operated by your typing at
the dreaded command line of raw net programs, picking from menus on services
such as Delphi, or clicking and pointing in the best of the new software, such as
the Pipeline. These tools include:

Ftp: File transfer protocol. A basic tool for downloading files from distant
computers.

Gopher: A program that retrieves files. It was first developed at the University
of Minnesota, and the name combines a reference to the perennially hapless Golden Gopher football teams with a pun on "go-fer." There are many gophers in
different locations now, and in some services you can simultaneously search all
"gopherspace."

Telnet: A program to make your computer behave as if it were a terminal   30
linked to a distant computer so you can use the programs and files there.

WAIS: Wide-area information server. A group of programs that work together to find information on different computers, from Mac to UNIX, according to "keywords" related to a topic.

Access Providers, or Gateways

Access providers are local services that provide you with a link to the Internet. Generally, they also offer their own selection of bulletin boards and chat
groups. In the real world, access providers are cruddy offices jammed with UNIX
boxes, big Suns, or DEC file-servers that act as brokers between your computer
and others, large and small, on the net.

Providers have flavor, like neighborhoods. They tend to reflect the qualities
of the cities or regions where they are located and the subcultures that make up
their membership.

1. *The WELL:* Marin County. Very *Whole Earth Catalog;* the original. Did tie-in to Woodstock anniversary.
2. *MindVox:* Manhattan cyberpunks nostalgic for a 1960s they never knew, impatient for reality to go virtual.
3. *Echo:* Manhattan downtown. More women than any other, and some female-only salons.

The Electronic Mailbox

All of the pieces of the larger net share three elements that reflect the overriding need of people on-line to sound off, gossip, and quibble.

E-mail: With nothing more than an AOL or CompuServe account, you can
send electronic mail to any E-address on the globe. Each of the on-line services has fairly straightforward mail to other members, and most can send to other services — from AOL to CompuServe, for instance. AOL's Internet gateway allows you to send mail only — not files — to net addresses.

Mailing lists. A step above E-mail is a mailing list to which you subscribe. Sign up on the "hey-joe" list, for instance, and new postings about Jimi Hendrix pop up in your E-mail. You subscribe by sending an E-mail message to hey-joe-request@ms.uky.edu. Many mailing lists include "archives" of older material. You can reach them by ftp, as for example, ftp ms.uky.edu, then look for publ/mailing.lists/hey-joe.

Forums or newsgroups: Called forums an AOL and CompuServe, newsgroups on the Internet, these are virtual bulletin boards where people of shared interests post news, queries, and opinions. These can be baseball fans, Deadheads, nanotech buffs, or investors in derivatives. You read, "post" a message, and wait for replies — or flames.

III. BEYOND INTERNET

The net can carry more than words, but for most people only if they download files of image and sound — fifteen-second snatches of songs, say, or even bits of film. You can download film trailers from AOL, for instance, but it will take you as long as it would to watch the film. Seeing the trailer for *Schindler's List* running in a little box at the edge of your computer is but one example of the many bizarre experiences to come in the multimedia world of the net. At info.tamu.edu, you can find the president's weekly Saturday radio address, around which millions do not arrange their weekend schedules. And last year, hardcore UNIX boys laboriously transmitted the first film on the net, an obscure title, *The Secret Life of Bees.* But the promise of full multimedia Internet lies in the World Wide Web.

The World Wide Web

"All else is gaslight," said the late conductor Herbert von Karajan after he first heard music on a compact disc. For longtime net denizens, the World Wide Web makes the weary world of gophers or telnet seem like vinyl.

The World Wide Web is a new way of exploring the Internet based on a formidable type of organization called hypertext, in which documents are linked to others by keywords that lead to other documents, and so on — often in a dizzying drop into lists and more lists. It's a combination of Lewis Carroll and *Finnegans Wake,* or a nightmare version of the outlines your junior high school teacher made you produce.

Start with "art" and work your way down to specific museums, then specific collections of Kandinsky or Picasso stored at sites that are physically located around the world. The Web is intended to be simpler to use than gopher or WAIS — so simple that it took only the subparticle physicists at the European Laboratory for Particle Physics to dream it up. So think of it as an information supercollider.

You can recognize a Web address by the prefix http://, from "hypertext transfer protocol." Web sites such as the Underground Music Archive often contain hypermedia — picture, sound, and even video files as well as words.

The Web can be difficult and disorienting. When NASA first sent spiders into space, the earliest webs they spun were awkward and misshapen. It took days before webs with the neat axes and tangents of earthbound arachnids began to appear. As with outer space, so with cyberspace, where the gravity of the traditional organization of words and images is absent.

To deal with the Web, you need new kinds of programs called browsers, of which the most famous is Mosaic.

Mosaic: The Mondo App

Sure, it's a cool technology, venture capitalists regularly say about any new development, but where are the *applications?*

The key application for the Web is Mosaic, a program that follows the strands of the Web from one "site," or "page," to another. Invariably described by net vets as "totally warm and fuzzy," it has developed a legend as "the mondo application" — the future of the net. Developed at the National Center for Supercomputing Applications (NCSA) in Champaign-Urbana, Illinois, Mosaic brings in the sounds and images of the net — if you have a powerful enough computer.

And it's free — sort of. You can download it from the NCSA, but it requires a SLIP or PPP connection to use it, and it can run painfully slow on most personal computers. A more robust commercial version, AIR Mosaic, comes with Internet in a Box.

Internet in a Box

It sounds like what everyone wants: the whole shebang, ready to roll. Internet in a Box (call 800-777-9638; $149) combines software for Internet access with an 800-number phone system called RAMP that sets up your connection to the net automatically in a promised five minutes. Some two hundred local access providers support the program, and you can use it anywhere in the country — albeit at high rates of almost $10 an hour — through SprintLink. But whether the box lives up to the promise of its name depends on how well the ambitious phone link works and how enthusiastically local providers support it.

IV. NET CULTURE

The Internet was born in 1969 with the creation of the ARPANET by the Defense Department's Advanced Research Projects Agency, which would later give us the Stealth fighter. The network linked four computer networks — at UCLA, the Stanford Research Institute, the University of Utah, and the University of California at Santa Barbara — to help computer researchers working around the country. The net grew until military functions split off as MILNET in 1983. And something strange happened: More than a way to ship technical files or scientific documents, the net became a means of communication. On its margins, just as beside the railroad or blacktop, a new culture began to sprout. That culture had everything to do with the fact that while the net had been built by professors, it would be run by sophomores. So Deadheads and Trekkies are disproportionately represented on newsgroup lists.

Crime: Can You Be Raped On-Line?

As on campus, jokers abound on the net, and not all of their pranks are merry. Not long ago, it was revealed that wily hackers had stored more than a thousand pornographic images on the computers at the Lawrence Livermore lab, well known for its nuclear-weapons research. The problem is not that your tax dollars are being wasted on hard-disk space for smut but that someone trying to download the image of Katrina the Princess of 69 in all her bit-mapped glory might accidentally get detailed plans for a multiple, independently targeted warhead system.   50

The net has long fostered a Woodstock-like spirit, mingling respect for the common good with that for individual rights of expression. This spirit is violated only hourly, by the shrill, the psychotic, the greedy.

Commercial services have their policies, too. AOL warns against such offenses as obscenity, chain letters, spamming, and general flaming. Prodigy is said to be developing "George Carlin software" to send through the files on search-and-destroy missions targeting seven or more words you can't type in (private, at least) cyberspace. If you do, you can "lose privilege" — that is, be bounced.

Other sins remain less easy to define. One AOL user charged that her ex was "stalking" her on-line — she didn't dare open her mailbox for fear she'd encounter another of his missives. And the phrase "on-line rape" has popped up in discussions of future net policy, a weird mingling of the philosophies of Jaron Lanier and Catharine MacKinnon. But the biggest offense on the net, with its happy anarchy, is commercialism. Laurence Canter and Martha Siegel, the two lawyers who ran an ad last year, have become as famous on the net as Bonnie and Clyde.

The Future of the Net

Be warned: As soon as you take to the net, you will encounter traffic jams. The sexier the software, the slower it runs on the net; the neater the site, the harder to get on. And just as we are running out of telephone numbers, the Internet is running out of IP addresses. So get ready for more notices like this one: "*UNTIL FURTHER NOTICE: Due to system and network load, the music archives at uwp.edu will no longer be made available via gopher.*"

Look for what Kevin Kelly, net visionary and author of *Out of Control,* calls "flash crowds" — hordes of on-liners following fashion from one hot site to the next.

Right now, programs such as Mosaic run slowly as they struggle to cram pictures and sounds through copper wire. Faster computers and modems will ease the problem, and cable will soon bring the net through a bigger information pipeline to your home. (Intel has already developed the means to do so.) But even before that happens, fervid netizens and websters will be demanding live audio, then video.   55

Already, bouncers are being posted in cyberspace. No one has complained, because the first users to be restricted are not human — the first barriers are being erected against software: the retrieval rodents and web worms. NO BOTS ALLOWED signs are springing up outside the most exclusive clubs on the net.

Get ready for the reaction, and the debate: Doesn't software have rights, too? If you think PC has gone too far, wait until you meet PC on your PC.

Wrong Ism

J. B. PRIESTLEY

THERE ARE THREE ISMS that we ought to consider very carefully — region-   1
alism, nationalism, internationalism. Of these three the one there is most fuss about, the one that starts men shouting and marching and shooting, the one that seems to have all the depth and thrust and fire, is of course nationalism. Nine people out of ten, I fancy, would say that of this trio it is the one that really counts, the big boss. Regionalism and internationalism, they would add, are comparatively small, shadowy, rather cranky. And I believe all this to be quite wrong. Like many another big boss, nationalism is largely bogus. It is like a bunch of flowers made of plastics.

The real flowers belong to regionalism. The mass of people everywhere may never have used the term. They are probably regionalists without knowing it. Because they have been brought up in a certain part of the world, they have formed perhaps quite unconsciously a deep attachment to its landscape and

---

▦ Cruising the I-Way: Jack In, Good Buddy ▦

You can't escape the metaphor: the Internet as the Interstate. In one way, the I-way metaphor is right: Being on-line is like driving. You can read the manual, but you have to try it to really learn. In another, though, it's misleading. The net today is less like the highway than like CB radio — rough-and-ready communication, highly verbal and personal, with the same mix of cracker populism and crackpot petulance, the same crossing of lines and overloading of channels — the same native American surrealism, in short. It's no accident that one of the most popular features of CompuServe is the CB simulator, especially the adult "channels," on which you can type dirty — or that the Internet has thousands of chat "channels."

Right now, the I-way is dominated by net vets who resemble truck drivers, running UNIX as if it were a big Kenworth, flipping family sedans out of the way with their slipstreams, leering down from their cabs at teenage girls in convertibles. They delight in "flaming newbies." And since the number of users on the net grows by 10 percent each month, most of us are newbies.

Like most truck drivers, too, those on the I-way see themselves as latter-day cowboys, pioneers on a new and lawless frontier. They like it like that: They associate the blank emptiness of a UNIX command line with the hazy, endless line of a Great Plains horizon. And they don't want the rest of us to move in. But we will. Civilization is coming — better programs, wider access, more bandwidth. We're settling the electronic frontier. Soon, we'll all be on-line.

---

speech, its traditional customs, its food and drink, its songs and jokes. (There are of course always the rebels, often intellectuals and writers, but they are not the mass of people.) They are rooted in their region. Indeed, without this attachment a man can have no roots.

So much of people's lives, from earliest childhood onwards, is deeply intertwined with the common life of the region, they cannot help feeling strongly about it. A threat to it is a knife pointing at the heart. How can life ever be the same if bullying strangers come to change everything? The form and colour, the very taste and smell of dear familiar things will be different, alien, life-destroying. It would be better to die fighting. And it is precisely this, the nourishing life of the region, for which common men have so often fought and died.

This attachment to the region exists on a level far deeper than that of any political hocus-pocus. When a man says "my country" with real feeling, he is thinking about his region, all that has made up his life, and not about that political entity, the nation. There can be some confusion here simply because some countries are so small — and ours is one of them — and so old, again like ours, that much of what is national is also regional.[1] Down the centuries, the nation,

---

[1] Priestley (1894–1984) was English. [Ed.]

itself, so comparatively small, has been able to attach to itself the feeling really created by the region. (Even so there is something left over, as most people in Yorkshire or Devon, for example, would tell you.) This probably explains the fervent patriotism developed early in small countries. The English were announcing that they were English in the Middle Ages, before nationalism had arrived elsewhere.

If we deduct from nationalism all that it has borrowed or stolen from region-   5
alism, what remains is mostly rubbish. The nation, as distinct from the region, is largely the creation of power-men and political manipulators. Almost all nation-alist movements are led by ambitious frustrated men determined to hold office. I am not blaming them. I would do the same if I were in their place and wanted power so badly. But nearly always they make use of the rich warm regional feel-ing, the emotional dynamo of the movement, while being almost untouched by it themselves. This is because they are not as a rule deeply loyal to any region themselves. Ambition and a love of power can eat like acid into the tissues of regional loyalty. It is hard, if not impossible, to retain a natural piety and yet be for ever playing both ends against the middle.

Being itself a power structure, devised by men of power, the nation tends to think and act in terms of power. What would benefit the real life of the region, where men, women and children actually live, is soon sacrificed for the power and prestige of the nation. (And the personal vanity of presidents and ministers themselves, which historians too often disregard.) Among the new nations of our time innumerable peasants and labourers must have found themselves being cut down from five square meals a week to three in order to provide unnecessary airlines, military forces that can only be used against them and nobody else, great conference halls and official yachts and the rest. The last traces of imperialism and colonialism may have to be removed from Asia and Africa, where men can no longer endure being condemned to a permanent inferiority by the colour of their skins; but even so, the modern world, the real world of our time, does not want and would be far better without more and more nations, busy creating for themselves the very paraphernalia that western Europe is now trying to abolish. You are compelled to answer more questions when trying to spend half a day in Cambodia than you are now travelling from the Hook of Holland to Syracuse.

This brings me to internationalism. I dislike this term, which I used only to complete the isms. It suggests financiers and dubious promoters living nowhere but in luxury hotels; a shallow world of entrepreneurs and impresarios. (Was it Sacha Guitry who said that impresarios were men who spoke many languages but all with a foreign accent?) The internationalism I have in mind here is best described as world civilisation. It is life considered on a global scale. Most of our communications and transport already exist on this high wide level. So do many other things from medicine to meteorology. Our astronomers and physicists (ex-cept where they have allowed themselves to be hush-hushed) work here. The UN special agencies, about which we hear far too little, have contributed more and more to this world civilisation. All the arts, when they are arts and not chunks of nationalist propaganda, naturally take their place in it. And it grows, widens, deepens, in spite of the fact that for every dollar, ruble, pound or franc spent in explaining and praising it, a thousand are spent by the nations explaining and praising themselves.

This world civilisation and regionalism can get along together, especially if we keep ourselves sharply aware of their quite different but equally important values and rewards. A man can make his contribution to world civilisation and yet remain strongly regional in feeling: I know several men of this sort. There is of course the danger — it is with us now — of the global style flattening out the regional, taking local form, colour, flavour, away for ever, disinheriting future generations, threatening them with sensuous poverty and a huge boredom. But to understand and appreciate regionalism is to be on guard against this danger. And we must therefore make a clear distinction between regionalism and nationalism.

It is nationalism that tries to check the growth of world civilisation. And nationalism, when taken on a global scale, is more aggressive and demanding now than it has ever been before. This in the giant powers is largely disguised by the endless fuss in public about rival ideologies, now a largely unreal quarrel. What is intensely real is the glaring nationalism. Even the desire to police the world is nationalistic in origin. (Only the world can police the world.) Moreover, the nation-states of today are for the most part far narrower in their outlook, far more inclined to allow prejudice against the foreigner to impoverish their own style of living, than the old imperial states were. It should be part of world civilisation that men with particular skills, perhaps the product of the very regionalism they are rebelling against, should be able to move easily from country to country, to exercise those skills, in anything from teaching the violin to running a new type of factory to managing an old hotel. But nationalism, especially of the newer sort, would rather see everything done badly than allow a few nonnationals to get to work. And people face a barrage of passports, visas, immigration controls, labour permits; and in this respect are worse off than they were in 1900. But even so, in spite of all that nationalism can do — so long as it keeps its nuclear bombs to itself — the internationalism I have in mind, slowly creating a world civilisation, cannot be checked.

Nevertheless, we are still backing the wrong ism. Almost all our money goes   10 on the middle one, nationalism, the rotten meat between the two healthy slices of bread. We need regionalism to give us roots and that very depth of feeling which nationalism unjustly and greedily claims for itself. We need internationalism to save the world and to broaden and heighten our civilisation. While regional man enriches the lives that international man is already working to keep secure and healthy, national man, drunk with power, demands our loyalty, money and applause, and poisons the very air with his dangerous nonsense.

The Revolution Has Just Begun

VÁCLAV HAVEL[1]

T WICE IN THIS CENTURY the world has been threatened by a catastrophe. Twice this catastrophe was born in Europe, and twice you Americans, along with others, were called upon to save Europe, the whole world and yourselves.

In the meantime, the U.S. became the most powerful nation on earth, and it understood the responsibility that flowed from this. But something else was happening as well. The Soviet Union appeared, grew and transformed the enormous sacrifices of its people suffering under totalitarian rule into a strength that, after World War II, made it the second most powerful nation in the world.

CREATING THE FAMILY OF MEN

All of this taught us to see the world in bipolar terms as two enormous forces — one a defender of freedom, the other a source of nightmares. Europe became the point of friction between these two powers, and thus it turned into a single enormous arsenal divided into two parts. In this process, one half of the arsenal became part of that nightmarish power, while the other, the free part, bordering on the ocean and having no wish to be driven into it, was compelled, together with you, to build a complicated security system to which we probably owe the fact that we still exist.

The totalitarian system in the Soviet Union and in most of its satellites is breaking down, and our nations are looking for a way to democracy and independence.

This, I am convinced, is a historically irreversible process and, as a result, Europe will begin again to seek its own identity without being compelled to be a divided armory any longer. Perhaps this will create the hope that sooner or later, your boys will no longer have to stand on guard for freedom in Europe or come to our rescue, because Europe will at last be able to stand guard over itself.

But that is still not the most important thing. The main thing is, it seems to me, that these revolutionary changes will enable us to escape from the rather antiquated straitjacket of this bipolar view of the world and to enter at last into an era of multipolarity in which all of us, large and small, former slaves and former masters, will be able to create what your great President Lincoln called "the family of men."

[1] Czech playwright and poet who became a spokesman for civil rights and democracy after the 1968 Soviet invasion of Czechoslovakia, despite continual surveillance and intimidation from the government and who played an important role in the reform of the Czechoslovakian government in 1989, being elected president of the new democratic government in 1990. [Ed.]

THE PATH OF PLURALISM

How can the U.S. help us today? My reply is as paradoxical as the whole of my life has been. You can help us most of all if you help the Soviet Union on its irreversible but immensely complicated road to democracy. It is far more complicated than the road open to its former European satellites. You yourselves know best how to support as rapidly as possible the nonviolent evolution of this enormous multinational body politic toward democracy and autonomy for all its people. Therefore, it is not fitting for me to offer you any advice.

I can only say that the sooner, the more quickly and the more peacefully the Soviet Union begins to move along the road toward genuine political pluralism, respect for the rights of the nations to their own integrity and to a working — that is, a market — economy, the better it will be not just for Czechs and Slovaks but for the whole world.

And the sooner you yourselves will be able to reduce the burden of the military budget borne by the American people. To put it metaphorically, the millions you give to the East today will soon return to you in the form of billions in savings. American soldiers shouldn't have to be separated from their mothers just because Europe is incapable of being a guarantor of world peace, which it ought to be in order to make some amends, at least, for having given the world two world wars.

THE LEGACY OF OPPRESSION

As long as people are people, democracy, in the full sense of the word, will always be no more than an ideal. In this sense, you too are merely approaching democracy. But you have one great advantage: You have been approaching democracy uninterruptedly for more than 200 years, and your journey toward the horizon has never been disrupted by a totalitarian system.

The communist type of totalitarian system has left both our nations, Czechs and Slovaks, as it has all the nations of the Soviet Union and the other countries the Soviet Union subjugated in its time, a legacy of countless dead, an infinite spectrum of human suffering, profound economic decline and, above all, enormous human humiliation. It has brought us horrors that fortunately you have not known.

It has given us something positive, a special capacity to look from time to time somewhat further than someone who has not undergone this bitter experience. A person who cannot move and lead a somewhat normal life because he is pinned under a boulder has more time to think about his hopes than someone who is not trapped that way.

What I'm trying to say is this: We must all learn many things from you, from how to educate our offspring, how to elect our representatives, all the way to how to organize our economic life so that it will lead to prosperity and not to poverty. But it doesn't have to be merely assistance from the well educated, powerful and wealthy to someone who has nothing and therefore has nothing to offer in return.

We too can offer something to you: our experience and the knowledge that   15
has come from it. The specific experience I'm talking about has given me one
certainty: Consciousness proceeds being, and not the other way around, as the
Marxists claim. For this reason, the salvation of this human world lies nowhere
else than in the human heart, in the human power to reflect, in human meekness
and in human responsibility.

A NEW WAY OF THINKING

Without a global revolution in the sphere of human consciousness, nothing
will change for the better in the sphere of our being as humans, and the catastrophe toward which this world is headed — be it ecological, social, demographic
or a general breakdown of civilization — will be unavoidable. If we are no longer
threatened by world war or by the danger that the absurd mountains of accumulated nuclear weapons might blow up the world, this does not mean that we
have definitely won. We are still incapable of understanding that the only genuine backbone of all our actions, if they are to be moral, is responsibility. Responsibility to something higher than my family, my country, my company, my
success — responsibility to the order of being where all our actions are indelibly
recorded and where and only where they will be properly judged.

I think that you Americans should understand this way of thinking. When
Thomas Jefferson wrote that "governments are instituted among men, deriving
their just powers from the consent of the governed," it was a simple and important act of the human spirit. What gave meaning to that act, however, was the
fact that the author backed it up with his life. It was not just his words, it was his
deeds as well.

Chapter 4
Identifying and Recording
a Conversation

Identifying a Conversation

Once you have found an issue you care to know more about, you should learn what others have said about this issue. To do so, you need to find a community that also cares about the issue (or that you think should care about it). In Chapter 3 I talked about how to identify communities and to locate sites of communication. I also encouraged you to go out and observe such sites. Once you have focused on a specific issue, you need to observe the conversation more systematically and record what different people have to say about your issue.

In a small community, it is not difficult to identify sites of communication or conversations taking place at those sites. When you and your friends are sitting around talking, for example, you become a site of communication for the community defined by your friendship for each other. There may be more than one conversation taking place, but you can generally follow the thread of what people are saying. If friends come in late, you can fill them in on what people have been talking about because you have "recorded" the conversation in your memory and can summarize it.

Some sites of communication are more complex, however, and require more sophisticated means of catching up on the conversation. In fact, some conversations are so large or have been going for so long that no one person has recorded the conversation in his or her memory. Some very formal kinds of conversations are, nonetheless, recorded in great detail. For instance, the Supreme Court is a site of communication for debating and deciding U.S. constitutional issues. The Court deals with a number of complex cases each year and has been doing so for more than two hundred years, much longer than anyone on the present court has been alive. Imagine the problems if the Court did not keep written records of its proceedings and decisions: The present justices would have to rely solely on what they had heard others say about past decisions. Writing, reading, and research have made it possible for people to follow the development of complex conversations such as I have described.

Because your life as a student revolves around academic conversations, let me use the academic community as a further example. One site of communication for academic conversations is the classroom or lecture hall. How do you record the ideas that are shared at this site? You take notes. You jot ideas down in your own words, summarize or outline extended lecture material, and quote meaningful phrases. The same principle applies when you record ideas shared at other academic sites of communication — journals, books, and documents — which are recorded, stored, indexed, and referenced in libraries. The college research library is one of the most complex sites of communication that you will encounter, and the books, journals, and documents it contains are themselves sites within the larger site. Imagine if there were no system for archiving and classifying all this information. It would be impossible to follow the thread of a conversation; you would have no idea if you had reviewed a representative sampling of viewpoints on a particular issue. Examining how conversations are organized within a library is essential for your success as a student. It can also give you some idea of how other conversations are archived and organized.

The Process of Library Research

What I call identifying and recording the conversations stored in a library is what most people would call library research. A university or research library can seem an overwhelming and forbidding place for newcomers. Most libraries are equipped with information desks and reference librarians, but if they are to assist you, you first need to know what questions to ask. It helps to understand the process of library research. One approach that some students take is to wander about the library hoping their eye will catch a title somewhat related to their topic. If you pulled down every book in the library, you would eventually find one related to your topic, but this is a very inefficient process, akin to finding out what happened at a city council meeting by calling everyone in the phone book. You could also ask a librarian, for example, "Does this library have any information on endangered species?" or look up "endangered species" in the card catalog or on-line catalog. This is slightly better than wandering around the library, but not by much, because the library may have hundreds of books, articles, and documents related in some way to endangered species. A more sensible approach is to learn how information is organized in a library.

Library research has three basic stages, as shown in Figure 4-1:

1. Finding background material on your topic
2. Narrowing your topic and forming an issue question
3. Finding research citations to use in your paper

Adapted from Ford, James E., "A General Research Model for Research Paper Introduction," *Literary Research Newsletter* 6 (1981): 6–15.

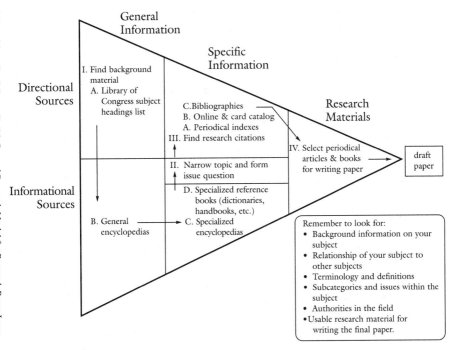

Figure 4-1   Research Strategy Model

Students are frequently tempted to skip the first two stages and try to go directly to the third, looking for books and articles to include in their final paper. But following the first two stages is more efficient and will save you time in the long run. The strategy outlined in this diagram applies not only to your college writing courses but to any kind of research project you undertake.

Library research begins with a topic or issue you wish to investigate. You may only have a vague notion of what you want to write about, perhaps something on biomedical ethics, water pollution, consumer product safety, or funding for the arts. You may have a more specific issue or controversy in mind. You may even have already formed an opinion on the issue and are looking for evidence to support what you want to say. Even if you have a specific issue question in mind, however, it is probably best to begin by examining that issue within a broader context. Once you can see how your issue fits within the context of other conversations, you will be able to narrow your discussion of the issue and write about it more intelligently. First, get caught up on the general conversation; then, focus on your particular issue. Begin with a topic area for your research rather than a specific question to answer or thesis to prove.

The best way to do the library research that will catch you up on the conversation is to begin with general sources and move on to more specific sources. There are two kinds of library source material: informational and directional. Informational sources are part of the conversation I described earlier. They contain actual information related to your topic. General information sources, such as encyclopedias, dictionaries, and other reference works, summarize what others have said; they review the major issues related to a topic, noting its major authors and contributors, and so are a quick way of catching up on the conversation. Particular scholarly communities and disciplines may also have their own encyclopedias, dictionaries, and reference works, containing more specific information. Journals, books, government documents, newspapers, and magazines are even more specific informational sources.

Directional sources help you locate informational sources and find out where academic conversations are taking place. Indexes, bibliographies, and catalogues are directional sources. As with informational sources, some directional sources are more specific than others, and some are related to particular scholarly disciplines.

▓ ▓ STAGE ONE: FINDING BACKGROUND MATERIAL

The Library of Congress Subject Heading Guide   Where you begin library research depends on your level of familiarity with your issue and the sites of conversation related to it. An experienced member of a scholarly community working in his or her field of expertise can bypass the preliminary steps of library research. A less experienced member of the community or a newcomer, however, will want to follow each step carefully. As a beginner, you should begin your research with the most general information and directional sources. First, consult the most general of all directional sources: *The Library of Congress Subject Heading Guide*. The three large red volumes of this guide are usually found near the reference desk, card catalogue, or computer terminals. The guide contains a list of terms used by the Library of Congress to catalog library materials. Many library catalogs use these same terms for subject searches. With this guide you can find some words used to describe your topic. If you have been following a conversation in a journal or magazine, you may already have some terms in mind. Jot down both general terms and more narrow terms. These will be important when you use other directional sources. Figure 4-2 shows a sample entry from the *Library of Congress Subject Headings* (LCSH).

Words that are printed in bold in the LCSH are subject headings you can use in other indexes organized according to the Library of Congress system. Card catalogs and on-line catalogs at many colleges, for example, use these terms as part of their indexing and cataloging system. Following each valid term is a list of other terms that are also used to describe the topic. These terms are useful for keyword searches and for searching databases that do not use the Library of Congress terms or on-line indexes that allow for both Library of Congress subject searches and keyword searches on any term. The two-letter codes identify these keywords related to Library of Congress terms. UF stands for "Used For." Library of Congress terms are "used for" — or substitute for — terms with this designation. In other words, a UF term won't show up in the Library of Con-

Cries *(May Subd Geog)*
  [GT3450]
  UF Street cries
       Street songs
  BT Cities and towns
       Manners and customs
       Sounds
       Street music and musicians
  NT Battle-cries
       Peddlers and peddling
Crile family *(Not Subd Geog)*
Crime *(May Subd Geog)*
  [HV6001-HV7220.5]
       Here are entered works on the occurrence
  of crime. Works on the discipline that studies
  the causes, detection and prevention of
  crime, and the treatment or punishment of
  criminals, are entered under Criminology.
  Works on the criminal justice system are
  entered under Criminal justice, Administra-
  tion of.
  UF City crime
       Crime and criminals
       Crimes
       Delinquency
       Urban crime
  BT Social problems
  RT Criminal justice, Administration
          of
       Criminal law
       Criminals
       Criminology
  SA *headings beginning with the*
          word Criminal
  NT Alcoholism and crime
       Computer crimes
       Crimes of passion
       Crimes without victims
       Drug abuse and crime
       Education and crime
       Employee crimes
       Fear of crime
       Hate crimes
       Hypnotism and crime
       Illegitimacy and crime
       Impostors and imposture
       Indians of North America—
          Crime
       Juvenile delinquency
       Mentally handicapped and crime
       Narcotics and crime
       Organized crime
       Parapsychology and crime
       Physically handicapped and
          crime
       Reading disability and crime
       Recidivism

       Rural crimes
       Sex crimes
       Suburban crimes
       Swindlers and swindling
       Unemployment and crime
       Violent crimes
       War and crime
  — Analysis
       USE Crime analysis
  — Authorship
       USE Crime writing
  — Classification
       UF Classification of crimes
  — Cross-cultural studies
  — Fiction
       UF Crime stories
  — Forecasting
       USE Crime forecasting
  — Law and legislation
       USE Criminal law
  — Prevention
       USE Crime prevention
  — Religious aspects
       [BL65.C7]
  — — Buddhism, [Christianity, etc.]
  — Sex differences
  — Statistical methods
       USE Criminal statistics
  — Statistics
       USE Criminal statistics
  — Study and teaching
       USE Criminology
Crime, Employee
  USE Employee crimes
Crime analysis *(May Subd Geog)*
  [HV7936.C88]
       Here are entered works on the examina-
  tion of data concerning criminal activity to
  assist in the planning, decision making,
  and administration of police and law
  enforcement work.
  UF Crime—Analysis
  BT Police administration
Crime and age
  [HV6163]
  UF Age and crime
  BT Age
  NT Aged—Crimes against
       Youth—Crimes against
Crime and alcoholism
  USE Alcoholism and crime
Crime and criminals
  USE Crime
       Criminals
Crime and criminals in mass media
  USE Crime in mass media
Crime and criminals in the Bible

1130

gress subject search (although it may show up in another keyword search). BT stands for "broader term." BT identifies a larger classification or more comprehensive topic than the term in bold. NT stands for "narrower term." NT identifies a more focused topic or subtopic. RT stands for "related term." An RT term is a cross-reference to similar subjects. SA stands for "see also" and refers you to other main headings in the LCSH. Terms following dashes are subdivisions of the main term; those in boldface are also valid LCSH terms when entered after the main term and two hyphens ("crime - fiction," for example). USE identifies a term that you should use instead of the term listed if you want to conduct a Library of Congress subject search. *May Subd Geog* at the main term means that a topic may be divided further by geographical area, usually by nation. For instance, the subject "crime" may be further divided into "Crime - United States" or "Crime - England." Notice that many terms are followed by a Library of Congress call number (one or two letters followed by a series of numbers and letters). These call numbers indicate where materials on this topic will be shelved in libraries following the Library of Congress system.

The LCSH is useful because it can suggest topics that you may not have thought of. It can also help you focus your topic and even find specific material on your topic. It gives a broad overview of the possibilities for research and provides a list of terms you can use for subject and keyword searches. These keywords are particularly useful if you have access to an on-line catalog or index.

Encyclopedias   The most general information sources are encyclopedias, such as the *Encyclopedia Britannica,* the *Encyclopedia Americana,* and *Collier's Encyclopedia.* Many libraries have on-line general encyclopedias, such as Grollier's or Compton's on-line encyclopedias. These save space, allow more possibilities for keyword searching, and often allow you to print or download the articles you need. They can also be updated quickly. They do not allow for the serendipitous discoveries that often result from browsing through a print encyclopedia, but you can benefit from using both kinds. Using the terms you found in the LCSH guide, you can search encyclopedias for information on your topic. If you find too much information, use a narrower term; if you find too little, use a broader term.

An encyclopedia article provides one author's summary of the scholarly conversation related to a topic. Encyclopedia articles are usually written by experienced members of an academic community. Remember, though, that they are one person's view of the conversation; although they are generally reliable, some experts may disagree with the information as presented.

As you read, begin to record information about the scholarly conversation taking place about your topic. Summarize the information you find. Write down the names of important contributors to the conversation and any informational sources (books, articles, and so forth) cited in the encyclopedia article. Look up unfamiliar terms in a dictionary. Remember to include full bibliographical information for material you record. Different scholarly communities use different styles, but you should generally record the author, title, place and date of publication, and page numbers. (For more on recording bibliographic information, see pages 136–137.)

Other general informational sources include almanacs and fact lists. *Facts on File*, for example, provides a yearly overview of significant news stories, and *Statistical Abstracts of the United States* gives all kinds of information (statistics, graphs, charts, tables) related to life in the United States.

Specialized Encyclopedias   After your survey of general directional and informational sources, the next step is to locate more specific ones. Specialized encyclopedias and indexes are often located together in the reference section of the library according to subject area or academic discipline. Examples of specialized informational sources include *The International Encyclopedia of Social Sciences,* the *Dictionary of American History,* the *Encyclopedia of World Art,* and the *McGraw-Hill Encyclopedia of Science and Technology.* A reference librarian can help you locate the specific sources you are looking for. (By now you should have some specific questions to ask.) The reference librarian usually has access to Sheehy's *Guide to Reference Works,* a directional source that lists reference works by subject area. (Check to see that your library has the works listed.) If your library has an on-line catalog, you can do a keyword search with a general term from your topic and a word such as "encyclopedia," "bibliography," "dictionary," or "index." For instance, if your topic is related to endangered species, you could do a keyword search on "endangered species and bibliography." Instead of finding every book or article with any information on endangered species, you would now find only bibliographies specific to your topic. Such specialized bibliographies can help you find specific articles and books on your topic rather quickly.

▨ ▨ STAGE TWO: NARROWING YOUR TOPIC

Once you have read several sources for background information, you should attempt to *intelligently* narrow your topic. General and specialized encyclopedias should have alerted you to subcategories of your topic on which you could focus your research. Understanding your topic from a variety of perspectives should help you select one aspect of the topic to research in greater detail. If the encyclopedias raised questions about that aspect of the topic, you can be confident that experts are also asking similar questions, and you can go forward assuming that there will probably be adequate research material to support your paper. Be sure to select an area that is of interest to you.

Identifying a Controversial Issue   In writing argumentatively, you will focus on an issue that is controversial, an issue about which people disagree. There will always be at least two opposing points of view on a controversial issue, but often there will be more. You may want to begin with an issue that you already care about or want to know more about. Or you may want to listen in on the conversation for awhile to see what issues arise.

As you define the issue you are going to analyze, resist the temptation to think of all controversies as two-sided: right/wrong, us/them, for/against, pro/con. Such dualistic thinking is popular in the United States, with its two main political factions: Republican/Democrat, conservative/liberal, anti-abortion/pro-choice, pro-business/pro-labor, and so on. Such binary thinking glosses over important distinctions and silences those who do not feel comfortable in either camp. As you analyze controversial issues, try to identify as many views as you can. Identifying a diversity of viewpoints will provide you with the most complete understanding of the issue and help you prepare an effective response. Remember that diversity is a strength. In order to articulate your own opinions and justify them with the best reasons, you need to hear a number of different viewpoints. After all, the opinion you ultimately embrace as your own may be one that you haven't encountered yet. You may change your mind about your beliefs once you hear what others have to say. And even if you don't change your mind, listening to others will help you understand why you believe the way you do and will give you good reasons for explaining your beliefs to others.

Forming an Issue Question   You can benefit greatly at this point by using any prewriting techniques you have learned in order to focus your topic. For example, you might brainstorm or freewrite about all of the background information you have accumulated; you can then look over this material and decide which ideas look most interesting or most promising. You might also want to try clustering your ideas to develop a sense of what information you need to be looking for in your research.

Your background research and narrowing of your topic should result in an issue question, a specific question that you want to answer in your research. This should be a question that is "at issue" for the community you are addressing. In other words, it should be a question that people care about and disagree about. Here are some examples of issue questions:

> Should Congress provide compensation to property owners who lose equity in their property because of the Endangered Species Act?
>
> Should the National Endowment for the Arts fund individual artists, or should all NEA grants be disbursed through state humanities councils?
>
> Do live television broadcasts of trials encroach on the defendant's right to a fair trial?

You phrase these issues as questions to answer so that you can be open to what other people have to say rather than merely look for evidence to support what you already believe. You might want to brainstorm about the format of your issue question — try several different phrasings of it to see which one creates a suffi-

ciently narrow area that will still allow room for developing important and interesting ideas in a paper. Once you have formed a specific issue question, you are
ready to read books and articles related to your topic to find answers to your
questions.

■ ■ STAGE THREE: FINDING RESEARCH MATERIAL

You have used background information to learn more about the conversation regarding your topic and to help narrow your topic to a workable focus. You
are now ready to begin locating research material (as opposed to background
material). With the subject terms you have defined from the LCSH guide and
from your background reading, you can look for particular books and journal
articles that respond to the issue question that you have formulated for your
paper.

Library Reference Systems   Libraries use alpha-numerical reference systems
to track academic conversations by topic. Knowing the Library of Congress or
Dewey Decimal number for your subject area will help in your search for information. Each system uses a general number or letter for the major topic classifications, and each of these classifications then has additional numbers or letters
for specific subdivisions. For instance, in the Library of Congress system, "P" is
used for the general classification "language and literature," while "PS" is used
for the subdivision "American literature" and "PR" for the subdivision "English
literature." Following is an overview of these reference systems.

Dewey Decimal System

000	General Works	500	Pure Science
100	Philosophy and Related Disciplines	600	Technology and Applied Science
		700	The Arts
200	Religion	800	Literature and Rhetoric
300	Social Sciences	900	General Geography and History
400	Language		

Library of Congress System

A	General Works, Polygraphy
B	Philosophy, Psychology, and Religion
C	Auxiliary Sciences of History (such as biography)
D	General and Old World History (except America)
E–F	American History
G	Geography, Anthropology, Manners and Customs, Folklore, Recreation
H	Social Science, Statistics, Economics, Sociology
J	Political Science
K	Law

L	Education
M	Music
N	Fine Arts
P	Language and Literature
Q	Science
R	Medicine
S	Agriculture, Plant and Animal Industry, Fish Culture, Fisheries, Hunting, Game Protection
T	Technology
U	Military Science
V	Naval Science
Z	Bibliography and Library Science

Subject Area Indexes   Below are some commonly used subject area indexes. Many of these are now available on-line, and some databases such as Infotrac, Newsbank, and Lexis/Nexis are only available on-line. Libraries use these to keep track of scholarly conversations in journals.

Commonly Used Subject Area Indexes

CURRENT EVENTS AND POPULAR MEDIA

1. *Reader's Guide to Periodical Literature*
2. *Social Sciences Index*
3. *Biography Index*
4. *Business Periodicals Index*
5. *General Science Index*
6. *New York Times Index*
7. *Wall Street Journal Index*
8. *Public Affairs Information Service* (PAIS)
9. Infotrac
10. Newsbank
11. Lexis/Nexis

EDUCATION

1. *Education Index*
2. *Current Index to Journals in Education*
3. ERIC (*Educational Resource Information Center*)

HISTORY AND HUMANITIES

1. *America: History and Life*
2. *Annual Bibliography of English Language and Literature*
3. *Historical Abstracts*
4. *Humanities Index*
5. *MLA International Bibliography*

NURSING AND MEDICINE

1. *Cumulative Index to Nursing and Allied Health Literature*
2. *Index Medicus*

PHILOSOPHY AND RELIGION

1. *Philosopher's Index*
2. *Religion Index One: Periodicals*

PSYCHOLOGY AND SOCIOLOGY

1. *Psychological Abstracts*
2. *Social Sciences Index*

GENERAL SCIENCE AND TECHNOLOGY

1. *Applied Science and Technology Index*
2. *Biological and Agricultural Index*
3. *General Science Index*

GOVERNMENT DOCUMENTS

1. *Congressional Abstracts*
2. *Monthly Catalog of U.S. Government Publications*

▓ ▓ THE WORKING BIBLIOGRAPHY

Using the card catalog or on-line catalog and appropriate subject area in-dexes should provide you with a working bibliography of books and articles re-lated to your topic. It is important to remember, however, that you are not looking just for information; you are looking for conversations. The books and articles you find are part of a context, a conversation about a particular issue. This conversation has a history, so as you examine your sources, try to learn as much as you can about the conversation of which these books and articles are a part and the communities that this conversation represents. Be careful not to take information from a source out of context (that is, out of its place in the conversation).

Recording the Conversation

▓ ▓ DOCUMENTING SOURCES

In academic communities, it is important that you document material you borrow from another writer (or bring from another community when it is not part of the common stock of knowledge of the community you are writing for). Documenting borrowed material allows your readers to locate your own writing within the context of a conversation and community and to identify your role as a contributor to that conversation. You readers will be able to identify the con-versations that you respond to and observe those conversations for themselves, understanding how you have extended or responded to other authors. In academic writing, there are three ways of recording and reporting what someone else has contributed to the conversation: quotation, summary, and paraphrase.

Quotation   Quotation, the word-for-word transcription of what someone else said or wrote, may seem like the simplest method of recording a source's ideas, but it requires painstaking attention to detail. You have to record everything exactly as it is found in your source. This can take a lot of time if you copy by hand. It is a bit quicker if you have a laptop computer or if you can find an electronic version of the original. Using the computer, you can simply cut and paste material to include in your own writing. Be very careful, though, to put quotation marks around anything you quote or to set off longer quotations as an indented block. Failure to do so constitutes plagiarism, an attempt to pass off the writing or ideas of others as your own. Plagiarizing distorts your contribution to the conversation, leading readers to believe that you play a more important role than you actually do. It is a type of fraud and is considered a serious breach in the academic community.

When you quote, you should also be careful to indicate where the material came from. Academic communities have developed different formats for documenting sources. Two of the most common are the MLA and the APA styles (named for the Modern Language Association and the American Psychological Association, two organizations within the academic community). You should find out from your instructor the style that is appropriate for your particular academic discipline. (Most college writing handbooks contain detailed information about documentation style.)

The MLA and APA styles call for "in-text" or "parenthetical" documentation. In this type of documentation, identifying information about the source is included in parentheses following the quoted material. MLA style includes the author's last name (if it has not been mentioned in the text) and the page number. APA style includes the author's last name, the year of publication, and the page number.

The following passages quote from the article "Employment-Based Health Insurance and Job Mobility," written by Brigitte C. Madrian, a Harvard economist. The first is in MLA style

```
Employers should note that "individuals with larger
families are less likely to leave their jobs if they have
health insurance than if they do not" (Madrian 52).
```

The documentation is in the parentheses following the quotation. It includes the author's last name and the page number of the source with no other punctuation. Notice that the period comes after the parenthetical documentation. This is because the parenthetical material is actually part of the sentence (so it comes before the period) but not part of the quotation (so it comes after the last set of quotation marks).

Here is an example of APA style.

```
Employers should note that "individuals with larger
families are less likely to leave their jobs if they have
health insurance than if they do not" (Madrian, 1994,
p. 27).
```

Again, the documentation is in the parentheses following the quotation. In APA style the author's last name, the year of publication, and the page number of the source are included, separated by commas. Notice that in APA style, the abbreviation "p." is used for "page" ("pp." for "pages"); MLA style doesn't use this abbreviation.

You should generally give some kind of context or background for anything you quote, bringing your reader up on the conversation from which you are quoting. You may want to mention the author's full name, along with a bit about his or her background and a summary of the context from which you are quoting. When you introduce a quotation with the author's name, this information does not need to be repeated in the parentheses. Here is an example. The first is in MLA style.

```
Brigitte Madrian, a Harvard economist, in her recent study
of the effects of health insurance on job mobility found
that "individuals with larger families are less likely to
leave their jobs if they have health insurance than if
they do not" (52).
```

Since the name of the author is given as part of the introduction to the quoted material, only the page number is included in the parentheses. Here is the same quotation following the APA format.

```
Brigitte Madrian's study of the effects of health
insurance on job mobility (1990) found that "individuals
with larger families are less likely to leave their jobs
if they have health insurance than if they do not"
(p. 52).
```

In APA style, it is typical for the year of publication (and author's last name, if not mentioned in the sentence) to follow the first mention of an article, with the page number following the actual quotation.

The previous two examples included the quoted material as part of a sentence that introduces that material. It is also possible for the quotation to follow a sentence, with a comma or colon introducing it. The following example uses MLA style.

> In a recent study, Brigitte Madrian, a Harvard economist, examined the effects of health insurance on job mobility: "Individuals with larger families are less likely to leave their jobs if they have health insurance than if they do not" (52).

It is even possible to interrupt quoted material with information about the context. This kind of interruption is set apart with commas. The following example uses APA style.

> "The majority of privately insured Americans obtain their health insurance through their own or a family member's employer," according to a recent study of the effects of health insurance on job mobility (Madrian, 1994). "The rationale for employers to provide health insurance is straightforward. By pooling the risks of individuals, employers can reduce adverse selection and lower administrative expenses" (p. 27).

Summary   Summary is another common method of recording and reporting information. In a summary, you extract the main ideas from a larger piece of writing and report them in a much briefer form. You should use your own words, although it is acceptable in writing a summary to use some key words and phrases from the original without setting them in quotation marks or to quote a memorable phrase. You may summarize a complete article or any part of it. As with quoted material, you must indicate where the summarized material came from using the appropriate style of documentation. Here is a summary of Brigitte Madrian's article on health insurance documented according to APA style.

> A recent study of the effects of health insurance on job mobility (Madrian, 1994) examined whether workers were "locked" into their jobs when their employers provided health insurance because prior medical conditions would not be insured if they left their jobs and had to obtain new coverage. For the years examined, this study found that in companies that provided health insurance the

```
number of workers who willingly chose to change jobs
decreased by 25 percent per year (p. 27-54).
```

Note that, as with quoted material, the period in the final sentence of the summary follows the parenthetical documentation.

When you write a summary, you should begin by previewing the essay: reading the first couple of paragraphs, the last few paragraphs, and the subheadings. Write down what you think the main ideas are in the essay, phrasing these ideas in your own words. Then read the article carefully and see how accurately you anticipated the writer's main ideas. Now try to summarize the main ideas of the writer. (The length of your summary depends on how much information from the writer you need.)

Paraphrase   Paraphrase is the third method of recording and reporting information from sources. In a paraphrase you rewrite a passage in your own words, preserving as much of the meaning of the original as you can. Think of paraphrase as an exercise in translation. You translate from the "language" of one community to the "language" of another. You may, for example, paraphrase a highly technical passage into language more familiar to nonspecialists or paraphrase highly formal language into more informal language. One method of paraphrasing is to read a passage carefully, cover it up, and then try to rewrite it in your own words. After you are finished, compare your paraphrase with the original. Cover the original again, revising your paraphrase to make sure that you have included the meaning of the original passage without using the actual language of the original. This may be difficult at first, but it will become easier as you become more skilled at rephrasing what others have said.

If this method does not work for you, then try the following two-step process. Substitute synonyms (words with similar meanings) for each key word of the original passage. Be sure that you look up in a dictionary any words that are unfamiliar to you. Choose the words you substitute carefully so that they fit together in terms of their connotations, level of formality, and familiarity. Don't just open a thesaurus and pick any word from the list. For some particularly technical or precise words in the original, you may need to substitute an entire phrase in order to capture the right meaning. In fact, unlike a summary, a paraphrase is often longer than the original. After substituting key words, revise the sentence and phrasal structure so that your paraphrase does not closely resemble the original.

As an example I will paraphrase the following passage from *The Communist Manifesto* by Karl Marx and Friedrich Engels:

> The bourgeoisie, wherever it has got the upper hand, has put an end to all feudal, patriarchal, idyllic relations. It has pitilessly torn asunder the motley feudal ties that bound man to his "natural superiors," and has left remaining no other nexus between man and man than naked self-interest, than callous "cash payment."

I will assume that I am using this passage in an essay addressed to a group that is not very familiar with the technical terminology of Marxist politics and economics, as well as other terms used in the passage, so that I need to paraphrase (or "translate") the passage to make the meaning more understandable. First, let's look up some of the unfamiliar terms. The following definitions come from Webster's Ninth New Collegiate Dictionary:

> *bourgeoisie:* the middle class or the social order dominated by the middle class

> *feudal:* relating to feudalism, the system of political organization prevailing in Europe from the 9th to about the 15th centuries, having as its basis the relation of lord to vassal with all land held in fee and as chief characteristics homage, the service of tenants under arms and in courts, wardship, and forfeiture

> *patriarchal:* related to patriarchy, a social organization marked by the supremacy of the father in the clan or family, the legal dependence of wives and children, and the reckoning of descent and inheritance in the male line

> *idyllic:* pleasing or picturesque in natural simplicity

> *torn asunder:* torn into parts

> *motley:* composed of diverse often incongruous elements

> *nexus:* a connection or link

> *callous:* feeling no emotion, feeling no sympathy for others

When writing a paraphrase you cannot simply substitute dictionary definitions such as these for the words of the original. You must always consider whether or not the author is using these words according to the meaning expressed in the dictionary. And you must still put the paraphrase in your own words. Still, the dictionary can help you with unfamiliar or technical terms. Here is my first attempt at substituting my words for those of Marx and Engels:

```
The middle class, wherever it has gained control, has
eliminated any associations between lord and subject,
father and family, or other natural ties. It has
mercilessly broken apart the odd mix of agreements between
the lord and his subjects that tied individuals to those
who ruled over them "by nature" and has left behind no
other connection between one individual and another than
merely looking out for oneself, than emotion-free
"monetary transaction."
```

In order to find some of these words, I consulted the dictionary. I also used a thesaurus to help me remember synonyms for words, but I was careful not to use any words from the thesaurus that I did not already know or that I did not look up in a dictionary to check for precise meaning.

Still, this paraphrase is not complete. It is only half of a paraphrase, relying too heavily on the structure and language of the original. Here is my attempt to recast the entire paragraph in my own words, using my own voice:

> In <u>The Communist Manifesto</u> Karl Marx and Friedrich Engels argue that whenever the middle class has gained control, it has done away with "natural" associations between individuals, such as those between lord and subject or father and family. They contend that the middle class mercilessly dissolved the odd mix of agreements found in the middle ages that tied individuals to those who ruled over them "by nature." It has eliminated every connection between one individual and another except for looking out for oneself in a cold-hearted "monetary transaction" (60).

Evaluate this paraphrase. Does it capture the meaning without relying too heavily on the language of the original passage? Is it more understandable than the original? What kind of community would this kind of paraphrase be appropriate for? Could you revise this paraphrase and make it even less formal? (Notice that my paraphrase is actually longer than the original.)

In the sample above, I introduced the paraphrased passage by noting its source and included in-text documentation just as I might in a research paper. It is extremely important to introduce summarized and paraphrased material. Readers know when quoted material begins because you indicate this with quotation marks; but because a summary or paraphrase is in your own words, readers have no way of knowing when the borrowed passage begins unless you introduce it in some way. You can introduce summarized or paraphrased material by using the author's name or phrases such as "According to one author," "Studies show," "Research indicates," and "Some claim." Your parenthetical documentation will indicate where a borrowed passage ends.

▧ ▧ DECIDING WHEN TO QUOTE, SUMMARIZE, OR PARAPHRASE

How do writers decide whether to quote, summarize, or paraphrase? Generally, beginning academic writers quote far too much, producing a paper that is more like a scrapbook of what others have said rather than a contribution to the academic conversation. You may want to quote in the following situations:

- when it is not only important to capture a writer's meaning but also the writer's language
- when the writer writes with unusual authority and you want to include that sense of authority in your own writing
- when you want to analyze a writer's exact words
- when you want to distance yourself from what a writer has said so that it is clear to your audience that this is the writer's view and not yours
- when the writer's words are famous or particularly memorable

In nearly every other case, it is best to summarize or paraphrase. Use summary when you need only the main idea from an essay or long passage. Paraphrase passages when you want to include as much meaning as you can but when the language itself is not particularly significant.

▓ ▓ TAKING RESEARCH NOTES

When you do library research, observing and recording academic conversations, it is important to keep careful notes. In the past, teachers encouraged students to keep these notes on 3 × 5 or 4 × 6 cards. I recycle paper by keeping notes on the back of half sheets of used office paper. These half sheets are less bulky than cards and fit neatly into a folder. They also give me room to write the things I need to. If you have a laptop computer, you can also save time by using it for taking notes. Just insert a page break for each new note and organize your notes into separate computer files.

Generally, you should keep two kinds of notes: bibliographic notes and content notes. The bibliographic note should provide publication information about the source you are using. For a book this would generally include the author's name, the title of the book, the place of publication, the publisher's name, and the year of publication. For a journal or magazine, this would generally include the author's name, the article title, the name of journal, the volume, the year, and the inclusive page numbers. When you write your final paper, a "Works Cited" or "References" page at the end of the essay includes this information for each source you quoted, summarized, or paraphrased in the essay.

Each documentation style has a particular form for reporting bibliographic information. Here are the forms for a book and for an academic journal in MLA style:

Book

Bardwick, Judith M. The Plateauing Trap. New York: AMACOM,
      1986.

Journal

Madrian, Brigitte C. "Employment-Based Health Insurance
   and Job Mobility: Is There Evidence of Job-Lock?"
   Quarterly Journal of Economics 109 (1994): 27-54.

Here are the forms for a book and a journal in APA style:

Book

Bardwick, J. M. (1986). The plateauing trap. New York:
   AMACOM.

Journal

Madrian, B. C. (1994). Employment-based health insurance
   and job mobility: Is there evidence of job-lock?
   Quarterly Journal of Economics, 109, 27-54.

(For a more complete list of MLA and APA formats, see Appendix B.)

Whatever documentation style you use, I recommend that you memorize at least the forms for a book and a scholarly journal and that you record the information for your bibliographic note in the proper form. Doing this will save you a lot of time when it is time to write the paper. Since the bibliographic note is the record of a "site" of conversation, you may also want to include whatever else you learned about the particular book, journal, magazine, or document, such as what you can discover about its readership or intended audience, its editorial policy, and any organizations affiliated with it. You will also want to include the call number and location of the source in the library.

The second type of note you need to take is a content note. This note contains information that you have learned from your source. It is difficult to copy out everything by hand, and photocopying every page you might need is expensive and really only postpones the process of note-taking. I would recommend the habit of taking notes in the form of summary, paraphrase, and occasional quotation. Use summary and paraphrase for most of the notes you take; use direct quotations sparingly. If you merely photocopy your sources or take all your notes as direct quotations, you will still have to summarize and paraphrase this material to include it in your essay. By taking most of your notes in the form of summary and paraphrase, you will save time in writing your essay and understand your research material better. Make sure that you include the information you will need to document this source in your essay: at least the author's name and the page number. You may also want to include a short title (if you are using more than one work by the same writer) or the year of publication (if you are using APA style).

Along with what you actually borrow from a source, you may want to include in your content notes any ideas you have about what you borrowed, perhaps your evaluation or response. I write my own ideas on the note within square brackets [like these] so that I can distinguish what I have borrowed from what is my own. (It is a typical practice to use square brackets in quoted material to indicate a comment from the writer who is quoting the passage.) If you think this might be confusing for you, use a separate card (or page break) and attribute the note to yourself.

Applying the Principles

▪ ▪ DOING LIBRARY RESEARCH

Now that you have learned something about how academic conversations are recorded and organized in libraries, you need to check out your own library and get involved in some research. First of all, keep in mind that the library is not only a site of communication for the academic community; it is in fact a community itself, so you'll need to know how to find your way around. You should be able to answer the following questions about your library:

- Where are the information desks located?
- What are the names of some librarians who could help me with my research?
- Where are the reference materials located? Is there a general reference area, or are reference materials spread throughout the library?
- Where is the card catalog or on-line catalog?
- Where are the books shelved?
- Where is the circulation desk? What do I have to do to obtain borrowing privileges?
- Where are current magazines and periodicals kept?
- Where are past issues of magazines or bound periodicals kept?
- Where are reserve materials kept? How can I get access to reserve materials?
- Where is the inter-library loan office? What procedure do I follow to obtain material from other libraries?
- Where are the copy machines?
- Where are places where I can read, write, and study? Is there a word processing or typing room?
- Where are audio-visual materials kept?
- Is there a rare book room or special collections area? Where is it located?
- What are the rules for using this library?

One way to analyze the library as a site of communication is to complete the preliminary work for a research topic. Select a topic area that you are interested in or a general issue that you feel strongly about and complete the following Background Study Guide. This is adapted from the background study guides prepared by Juliene Butler and Nancy Tidwell, two librarians at Brigham Young University.

Background Study Guide

This study guide is intended to lead you to sources that will (1) provide background information on your topic; (2) assist you in narrowing your topic; and (3) guide you in finding appropriate research materials for your paper.

As you begin, keep your subject general (so you can gather background information and gain understanding), but be alert to *issues* in the field (so you can later narrow your research to a specific issue and discuss it in your paper). As you read for background information, keep these questions in mind: What seem to be the most important questions the people who write about this subject are asking? Which of the issues discussed are of the greatest personal interest to you?

I. FINDING BACKGROUND MATERIAL

As you read background material, look for the history of your topic, relationships between your topic and other topics, issues within the topic, authorities in the field, and special terminology and definitions.

A. *Finding Subject Headings for Your Topic*

Go to the *Library of Congress Subject Headings* list at the General Reference Desk or near the card catalog, and look up some key words describing your topic area. Use both broad and narrow subject headings you could use in researching this topic. Note the Library of Congress classification number used for your topic: _____.

SUBJECT HEADINGS

_____   _____   _____

_____   _____   _____

_____   _____   _____

B. Searching General Encyclopedias

You can use any general encyclopedia to get background information. Using the index volume look up general terms describing your topic as well as more specific subtopics (narrower terms) that you found in the *Library of Congress Subject Headings* list. Examine any articles that may be of interest to you. These articles supply background information, names of authorities, and bibliographies. List below the authorities you find in general and specialized reference sources. Then list the encyclopedias you used and bibliographic references you may wish to consult.

AUTHORITIES IN THE FIELD

_____ _____ _____

_____ _____ _____

_____ _____ _____

C. Using Specialized Reference Books on Your Subject

1. Ask your reference librarian for general reference books on your subject. Read all articles in them relevant to your subtopic. You will find more detailed background information and learn of more issues in the field. List titles and bibliographic information for any of the sources you consult.

2. To find other specialized reference books (dictionaries, and so forth):

- Browse the reference collection shelves near the specialized encyclopedias you have been using. Look for dictionaries, handbooks, and so forth that will provide additional background information on your topic.
- Go to your on-line or card catalog and enter a subject search under the subject headings you have chosen from the *Library of Congress Subject Headings* list. Add the keywords "Dictionaries" or "Handbooks" to your search.
- If you are having trouble locating specialized reference books for your topic, ask a librarian for help.

GENERAL AND SPECIALIZED REFERENCE BOOKS
CONSULTED FOR BACKGROUND INFORMATION

_____

_____

_____

_____

RELEVANT BOOKS AND ARTICLES FROM BIBLIOGRAPHIES
IN ENCYCLOPEDIAS OR FROM OTHER REFERENCE BOOKS

_____

_____

_____

_____

_____

POSSIBLE RESEARCH TOPICS

_____

_____

II. FORMING AN ISSUE QUESTION

Your reading so far should have given you some background about your topic, an idea of the relationship of your topic to other topics, and some possible issues for research, as well as relevant terms and definitions and the names of some authorities. Now select an area of interest to you and formulate an issue question.

Sample Issue Question: "Are tests of mental health reliable?"

YOUR ISSUE QUESTION

_____

_____

_____

III. DOING THE RESEARCH

After gathering background information and formulating a research question, you are ready to turn to the library's on-line catalog or card catalog and to relevant periodicals indexes. Before you consult these sources, return to the *Library of Congress Subject Headings* list with your specific issue in mind. Review the subject headings to find those most appropriate for your narrower topic. Check all of your subject headings. Be aware that not all indexes use *Library of Congress Subject Headings* and you may need to use alternate terminology.

A. Using Specialized Indexes

List several articles you find in specialized indexes that you could use to write a research paper on your specific issue. (For a list of specialized indexes, see pages 128–129.) Include complete bibliographic information for each article. If the journal title is abbreviated in the index, be sure to check the key to journal abbreviations in the index's preface.

RELEVANT ARTICLES FROM SPECIALIZED INDEXES

_____

_____

_____

_____

B. Using the On-Line or Card Catalog

Find books that are related to your issue. Try finding specific titles contained in encyclopedia bibliographies, as well as books written by authorities on your subject. Try a keyword search to see if there are additional books on your topic. List the complete bibliographic information and call number for a few books you may want to use in writing a research paper on your issue.

BOOKS TO BE USED

_____

_____

_____

_____

C. Using Bibliographies

If you have trouble finding books or articles on your topic, do an on-line subject search with the additional keyword "bibliography." You may wish to consult the *Bibliographic Index* to locate additional bibliographies.

ADDITIONAL BIBLIOGRAPHIES (IF NEEDED)

_____

_____

The Background Study Guide should give you a good overview of the possibilities for your topic. After you have completed this guide, you should be prepared to follow the research strategy outlined in Figure 4-2, following your topic from general sources to more specific sources. This guide gives you a systematic approach to identifying and recording the conversations from various communities on the issue that interests you.

▒ ▒ IDENTIFYING AND RECORDING CONVERSATIONS FROM OTHER COMMUNITIES

The survey I've given here of library research describes one way to identify and record conversations for academic communities, but there are many other communities besides academic communities. The following readings describe how you might record conversations for two of these other communities. The first essay describes "lurking," the process of listening in on an electronic conversation before joining in yourself. The second essay describe how folklorists gather information from oral traditions.

Lurking

J. C. HERZ

I LURK FOR weeks.
Lurkers — that's what they call people on the Net who don't make any noise. Lurkers don't register on the Net. Not even a blip. And there are tens of thousands of them, literally the silent majority, peering down from the gallery.

Lurking is considered unsporting here in cyberspace (this is, after all, a theater of verbal flamboyance). But the number crunchers who crank out quasi-Arbitron ratings of Usenet newsgroups estimate that lurkers outnumber their chatty counterparts ten to one. Even here, most people are content to be part of the grand, high-beamed woodwork. Virtual wallflowers.

Lurking is a larval phase in the nethead life cycle. It's that spooky, voyeuristic time when you haven't got your bearings yet, but you're fascinated enough to browse with bovine contentment on the grassy pastures of online discourse. Concealed, you can sit back and binge on ASCII text, guzzling it faster than you've ever absorbed information in your life. You inhale information. And all the while, you're completely invisible. Lurking is like one of those Sunday-night movies on network TV where a guy is struck by lightning or toxic waste and becomes Captain Undetectable, suddenly able to overhear boardroom conversations and sneak into the lingerie dressing room at Macy's at a single bound. People get into fights, yell and scream at each other, and they're completely oblivious to you, in your front-row seat. Transparency has its privileges.

But after a while, the novelty of eavesdropping wears off. The learning curve 5 flattens out. You're bloated with other people's thoughts, and you know enough lingo not to embarrass yourself. So you say something. Anything. On some newsgroup. Any newsgroup. Just a few sentences. Nothing major.

And then you press a button, and your words come out the other side of the pipe. An offhand comment that lit up only one screen has circumnavigated the globe. One keystroke sends duplicates to Auckland, Helsinki, Pretoria, and a few hundred polytechnic colleges in the American Midwest.

This takes a few seconds.

And then, a few hours later, you pick up a response from some math major in Ontario — another rabbit out of the hat — and you're rolling. You have successfully evolved from larval lurker to the pupal nethead phase: novice poster (a creature with wriggly little legs but no wings). From there, it's just a matter of picking up speed and justifying sporadic editorials at the expense of school and state.

This is not a problem, as it allows me to avenge all those other frivolous uses of my tuition and tax dollars.

And in the midst of all this Netsurfing, it doesn't seem to matter that I've 10 graduated. It doesn't matter where I am, physically (in this case, Florida). I'm still on the Net, and it's seamless. It's absolutely continuous. I've moved, but I'm still *here*.

The concept of "here" is doing a slow, graceful back flip.

Documenting Folklore

WILLIAM A. WILSON

N OT LONG AGO I attended an informal dinner party with a number of fac- 1 ulty members and spouses. Midway through dinner the associate dean of my college said, "Bert, tell us some folklore." I replied that I would rather experience folklore than tell it. He looked at me blankly for a moment and then turned his attention to the obviously more intelligent faculty member seated across the table. They were soon engaged in an animated discussion of Southeast Asians who kill and eat their own dogs as well as those of their unwary neighbors. A few minutes later, as we complimented our hostess on the excellent fish she had just served, her husband, a fine poet and an even better storyteller, told us of another serving of fish at another dinner party in his native Wales. An up-and-coming young businessman and his wife, friends of a relative of our host, had thrown an elaborate party which they were sure would guarantee the husband's entry into the elite business circles in their community. A few minutes before the guests arrived, the family cat jumped on the table and ate a hole in the beautifully prepared and garnished salmon which was to serve as the dinner's main course. Horrified, the wife threw the cat outside and camouflaged the hole with parsley and other condiments. The party was a success — no one discovered the damage. Convinced that a good reputation among his colleagues was now assured, the husband bade farewell to the last guest and then walked outside, where he discovered the cat dead by the driveway. Mortified, he called everyone who had attended the party, confessed that they, with the cat, had evidently eaten spoiled fish, and urged them to rush to the hospital to have their stomachs pumped. The next morning, as the husband was contemplating his ruined career, his neighbor came by and apologized for having run over and killed the cat the night before. So as not to bother the dinner guests, he explained, he had quietly placed the cat by the driveway and waited until morning to tell what he had done. The story both shocked and amused the people at our dinner party. Most of these aspiring professionals felt genuine sympathy over the tragedy which had befallen the aspiring businessman. I smiled at my wife but said nothing.

The next day I xeroxed a story called "The Poisoned Pussy Cat at the Party" from Jan Brunvand's *The Vanishing Hitchhiker: American Urban Legends and Their Meanings,*[1] and copied an entire article from *Western Folklore,*[2] which discussed widely told stories about Southeast Asians stealing and eating dogs. On a piece of paper, I scribbled, "See what I mean!" and sent the note and the xeroxed pieces to the associate dean. He replied that he did now see and that in the future he would be careful what he said around me.

More than almost any other subject, folklore must be experienced directly in actual life, as I experienced these narratives, to be properly understood. In twenty years of teaching, I have discovered that my students can listen to my lectures, can read assigned books and essays on the subject, and can still leave the course not understanding folklore unless they have encountered it in the actual settings in which it is performed. I encourage students to achieve this end by keeping their eyes and ears open to what is going on around them — even to pay close attention to dinner-party talk; and I make sure they do this by requiring them to submit, first to me and then to the university archive, folklore they have collected themselves. Writing up these collections carefully enough to help potential archive users understand the substance and significance of the material submitted requires students to look more analytically at the folklore which surrounds them than they might have otherwise. The byproduct of this collecting, of course, is the development of folklore archives to support folklore research. But the main benefit is the increased understanding that comes to the students themselves.

If you are a beginning collector in search of this understanding, you will want to work closely with your teacher or with the archivist to whom you will submit your work. What follows is designed to supplement, not supplant, what they tell you. As you face for the first time the somewhat bewildering task of actually collecting and documenting some of the subject matter you will study, you must develop fairly clear notions about where to collect, what to collect, how to collect, and how to write up your data.

THE TRADITION-BEARERS

The essays in this book should have taught you that the study of folklore   5 seldom leads to the strange and exotic, but rather to much of what you have already known and experienced but not recognized as folklore. The essays should also have shown you that folklore is transmitted through time and space, not just by old, rural, uneducated, and ethnically different people, as is often believed to be the case, but by the doctor next door, by the fellow computer programmer at work, by the members of your religious congregation, by your younger brothers and sisters, by friends at a dinner party, and often by yourself. To collect folklore, then, you needn't pack your bags and head for some exotic place (as exciting as that might be); the lore you are after may be no further away than your workplace, your church, your mother's kitchen, your sister's playground, a casual gathering of friends, or your own memory.

As you try to decide where and from whom to collect, think of the different social identities (shaped by the social groups to which you belong) which make up your own personality. You are probably a student. You may belong to a religious group and live in a constant swirl of religious traditions and religious legends. You may have learned to view the world through ethnic or immigrant eyes. You probably have hobbies. You may already belong to an occupational group and may have learned much of what you must know to succeed not from job manuals but from traditional knowledge passed from person to person at work. You may live in a small, homogeneous community. You belong to a family. You have been a child and may still have close ties with children. Think for a moment of the rhymes, the chants, the songs, the games, the riddles, the superstitions, the traditional rules of conduct, and the taboos which you could collect from these youngsters with little difficulty. Other groups you are familiar with share equally rich lore. Though it is possible, and often rewarding, to collect from members of social groups different from your own, the price you will have to pay to establish rapport, win trust, and avoid violation of cultural taboos may be too high for the beginner. You will probably be more successful if you will do your first collecting among people you know. Once you have mastered collecting techniques and gained a better understanding of folklore in general, then you can turn your attention to people whose lifestyles and world views differ from your own.

Folklorists customarily refer to the people from whom they collect, whether from their own groups or not, as "informants"; some prefer a more deferential word like "consultants." What you should remember, whatever term you use, is that the people sharing their knowledge with you are the tradition-bearers and should be treated with respect. That means you must never collect from them in secret and without their permission. . . .

THE TRADITIONAL WORLD

As you think about the particular social group from which you wish to collect, try to determine what is traditional within that group. What are the behavioral consistencies and continuities? Ask yourselves as many questions as you can: Are there rites to initiate new members? Are there superstitions and taboos connected with the group? Are there stories of group heroes and anti-heroes? Are there jokes and anecdotes that ridicule outsiders with whom group members must carry on social exchange (doctors versus patients, for example)? Are there jokes about members of subgroups within the same larger social organization (doctors versus nurses)? Do group members wear distinctive clothing, eat distinctive food, use a distinctive, and often highly specialized vocabulary? Is there a traditional code of conduct? Are there ways of punishing violators of the code? And so on.

You may find it useful to divide the folklore these questions will call forth into three broad categories: things people make with words (verbal lore), things they make with their hands (material lore), and things they make with their actions (customary lore). Such a division is, of course, highly arbitrary, but it does help order the materials of folklore and get you thinking about what you could most profitably collect. The following lists drawn from these categories suggest some, but certainly not all, the folklore awaiting the collector's hand:

- *Things people make with words (verbal lore):* Ballads, lyrical songs, legends, folktales, jokes, proverbs, riddles, chants, curses, insults, retorts, teases, toasts, tongue twisters, greetings, leave-takings, autograph-book verses, limericks, graffiti, epitaphs.
- *Things people make with their hands (material lore):* Houses, barns, fences, gardens, tools, toys, tombstones, foods, costumes, and things stitched, woven, whittled, quilted, braided, and sculpted.
- *Things people make with their actions (customary lore):* Dances, instrumental music, gestures, pranks, games, work processes, rituals, community and family celebrations such as weddings, birthdays, anniversaries, funerals, holidays, and religious ceremonies.

Many forms of folklore, of course, overlap these categories. For example, a song is an item of verbal lore and a quilt material lore, but the singing of the song and the making of the quilt are customary practices. In many folklore events, all three media merge. At a birthday celebration, the making and decorating of the cake are customary practices, and the cake itself is an item of material lore; the singing of the birthday song is a customary practice, and the song is an item of verbal lore. What this means, as we shall see, is that you really can't, or shouldn't, collect individual forms of folklore isolated from the other forms

10

that surround them. You can, obviously, record only the words and music of a birthday song, but if you do not describe the setting in which the song is performed, including at least a brief description of the other forms of folklore also present, your recording really will not help you or a potential archive user properly understand the significance of the song in the lives of its performers.

COLLECTING FOLKLORE

This brings us to the issue of how actually to collect the folklore, how to record it so that archive users will recognize the importance of the lore to those who express it.

You will probably do a better job of collecting if you are fortunate enough to be present when folklore is performed naturally, without any prompting from you. Sometimes this happens by accident, as it did with me at the dinner party. More often you can arrange to be present where you know the kind of folklore you are interested in is likely to occur — at a bridal party, for example, where you will collect wedding or shower games. At times you may be able to bring a number of people together who will probably generate the lore you are after. If you arrange a skiing party, you will surely hear a lot of skiers' lore before the evening is over.

The value of this kind of "participant observation" is that you have the opportunity to observe firsthand what sparked the performance of a particular item of folklore, how successful the performance was, and what impact it had on the audience (including the impact it had on you). When you write up the event for submission to the archive, you may first want to interview other members of the audience for their responses to the performance, but, if you have observed carefully, most of what you need to describe of the social setting will already be in your own head.

The difficulty with this kind of collecting is that in many instances you will not be able to record the actual performance as it occurs. You can, of course, set up a tape recorder in advance at a bridal shower or a skiing party and record what takes place there. But if you hear a good story at a dinner party, you will have to go back to the narrator later and ask him to tell you the story again. When you do this, you may want to bring along a couple of people who have not heard the story before so the narrator's retelling will be as spontaneous as possible.

Much of the collecting you do will be by "direct interviewing" from the beginning. Once you have decided what kind of lore you wish to collect, then you must determine which people are most likely to possess the information you are after. As you collect using this method, you will be collecting folklore not from firsthand observation but from other people who were firsthand observers — from somebody else who has been at a bridal shower, skiing party, or dinner party. In this instance, you will have little trouble recording the folklore but will have to work much harder to get the necessary contextual background. You will have to elicit from the person who was present at the folklore performance what you would have observed had you been there yourself.

15

Don't hesitate at times to interview yourself. Without reaching far into memory, you should remember all kinds of folklore events in which you have taken part. You may never be able to discover completely how a folklore performance affected someone else, but you do know how participation in folklore events affected you. If you were once initiated into a fraternal order, you can not only describe the initiation, but tell how it made you feel. Some of our best contextual data come this way.

As you begin to gather material, you should understand at the outset that you can't record *all* the information every potential archive user may one day need to interpret a body of lore. This is why serious folklorists, while using archive data, will collect much of their material in the field — it's the only way to get exactly what they want. But you can record enough data to make your document useful. No matter what kind of lore you collect, you should always ask yourself a number of important questions. First, what is there about this lore that is pleasing? What makes it artistically powerful, or persuasive? Second, how does the lore function in the lives of the people who possess it? What needs does it meet in their lives? Third, what does the lore tell us about the values and attitudes of individuals and the groups to which they belong?

The Art of Folklore

In many ways the performance of folklore could be called an exercise in behavior modification. Through the things people make with their words, hands, and actions, they attempt to create a social world more to their own liking. When they tell a story, or make a quilt, or perform an initiation ceremony, they are usually attempting, through the power of artistically successful forms, to influence the way people act, including at times themselves. We cannot hope to understand the artistic impact of these forms unless they are recorded as precisely as possible as they live in actual performance.

Verbal lore   To capture the art of verbal lore you should, where possible, record your material with a tape recorder, especially free narrative forms in which the wording and presentational style may change strikingly from telling to telling. It is possible to take down material with pen or pencil, but this usually impedes the performance and brings you a truncated bit of reality. The following tape-recorded "scary story," told by an exuberant fourteen-year-old girl at summer camp, captures the essence of the real narrative with an exactness seldom matched in handwritten recordings:

> There was these couples that ran away from home to get married, and they were driving out on the desert, and all of a sudden he ranned out of gas, and she says, "Well, I told you to get some gas at that last town, but you just wouldn't listen."
>
>   And he goes, "Well, I'll walk back and get some." And he goes, "Now lock all the doors and windows, because they've heard about this hook man who goes around the desert trying to kill people." And he goes, "Now lock all the doors and windows and don't let it open for anyone or anything that you hear."

And so she locked them all and started listening to the radio. And she heard more about that hooked man that went around killing people. And so she got really scared. So she turned it off and she fell asleep. And during the night she woke up and she heard a scratching sound. And, and she got kind of worked up about that and so, so she just went back to sleep. And all of a sudden she woke up and she was wondering what woke her up. And there was that hook man outside, and he was sitting there trying to get in the car. And she just kind of got really scared and everything, but she didn't dare try to get out of the car or move. And so she fell asleep just sitting there.

And so, when she woke up again he was gone, but there was still that swishing and thumping sound kind of on the roof of the car, but she didn't dare open it.

Pretty soon she was getting worried about her boyfriend because he hadn't come back all night. And so she fell asleep again because she was really tired.

And pretty soon a cop came — it was in the morning — and he sat there knocking on the windows. And she woke up and she saw the cop and, and he goes, "Open the door."

And so she opened the door.

And he goes, "What do you know about this?"

And she goes, "Know about what?"

And he pointed in this tree above their car — they parked by a tree. And there was the guy, there was her boyfriend hooked to the tree, and he'd been all clawed up by that hooked man.[3]

One of the values of the tape recorder is that it frees you to write down   20
information which *should* be recorded on a note pad, information about the circumstances of the storytelling situation: the setting in which the story was told; the nature of the audience; movements and hand gestures made during the telling; responses and promptings of the audience; everything, in short, to help the reader of your document not only hear the story but also visualize the setting in which it was related.

While the collector of the above item claimed to have recorded it word-for-word as it was told, I suspect that a few false starts and an occasional "uh" were edited out. Many collectors of oral documents, in fact, encourage editing. Folklorists do not, at least not for the archive document. It should be recorded just as it was spoken. If one later wishes to edit the piece for publication, at least the original remains available for scrutiny in the archive. Above all, when you prepare a document for archive submission, be sure to tell whether the item recorded is a verbatim transcription, an edited transcription (tell the extent of the editing), a close (but not totally accurate) shorthand recording, or a paraphrase of the original.

Good transcriptions are hard to make from unclear tape recordings. The bibliographical section following this essay will guide you to sources which will instruct you in the proper use of recording devices — tape recorders, cameras, video machines. But you should understand that you needn't be an expert or own expensive equipment to get a satisfactory recording. You must, however, use a machine with a separable microphone (in-machine microphones record mostly the whirling of the drive belts), keep the microphone within a foot of the speaker's mouth, and avoid touching or moving the microphone wire during the recording (each stroke of the wire will be transmitted to the tape).

Material lore   Beginning folklore collectors seldom focus on material lore — not because the things people make with their hands are any less worthy of study, but because accurately documenting them is a difficult task not easily achieved by the novice. This is not to say that if you are interested in ranch fences, quilts, barn styles, or sculpted gravestone motifs, you should not set out to document them. But you should realize that the task will not be particularly easy.

To help archive users understand what is artistically pleasing about the artifacts you document, you must begin with accurate pictures of the objects. Occasionally, you can record these pictures with line drawings just as you can occasionally record verbal lore with a pencil. I have seen excellent sketches of folk toys — rubber guns, sling shots, clothespin pistols, handkerchief dolls, cootie catchers — which vividly depict these objects. But in most instances, you will need to record material culture with a camera, and a good one at that, preferably a 35-mm, single-lens reflex camera which can be set for varying light intensities and distances.

You may take either color slides or black-and-white prints. Just as your sound recordings will reveal narrative texture, so too must these pictures display the stylistic and textural features of the artifacts being photographed. That means you will need to take a number of shots of the same object. If you were documenting a quilt, you would want a photograph of the entire quilt so that the overall design would be clear; you would take a close-up of individual blocks in the quilt; and you would want a still closer shot of the needlework in the block. If possible, you would also take pictures of different stages in the quilt making, from assembling the quilting frames to removing the quilt at its completion; and, because material objects are made to be used, you ought to get a picture of the quilt on the bed for which it was made.

Through your photographs, you should give an accurate view of material artifacts as they exist in actual life. To do this, you will have to do more than take pictures. You will need also to submit written texts that explain in considerable detail what appears in the pictures. A photograph of a well-crafted saddle, for example, without an explanation of its different parts and their functions, will be of limited value.

Customary lore   If the pleasure derived from verbal and material folklore comes principally from hearing and seeing, the artistic satisfaction derived from customary lore results primarily from participating in action. Customary practices range broadly across the full spectrum of human activity, but they tend to focus on ceremonies and festive events which tie people more closely to their family, ethnic, religious, occupational, and regional groups; on rites of passage which move people through transitional stages of life such as birth, puberty, marriage, incorporation into new social groups, and death; and on work processes which make easier and more enjoyable the hours people spend earning their bread.

Customary lore is a good place to begin collecting because you will often have to go no further than your own memory and because attempting to understand the significance of the traditional activities which make up your life will help you discover significance in the practices you collect from others. The following excerpt from a Swiss-American student describing Swiss Independence Day (August 1) in her Minnesota community should stir memories of important ceremonial events you could record from your own life:

> Between one and two hundred Swiss-Americans will gather at one of the homes (lately, my family's) and sing traditional songs, play traditional music, dance, eat bratwurst, good Swiss bread and cheese, and drink wine. As the sun sets, the highlight of the evening is reached. A huge bonfire is lit, and everyone gathers around it to soak up its warmth and glow and to sing late into the night — until the fire has died down to a pile of glowing coals.
>
> The creation of this bonfire is a task undertaken with care and great enthusiasm. The men build it, using scrap lumber and carefully balancing and arranging them teepee style till the structure is about 10–15 feet high. The lighting of it is made to be spectacular (with the help of gasoline) and worthy of the long "oohs" and "ahhs" it inevitably gets.
>
> The bonfire is a very old tradition in Switzerland for celebrating Independence Day. Neighborhoods and towns will get together to create one. It is important for the Swiss in America to continue to celebrate the day in this way, for the very reason of being so far from their homeland. The closeness, the oneness, the nostalgic comfort that building and standing 'round the fire fosters is an important binding force among the Swiss-American group.

When you collect customary practices, the camera will once again serve as a useful tool to record steps in processes like branding cattle, felling trees, preserving food, playing games, and celebrating Christmas. But you must, above all, observe keenly and describe accurately the action itself and the interplay of people involved in the event described. The following description of a fraternity birthday celebration, witnessed for the first time by a new pledge, catches in exemplary fashion both the actions and the joyful spirit of the occasion:

> After everyone had finished dinner, one of the brothers started to sneak away from the table, at which time another brother yelled out that it was that guy's birthday. Everybody grabbed him and dragged him into the living room (he didn't fight too hard). Everyone was having a fun time of it. They put the guy face down on a table and then carried out the following rite, which I have recorded as I witnessed it:
>
> Every brother got the chance to paddle the birthday brother. The paddles were the ones given by the pledges to their Big Brothers. [This point needs further explanation.] Every brother had a favorite paddle and talked about how each one was most effective at inflicting pain (much to the dismay of the birthday brother). The brothers got their chances alphabetically. They were allowed one swat apiece, but the swing was only allowed from the wrist (so as not to do much damage). A painful swat could still be achieved by most. Most of the swatters

would put up the act that they were about to wail on the birthday brother. Some of them would, but others would take it easy and just let the paddle flop down. When hit hard, the swattee would cry out pledges for vengeance. When hit softly, he usually called the swatter a gentleman and gave him sincere thanks. After everyone got their chance, somebody gave the birthday brother a beer. Then they all started singing the following song while they shook his hand:

> Happy birthday to you; happy birthday to you.
> Happy birthday dear _____; happy birthday to you.
> May you live a thousand years.
> May you drink a thousand beers.
> Get plastered, you bastard; happy birthday to you.

After the song, everyone joined in the following cheer:

> Rah, rah, rah, Phi Kappa Tau!
> Live or die for Phi Kappa Tau! Rah!

Meaning and aesthetic judgments: As you record data to help the archive user better understand the meaning or artistic significance of the material collected, try to give the tradition-bearer's own point of view, not yours, of why something is meaningful or aesthetically pleasing. People who sing working songs, braid hackamores, and ritually celebrate the birth of a child know what pleases them and what does not. And if you ask the right questions, they will tell you.

This is not a particularly easy task. If someone tells you a moving family story about her grandparents keeping the bodies of children dead from the flu in the woodshed until the weather finally warmed enough in the spring to dig the frozen ground, and you respond by asking, "What does that story mean to you?" you will probably be considered both stupid and bad-mannered. But if you can get her talking about the occasion on which she heard the story, those on which she tells it, and her reasons for telling it, you should gain a fair notion of what the story *means* to her. Similarly, if you can get a quilter to tell you why she chooses certain colors for her patterns, a housewife to explain why she arranges food on the table in a given way, a rancher to explain why he prefers to rope calves for branding instead of using a cattle chute, you will have recorded at least some aesthetic judgments. These judgments, to be sure, are usually shaped by the tradition-bearer's larger community or social group, but the group aesthetic can be generalized only after the responses of numerous individuals have been documented and archived.

You will discover that while the people you interview, like everyone else, make artistic judgments on formal criteria (the pleasing interrelationship of parts), they also judge folklore creations on functional and associational grounds. A rawhide rocking chair that does not "set well," or does not rock (function) properly, will not be judged artistically successful by the craftsman and his community, no matter how handsome it might appear to the outsider. Similarly, folklore which does not call forth the proper associations will probably not be valued as much as that which does. Children insist on celebrating Christmas the same way each year because doing so brings forth pleasant memories of Christmases past. A housewife continues to use the same decorative pattern in her pie crusts, not because the pattern itself particularly pleases her but because she learned it from her mother as a child and almost feels her mother's presence as she now decorates her own pies.

When I asked a quilter one day which of all the wonderful quilts she had shown me she liked best, she picked out one which to me seemed no more distinctive than the rest. She then explained that she had made the quilt while recovering from an arthritis attack and had hurt more during the quilting than she ever had before. The quilt reminded her of her triumph over pain — and was therefore beautiful. A young woman in my folklore class, expecting her second child and experiencing considerable discomfort, collected and submitted a joke which she found especially funny. It was a joke about a pain machine that supposedly transferred the pains from a woman in labor to the father of the child. The night the baby was due, the doctor hooked husband and wife up to the machine and, as the labor intensified, gradually turned the machine up to its limit. The wife's pains disappeared, but for some reason the husband felt no discomfort himself. The baby safely delivered, the husband returned home, opened the door, and found the milkman dead on the kitchen floor. I thought the joke passingly funny because of the cuckolding of the husband and because of the surprise ending. My student commented, "I found this joke to be very funny. It is funny because it demonstrates to women that men cannot stand as much pain as a woman even though they think they can." As you collect and document folklore, you must discover, through careful questioning, the *tradition-bearer's view* of why the quilt is beautiful or the joke is funny.

The Social Function of Folklore

Folklore persists through time and space because the things people traditionally make with their words, hands, and actions continue to give pleasure and satisfy artistic impulses common to the species. Folklore persists also because it continues to meet basic human needs. This means that to properly document folklore you will have to record not just a proverb, or a recipe, or a game, or a story about a poisoned cat at a dinner party, but also the social settings in which these items were performed — not just what was said or made or done, but also the circumstances that generated the performances and the participants' responses to them. The following description of a recitation of traditional rhyme points the direction you should take:

> Sara [age 62, the collector's maternal aunt, a Swedish immigrant] currently babysits small children in her home for a living. She enjoys her work because she is always around children and always says that she's just a kid herself.
>
> Sara is one of the funniest ladies I've ever known. She's always joking about how she's going on a diet and that we won't even recognize her when we see her next. She has a lot of funny rhymes and a poem for every occasion.
>
> One Thanksgiving Day (last year) she came to Idaho for dinner in Pocatello. We were all just finished with dinner and everyone was letting out their moans

and groans from eating too much. Nobody was saying too much at the time because of the agony of bloating ourselves. We were all family members, my mom and dad, some of my sisters, and about three cousins. The little incident that happened wouldn't have been nearly as funny if a couple of our friends (non-family members who are considered "high class") had not been there.

What happened was that Sara let go with a *loud* burp. I quickly looked over to see the expressions on the faces of the "high class" friends. It was a little embarrassing for us all, but Sara really smoothed things out well when she said this little rhyme immediately afterwards:

> It's better to burp and bear the shame,
> Than not to burp and bear the pain!

After she said it, we *all* had a good laugh, even the two friends who normally wouldn't laugh at such a thing.

Note what the collector has told us in this description. We know a little about Sara's personality; we know what the occasion for the gathering was; we know who was present and something about the way they related to each other; we are aware of the embarrassment caused by the burp; we learn how Sara dealt with the embarrassment through reciting a traditional rhyme; and we learn what impact the recitation had on the others.

Because of what the collector has told us about the social setting in which the rhyme was used, we can now move beyond the rhyme, which by itself could be dismissed as an interesting bit of trivia, toward a better understanding of the way folklore, skillfully used, can help people affect the social environment to their own advantage. One description of one rhyme will not bring us to this end, but enough good descriptions of enough folklore performances will. Again, this is the function of an archive, to keep on file the folklore you collect until enough of it is available to move from descriptions of individual folklore performances to generalizations about folklore's larger social uses.

Just as you should let those from whom you collect interpret their folklore, so, too, should you allow them to comment on their reasons for performing it. I once listened to a tape-recorded story of a family supernatural legend in which the narrator became so emotionally involved in the story that she broke into tears. When the narration ended, the collector, evidently remembering that she was supposed to record information about her informant's attitude toward her narratives, asked, "Now, do you believe the story?" The woman was highly offended, and rightly so. Of course, you will want to know what the tradition-bearers believe about their material, but if you will listen to and observe their performances carefully enough, and if you will get them to describe the social settings in which they have performed, or might perform, their lore, then you won't have to ask boorish questions to get your information. Certainly in the following illustration there can be little doubt about the attitude of the tradition-bearer, a rodeo cowboy, toward the tradition he describes:

> Many competing cowboys like myself believe and practice this rule whenever competing in a rodeo. The belief is that if you have ever been injured in a certain piece of clothing, whether it be a pair of stockings, Levis, or a shirt, then this

article of clothing has been cleansed of bad luck and now every time you wear it, it shall bring you luck.

I got in a fight on a Friday night several years ago, and I was beat rather badly by my opponent. But I was to compete in a jackpot rodeo on the following morning, even though I hurt everywhere. So I took the opportunity to wear a pair of "Wrangler Jeans" that I had been beat up in the night before, feeling that it would be a good omen. And I won the jackpot with one of the classiest bareback rides I have ever made.

The Cultural Background of Folklore

Perhaps the most difficult data to collect is that which places folklore in its larger cultural context. And in this instance, collecting from your peers may be a disadvantage, primarily because the tradition-bearers from whom you collect will probably speak a cultural language you already understand; and further, trapped by your mutual understanding, you may feel little need to explain the language for the cultural outsiders who may one day study your collection. For example, the following supernatural legend from Mormon tradition will be rich in meaning for most Mormons but may make little sense to non-Mormons:

> This man and woman was going through the temple doing work for the dead, and they got out to Salt Lake, and they had kids. And at the last minute the babysitter didn't come, and so they had to take their kids to the temple with them. And they were standing outside the temple waiting to get in, and they didn't know what they were going to do with their kids. There was no one around there they could leave them with, and they didn't know what they were going to do with them. While they were standing there, this strange man and woman came up to them and introduced themselves and said they would tend their kids while they went through the temple. The man and woman tended their kids, and the couple went in and did work for the dead, and that couple tending their kids turned out to be the couple they did the work for. When they came out of the temple, the man and woman were no longer there.

The individual who collected this narrative submitted it to the archive with the name of the teller attached plus a brief description of the storytelling setting, but with no information to help the non-Mormon user of the archive understand what is really happening in the story and happening in the minds of those who tell and listen to it. He should have included a statement something like this:

> Mormons believe they have an obligation to save not only themselves and, through missionary work, their neighbors, but also all their kinsmen who have died without benefit of gospel law. Thus, they seek the names of their ancestors through genealogical research and then in their sacred temples vicariously perform for these ancestors all the saving ordinances of their gospel. In this particular narrative, the couple evidently came "out to Salt Lake" to participate in temple activity because one of the church's limited number of temples is located there. The man and woman who tend the baby are spirits of the dead who have probably long been waiting for saving ordinance work to be performed on their

behalf. In a neat turn, the deceased husband and wife take care of the physical needs of the baby while the baby's parents attend to their spiritual needs. A story like this will be considered very sacred to many Mormons and should be treated with respect.

As any Mormon readers of these lines will know, we could still say a good deal more about this story, but the above information should place it in a cultural context making it at least partially intelligible to non-Mormons.   40

As you record cultural data for your folklore documentation, you should always ask what behaviors, ideas, and concepts people bring to the social setting in which a folklore performance takes place. And then you should include your answers to these questions in your document. What attitudes about Southeast Asians, for example, did the member of the dinner party bring to the discussion of Southeast Asians eating dogs? What feelings about the importance of national heritage did Swiss-Americans in Minnesota bring to their celebration of Swiss Independence Day? What concept of salvation did the teller of the temple story bring to his narration?

If you are collecting from members of your own group, you may already know the answers to these questions and can pull from your own head the information necessary to make the folklore clear to an outsider. If you are not a part of the group, you will have to get this information by learning as much about the group as possible before you begin collecting and then by asking the tradition-bearers themselves to explain what you do not understand in the folklore they give you. In the illustration above, asking no more than "What's the difference between a temple and a regular house of worship?" and "What is 'work for the dead'?" would probably produce enough information to make the story understandable.

Because the controlling concepts and the value center of any group are, in the final analysis, the composite concepts and values of individuals in the group, you will need to record as much information as possible about the tradition-bearers themselves. You should elicit information that relates directly to the lore being collected — ethnic attitudes from people who tell ethnic jokes — but you should also gather general information: sex, age, ethnic ancestry, education, religion, occupation, hobbies, and so on. And it's probably better to record too much than too little, since you can't know the uses to which your collections might be put in the future. Writing down the occupation of a teller of sexist jokes may seem unnecessary at the moment of collecting, but to the researcher who will one day use your material to study sex role attitudes of different male occupational groups, such information will prove crucial.

THE FOLKLORE DOCUMENT

Once you have brought together the kinds of data discussed in the sections above, your final task will be to write up your material for submission to the folklore archive. You should visit the archive to see where your collections will finally be located, to glimpse the range of materials filed there, to gain a better understanding of the contribution you can really make through careful work, and especially, to review the documentary forms used by the archive. In the absence of specific requirements from the archive or from your instructor, you may want to use the format below (a format used, in varying degrees, by a number of university archives). Remember that your ultimate goal is to capture on paper what took place in a particular folklore performance. Let the format be your servant, not your master. Follow it as closely as possible, but alter it if necessary to meet the demands of the material collected.

1. In the upper right-hand corner, in three lines, put the name of the in-   45
formant, the place the lore was collected, and the date it was collected. If you submit lore culled from your own memory, write "Myself" for the informant's name and then record where and when you learned the lore.

2. In the upper left-hand corner put the form of folklore collected and, when possible, a title for the lore which suggests its content.

3. Three spaces below the title, at the left-hand margin, write "Informant Data:" and then give general biographical information about the informant and any details, including personal comments, which would give a clearer picture of the informant's relationship to and understanding of the folklore recorded. If you are your own informant, give the same kinds of details about yourself as you would for someone else.

4. Three spaces further down, at the left-hand margin, write "Contextual Data:" and then give both the social and cultural context for the folklore.

Under social context describe the circumstances under which you collected the folklore and under which your informant originally learned it, focusing, as already noted, on such things as the people present when the folklore performance occurred, the circumstances that generated the performance, the way people present participated in or influenced the performance, and the impact of the performance on them. Be sure to indicate if the folklore is normally performed at specific times and before certain people (at family reunions, for instance, or before women only). Other methods failing, you can often get good information about the social uses of folklore by asking for a description of a hypothetical context in which the informant might tell a particular story or take part in a particular ritual. Under cultural context, give information about the informant's culture which would make the folklore understandable to outsiders.

5. Three spaces further down, at the left-hand margin, write "Item:" and   50
then present the folklore collected. Be sure to tell how the lore was recorded and to what extent the words on paper faithfully follow or depart from those of the informant.

If you collect folksongs, try to record both words and music. Put at least one verse directly under the music.

If you submit line drawings or diagrams of steps in an action (finger games, for example), test the accuracy of these drawings before you submit them; see if a friend can perform the actions you have illustrated in the drawing.

If you collect folk speech, or jargon, explain the words and expressions submitted and use them in sentences which communicate the meaning.

If you submit photographs or slides, clearly identify each one and key it to the accompanying written document.

6. In the bottom right-hand corner, give your name and age, your home address (including street number), your school address if you wish, your university (if applicable), the course for which you are submitting the folklore (if applicable), and the semester or quarter and year (if applicable).

55

Each folklore document submitted to the archive, then, should contain the following:

Genre	Name of the informant
Title	Place the folklore was collected
	Date the folklore was collected

Informant Data:

Contextual Data:
    Social Context:
    Cultural Context:

Text:

Your name and age
Your home address
Your school address
Your school
Course number
Semester/quarter and year

The three examples given below (drawn from Utah State University and Brigham Young University Folklore Archives) follow the format quite closely: each does a reasonably credible job of describing the folklore submitted, although each could be improved.

The collector/informant of Sample #1 describes well enough the hunting practice he witnessed, but does not comment on its impact on him personally, something he could easily have told us since he serves as his own informant. How does he feel about hunting in general? Does he share the attitude of his companions about the manliness of the sport? What kind of verbal teasing accompanies the shooting of the clothing? Did others (insiders) in the party who failed to bag a deer shoot up their clothing? How did they seem to respond to the ritual? Was he, an outsider, treated differently from them? Did he actually shoot his own hat or coat? How did this make him feel? Did he wear the wounded article of clothing during the year? When and where? How did this make him feel? Did he go hunting again?

(Sample #1)

Hunting Custom | Myself
"Shooting Hunting Clothing" | Spanish Fork, Utah
| October 1979

Informant Data:
Walter M. Jones was born in Richland, Washington, on July 8, 1960. His father was in the military and moved around the country a lot. Walter's background is basically western. His family origins are northern European. He is a member of the LDS (Mormon) church. Walter is married and is a junior at Brigham Young University.

Contextual Data:
Walter attended BYU back in 1978 and 1979, before entering the armed forces. He lived with a family in Spanish Fork, Utah, and became very close to them. During the month of October, Utah holds its annual deer hunt. The family in Spanish Fork participated in the hunt the same way as most residents of the state, with much enthusiasm. The family invited Walter to participate, and he went along. He had never been on a deer hunt and was ignorant of the great fervor that surrounds it. He and a few others in the hunting party did not shoot a deer and had to go through the punishment described below. The members of the group are a hardy bunch who pride themselves on being very manly. Not bagging a deer is considered not manly, and the person committing the sin is humiliated as a means of punishment. The evidence of humiliation is worn throughout the year to prompt the individual to do a better job in hunting next year.

Item:
If, at the end of the deer hunt, a person hasn't killed a deer, he must take off his hat or coat and lay it on the ground. He is then ordered to shoot the article of clothing and put it back on. When you wear the hat or coat, then everyone will know that you didn't get a deer. The only way to earn the right to wear a good hat or coat is to shoot a deer the next hunt.

Walter G. Jones
373 N. 400 W.
Provo, Utah
Brigham Young University
English 391   Fall 1985

The collector of Sample #2 records not only a belief (superstition), but also a story (in the informant's own words) about the belief. Whether the informant has actually "gotten over" the experience related we may never know, but at least we know, through her excellent little narrative, how it once affected her behavior. Beyond the narrative itself, we do not learn much about the informant and the role of folk belief in her life and in the rural Mormon community where she lived. For people who may have never seen anything but a gas or electric clothes dryer, the collector probably should have explained "leaving clothes out on the line."

(Sample #2)

Belief   Chris Sorenson
"Diapers on Clothesline"   Logan, Utah
                                                               Feb. 5, 1983

Informant Data:
Chris Sorenson, 51, was born (1932) and raised in Roosevelt, Utah. She is an active member of the Mormon church. She has two children and four grandchildren. She presently owns and manages a dress shop. She has a heart of gold and would give anything to her family if she thought it would make them happy.

Contextual Data:
Chris said she heard this a long time ago, when she was about seven. What happened made a big impression on her. She says she knows the event could not really have happened, but it took her a long time to get over it. This is what she said, taken down in shorthand as she spoke:

"When I was little, people told me that if anyone left their clothes out on the line over New Year's Eve, someone in their family would die during the year. One year me and a few of my friends were talking and one of them said, 'I don't believe it, and just to prove it, I'm gonna leave ours out.' In those days we used to have to leave the clothes on the line for quite a few days before they were dry, especially during the winter. Anyway, this girl left their clothes out over New Year's, and a few months later her brother died. This made a really big impression on me. For many years I'd call around to everyone in the family on New Year's Eve and remind them to get their clothes in."

Item:
If you leave your clothes on the line on New Year's Eve, someone in the family will die the coming year.

                                                               Mary Sorenson
                                                               234 Maple
                                                               Logan, Utah
                                                               Utah State University
                                                               Hist 423   Winter 1983

The collector of Sample #3 gives fairly good information about the social setting but very weak information about the cultural background. He describes the informant's religious feelings and activity, though he does not explain how someone of Jewish ancestry happens to be a Mormon. He describes the natural setting in which the informant told his story, elicits a good statement of the contexts in which the informant would recount the story, and gets at the intensity of the informant's feeling about the story, partly through an ill-advised question which brought informative results. He should also have asked the informant to describe the circumstances under which he originally learned the story. Further, since the collector is Mormon himself, and was a participant observer during the narration, he should have said something about his own response to the event.

The collector tells us almost nothing about the culture which shapes and gives meaning to the narrative. What are a mission (a two-year proselytizing endeavor), an elder (an office in the lay priesthood), a ward (a local congregation), a sacrament meeting (the weekly ward meeting in which the sacrament ordinance is administered and certain members are assigned in advance to give inspirational talks), and the Nephites (ancient American followers of Christ who, according to Mormon tradition, wander the earth helping the faithful in time of need)? Why does the collector call this account a Nephite story when the word "Nephite" is not mentioned in the narrative itself?

Finally, the collector has not just relied on his memory of the story told in the church meeting but has correctly gone to the teller later and had him tell the story again. Unfortunately, he has not recorded the story on tape, and we are therefore denied a verbatim transcription.

(Sample #3)

Legend	Chad Newman
"Nephite Story: Missionaries Rescued"	Pasadena, California
	September 1970

Informant Data:
Chad Newman is my brother-in-law. He was born in Pasadena, California, in 1948 and has lived there all his life. He is currently in electrical engineering at Utah State University in Logan, Utah. He is of Jewish ancestry, but no one in his family practices Judaism, and all but his father are active members of the Mormon church. Chad has not served as a missionary, but he is an elder and at USU lives in the Delta Phi house, built by the church and run by the "returned missionary" fraternity. His home address is 5473 Cheery Pl., Pasadena, California.

Contextual Data:
Chad told this story as part of a talk he gave in sacrament meeting in the Pasadena Ward, as an illustration of the ability of the Lord to protect those who place their faith in Him and live good lives. As nearly as I could tell, everyone present took the story in the way he intended it. Of course, I can not be sure if they all believed it to be a true story, but Chad himself was completely sure of its veracity. I later asked him (somewhat ill-advisedly, as it turned out) if he really believed it, to his immediate indignation. He said he knew it was true because it had happened to a companion of someone a friend of his had known in the mission field. He said he didn't know very many Nephite stories, so he couldn't be sure if they were all true, but that he very definitely does believe the Nephites are somewhere here on the earth and have a mission to perform such as told in this story. When asked when and where else he would tell this story, Chad said only to people who were members of the church and who would probably believe in the Nephites and understand what their purpose was.

Item:

[I have recorded the story here not exactly as Chad told it in that particular sacrament meeting, but as he told it to me again in September 1970. I took notes as he told it, and it is close to his version, but mainly in my own words.]

Two missionaries in the Canadian Mission were driving home from a discussion meeting one day and there was quite a bad storm going. They were clear out in the middle of nowhere when their car broke down, and they were unable to repair it. They decided that they would just freeze to death if they stayed there, so they got out of the car and started walking down the road. After a couple of hours they were pretty badly frozen anyway and could tell they weren't going to be able to go much farther. Just then they heard a car coming behind them. It stopped and the man opened the door, and they got into the back seat. They were so cold they just laid down on the floor and didn't even look at the man. Finally they came to a service station, and the man stopped the car at the side of the road to let them out. They got out and stumbled over to the station, but they still hadn't really got a look at the man in the car. When they got up to the station, the attendant looked surprised, and asked where they had come from. They said, "From the car that had just stopped out in front." He said, "There hasn't been any car come along here for a couple of hours." They went out to the road and looked, but there weren't even any tire tracks.

Bill Henry
Route 1, Box 212
Moses Lake, Washington

364 E. 8974 S. #7
Provo, Utah
Brigham Young University
English 391   Spring 1971

CONCLUSION

I have not yet documented the story of the poisoned cat that I heard at the dinner party, but I intend to. I have arranged a gathering at my house, have invited my poet friend, and will ask him to tell the story again, this time with a tape recorder turning. If I am then able to follow the instructions I have given above, I will soon turn into the archive a document which may one day prove valuable to a researcher interested in contemporary legends. And I will in the process have increased my own understanding of folklore and its significance in people's lives. Through collecting and documenting folklore, you too can make an important contribution to folklore research and, in the process, increase your understanding of what it means to be human.

NOTES

1. Jan Harold Brunvand, *The Vanishing Hitchhiker: American Urban Legends and their Meanings* (New York: W. W. Norton & Company, Inc., 1981), 112.

2. Florence E. Baer, "'Give me . . . your huddled masses': Anti-Vietnamese

Refugee Lore and the 'Image of Limited Good,'" *Western Folklore* 61 (1982): 275–91.

3. All examples quoted in this paper are from student collections on file at the Brigham Young University Folklore Archives, Provo, Utah 84602.

FURTHER READINGS

An early but valuable guide to collecting folklore is Kenneth S. Goldstein, *A Guide for Field Workers in Folklore* (Hatboro, Penn.: Folklore Associates, 1964); its discussion of mechanical recording equipment is badly outdated, but its treatment of different interview methods is still instructive. The most complete and up-to-date work on collecting is Bruce Jackson, *Fieldwork* (Urbana, Ill.: University of Illinois Press, scheduled for release in the spring of 1987); this book, which I have seen in manuscript, covers in great detail major steps in collecting: planning, finding informants, interviewing, using mechanical equipment, and keeping records; it also discusses the ethics of collecting and gives good advice on obtaining releases. For the collector of verbal lore, one of the most useful works is Edward D. Ives. *The Tape-Recorded Interview: A Manual for Field Workers in Folklore and Oral History* (Knoxville, Tenn.: The University of Tennessee Press, 1974); particularly helpful are Ives's careful instructions on using tape recorders and his discussions of transcribing, processing, and preparing manuscripts for archive submission. For the collector of visual materials, a good work is John Collier, Jr., *Visual Anthropology: Photography as a Research Method* (New York: Holt, Rinehard, & Winston, Inc., 1967). To move beyond technique and to gain better understanding of the ways collectors and informants interrelate and together shape the document collected, every beginning field-worker should read Robert A. Georges and Michael O. Jones, *People Studying People: The Human Element in Fieldwork* (Berkeley, Cal.: University of California Press, 1980).

Introductory folklore textbooks and manuals often contain sections on collecting and documenting folklore which are helpful to the beginner. One of the best of these, "The Methods of Folklore Study," in Richard M. Dorson, ed., *Folklore and Folklife: An Introduction* (Chicago: The University of Chicago Press, 1972), 405–533, contains good essays on archiving and on the techniques of collecting different forms of folklore — music, narrative, material culture — and provides bibliographies for further reading. Two fine chapters, "Being a Folklorist" and "Folklore Research," in Barre Toelken, *The Dynamics of Folklore* (Boston: Houghton Mifflin Co., 1979), 263–329, briefly survey major steps in collecting and documenting folklore and, once again, include valuable bibliographical notes.

Journal articles are too numerous and varied to list here. (See the bibliographical references in the works cited above.) But two articles every first-time collector ought to read are Alan Dundes, "Texture, Text, and Context," *Southern Folklore Quarterly* 28 (1964): 251–65, which, though dated, was one of the first pieces to plead for the recording of both the folklore text and its social setting; and James E. Myers, "Unleashing the Untrained: Some Observations on Student Ethnographers," *Human Organization* 28 (1969): 155–59, which describes in humorous detail the pitfalls awaiting the student collector, but nevertheless argues in favor of student collecting.

Chapter 5

Evaluating Arguments

Arguing in Communities

▪ ▪ DIFFERENCE

If you could grow to maturity and live completely isolated from other human beings, then you would probably never have a need for language — or for arguing either. But even those who isolate themselves completely from society must at some time have experienced what it means to live in a community and to participate in the life of that community, even if only the family community. Part of living in a community is arguing. Why is this so? Even though members of a community have something in common — that which defines them as a group — there is also much that divides them. Although humans are genetically similar, no two humans are physically identical. And although we have many similar experiences as humans, no two humans have experienced the world in the exact same way. Each person is unique. Even in a family where genetic similarities are strong and where members share many experiences, children can turn out quite different.

Our language divides us as well. George Bernard Shaw once joked that England and the United States are two countries divided by a common language. Actually, you could make the same comment about any community. Language makes understanding and community possible. It allows us to bond with each other and to share our beliefs and values. But language can also create misunderstanding, confusion, and division. Even in a community that supposedly speaks one language (like English or French or Mandarin), differences in language ability and in people's notions of what words "mean" can often lead to misunderstandings. The miracle of language is that we are able to communicate with each other at all.

The problem of difference within a community is compounded by the fact

165

that most of us belong to a number of different communities. Since communities are made up of unique individuals, communities are themselves unique. Each community also has its own language and its own rules. If individuals who speak the same language misunderstand each other on occasion, imagine the even greater potential for misunderstanding that exists among communities that speak different languages.

▪ ▪ RESPONDING TO DIFFERENCE

As human beings we have much in common. Our genetic makeup, our experiences, and our language are similar enough that we can communicate and cooperate. But our diversity insures that within any community, there will be some disagreement and difference of opinion. Even within families or groups of close friends — where people identify with each other most closely — there are bound to be disagreements. These disagreements can obviously be even greater within larger communities or between one community and another.

Where there are disagreements or differences, there may be conflicts — even among individuals or communities that have much in common. Some conflict is normal within any community. One way to resolve differences is through force: punishing, silencing, or expelling members of the community that disagree or dissent. This force may be exerted by powerful members of the community, by vote of the majority, through the power of law, through military or physical strength, or through subtle pressure from peers to conform or risk ridicule and alienation. Individuals who dissent or disagree may choose either to fall in line, to accept the punishment and continue to dissent, or to withdraw from the community altogether. Most communities acknowledge what they consider to be a legitimate use of force. For instance, a sports team may suspend or waive athletes for violating team rules. A church may deny membership to those who refuse to acknowledge certain beliefs or undergo certain rituals. A country may imprison or even execute those who violate the laws of that country. However, the use of force, if taken to an extreme, can become the kind of totalitarian intolerance that led to the Holocaust in Germany and Poland, the "killing fields" of Cambodia, and "ethnic cleansing" in Bosnia.

A lot of the conflict that results in violence, terrorism, and manipulation could often be avoided if people learned how to negotiate their differences. One way to negotiate difference is to learn to live with it. Learning to live with difference is not necessarily a bad solution. Members of a community can "agree to disagree" as long as they can accept the consequences of leaving the disagreement unresolved. For instance, members of a church congregation may disagree about political issues but still agree on the religious issues that define them as a community. In the same way, members of a political party may have differing religious views. Rather than arguing politics in church or religion at a party meeting, members may agree to disagree. Members of a community may even disagree about those issues that define the community and yet be willing to acknowledge the right of others to hold opposing opinions and still remain part of the community. When people agree to disagree, arguing can clarify where the disagreement lies and solidify the agreement to live with difference. Arguing may even reveal common beliefs that the parties involved had not recognized before. When taken to an extreme, however, accepting difference of every kind can lead to anarchy, apathy, inertia, and the dissolution of the community.

Another way to negotiate difference is to use the power of communication and persuasion to work toward consensus or compromise. Threats of force may cause people to change their opinions and actions, but they may do so grudgingly, resenting those who have threatened them. Negotiation and persuasion, on the other hand, cause people to change their opinions willingly. Ideally, negotiation is a decision-making process that involves everyone concerned in a forum of free and open debate, each presenting his or her opinion in good faith, willing to abide by the consensus or compromise that results from the negotiation. Arguing in this manner serves the purpose of resolving diverse opinions into a synthesis that is essentially agreeable to all.

Unfortunately, not everyone is willing to negotiate in good faith, and persuasion can also be a device to manipulate, deceive, or entrap. Some members may be more intent on getting what they want than on working for the good of the community. So the abuse of persuasion can be just as dangerous as the abuse of force — and more subtle.

Despite pressures to conform, some differences will always exist. It is these differences that give individuals their identity within a community and that give communities their identity separate from other communities. Our boundaries define us. If we always agreed with one another on everything, there would be no individuality and no identity. Healthy communities choose to live with some differences and resolve others. A community that absolutely refuses to tolerate any difference rapidly becomes a community of one. But a community that tolerates everything or encourages difference to the point of divisiveness and anarchy risks losing the commonality that defines it as a community.

As long as the community is not torn apart, difference and diversity can be the strength of a community. Rather than eliminating difference, we should learn to accept some of our differences, resolve others, and cooperate with one another in the life of the community. Learning to negotiate our differences is particularly important in a democratic society, which attempts to allow the majority the right to rule and at the same time protect the rights of those who disagree with the majority opinion: to build consensus, but allow individualism. Debate and discussion — arguing — should play an important role in the democratic process.

Arguing allows individuals to negotiate their differences in ways that are "reasonable." Being reasonable means resorting to reasons — justifying, clarifying, and explaining without resorting to violence, trying to find a solution to a conflict that all parties can agree on without being compelled to. This is, of course, an ideal that is rarely realized. But perhaps many more conflicts could be resolved peacefully if community members understood something about the process of "reasoning," of negotiating on the basis of reasons. Such a process is necessary if we are ever to coexist and survive as humans. We must learn to live together reasonably, accepting some of our differences and negotiating others. It may be the hope for humanity.

▓ ▓ ARGUING IN ACADEMIC COMMUNITIES

As you read David Russell's essay in Chapter 3 on academic communities, you may have begun to think about the communities that exist at your school. A college or university is made up of different departments, divisions, programs, majors, and disciplines. A college is really a community made up of smaller communities. In fact, the word *college* is related to the word *collection*. A college is a group of individuals and communities that gather to learn together. Each community in a college has its own body of shared knowledge, its own approaches to learning, and its own peculiar way of talking and writing about knowledge. But some features of academic discourse are common among many communities at many different schools. They may not actually show up in all of your educational experiences at school, but they are expectations shared by many of your instructors. In a sense, a college or university tries to perpetuate an ideal of community discourse about knowledge. First of all, the function of a college is to inquire, to pose questions and seek answers to questions. This is what many of your professors mean by "research." Most professors spend at least some of their time in the active search for knowledge, and many will expect you to participate in the active search for knowledge as well. Second, a college exists to share knowledge. This takes place in the classroom, of course, but scholars also attend seminars, conferences, and meetings where they share the knowledge they have gained with each other. Scholars also share knowledge with one another by publishing academic books and articles.

Usually, there is a lot of debate and arguing taking place at a college or university, but this is the way it should be. No one has a monopoly on knowledge, and no one is right all of the time. Scholars usually welcome open discussion and scrutiny of their views, realizing that the process of arguing is a process of creating and supporting the common knowledge of the community.

Because a college is designed to promote inquiry and the sharing of knowledge, scholars try to value a diversity of opinion. They try not to ignore or reject others' views just because they are challenging or different. They know that new and challenging ideas can help them strengthen their own opinions and may even force them to change their opinions. Scholars welcome true or useful ideas from any source. And because no one is right all of the time, scholars learn to exercise judgment, evaluating and assessing opinions before accepting or rejecting them. They learn to critique and criticize. In their popular sense, these words may have negative connotations; someone who is "critical" of others may just be mean and nasty. But the root of the words *critical, critique,* and *criticize* is a Greek word meaning "to judge" or "weigh." When scholars are "critical," they weigh ideas against one another to see which is most reasonable. This type of critical judgment is the basis for a liberal or "liberating" education. Arguing is an important part of exercising critical judgment in an academic setting because it involves the search for reasons and the attempt to clarify.

I know that I've presented an ideal picture of how arguing can work in the college community. It doesn't always happen this way. Debates and discussions in the college community can be just as rancorous as debates in the public sphere. Deceptions, manipulation, intimidation, and petty quarreling all happen on occasion. But my hope in writing this book is that understanding something about the nature of arguments can improve the quality of debates in all kinds of communities, including the communities you belong to as a college student. Who knows, maybe you'll even be able to get along better with your roommate.

■ ■ A GENERAL METHOD FOR ARGUING IN COMMUNITIES

Since communities are so different from one another and each argument has its particular complexities, it is difficult to propose a general method for engaging all arguments. Much depends upon your ability to analyze and understand the features of the particular community you find yourself in. Still, as I pointed out in Chapter 1, arguments found in all communities do have some features in common, so there is a process that may assist you in your task of joining the conversation:

- Identify a controversial issue or claim you want to know more about.
- Identify a community that discusses or cares about this issue (or that should care).
- Understand the organization of the community and your place within that organization.
- Locate "sites" of conversation.
- Identify and record the conversation going on about your issue.
- Analyze and evaluate the various arguments being made about the issue.
- Find or create a place from which you can contribute to the conversation.

Remember, though, that this is a process rather than a method or procedure. It is intended to be flexible and may be somewhat different for different issues or different communities. For instance, the steps may not always follow the same order. You may already have formed your opinion on an issue, but you should still try to find out what others have said. Or you may belong to a community that cares about the issue. Also, you may not need to go through every step. If you already have a good sense of the community and the sites of conversation for a particular issue, you may only need to go through the final few steps of the process.

In order to use argumentation to resolve differences within communities, it is important to apply the following questions based on those for analyzing an argument in Chapter 1:

What is the issue?

What claims do people make about the issue?

What kind of claims are they?

What reasons do people give to support those claims?

What assumptions are implied by these reasons?

What additional reasons or claims of reasons support the point made in the reasons and assumptions?

Where do I agree or disagree with this argument?

Analyzing an argument in this way helps you to evaluate and respond to the argument. If it is a convincing argument, then the process of analysis may give you good reasons to believe as you do or may cause you to change your opinion. If the argument is not convincing, then you are in a position to respond with a better argument or to help others see the weaknesses in the argument. When pursued in the proper manner, in a spirit of cooperation, such analysis may resolve conflicts within a community (not necessarily removing disagreements, but perhaps helping members to accept differences or to understand why others hold the opinions they do). Ethical persuasion presupposes an investigation of evidence, an examination of assumptions, a commitment to values, and, most of all, a commitment to the membership of the community, to taking responsibility for the effects of one's attempts at persuasion. It requires a realization that truth is created and sustained by the community, that it depends upon compromise and adherence, and that people may still disagree and remain faithful members of the community. It requires that you focus on ideas rather than on individuals and that you respect others. Questioning long-held assumptions can create tension and conflict in a community. Sometimes the community resolves this tension through force or violence, persecuting those who dare to question the "common sense" of the community. Responding through violence may solve the conflict, but no learning or self-awareness results. When a community responds to questioning by allowing for debate and discussion in a spirit of good will, there may still be tension, but negotiating this tension will lead to new levels of understanding and ultimately strengthen the community.

Analyzing and Evaluating Arguments

In Chapters 1 and 2, I described the elements of persuasion (logos, ethos, and pathos) and the structure of arguments (claims, reasons, and assumptions). Once you have identified a community (Chapter 3) and observed a site of conversation, identified a controversial issue, and begun to record what other people are saying about that issue (Chapter 4), you are ready to analyze and evaluate the arguments being made. This process of evaluation is an important part of clarifying your own opinion, and it also helps you understand where you might contribute to the conversation.

EVALUATING ETHOS

In Chapter 1, I defined ethos as the credibility of a speaker or writer based on how the community perceives his or her character. Some of a writer's credibility comes from the position or status the writer holds in the community, and some is achieved by the writer's use of language. (You may want to review the discussion of ethos in Chapter 2.)

As you analyze how a writer uses language to achieve credibility, consider whether the writer's methods are legitimate or whether they are manipulative in any way. Pay particular attention to differences between the writer's reputation in the community and the image he or she presents in the argument. This kind of difference, popularly called a "credibility gap," occurs when a writer sounds credible but does not have a reputation or occupy a position which supports that credibility. Such a gap occurs, for instance, when someone pretends to be an expert or authority but really is not; this is called an *appeal to false authority*. Michael Jordan may be an expert on basketball shoes — at least, he knows what it is like to play a lot in basketball shoes. But does being a basketball player make him an expert on cola drinks? Does credibly playing a doctor on television enable an actor to recommend the brand of pain-reliever you should buy? Does the fact that Ed McMahon worked with Johnny Carson or hosts *Star Search* mean that you should take his advice about life insurance?

EVALUATING PATHOS

The appeal to emotions is an important part of persuasive writing because it is often the emotional impact of an argument that inspires people to act rather than just to change their opinions. Still, appeals to the emotions are often manipulative. In Chapter 2 I described common strategies used to create an emotional response in an audience.

As you analyze an author's appeal to emotion or when you find yourself responding emotionally to an argument, consider whether the emotions you are feeling are appropriate to the situation. When politicians drape themselves in the flag, talk about their immigrant parents, rehearse their war experiences, or have their pictures taken playing football with a group of kids, they are trying associate themselves with how we feel about our country, our families, and our childhood. But do these emotions necessarily have anything to do with a politician's political view?

▓ ▪ EVALUATING LOGOS

Remember that logos is the attempt to justify or explain a claim through reasons. Because of its appeal to reason, logos involves arguing. An argument is a claim supported by reasons and assumptions. The first step in analyzing logos is to identify the parts of the argument: the claim, reasons, and assumptions. Once you have identified the parts of the argument, ask the following questions to evaluate the quality of the argument:

1. Is the claim an idea? Does it state an assertion in a complete sentence?
2. Does it answer a question that is at issue for the community?
3. Is it framed in precise language? If it is your own claim, does it say exactly what you mean?
4. Is it justified by reasons and assumptions that are acceptable to the community being addressed?
5. Is it justified by reasons and assumptions that are acceptable to you?

If you answer "no" to any of these questions, then you have found a place where you can respond to the claim. If it is your own claim, then you have found where your argument needs to be revised. If you can answer "yes" to these questions, then you are ready to evaluate the reasons that are used to justify or explain the claim. Here are some questions to ask when evaluating a reason:

1. Is the reason an idea? Does it state an assertion in a complete sentence?
2. Does it answer the question "What makes the claim true?"
3. Is it framed in precise language? If it is your own claim, does it say exactly what you mean?
4. Can you identify the assumptions that allow you to make the logical connection between the claim and reason?
5. Will the community accept the reason, or does it need to be supported with additional reasons?
6. Do you accept the reason?

Again, if your answer to any of these questions is "no," you have discovered a place where you can respond to those who are using this reason to support their claim. If the reason is your own, then you have discovered a place where you can revise and improve your argument. If you can answer "yes" to the above questions, then you need to evaluate each of the assumptions you identified in response to Question 4:

1. Is the assumption an idea? Does it state an assertion in a complete sentence?
2. Does it answer the question "If the reason is true, then what else must be true for the claim to be true?"
3. If stated, is it framed in precise language? If implied, can it be reconstructed in precise terms?
4. Will the community accept the assumption, or does it need to be supported with additional reasons?
5. Do you accept the assumption?

▨ ▨ FALLACIES IN REASONING

Some arguments sound persuasive but actually contain assumptions most people wouldn't accept if they stopped to think. Such arguments are called "logical fallacies." Even though they are based on faulty reasoning, logical fallacies show up frequently because they are easy arguments to make and at first seem true. Many of them are persuasive because they resemble legitimate arguments.

Hasty Generalization/Sweeping Generalization   A hasty generalization is another name for "jumping to conclusions." It is a conclusion formed on very little evidence. Here is an example:

> The country is probably going into a recession because they laid off five people at my office.

The assumption in this argument is that a few people being laid off at one office is a sure sign of a coming recession. But in fact the economy is so large and complex that five people being laid off would have little effect at all. This conclusion requires more evidence.

A sweeping generalization, which is similar to a hasty generalization, involves applying a statement that is true for one particular situation to another situation without considering how the situations might be different. Here is an example:

> My accounting degree really prepared me well for law school. Everyone who wants to go to law school should major in accounting.

The assumption in this argument is that what is true for the writer is true for everyone. The argument ignores important differences among students: Some people feel well prepared for law school after studying English, political science, or philosophy.

Guilt by Association   One really ugly form of sweeping generalization involves grouping individuals together and stereotyping all members of the group based on how some members of the group behave. This is called "guilt by association." For instance, a neighbor of mine said he didn't like the fact that an Asian family had moved into our neighborhood because he had worked with some Chinese people and found them untrustworthy. He assumed that because he didn't trust some Chinese people, he couldn't trust anyone Chinese. He also assumed that anyone with Asian features must be Chinese. (This particular family was Vietnamese.)

False Dilemma   The false dilemma, or "either/or" fallacy, involves trying to force readers to accept a conclusion by presenting only two options, one of which is clearly more desirable than the other. Rarely are there only two possibilities. I have to admit, however, that my wife and I often use this strategy with our little boy: "Do you want to finish your dinner or go straight to bed?" "Hard sell" salespersons and negotiators often use the false dilemma to try and close a deal: "Do you want to pay cash or credit for that?" (eliminating the option that you may not want to buy at all); "If you don't act now, you will never get another chance!"; "Would you rather buy whole life insurance or risk leaving your family without any income?"

Non Sequitur   I mentioned non sequiturs in Chapter 1, but it is worth touching on them again. This Latin phrase means "it does not follow" and refers to a conclusion that has no apparent connection to the reasons. Here is an example: "This restaurant is no good because it's raining outside." There is no clear connection here between the claim (this restaurant is no good) and the reason (it's raining outside). Non sequiturs are often used in advertising. For example, a car may be pictured with a beautiful woman, the implied argument being "You should buy this car because of this beautiful woman." But there is really no clear connection between the conclusion and the reason. In other words, it is not possible to identify an assumption or chain of reasons that would link the reason and conclusion in a sensible way.

Fallacious Appeal to Emotion   In Chapter 2 I described how the appeal to emotions is an important and legitimate part of any argument. But when an emotional issue is raised as a distraction from the issue under discussion, then it is a fallacious appeal to emotion. Teachers occasionally hear fallacious appeals to emotion from their students. I once had a student who missed a lot of class and skipped some major assignments; he turned in a final paper, but it showed signs of being thrown together at the last minute. When I told him he wouldn't be passing the class, he talked about how angry his parents would be if he lost his scholarship. His implied argument was "You should give me a passing grade because my parents will be mad at me," based on the assumption that performance in college courses should be measured by how parents will react to final grades. This assumption was unacceptable to me, but the student was hoping that the vividness of his emotional appeal would distract me from the flimsiness of the argument.

Begging the Question   This term describes an argument in which the reason is really no more than a restatement of the conclusion. For example, "You should exercise because it is good for you" is just another way of saying "You should exercise because you should exercise." A writer also begs the question when he or she offers a conclusion without adequate support or uses reasons or assumptions that are just as controversial as the conclusion. Consider the familiar argument "Abortion is wrong because it is murder." This argument doesn't really advance the conversation about abortion because it offers as a reason one of the primary points of contention in the abortion issue: that a fetus is really an individual life which can be "murdered."

Appeal to Ignorance   The burden of supporting an argument falls on the person making it. A writer who makes an appeal to ignorance refuses to accept this burden of proof. Here is an example: "Bigfoot, the Loch Ness monster, and extraterrestrials must really exist because no one has ever proved that they don't." In fact, those who make the claim "Bigfoot exists" are the ones who need to support the claim. It would be a mistake, however, to assume that "Bigfoot does not exist" just because you don't accept the argument that he does. "Bigfoot does not exist" is also a claim that carries with it a burden of proof.

Stacking the Deck   Gamblers "stack the deck" in their favor by arranging the cards so that they will win. Writers "stack the deck" by ignoring any evidence or arguments that don't support their position. I once experienced "stacking the deck" when I went to buy a used car. The man trying to sell me the car talked only about how wonderful the car was. After I bought the car, another man tried to sell me an extended warranty by pointing out all the things that could break down.

Dicto Simpliciter   This fallacy (the Latin phrase means "simple speech") occurs when a writer applies statements that are true in simple cases to more complex cases without qualifying the statements. Here is an example: "Jogging is good for you. Everybody ought to jog every day." It is true *all other things being equal* that jogging is good for humans. But some people may have conditions that make jogging harmful or inappropriate.

Personal Attack   Questioning a person's character or credibility is not necessarily fallacious. It becomes so when the attack on a person's character is used as a distraction from the real issue at hand. For instance, it would not be fallacious to attack a scientist's experimental results because you had reason to believe he or she had falsified some data; an attack would be fallacious, however, if you based it on the fact that he or she had a string of outstanding parking tickets.

Some politicians use personal attacks as part of their campaign strategy. A politician may rake up an opponent's past behavior, even things the opponent did when he or she was quite young, for anything that might damage the opponent's public image. Sometimes, politicians will even point to the irresponsible behavior of an opponent's relatives (siblings, children, or in-laws) as a way of attacking that opponent's current credibility.

Poisoning the Well   A writer who "poisons the well" presents an argument in such an emotionally biased way that it is difficult for a critic to respond without looking dishonest or immoral. This strategy is also meant as a distraction from the real issue and may involve personal attacks or fallacious appeals to emotion. Here's an example: "Of course, this liar will tell you that he didn't steal my stuff. You can't believe a thief. Go ahead and ask him; he'll deny it." How is the accused supposed to respond? The very act of asserting innocence can be construed as a sign of guilt. The emotional and manipulative nature of the language in this case is a distraction from the real issue: Who is guilty of stealing?

Appeal to Force/Appeal to Reward   The appeal to force is another name for a threat. A threat diverts attention from the real issue to the negative consequences of not accepting an argument. Extortion, blackmail, intimidation, and sexual harassment are all examples of threats. The appeal to reward is just the opposite of a threat, diverting attention from the issue to what will be gained by accepting the point of view. Buying votes, trading favors, and bribery are all examples of the appeal to reward.

Ad Populum   This Latin phrase means "to the people." It is also known as the "bandwagon appeal." Here is an example: "It is all right for me to cheat on my taxes because everyone else does it." The assumption in this argument is that "just because something is popular or common it is right." This fallacy ignores the fact that the majority may be wrong.

Complex or Loaded Question   A complex question is really two questions phrased as one: A famous example is "Have you stopped beating your wife?" The two questions phrased here as one are "Have you ever beat your wife?" and "If so, have you stopped?" As the question is phrased, answering either "yes" or "no" will get a husband in trouble: "Yes (I used to beat her)"; "No (I still beat her)."

Post Hoc, Ergo Propter Hoc   This Latin phrase means "after this, therefore because of this" and refers to an error in reasoning based on the assumption that just because one event follows another, the first caused the second. A lot of superstitions originate in this fallacy. A person walks under a ladder, and a bucket of paint falls on his head, so he tells people that walking under a ladder brings bad luck. The problem is that walking under the ladder did not cause the bucket to fall; further, to jump to the conclusion that there is a connection between ladders and bad luck is a hasty generalization.

Oversimplified Cause   This fallacy is similar to the post hoc fallacy. It occurs when a writer tries to reduce a complex event or phenomenon to one simple cause. When Dan Quayle blamed the television show *Murphy Brown* for the breakdown of the American family, he reduced a complex social phenomenon to a ridiculously simple cause. The same fallacy occurred when people blamed talk radio programs for the bombing in Oklahoma City in 1995.

Red Herring   The name of this fallacy probably comes from a trick once used by escaping prisoners: dragging a fish across their path of escape to throw dogs off the scent. A red herring is any attempt to draw attention away from the issue at hand by raising irrelevant issues. Here is an example: "I don't think the president's economic plan is a good idea. I mean, what is he going to do about the violence in our inner cities?"

False Analogy   An analogy is a powerful persuasive tool because it presents an argument in interesting and memorable terms. An analogy becomes fallacious, however, when the differences between the things being compared are greater than the similarities. When the United States got involved in a war against communists in Korea and Vietnam, government leaders justified their actions by referring to the "domino theory." According to this theory, if communists were allowed to take over one country, neighboring countries would also fall to communism like a line of dominoes until the whole democratic world was at risk. This analogy is a powerful and memorable image, but it ignores the fact that international politics is much more complex than a game of dominoes.

Applying the Principles

▦ ▦ EVALUATING STATISTICAL ARGUMENTS

Our society places a great deal of trust in statistics, which are really just another way of describing our experience. Statistics help us count and quantify certain aspects of the world we live in and allow us to say something about the collective experience of a community. But just because they are subject to mathematical principles, statistics are still not absolute truth. Some experiences cannot be counted and measured, and the quality of an argument based on statistics depends on how the information was gathered and interpreted. Statistics can be deceiving. For instance, there are problems with averaging. The *average,* or mean, for a group is calculated by adding together the data relating to each member of the group and then dividing that total by the number of members. If you want to calculate the average weight of a football team's defensive line, for example, you take the weight of each player and add them together; then you divide that total weight by the number of players on the defensive line. When there are great differences among the numbers being totaled, averages can be deceiving. Let's say that the average weight of the defensive line is 300 pounds (a total of 1200 pounds divided by four players). Sounds like a nightmare for the opposing quarterback. But suppose the weight is distributed as follows:

left end	450 pounds
left tackle	450 pounds
right tackle	150 pounds
right end	150 pounds

Now it sounds like a quarterback's dream. The opposing team can play to the right side of the defensive line and run right over those 150-pounders or play to the left side and run right past those 450-pounders.

As this example suggests, it is always important to know how the numbers being averaged are distributed among the members of the group. Take average income, as another example. If it is reported that the average yearly income for a household of four is $35,000, you should not assume that most households of four actually make that much. There are individuals in the United States who make millions of dollars annually, and these pull the "average" income above the average household's income. To evaluate the figure, it might help to know the *median*, the level at which half the incomes are higher and half are lower, or the *mode*, the income that shows up most frequently.

Averages can also be deceiving when there are only a few numbers being averaged. If two students take a class and one gets an A while the other fails, then the average grade for that class is C. But that average doesn't really say much about the performance of the class: There are too few numbers being averaged.

Percentages can be deceiving as well. A percentage is calculated by dividing a part of a group by the total number of members in the group (for example, $50 \div 200 = .25$). A percentage is always expressed as a part of one hundred, so .25 is 25/100, or 25 percent. When dealing with percentages, it is always important to know the "raw" numbers from which they are calculated. A percentage is particularly deceiving when it is calculated from only a few numbers. Suppose that you ask three of your classmates what kind of music they prefer, and two of them tell you country music, while the third mentions jazz. Based on this you could say that almost 70 percent of the students you surveyed at your school prefer country music, but the number would be deceiving because you only surveyed three students.

Even raw numbers can be deceiving. It doesn't mean much to take second place, for instance, if there are only two competitors in the contest. Raw numbers have to be put in some context. If your school reports that 300 students flunked out last year, is that good or bad? It depends. How many have flunked out in previous years? Maybe 300 represents a real improvement. How many students attend your school? If the total student body is 50,000, 300 dropouts might not be too bad. For a school with 1,500 students, however, a dropout rate of 300 looks much worse.

Sometimes statistics are intentionally used to mislead or deceive. When an ad claims that a "new, improved" toothpaste is "twice as good" (or 200 percent better), what does that mean? Twice as good as it was before? Twice as good as other brands? Twice as good in one or two ways? What information has been omitted from an ad like this? As noted earlier, admitting only information that proves your case while ignoring other statistical information is a fallacy called "stacking the deck."

When evaluating statistics, it may help to ask questions such as these:

How have the statistics been gathered?

What can one really conclude from these statistics?

Is any information missing?

Is the experience these statistics quantify reliable? Is it an experience that can be quantified?

The following two essays discuss some errors in reasoning to look out for when writers use statistics and graphs.

The Numbers Racket: How Polls and Statistics Lie

STEPHEN BUDIANSKY

S TATISTICS ARE an American obsession. In an election year, they become a   1
positive mania. The poll data pour in daily on everything a person could
conceivably have an opinion about — and some things it's hard to imagine anyone having an opinion about. One recent survey reports that by a narrow, 42–
to–40 margin, American women believe the First Lady should be active in "all"
as opposed to "just some" aspects of presidential business.

It's not just polls. Numbers of every description have become the currency
of American life. Politicians and advocacy groups burnish their positions with
them, sports commentators dissect them, advertisers bombard us with them,
corporations make multimillion-dollar decisions based on them. The Census Bureau used to count just people; now, it tabulates everything from coffee consumption to the number of coin-operated videogames. School-reform advocates
once pressed their case with anecdotes of ill-trained teachers and out-of-date
textbooks; now, they cite scores on the 50 million or more standardized tests
that are administered to elementary and high-school students each year. A campaign against drugs that swept the country in the 1930s featured lurid tales of
marijuana-crazed children killing their parents; today's war on drugs features
lurid numbers of drug profits.

"Numbers suggest understanding," says Peter Reuter, an economist at the
RAND Corporation. "People believe that you can't have a policy debate if you
don't have numbers."

But that faith in numbers means that all too rarely is the truth behind the
numbers questioned — and all too easily are they manipulated. Whatever your
position, a statistic is available to back it up. Crime? It's going down. Except,
that is, if you're a law-enforcement official pleading for a higher budget. Then
crime is going up. The crisis in education? School superintendents can prove it's
not their fault. A new study shows that students' test scores are above the national average. Everywhere. The explosive issues of abortion and gun control? A
majority of Americans, polls clearly show, are against both. A majority are also
for them. Take your pick.

THE NUMBER THAT WOULD NOT DIE

Numbers concocted to support a position may be complete guesses — but   5
once in the public record, they take on a life of their own that belies their shadowy origins. Take the figure of $140 billion for the size of the U.S. illegal-drug-
trafficking industry. In its various incarnations, this figure has been cited in
countless newspaper articles, in congressional testimony, in speeches by attorneys general and most prominently this year by Representative Charles Rangel
(D–N.Y.), chairman of the House Select Committee on Narcotics Abuse and
Control, in his push for an expanded war on drugs. Not only is it a large number,

it's also a seemingly precise number — 140, not 100 or 150 — that implies some real knowledge of the scope of the problem. But where does it come from? The figure seems to have originated in 1978, when the National Narcotics Intelligence Consumers Committee, the government unit once charged with keeping track of such things, put the drug trade at $50 billion. It jumped mysteriously to $80 billion in 1980. After some internal wrangling — and much external criticism — NNICC quietly dropped the estimate a few years ago. But then the cause was taken up by Rangel's committee. John Cusack, the panel's former staff director, recalls that when he noticed that the NNICC estimate had risen to $90 billion by 1982, "adding $10 billion a year seemed to make sense" — and that's what the committee has done ever since. The figure "is not scientifically accurate," admits Cusack, now a drug consultant to the Attorney General of the Bahamas. "It's an educated guess."

THE VANISHING DEFICIT

If there were any doubt about the power that statistics have come to command, consider last October's stock-market crash — triggered in large measure by the release of government trade figures showing a deficit $1.5 billion greater than Wall Street expected. Never mind that trade figures are notoriously unreliable because of the difficulty of tracking our own exports and the flow of capital. It was a number, it came from the government — and that was enough to base billions of dollars in financial decisions upon. That market-crashing trade figure has since been revised downward — by $1.3 billion.

The abuse of numbers is almost a matter of course in the burgeoning business of polling. Even many of the major polling firms routinely do work for interest groups that are interested in one thing only: getting a poll that supports their position. The essence of such "tactical polling" — as the member of one Washington advocacy group unabashedly termed it — is to phrase questions or sequences of questions in a way that leads respondents to the "right" response.

Studies have shown how easy that can be to do. A 1978 CBS– *New York Times* poll, for example, asked: "Do you agree or disagree that the federal government ought to help people get medical care at low cost?" When 81 percent agreed, the results were reported as evidence of support for an expanded federal government. But critics pointed out that it was absurd to draw that conclusion without having presented an alternative. To prove the point, the North American Newspaper Alliance conducted another poll that asked the same question, substituting the words "private enterprise" for "federal government" — and found that 71 percent agreed with *that* proposition.

So it's not surprising that groups with an ax to grind manage to get the results they pay for (see "How to Skew a Poll" — on pages 182–183). "It is genuinely becoming 'pollster wars' out there," says Democratic pollster Alan Secrest. "Too many people are playing fast and loose with polling data. It is unconscionable, but understandable with so much at stake." Adds Mervin Field, head of the respected Field Research Corporation: "There's a real danger. Legislation is being tailored and the public manipulated with these polls."

This year's political primaries have shown the power of numbers as never   10
before. Thomas Patterson, professor of political science at Syracuse University, warns that coverage of the candidates is being dictated to a dangerous degree by poll results — and some extremely shoddy poll results at that. "There is a poll craziness out there. If you are high in the polls, you almost automatically have some good things said about you in the press." Adds Everett Ladd, director of the Roper Center for Public Opinion Research at the University of Connecticut: "The numbers contribute to a misplaced concreteness."

The trouble is that in the frenzied media competition over polling, little distinction is made between good polls and bad polls, and many news organizations aren't willing to spend the money on the extra effort needed to eliminate biases in their polls — using an adequate sample group, taking the trouble to reach everyone in that sample group even if it means calling back repeatedly, and phrasing questions properly. "Any damn fool with 10 phones and a typewriter thinks he can conduct a poll," says Warren Mitofsky, director of elections and surveys for CBS News.

OFF BY A MILE

Even a casual glance at the contradictory poll results of this political year demonstrates that the uncertainties far surpass the standard 3-percent-plus-or-minus warning. For example, an NBC news poll a month before the New Hampshire primary had Michael Dukakis trailing Richard Gephardt 18 points to 19. A *Los Angeles Times* poll conducted the same day showed Dukakis leading 37 to 8. The actual result: Dukakis 36, Gephardt 20. In fact, the usual plus-or-minus warning only refers to the smallest source of possible error — the probability that a randomly chosen sample group differs from the population as a whole. It doesn't account for the fact that people may refuse to answer, may lie or may be influenced by leading questions.

The media fascination with polls is part and parcel of the wider fascination with statistics of all kinds. Numbers seem concrete; numbers seem objective. "It is a safe kind of journalism. You can't generally be accused of ideological or political bias," says Michael Jay Robinson, a consultant to the Gallup-Times Mirror survey.

The case of all test scores being above average (see "Statistical Myths" on page 184) is a classic example — both of the political impact of unsubstantiated numbers and of the many ways available to manipulate statistics. For several years, virtually every state's department of education and even most urban school districts had reported in glowing terms that their students had scored above the national average on standardized reading, writing and math tests. Obviously, if the average really had been an average, some states would have had to be below it. It turned out that the "average" was calculated using a skewed sample

■ How to Skew a Poll: Loaded Questions and Other Tricks ■

Even polls taken at the same time can produce dramatically different results depending on how the question is phrased. Some examples:

CONTRA AID

Aid the rebels in Nicaragua "to prevent Communist influence from spreading"?

Assist "the people trying to overthrow the government of Nicaragua"?

(Yankelovich-Clancy-Shulman poll for *Time*)

(CBS-*New York Times* poll)

ABORTION

Constitutional amendment "prohibiting abortion"?

Constitutional amendment "protecting the life of the unborn"?

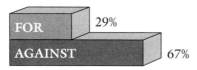

(*New York Times* poll)

GUN CONTROL

Waiting period and background check before guns can be sold?

"National gun-registration program costing about 20% of all dollars now spent on crime control?"

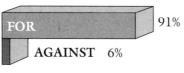
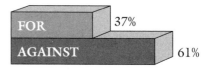

(Gallup Poll)

(Write-in poll for National Rifle Association)

WELFARE

"Are we spending too much, too little, or about the right amount on welfare?"

"Are we spending too much, too little, or about the right amount on assisitance to the poor?"

(Survey of the National Opinion Research Center of the University of Chicago)

What does it mean when a poll says "margin of error of plus or minus 3 percent?" Not as much as most people think. That standard warning label refers only to the most obvious possible source of error — the statistical chance that a perfect, randomly selected sample doesn't reflect the country as a whole. In practice, political polls are off by an average of 5.7 percent, according to polling consultant Irving Crespi of Princeton, N.J.; one third are off by more than 6.4 percent.

Loaded questions, such as those above, are one way results can be tilted. Some other major sources of error:

The Skewed Sample

Women answer the phone 70 percent of the time. A poll that doesn't take that into account by making extra calls to get enough men is likely to be slanted. But biases can slip in by much less obvious ways. A test poll conducted in the 1984 presidential election found that if the poll were halted after interviewing only those subjects who could be reached on the first try, Reagan showed a 3-percentage point lead over Mondale. But when interviewers made a determined effort to reach everyone on their lists of randomly selected subjects — calling some as many as 30 times before finally reaching them — Reagan showed a 13 percent lead, much closer to the actual election result. As it turned out, people who were planning to vote Republican were simply less likely to be at home.

The Ignorance Factor

Not many people want to appear unpatriotic, uninformed or socially unacceptable. So when the pollster calls, they say they intend to vote when they don't, offer what they believe are less controversial opinions, or express a view — any view — to cover up their ignorance of an issue. One study found that almost a third of respondents offered opinions when asked about the nonexistent "Public Affairs Act."

The "Pseudo Poll"

The least reliable polls are not even polls at all — experts call them "pseudo polls" because they don't even make an attempt at surveying a random sample. AT&T has been marketing call-in polls using its area-code 900 numbers. TV stations ask viewers to call one number to register a "Yes" vote, another for "No." The results are then tallied and aired. The trouble is that only those who feel strongly enough to spend the 50 cents AT&T charges for each call are likely to phone in — hardly a representative sample.

group that included students with learning disabilities. It also was seven years out of date, and thus failed to reflect an overall rise in the average that had taken place.

Such fiddling with the sample group is in fact one of the most common ways to tease a desired result out of an otherwise valid statistic. That's how partisans on both sides of the 65-mile-per-hour-speed-limit debate were able to use the same data to prove their case. Depending on which states you include in

---

▧ Statistical Myths ▧

All Children Are Above Average

Test scores are up. Children are scoring above the national norm in reading and math. The education crisis is over.

Dr. John Cannell of Beaver, W. Va., smelled a rat. A family physician, he was troubled by the low self-esteem of his teenage patients. Many had apparently been assigned to grade levels beyond their academic abilities. So how could West Virginia be above the national average?

Simple: *All* states are above average. One reason is that the sample group of students that was used to establish the "average" had been required to take all of the tests — but when schools later administered the tests, they could pick only those tests that best matched their curricula. "The testing industry wants to sell lots of tests, and the school superintendents desperately need high and improving scores," says Cannell. "Nobody is disappointed."

3 Million Americans Are Homeless

While homeless advocates fiercely defend this number, it has a strange history. In 1980, homeless advocate Mitch Snyder conducted interviews with local agencies, and listed estimates of the number of homeless in 14 cities. The numbers ranged from a few hundredths of a percent in some cities to 1 percent in a few cases. Whiles he made no national estimate at that time, by 1982, Snyder was claiming that his 1980 survey had found that "1 percent of the population, or 2.2 million people, lacked shelter." He went on to say that the number "could" reach 3 million in 1983. That number was picked up and widely quoted.

More-scientific surveys have found the number to be 8 to 10 times too large. Part of the discrepancy is also due to advocates' having included in their definition of the "homeless" people who live in substandard housing. But Snyder subsequently told a congressional hearing: "These numbers are in fact meaningless. We have tried to satisfy your gnawing curiosity for a number because we are Americans with Western little minds that have to quantify everything in sight, whether we can or not."

---

the sample, you can prove that the higher speed limit has caused more traffic fatalities — or fewer fatalities.

A variation on that theme is regularly practiced by environmental activists who discover a cancer "hot spot," or political reporters who discover a "key" county that always picks the winner in presidential elections. But pure chance alone will dictate that some areas will have a much higher cancer rate than the average (just as some will have a much lower rate). And while picking the right presidential candidate in 10 straight elections might seem remarkable, someone who voted by tossing a coin would have 1 chance in 1,024 of duplicating that feat. With more than 3,000 counties in the country, those odds don't seem so long.

Why are we so impressed by numbers? "Human judgment and intuition are fallible," says Stanford University psychology Prof. Amos Tversky. Some of the errors people make in interpreting statistics in fact fall into definable patterns. One rule is that losses loom larger than gains. People are more willing to support public-health programs when told of the numbers of lives that would be lost without it — as opposed to lives saved by it. Psychologists have also found that people rarely question the context of numbers — as in accepting the statement that a detergent is "35 percent better" without asking, "35 percent better than what?"

But most important, numbers have taken on the role of the compelling anecdote — the story that people take to repeating without ever asking where it came from. Numbers that begin their lives as total guesses often persist for years, being quoted and requoted — usually for a lack of any more-reliable data. (The 3 million homeless people in the U.S. is one such famous statistic that would not die; see "Statistical Myths.")

FOOLING THE PROS

Number blindness even besets people who should be experts. That mainstay of economic statistics, the gross national product, is the basis of countless economic projections. Yet it is a number fraught with uncertainties. At times recently, it has even showed economic growth dramatically slowing when it was really accelerating. Frank de Leeuw, chief statistician for the Bureau of Economic Analysis that puts together the figure, admits that the GNP estimates err, on average, by almost 2 percentage points. One reason: The data that go into the figure are still heavily tilted toward industries that were dominant in the 1930s and 1940s; it is a poor measure of the newly ascendant service industries.

Those who make multimillion-dollar decisions every day have been no less susceptible to the allure of numbers. When General Foods decided to launch a new instant-drink mix called Great Shakes, it test marketed it in several cities with what appeared to be a resounding success. Customers, the numbers showed, seemed to be enthusiastically purchasing all of the various flavors. General Foods immediately launched it nationally — to a resounding thud. The company finally pieced together what had happened: Customers were trying one flavor after another, hoping that the next one surely would taste better than the last. When they had run through them all, they stopped buying any of them. "There's an overreliance on numbers," says Bruce Meyers, marketing-research director of the BBD&O advertising agency. "Any research should be an aid to judgment, not a replacement for it." But here's one number that shows what American business thinks of that advice: The survey-research industry now earns more than $2 billion a year — and is growing at a rate of about 15 percent a year.

20

from Doublespeak

WILLIAM LUTZ

BEWARE OF THE POLLS

S TATISTICAL DOUBLESPEAK is a particularly effective form of doublespeak, since statistics are not likely to be closely scrutinized. Moreover, we tend to think that numbers are more concrete, more "real" than mere words. Quantify something and you give it a precision, a reality it did not have before.

We live in an age where people love numbers. Computer printouts are "reality." You identify yourself with your Social Security number; your American Express, MasterCard, or Visa number, your driver's license number; your telephone number (with area code first); your zip code. Three out of four doctors recommend something, we are told; a recent poll reveals 52.3 percent are opposed; Nielsen gives the new television program a 9.2; the movie grossed $122 million.

Baseball produces not just athletic contests but an infinity of statistics, which all true fans love to quote endlessly. Crowds at football and basketball games chant, "We're number one!" while the Dow Jones index measures daily our economic health and well-being. Millions of people legally (and illegally) play the daily number. Millions of pocket calculators are sold every year. The list could go on to include the body count of Vietnam and the numbers of nuclear warheads and intercontinental ballistic missiles cited as the measure of national security.

The computer scientist, the mathematician, the statistician, and the accountant all deal with "reality," while the poet, the writer, the wordsmith deal with, well, just words. You may find, however, that the world of numbers is not as accurate as you think it is, especially the world of the public opinion poll.

If you believe in public opinion polls, I've got a bridge you might like to buy. Depending upon which poll you believed just before the New Hampshire primary in February 1988, you would have known that Robert Dole would beat George Bush 35 percent to 27 (Gallup); or Dole would win 32 percent to Bush's 28 percent (*Boston Globe*); or that Dole and Bush were even at 32 percent each (ABC-*Washington Post*); or Bush would win 32 percent to Dole's 30 (WBZ-TV); or Bush would win 34 percent to Dole's 30 percent (CBS-*New York Times*). Of course, George Bush won the actual vote 38 percent to 29 percent.

Things weren't much better on the Democratic side, either. While most primary polls were correct in identifying Michael Dukakis as the winner, the margin of victory varied from 47 percent to 38 percent. Dukakis won with 36 percent of the vote. For second place, though, the polls really missed the call. Two had Paul Simon ahead of Richard Gephardt for second place, while a third had the two tied and the others had Simon behind by a thin margin. In the actual vote, Simon finished third, with 17 percent of the vote, while Gephardt finished second with

20 percent. No one predicted Gephardt's 20 percent of the vote, *not even the surveys of voters leaving the polling places after they had voted.* This last point should not be overlooked, for it reminds us that no poll is worth anything unless people tell the pollster the truth. Since no pollster can ever know whether or not people are telling the truth, how can we ever be sure of any poll?

Things didn't improve during the presidential campaign either. In August, 1988, before the Republican National Convention, seven polls gave seven different answers to the question of who was ahead. The CBS-*New York Times* poll had Dukakis leading Bush 50 percent to 33 percent, while a poll taken by KRC Communications/Research had Dukakis ahead only 45 percent to 44 percent. When the ABC News poll came out with Bush ahead 49 percent to 46 percent, many people in the polling business discounted the results. ABC promptly took another poll three days later which showed Dukakis ahead 55 percent to 40 percent. That was more like it, said the other professional poll takers.

Even as presented, such polls are deceptive. Any poll has a margin of error inherent in it, but pollsters don't discuss that margin very much. They like their polls to have an air of precision and certainty about them. The KRC polls just mentioned had a margin of error of plus or minus 4 percent. This means that, in the first poll KRC took Dukakis really had anywhere from 49 to 41 percent, while Bush had anywhere from 48 to 40 percent. In other words, Dukakis could have been ahead 49 to 40 percent, or Bush could have been ahead 48 to 41 percent. The poll didn't tell you anything.

Polls have become important commodities to be sold. Television news programs and newspapers use polls to show that they have the inside information, thus boosting their ratings and their circulation. Also, the more dramatic or unexpected the results of a poll, the better the chances the poll will be featured prominently on the evening news program. In addition to all this hype and use of polls as news, politicians, corporations, special-interest groups, and others have vested interests in the results of particular polls. Such people and groups have been known to design and conduct polls that will produce the results they want. In other words, polls can be and are a source of a lot of doublespeak.

How do you read a poll? Actually, it's not all that hard, but the problem is 10 that most poll results don't give you enough information to tell whether the poll is worth anything. In order to evaluate the results of a poll, you need to know the wording of the question or questions asked by the poll taker, when the poll was taken, how many people responded, how the poll was conducted, who was polled, how many people were polled, and how they were selected. That's a lot of information, and rarely does a poll ever give you more than just the results.

In 1967, two members of Congress asked their constituents the following question: "Do you approve of the recent decision to extend bombing raids in North Vietnam aimed at the strategic supply depots around Hanoi and Haiphong?" Sixty-five percent said yes. When asked, "Do you believe the U.S. should bomb Hanoi and Haiphong?" however, only 14 percent said yes. In 1973, when Congress was considering articles of impeachment against President Nixon, a Gallup poll asked the question, "Do you think President Nixon should be impeached and compelled to leave the Presidency, or not?" Only 30 percent said yes to this question. They were then asked, "Do you think the President should be tried and removed from office if found guilty?" To this, 57 percent said yes.

The most popular form of polling these days is the telephone poll, where a few hundred people are called on the telephone and asked a couple of questions. The results are then broadcast the next day. The two ABC polls mentioned earlier were based on telephoning 384 and 382 people, respectively. Just remember that the U.S. population is over 245 million.

According to Dennis Haack, president of Statistical Consultants, a statistical research company in Lexington, Kentucky,

> most national surveys are not very accurate measures of public opinion. Opinion polls are no more accurate than indicated by their inability to predict Reagan's landslide in 1980 or Truman's win in 1948. The polls were wrong then and they have been wrong many other times when they tried to measure public opinion. The difference is that with elections we find out for sure if the polls were wrong; but for nonelection opinion polls there is no day of reckoning. We never know for sure how well surveys measure opinion when elections are not involved. I don't have much confidence in nonelection opinion surveys.

THE DOUBLESPEAK OF GRAPHS

Just as polls seem to present concrete, specific evidence, so do graphs and charts present information visually in a way that appears unambiguous and dramatically clear. But, just as polls leave a lot of necessary information out, so can graphs and charts, resulting in doublespeak. You have to ask a lot of questions if you really want to understand a graph or chart.

In 1981 President Reagan went on television to argue that citizens would   15
be paying a lot more in taxes under a Democratic bill than under his bill. To prove his point, he used a chart that appeared to show a dramatic and very big difference between the results of each bill (see Figure 1). But the president's chart was doublespeak, because it was deliberately designed to be misleading. Pointing to his chart, President Reagan said, "This red space between the two lines is the tax money that will remain in your pockets if our bill passes, and it's the amount that will leave your pockets if their bill is passed. On the one hand, you see a genuine and lasting commitment to the future of working Americans. On the other, just another empty promise." That was a pretty dramatic statement, considering that the maximum difference between the two bills, after five years, would have been $217.

The president's chart showed a deceptively dramatic difference because his chart had no figures on the dollar scale and no numbers for years except 1982 and 1986. The difference in tax payments was exaggerated in the president's chart by "squashing" or tightening the time scale as much as possible, while stretching the dollar scale, starting with an oddly unrounded $2,150 and winding up at $2,400. Thus, the chart had no perspective. Using the proper method

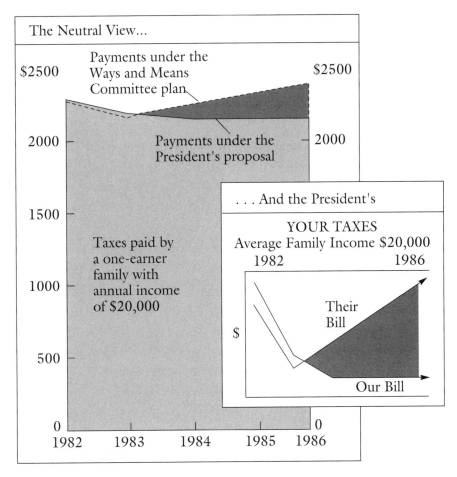

The Neutral View...

$2500 Payments under the
       Ways and Means
       Committee plan

$2500

2000   Payments under the   2000
                    President's proposal

                                    . . . And the President's

1500
                                        YOUR TAXES
                                Average Family Income $20,000
          Taxes paid by   1982   1986
          a one-earner
          family with
1000   annual income   Their
          of $20,000   Bill

                                  $

 500
                                                    Our Bill

   0   0
     1982   1983   1984   1985   1986

Figure 1   President Reagan's misleading and biased chart, compared with a neutral presentation regarding the same tax proposals.

for constructing a chart would have meant starting at $0 and going up to the first round number after the highest point in the chart, as done in the "neutral view" in Figure 1. Using that method, the $217 seems rather small in a total tax bill of $2,385.

What happened to the numbers on the president's chart? "The chart we sent over to the White House had all the numbers on it," said Marlin Fitzwater, then a press officer in the Treasury Department. Senior White House spokesperson David Gergen said, "We took them off. We were trying to get a point across, not the absolute numbers." So much for honesty.

In 1988 the Department of Education issued a graph that seemed to prove that there was a direct connection between the rise in elementary and secondary school spending and the decline in scores on the Scholastic Aptitude Test (see

Elementary/Secondary Education Spending
and Achievement: 1963–1988

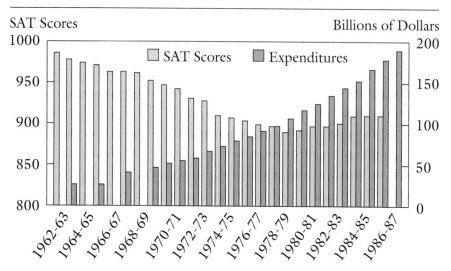

Figure 2   Misleading graph from the Department of Education, showing school spending relative to SAT scores.

Figure 2). The Reagan Administration had been arguing that spending more money doesn't improve education and may even make it worse. But the chart was doublespeak. First, it used current dollars rather than constant dollars, adjusted for inflation. Because each year it takes more money to buy the same things, charts are supposed to adjust for that increase so the measure of dollars remains constant over the years illustrated in the chart. If the Department of Education had figured in inflation over the years on the chart, it would have shown that the amount of constant dollars spent on education had increased modestly from 1970 to 1986, as Figure 3 on page 191 shows.

Second, scores on the Scholastic Aptitude Test go from 400 to 1,600, yet the graph used by the Education Department (Figure 2) used a score range of only 800 to 1,000. By limiting the range of scores on its graph, the department showed what appeared to be a severe decline in scores. A properly prepared graph, shown in Figure 4 on page 191, shows a much more gradual decline.

The Department of Education's presentation is a good example of diagrammatic doublespeak. Without all the information you need in order to understand the chart, you can be easily misled, which of course was the purpose of the chart. You should always be skeptical whenever you see a graph or chart being used to present information, because these things are nothing more than the visual presentation of statistical information. And as for statistics, remember what Benjamin Disraeli is supposed to have said: "There are three kinds of lies — lies, damn lies, and statistics."   20

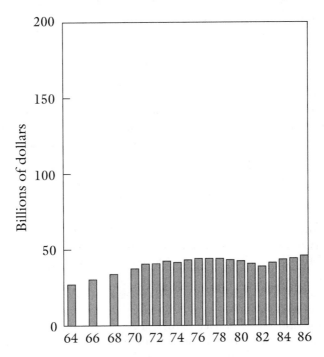

Figure 3   Elementary/secondary education spending in constant dollars (billions).

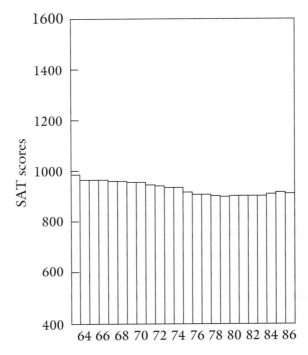

Figure 4   SAT scores, 1963–1986.

Two Views of Intelligence

The following set of essays provide an example of authors evaluating arguments. Both writers address the same issue, the relationship between race and IQ, but they come to very different conclusions. As you read these articles, consider the following questions:

1. What kind of ethos does each author construct? How credible does each writer sound? What specific techniques does each writer use to sound credible?
2. Does either writer use appeals to emotion? If so, what emotions does the writer try to invoke? How effective is the use of appeals to emotion?
3. What is the claim of each essay? How effectively does each writer state his claim?
4. What reasons does each writer give to support his claim? How effectively are these reasons stated? How convincing are they for you?
5. What assumptions are implied in these arguments? Are any of these assumptions stated explicitly or supported with evidence? To what extent do you accept each writer's assumptions?
6. Why don't these writer's agree with each other? In other words, what point is at issue for each writer?

Racist Arguments and IQ

STEPHEN JAY GOULD

L OUIS AGASSIZ, the greatest biologist of mid-nineteenth-century America,   1
argued that God had created blacks and whites as separate species. The defenders of slavery took much comfort from his assertion, for biblical proscriptions of charity and equality did not have to extend across a species boundary. What could an abolitionist say? Science had shone its cold and dispassionate light upon the subject; Christian hope and sentimentality could not refute it.

Similar arguments, carrying the apparent sanction of science, have been continually invoked in attempts to equate egalitarianism with sentimental hope and emotional blindness. People who are unaware of this historical pattern tend to accept each recurrence at face value: that is, they assume that each statement arises from the "data" actually presented, rather than from the social conditions that truly inspire it.

The racist arguments of the nineteenth century were based primarily on craniometry, the measurement of human skulls. Today, these contentions stand totally discredited. What craniometry was to the nineteenth century, intelligence testing has been to the twentieth. The victory of the eugenics movement in the Immigration Restriction Act of 1924 signaled its first unfortunate effect — for the severe restriction upon non-Europeans and upon southern and eastern Europeans gained much support from results of the first extensive and uniform application of intelligence tests in America — the Army Mental Tests of World War I. These tests were engineered and administered by psychologist Robert M. Yerkes, who concluded that "education alone will not place the negro [*sic*] race on a par with its Caucasian competitors." It is now clear that Yerkes and his colleagues knew no way to separate genetic from environmental components in postulating causes for different performances on the tests.

The latest episode of this recurring drama began in 1969, when Arthur Jensen published an article entitled, "How Much Can We Boost IQ and Scholastic Achievement?" in the *Harvard Educational Review*. Again, the claim went forward that new and uncomfortable information had come to light, and that science had to speak the "truth" even if it refuted some cherished notions of a liberal philosophy. But again, I shall argue, Jensen had no new data; and what he did present was flawed beyond repair by inconsistencies and illogical claims.

Jensen assumes that IQ tests adequately measure something we may call "intelligence." He then attempts to tease apart the genetic and environmental factors causing differences in performance. He does this primarily by relying upon the one natural experiment we possess: identical twins reared apart — for differences in IQ between genetically identical people can only be environmental. The average difference in IQ for identical twins is less than the difference for two unrelated individuals raised in similarly varied environments. From the data on twins, Jensen obtains an estimate of environmental influence. He concludes that IQ has a heritability of about 0.8 (or 80 percent) *within* the population of American and European whites. The average difference between American whites and blacks is 15 IQ points (one standard deviation). He asserts that this difference is too large to attribute to environment, given the high heritability of IQ. Lest anyone think that Jensen writes in the tradition of abstract scholarship, I merely quote the first line of his famous work: "Compensatory education has been tried, and it apparently has failed."

I believe that this argument can be refuted in a "hierarchical" fashion — that is, we can discredit it at one level and then show that it fails at a more inclusive level even if we allow Jensen's argument for the first two levels:

Level 1: The equation of IQ with intelligence. Who knows what IQ measures? It is a good predictor of "success" in school, but is such success a result of intelligence, apple polishing, or the assimilation of values that the leaders of society prefer? Some psychologists get around this argument by defining intelligence operationally as the scores attained on "intelligence" tests. A neat trick. But at this point, the technical definition of intelligence has strayed so far from the vernacular that we can no longer define the issue. But let me allow (although I don't believe it), for the sake of argument, that IQ measures some meaningful aspect of intelligence in its vernacular sense.

Level 2: The heritability of IQ. Here again, we encounter a confusion between vernacular and technical meanings of the same word. "Inherited," to a layman, means "fixed," "inexorable," or "unchangeable." To a geneticist, "Inherited" refers to an estimate of similarity between related individuals based on genes held in common. It carries no implications of inevitability or of immutable entities beyond the reach of environmental influence. Eyeglasses correct a variety of inherited problems in vision; insulin can check diabetes.

Jensen insists that IQ is 80 percent heritable. Princeton psychologist Leon J. Kamin has done the dog-work of meticulously checking through details of the twin studies that form the basis of this estimate. He has found an astonishing number of inconsistencies and downright inaccuracies. For example, the late Sir Cyril Burt, who generated the largest body of data on identical twins reared apart, pursued his studies of intelligence for more than forty years. Although he increased his sample sizes in a variety of "improved" versions, some of his correlation coefficients remain unchanged to the third decimal place — a statistically impossible situation. IQ depends in part upon sex and age; and other studies did not standardize properly for them. An improper correction may produce higher values between twins not because they hold genes for intelligence in common, but simply because they share the same sex and age. The data are so flawed that no valid estimate for the heritability of IQ can be drawn at all. But let me assume (although no data support it), for the sake of argument, that the heritability of IQ is as high as 0.8.

Level 3: The confusion of within- and between-group variation. Jensen   10
draws a causal connection between his two major assertions — that the within-group heritability of IQ is 0.8 for American whites, and that the mean difference in IQ between American blacks and whites is 15 points. He assumes that the black "deficit" is largely genetic in origin because IQ is so highly heritable. This is a *non sequitur* of the worst possible kind — for there is no necessary relationship between heritability within a group and differences in mean values of two separate groups.

A simple example will suffice to illustrate this flaw in Jensen's argument. Height has a much higher heritability within groups than anyone has ever claimed for IQ. Suppose that height has a mean value of five feet two inches and a heritability of 0.9 (a realistic value) within a group of nutritionally deprived Indian farmers. High heritability simply means that short farmers will tend to have short offspring, and tall farmers tall offspring. It says nothing whatever against the possibility that proper nutrition could raise the mean height to six feet (taller than average white Americans). It only means that, in this improved status, farmers shorter than average (they may now be five feet ten inches) would still tend to have shorter than average children.

I do not claim that intelligence, however defined, has no genetic basis — I regard it as trivially true, uninteresting, and unimportant that it does. The expression of any trait represents a complex interaction of heredity and environment. Our job is simply to provide the best environmental situation for the realization of valued potential in all individuals. I merely point out that a specific claim purporting to demonstrate a mean genetic deficiency in the intelligence of American blacks rests upon no new facts whatever and can cite no valid data in its support. It is just as likely that blacks have a genetic advantage over whites. And, either way, it doesn't matter a damn. An individual can't be judged by his group mean.

If current biological determinism in the study of human intelligence rests upon no new facts (actually, no facts at all), then why has it become so popular of late? The answer must be social and political. The 1960s were good years for liberalism; a fair amount of money was spent on poverty programs and relatively little happened. Enter new leaders and new priorities. Why didn't the earlier programs work? Two possibilities are open: (1) We didn't spend enough money, we didn't make sufficiently creative efforts, or (and this makes any established leader jittery) we cannot solve these problems without a fundamental social and economic transformation of society; or (2) the programs failed because their recipients are inherently what they are — blaming the victims. Now, which alternative will be chosen by men in power in an age of retrenchment?

I have shown, I hope, that biological determinism is not simply an amusing matter for clever cocktail party comments about the human animal. It is a general notion with important philosophical implications and major political consequences. As John Stuart Mill wrote, in a statement that should be the motto of the opposition: "Of all the vulgar modes of escaping from the consideration of the effect of social and moral influences upon the human mind, the most vulgar is that of attributing the diversities of conduct and character to inherent natural differences."

from *The Bell Curve*

RICHARD J. HERRNSTEIN and CHARLES MURRAY

INTELLIGENCE REDUX

A s FAR AS PUBLIC DISCUSSION is concerned, this collection of beliefs, with some variations, remains the state of wisdom about cognitive abilities and IQ tests. It bears almost no relation to the current state of knowledge among scholars in the field, however, and therein lies a tale. The dialogue about testing has been conducted at two levels during the last two decades — the visible one played out in the press and the subterranean one played out in the technical journals and books.

The case of Arthur Jensen is illustrative. To the public, he surfaced briefly, published an article that was discredited, and fell back into obscurity. Within the world of psychometrics,[1] however, he continued to be one of the profession's

---

[1] The quantitative measurement of mental abilities such as intelligence. [Ed.]

most prolific scholars, respected for his meticulous research by colleagues of every theoretical stripe. Jensen had not recanted. He continued to build on the same empirical findings that had gotten him into such trouble in the 1960s, but primarily in technical publications, where no one outside the profession had to notice. The same thing was happening throughout psychometrics. In the 1970s, scholars observed that colleagues who tried to say publicly that IQ tests had merit, or that intelligence was substantially inherited, or even that intelligence existed as a definable and measurable human quality, paid too high a price. Their careers, family lives, relationships with colleagues, and even physical safety could be jeopardized by speaking out. Why speak out when there was no compelling reason to do so? Research on cognitive abilities continued to flourish, but only in the sanctuary of the ivory tower.

In this cloistered environment, the continuing debate about intelligence was conducted much as debates are conducted within any other academic discipline. The public controversy had surfaced some genuine issues, and the competing parties set about trying to resolve them. Controversial hypotheses were put to the test. Sometimes they were confirmed, sometimes rejected. Often they led to new questions, which were then explored. Substantial progress was made. Many of the issues that created such a public furor in the 1970s were resolved, and the study of cognitive abilities went on to explore new areas.

This is not to say that controversy has ended, only that the controversy within the professional intelligence testing community is much different from that outside it. The issues that seem most salient in articles in the popular press (Isn't intelligence determined mostly by environment? Aren't the tests useless because they're biased?) are not major topics of debate within the profession. On many of the publicly discussed questions, a scholarly consensus has been reached. Rather, the contending parties within the professional community divide along other lines. By the early 1990s, they could be roughly divided into three factions for our purposes: the classicists, the revisionists, and the radicals.

The Classicists: Intelligence as a Structure

The classicists work within the tradition begun by Spearman, seeking to identify the components of intelligence much as physicists seek to identify the structure of the atom. As of the 1990s, the classicists are for practical purposes unanimous in accepting that g sits at the center of the structure in a dominating position — not just as an artifact of statistical manipulation but as an expression of a core human mental ability much like the ability Spearman identified at the turn of the century.[2] In their view, g is one of the most thoroughly demonstrated entities in the behavioral sciences and one of the most powerful for understanding socially significant human variation.

[2] In 1904 British army officer Charles Spearman claimed to have discovered a general factor in intelligence, a single mental ability that governed all other cognitive processes. He called this ability "g" for "general intelligence." [Ed.]

The classicists took a long time to reach this level of consensus. The ink on Spearman's first article on the topic in 1904 was barely dry before others were arguing that intellectual ability could not be adequately captured by g or by any other unitary quantity — and understandably so, for common sense rebels against the idea that something so important about people as their intellects can be captured even roughly by variations in a single quantity. Many of the famous names in the history of psychometrics challenged the reality of g, starting with Galton's most eminent early disciple, Karl Pearson, and continuing with many other creative and influential psychometricians.

In diverse ways, they sought the grail of a set of primary and mutually independent mental abilities. For Spearman, there was just one such primary ability, g. For Raymond Cattell, there are two kinds of g, *crystallized* and *fluid,* with crystallized g being general intelligence transformed into the skills of one's own culture, and fluid g being the all-purpose intellectual capacity for which the crystallized skills are formed. In Louis Thurstone's theory of intelligence, there are a half-dozen or so *primary mental abilities,* such as verbal, quantitative, spatial, and the like. In Philip Vernon's theory, intellectual capacities are arranged in a hierarchy with g at its apex; in Joy Guilford's, the structure of intellect is refined into 120 or more intellectual components. The theoretical alternatives to unitary, general intelligence have come in many sizes, shapes, and degrees of plausibility.

Many of these efforts proved to have lasting value. For example, Cattell's distinction between fluid and crystallized intelligence remains a useful conceptual contrast, just as other work has done much to clarify what lies in the domain of specific abilities that g cannot account for. But no one has been able to devise a set of tests that do not reveal a large general factor of intellectual ability — in other words, something very like Spearman's g. Furthermore, the classicists point out, the best standardized tests, such as a modern IQ test, do a reasonably good job of measuring g. When properly administered, the tests are not measurably biased against socioeconomic, ethnic, or racial subgroups. They predict a wide variety of socially important outcomes.

This is not the same as saying that the classicists are satisfied with their understanding of intelligence. g is a statistical entity, and current research is probing the underlying neurologic basis for it. Arthur Jensen, the archetypal classicist, has been active in this effort for the last decade, returning to Galton's intuition that performance on elementary cognitive tasks, such as reaction time in recognizing simple patterns of lights and shapes, provides an entry point into understanding the physiology of g.

The Revisionists: Intelligence as Information Processing

A theory of intelligence need not be structural. The emphasis may be on process rather than on structure. In other words, it may try to figure out what a person is *doing* when exercising his or her intelligence, rather than what elements of intelligence are put together. The great Swiss psychologist, Jean Piaget, started his career in Alfred Binet's laboratory trying to adapt Cyril Burt's intelligence tests for Parisian children. Piaget discovered quickly that he was less interested in how well the children did than in what errors they made. Errors revealed what the underlying processes of thought must have been, Piaget believed. It was the processes of intelligence that fascinated him during his long and illustrious career, which led in time to his theory of the stages of cognitive development.

Starting in the 1960s, research on human cognition became the preoccupation of experimental psychologists, displacing the animal learning experiments of the earlier period. It was inevitable that the new experimentalists would turn to the study of human intelligence in natural settings. John B. Carroll and Earl B. Hunt led the way from the cognition laboratory to the study of human intelligence in everyday life. Today Yale psychologist Robert Sternberg is among the leaders of this development.

The revisionists share much with the classicists. They accept that a general mental ability much like Spearman's *g* has to be incorporated into any theory of the structure of intelligence, although they would not agree that it accounts for as much of the intellectual variation among people as many classicists claim. They use many of the same statistical tools as the classicists and are prepared to subject their work to the same standards of rigor. Where they differ with the classicists, however, is their attitude toward intellectual structure and the tests used to measure it.

Yes, the revisionists argue, human intelligence has a structure, but is it worth investing all that effort in discovering what it is? The preoccupation with structure has engendered preoccupation with summary scores, the revisionists say. That, after all, is what an IQ score represents: a composite of scores that individually measure quite distinct intellectual processes. "Of course," Sternberg writes, "a tester can always average over multiple scores. But are such averages revealing, or do they camouflage more than they reveal? If a person is a wonderful visualizer but can barely compose a sentence, and another person can write glowing prose but cannot begin to visualize the simplest spatial images, what do you really learn about these two people if they are reported to have the same IQ?"

By focusing on processes, the revisionists argue, they are working richer veins than are those who search for static structure. What really counts about intelligence are the ways in which people process the information they receive. What problem-solving mechanisms do they employ? How do they trade off speed and accuracy? How do they combine different problem-solving resources into a strategy? Sternberg has fashioned his own thinking on this topic into what he calls a "triarchy of intelligence," or "three aspects of human information processing."

The first part of Sternberg's triarchy attempts to describe the internal architecture of intellectual functioning, the means by which humans translate sensory inputs into mental representations, allocate mental resources, infer conclusions from raw material, and acquire skills. This architectural component of Sternberg's theory bears a family resemblance to the classicists' view of the dimensions of intelligence, but it emphasizes process over structure.

The second part of the triarchic theory addresses the role of intelligence in routinizing performance, starting with completely novel tasks that test a person's insightfulness, flexibility, and creativity, and eventually converting them to routine tasks that can be done without conscious thought. Understand this process, Sternberg argues, and we have leverage not just for measuring intelligence but for improving it.

The third part of Sternberg's triarchy attacks the question that has been central to the controversy over intelligence tests: the relationship of intelligence to the real world in which people function. In Sternberg's view, people function by means of three mechanisms: *adaptation* (roughly, trying to make the best of the situation), *shaping* the external environment so that it conforms more closely to the desired state of affairs, or *selecting* a new environment altogether. Sternberg laments the inadequacies of traditional intelligence tests in capturing this real-world aspect of intelligence and seeks to develop tests that will do so — and, in addition, lead to techniques for teaching people to raise their intelligence.

The Radicals: The Theory of Multiple Intelligences

Walter Lippman's hostility toward intelligence testing was grounded in his belief that this most important of all human qualities was too diverse, too complex, too changeable, too dependent on cultural context, and, above all, too subjective to be measured by answers to a mere list of test questions. Intelligence seemed to him, as it does to many other thoughtful people who are not themselves expert in testing, more like beauty or justice than height or weight. Before something can be measured, it must be defined, this argument goes. And the problems of definition for beauty, justice, or intelligence are insuperable. To people who hold these views, the claims of the intelligence testers seem naive at best and vicious at worst. These views, which are generally advanced primarily by nonspecialists, have found an influential spokesman from the academy, which is mainly why we include them here. We refer here to the theory of multiple intelligences formulated by Howard Gardner, a Harvard psychologist.

Gardner's general definition of intelligent behavior does not seem radical at all. For Gardner, as for many other thinkers on intelligence, the notion of problem solving is central. "A human intellectual competence must entail a set of skills of problem solving," he writes, "enabling the individual to *resolve genuine problems or difficulties* that he or she encounters and, when appropriate, to create an effective product — and also must entail the potential for *finding or creating problems* — thereby laying the groundwork for the acquisition of new knowledge."

Gardner's view is radical (a word he uses himself to describe his theory) in that he rejects, virtually without qualification, the notion of a general intelligence factor, which is to say that he denies g. Instead, he argues the case for seven distinct intelligences: linguistic, musical, logical-mathematical, spatial, bodily-kinesthetic, and two forms of "personal intelligence," the intrapersonal and the interpersonal, each based on its own unique computational capacity. Gardner rejects the criticism that he has merely redefined the word *intelligence* by broadening it to include what may more properly be called talents: "I place no particular premium on the word *intelligence,* but I do place great importance on the equivalence of various human faculties," he writes, "If critics [of his theory] were willing to label language and logical thinking as talents as well, and to remove these from the pedestal they currently occupy, then I would be happy to speak of multiple talents."

Gardner's approach is also radical in that he does not defend his theory with quantitative data. He draws on findings from anthropology to zoology in his narrative, but, in a field that has been intensely quantitative since its inception, Gardner's work is uniquely devoid of psychometric or other quantitative evidence. He dismisses factor analysis: "[G]iven the same set of data, it is possible, using one set of factor-analytic procedures, to come up with a picture that supports the idea of a 'g' factor; using another equally valid method of statistical analysis, it is possible to support the notion of a family of relatively discrete mental abilities." He is untroubled by the fact that tests of the varying intelligences in his theory seem to be intercorrelated: "I fear . . . that I cannot accept these correlations at face value. Nearly all current tests are so devised that they call principally upon linguistic and logical facility. . . . Accordingly, individuals with these skills are likely to do well even in tests of musical or spatial abilities, while those who are not especially facile linguistically and logically are likely to be impaled on such standardized tests." And in general, he invites his readers to disregard the thorny complexities of the classical and revisionist approaches: "When it comes to the interpretation of intelligence testing, we are faced with an issue of taste or preference rather than one on which scientific closure is likely to be reached."

THE PERSPECTIVE OF THIS BOOK

Given these different ways of understanding intelligence, you will naturally ask where our sympathies lie and how they shape this book.

We will be drawing most heavily from the classical tradition. That body of scholarship represents an immense and rigorously analyzed body of knowledge. By accepted standards of what constitutes scientific evidence and scientific proof, the classical tradition has in our view given the world a treasure of information that has been largely ignored in trying to understand contemporary policy issues. Moreover, because our topic is the relationship of human abilities to public policy, we will be dealing in relationships that are based on aggregated data, which is where the classical tradition has the most to offer. Perhaps an example will illustrate what we mean.

Suppose that the question at issue regards individuals: "Given two 11 year olds, one with an IQ of 110 and one with an IQ of 90, what can you tell us about the differences between those two children?" The answer must be phrased very tentatively. On many important topics, the answer must be, "We can tell you nothing with any confidence." It is well worth a guidance counselor's time to know what these individual scores are, but only in combination with a variety of other information about the child's personality, talents, and background. The individual's IQ score all by itself is a useful tool but a limited one.

Suppose instead that the question at issue is: "Given two sixth-grade classes, one for which the average IQ is 110 and the other for which it is 90, what can you tell us about the difference between those two classes and their average prospects for the future?" Now there is a great deal to be said, and it can be said with considerable confidence — not about any one person in either class but about average outcomes that are important to the school, educational policy in general, and society writ large. The data accumulated under the classical tradition are extremely rich in this regard, as will become evident in subsequent chapters.

If instead we were more concerned with the development of cognitive processes than with aggregate social and economic outcomes, we would correspondingly spend more time discussing the work of the revisionists. That we do not reflects our focus, not a dismissal of their work.

With regard to the radicals and the theory of multiple intelligences, we share some common ground. Socially significant individual differences include a wide range of human talents that do not fit within the classical conception of intelligence. For certain spheres of life, they matter profoundly. And even beyond intelligence and talents, people vary temperamentally, in personality, style, and character. But we confess to reservations about using the word *intelligence* to describe such factors as musical abilities, kinesthetic abilities, or personal skills. It is easy to understand how intelligence (ordinarily understood) is part of some aspects of each of those human qualities — obviously, Bach was engaging in intelligent activity, and so was Ted Williams, and so is a good used-car salesman — but the part intelligence plays in these activities is captured fairly well by intelligence as the classicists and revisionists conceive of it. In the case of music and kinesthetics, *talent* is a word with a domain and weight of its own, and we are unclear why we gain anything by discarding it in favor of another word, *intelligence,* that has had another domain and weight. In the case of intrapersonal and interpersonal skills, conventional intelligence may play some role, and, to the extent that other human qualities matter, words like *sensitivity, charm, persuasiveness, insight* — the list could go on and on — have accumulated over the centuries to describe them. We lose precision by using the word *intelligence* to cover them all. Similarly, the effect that an artist or an athlete or a salesman creates is complex, with some aspects that may be dominated by specific endowments or capacities, others that may be the product of learned technique, others that may be linked to desires and drives, and still others that are characteristic of the kind of cognitive ability denoted by intelligence. Why try to make *intelligence* do triple or quadruple duty?

We agree emphatically with Howard Gardner, however, that the concept of intelligence has taken on a much higher place in the pantheon of human virtues than it deserves. One of the most insidious but also widespread errors regarding

IQ, especially among people who have high IQs, is the assumption that another person's intelligence can be inferred from casual interactions. Many people conclude that if they see someone who is sensitive, humorous, and talks fluently, the person must surely have an above-average IQ.

This identification of IQ with attractive human qualities in general is unfortunate and wrong. Statistically, there is often a modest correlation with such qualities. But modest correlations are of little use in sizing up other individuals one by one. For example, a person can have a terrific sense of humor without giving you a clue about where he is within thirty points on the IQ scale. Or a plumber with a measured IQ of 100 — only an average IQ — can know a great deal about the functioning of plumbing systems. He may be able to diagnose problems, discuss them articulately, make shrewd decisions about how to fix them, and, while he is working, make some pithy remarks about the president's recent speech.

At the same time, high intelligence has earmarks that correspond to a first 30 approximation to the commonly understood meaning of *smart*. In our experience, people do not use *smart* to mean (necessarily) that a person is prudent or knowledgeable but rather to refer to qualities of mental quickness and complexity that do in fact show up in high test scores. To return to our examples: Many witty people do not have unusually high test scores, but someone who regularly tosses off impromptu complex puns probably does (which does not necessarily mean that such puns are very funny, we hasten to add). If the plumber runs into a problem he has never seen before and diagnoses its source through inferences from what he does know, he probably has an IQ of more than 100 after all. In this, language tends to reflect real differences: In everyday language, people who are called very smart tend to have high IQs.

All of this is another way of making a point so important that we will italicize it now and repeat elsewhere: *Measures of intelligence have reliable statistical relationships with important social phenomena, but they are a limited tool for deciding what to make of any given individual.* Repeat it we must, for one of the problems of writing about intelligence is how to remind readers often enough how little an IQ score tells about whether the human being next to you is someone whom you will admire or cherish. This thing we know as IQ is important but not a synonym for human excellence.

Howard Gardner has also convinced us that the word *intelligence* carries with it undue affect and political baggage. It is still a useful word, but we shall subsequently employ the more neutral term *cognitive ability* as often as possible to refer to the concept that we have hitherto called *intelligence,* just as we will use *IQ* as a generic synonym for *intelligence test score.* Since *cognitive ability* is an uneuphonious phrase, we lapse often so as to make the text readable. But at least we hope that it will help you think of *intelligence* as just a noun, not an accolade.

We have said that we will be drawing most heavily on data from the classical tradition. That implies that we also accept certain conclusions undergirding that tradition. To draw the strands of our perspective together and to set the stage for the rest of the book, let us set them down explicitly. Here are six conclusions

> ## ▨ Idiot Savants and Other Anomalies ▨
>
> To add one final complication, it is also known that some people with low measured IQ occasionally engage in highly developed, complex cognitive tasks. So-called idiot savants can (for example) tell you on what day Easter occurred in any of the past or future two thousand years. There are also many less exotic examples. For example, a study of successful track bettors revealed that some of them who used extremely complicated betting systems had below-average IQs and that IQ was not correlated with success. The trick in interpreting such results is to keep separate two questions: (1) If one selects people who have already demonstrated an obsession and success with racetrack betting systems, will one find a relationship with IQ (the topic of the study in question)? versus (2) if one selects a thousand people at random and asks them to develop racetrack betting systems, will there be a relationship with IQ (in broad terms, the topic of this book)?

regarding tests of cognitive ability, drawn from the classical tradition, that are by now beyond significant technical dispute:

1. There is such a thing as a general factor of cognitive ability on which human beings differ.
2. All standardized tests of academic aptitude or achievement measure this general factor to some degree, but IQ tests expressly designed for that purpose measure it most accurately.
3. IQ scores match, to the first degree, whatever it is that people mean when they use the word *intelligent* or *smart* in ordinary language.
4. IQ scores are stable, although not perfectly so, over much of a person's life.
5. Properly administered IQ tests are not demonstrably biased against social, economic, ethnic, or racial groups.
6. Cognitive ability is substantially heritable, apparently no less than 40 percent and no more than 80 percent.

All six points have an inverse worth noting. For example, some people's scores change a lot; cognitive ability is not synonymous with test scores or with a single general mental factor, and so on. When we say that all are "beyond significant technical dispute," we mean, in effect, that if you gathered the top experts on testing and cognitive ability, drawn from all points of view, to argue over these points, away from television cameras and reporters, it would quickly become apparent that a consensus already exists on all of the points, in some cases amounting to near unanimity. And although dispute would ensue about some of the points, one side — the side represented by the way the points are stated — would have a clear preponderance of evidence favoring it, and those of another viewpoint would be forced to lean heavily on isolated studies showing anomalous results.

This does not mean that the experts should leave the room with their differences resolved. All six points can be accurate as general rules and still leave room for differences in the theoretical and practical conclusions that people of different values and perspectives draw from them (and from the mass of material about cognitive ability and testing not incorporated in the six points). Radicals in the Gardner mold might still balk at all the attention being paid to intelligence as the tests measure it. But these points, in themselves, are squarely in the middle of the scientific road.

Chapter 6
Joining the Conversation

Identifying a Starting Point

By this point, you should understand how to identify, analyze, and evaluate arguments. The next step is to join a conversation yourself, constructing arguments of your own using all the means of persuasion. The best arguments are those that are part of a conversation, that respond to issues facing a real community. To join the conversation in a meaningful way, you need to identify a place where you can enter the conversation. Your response may originate in a disagreement or controversy that already exists in the community, or you may wish to present a position that has not been presented at all. In the process of listening to others and recording and evaluating their ideas, you may have found gaps in their reasoning, areas that have not been considered. These would be natural points to enter the conversation. It is difficult, however, to describe exactly how to identify a proper time and place for you to add your voice to the conversation. Usually, when you really try to get involved in the intellectual life of a community, the opportunities present themselves.

Exploring and Rehearsing

■ ■ FREEWRITING

Identifying a starting point — a place to enter the conversation — is the first step in responding. The next step is exploring and rehearsing your response, discovering in writing what you want to say and what you really think. One way to begin is with freewriting or "rush" writing. In rush writing, you set a designated amount of time — five minutes, for instance — and then write down anything that comes into your mind, whether it pertains to the issue or not. If you can't think of anything to write, then write about your writer's block. The important thing is that you get words down on the paper. After all, even the longest journey must begin with the first step, and that first step is often the hardest. Rush writing will help you get the writing process going.

▪ ▪ MAPPING AND CLUSTERING

You might also try to represent your ideas visually, using mapping or clustering. With mapping, you sketch or outline your argument. Unlike a formal outline, which uses a system of numbers and letters to show the relationships among ideas, mapping is much more informal. It resembles a constructive kind of doodling. You may draw pictures to represent parts of your argument, with captions to describe these parts. You might also try mapping your ideas as a branching tree. Clustering is a type of mapping that you begin by writing down your topic or issue in a circle at the center of a sheet of paper. You then jot down as many words and ideas related to this topic as you can, anywhere on the paper. After you are done, you group or "cluster" these ideas together, drawing lines between those that are related.

▪ ▪ BRAINSTORMING

Another way to get started is by brainstorming, which is usually a group activity, often used to suggest solutions to a problem. (Clustering and mapping are forms of brainstorming you can do by yourself.) In brainstorming, a group decides on a subject, and then members call out anything they can think of related to the subject. One member is assigned to write these responses down, not omitting anything no matter how ridiculous. A brainstorming session usually lasts for a specified amount of time, such as five or ten minutes. After the brainstorming is finished, the group discusses and evaluates the ideas and suggestions, trying to determine the best one. If the group is not satisfied with any of the responses, the brainstorming session may be repeated.

▪ ▪ CLASSICAL ARGUMENT

At some point, your ideas need to take a more coherent shape. Some writers like writing a "discovery draft," an essay that takes its own form as the writer follows out the implications of his or her topic and ideas. Another way of discovering what you believe is to draft your ideas in the form of a traditional argument, to make a claim and attempt to support it with reasons. This is usually done in the form of an essay, but you can also draft a formal outline of the argument as a way of organizing your thinking.

Classical argument is the form taken by a lot of academic writing, and it is often used by philosophers as a way of exploring and evaluating their ideas. To begin, you might summarize the situation that leads you to make your claim, the "space" in the conversation that your argument is going to fill. In academic writing this usually serves as the introduction of an essay. At the end of your introduction, you should state your claim. In academic writing, this is called the thesis of the essay. Your thesis may also include the reasons you will present to support your claim, possible objections to your thesis, and perhaps even your response to these objections. Here is an example: "Although some activists are concerned about the effect that tax reform would have on the poor, introducing a flat rate tax is a good idea because such a tax would make the government more efficient and will have long-term benefits for the economy." In this sample thesis, there are one claim (introducing a flat rate tax is a good idea) and two reasons (such a tax would make the government more efficient and will have long-term benefits for the economy). This thesis also states a possible reservation or objection (some activists are concerned about the effect that tax reform would have on the poor).

After the introduction, the body of a classical argument essay contains two sections. In the first of these, you present and support each of your reasons as best you can. You may also wish to identify and support the assumptions implied by your reasons. In the second section of the body, you respond to possible objections to your argument. A classical argument typically concludes with a review of the major points that have been made, a discussion of what this argument adds to the conversation, or a presentation of the action those who accept the argument should take. Here is an overview of the classical argument:

Introduction: background, context, review of the conversation

Thesis: statement of claim and reasons

Support of reasons and assumptions

Answers to possible objections

Conclusion: review of major points, the contribution of this argument, call to action

Revising

Remember that in the exploration and rehearsal stage you are your own audience. You are trying to frame your ideas for yourself, to express to yourself why you believe what you do. Your writing up to now is not necessarily in the form best suited to presenting your ideas to others. Unless you are an exceptionally precise thinker and writer, you will need to revise your arguments as you go along. Revision is an important part of exploration and rehearsal. It is through revision that you discover what you are really trying to say. One activity that will help you find revisions to your argument is the "doubting game." In this activity you pretend that you hold a position in opposition to the one you are claiming; you then try to support that opposing position and also answer possible objections (including the reasons you are offering for your true position). This activity may cause you to rethink your original position. You may decide that it needs to be modified or even that it is not worth defending at all. You may even be led to a new position that you can support with more confidence. Whether or not you modify or reverse your original opinion, the doubting game will help you find places where your argument is poorly supported or explained and suggest possibilities for revision.

Although you are writing for yourself at this stage, you may still want to share your argument with others. They may help you think of reasons or evidence you omitted and raise possible objections that you did not anticipate. They may also help you take a critical stance toward your argument, helping you to discover where it needs reinforcing. Often, when writers spend a lot of time with an essay, it grows so familiar that they have difficulty seeing its shortcomings. Getting someone else's perspective can help; best is to seek a number of perspectives that are quite different from your own — the more diverse, the better.

Adapting to the Community

Once you have framed your ideas to your own satisfaction, it is time to go public, to make your ideas available to the community. Doing so means adapting your argument to the needs of that community, and here is where your argument gains its persuasive power. Adapting an argument to a community involves finding community-based reasons, organizing the argument for its audience, and following the conventions of the site of communication chosen for presenting the argument.

▦ ▦ FINDING COMMUNITY-BASED REASONS

In the process of analyzing arguments, you may begin to feel that any claim can be called into question. In addition, reasons and assumptions can themselves become claims in need of additional support, leading to a chain of reasoning with no apparent solid intellectual ground upon which you can build with any certainty. Where does the justifying come to an end? Couldn't a stubborn person keep asking for more and more support, disputing every statement in an argument, asking — as a young child does — "Why? Why? Why?" If one wants to be stubborn, yes; but such orneriness becomes ridiculous after awhile. When arguments have a context, when they are a meaningful part of the life of a community, then at some point they can be grounded in what the community accepts as credible, authoritative, or true — the common sense or common knowledge of the community. This stock of knowledge differs from one community to another, and not all members of any community completely agree on that community's "common knowledge." This is why disagreements arise in the first place. But still there are statements and beliefs that most members of a community accept as true, and an argument will be persuasive only when the reasons and assumptions that justify the claim are grounded in this core of common belief. Reasons grounded in the common beliefs of the community are called "community-based reasons."

The danger in relying on community-based reasons and adapting your argument to the needs of the community is that you may compromise the integrity of your own views. In other words, you may end up telling people what they want to hear rather than what you really believe. Some people can accept being insincere or deceitful, and telling people what they want to hear may help them get what they want in the short run. But insincerity and deceit are usually discovered eventually. If you want to make a long-term commitment and any real contribution to a community, you should be wary of such compromises. The trick is to find reasons that the community will find persuasive and that you can accept and believe in. These may not be the most compelling reasons for you, but they will be the most compelling for those you are addressing.

I once had a student writing an essay about a controversy in the small town she came from. A town ordinance forbid the consumption and sale of alcohol in city parks. Some citizens wanted to change the ordinance to make the sale and consumption of alcohol legal by special permit. The intent of this proposed change was to make it possible for the town to attract concerts to the city parks, which many felt would help the town's economy. At the same time, influential religious groups in the town opposed the change because public drinking violated their religious beliefs or because they believed that such access to alcohol would destroy the morality of the town, making it an unhealthy place to raise a family. These groups argued that giving in on this drinking law would open the door to all other kinds of compromises in the name of economic development.

The issue had polarized the town. Supporters of the change saw members of the religious groups as being self-righteous and judgmental or as trying to protect their own economic interests. When my student wrote her discovery draft (her argument for herself), she sided with those who objected to the proposed change on religious and moral grounds. But she realized that because the town was so polarized, these reasons might not be convincing to the community as a whole or to the town council.

Being an emergency room nurse at the local hospital, which was in a neighboring city that did allow the sale of alcohol for park concerts, she knew that on concert nights the emergency room was overloaded with concert-goers who had had too much too drink or had run into trouble with those who had. Her own son had even had to wait for emergency medical care on a concert night. So in her draft she argued that allowing alcohol at concerts in her town — as well as the neighboring town — would overload the local medical system and ultimately cost the town much more than it would gain in human as well as monetary terms.

Even though this was not the most compelling reason for my student, it was a reason that she nonetheless believed in strongly and one that added a new dimension to the debate, an argument centered in the common values of the community. After all, who would deny the value of reliable medical care?

Here is another example of finding community-based reasons. A few years ago the State of Utah voted on a proposition to allow individual counties to decide whether to legalize gambling between individuals (on sporting events, horse racing, and "friendly" games of chance). At the time such gambling was illegal under state law, but a majority of citizens in several counties favored legalizing gambling between individuals because of the economic benefits they felt it would bring to their communities.

The religious groups in the state opposed the proposition. They felt that gambling of any sort was immoral. But these groups realized that the immorality of gambling was not the best community-based reason because it would polarize the state along religious lines. So these groups argued instead that legalizing gambling would actually bring economic problems to the state. They used the examples of other states, such as Wyoming, that had relaxed their gambling laws and showed how the economic costs of doing so had outweighed any benefits. Even though the most compelling reason for these religious groups was that they considered gambling immoral, they could still accept the argument about economic harm. The argument about economic harm was a community-based reason because it relied on one of the values held by the proponents of gambling, showing how their proposal actually ran counter to that value.

The proposition was defeated by an overwhelming majority of voters, some of whom may have believed it was immoral, some of whom may have been persuaded of the argument about economic disadvantages. Some claimed that they voted against the proposition because they felt its proponents were self-serving in basing their argument on economic benefits. In other words, the proponents of the gambling proposition made the mistake of arguing for the reason that they found most convincing rather than finding community-based reasons. Rather than arguing for economic benefits, they might have been more successful had they argued for the importance of local government; the proposition did not actually legalize gambling, but only made it possible for individual counties to determine the issue locally. If they had argued that the issue was not gambling but rather decentralization of government, this value might have had wider appeal.

■ ■ ORGANIZING THE ARGUMENT

The structure of your argument, with its claim, chains of reasons, and assumptions, can become the structure for your essay or your presentation of that argument. In a classical argument, for instance, the organization of the essay follows the basic structure of the argument. And, as I mentioned earlier, classical argument is frequently used in academic writing. But there are other ways of organizing an argument that you may find useful in adapting your argument to a particular audience. You may also find these other patterns of organization to be interesting alternatives to the traditional academic essay.

In organizing your argument, you need to make some inferences about your audience. The audience for your writing is not exactly the same as the community. Rather, the audience is made up of those who participate in the conversation you are joining, and it will generally be only a part of the larger community. Take the national community, for instance. There are not really any sites of communication that include everyone who lives in the United States. Even if you were to broadcast your message on all the major networks, you would only reach those who have televisions — actually, only those who have their televisions on and are watching a major network. Likewise, if you published your argument in the *Wall Street Journal* or *New York Times,* you would reach a large number of people but only those who read these newspapers — and actually took the time to read your piece — not the full community.

As you adapt your argument to an audience, remember that you are adapting your argument to those who participate in the particular conversation you are joining. In a sense, this audience is a smaller community within the larger community to which you all belong, so in joining a conversation and adapting your argument to the needs of a particular audience, you may think of yourself as joining a new community with its own organization and conversations. The more you know about this audience the better. The following questions may help you understand your audience:

1. Whom are you addressing? Who participates in the conversation?
2. How much do they know or care about your topic?
3. What is your audience's current attitude?
4. What values and opinions do you share with your audience?
5. How do your views differ from the views of your audience?

Answering these questions will help you understand the relationship of your position to the positions held by members of your audience. (The audience may be quite complex and represent a number of opinions.)

You need to determine the relationship of the audience's opinions to your own. Let's call those with whom you basically agree your "in-group." Those who hold an opinion much different from yours are your "out-group." Between your opinion and the opinion of your out-group lies a spectrum of opinions, including those who share your position to a certain degree but not as fully as you and your in-group do. The following diagram shows a simple relationship:

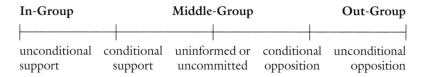

In-Group		Middle-Group		Out-Group
unconditional support	conditional support	uninformed or uncommitted	conditional opposition	unconditional opposition

At one extreme your out-group is characterized by "unconditional opposition." This group is completely opposed to your position, able to offer strong reasons to support its opposition, and reluctant to make any show of support or conciliation toward your view. At the other extreme, your in-group, those most closely associated with your position, offers unconditional support and is able to offer strong reason for that support. Between these two positions lie other positions. A less extreme out-group will be characterized by conditional opposition, opposing your view but perhaps unable to offer strong reasons for its opposition or willing to concede some support for your position. Likewise, a less extreme in-group will be characterized by conditional support, unable perhaps to offer strong reasons for that support or to commit fully to your view. In the middle are those who have not made much of a commitment either way or who may not know much about the issue.

In another situation you and your in-group may represent a middle ground between what you consider two extreme positions. Here is a diagram of that situation:

When the audience holds multiple opinions, you may come up with a more complex diagram, particularly if you try to represent the relationship of these different groups to one another as well as to you and your in-group:

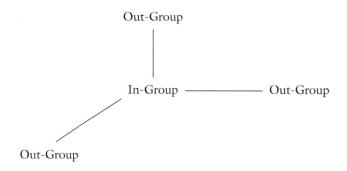

In this diagram the two out-groups on the right agree with each other more than they agree with the out-group on the left. The in-group position lies somewhere between the positions of the two groups on the left and the one on the right.

You will define these groups in relation to you and the issue you are arguing. They are not absolute: Another writer might define them differently, as you yourself might when writing about another issue. Your out-group on one issue might become your in-group on another. This type of grouping is also not meant to be judgmental or evaluative, and you might in fact sympathize with people in your out-group on a particular issue. The model is merely designed to help you analyze different kinds of audiences.

Once you have mapped out the relationship of your position to the various positions your audience holds, you are ready to select a structure that best addresses the needs of that particular audience. In doing this, you will need to consider the dominant positions in your audience, adapting your argument as well as you can to any other positions.

This process is not scientific or precise; it is an art and requires judgment, experience, and skill on the part of the writer. Because the process is not exact, even the most skilled writers sometimes misunderstand their audience or fail to be persuasive. Still, seeking to understand your audience and to adapt your argument to the needs of that audience should improve your ability to make a meaningful contribution to the conversation.

Following are a few common patterns for organizing an argument and adapting it to the needs of an audience.

Classical Argument   I have already outlined a classical argument. It begins with an introduction that provides some context: a question, a quotation, an anecdote, some historical background, the social context, some factual information, or a narration of events. Because the audience may not initially be very interested in the topic, you may also need to generate some interest in the introduction. The introduction typically includes a thesis statement, a statement of the claim, and major reasons. The body of the essay consists of two sections, one supporting the claim and one answering possible objections to the claim. The conclusion often summarizes the main points of the argument or calls for some kind of action. The conclusion occasionally includes an emotional appeal of some sort to give the argument presence.

In classical argument, writers try to demonstrate objectivity and impartiality, showing both sides of an issue. This type of structure works best with a middle group, one that is relatively uncommitted or uninformed. When addressing a middle group, it generally helps to show both sides of the issue; otherwise, the audience may think you are just doing a sales job. This approach also prepares your audience for possible objections to your argument.

Delayed Thesis   An argument with a delayed thesis is like a classical argument in reverse because the thesis comes at the end. The delayed thesis is particularly appropriate for an audience that is opposed to your position — and might not even listen to your argument if they knew your position from the beginning — but that might be willing to accept your position once they have heard your reasoning.

A delayed thesis argument generally begins by discussing assumptions, values, or definitions the audience holds in common. The writer then shows how these common assumptions provide support for a set of beliefs that will become the chain of reasons to support the claim. Like a classical argument, a delayed thesis essay is organized around reasons and assumptions, but the chain of reasoning leads the audience to the claim or thesis at the end.

The delayed thesis argument may also begin with objections to the claim. Then the writer answers these objections and leads the audience through the chain of reasons that support the claim. Such a pattern might work, for instance, when a moderate Republican advocate addresses moderate Democratic opponents on the subject of welfare reform. If the claim were presented at the beginning of the argument, such an audience's initial reaction might be so hostile that the subsequent reasoning would be ignored. But after considering the writer's reasoning, a Democratic audience might be willing to accept the Republican proposal when it is presented at the end.

A delayed thesis argument requires a fair amount of skill on the part of the writer because it doesn't follow a set form or pattern. In addition, the writer must maintain the interest and the assent of his or her audience throughout, without giving a sense that the audience is being manipulated or "trapped."

Conciliatory Argument   The conciliatory argument is closely related to the delayed thesis argument. It also begins by discussing common assumptions, values, or definitions, but it does not move on to any statement of the author's claim. The goal of this kind of argument is to move the audience from a position of unconditional opposition to a more moderate position, even one of conditional support. The writer tries to build a basis for further conversation, establishing some common ground with the audience in order to win a degree of consent.

This kind of argument is most effective when a writer is addressing his or her most extreme out-group. It might work, for instance, when an advocate for tolerance of homosexuality addresses fundamentalist Christians. The positions of the two are so far apart that the audience would probably not even accept a delayed thesis. But perhaps the writer could open the possibility for dialogue by emphasizing common ground (however remote from the actual issue) and arguing for an assumption, value, or belief that could lay the groundwork for future discussion. For example, he or she could argue for a common belief in the right to privacy and tolerance for difference without every mentioning homosexuality, perhaps discussing the persecution endured in the past by religious minorities. This argument would not convince its audience to support gay rights, but it might move the audience toward a more moderate position in relation to the writer's position.

Motivational Arguments   The prime concern in addressing an in-group is to build motivation and inspire members to action. An in-group already agrees with the writer's position but may not be motivated to act or respond. There are many ways to build motivation, all generally involving an appeal to a common vision or common set of values. In addition, the emotional appeal is often central to a motivational argument. Most advertisements are motivational arguments, trying to move us to acquire things we already want or value. A lot of religious discourse, such as preaching, is also motivational: A preacher describes a religious or moral vision and encourages those who accept this vision to change their behavior. Some business consultants have made millions of dollars because of their ability to deliver motivational arguments.

Monroe's motivated sequence is one type of motivational argument. It begins with the description of a need or a problem. In the next section the writer describes the negative effects or consequences of that need or problem, trying to make it real for the audience, to give it presence. The writer then presents a way to fill the need or solve the problem, followed by a description of a "vision" of this solution, how things would be better if the solution were put in place. The argument ends with a specific action that readers can take to contribute to the solution: making a phone call, writing a letter, contributing money, making an immediate change in behavior, making a commitment, signing a contract, and so on. The motivational argument usually includes the means to take the action. For instance, if the argument ends by asking you to write to your senator or representative, it will also include the names and addresses of those you should write to, and perhaps even a sample letter. If the argument ends by asking you to make an immediate change in your behavior, it might include a step-by-step guide for doing so. If you are to make a phone call, the argument will include the phone number and an example of what you should say.

Rogerian Argument   Rogerian argument is based on the theories of psychologist Carl Rogers. Rogers developed a theory of negotiation and conflict management that was nonconfrontational, nonjudgmental, and cooperative. This type of argument works well when you find yourself in the position of mediator, trying to bring two opposing groups together, or when you want to establish common ground between your in-group and an out-group.

Rogerian argument begins with a description of the context for the argument and a brief statement summarizing the various positions. All parties should agree that the mediator has stated their position accurately. In the next section, the mediator tries to outline each position as clearly as possible, without passing judgment on any position or seeking to favor one side over the other. Again, this description should be one that all parties can accept as accurate. The third section attempts to describe assumptions, values, and definitions that the different parties share. The argument concludes with a presentation of claims that all the parties can accept based on what they share.

A Rogerian argument may not bring the differing parties into complete agreement, but it will at least show precisely where they disagree and what they have in common. A Rogerian argument may result in an agreement to disagree, but at least it will be an informed disagreement.

Rogerian argument is an excellent way to begin a dialogue among parties that might not get together otherwise. Its success depends upon the ability of the mediator to describe the various positions and what the differing parties have in common, in terms that everyone will agree to. This type of argument works with groups whose interests seem to be in serious conflict, such as the parties to a labor dispute or at a diplomatic summit. A careful Rogerian argument can help stalemated groups begin talking.

Option Three   The term *option three* was coined by William Safire, a political columnist and language expert for the *New York Times*. He first identified this argument in political and corporate strategies for negotiation. The option three argument is related to Rogerian argument in form, but its goal is quite different: It is used when a writer is trying to appeal to a moderate group that lies between two extreme out-groups:

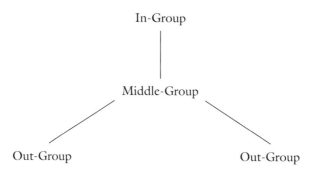

In this case the writer is not a mediator trying to bring two extreme groups together. Instead, the writer rejects both groups and presents a more moderate third option. In a sense the writer creates an in-group of those who are leaning toward one or the other extremes or who are uncommitted.

An option three argument follows a form similar to Rogerian argument with a few important differences. Like Rogerian argument, an option three argument begins by describing the controversy, its context and the positions that are currently set forth. In the next section, the writer describes each extreme position in detail, showing its weaknesses and disadvantages. In the third section, the writer describes the beliefs, values, and definitions that he or she shares with the audience (a more moderate group, a potential in-group for the author). The writer then presents a third option that lies between the two extremes, a position that builds on what he or she and the audience share.

The option three argument is often used in political campaigns when candidates try to identify with the political center, hoping to win votes from both parties. The option three is also used in the corporate world when a company, for instance, wants to show its stockholders that it is steering a middle course between two extremes.

▪ ▪ FOLLOWING THE CONVENTIONS

When you adapt your argument to the needs of an audience, you need to be careful to follow the conventions that guide the particular conversation you are joining. Each site of communication has its own types of discourse, its own rules governing what is and is not acceptable or understandable, and its own recognized experts and authorities. Generally, the more you conform to a community's conventions, the more credibility you will have with that community and the more persuasive you will be.

When you observe a site of conversation, pay attention not only to what people say, but also to how they say it. Pay particular attention to those who are recognized as experts or authorities.

How do they organize their arguments?

What kind of language do they use?

What kind of evidence do they use?

How do they incorporate what others have said into their own arguments?

What kind of ethos do they construct?

How do they use emotional appeals and give their arguments presence?

Newcomers to a community often learn to become accepted by imitating more experienced and respected members of the community. Very young children imitate their parents. Teenagers imitate members of their peer group. Aspiring artists or athletes may imitate the style of a master or champion. The same is true of those who are joining the community defined by a site of conversation: You can become accepted by imitating others around you. At the same time, however, you risk losing some of your identity and integrity if you merely follow what others have done and tell others what they want to hear. There is a balance between following the conventions of a conversation and preserving your own voice. Maintaining this balance is part of the whole tension between the individual and the community that characterizes living in a community and makes arguing such an important part of that life.

There are also those who are persuasive by deviating intentionally from the conventions of the conversation, who bring attention to an issue by presenting it in a surprising or unexpected way. I call this process "troping." The word *trope* comes from a Greek word that means "turning." Troping is a turning away from what is normally expected. Humorists, satirists, cartoonists, artists, poets, fiction writers, dramatists, and others often use troping as a form of arguing. They intentionally violate what is normally expected in order to draw attention to what they are saying. For instance, in his essay "A Modest Proposal" eighteenth-century satirist Jonathan Swift used biting irony, a trope that violated what his audience would have considered normal and appropriate, in order to draw attention to the plight of the Irish poor. Bill Watterson, the creator of the cartoon "Calvin and Hobbes," draws attention to the adult world by reducing it to the world of the playground and portraying it in the interactions between a young boy and his imaginary tiger. Science fiction writers draw attention to contemporary society by showing the problems that exist in future societies where the logical consequences of our behavior are played out. Arguments like these, when skillfully presented, have a devastating effect. But such arguments can backfire when they are not presented well or when the artist is not sufficiently tuned in to the community's cultural norms to deviate from them effectively. As a beginner you will probably have more success by adhering to the conventions of the community. You have to understand the rules before you can break them.

Applying the Principles

▪▪ AN INVITATION TO JOIN THE CONVERSATION

Throughout your academic career, you will be asked to respond to assignments and to write essays. Most of this writing will be in response to the classroom community you find yourself in. You can use the principles I have outlined to contribute to this classroom community. Analyze the organization of the classroom, your relationship to your teacher and to other students. Identify and analyze the classroom as a site of conversation. Observe how members of the community use language, and analyze the typical forms of writing that take place in this classroom community: in-class essays, research papers, lab reports, response papers, critical analyses, and so on. Then prepare to join the conversation as it is structured in your classroom.

Despite the fact that much of your writing in college is directed toward the classroom, I hope that you will try to make meaningful contributions to communities outside the classroom as well, not only while you are a student but also after you leave the university. Arguing is an important part of living in any community, and learning how to argue effectively and appropriately should make you a more responsible and integral member of any community you seek to join. Communities need leaders, and leaders — those who try to make a difference in the life of the community — are often those who have learned the power of language and the role it plays in community life.

▪▪ THREE VIEWS ON JOINING A COMMUNITY

The three essays that follow all describe what it's like for newcomers to enter a community. Bill Wodraska writes about moving from the city to the country and trying to master the art of "hunkering." Roberta Maynard gives advice to business executives on helping new managers make the transition into their new corporate communities. J. C. Herz talks about the effects on the Internet community of a massive influx of new members (called "newbies"). Each of these articles describes the conflict and confusion that can arise when new members enter a community, and each one outlines the role of language and communication in joining a community. As you read these essays, consider the following questions:

1. Have you ever had the experience of being a newcomer to a community? If so, what was your experience?
2. Have you ever had the experience of being a long-standing member of a community? What was it like when someone new tried to join?
3. To what extent does language distinguish new members of a community from long-standing members? How does one go about learning the language of a community?
4. What kinds of conflict can arise when newcomers try to join a community? How do communities typically resolve these conflicts? How should communities resolve these conflicts?

The Gentle Art of Hunkering

BILL WODRASKA

A LL OF US who move to the country are trying to make successful new lives for ourselves. But I conjecture that some of us will fail because we don't *hunker* . . . and never learn how.

On one level, hunkering is the squatting-on-the-haunches posture assumed by many countryfolk outdoors, especially when there's something serious to discuss or ponder. But the art of hunkering goes far beyond physical posture to encompass tact, sensitivity, and all the other aspects of effective communication between human beings. And I believe that mastering this skill just might be the key to successful living in a rural area.

Say you need to know when to plant strawberries, how deep to sink a fence posthole, or the answer to any one of a thousand other day-to-day questions. No amount of reading — even in MOTHER[1] — is going to provide you with *all* the information you need. Occasionally, you'll require on-the-spot aid and advice . . . and what better source is there than your neighbor who most likely met up with and solved the same problem 40 years ago?

OK, you're willing to ask for assistance. That's half the battle, but only half . . . because that man up the road is not an automated teaching device but a human being. And if he thinks you're nothing but an imported city slicker or stuck-up "foreigner" (who should have stayed where you came from), he won't lift a finger for you.

So my first suggestion is to rid yourself of any notion that you're "bringing

[1] *Mother Earth News,* which calls itself "the original country magazine."

yourself down to the level of the local people." True, you may be better educated, more widely traveled and perhaps even wealthier than your new neighbors. *But you're the one going to them for help and advice, not the other way
around.* Their experience has made them experts at the kind of life you're seeking. You aren't lowering yourself in this interaction . . . you're just *moving over*
toward the other fellow's position. I hope that point seems obvious to you. It
took a devil of a long time for *me* to learn it!

With that basic ground rule established, let's say you're approaching Ed
Hopkins — the owner of the next farm over — with a specific problem: You
need to know who owns the fence between your field and his. Although you
might view your visit as a fairly straightforward errand, Ed sees the transaction in
a somewhat different light. You need only some basic information, but he wants
to know who you are, where you come from, what you're doing over there on
the old McAllister place, and the identity of those other people living with you.
That's the conversational small change he'll spend talking down at the store with
his cronies . . . and that's part of the price you have to pay for what you want to
know. It's no use bemoaning the infringement on your precious privacy. The
"nosiness" of rural neighbors is inevitable. If you want perfect isolation, you
might be able to get it in a warrenlike Manhattan apartment house, but you
won't in the country.

So you find your neighbor in his driveway, fiddling with his hay baler . . .
and, willy-nilly, you start getting your message across even before you open your
mouth. The speed with which you walk up to him, the expression on your face,
whether you're smiling or not, your posture, and the way you hold your arms all
speak volumes about your intentions toward him. You can appear hostile and
threatening — by closing the distance between Ed and yourself too rapidly —
or you can be diffident and respectful in your advance. Bear down on your neighbor with a tense, clenched manner and you've created an atmosphere that makes
it easy for him to dislike you. But draw near in a relaxed, easygoing, candid
fashion . . . and you're in business.

You need to move in slowly and know when to stop (Ed's body language
will tell you) to avoid his recoiling away from you. Also, take care not to be too
aggressive when you look at your neighbor. Good communication calls for a
frank, nonfurtive meeting of the eyes, but it's possible to have too much of a
good thing. If you don't shift your gaze just before or just after Ed does, he'll
regard your stare — at least on some subconscious level — either as insolence or
as a downright threat.

If you think my description sounds a bit overdone, please recall one fact:
Although the city person may have dozens of contacts with strangers every
day, the country dweller may go for weeks without seeing anyone but family
and longtime friends. What is a casual meeting for you may be an event for
him or her.

Now, what do you say when you do open the conversation, and how do you   10
say it? Chances are — rural communication systems being what they are — Ed
already knows your name and something about you . . . but it won't hurt to

introduce yourself with a smile and a "Good morning, Mr. Hopkins." (If you don't know his name, "sir" will do nicely.) Then you'll want to observe the universal rapport-breeding ritual of brief chitchat about the weather and the crops.

These preliminaries serve not only to break the ice but also to give you an idea of Ed's reactions to you and your approach. If he's sullen, cold, and defensive, you'll have to work on building a warmer climate before popping your question. On the other hand, if he's friendly and receptive, much of the work is done.

What judgment Ed will make of you will depend, at least in part, on *how* you talk during this meeting and those to come. Your voice needs to be low, slow, modulated, and friendly . . . not brisk or clipped. Also, although your natural tendency may be to ask your question and get out of there, this just can't be done in rural intercourse. If you're like me, you may have to continually force yourself to take your time about coming to the point, to slow your speech, and even to allow occasional silences. It seems to me — though I have no real evidence for my belief — that countryfolk are less upset than city dwellers by lapses in conversation, and they feel less need to fill the pauses with idle chatter.

Now what can be said about the point itself; that is, the phrasing of your question or request? Probably best is an indirect form that gives Ed an out and leaves him the option of helping you or not, rather than putting him into a situation he has to wiggle away from. Master such phrasing as "Say, I've been wondering how . . ." instead of "Do you know how . . ." and "Do you know anyone who might . . ." instead of "Will you . . ." When you use these graceful and considerate forms, Ed can back out easily — turn you down — without feeling like an ogre. In addition, he has the option of referring you to someone else better able to handle the problem if he's unwilling, or unable, to help you himself.

Moreover, your query or request ought to be just as specific and well thought out as you can make it. After all, your accent may be strange, your appearance distracting, and your question somewhat out of the ordinary. You want to avoid confusing Mr. Hopkins. There's nothing quite so pitiful as two people talking at each other when neither has anything but the haziest idea of what the other is driving at.

And don't be surprised if your neighbor prefers to transact business outside in good weather . . . probably hunkered down in the yard. After some practice the position is comfortable, and the conversation is less strained outdoors than it would be sitting stiffly in the parlor. When you find yourself quite automatically lowering yourself to your haunches and looking for something to do with your hands (twisting a piece of grass or baling twine, poking at the gravel, or maybe drawing designs in the dust with a stick), you're on your way to productive rural communication.

Finally, when you have the information you need, don't break off the contact abruptly as you might with a clerk or TV repairman. The code of rural neighborliness requires more than perfunctory conversation before taking leave. (And who knows but that you'll find out something you hadn't thought to ask?) This brings up the necessity for having contact with your neighbors at times when you *don't* need anything from them, just to be neighborly. You'll probably have to take the initiative for the first visits on yourself.

Eventually — if you're going about all this in the right way and the folks nearby come to like you as a person — you'll find yourself being tested in a friendly, nonmalevolent way. You may be invited to swallow a raw clam (as I was by French-speaking clam diggers in New Brunswick) or to try your hand at some demanding chore like tobacco stripping. The point here is not whether you "pass" or "fail" the test but whether you play the game with grace and goodwill. You may bungle the "job," but if you're willing to laugh at your own ineptness and not take your own dignity too seriously, you'll prove the stuff you're made of and come through the *initiation* in good style.

Finally, consider this summation of the art of hunkering written many years ago by Horace Kephart, a man who made a new life for himself among the people of the southern Appalachians:

> Tact . . . implies the will and the insight to put yourself truly in the other man's place. Imagine yourself born, bred, circumstanced like him. It implies, also, the courtesy of doing as you would be done by if you were in that fellow's shoes. No arrogance, no condescension, but man to man on a footing of equal manliness.

Help Newcomers Learn the Ropes

ROBERTA MAYNARD

I F THE JOB of training a first-time manager has ever fallen to you and you were tempted to say "sink or swim," you are not alone. Many senior managers who learned the hard way think newcomers should do the same. Others see the training process as tedious and too time-consuming. Many just don't know how to do it.

But the benefits of a training program far outweigh any inconvenience it may cause. For the newcomer, a training program provides a smooth transition, the tools needed to do the job, and a means to find the way around without the frustration that often accompanies a new job. For the company, a uniform approach to training translates into shared goals among its managers. Moreover, trained employees become good managers, which buoys employees' morale and reduces turnover.

There is no training method that is the one and only right way to do it, but most successful trainers agree that training should be focused on teaching what the job is, not on how to do it.

The place to start is with the objectives of the position, says Bob Burden, executive vice president of Alexander and Alexander Benefits Services, Inc., a

1

Chicago-based consulting firm. "Is it to make 30 percent profit on the bottom line? Is it to make 50 burgers in 50 minutes? Define it. From there, go to the specifics of the operation. Communicate what needs to be done to achieve those objectives."

Provide standards and goals. Help newcomers understand their roles and what everyone expects — other managers, customers, and employees.

You might arrange for new managers — particularly those hired from the outside — to spend some time in every type of job they will supervise.

Or have the trainees trade places for a week with other managers with whom they will regularly interact. This exercise helps give newcomers a picture of the whole operation.

Training must take a back seat to schedules and business demands, to some extent, so care must be taken to keep it from falling through the cracks. For that reason, and to ensure consistency and thoroughness, you need a plan.

"As a manager, you have to have a semiformal plan to take new managers from point A to point B," says Burden. "I feel that operations skills are paramount, so I recommend focusing on those. Without them, [managers] can't do the job. You can address particular areas of weakness, such as speaking in public, with specific courses later on."

The plan should identify the areas to cover, and it's a good idea to make new managers part of the process. One approach is to ask newcomers what is most important and then spend a defined period of time working on that area. Schedule a meeting with each newcomer for one week later to discuss it. Another method is to get new managers to think about the kind of manager they want to be and the kind of experiences they want to have. Then, work backward to a plan designed to meet those goals.

With either approach, you are making the managers responsible for their own training.

The training should cover the legal aspects of managing, including hiring, firing, and interviewing.

Regularly question the new manager on what is being learned, not only about the specifics of the job but also about the company's structure and philosophy. To help reinforce what has been learned and to determine how the training is going, you could ask questions such as "What have you learned in the past week about your customers?" and "Tell me about the function of the marketing department."

After a period of regular supervision, there should be a weaning process, says Phil Barry, president of Compro Insurance Services, Inc., based in San Jose, Calif. Barry employs 60 people, 10 of whom are managers, and has been training managers for more than 24 years. "You may want to jointly do a lot of duties, such as performance evaluations," he says. "Have the new manager write out the evaluation and explain it. Initially, the senior and junior managers together conduct the interview. In the next phase, they review the process with you, but they alone conduct the interview. And, finally, they manage the entire process, with you available if needed. You can use the same technique for hiring or completing department budgets."

Barry also finds it helpful to let new managers sit in occasionally on meetings   15
one level higher to gain a larger perspective on the business. "It's a way of inspiring," he says. "It says that we communicate and that we are not secretive."

To maintain communication, the new manager and trainer should meet for an hour once or twice a month. These should be informal sessions to see how the manager is doing. To emphasize the importance of this training to the operation, the owner might sit in on every fourth meeting.

Interruptions in the workplace impede discussion, so it can be helpful to get out of the shop for training meetings. "To even find time to talk about our work is an enormous commitment for small companies," says Ronald E. Galbraith, whose management company, Management 21, in Nashville, Tenn., has 37 employees. "We often think it is not a productive use of time to take people out of the office, but that's exactly the way we learn to be more productive."

Galbraith adds: "Even though I know this myself, I still must make an effort to close my office for a half-day retreat." But the effort is worth it, he adds. The training sessions he schedules allow him and his employees time to be creative and reflect on work-related problems.

Because small businesses rely heavily, if not solely, on the informal, mentor approach to preparing new managers, the senior managers must be evaluated and chosen with care.

Says Bob Burden: "I think a management trainer has to have a quality of   20
openness — the ability to communicate both the positives and the negatives about the job and to be open enough to take suggestions about how to improve the operation. Also, there has to be a high level of integrity. The senior manager has to be completely honest with himself as to the information being imparted and not operate out of fear that the trainee will do a better job.

"Finally, the senior manager needs to give the new person the flexibility to achieve the end result the way they want to do it. Some managers have difficulty acknowledging that there are different management styles and different solutions."

Frequently, senior managers who have been successful using their own methods are biased in favor of them. They tend to tell trainees the answers rather than help them figure out the answers for themselves. And some senior managers are reluctant to give authority and freedom to the new manager.

"In their roles as mentors and trainers, managers must be careful not to create dependency rather than independence," says Galbraith. "You're not trying to clone someone with mentoring. The process should be collaborative."

One way to foster that result is to present an objective, such as "reduce turnover by 50 percent during the coming year." Get the new manager to think about how to achieve that goal, and work with the manager to achieve it.

Some managers guard their turf. They "feel their ultimate job security is that   25
no one else can do what they do. This is a commonly held belief, but it is a

myth," says Larry Malone, senior associate in the human resources management division of CSRI, a management consulting firm in Santa Clara, Calif. "Managers who believe this need to examine their attitudes," he says. "In order to develop a competent new manager and to free themselves up for their own personal growth, they need to reprogram.

"All managers should be responsible for making sure that things can be done without them. They should be committed to some extent to documenting the technical parts of the job — not a list of duties, but the responsibilities and activities necessary to achieve them. When managers view their responsibilities collectively, that's when a company grows. And the subordinate is seeing growth instead of working for someone with a personal security problem."

The philosophy of sharing information — or not sharing it — starts at the top, as part of the mission or strategy of the company. It is the owner's responsibility, says Malone, to have this heartfelt goal and convey it to the managers.

"You want to be sure you're conveying, as a company, that you want all your managers and supervisors to be successful," he says, "and that the company will deliver all resources possible to that new manager."

Whether training one's own successor or a first-time manager, the senior manager's challenge is to be honest as well as dedicated to the growth of someone who, properly trained, may bring to the company energy, enthusiasm, and creativity.

The Newbies Are Coming! The Newbies Are Coming!

J. C. HERZ

This is the snobbery of the people on the Mayflower looking down their noses at the people who came over ON THE SECOND BOAT!

— MITCH KAPOR

H ERE'S A SCARY thought," says the Great Grendel-Khan. "The vast majority of the net is made up of educated individuals. What will happen to the net when just anyone can loggin? Personally, I don't think that you should 'weep' for joy as beer-drinking-WWF-loving-Home-Shopping-Network-watching-high-school-Burger-King-dropouts loggin. I think you will see a retreat from these type of people. Those that loggin now will flee to places like the well or mindvox, where they will pay to be separated from the chattel."

The newbies are coming! The newbies are coming!

New users are flooding onto the Net at the rate of a million per month. And from what I've seen, old-timers would just as soon they stay home. The Net is the most perfect form of anarchy to come along since the Golden Horde stomped through central Asia, and many Net veterans would prefer it stay that way. The Net works, they argue. Don't mess with it.

And it does work, for the most part. But the population explosion is putting a lot of stress on the system. Not so much the physical system of hardware and phone lines, but the social structure is beginning to fray. Noise levels are up. Signal quality is down. The fringe cachet of the place is being engulfed by a wave of ill-informed mainstreamers. Basically, the Net is turning into post-grunge Seattle.

Even die-hard Net addicts now admit that it's impossible to wade through the daily traffic. We have on our hands what Steve Crocker, an armchair Net sociologist at Youngstown State University, calls a "human bandwidth problem." The hardware is whirring away just fine (for now), but the danger of human overload is more serious. "A limiting factor in the usefulness of the Net to individuals is the inability of a person to read more than a minute fraction of even the news they are actually interested in," he says. "I think we all have wished that the Net were more universal. We are vastly underrepresented in areas such as poor people, industrial workers, housewives, young children, policy makers, and senior professionals. We need to find effective means of outreach to all these groups, and more. And that's only in North America. The extension of the Net into the Third World is a problem, parallel in some ways to that of including the poor and undereducated of North America."

The Net's anti-establishment politics are contradictory. Most of us realize that the Net is an elite community, and the idea of expansion in the name of social justice is appealing. On the other hand, veterans cherish the Net's fast-fading underground flavor and their own edge status. Very few people are against universal access per se, but the attitude is: send us your tired unwired masses yearning to post free, just as long as they're hip, tech-savvy, and think like us. Anything that puts the Net's unique vibe in jeopardy is considered noise, or worse, cultural pollution.

"As we expand," says Crocker, "there is a danger of having the cultural traditions which have been developed by trial and error over the years overwhelmed. These customs, although not perfect, have by and large been successful in allowing the Net to WORK. A first approximation suggestion would be to attempt to manage Net expansion in such a way that at any given moment, the population of Net citizens on-line for less than (say) 6 months should constitute a minority of the total Net population. This will allow our culture to evolve in a somewhat orderly way, rather than simply being swept away by ignorance, well intentioned or otherwise."

The problem with this plan is that there is no border control. There is no Digital Department of Immigration and Naturalization to monitor the cultural temperature of the net and limit the influx of aliens, whom he defines as "the Bad Guys, The Net-Fascists, the Conspiracy, the Reactionaries, the FBI/CIA/NSA/IRS/ETC, the Politically Correct Liberals, the Corporate Culture, the Yuppies, the Media Elite, the Entertainment Industry, the Mindless, and anyone

5

else who we can agree by consensus ought not to be allowed to dominate our consciousness, our culture or our Net." For the first time, a highly educated elite has rallied to protect the fragile culture of a tribe under siege from the outside world, and the tribe is us.

The immediate reaction when the newsmagazine-driven wave of colonizers landed was to haze them in hopes that they would frighten easily, wither, and fade away. But the algal bloom of newbie bashing could only last so long before the old guard flame brigade started running short of lighter fluid. Gradually, they realized that trying to frighten away newcomers was like tossing deck chairs off the *Titanic* in hopes that it would regain buoyancy. Besides, there was another strategy, less combative and possibly more effective: ASSIMILATE THEM.

Newbie reception has shifted somewhat. Fresh arrivals don't get the red car- 10
pet treatment by any means, but they aren't told "Newbie go home" either. A kinder, gentler sandbagging strategy is in force: educate the newbies. Convert them. Make them swear allegiance to the goddess of discord, Pop-Tarts, Kibo, and the Electronic Frontier Foundation, then put them on patrol for other greenhorns, because after all, newbies aren't evil. They're just ignorant.

Bringing newbies into the fold is especially important in light of the latest wave of invaders, the conquistadors who come not to settle but to mine, rape, and pillage the Net for every cent it's worth.

Yes, friends, I'm talking about corporate advertisers (savvy doublethink allows us to embrace their language even as we burn them in effigy).

Something must be done about these people, lest we all wash away in the tide of junk e-mail and postvertisements. This much is agreed — it's the closest thing to unanimity in Net history. But no one seems to know what is to be done or who is going to do it, or even the appropriate venue to stage some show of Net consensus.

Chris Keroack at Hampshire College suggests that the Net meet advertisers on their own turf. "The text of a full-page ad in the New York Times, Boston Globe, Chicago Sun-Times and other major newspapers as yet to be determined would be composed as a public service announcement to all those who want to advertise on the 'hip new information superhighway.' It would serve as a wake-up call to those who tend to blunder into new technologies and places without adequately researching them first, and if it stops even one major company from blindly advertising and generally harassing Internet/Usenet users, then it will have served its purpose.

"A regular print media campaign MAKES SENSE. Consider: would you try 15
to caution drivers who drive too fast by putting up lengthy advertisements on highway billboards? No. Similarly, calls to read the FAQ for a group, or to obey basic nettiquette, are wasted on people who only want to know how to get their message out there." Again, the problem is how to arrange logistics in an anarchy. If everyone on the Net gave their *literal* two cents for a change, we'd have quite a piggy bank. But collecting those pennies is one hell of a job.

Keroack is right about one thing, though. "Until it is universally recognized that the Internet is a CULTURE and not just a mechanical, soulless means for the transmission of information, people will have to be reminded that there are rules and customs here just as in any other group of people."

Netiquette isn't just a set of social conventions. It's a political issue. Net customs are important, because they have allowed us to participate in a truly democratic mass medium, and that's something worth defending. As Crocker of Youngstown State says, "It does not take a rocket scientist to realize that 'they' decide what appears in newspapers, magazines, books, and on radio and TV, whereas WE decide what will appear on the Net. . . . Ultimately, we may actually realize the ideal of the old New Left (and the Founding Fathers!), of democratic participation of the people in shaping political programs. I keep coming back to the image of old Ben Franklin and his printing press. Franklin understood that the British Empire was a dinosaur. Its bandwidth was no longer sufficient to support the extent of its body. So he used the innovative medium of his time to CREATE bandwidth, thus setting into motion a form of social organization which could move faster and plan smarter than its obsolete competitor. So today we have the Net, the last accidentally uncensored mass medium in existence. Is it a toy of the rich and the ivory tower, or is it potent? . . . Will we allow ourselves to be possessed by the vision of a Net whose purpose is to help create and support HEROES? Or will we dismiss it all with a keystroke, and get back to the REAL FUN STUFF on alt.flame.joe.schmuck.the.world's.greatest.poophead?"

This question lies at the root of newbiephobia. The nightmare is that newcomers, once they discover the Net's more trivial kicks, will lose sight of its broader potential. There will be enough newbies on-line to hijack the culture, and when they get lost in the bullshit, they'll drag the whole shooting match down with them. A precious opportunity will be lost forever, and Big Corporate Media suits will lean back in their executive swivel seats and breathe a sigh of relief.

That's the fear. That's the impetus behind newbie bashing. That's also why Net veterans are now turning evangelist. If you can't drive them away, the reasoning goes, bring them on board. And make them row. Because the way things are heading, we're going to need lots of warm bodies down in the galley.

▪ ▪ TROPING

The final essay in this chapter is an example of what I've called "troping," or argument by indirection. Here, Horace Miner argues that Americans are too obsessed with their bodies. Rather than argue this point in a straightforward manner, however, he uses the persona of an anthropologist exploring the rituals of an unfamiliar culture, an approach that makes ordinary parts of our lives seem strange. This strangeness draws our attention to what we take for granted and allows Miner to make his point more effectively than in a straightforward argument.

Body Ritual among the Nacirema

HORACE MINER

T HE ANTHROPOLOGIST has become so familiar with the diversity of ways in   1
which different peoples behave in similar situations that he is not apt to be
surprised by even the most exotic customs. In fact, if all of the logically possible
combinations of behavior have not been found somewhere in the world, he is
apt to suspect that they must be present in some yet undescribed tribe. This
point has, in fact, been expressed with respect to clan organization by Murdock
(1949: 71). In this light, the magical beliefs and practices of the Nacirema present such unusual aspects that it seems desirable to describe them as an example
of the extremes to which human behavior can go.

Professor Linton first brought the ritual of the Nacirema to the attention of
anthropologists twenty years ago (1936: 326), but the culture of this people is
still very poorly understood. They are a North American group living in the territory between the Canadian Cree, the Yaqui and Tarahumare of Mexico, and
the Carib and Arawak of the Antilles. Little is known of their origin, although
tradition states that they came from the east. According to Nacirema mythology,
their nation was originated by a culture hero, Notgnihsaw, who is otherwise
known for two great feats of strength — the throwing of a piece of wampum
across the river Pa-To-Mac and the chopping down of a cherry tree in which the
Spirit of Truth resided.

Nacirema culture is characterized by a highly developed market economy
which has evolved in a rich natural habitat. While much of the people's time is
devoted to economic pursuits, a large part of these labors and a considerable
portion of the day are spent in ritual activity. The focus of this activity is the
human body, the appearance and health of which loom as a dominant concern
in the ethos of the people. While such a concern is certainly not unusual, its
ceremonial aspects and associated philosophy are unique.

The fundamental belief underlying the whole system appears to be that the
human body is ugly and that its natural tendency is to debility and disease. In-
carcerated in such a body, man's only hope is to avert these characteristics
through the use of the powerful influences of ritual and ceremony. Every household has one or more shrines devoted to this purpose. The more powerful individuals in the society have several shrines in their houses and, in fact, the
opulence of a house is often referred to in terms of the number of such ritual
centers it possesses. Most houses are of wattle and daub construction, but the
shrine rooms of the more wealthy are walled with stone. Poorer families imitate
the rich by applying pottery plaques to their shrine walls.

While each family has at least one such shrine, the rituals associated with it   5
are not family ceremonies but are private and secret. The rites are normally only
discussed with children, and then only during the period when they are being

initiated into these mysteries. I was able, however, to establish sufficient rapport with the natives to examine these shrines and to have the rituals described to me.

The focal point of the shrine is a box or chest which is built into the wall. In this chest are kept the many charms and magical potions without which no native believes he could live. These preparations are secured from a variety of specialized practitioners. The most powerful of these are the medicine men, whose assistance must be rewarded with substantial gifts. However, the medicine men do not provide the curative potions for their clients, but decide what the ingredients should be and then write them down in an ancient and secret language. This writing is understood only by the medicine men and the herbalists who, for another gift, provide the required charm.

The charm is not disposed of after it has served its purpose, but is placed in the charm-box of the household shrine. As these magical materials are specific for certain ills, and the real or imagined maladies of the people are many, the charm-box is usually full to overflowing. The magical packets are so numerous that people forget what their purposes were and fear to use them again. While the natives are very vague on this point, we can only assume that the idea in retaining all the old magical materials is that their presence in the charm-box, before which the body rituals are conducted, will in some way protect the worshipper.

Beneath the charm-box is a small font. Each day every member of the family, in succession, enters the shrine room, bows his head before the charm-box, mingles different sorts of holy water in the font, and proceeds with a brief rite of ablution. The holy waters are secured from the Water Temple of the community, where the priests conduct elaborate ceremonies to make the liquid ritually pure.

In the hierarchy of magical practitioners, and below the medicine men in prestige, are specialists whose designation is best translated "holy-mouth-men." The Nacirema have an almost pathological horror of and fascination with the mouth, the condition of which is believed to have a supernatural influence on all social relationships. Were it not for the rituals of the mouth, they believe that their teeth would fall out, their gums bleed, their jaws shrink, their friends desert them, and their lovers reject them. They also believe that a strong relationship exists between oral and moral characteristics. For example, there is a ritual ablution of the mouth for children which is supposed to improve their moral fiber.

The daily body ritual performed by everyone includes a mouth-rite. Despite   10
the fact that these people are so punctilious about care of the mouth, this rite involves a practice which strikes the uninitiated stranger as revolting. It was reported to me that the ritual consists of inserting a small bundle of hog hairs into the mouth, along with certain magical powders, and then moving the bundle in a highly formalized series of gestures.

In addition to the private mouth-rite, the people seek out a holy-mouth-man once or twice a year. These practitioners have an impressive set of paraphernalia, consisting of a variety of augers, awls, probes, and prods. The use of these objects in the exorcism of the evils of the mouth involves almost unbelievable ritual torture of the client. The holy-mouth-man opens the client's mouth and, using the above mentioned tools, enlarges any holes which decay may have created in the teeth. Magical materials are put into these holes. If there are no naturally occurring holes in the teeth, large sections of one or more teeth are gouged out so that the supernatural substance can be applied. In the client's view, the purpose of these ministrations is to arrest decay and to draw friends. The extremely sacred and traditional character of the rite is evident in the fact that the natives return to the holy-mouth-men year after year, despite the fact that their teeth continue to decay.

It is to be hoped that, when a thorough study of the Nacirema is made, there will be careful inquiry into the personality structures of these people. One has but to watch the gleam in the eye of a holy-mouth-man, as he jabs an awl into an exposed nerve, to suspect that a certain amount of sadism is involved. If this can be established, a very interesting pattern emerges, for most of the population shows definite masochistic tendencies. It was to these that Professor Linton referred in discussing a distinctive part of the daily body ritual which is performed only by men. This part of the rite involves scraping and lacerating the surface of the face with a sharp instrument. Special women's rites are performed only four times during each lunar month, but what they lack in frequency is made up in barbarity. As part of this ceremony, women bake their heads in small ovens for about an hour. The theoretically interesting point is that what seems to be a preponderantly masochistic people have developed sadistic specialists.

The medicine men have an imposing temple, or *latipso,* in every community of any size. The more elaborate ceremonies required to treat very sick patients can only be performed at this temple. These ceremonies involve not only the thaumaturge but a permanent group of vestal maidens who move sedately about the temple chambers in distinctive costume and headdress.

The *latipso* ceremonies are so harsh that it is phenomenal that a fair proportion of the really sick natives who enter the temple ever recover. Small children whose indoctrination is still incomplete have been known to resist attempts to take them to the temple because "that is where you go to die." Despite this fact, sick adults are not only willing but eager to undergo the protracted ritual purification, if they can afford to do so. No matter how ill the supplicant or how grave the emergency, the guardians of many temples will not admit a client if he cannot give a rich gift to the custodian. Even after one has gained admission and survived the ceremonies, the guardians will not permit the neophyte to leave until he makes still another gift.

The supplicant entering the Temple is first stripped of all his or her clothes.   15
In every-day life the Nacirema avoids exposure of his body and its natural functions. Bathing and excretory acts are performed only in the secrecy of the household shrine, where they are ritualized as part of the body-rites. Psychological shock results from the fact that body secrecy is suddenly lost upon entry into the *latipso.* A man, whose own wife has never seen him in an excretory act, suddenly finds himself naked and assisted by a vestal maiden while he performs his natural functions into a sacred vessel. This sort of ceremonial treatment is necessitated by the fact that the excreta are used by a diviner to ascertain the course and

nature of the client's sickness. Female clients, on the other hand, find their naked bodies are subjected to the scrutiny, manipulation and prodding of the medicine man.

Few supplicants in the temple are well enough to do anything but lie on their hard beds. The daily ceremonies, like the rites of the holy-mouth-men, involve discomfort and torture. With ritual precision, the vestals awaken their miserable charges each dawn and roll them about on their beds of pain while performing ablutions, in the formal movements of which the maidens are highly trained. At other times they insert magic wands in the supplicant's mouth or force him to eat substances which are supposed to be healing. From time to time the medicine men come to their clients and jab magically treated needles into their flesh. The fact that these temple ceremonies may not cure, and may even kill the neophyte, in no way decreases the people's faith in the medicine men.

There remains one other kind of practitioner, known as a "listener." This witch-doctor has the power to exorcise the devils that lodge in the heads of people who have been bewitched. The Nacirema believe that parents bewitch their own children. Mothers are particularly suspected of putting a curse on children while teaching them the secret body rituals. The counter-magic of the witch-doctor is unusual in its lack of ritual. The patient simply tells the "listener" all his troubles and fears, beginning with the earliest difficulties he can remember. The memory displayed by the Nacirema in these exorcism sessions is truly remarkable. It is not uncommon for the patient to bemoan the rejection he felt upon being weaned as a babe, and a few individuals even see their troubles going back to the traumatic effects of their own birth.

In conclusion, mention must be made of certain practices which have their base in native esthetics but which depend upon the pervasive aversion to the natural body and its functions. There are ritual fasts to make fat people thin and ceremonial feasts to make thin people fat. Still other rites are used to make women's breasts larger if they are small, and smaller if they are large. General dissatisfaction with breast shape is symbolized in the fact that the ideal form is virtually outside the range of human variation. A few women afflicted with almost inhuman hypermammary development are so idolized that they make a handsome living by simply going from village to village and permitting the natives to stare at them for a fee.

Reference has already been made to the fact that excretory functions are ritualized, routinized, and relegated to secrecy. Natural reproductive functions are similarly distorted. Intercourse is taboo as a topic and scheduled as an act. Efforts are made to avoid pregnancy by the use of magical materials or by limiting intercourse to certain phases of the moon. Conception is actually very infrequent. When pregnant, women dress so as to hide their condition. Parturition takes place in secret, without friends or relatives to assist, and the majority of women do not nurse their infants.

Our review of the ritual life of the Nacirema has certainly shown them to be magic-ridden people. It is hard to understand how they have managed to exist so long under the burdens which they have imposed upon themselves. But even

20

such exotic customs as these take on real meaning when they are viewed with the insight provided by Malinowski when he wrote (1948: 70):

> Looking from far and above, from our high places of safety in the developed civilization, it is easy to see all the crudity and irrelevance of magic. But without its power and guidance early man could not have mastered his practical difficulties as he has done, nor could man have advanced to the higher stages of civilization.

REFERENCES CITED

Linton, Ralph. (1936). *The Study of Man*. New York: D. Appleton Century Co.

Malinowski, Bronislaw. (1948). *Magic, Science, and Religion*. Glencoe: The Free Press.

Murdock, George P. (1949). *Social Structure*. New York: The Macmillan Co.

PART TWO

Types of Claims

Chapter 7

Arguing Claims about Existence

Our Differences about Experience

Our most immediate means of knowing the world around us is through our experience. Our senses constantly provide our brains with information about our environment, and we also experience our own thoughts and emotions inspired by that information. Sometimes, however, our experience of the world can mislead us. Perhaps we don't have enough sensory data to form correct conclusions. Perhaps we don't reflect sufficiently on the data we have received and so form false notions about our experience. Most all people on occasion hear things that do not exist or see optical illusions. Seeing should not always mean believing. Yet, to interpret experience, most of us rely primarily on data from our physical senses or on reports of experience in print or pictures.

We usually consume this material uncritically because we lack the time or inclination to question every bit of reported data that comes to us. The scholarly community, however, attempts to scrutinize experience a bit more carefully. In fact, much of the writing you will do during your university career will involve writing about questions of existence and causality. Although it would be foolish to discount our experience of the world entirely, it is healthy occasionally to reflect on experience critically: What am I experiencing? What is causing this event? How can I understand it?

■ ■ FACT AND OPINION

Because our human bodies are similar, we all share some of the same experiences. We all shiver when it gets cold enough or sweat when it gets hot. We all sleep and eat. We know what it's like to be tired. When a community comes to a general agreement about experience, that agreement is called a "fact," something that is accepted as true about the world of experience. But because each person is also unique, we each experience the world around us somewhat differently. We have different bodies. We have each had a different upbringing. We may speak different languages or varieties of the same language: We each have at least a somewhat different perspective of the world. Often, these differences are slight, but different perspectives of the world — separate ways of experiencing reality — can lead to disagreements within a community. When there is disagreement about the world of experience, then the various divergent interpretations are called "opinions" rather than facts. Opinions are less certain and less accepted in a community than facts are. Being less accepted, however, does not make an opinion less true; it is simply under dispute. Some of today's opinions may well be tomorrow's facts. And because our experience of the world is imperfect, what we accept as facts today may not be accepted in the future. New data and analysis can change our perception of what is real and true.

▪▪ PAST, PRESENT, AND FUTURE

We often disagree about things that happened in the past. To know what happened in the past, we must rely either on our own memories or on someone else's report of past experience. And in addition to the fact that we all experience reality somewhat differently, we all have selective (and somewhat imperfect) memories. For example, my wife and I recall our first date differently. She remembers things that I don't, such as what she wore and where we went. I tend to remember what we ate. Occasionally, we disagree about particular details of other experiences: what we wore, where we went, what we did, who said what.

People can also disagree about present experiences. Someone asks, "Is it cold in here or is it just me?," and a debate ensues about whether or not it's cold enough to close the windows. A thermometer can provide a quantifiable reading of the temperature, but knowing that it is 78 degrees generally won't change the fact that someone's hands are cold.

In addition people disagree about what will happen in the future. Where I grew up, farmers were always talking about the weather: Will it rain today? Do you expect a heavy winter? Their attempts to predict the weather could lead to some lively debates. Investors disagree about what will happen in the future in financial markets. Civil engineers disagree about the effect that a future earthquake might have on buildings, roads, and bridges. Environmental biologists and developers disagree about the effect that a new subdivision will have on the habitat of a threatened species.

▪▪ QUESTIONS ABOUT EXPERIENCE

Journalists are taught to ask six questions about experience: who? what? when? where? why? how? These questions are designed to help record experience in a complete and detailed way. They are also among the most basic questions we all ask about experience. The first four ask about the existence and nature of an experience. The final two address causality, the relationship between causes and effects. This chapter focuses on questions of existence. Chapter 8 discusses questions of causality.

Questions about Existence

The most basic of all questions about existence is whether something exists at all: Did it happen? Is it happening now? Will it happen again? Did it used to exist? Does it exist now? Will it ever exist? Here are some examples of specific questions about existence:

Do paranormal phenomena exist?

Are UFOs real?

Does ESP exist?

Is there a God?

Has someone been in my room?

Does she have cancer?

Did the accused kill the victim?

An answer to any of the questions above would be a statement affirming or denying a state of existence. This kind of statement is a claim about existence. When members of a community disagree about the state of existence there will be opposing claims:

Yes, there is a God. No, there is not a God.

Yes, the accused did kill the victim. No, the accused did not.

Someone has been in my room. No one has been in your room.

Some questions about existence relate to the nature of reality—not whether an event or object exists, but rather how we can describe this event or object: What kind? What size? How much? How many? How long? Here are some examples of questions about the nature of reality:

Is that car green?

How large is the national debt?

Is Japan a world power?

Does Israel treat Palestinians fairly?

How serious a problem is nuclear proliferation?

How harmful is alcohol for humans?

Questions about existence can relate to questions about symbols and language. For instance, arguing whether Japan is a world power may depend on how different parties define "world power." Then the argument becomes one about language as well as existence. But if all concerned agree on the definition of "world power," then the argument is simply about the nature of our experience of Japan: Does Japan fit the definition of "world power" on which we all agree?

Some questions about existence are so complex that the community as a whole will never come to complete agreement about them (for example, questions of the existence, power, and nature of a supreme being). But even if we cannot come to complete agreement about such complex issues of existence, we may be able to understand more clearly why we disagree, and we may then be able better to accept one another despite our differences.

▧ ▧ ARGUING ABOUT EXISTENCE AND THE NATURE OF REALITY

Because questions about existence and the nature of reality are so closely related, I have chosen to treat them together. We come to know that something exists in the same ways we come to know the nature of that object: through direct physical experience, introspection (inner experience), memory, and reports of the experiences of others.

As I mentioned before, although these ways of understanding experience serve us well most of the time, each can occasionally lead us to form false or incomplete impressions of reality. Francis Bacon, a contemporary of Shakespeare and a proponent of the scientific method, explained some of the problems of understanding experience in his *Novum Organum*, written in 1620. In the following excerpt from that work, Bacon describes the "idols" or "false notions" that humans form about experience.

The Four Idols

FRANCIS BACON

T HE IDOLS AND FALSE NOTIONS which are now in possession of the human   1
understanding, and have taken deep root therein, not only so beset men's minds that truth can hardly find entrance, but even after entrance is obtained, they will again in the very instauration of the sciences meet and trouble us, unless men being forewarned of the danger fortify themselves as far as may be against their assaults.

There are four classes of idols which beset men's minds. To these for distinction's sake I have assigned names—calling the first class *Idols of the Tribe;* the second, *Idols of the Cave;* the third, *Idols of the Marketplace;* the fourth, *Idols of the Theater.*

The formation of ideas and axioms by true induction is no doubt the proper remedy to be applied for the keeping off and clearing away of idols. To point them out, however, is of great use, for the doctrine of idols is to the interpretation of nature what the doctrine of the refutation of sophisms is to common logic.

The *Idols of the Tribe* have their foundation in human nature itself, and in the tribe or race of men. For it is a false assertion that the sense of man is the measure of things. On the contrary, all perceptions as well of the sense as of the mind are according to the measure of the individual and not according to the measure of the universe. And the human understanding is like a false mirror, which, receiving rays irregularly, distorts and discolors the nature of things by mingling its own nature with it.

The *Idols of the Cave* are the idols of the individual man. For everyone (besides the errors common to human nature in general) has a cave or den of his own, which refracts and discolors the light of nature; owing either to his own proper and peculiar nature; or to his education and conversation with others; or to the reading of books, and the authority of those whom he esteems and admires; or to the differences of impressions, accordingly as they take place in a mind preoccupied or predisposed or in a mind indifferent and settled; or the like. So that the spirit of man (according as it is meted out to different individuals) is in fact a thing variable and full of perturbation, and governed as it were by chance. Whence it was well observed by Heraclitus[1] that men look for sciences in their own lesser worlds, and not in the greater or common world.

There are also idols formed by the intercourse and association of men with each other, which I call *Idols of the Marketplace,* on account of the commerce and consort of men there. For it is by discourse that men associate; and words are imposed according to the apprehension of the vulgar. And therefore the ill and unfit choice of words wonderfully obstructs the understanding. Nor do the definitions or explanations wherewith in some things learned men are wont to guard and defend themselves, by any means set the matter right. But words plainly force and overrule the understanding, and throw all into confusion and lead men away into numberless empty controversies and idle fancies.

Lastly, there are idols which have immigrated into men's minds from the various dogmas of philosophies, and also from wrong laws of demonstration. These I call *Idols of the Theater;* because in my judgment all the received systems are but so many stage-plays, representing worlds of their own creation after an unreal and scenic fashion. Nor is it only of the systems now in vogue, or only of the ancient sects and philosophies, that I speak; for many more plays of the same kind may yet be composed and in like artificial manner set forth; seeing that

5

---

[1] Greek philosopher (540?–475? BC), considered by many to be the founder of metaphysics, the study of reality beyond the physical world. He believed that the essential element in all things was fire and that physical reality was constantly changing. [Ed.]

errors the most widely different have nevertheless causes for the most part alike. Neither again do I mean this only of entire systems, but also of many principles and axioms in science, which by tradition, credulity, and negligence have come to be received.

In short, Bacon suggests four ways that humans draw false conclusions from their experience of the world:

The idols of the tribe: Our bodies and minds provide us with imperfect information about reality.

The idols of the cave: Our individual backgrounds and perspectives color our perceptions of reality.

The idols of the marketplace: Language affects how we perceive the world.

The idols of the theater: Theories about the nature of reality affect our perceptions.

One difficulty in learning about the world through direct experience is that the moment of direct experience — the present — is constantly becoming the past. Whenever present experience becomes past experience, we have to rely on our memories. Generally, our memories serve us quite well — particularly given that we do very little to train our memories. But, as attorneys are quick to point out in television courtroom dramas, memory is always imperfect. The problem is due partly to our imperfect perception of experience, as described by Bacon, and to the disorganized and chaotic state of memory itself. Problems also stem from the fact that we often remember what we want to remember — the way we want it to be remembered. In other words, our memories reconstruct reality, no matter how careful we are to remember the "truth." One of the great values of keeping a journal is that doing so allows us to compare a report of an experience written shortly after it happened with our memory of the experience months or years later.

▪▪ EXPERIENCE AS EVIDENCE IN SCHOLARLY WRITING

Scholars tend to have a healthy distrust of direct experience, personal introspection, and memory. They try to discount their own perceptions and postpone judgment on a subject until they have gathered sufficient objective data on which to base their findings. But scholars also realize that personal observation and reflection are valuable sources of information about the world. One way for scientists to gather data is to go out into the field and experience an event firsthand. Usually, they observe with some purpose in mind, organizing their observations by looking for answers to a particular question; sometimes, however, scientists observe with no particular question or purpose other than to see what turns up. Scientists pay attention not only to *what* they are observing but also to *how* they are observing. Familiar with the limitations of sensory experience and memory, scientists improve their powers of observation and reflection by keeping field notes or a log book, carefully recording what they observe. A log is usually organized by date and time. Scientists may also use various instruments to gather more data than they can through their senses and then record these data in log books along with their own observations. Personal *journals* can provide opportunities for reflection as well as observation. Henry David Thoreau kept a detailed journal of his experiences with nature and used his journal to compose *Walden,* his 1854 treatise on the relationship between humans and the natural world. Prolific inventor Thomas Edison wrote hundreds of pages a day in his journal to keep track of all of his discoveries and ideas.

An *ethnography* is a particular kind of field report, a systematic record of one's experience of another community. It usually combines an ethnographer's personal observation and reflection with hard data and reports of experience from members of the community. Similar to an ethnography, a *case study* is the systematic observation of a particular event or object. Psychologists, sociologists, and journalists rely heavily on case studies. These kinds of studies suggest possibilities for generalizing, but there is a danger of hasty generalization or overgeneralization: Is the example studied typical? Are there countering examples? How accurate are the observations? Case studies usually are more reliable when there are multiple observers of multiple cases and if cases are used along with other kinds of evidence. At their best cases and examples can be quite persuasive because they offer vivid portrayals of particular experience, giving an argument presence and making it seem more real and human.

▦ ▦ REPORTED EXPERIENCE

Reported experience offers some of the immediacy and authenticity of direct experience. Primary sources or eyewitnesses can provide numerous specific details along with the credibility of personal testimony. But scholars approach the reported experience of others with a degree of skepticism, asking questions such as the following to determine a report's reliability:

1. Is the source reliable, fair, responsible, and capable? Does the source have a personal interest or obvious bias?
2. Is this a primary source or a "report of a report"?
3. How far removed was the source from the event? To what extent is the source relying upon memory?
4. Are the statements in the report consistent with one another and with other reports and evidence?
5. Are the statements verifiable?
6. Is all relevant evidence included?
7. Is the language detailed, specific, and clear?

As Bacon points out, humans have a tendency to select details from experience to fit our own biases and conceptions of reality. We often see what we want to see.

This tendency to report experience selectively is evident in the following conflicting eyewitness accounts of the Battle of Lexington at the start of the American Revolution. Tension between the British army and the colonists had been building for some time when shots were fired at Lexington, Massachusetts, on April 19, 1775. Known as "the shot heard round the world," this incident was the first armed conflict of the revolution. The first account is by Thomas Fessenden, a colonist:

> *Lexington, April 23, 1775*
> I, Thomas Fessenden, of lawful age, testify and declare, that being in a pasture near the meeting-house at said Lexington, on Wednesday, last, at about half an hour before sunrise, . . . I saw three officers on horseback advance to the front of said Regulars, when one of them being within six rods of the said Militia, cried out, "Disperse, you rebels, immediately"; on which he brandished his sword over his head three times; meanwhile the second officer, who was about two rods behind him, fired a pistol pointed at said Militia, and the Regulars kept huzzaing till he had finished brandishing his sword, and when he had thus finished brandishing his sword, he pointed it down towards said Militia, and immediately the said Regulars fired a volley at the Militia and then I ran off, as fast as I could, while they continued firing till I got out of their reach. I further testify, that as soon as ever the officer cried "Disperse, you rebels," the said Company of Militia dispersed every way as fast as they could, and while they were dispersing the Regulars kept firing at them incessantly, and further saith not.
>
> THOMAS FESSENDEN

Here is an account of the same event from the diary of a John Barker, a British officer:

> 19th. At 2 o'clock we began our march by wading through a very long ford up to our Middles: after going a few miles we took 3 or 4 People who were going off to give intelligence; about 5 miles on this side of a Town called Lexington, which lay in our road, we heard there were some hundreds of People collected together intending to oppose us and stop our going on; at 5 o'clock we arrived there, and saw a number of People, I believe between 2 and 300, formed in a Common in the middle of the Town; we still continued advancing, keeping prepared against an attack tho' without intending to attack them; but, on our coming near them they fired one or two shots, upon which our Men without any orders, rushed in upon them, fired and put 'em to flight; several of them were killed, we cou'd not tell how many, because they were got behind Walls and into the Woods; We had a Man of the 10th light Infantry wounded, nobody else hurt. We then formed on the Common, but with some difficulty, the Men were so wild they cou'd hear no orders; we waited a considerable time there, and at length proceed on our way to Concord. . . .

Who fired the first shots? Were the British ordered to fire by their officers, or did they fire on their own? Did the colonists disperse after the order of the British officers? Did the soldiers fire on the colonists after they began to disperse? Because of the differing eyewitness accounts, historians are still uncertain about what exactly transpired at Lexington. These two witnesses, for example, were probably not lying. The first was giving sworn testimony before a magistrate; the second was writing in his personal diary. The fact is that each saw and remembered a different sequence of events because his experience was filtered through his own individual perspective, position, and biases.

In addition to the selectivity of memory, direct experience of an event is limited by the observer's physical position in time and space or limited powers of observation: Some people have keener senses or longer attention spans than others. And, of course, the possibility exists that someone may knowingly give a false account. Sometimes what we take to be "facts" can be difficult to establish as true or false.

The difficulty of determining the truth of reported experience is greatest when the source of that report is lost or when the report has been passed from person to person. This is why scholars favor primary sources and are wary of claims where no source is disclosed: "Scientists say . . . ," "They say . . . ," "We know . . . ." You may have played a party game in which one person whispers a message to someone else who whispers it to another until the message has been passed from person to person around the room. Usually, the message has become quite distorted by the time it reaches the final person. When a message contains complex, detailed, or ambiguous information, the distortion over time can be even greater.

Written testimony or an eyewitness report is one way of reporting experience. Another common form of reported experience is an interview. An interview has the advantage of face-to-face contact, allowing the interviewer to observe the body language of the source. But the quality of an interview depends not only on the quality of the source; the quality of the questions being asked is also important. Open-ended questions — such as the journalist's who?, what?, when?, where?, why?, and how? — invite detailed responses. Questions answered "yes" or "no" invite commitment and confirmation from the source. Many interviewers like to ask questions in a particular sequence in order to determine the quality of the source and put him or her at ease. They begin with easy factual questions concerning background information, personal history, definitions, and key concepts, for example. They then ask application questions that require a more elaborate response, inquiring about how things work, causes and effects, comparisons and analogies, relationships among ideas, interpretation and predictions. They progress finally to questions that require judgment and commitment, asking about the source's views of right and wrong, good and bad, and his or her recommendations, reactions, and evaluation. These final questions reveal the values of the person being interviewed.

When evaluating a published interview, it is important to know how it was conducted. Who did the interviewing? What questions were asked? In what order? How were the responses recorded? It is also important to know how the interview is reported. Is it a verbatim question-and-answer report of the interview or an edited transcript or summary? What was left out of the reporting?

Another form of reported experience common in scholarly writing and journalism is the survey or questionnaire. Surveys and questionnaires are a way of gathering a number of people's reports of their experience. The usefulness of surveys and questionnaires lies in their ability to sample a large amount of reported experience. Surveys also add the dimension of community. But it is important to remember that questionnaires record perceptions and reports, not actual experience. Surveys and questionnaires have the same limitations as other types of reported experience: Their quality depends on respondents answering honestly and reporting their experiences accurately. Surveyers must also avoid questions that skew the results with loaded questions or emotion-laden words that may prejudice respondents:

Should cold-blooded killers be executed?

Do you favor tax-and-spend liberalism or Republican fiscal responsibility?

Are you pro-life or in favor of killing babies?

Would you hire someone who was convicted of a felony?

Questions that are too vague or too rigid leave people unsure how to respond:

Are you happy?

Do you believe in angels?

Is your favorite sport baseball or hockey?

Are you in favor of health care reform?

Questions that use absolute terms leave no middle ground for respondents: Do you always eat out or never eat out? To allow greater flexibility, many surveyers use a *Likert scale,* a scale that allows for a range of answers (strongly disagree, disagree, unsure, agree, strongly agree) or allow respondents to rank their response on a numerical scale: How often do you eat out? Never, seldom, sometimes, often, always.

When evaluating data from a survey or questionnaire, it is important to ask how the survey was conducted:

1. Did the surveyers explain the purpose of the survey?
2. Did they give clear, concise directions?
3. Is the survey free from personal bias and slanted terms?
4. Does it include words the respondents will understand?
5. Is there a clear range of choices?
6. Did researchers adhere to acknowledged ethical standards for human subject research, such as not conducting research on vulnerable populations (for example, the mentally disabled), informing participants of the nature of the research, gaining informed consent, and making the results and report of the research available to the participants?
7. Were respondents selected to reflect an accurate sample of the population?

Many news programs today conduct telephone polls by asking people to call in and register their opinions according to the number they choose to dial. People who respond to such polls are probably more interested in the issue under question than a randomly selected group would be. Most of these programs are careful to point out that the poll is not "scientific," yet they still report the outcomes as if the data can be meaningfully interpreted.

Does the means of contacting respondents affect their responses? When Franklin Roosevelt was running for president against Herbert Hoover in 1932, the Gallop organization surveyed people by phone about their presidential preference. This data predicted a Hoover victory; yet Roosevelt won overwhelmingly because he had strong support among the many people during the Depression who were too poor to own a telephone.

▪ ▪ MAKING INFERENCES ABOUT EXPERIENCE

Some phenomena are difficult, or even impossible, for humans to experience directly without the aid of instruments that extend the physical senses. For example, scientists know of the existence of microorganisms and far away galaxies only through the aid of instruments that extend the power of sight. Weather satellites provide a perspective on the planet that no one but an astronaut could otherwise enjoy. Cameras allow us to observe phenomena that are too fast or too slow for the unaided human eye to follow. Instruments such as these can give us more data about experience than we would have through our physical senses alone, but even the most finely tuned scientific instruments cannot provide a complete picture of experience. Experience is too complex. And the data that these instruments provide must still be interpreted by humans.

Sometimes, even with the most sensitive instruments, humans cannot experience a phenomenon directly. For experience of the past or the future, we must rely upon "signs" or "evidence" that something occurred or existed or that something is likely to occur. *Jurassic Park* aside, no one has direct experience of dinosaurs, yet scientists don't doubt that such creatures existed because they left clear evidence: fossilized bones, teeth, eggs (some with fossilized embryos), footprints, skin impressions, DNA strands. The evidence is adequate (for the community of scientists) to eliminate any doubt about the existence of dinosaurs. But scientists still disagree about the nature of dinosaurs. Were they warm-blooded or cold-blooded? Are they more closely related to birds or lizards? Did they travel alone or in herds?

Even some phenomena in the present are too large or too small or too far away for humans to experience them directly — even with sensitive instruments. In such cases, we must "infer" their existence from what evidence is available. Most scientists believe, for example, that black holes exist, but this belief is based on inferences rather than direct observation of black holes.

Reports, reports of reports, and inferences all involve claims about existence. These are what people commonly call "facts" although it should be clear by now that there is a fair amount of interpretation in any report of experience. Take the hole in the ozone, for example. The layer of ozone around the earth is so large and remote that humans cannot experience it directly. Scientists must rely on instruments to gather data about the ozone, and then they make inferences based on these data. Is there actually a hole in the ozone? Does it exist? If it does exist, what is the nature of this ozone hole? Is it growing? Does it threaten the planet? Different experts will have different answers to these questions of "fact," of existence.

Applying the Principles

▓ ▓ TWO VIEWS OF EYEWITNESS TESTIMONY

The following two essays discuss the reliability and unreliability of eyewitness testimony. The first is by a psychologist, Elizabeth F. Loftus, who speculates about whether it is possible for eyewitnesses to provide completely objective reports. The second is by Barry Winston, a practicing defense attorney. Winston talks about the consequences of believing too much in the objectivity of legal testimony. As you read these essays, consider the following questions:

1. What makes some witnesses more reliable or believable than others?
2. How often do you have to rely on accounts given by others? Do you tend to believe these accounts? What makes you believe some people more than others?
3. What happens when two people who experienced the same event disagree with one another? Is one of them necessarily lying or mistaken?
4. What should be the role of eyewitness testimony in legal cases?

Eyewitnesses: Essential but Unreliable

ELIZABETH F. LOFTUS

T HE LADIES AND GENTLEMEN of William Bernard Jackson's jury decided 1 that he was guilty of rape. They made a serious mistake, and before it was discovered, Jackson had spent five years in prison. There he suffered numerous indignities and occasional attacks until the police discovered that another man, who looked very much like Jackson, had committed the rapes.

If you had been on the jury, you would probably have voted for conviction too. Two women had positively identified Jackson as the man who had raped them in September and October of 1977. The October victim was asked on the witness stand, "Is there any doubt in your mind as to whether this man you have identified here is the man who had the sexual activity with you on October 3, 1977?" She answered "No doubt." "Could you be mistaken?" the prosecutor asked. "No, I am not mistaken," the victim stated confidently. Jackson and other defense witnesses testified that he was home when the rapes occurred. But the jury didn't believe him or them.

This is just one of the many documented cases of mistaken eyewitness testimony that have had tragic consequences. In 1981, Steve Titus of Seattle was convicted of raping a 17-year-old woman on a secluded road; the following year he was proven to be innocent. Titus was luckier than Jackson; he never went to prison. However, Aaron Lee Owens of Oakland, California, was not as fortunate. He spent nine years in a prison for a double murder that he didn't commit. In these cases, and many others, eyewitnesses testified against the defendants, and jurors believed them.

One reason most of us, as jurors, place so much faith in eyewitness testimony is that we are unaware of how many factors influence its accuracy. To name just a few: what questions witnesses are asked by police and how the questions are phrased; the difficulty people have in distinguishing among people of other races; whether witnesses have seen photos of suspects before viewing the lineup from which they pick out the person they say committed the crime; the size, composition and type (live or photo) of the lineup itself.

I know of seven studies that assess what ordinary citizens believe about eye- 5 witness memory. One common misconception is that police officers make better witnesses than the rest of us. As part of a larger study, my colleagues and I asked 541 registered voters in Dade County, Florida, "Do you think that the memory of law enforcement agents is better than the memory of the average citizen?" Half said yes, 38 percent said no and the rest had no opinion. When A. Daniel Yarmey of the University of Guelph asked judges, lawyers, and policemen a similar question, 63 percent of the legal officials and half the police agreed that "The policeman will be superior to the civilian" in identifying robbers.

This faith in police testimony is not supported by research. Several years ago, psychologists A. H. Tinkner and E. Christopher Poulton showed a film depicting a street scene to 24 police officers and 156 civilians. The subjects were asked to watch for particular people in the film and to report instances of crimes, such as petty theft. The researchers found that the officers reported more alleged thefts than the civilians but that when it came to detecting actual crimes, the civilians did just as well.

More recently, British researcher Peter B. Ainsworth showed a 20-minute videotape to police officers and civilians. The tape depicted a number of staged criminal offenses, suspicious circumstances and traffic offenses at an urban street corner. No significant differences were found between the police and civilians in the total number of incidents reported. Apparently neither their initial training nor subsequent experience increases the ability of the police to be accurate witnesses.

Studies by others and myself have uncovered other common misconceptions about eyewitness testimony. They include:

- *Witnesses remember the details of a violent crime better than those of a nonviolent one.* Research shows just the opposite: The added stress that violence creates clouds our perceptions.
- *Witnesses are as likely to underestimate the duration of a crime as to overestimate it.* In fact, witnesses almost invariably think a crime took longer than it did. The more violent and stressful the crime, the more witnesses overestimate its duration.
- *The more confident a witness seems, the more accurate the testimony is likely to be.* Research suggests that there may be little or no relationship between confidence and accuracy, especially when viewing conditions are poor.

The unreliability of confidence as a guide to accuracy has been demonstrated outside of the courtroom too; one example is provided by accounts of an aircraft accident that killed nine people several years ago. According to *Flying* magazine, several people had seen the airplane just before impact, and one of them was certain that "it was heading right toward the ground, straight down." This witness was profoundly wrong, as shown by several photographs taken of the crash site that made it clear that the airplane hit flat and at a low enough angle to skid for almost 1,000 feet.

Despite the inaccuracies of eyewitness testimony, we can't afford to exclude   10
it legally or ignore it as jurors. Sometimes, as in cases of rape, it is the only evidence available, and it is often correct. The question remains, what can we do to give jurors a better understanding of the uses and pitfalls of such testimony? Judges sometimes give the jury a list of instructions on the pitfalls of eyewitness testimony. But this method has not proved satisfactory, probably because, as studies show, jurors either do not listen or do not understand the instructions.

Another solution, when judges permit, is to call a psychologist as an expert witness to explain how the human memory works and describe the experimental findings that apply to the case at hand. How this can affect a case is shown by a murder trial in California two years ago. On April 1, 1981, two young men were walking along Polk Street in San Francisco at about 5:30 in the evening. A car stopped near them and the driver, a man in his 40s, motioned one of the men to get in, which he did. The car drove off. Up to this point, nothing appeared unusual. The area was known as a place where prostitutes hang out; in fact, the young man who got in the car was there hustling for "tricks." Three days later, he was found strangled in a wooded area some 75 miles south of San Francisco.

Five weeks later, the victim's friend was shown a six-person lineup and picked out a 47-year-old I'll call D. The quick selection of D's photograph, along with the strong emotional reaction that accompanied it (the friend became ill when he saw the photo), convinced the police that they had their man. D was tried for murder.

At his trial, the defense lawyer introduced expert testimony by a psychologist on the factors that made accurate perception and memory difficult. For example, in the late afternoon of April 1, the witness had been using marijuana, a substance likely to blur his initial perceptions and his memory of them. Furthermore, just before viewing the lineup, the witness had seen a photograph of D on a desk in the police station, an incident that could have influenced his selection. During the five weeks between April 1 and the time he saw the photographs, the witness had talked about and been questioned repeatedly about the crime, circumstances that often contaminate memory.

In the end, the jury was unable to reach a verdict. It is difficult to assess the impact of any one bit of testimony on a particular verdict. We can only speculate that the psychologist's testimony may have made the jury more cautious about accepting the eyewitness testimony. This idea is supported by recent studies showing that such expert testimony generally increases the deliberation time jurors devote to eyewitness aspects of a case.

Expert testimony on eyewitness reliability is controversial. It has its advocates and enemies in both the legal and psychological professions. For example, several judicial arguments are used routinely to exclude the testimony. One is that it "invades the province of the jury," meaning that it is the jury's job, not an expert's, to decide whether a particular witness was in a position to see, hear and remember what is being claimed in court. Another reason judges sometimes exclude such testimony is that the question of eyewitness reliability is "not beyond the knowledge and experience of a juror" and thus is not a proper subject matter for expert testimony.

In virtually all the cases in which a judge has prohibited the jury from hearing expert testimony, the higher courts have upheld the decision, and in some cases have driven home the point with negative comments about the use of psychologists. In a recent case in California, *People v. Plasencia,* Nick Plasencia Jr. was found guilty of robbery and other crimes in Los Angeles County. He had tried to introduce the testimony of a psychologist on eyewitness reliability, but the judge refused to admit it, saying that "the subject matter about which (the expert) sought to testify was too conjectural and too speculative to support any opinion he would offer." The appellate court upheld Plasencia's conviction and made known its strong feelings about the psychological testimony:

> Since our society has not reached the point where all human conduct is videotaped for later replay, resolution of disputes in our court system depends almost entirely on the testimony of witnesses who recount their observations of a myriad of events.
>
> These events include matters in both the criminal and civil areas of the law. The accuracy of a witness's testimony of course depends on factors which are as variable and complex as human nature itself. . . . The cornerstone of our system remains our belief in the wisdom and integrity of the jury system and the ability of 12 jurors to determine the accuracy of witnesses' testimony. The system has served us well. . . .
>
> It takes no expert to tell us that for various reasons, people can be mistaken about identity, or even the exact details of an observed event. Yet to present these commonly accepted and known facts in the form of an expert opinion, which opinion does nothing more than generally question the validity of one form of traditionally accepted evidence, would exaggerate the significance of that testimony and give a "scientific aura" to a very unscientific matter.
>
> The fact remains, in spite of the universally recognized fallibility of human

15

beings, persons do, on many occasions, correctly identify individuals. Evidence that under contrived test conditions, or even in real-life situations, certain persons totally unconnected with this case have been mistaken in their identification of individuals is no more relevant than evidence that in other cases, witnesses totally unconnected with this event have lied.

It seems beyond question that the identifications in this case were correct. We find no abuse of discretion in the trial court's rejecting the proffered testimony.

Quite the opposite view was expressed by the Arizona Supreme Court in *State v. Chapple.* At the original trial, defendant Dolan Chapple had been convicted of three counts of murder and two drug-trafficking charges, chiefly on the testimony of two witnesses who identified him at the trial. Earlier they had selected him from photographs shown them by the police more than a year after the crime.

Chapple's lawyer tried to introduce expert psychological testimony on the accuracy of such identification. The judge refused to permit it on the grounds that the testimony would pertain only to matters "within the common experience" of jurors. The high court disagreed, maintaining that expert testimony would have provided scientific data on such pertinent matters as the accuracy of delayed identification, the effect of stress on perception and the relationship between witness confidence and accuracy. "We cannot assume," the court added, "that the average juror would be aware of the variables concerning identification and memory" about which the expert would have testified. Chapple's conviction was reversed, and he has been granted a new trial.

Like lawyers and judges, psychologists disagree on whether expert testimony is a good solution to the eyewitness problem. Two of the most outspoken critics are Michael McCloskey and Howard Egeth of The Johns Hopkins University. These experimental psychologists offer four reasons why they believe that expert testimony on eyewitness reliability is a poor idea. They say that there is no evidence that such testimony is needed; that the data base on which the expert must rely is not sufficiently well-developed; and that conflicting public testimony between experts would tarnish the profession's image. Given this sorry state of affairs, they argue, psychologists may do more harm than good by intruding into judicial proceedings.

Obviously, many psychologists disagree with this assessment and believe that both the law and psychology gain from mutual interaction. In the area of eyewitness testimony, information supplied by psychologists to lawyers has stimulated responses that have suggested a number of important ideas for future research.   20

For example, psychologists need to learn more about the ideas that the rest of us have about the operation of human perception and memory. When these ideas are wrong, psychologists need to devise ways to educate us so that the judgments we make as jurors will be more fully informed and more fair. Only through this give-and-take, and occasional biting controversy, will progress be made. It is too late to help William Jackson, or Steve Titus, or Aaron Lee Owens, but it is not yet too late for the rest of us.

Stranger Than True: Why I Defend Guilty Clients

BARRY WINSTON

L ET ME TELL YOU a story. A true story. The court records are all there if 1
anyone wants to check. It's three years ago. I'm sitting in my office, staring out the window, when I get a call from a lawyer I hardly know. Tax lawyer.
Some kid is in trouble and would I be interested in helping him out? He's
charged with manslaughter, a felony, and driving under the influence. I tell him
sure, have the kid call me.

So the kid calls and makes an appointment to see me. He's a nice kid, fresh
out of college, and he's come down here to spend some time with his older sister,
who's in med school. One day she tells him they're invited to a cookout with
some friends of hers. She's going directly from class and he's going to take her
car and meet her there. It's way out in the country, but he gets there before she
does, introduces himself around, and pops a beer. She shows up after a while and
he pops another beer. Then he eats a hamburger and drinks a third beer. At some
point his sister says, "Well, it's about time to go," and they head for the car.

And, the kid tells me, sitting there in my office, the next thing he remembers, he's waking up in a hospital room, hurting like hell, bandages and casts all
over him, and somebody is telling him he's charged with manslaughter and DUI
because he wrecked his sister's car, killed her in the process, and blew fourteen
on the Breathalyzer. I ask him what the hell he means by "the next thing he
remembers," and he looks me straight in the eye and says he can't remember
anything from the time they leave the cookout until he wakes up in the hospital.
He tells me the doctors say he has post-retrograde amnesia. I say of course I
believe him, but I'm worried about finding a judge who'll believe him.

I agree to represent him and send somebody for a copy of the wreck report.
It says there are four witnesses: a couple in a car going the other way who passed
the kid and his sister just before their car ran off the road, the guy whose front
yard they landed in, and the trooper who investigated. I call the guy whose yard
they ended up in. He isn't home. I leave word. Then I call the couple. The wife
agrees to come in the next day with her husband. While I'm talking to her, the
first guy calls. I call him back, introduce myself, tell him I'm representing the kid
and need to talk to him about the accident. He hems and haws, and I figure he's
one of those people who think it's against the law to talk to defense lawyers. I
say the D.A. will tell him it's O.K. to talk to me, but he doesn't have to. I give
him the name and number of the D.A. and he says he'll call me back.

Then I go out and hunt up the trooper. He tells me the whole story. The 5
kid and his sister are coming into town on Smith Level Road, after it turns from
fifty-five to forty-five. The Thornes — the couple — are heading out of town.
They say this sports car passes them, going the other way, right after that bad
turn just south of the new subdivision. They say it's going like a striped-ass ape,
at least sixty-five or seventy. Mrs. Thorne turns around to look and Mr. Thorne
watches in the rear-view mirror. They both see the same thing: Halfway into the

curve, the car runs off the road on the right, whips back onto the road, spins, runs off on the left, and disappears. They turn around in the first driveway they come to and start back, both terrified of what they're going to find. By this time, Trooper Johnson says, the guy whose front yard the car has ended up in has pulled the kid and his sister out of the wreck and started CPR on the girl. Turns out he's an emergency medical technician. Holloway, that's his name. Johnson tells me that Holloway says he's sitting in his front room, watching television, when he hears a hell of a crash in his yard. He runs outside and finds the car flipped over, and so he pulls the kid out from the driver's side, the girl from the other side. She dies in his arms.

And that, says Trooper Johnson, is that. The kid's blood/alcohol content was fourteen, he was going way too fast, and the girl is dead. He had to charge him. It's a shame, he seems a nice kid, it was his own sister and all, but what the hell can he do, right?

The next day the Thornes come in, and they confirm everything Johnson said. By now things are looking not so hot for my client, and I'm thinking it's about time to have a little chat with the D.A. But Holloway still hasn't called me back, so I call him. Not home. Leave word. No call. I wait a couple of days and call again. Finally I get him on the phone. He's very agitated, and won't talk to me except to say that he doesn't have to talk to me.

I know I better look for a deal, so I go to the D.A. He's very sympathetic. But. There's only so far you can get on sympathy. A young woman is dead, promising career cut short, all because somebody has too much to drink and drives. The kid has to pay. Not, the D.A. says, with jail time. But he's got to plead guilty to two misdemeanors: death by vehicle and driving under the influence. That means probation, a big fine. Several thousand dollars. Still, it's hard for me to criticize the D.A. After all, he's probably going to have the MADD mothers all over him because of reducing the felony to a misdemeanor.

On the day of the trial, I get to court a few minutes early. There are the Thornes and Trooper Johnson, and someone I assume is Holloway. Sure enough, when this guy sees me, he comes over and introduces himself and starts right in: "I just want you to know how serious all this drinking and driving really is," he says. "If those young people hadn't been drinking and driving that night, that poor young girl would be alive today." Now, I'm trying to hold my temper when I spot the D.A. I bolt across the room, grab him by the arm, and say, "We gotta talk. Why the hell have you got all those people here? That jerk Holloway. Surely to God you're not going to call him as a witness. This is a guilty plea! My client's parents are sitting out there. You don't need to put them through a dog-and-pony show."

The D.A. looks at me and says, "Man, I'm sorry, but in a case like this, I gotta put on witnesses. Weird Wally is on the bench. If I try to go without witnesses, he might throw me out."

The D.A. calls his first witness. Trooper Johnson identifies himself, tells about being called to the scene of the accident, and describes what he found when he got there and what everybody told him. After he finishes, the judge looks at me. "No questions," I say. Then the D.A. calls Holloway. He describes

10

the noise, running out of the house, the upside-down car in his yard, pulling my client out of the window on the left side of the car and then going around to the other side for the girl. When he gets to this part, he really hits his stride. He describes, in minute detail, the injuries he saw and what he did to try and save her life. And then he tells, breath by breath, how she died in his arms.

The D.A. says, "No further questions, your Honor." The judge looks at me. I shake my head, and he says to Holloway. "You may step down."

One of those awful silences hangs there, and nothing happens for a minute. Holloway doesn't move. Then he looks at me, and at the D.A., and then at the judge. He says, "Can I say something else, your Honor?"

All my bells are ringing at once, and my gut is screaming at me, Object! Object! I'm trying to decide in three quarters of a second whether it'll be worse to listen to a lecture on the evils of drink from this jerk Holloway or piss off the judge by objecting. But all I say is, "No objections, your Honor." The judge smiles at me, then at Holloway, and says, "Very well, Mr. Holloway. What did you wish to say?"

It all comes in a rush. "Well, you see, your Honor," Holloway says, "it was just like I told Trooper Johnson. It all happened so fast. I heard the noise, and I came running out, and it was night, and I was excited, and the next morning, when I had a chance to think about it, I figured out what had happened, but by then I'd already told Trooper Johnson and I didn't know what to do, but you see, the car, it was upside down, and I did pull that boy out of the left-hand window, but don't you see, the car was upside down, and if you turned it over on its wheels like it's supposed to be, the left-hand side is really on the right-hand side, and your Honor, that boy wasn't driving that car at all. It was the girl that was driving, and when I had a chance to think about it the next morning, I realized that I'd told Trooper Johnson wrong, and I was scared and I didn't know what to do, and that's why" — and now he's looking right at me — "why I wouldn't talk to you." 15

Naturally, the defendant is allowed to withdraw his guilty plea. The charges are dismissed, and the kid and his parents and I go into one of the back rooms in the courthouse and sit there looking at one another for a while. Finally, we recover enough to mumble some Oh my Gods and Thank yous and You're welcomes. And that's why I can stand to represent somebody when I know he's guilty.

▪ ▪ TWO HOAXES

Consider the following two essays. In the first P. J. Wingate reports a trick that H. L. Mencken, the famous Baltimore journalist, played on an unsuspecting public. In the second Barry O'Neill uncovers the true source of a widely reported education survey. As you read, consider the following questions:

1. Have you ever encountered the "hoaxes" reported here? If so, did you accept them to be true or find them suspicious?
2. Are you familiar with any other popular beliefs that have no basis in reality?

3. How is misinformation like this spread? What potential do the mass media have for spreading misinformation in addition to information?
4. How can you know if the information you are receiving from others or through the media is accurate?

The Philosophy of H. L. Mencken

P. J. WINGATE

D URING THE 1920's, when he was at the peak of his literary fame, H. L.   1
Mencken became widely known as the "Sage of Baltimore." Mencken was busy in those days editing *The American Mercury* and preparing revised editions of his most famous book, *The American Language,* and he made no comment on being called a sage; but when some people began to call him the "Baltimore Philosopher" he objected.

In 1927 he wrote an essay called "On Metaphysicians," which was Mencken's word for philosophers, and in it made clear that he did not want to be known as a philosopher. He started his essay by saying that when Baltimore got too hot for what he called "serious mental activity," he always took a couple of weeks off for a "rereading of the so-called philosophical classics with a glance or two at the latest compositions of the extant philosophers."

He explained his annual trip into the forests of philosophy by saying:

> There is somewhere down in my recesses an obscure conviction that I owe a duty to my customers, who look to me to flatter them with occasional dark references to Aristotle, Spinoza and the categorical imperative. Out of this business, despite the high austerity, I always carry away the feeling that I have had a hell of a time. That is, I carry away the feeling that the art and mystery of philosophy as it is practiced in the world of professional philosophers, is largely moonshine and wind music — or, to borrow Henry Ford's searching term, bunk.

"Since the dawn of time," he continued,

> they have been trying to get order and method into the thinking of Homo Sapiens, and Homo Sapiens, if he thinks at all, is still a brother to the lowly ass . . . even to the ears and the bray. I include the philosophers themselves unanimously and especially. True enough, one arises now and then who somehow manages to be charming and even plausible. I point to Plato, to Nietzsche, to Schopenhauer. But it is always as a poet or politician, not as a philosopher. The genuine professional, sticking to his gloomy speculations is as dull as a table of logarithms. What man in human history ever wrote worse than Kant?

Mencken then went on to define the problem with philosophers this way: "What reduces all philosophers to incoherence and folly, soon or late, is the lure of the absolute. . . . For the absolute, of course, is a mere banshee, a concept without substance or reality. No such thing exists."

Mencken's long experience as a reporter and editor probably was what caused him to feel so strongly that absolute truth did not exist. He knew from sad experience with newspapers how difficult it was to come by the facts of events as recent as yesterday. 5

Mencken's own part in the history of the bathtub in America was a case in point. A great amount had been written about bathtubs in ancient Greece and Rome, but when Mencken became interested in them he found that nothing at all had ever been written about bathtubs in America. So he wrote the first piece on the subject and had it published in the New York *Evening Mail* of 28 December 1917.

He called his piece "A Neglected Anniversary" because he said no attention had been given to the seventy-fifth anniversary of the installation of the first true bathtub — one with pipes carrying in hot and cold water and others to carry away the spent water — ever set up in the United States.

This bathtub, Mencken reported, had been completed on December 20, 1842, in the home of Adam Thompson, a Cincinnati grain merchant who shipped much of his grain to England. During trips to visit customers in England, Thompson became familiar with bathtubs and decided to install one in his own home.

Thompson's tub was a large thing made of mahogany wood and lined with lead so that it weighed 1750 pounds. It was supplied with water from a third floor tank and some of the water was heated by running it through a long copper coil in the chimney of the fireplace. Thompson liked his new tub and invited several other wealthy Cincinnatians to try a bath in it. They liked it too and soon there were several bathtubs in Cincinnati and the newspapers there ran stories about these tubs.

Whereupon a surprising reaction to use of the bathtub occurred. 10

"On the one hand," Mencken wrote, "it was denounced as an epicurean and obnoxious toy from England, designed to corrupt the democratic simplicity of the republic, and on the other hand it was attacked by the medical faculty as dangerous to health."

Mencken went on to quote from the *Western Medical Repository* of April 23, 1843, which called the bathtub a certain inviter of "phthisic rheumatic fevers, inflammation of the lungs and the whole category of zymotic diseases."

Nevertheless, news about the bathtub spread and soon tubs were being installed in other cities which developed controversies of their own. Hartford, Providence, Charleston (South Carolina), and Wilmington (Delaware) all put special water taxes on homes with bathtubs, Mencken reported, and Boston in 1845 made bathing unlawful except upon medical advice. But this ordinance was never enforced and was repealed in 1862. The repeal was a slow reaction to the fact that the American Medical Association had met in Boston in 1852. A poll of the membership showed that nearly all the doctors present then thought bathing was harmless, and twenty per cent advocated it as beneficial.

However, the thing which really caused the bathtub to flourish in America, Mencken reported, was the example set by President Millard Fillmore. Fillmore had visited Cincinnati on a political tour in 1850 and had taken a bath in the original Thompson tub. To quote Mencken: "Experiencing no ill effects, he became an ardent advocate of the new invention" and when he succeeded to the Presidency, after Taylor died on July 9, 1850, he had his Secretary of War, General Conrad, install one in the White House.

"This action," Mencken reported, "revived the old controversy and its opponents made much of the fact that there was no bathtub at Mt. Vernon or Monticello, and all the Presidents and magnificos of the past had got along without such monarchial luxuries."

Nevertheless, the bathtub prospered greatly after Fillmore's term as President and by 1860, according to newspaper advertisements, every hotel in New York had a bathtub and some had two or even three.

Mencken closed his story for the *Evening Mail* this way: "So much for the history of the bathtub in America. One is astonished, on looking into it, to find that so little of it has been recorded. The literature, in fact, is almost nil. But perhaps this brief sketch will encourage other inquiries and so lay the foundation for an adequate celebration of the Centennial in 1942."

However, for the next nine years, no one wrote anything else about the bathtub, although Mencken's account was reprinted in over a hundred magazines and newspapers, and excerpts from it appeared in history books and encyclopedias. One item in particular — Fillmore's installation of the first White House bathtub — fascinated historians and it was recorded in a multitude of places. Fillmore, in fact, became known during the 1920's as "the first clean president."

Then almost a decade after he wrote his story for the New York *Evening Mail*, Mencken wrote a follow-up piece which appeared in the *Chicago Tribune* of May 23, 1926. In this new story Mencken admitted that the first piece was totally a product of his own imagination.

"This article," he wrote in the *Tribune* story, "was a tissue of absurdities, all of them deliberate and most of them obvious. If there were any facts in it they got there accidentally and against my design."

Mencken went on to say that he had liked his fabrication and was at first pleased when so many newspapers across the country reprinted it. Then he became alarmed because "I began to encounter my preposterous "facts" in the writings of other men. They began to be used by chiropractors and other such quacks as evidence of the stupidity of medical men. They began to be cited by medical men as proof of the progress of public hygiene. They got into the learned journals. They were alluded to on the floor of Congress. They crossed the ocean and were discussed solemnly in England and on the continent. Today, I believe they are accepted as gospel everywhere on earth. To question them becomes as hazardous as to question the Norman invasion."

This exposé, itself, was reprinted in twenty or thirty major newspapers and then a very curious situation developed. No one paid any attention to this exposé. Two weeks later the *Boston Herald* reprinted the original hoax as an interesting piece of American history. Of course, no one corrected the history books which had faithfully reproduced parts of it, particularly the item about Millard Fillmore putting in the first White House bathtub.

Mencken made one more attempt to debunk his bathtub hoax and on July 25, 1926, wrote another piece on the subject for the Chicago *Tribune,* once again calling his original story a fake.

Again, very few people apparently paid any attention to the exposé and the original story kept right on gaining credibility and acceptance. And it kept on doing so long after Mencken died.

Dr. Daniel Boorstin, Librarian of the Library of Congress, for example, in-   25
cluded the most intriguing of Mencken's "facts" in his scholarly book *The Americans — The Democratic Experience* published by Random House in 1973. On page 353 Dr. Boorstin wrote: "In 1851 when President Millard Fillmore reputedly installed the first permanent bathtub and water closet in the White House he was criticized for doing something that was 'both unsanitary and undemocratic.'"

Dozens of other authors have done the same thing, the two most recent being Barbara Seuling in 1978 and Paul Boller in 1981. Boller's book, called *Presidential Anecdotes,* was published by the Oxford University Press.

Also, all three of the national television networks reported in 1976, on January 7 the occasion of Fillmore's birthday, that he had installed the first White House bathtub.

All this has occurred despite the fact that many newspapers have exposed Mencken's fake over the years. For example, on January 4, 1977, the Washington *Post* exposed it once more but the *Post* closed its story on a note of optimism.

"Will this current account," the *Post* asked, "destroy one of the nation's most charming myths? Certainly not. It will not even slow it up any more than a single grape placed on the railroad tracks would slow up a freight train."

"So on January 7, let all true patriots retire to their bathrooms, fill up the   30
tub with champagne, invite the neighbors in, and drink a toast to Millard Fillmore, statesman, scholar, patriot, and the finest plumber who ever lived in the White House."

The Philadelphia *Inquirer* of January 7, 1977, carried a similar story which was headlined: "A Dirty Story. Fillmore's Still in That Tub."

And so it goes. The original hoax has become indestructible while all attempts to correct it go nowhere.

Mencken explained all this in his essay which he called "Hymn To The Truth" written for the Chicago *Tribune* in 1926.

"No normal human being," he wrote, "wants to hear the truth. It is the passion of a small and aberrant minority of men, most of them pathological. They are hated for telling it while they live, and when they die are swiftly forgotten. What remains to the world, in the field of wisdom, is a series of long-tested and solidly agreeable lies."

In another essay called "The Art Eternal" Mencken stated his views in a   35 somewhat similar manner and said that Americans were particularly resentful of the truth.

"A Galileo,"[1] he wrote, "could no more be elected President of the United States than he could be elected Pope of Rome. Both high posts are reserved for men favored by God with an extraordinary genius for swathing the bitter facts of life in bandages of soft illusion."

Mencken closed his 1927 essay on philosophers this way:

> There is no record in human history of a happy philosopher: They exist only in romantic legend. Practically all of them have turned their children out of doors and beaten their wives. And no wonder! If you want to find out how a philosopher feels when he is engaged in the practice of his profession, go to the nearest zoo and watch a chimpanzee at the weary and hopeless job of chasing fleas. Both suffer damnably and neither can win.

So it is clear why Mencken did not wish to be called a philosopher.

Nevertheless, he had a philosophy of his own. Mencken believed that the list of eternal truths is a very short one and if a man happens to come across what he believes to be one of these eternal truths, he still should not take it too seriously.

The History of a Hoax

BARRY O'NEILL

W E OFTEN DEFINE ourselves more by our misdeeds than by our accomplish-   1
ments. Twenty years after my father died, I leafed through his school diaries and found a side of him that I hadn't known. The events he considered worth recording weren't his successes but the trouble he got into: "fought with Jimmy Egan," "running in hall, broke statue of Virgin Mary," "teacher took my slingshot."

For many worried adults, the offenses of young people have become a measure of America's well-being. Last April someone tacked a survey on a Yale bulletin board comparing the top problems of public schools in the 1940's and 1980's. In the 40's the problems were: 1. talking; 2. chewing gum; 3. making noise; 4. running in the halls; 5. getting out of turn in line; 6. wearing improper clothing; 7. not putting paper in wastebasket.

The top problems in the 80's had become: 1. drug abuse; 2. alcohol abuse; 3. pregnancy; 4. suicide; 5. rape; 6. robbery; 7. assault.

---

[1] Galileo Galilei (1564–1642) used the telescope to view the moons of Jupiter, supporting Copernicus's theory that the earth circles the sun rather than the sun circling the earth. Some influential church leaders claimed that his teachings violated Christian doctrine. He was imprisoned for refusing to deny his findings.

Something stopped me. The old-time problems seemed too trivial, the contrast between then and now too tidy. My father could have bested the 1940 list any day, and in my own school years I worried about bullies starting fistfights or stealing my lunch, not kids cutting in line at the drinking fountain. A 1984 Gallup poll asking teachers to name the biggest school problems recorded the top two as parent apathy and lack of financial support, but drugs were near the bottom. In 1991 the National Center for Education Statistics asked specifically about discipline and safety issues, and educators' prime complaints were tardiness, absenteeism and fighting. Again drugs fell near the bottom, well below tobacco.

Puzzled by these inconsistencies, I tried to locate the source of the list of   5 school problems. The list on the bulletin board had been taken from a book published by the Young & Rubicam Foundation, an arm of the ad agency that created the slogan "A mind is a terrible thing to waste." But it attributed the research to the California Department of Education. I scoured computer bibliographies and data bases, but could find no specific title or date or author. I began to suspect that the lists were folklore, like the famous alligators crawling through New York's sewers.

If so, they were a rare variety, folklore of the eminent and powerful. William Bennett, a former Secretary of Education, used them in television talks, editorials and speeches to promote *The Index of Leading Cultural Indicators,* his 1993 book on America's moral decay. The lists were not just the oratory of conservatives: Anna Quindlen, Herb Caen and Carl Rowan included them in their columns. A former Harvard president, Derek Bok, recounted the lists to the Harvard Club of Chicago. Joseph Fernandez, former chancellor of New York City's schools, used them to argue for his curriculum reforms, and the publisher Mortimer Zuckerman saw them as an outgrowth of television violence. Dr. Joycelyn Elders, then the Surgeon General nominee, said they showed the need for social-service and health programs.

Senators, mayors, state education officials, university professors, deans — these were notables who would never stand up to announce the discovery of alligators underneath New York, but they accepted the lists as factual. They were reported in all the major news magazines. In addition to the Quindlen column, *The New York Times* printed them five times (not as fact but in quotes of various people), and they became commonplace in grass-roots America, popping up in Dear Abby, Ann Landers and countless letters to the editor. They have become the most quoted "results" of educational research, and possibly the most influential.

We will never know who first said "Let's do lunch," but this was a different case — an item from popular culture that had circulated widely through the news media, leaving a traceable record. I was determined to find its origin.

I wrote letters to users asking them where they had found their versions, and paged through educational journals looking for the originator. After several months I found him. As I had suspected, his lists were not scientifically valid, but neither were they hoaxes. He had offered them simply as his opinion, never meaning to hoodwink the experts. It was later users who added background details, like William Bennett's elaboration about an "ongoing" survey asking teachers "the same question" over the years.

Some felt free to modify the lists. Rush Limbaugh, for example, cited the 10 authority of Bennett but added a few school offenses of his own. Others advanced the date, making the results sound more current; in November 1992, when *The Wall Street Journal* reprinted the lists from the *CQ Researcher,* the modern survey's date jumped from 1980 to 1990. If there was any hoaxing, it was users hoaxing themselves.

Their originator was T. Cullen Davis of Fort Worth, a born-again Christian who devised the lists as a fundamentalist attack on public schools. Davis was born again through a remarkable course of events. He and his brother Ken had built the family business in oil equipment into a billion-dollar conglomerate, but in 1976 Cullen was arrested for a double murder, accused of shooting his step-daughter and the lover of his estranged wife. The sensational trials, which featured lurid tales of his wife's drug and sex parties at his mansion, became the talk of bridge tables and barrooms across Texas.

After his acquittals, Davis turned from the fast life to Christianity. One night at his home, he and James Robison, a television evangelist, took hammers to Davis's million-dollar collection of jade and ivory statues, smashing them as false religion. He plunged into a reading program on public schools, fought plans for sex education and lobbied for the teaching of creationism.

Sometime around 1982, Davis constructed the lists and passed them around to other fundamentalists. His 1940 offenses were close to the seven on the Yale bulletin board: 1. talking; 2. chewing gum; 3. running in the halls; 4. wearing improper clothing; 5. making noise; 6. not putting paper in wastebaskets; 7. getting out of turn in line. But he listed 20 modern problems: 1. rape; 2. robbery; 3. assault; 4. personal theft; 5. burglary; 6. drug abuse; 7. arson; 8. bombings; 9. alcohol abuse; 10. carrying of weapons; 11. absenteeism; 12. vandalism; 13. murder; 14. extortion; 15. gang warfare; 16. pregnancies; 17. abortions; 18. suicide; 19. venereal disease; 20. lying and cheating.

I asked him how he had arrived at his items. "They weren't done from a scientific survey," he told me. "How did I know what the offenses in the schools were in 1940? I was there. How do I know what they are now? I read the newspapers."

His recollection that he formed the lists entirely from scratch must be faulty. 15 His first 10 modern offenses are almost identical in wording to items on a questionnaire from a survey by the National Center for Education Statistics, which asked principals whether they had reported certain *crimes* in their schools during a five-month period in 1974–75. This survey was published in the Safe School study of 1977–78, which was widely distributed. Rape, robbery and assault held the top places not because they were the top problems, but because the researchers used a standard ordering in crime reports: first crimes against people, then crimes against property, then others. Curiously, murder does not appear among the serious items at the head of Davis's modern list. It shows up only after playing hooky and vandalizing. The reason is that the survey relied upon a list of crimes for which researchers could interview the victims, so murder obviously was left off.

Thus, Davis's modern list is made up not of survey answers but of the questions. His list of 1940 problems, however, seems genuinely to date from that time. It is close to the wording of a 1943 list in a Texas teachers' magazine and fits with dozens of old research reports collecting teachers' most common classroom problems. Talking usually ranked high and gum-chewing close behind.

Davis's 1940 list may be based on real data, but it cannot in any event be compared with his 1980's list. It gave the answers to a discipline, while the new list was an inventory of crimes. You can't learn how times have changed if you change your question.

In the early 1980's some of Davis's conservative colleagues took up his creation. The Rev. Tim LaHaye put the lists in a book promoting family values, and the anti-feminist activist Phyllis Schlafly used the idea in an essay about her school days. The lists gained wide circulation in the fundamentalist community when they appeared in a newsletter published by Mel and Norma Gabler. These were the education activists who gained national fame for pressuring the Texas state textbook committee to purchase books that promote creationism, patriotism and a Christian life style. In their newsletter they reordered the old problems and shrank the new list to 17, knocking out lying and cheating, personal theft and weapons.

In 1984 David Balsiger, then of Costa Mesa, Calif., picked up the Gablers' version for the *Presidential Biblical Scoreboard,* a glossy magazine that rated presidential candidates on how closely their platforms followed biblical teachings. Although the print run for the *Scoreboard* was around two million, the lists had little visibility outside conservative religious circles. To gain wider circulation, they needed the imprimatur of a credible publication. That came, in a backhanded way, in March 1985, when *Harper's* printed the *Scoreboard's* version as a curious piece of Americana. *Harper's* slipped in clues that the lists were unscientific, noting that the *Scoreboard* wanted readers to "vote conscientiously for godly rule." Nevertheless, in April the Governor of California, George Deukmajian, included the lists in an address warmly received by the California Sheriff's Association.

Mary Weaver, a program administrator at the California Department of Education, circulated the table from *Harper's* in a March memo to her guidance and counseling staff, and used it for workshops on discipline and safety. The department had set up a liaison group with the police across the state, and a police officer from Fullerton began presenting the lists in talks in his home community.

Simply by quoting the lists the Fullerton police and the California Department of Education put their stamp on them, and many would later claim that they were the originators. This is the best-source-yet rule. The most credible party to date to recite or publish the lists becomes their source. Following the best-source-yet rule, various later users would say that the survey was compiled by CBS News, the CQ Researcher or the Heritage Foundation, whose staff, according to John McCaslin of *The Washington Times*, found the 1940 offenses in an old survey.

During their time in Fullerton the lists underwent a crucial change — the drug shift. The public was alarmed about teen-age drug use, which a Gallup poll rated the public's No. 1 worry about schools. The modern list could ride this concern if drugs were moved to the top. Most users had not explicitly claimed that the items were in order of worst first, so shifting them around seemed permissible. The four self-destructive offenses — drugs, alcohol, pregnancy and suicide — got promoted as a block, and rape, robbery and assault fell to fifth, sixth and seventh. My earliest record of the new ranking comes from a January 1986 meeting in a Fullerton junior high school. Most recent lists feature the drug shift, a clue that they descended from the Fullerton version.

According to a University of Michigan study, drug use by high-school seniors dropped by about one-half between 1980 and 1990. But the public thought just the opposite was true. In Gallup polls over the decade, the proportion of respondents naming drugs as an important school problem rose from 14 percent to 38 percent. In other words, when drug use was most severe, the school lists were sounding the klaxon about rape, robbery and assault, and they focused on drugs just as students were using them less. The experts and reporters repeating the lists were not providing the public with real information, just reflecting public opinion back to the public.

In 1986, with pseudo-credentials from California educators and the Fullerton police, and a new look from the drug shift, the lists of school problems spread across the country. They popped up frequently in the literature of the anti-drug movement, which became another crucial conduit from the religious right to the mainstream.

The first national writer to publish the list as factual was George Will, in his *Newsweek* column of Jan. 5, 1987. He gave no source. A month later a CBS News reporter, Bernard Goldberg, featured them in a story about child criminals. Will's and Goldberg's modern lists were cut to seven: drug abuse, alcohol abuse, pregnancy, suicide, rape, robbery, assault. Fundamentalists wanted to leave no sin unmentioned, but trimming the list gave it wider appeal. Seven elements seem to be the approximate limit to people's apprehension, according to George Miller, a psychologist. There are seven colors in the rainbow, seven deadly sins and seven wonders of the world, among many other examples. Seven versus seven gave a balanced comparison of old and new, and let some public speakers go sideways across the columns, contrasting yesterday's abuse of chewing gum against today's drugs and alcohol abuse.

CBS News changed the wording slightly, and this became the preferred form among the elite, like Senator John Glenn, whose speech was picked up by the CQ Researcher for an article later copied by *The Wall Street Journal* and *The International Herald Tribune*. In a 1989 syndicated documentary on youth morals, Tom Selleck delivered the CBS News version of the list "like a punch in the solar plexus," according to one reviewer, and he also changed the wording slightly, generating another family of the lists.

Time magazine's 10-item version in 1988 included "bombings" as a top problem. F.B.I. data for 1987 show that the total reputed damage done by bombs to all the schools and universities across America was only $30,000, just a drop in the budget. So many in the news media had seen the lists so often that they assumed they were valid.

After collecting close to 250 versions of the lists, I tackled a harder question: Why have Americans found them so attractive? One clue is the way they change, like a folk song or folk tale, as they are passed on. When people hear an item of folklore they remember its core emotional meaning, not its exact words, so when they want to reproduce it they reconstruct it around that meaning. The elements of a folklore item that are not essential to this meaning change or fall away. Those that endure through successive versions often reveal its emotional significance for the group.

The items on the original 1940 list have hardly changed at all. Constant also is the location in the public schools. The date of the old list is semi-stable, usually 1940, although it has been put at anywhere from "the Depression" (Ross Perot) to "five years ago." The modern problems usually stay in the recent past, so their date moves forward as time passes.

The feature that varies widely, sometimes even slips away, is just what the inventory represents. If it is the answer, what is the question? Sometimes the lists are "top" problems, sometimes discipline problems, offenses or worries. None of these categories fit all the items, but no one seems to mind calling suicide a discipline problem. Logically an answer should be judged against its question, but at its core the list is an emotional expression, not a logical assertion. 30

In fact, the school lists are remarkably close to the Puritan jeremiads of 300 years ago, and what made them the rage then may be working for the school lists now. Jeremiads were formulaic political sermons. First the preacher reminded the congregation of its covenant with God and God's blessings on their ancestors; next, he catalogued the afflictions of the day, like Indian wars, fires or caterpillar plagues, or, in later versions, the congregation's evil habits. These were God's punishment for breaking the covenant and his warning to them to reform. Finally, he called for a renewal, after which God would grant them fulfillment.

In their nostalgic contrast of then and now, the school lists constitute a jeremiad. On their face they are criticizing schools but their real target, like the jeremiad's, is society in general. They place drugs, pregnancy, rape or suicide as problems in the public schools. But is a typical school more hazardous or immoral than its surrounding area? Blaming the schools is illogical, but it is rhetorically right, since responsibility for schools falls on all Americans.

The second and third generations of Puritans felt a tension, for which the jeremiad provided a release. Their religion had sanctioned ambition for the good of the community, but now that virtue was promoting greed, worldliness and sin. Springing from a "grief and a sickness of soul," says Perry Miller, the great scholar of Puritan intellectual history, the Puritans' sermons were "professions of a society that knew it was doing wrong, but could not help itself, because the wrong thing was also the right thing." Through public lamentations, they paid tribute to their sense of guilt over betraying their ancestors' ideals.

Americans today regard their country as the richest, freest and fairest, with the best social system, but cannot square this with the social problems of America's youth. And what does this disorder promise for the future? The tension felt by modern Americans, like that of the Puritans, demands release. The school lists are a collective moan of anxiety over the gap between ideals and reality. When Puritans or modern Americans enumerate their faults, they are declaring their dedication to their ideals, reassuring each other that at least their goals remain high.

The spread of the school lists proves that jeremiads, at least, are not in decline. The lists are not facts but a fundamental expression of attitudes and emotions. They overlook the successes of American public education, its great expansion since 1940 and its high quality despite taxpayer resistance. The lists' broad sweep ignores that some public schools are devastated by violence and substance abuse and others hardly touched at all. They should not guide our choices on education policy.

▪ ▪ THE MEDIA AND REPORTED EXPERIENCE

The next set of readings focuses on the power of mass media, such as television, to shape our perceptions of reality and to create experience. The word *media* is the plural form of the *medium,* a word that comes from a Latin word meaning "middle." A medium is "in the middle" of the receiver and direct experience. In other words, a medium provides a selection and representation of experience, not experience itself. For instance, television provides images and sounds that you could not experience in any other way. During a typical news program, you can see footage from combat zones, crime scenes, and sporting events. You get satellite views of the weather and stock reports. All these images are accompanied by "expert" testimony to explain what you are seeing and experiencing. But what happens when viewers forget that television is *mediated* experience? As you read the following essays, consider these questions:

1. How would you answer the question posed by Neil Postman: "What is T.V. News?"
2. How often do you watch television, listen to radio, or read a newspaper? How is each of these media different from the others? What kind of information do you get from each?
3. How much confidence do you have in the media? Do you generally believe what you see on television, hear on the radio, or read in the newspaper?
4. What effect do you think the media have on public opinion about events such as the 1990 Gulf War?
5. Have the media ever covered a subject or event that you know quite well? If so, how closely did this coverage match your own experience?

What Is News?

NEIL POSTMAN and STEVE POWERS

ALL THIS TALK about news — what is it? We turn to this question because unless a television viewer has considered it, he or she is in danger of too easily accepting someone else's definition — for example, a definition supplied by the news director of a television station; or, even worse, a definition imposed by important advertisers. The question, in any case, is not a simple one, and it is even possible that many journalists and advertisers have not thought deeply about it.

A simplistic definition of news can be drawn by paraphrasing Justice Oliver Wendell Holmes's famous definition of the law. The law, Holmes said, is what the courts say it is. Nothing more. Nothing less. In similar fashion, we might say that the news is what news directors and journalists say it is. In other words, when you turn on your television set to watch a network or local news show, whatever is on is, by definition, the news. But if we were to take that approach, on what basis would we say that we haven't been told enough? Or that a story that should have been covered wasn't? Or that too many stories of a certain type were included? Or that a reporter gave a flagrantly biased account?

If objections of this kind are raised by viewers, then they must have some conception of the news that the news show has not fulfilled. Most people, in fact, do have such a conception, although they are not always fully conscious of what it is. When people are asked "What is the news?," the most frequent answer given is that the news is "what happened that day." This is a rather silly answer since even those who give it can easily be made to see that an uncountable number of things happen during the course of a day, including what you had for breakfast, that could hardly be classified as news by any definition. In modifying their answer, most will add that the news is "important and interesting things that happened that day." This helps a little but leaves open the question of what is "important and interesting" and how that is decided. Embedded somewhere in one's understanding of the phrase "important and interesting events" is one's definition of "the news."

Of course, some people will say that the question of what is important and interesting is not in the least problematic. What the President says or does is important; wars are important, rebellions, employment figures, elections, appointments to the Supreme Court. Really? We doubt that even the President believes everything he says is important. (Let us take, for example, President Bush's remark that he doesn't like broccoli.) There are, as we write, more than forty wars and rebellions going on somewhere in the world. Not even *The New York Times*, which claims to be the "newspaper of public record," reports on all of them, or even most. Are elections important? Maybe. But we doubt you'd be interested in the election in Iowa's Third Congressional District — unless you happen to live there. Some readers will remember the famous comedy routine of the 2,000-Year-Old Man who was discovered in the imaginations of Carl Reiner and Mel Brooks. Upon being asked what he believed to be the greatest invention of humankind during his life span, the 2,000-Year-Old Man replied unhesitatingly, "Saran Wrap." Now, there is a great deal to be said for Saran Wrap. We suspect that in the long run it may prove more useful to the well-being of most of us than a number of inventions that are daily given widespread publicity in the news media. Yet it is fair to say that no one except its manufacturer knows the date of Saran Wrap's invention, or even cares much to know. Saran Wrap is not news. The color of Liz Taylor's wrap is. Or so some people believe.

On the day Marilyn Monroe committed suicide, so did many other people,   5
some of whose reasons may have been as engrossing as, and perhaps more significant than, Miss Monroe's. But we shall never know about these people or their reasons; the journalists at CBS or NBC or *The New York Times* simply took no notice of them. Several people, we are sure, also committed suicide on the very day in 1991 when the New York Giants won the Super Bowl. We shall never learn about these people either, however instructive or interesting their stories may have been.

What we are driving at is this: "Importance" is a judgment people make. Of course, there are some events — the assassination of a president, an earthquake, etc. — that have near-universal interest and consequences. But most news does not inhere in the event. An event *becomes* news. And it becomes news because it is selected for notice out of the buzzing, booming confusion around us. This may seem a fairly obvious point but keep in mind that many people believe that the news is always "out there," waiting to be gathered or collected. In fact, the news is more often *made* rather than gathered. And it is made on the basis of what the journalist thinks important or what the journalist thinks the audience thinks is important or interesting. It can get pretty complicated. Is a story about a killing in Northern Ireland more important than one about a killing in Morocco? The journalist might not think so, but the audience might. Which story will become the news? And once selected, what point of view and details are to be included? After all, once a journalist has chosen an event to be news, he or she must also choose what is worth seeing, what is worth neglecting, and what is worth remembering or forgetting. This is simply another way of saying that every news story is a reflection of the reporter who tells the story. The reporter's previous assumptions about what is "out there" edit what he or she thinks is there. For example, many journalists believe that what is called "the intifada" is newsworthy. Let us suppose that a fourteen-year-old Palestinian boy hurls a Molotov cocktail at two eighteen-year-old Israeli soldiers. The explosion knocks one of the soldiers down and damages his left eye. The other soldier, terrified, fires a shot at the Palestinian that kills him instantly. The injured soldier eventually loses the sight of his eye. What details should be included in reporting this event? Is the age of the Palestinian relevant? Are the ages of the Israeli soldiers relevant? Is the injury to the soldier relevant? Was the act of the Palestinian provoked by the mere presence of Israeli soldiers? Was the act therefore justified? Is the shooting justified? Is the state of mind of the shooter relevant?

The answers to all of these questions, as well as to other questions about the event, depend entirely on the point of view of the journalist. You might think this is an exaggeration, that reporters, irrespective of their assumptions, can at least get the facts straight. But what are "facts"? In A. J. Liebling's book *The Press,* he gives a classic example of the problematic nature of "facts." On the same day, some years ago, both the *Wall Street Journal* and the now-defunct *World Telegram and Sun* featured a story about the streets of Moscow. Here is what the *Wall Street Journal* reporter wrote:

> The streets of central Moscow are, as the guidebooks say, clean and neat; so is the famed subway. They are so because of an army of women with brooms, pans, and carts who thus earn their 35 rubles a month in lieu of "relief"; in all Moscow we never saw a mechanical street-sweeper.

Here is what the *World Telegram and Sun* reporter wrote:

> Four years ago [in Moscow] women by the hundreds swept big city streets. Now you rarely see more than a dozen. The streets are kept clean with giant brushing and sprinkling machines.

Well, which is it? Can a dozen women look like an army? Are there giant machines cleaning the streets of Moscow or are there not? How can two trained journalists see events so differently? Well, one of them worked for the *Wall Street Journal,* and when these stories were written, it was the policy of the *Journal* to highlight the contrast between the primitive Russian economy and the sophisticated American economy. (It still is.) Does this mean the reporter for the *Journal* was lying? We doubt it. Each of our senses is a remarkably astute censor. We see what we expect to see; often, we focus on what we are paid to see. And those who pay us to see usually expect us to accept their notions not only of what is important but of what are important details.

That fact poses some difficult problems for those of us trying to make sense of the news we are given. One of these problems is indicated by a proposal, made years ago, by the great French writer Albert Camus. Camus wished to establish "a control newspaper." The newspaper would come out one hour after all the others and would contain estimates of the percentage of truth in each of their stories. In Camus's words: "We'd have complete dossiers on the interests, policies, and idiosyncrasies of the owners. Then we'd have a dossier on every journalist in the world. The interests, prejudices, and quirks of the owner would equal Z. The prejudices, quirks, and private interests of the journalist Y. Z times Y would give you X, the probable amount of truth in the story" (quoted in *The Press* by A. J. Liebling, p. 22n).

Camus was either a reckless mathematician or else he simply neglected to say   10
why and how multiplying Z and Y would tell us what we need to know. (Why not add or divide them?) Nor did he discuss the problem of how to estimate the reliability of those doing the estimating. In any case, Camus died before he had a chance to publish such a newspaper, leaving each one of us to be our own "control center." Nonetheless, we can't help thinking how Camus's idea might be applied to television. Imagine how informative it would be if there were a five-minute television program that went on immediately after each television news

show. The host might say something like this: "To begin with, this station is owned by Gary Farnsworth, who is also the president of Bontel Limited, the principal stockholder of which is the Sultan of Bahrain. Bontel Limited owns three Japanese electronic companies, two oil companies, the entire country of Upper Volta, and the western part of Romania. The anchorman on the television show earns $800,000 a year; his portfolio includes holdings in a major computer firm. He has a bachelor's degree in journalism from the University of Arkansas but was a C+ student, has never taken a course in political science, and speaks no language other than English. Last year, he read only two books — a biography of Cary Grant and a book of popular psychology called *Why Am I So Wonderful?* The reporter who covered the story on Yugoslavia speaks Serbo-Croatian, has a degree in international relations, and has had a Neiman Fellowship at Harvard University."

We think this kind of information would be helpful to a viewer although not for the same reason Camus did. Such information would not give an estimate of the "truth probability" of stories but it would suggest possible patterns of influence reflected in the news. After all, what is important to a person whose boss owns several oil companies might not be important to a person who doesn't even have a boss, who is unemployed. Similarly, what a reporter who does not know the language of the people he or she reports on can see and understand will probably be different from the perceptions of another reporter who knows the language well.

What we are saying is that to answer the question "What is news?" a viewer must know something about the political beliefs and economic situation of those who provide the news. The viewer is then in a position to know why certain events are considered important by those in charge of television news and may compare those judgments with his or her own.

But here's another problem. As we have implied, even oil magnates and poorly prepared journalists do not consult, exclusively, their own interests in selecting the "truths" they will tell. Since they want people to watch their shows, they also try to determine what audiences think is important and interesting. There is, in fact, a point of view that argues against journalists imposing their own sense of significance on an audience. In this view, television news should consist only of those events that would interest the audience. The journalists must keep their own opinions to themselves. The response to this is that many viewers depend on journalists to advise them of what is important. Besides, even if journalists were mere followers of public interest, not all members of the audience agree on what they wish to know. For example, we do not happen to think that Liz Taylor's adventures in marriage were or are of any importance whatsoever to anyone but her and Michael Wilding, Nicky Hilton, Mike Todd, Eddie Fisher, Richard Burton, John Warner, Larry Fortensky, and, of course, Debbie Reynolds and Sybil Burton. Obviously, most people don't agree, which is why an announcement of her intention to marry again is featured on every television news show. What's our point? A viewer must not only know what he or she thinks is significant but what others believe is significant as well.

It is a matter to be seriously considered. You may conclude, for example, that other people do not have a profound conception of what is significant. You may even be contemptuous of the taste or interests of others. On the other hand, you may fully share the sense of significance held by a majority of people. It is not our purpose here to instruct you or anyone else in what is to be regarded as a significant event. We are saying that in considering the question "What is news?" a viewer must always take into account his or her relationship to a larger audience. Television is a mass medium, which means that a television news show is not intended for you alone. It is public communication, and the viewer needs to have some knowledge and opinions about "the public." It is a common complaint of individuals that television news rarely includes stories about some special interest. We know a man, for example, who emigrated from Switzerland thirty years ago. He is an American citizen but retains a lively interest in his native land. "Why," he asked us, "are there never any stories about Switzerland?" "Because," we had to reply, "no one but you and a few others have any interest in Switzerland." "That's too bad," he replied. "Switzerland is an interesting country." We agree. But most Americans have not been in Switzerland, probably believe not much happens in Switzerland, do not have many relatives in Switzerland, and would much rather know about what some English lord has to say about the world's economy than what a Swiss banker thinks. Maybe they are right, maybe not. Judging the public mind is always risky.

And this leads to another difficulty in answering the question "What is news?" Some might agree with us that Liz Taylor's adventures in marriage do not constitute significant events but that they ought to be included in a news show precisely for that reason. Her experiences, they may say, are amusing or diverting, certainly engrossing. In other words, the purpose of news should be to give people pleasure, at least to the extent that it takes their minds off their own troubles. We have heard people say that getting through the day is difficult enough, filled with tension, anxiety, and often disappointment. When they turn on the news, they want relief, not aggravation. It is also said that whether entertaining or not, stories about the lives of celebrities should be included because they are instructive; they reveal a great deal about our society — its mores, values, ideals. Mark Twain once remarked that news is history in its first and best form. The American poet Ezra Pound added an interesting idea to that. He defined literature as news that *stays* news. Among other things, Pound meant that the staff of literature originates not in stories about the World Bank or an armistice agreement but in those simple, repeatable tales that reflect the pain, confusion, or exaltations that are constant in human experience, and touch us at the deepest levels. For example, consider the death of Michael Landon. Who was Michael Landon to you, or you to Michael Landon that you should have been told so much about him when he died? Here is a possible answer: Michael Landon was rich, decent, handsome, young, and successful. Suddenly, very nearly without warning, he was struck down at the height of his powers and fame. Why? What are we to make of it? Why him? It is like some Old Testament parable; these questions were raised five thousand years ago and we still raise them today. It is the kind of story that *stays* news, and that is why it must be given prominence. Or so some people believe.

What about the kind of news that doesn't stay news, that is neither the stuff of history nor literature — the fires, rapes, and murders that are daily featured on local television news? Who has decided that they are important, and why? One cynical answer is that they are there because viewers take comfort in the realization that *they* have escaped disaster. At least for that day. It doesn't matter who in particular was murdered; the viewer wasn't. We tune in to find out how lucky we are, and go to sleep with the pleasure of knowing that we have survived. A somewhat different answer goes this way: it is the task of the news story to provide a daily accounting of the progress of society. This can be done in many ways, some of them abstract (for example, a report on the state of unemployment), some of them concrete (for example, reports on particularly gruesome murders). These reports, especially those of a concrete nature, are the daily facts from which the audience is expected to draw appropriate conclusions about the question "What kind of society am I a member of?" Studies conducted by Professor George Gerbner and his associates at the University of Pennsylvania have shown that people who are heavy television viewers, including viewers of television news shows, believe their communities are much more dangerous than do light television viewers. Television news, in other words, tends to frighten people. The question is, "Ought they to be frightened?," which is to ask, "Is the news an accurate portrayal of where we are as a society?" Which leads to another question, "Is it possible for daily news to give such a picture?" Many journalists believe it is possible. Some are skeptical. The early-twentieth-century journalist Lincoln Steffens proved that he could create a "crime wave" anytime he wanted by simply writing about all the crimes that normally occur in a large city during the course of a month. He could also end the crime wave by not writing about them. If crime waves can be "manufactured" by journalists, then how accurate are news shows in depicting the condition of a society? Besides, murders, rapes, and fires (even unemployment figures) are not the only way to assess the progress (or regress) of a society. Why are there so few television stories about symphonies that have been composed, novels written, scientific problems solved, and a thousand other creative acts that occur during the course of a month? Were television news to be filled with these events, we would not be frightened. We would, in fact, be inspired, optimistic, cheerful.

One answer is as follows: These events make poor television news because there is so little to show about them. In the judgment of most editors, people *watch* television. And what they are interested in watching are exciting, intriguing, even exotic pictures. Suppose a scientist has developed a new theory about how to measure with more exactitude the speed with which heavenly objects are moving away from the earth. It is difficult to televise a theory, especially if it involves complex mathematics. You can show the scientist talking about his theory but that would not make for good television and too much of it would drive viewers to other stations. In any case, the news show could only give the scientist twenty seconds of air time because time is an important commodity. Newspapers and magazines sell space, which is not without its limitations for a commercial enterprise. But space can be expanded. Television sells time, and time cannot be expanded. This means that whatever else is neglected, commercials cannot be. Which leads to another possible answer to the question "What is news?" News, we might say, may be history in its first and best form, or the stuff of literature, or a record of the condition of a society, or the expression of the passions of a public, or the prejudices of journalists. It may be all of these things, but in its worst form it can also be mainly a "filler," a "come-on" to keep the viewer's attention until the commercials come. Certain producers have learned that by pandering to the audience, by eschewing solid news and replacing it with leering sensationalism, they can subvert the news by presenting a "television commercial show" that is interrupted by news.

All of which leads us to reiterate, first, that there are no simple answers to the question "What is news?" and, second, that it is not our purpose to tell you what you ought to believe about the question. The purpose of this chapter is to arouse your interest in thinking *about* the question. Your answers are to be found by knowing what you feel is significant and how your sense of the significant conforms with or departs from that of others, including broadcasters, their bosses, and their audiences. Answers are to be found in your ideas about the purposes of public communication, and in your judgment of the kind of society you live in and wish to live in. We cannot provide answers to these questions. But you also need to know something about the problems, limitations, traditions, motivations, and, yes, even the delusions of the television news industry. That's where we can help you to know how to watch a television news show.

Portions of the Gulf War Were Brought to You by . . . the Folks at Hill and Knowlton

MORGAN STRONG

B Y NOW, it is well known that some portions of the Persian Gulf war effort were stage-managed in an effort to rally public opinion for military action against Iraq. The two leading television newsmagazines, ABC's *20/20* and CBS's *60 Minutes,* devoted segments last month to the fact that an emotional appeal in 1990 before a Congressional caucus hearing, supposedly by an anonymous Kuwaiti refugee girl called Nayirah, was, in fact, delivered by the daughter of Kuwait's ambassador to the U.S. Both stories followed a *New York Times* op-ed piece that exposed Nayirah's true identity, by John R. MacArthur, publisher of *Harper's Magazine.*

Further, it was revealed that the public-relations firm of Hill and Knowlton, headed at the time by Craig Fuller, former chief of staff to George Bush when he was Vice President, helped to package and rehearse the young woman's appearance on behalf of their client, Citizens for a Free Kuwait, an exile organization primarily funded by the Emir of Kuwait. Nayirah's testimony was that Iraqi soldiers had stormed hospitals and torn newborn babies from their incubators, leaving them to die. Her story, which received wide network coverage — and was invoked on numerous occasions by President Bush — had, in fact, been rehearsed before video cameras by Hill and Knowlton. But according to Kuwaiti doctors interviewed by *20/20* and *60 Minutes,* no such incident had occurred.

If this had been the only occurrence of packaged war reporting broadcast in the heat of war hysteria, it might be excusable. But what I found during my long stint in Saudi Arabia (I was a consultant for both PBS's *Frontline* and England's Thames Television) was a far more systematic manipulation of news by the PR firm than is generally known:

1. Following the August 1990 invasion of Kuwait by Iraq, refugees with stories about conditions in their country were selected and coached by Hill and Knowlton. Those with the most compelling tales — and the ones most in keeping with the agenda of Hill and Knowlton's client — were made available to news organizations, thus limiting journalists' ability to independently assess claims of brutalities. Indeed, the PR firm's operatives were given free rein to travel unescorted throughout Saudi Arabia, while journalists were severely restricted.

2. Hill and Knowlton also was the source for a large number of the amateur videos shot inside Kuwait and smuggled out. The videos were collected, screened and edited at the PR firm's TV studios in the Saudi capital, Riyadh, and in the coastal city of Dharan. The packaged videotapes were then distributed free of charge to the networks, ostensibly by Citizens for a Free Kuwait. In the U.S., Hill and Knowlton also distributed the tapes to affiliated and independent stations.

3. A second woman who was identified as simply another Kuwaiti refugee, and who made an appearance before a widely televised session of the UN Security Council on Nov. 27, 1990, turned out to be a close relative of a senior Kuwaiti official. The woman, Fatima Fahed, came before the world body as it was debating the use of force to oust the Iraqis from Kuwait. She gave harrowing details of Iraqi atrocities inside her country.

What was not reported is that Fahed was, in fact, the wife of Sulaiman Al-Mutawa, Kuwait's minister of planning, and herself a well-known TV personality in Kuwait. Surprised that a high-profile Kuwaiti could be labeled, and accepted, as just another "refugee," I asked one of the leaders of Citizens for a Free Kuwait, Fawzi Al-Sultan, why Fahed had been chosen to speak to the UN. "Because of her professional experience," he said, "she is more believable."

But, like the story related by Nayirah, Fahed's testimony was not necessarily true. In testifying to the UN, she implied that her information was firsthand. "Such stories . . . I personally have experienced," she said. But when I had interviewed her in Jedda, Saudi Arabia, *before* her UN appearance, she told me that she had *no* firsthand knowledge of the events she was describing. Some weeks later, in advance of her UN testimony, she and other witnesses were coached —

5

including rehearsals, wardrobe and prepared scripts — extensively by employees of Hill and Knowlton.

4. A tape from inside Kuwait, supplied to journalists by the PR firm before the U.S.-led invasion, purported to show peaceful Kuwaiti demonstrators being fired upon by the occupying Iraqi troops.

But, on the ground in Saudi Arabia, I managed to interview a Kuwaiti refu-   10
gee present at the demonstration whose story was quite different. The man, a Kuwaiti policeman, said that no demonstrators were injured, and that gunshots captured on tape were, in fact, those of Iraqi troops firing on nearby resistance fighters, who had fired first at the Iraqis. When I asked him to appear on camera and tell the true story, he refused. "I do not want to harm the resistance," he said.

None of this is to suggest that the Iraqis did not perpetrate atrocities while occupying Kuwait, nor does it underestimate the difficulties facing the media in obtaining original material under censorship conditions. However, these examples are but a few of the incidents of outright misinformation that found their way onto the network news. It is an inescapable fact that much of what Americans saw on their news broadcasts, especially leading up to the Allied offensive against Iraqi-occupied Kuwait, was in large measure the contrivance of a public-relations firm.

The Media's Image of Arabs

JACK G. SHAHEEN

A MERICA'S BOGYMAN is the Arab. Until the nightly news brought us TV   1
pictures of Palestinian boys being punched and beaten, almost all portraits of Arabs seen in America were dangerously threatening. Arabs were either billionaires or bombers — rarely victims. They were hardly ever seen as ordinary people practicing law, driving taxis, singing lullabies or healing the sick. Though TV news may portray them more sympathetically now, the absence of positive media images nurtures suspicion and stereotype. As an Arab-American, I have found that ugly caricatures have had an enduring impact on my family.

I was sheltered from prejudicial portraits at first. My parents came from Lebanon in the 1920s; they met and married in America. Our home in the steel city of Clairton, Pa., was a center for ethnic sharing — black, white, Jew and gentile. There was only one major source of media images then, at the State movie theater where I was lucky enough to get a part-time job as an usher. But in the late 1940s, Westerns and war movies were popular, not Middle Eastern dramas. Memories of World War II were fresh, and the screen heavies were the Japanese and the Germans. True to the cliché of the times, the only good Indian was a dead Indian. But when I mimicked or mocked the bad guys, my mother cautioned me. She explained that stereotypes blur our vision and corrupt the imagination. "Have compassion for all people, Jackie," she said. "This way, you'll learn to experience the joy of accepting people as they are, and not as they appear in films. Stereotypes hurt."

Mother was right. I can remember the Saturday afternoon when my son, Michael, who was seven, and my daughter, Michele, six, suddenly called out: "Daddy, Daddy, they've got some bad Arabs on TV." They were watching that great American morality play, TV wrestling. Akbar the Great, who liked to hear the cracking of bones, and Abdullah the Butcher, a dirty fighter who liked to inflict pain, were pinning their foes with "camel locks." From that day on, I knew I had to try to neutralize the media caricatures.

It hasn't been easy. With my children, I have watched animated heroes Heckle and Jeckle pull the rug from under "Ali Boo-Boo, the Desert Rat," and Laverne and Shirley stop "Sheik Ha-Mean-Ie" from conquering "the U.S. and the world." I have read comic books like the *Fantastic Four* and *G.I. Combat* whose characters have sketched Arabs as "low-lifes" and "human hyenas." Negative stereotypes were everywhere. A dictionary informed my youngsters that an Arab is a "vagabond, drifter, hobo and vagrant." Whatever happened, my wife wondered, to Aladdin's good genie?

To a child, the world is simple: good versus evil. But my children and others   5
with Arab roots grew up without ever having seen a humane Arab on the silver screen, someone to pattern their lives after. Is it easier for a camel to go through the eye of a needle than for a screen Arab to appear as a genuine human being?

Hollywood producers must have an instant Ali Baba kit that contains scimitars, veils, sunglasses and such Arab clothing as *chadors* and *kufiyahs.* In the mythical "Ay-rabland," oil wells, tents, mosques, goats and shepherds prevail. Between the sand dunes, the camera focuses on a mock-up of a palace from "Arabian Nights" — or a military air base. Recent movies suggest that Americans are at war with Arabs, forgetting the fact that out of 32 Arab nations, America is friendly with 19 of them. And in *Wanted Dead or Alive,* a movie that starred Gene Simmons, the leader of the rock group Kiss, the war comes home when an Arab terrorist comes to the United States dressed as a rabbi and, among other things, conspires with Arab-Americans to poison the people of Los Angeles. The movie was released last year.

The Arab remains American culture's favorite whipping boy. In his memoirs, Terrel Bell, Ronald Reagan's first secretary of education, writes about an "apparent bias among mid-level, right-wing staffers at the White House" who dismissed Arabs as "sand niggers." Sadly, the racial slurs continue. At a recent teacher's conference, I met a woman from Sioux Falls, S.D., who told me about the persistence of discrimination. She was in the process of adopting a baby when an agency staffer warned her that the infant had a problem. When she asked whether the child was mentally ill, or physically handicapped, there was silence. Finally, the worker said: "The baby is Jordanian."

To me, the Arab demon of today is much like the Jewish demon of yesterday.

We deplore the false portrait of Jews as a swarthy menace. Yet a similar portrait has been accepted and transferred to another group of Semites — the Arabs. Print and broadcast journalists have started to challenge this stereotype. They are now revealing more humane images of Palestinian Arabs, a people who traditionally suffered from the myth that Palestinian equals terrorist. Others could follow that lead and retire the stereotypical Arab to a media Valhalla.

It would be a step in the right direction if movie and TV producers developed characters modeled after real-life Arab-Americans. We could then see a White House correspondent like Helen Thomas, whose father came from Lebanon, in *The Golden Girls*, a heart surgeon patterned after Dr. Michael DeBakey on *St. Elsewhere*, or a Syrian-American playing tournament chess like Yasser Seirawan, the Seattle grandmaster.

Politicians, too, should speak out against the cardboard caricatures. They should refer to Arabs as friends, not just as moderates. And religious leaders could state that Islam like Christianity and Judaism maintains that all mankind is one family in the care of God. When all imagemakers rightfully begin to treat Arabs and all other minorities with respect and dignity, we may begin to unlearn our prejudices.

Chapter 8

Arguing Claims about Causality

Types of Causes

Causality refers to a relationship between events in which an earlier event somehow causes or influences a later event or in which a later event somehow explains an earlier one. It is a statement about existence to say "The king died and then the queen died." The later event in this sequence merely follows the earlier one in time. But it is a statement about causality to say "The king died and so the queen died." This statement asserts that the death of the king (the earlier event) caused or influenced the death of the queen (the later event). Like questions about existence, questions about causality can focus on the past, present, or future: Why did this happen? Why is it happening now? Why will this happen again?

Unlike questions about existence, which are about whether an event or phenomenon occurred or about the nature of an event or phenomenon, questions about causality are about the relationship between two or more events or phenomena and between causes and effects. Did one cause the other? Did the second result from the first? Are they in some way connected? Here are sample questions about causality:

What causes homosexuality?

How does work affect the family?

What are the causes of poverty?

How can famine in Africa be reduced?

How will dismantling apartheid affect South Africa's future?

What role does Christianity play in Central America?

What are the causes of terrorism?

279

Complex decisions may involve questions of existence and causality. In a murder case the jury may need to consider how a killing occurred (causality), whether the killing was premeditated (existence), what motivated the killing (causality), and whether the accused killed the victim (existence). Understanding the differences between these two kinds of questions about experience can help us to solve a lot of misunderstandings and negotiate some of the disagreements about experience that inevitably arise in community.

A number of relationships are included under the term "causality":

- A *sufficient cause* describes a relationship in which, under normal conditions, one event or phenomenon (the sufficient cause) is always followed by a second: Something dropped from a height falls to the ground. Water that reaches 100 degrees celsius begins to boil.

- A *necessary cause* is an event or phenomenon that must exist for a second to occur but that is not sufficient in itself to cause the second. Heat, fuel, and oxygen are all necessary for a fire to burn, but no one of these can cause a fire by itself. A combination of necessary causes can become a sufficient cause. The right combination of heat, fuel, and oxygen will cause a fire to start all by itself.

- A *constraint* is a necessary element that, when removed, allows an event to occur. For instance, the relatively moderate communist government of Yugoslavia maintained peace amid ethnic tension for years. When the communists lost power, the constraint on ethnic violence was removed, and war erupted in Bosnia. The government didn't cause the ethnic unrest or violence. Instead, the communist government constrained the forces that resulted in violence when that constraint was removed.

- A *contributing cause* is something that may enable or influence a second event or phenomenon but that is not necessary or sufficient to cause the second. Snow on a road may enable an automobile accident, but snow does not cause the accident by itself. Nor is it a necessary condition for auto accidents; accidents occur without the presence of snow.

- A *correlation* is a relationship between two events or phenomena that occur together without it being clear whether one caused the other or whether both resulted from a third cause. For instance, philosophy majors have a higher rate of acceptance into law school than students with other undergraduate majors. The two phenomena are correlated. But does studying philosophy better prepare students for law school, or are students who choose to study philosophy naturally attuned to what law schools look for? Another correlation is between nearsightedness (the ability to see near objects better than distant objects) and reading ability. But does nearsightedness encourage reading (a preference for close tasks), or does excessive reading lead to nearsightedness? (Just notice how many English teachers wear glasses.)

- An *agent* is an individual who takes purposeful action to bring about a change: a person walking across a room to turn off a television, eating, throwing a baseball, playing the piano; a dog begging for food; a cat brushing up against a person's leg. All of these examples describe purposeful motion, motion with an intention to change some event or phenomenon.

- An *instrument* or *agency* is the means by which an agent can cause something to happen. The National Rifle Association makes this distinction in its famous line "Guns don't kill people. People kill people." People are the necessary agents for firing guns to kill others. A gun is the instrument or agency.
- A *logical cause* justifies or explains a situation. The "reason" in an argument that justifies a claim is a logical cause: You can't have any candy because you haven't eaten your dinner (the assumption is that you can only have candy after dinner).
- A *purpose* is a cause that follows what it causes, with the later event or phenomenon serving as the purpose of the earlier one: If you go to the refrigerator to get something to eat, you could think of yourself as an agent causing the motion that takes you to the refrigerator, but you could also think of your purpose or intention as a cause (getting something to satisfy your hunger).

The following terms signal a statement about causality:

X has the effect of

X facilitates

X leads to

X influences

X is a factor in

X is linked to

because of X

X deters

as a result of X

X increases the likelihood that

X determines

X contributes to

X causes

Arguing about Causality

Arguing about causality is always a tricky affair. Causes are rarely self-evident. The fact that one event or phenomenon follows another does not mean that the first caused the second. Such an assumption is a *post hoc* fallacy (see Chapter 5), from the Latin *post hoc, ergo propter hoc* ("after this, therefore because of this"). Many superstitions arise from this fallacy. A black cat crosses your path on your way to school, and later that day you fail your chemistry test. Did the black cat bring you bad luck, or are there other possible causes? Experience is so complex and chaotic that the numbers of factors involved in a single event are usually multiple and changing. Rarely is causality as neat as one pool ball striking another and causing it to move.

Although knowledge of causal relationships is rarely absolute, some causal arguments are more believable or persuasive than others. Causal statements are based on probability and are more or less convincing depending on the reasons used to support them. Causal statements are usually most convincing when the cause and the effect are close to one another in time and space, when the event or phenomenon can be observed repeatedly, when the cause can be isolated by experiment, when there is a clear explanation of how one event or phenomenon leads to another, or when one can reason by analogy from a similar situation where the causes are known. Simpler explanations are usually more convincing than more complicated explanations (though complicated ones may in fact be true); such explanations are "models" or "theories" of the mechanism for the causal relationship.

To summarize, here are the most common ways to argue for a causal relationship:

1. Provide a model or theory to explain the mechanism for causation.
2. Use inductive methods, such as scientific experiments or statistical research, to show a probable link.
3. Use an analogous situation, a precedent or similar case, in which the causes are known.

▦ ▦ PROVIDING A MODEL OR THEORY TO EXPLAIN CAUSALITY

A model or a theory is a detailed explanation of how something works. For instance, a car's engine is a complex series of causes and effects designed to be controlled by a human agent (the driver). The engineer's design for the engine is the model or theory describing how this complex system works. The theory of evolution describes an extremely complex system of causes and effects to explain changes in life forms over time. Whenever you plan something or act with purpose, you are using a model or theory to predict the possible outcomes of your actions. With many human actions, however, the model for action is so internalized as to be automatic. For example, I don't have to plan how to get from the couch to the cupboard to find something to eat, but my one-year-old son develops all kinds of plans for getting to the cupboard. His actions are based on models and theories.

Sometimes there can be more than one theory to explain the causes of the same event. For instance, in a court trial, lawyers may disagree about what brought about the defendant's actions. The prosecution might argue that the defendant was an agent who acted intentionally and should therefore be considered guilty. The defense might argue that the defendant is legally insane and that the defendant's mental state caused the criminal behavior. This kind of debate requires some kind of model or theory about the human mind and the relationship between the mind and behavior. It also requires theories about action, intention, and guilt. The debate, in this case, might focus on the validity of the theories or else on the applicability of the theories to the defendant.

The debate surrounding the theory of organic evolution provides another example of a disagreement about models and theories. Life on earth is constantly changing, and it had to originate somewhere. Evolutionary biologists try to develop models that will explain the creation of the earth according to the standards of scientific proof. Some Christian theologians try to explain the origin of the earth by referring to the Bible as an authoritative text, using models that meet the standards of religious or spiritual truth. These models come into conflict because scientists and theologians do not agree on a common set of criteria for evaluating truth.

What happens when scientists themselves disagree about the models or theories used to explain causality? Generally, scientists favor a theory that explains phenomena in the most comprehensive way. For two theories that both explain equally well, scientists tend to favor the simpler one.

USING INDUCTIVE METHODS

A *laboratory experiment* recreates direct experience in a controlled environment. Its validity relies on the similarity between the controlled environment and the event or phenomenon being recreated and on the ability of the scientists conducting the experiment to observe and record data. Experiments often use instruments to provide data not accessible to the unaided physical senses, data that must be interpreted by the scientists. Accurate observation and interpretation require precise language as well. The strength of an experiment lies in its ability to repeat conditions that will verify observations. Similar conditions should lead to similar results and conclusions. A formal experiment has a control group and a variable group. The control and the variable group should be exactly the same except for those elements that are the object of study.

USING AN ANALOGY, PRECEDENT, OR SIMILAR CASE

A third way to argue for a causal relationship to identify a precedent or similar case in which the causes are known and then make an analogy between that case and another where the causes are less certain. Arguing by analogy is difficult because analogies depend on similarities and any analogy contains some dissimilarities. Because there are always differences between two similar cases, the strength of an analogy depends upon the similarities being more important than those differences. If the audience does not accept the assumption that the two cases are similar, the writer must support the analogy. One way to do so is to point out a number of specific similarities, based on the assumption that the two cases will be similar in other ways as well. Another way to support an analogy is to show that the two cases are similar in essential ways, even though they may be different in a number of other ways. The writer then has the burden of showing why these similarities are essential.

The danger in using an analogy is making a *false comparison*. A false comparison is a logical fallacy in which an analogy is made between two cases that are really more different than similar or that are different in essential ways. To test the similarities between two cases, try the following. First of all, list the features of each of the cases you are comparing. Then identify the features that they share. Finally, determine whether the two cases are more similar or different in terms of the features they share. For instance, many writers have compared the war in Bosnia to the Vietnam War. The first step in testing this comparison is to list the features of the two wars. In what ways can a modern war be described? Here are some possibilities: level of U.S. involvement, level of United Nations involvement, types of weapons and tactics used, risk to U.S. security, risks to European security, number of civilian casualties, ideological differences, involvement of other countries. The next step is to compare the two wars according to the features listed. Is the level of U.S. involvement in Bosnia and Vietnam similar or different? Are the weapons and tactics similar or different? Is the risk to U.S. security similar or different? After asking about similarity or difference for each of the features, you can evaluate the similarities and differences to determine whether the war in Bosnia and the war in Vietnam are more similar than different or are similar in essential ways. If the audience accepts the similarities between the two wars, one could then argue that the results of U.S. involvement in Bosnia would be similar to the results of U.S. involvement in Vietnam.

Applying the Principles

▓ ▓ HOW SCIENTIFIC KNOWLEDGE IS MADE

As a student, I assumed that scientific knowledge was somehow more real and reliable than other forms of knowledge. To me, science was "hard" and "exact." It dealt with things that could be counted and that obeyed natural laws and principles. But then my only experience with science and scientists had been in classrooms, through textbooks, or through the representation of science in the media. My textbooks presented scientific knowledge as a collection of facts and theories that I should master, not question or dispute. These books also described the scientific method as a fairly straight-forward process: A scientist forms a hypothesis based on a theory or model, designs an experiment to test that hypothesis, conducts that experiment, and analyzes the results. I had heard that scientists often worked together on projects and tried to replicate and evaluate one another's results. But is science always exact? Do scientists always follow the scientific method as it is described in textbooks? The next set of readings challenges the idea that the pursuit of scientific knowledge is always objective, orderly, and exact. The first comes from Thomas Kuhn's significant book on the history of science, *The Structure of Scientific Revolutions*. Kuhn examines why many scientific discoveries were not accepted by the scientists of the time. The second essay comes from *Golem: What Everyone Should Know About Science* by Harry Collins and Trevor Pinch. These authors provide a series of cases showing that scientists do not always follow the scientific method and that economic concerns, personal prejudices and jealousies, and debates and disagreements can affect how scientific knowledge is made. As you read these essays, consider the following questions:

1. How would you define "science"? Can what counts as science differ from one community to another?
2. How reliable is scientific knowledge? How is scientific knowledge evaluated?
3. How do you think scientific knowledge is made?
4. How is science presented in your classrooms and textbooks? How is science presented in the media?
5. What role do argumentation and persuasion play in the making of scientific knowledge?

The Historical Structure of Scientific Discovery

THOMAS KUHN

M Y OBJECT IN THIS ARTICLE is to isolate and illuminate one small part of what I take to be a continuing historiographic revolution in the study of science. The structure of scientific discovery is my particular topic, and I can best approach it by pointing out that the subject itself may well seem extraordinarily odd. Both scientists and, until quite recently, historians have ordinarily viewed discovery as the sort of event which, though it may have preconditions and surely has consequences, is itself without internal structure. Rather than being seen as a complex development extended both in space and time, discovering something has usually seemed to be a unitary event, one which, like seeing something, happens to an individual at a specifiable time and place.

This view of the nature of discovery has, I suspect, deep roots in the nature of the scientific community. One of the few historical elements recurrent in the textbooks from which the prospective scientist learns his field is the attribution of particular natural phenomena to the historical personages who first discovered them. As a result of this and other aspects of their training, discovery becomes for many scientists an important goal. To make a discovery is to achieve one of the closest approximations to a property right that the scientific career affords. Professional prestige is often closely associated with these acquisitions. Small wonder, then, that acrimonious disputes about priority and independence in discovery have often marred the normally placid tenor of scientific communication. Even less wonder that many historians of science have seen the individual discovery as an appropriate unit with which to measure scientific progress and have devoted much time and skill to determining what man made which discovery at what point in time. If the study of discovery has a surprise to offer, it is only that, despite the immense energy and ingenuity expended upon it, neither polemic nor painstaking scholarship has often succeeded in pinpointing the time and place at which a given discovery could properly be said to have "been made."

That failure, both of argument and of research, suggests the thesis that I now wish to develop. Many scientific discoveries, particularly the most interesting and important, are not the sort of event about which the questions "Where?" and, more particularly, "When?" can appropriately be asked. Even if all conceivable data were at hand, those questions would not regularly possess answers. That we are persistently driven to ask them nonetheless is symptomatic of a fundamental inappropriateness in our image of discovery. That inappropriateness is here my main concern, but I approach it by considering first the historical problem presented by the attempt to date and to place a major class of fundamental discoveries.

The troublesome class consists of those discoveries — including oxygen, the electric current, X rays, and the electron — which could not be predicted from accepted theory in advance and which therefore caught the assembled profession by surprise. That kind of discovery will shortly be my exclusive concern, but it will help first to note that there is another sort and one which presents very few of the same problems. Into this second class of discoveries fall the neutrino, radio waves, and the elements which filled empty places in the periodic table. The existence of all these objects had been predicted from theory before they were discovered, and the men who made the discoveries therefore knew from the start what to look for. That foreknowledge did not make their task less demanding or less interesting, but it did provide criteria which told them when their goal had been reached. As a result, there have been few priority debates over discoveries of this second sort, and only a paucity of data can prevent the historian from ascribing them to a particular time and place. Those facts help to isolate the difficulties we encounter as we return to the troublesome discoveries of the first class. In the cases that most concern us here there are no benchmarks to inform either the scientist or the historian when the job of discovery has been done.

As an illustration of this fundamental problem and its consequences, consider first the discovery of oxygen. Because it has repeatedly been studied, often with exemplary care and skill, that discovery is unlikely to offer any purely factual

5

surprises. Therefore it is particularly well suited to clarify points of principle. At least three scientists — Carl Scheele, Joseph Priestley, and Antoine Lavoisier — have a legitimate claim to this discovery, and polemicists have occasionally entered the same claim for Pierre Bayen. Scheele's work, though it was almost certainly completed before the relevant researches of Priestley and Lavoisier, was not made public until their work was well known. Therefore it had no apparent causal role, and I shall simplify my story by omitting it. Instead, I pick up the main route to the discovery of oxygen with the work of Bayen, who, sometime before March 1774, discovered that red precipitate of mercury (HgO) could, by heating, be made to yield a gas. That aeriform product Bayen identified as fixed air (CO_2), a substance made familiar to most pneumatic chemists by the earlier work of Joseph Black. A variety of other substances were known to yield the same gas.

At the beginning of August 1774, a few months after Bayen's work had appeared, Joseph Priestley repeated the experiment, though probably independently. Priestley, however, observed that the gaseous product would support combustion and therefore changed the identification. For him the gas obtained on heating red precipitate was nitrous air (N_2O), a substance that he had himself discovered more than two years before. Later in the same month Priestley made a trip to Paris and there informed Lavoisier of the new reaction. The latter repeated the experiment once more, both in November 1774 and in February 1775. But, because he used tests somewhat more elaborate than Priestley's, Lavoisier again changed the identification. For him, as of May 1775, the gas released by red precipitate was neither fixed air nor nitrous air. Instead, it was "[atmospheric] air itself entire without alteration . . . even to the point that . . . it comes out more pure." Meanwhile, however, Priestley had also been at work, and, before the beginning of March 1775, he, too, had concluded that the gas must be "common air." Until this point all of the men who had produced a gas from red precipitate of mercury had identified it with some previously known species.

The remainder of this story of discovery is briefly told. During March 1775 Priestley discovered that his gas was in several respects very much "better" than common air, and he therefore reidentified the gas once more, this time calling it "dephlogisticated air," that is, atmospheric air deprived of its normal complement of phlogiston. This conclusion Priestley published in the *Philosophical Transactions*, and it was apparently that publication which led Lavoisier to reexamine his own results. The reexamination began during February 1776 and within a year had led Lavoisier to the conclusion that the gas was actually a separable component of the atmospheric air which both he and Priestley had previously thought of as homogeneous. With this point reached, with the gas recognized as an irreducibly distinct species, we may conclude that the discovery of oxygen had been completed.

But to return to my initial question, when shall we say that oxygen was discovered and what criteria shall be used in answering that question? If discovering oxygen is simply holding an impure sample in one's hands, then the gas had been "discovered" in antiquity by the first man who ever bottled atmospheric air. Undoubtedly, for an experimental criterion, we must at least require a relatively pure sample like that obtained by Priestley in August 1774. But during 1774 Priestley was unaware that he had discovered anything except a new way to produce a relatively familiar species. Throughout that year his "discovery" is scarcely distinguishable from the one made earlier by Bayen, and neither case is quite distinct from that of the Reverend Stephen Hales, who had obtained the same gas more than forty years before. Apparently to discover something one must also be aware of the discovery and know as well what it is that one has discovered.

But, that being the case, how much must one know? Had Priestley come close enough when he identified the gas as nitrous air? If not, was either he or Lavoisier significantly closer when he changed the identification to common air? And what are we to say about Priestley's next identification, the one made in March 1775? Dephlogisticated air is still not oxygen or even, for the phlogistic chemist, a quite unexpected sort of gas. Rather it is a particularly pure atmospheric air. Presumably, then, we wait for Lavoisier's work in 1776 and 1777, work which led him not merely to isolate the gas but to see what it was. Yet even that decision can be questioned, for in 1777 and to the end of his life Lavoisier insisted that oxygen was an atomic "principle of acidity" and that oxygen *gas* was formed only when that "principle" united with caloric, the matter of heat. Shall we therefore say that oxygen had not yet been discovered in 1777? Some may be tempted to do so. But the principle of acidity was not banished from chemistry until after 1810 and caloric lingered on until the 1860s. Oxygen had, however, become a standard chemical substance long before either of those dates. Furthermore, what is perhaps the key point, it would probably have gained that status on the basis of Priestley's work alone without benefit of Lavoisier's still partial reinterpretation.

I conclude that we need a new vocabulary and new concepts for analyzing 10
events like the discovery of oxygen. Though undoubtedly correct, the sentence "Oxygen was discovered" misleads by suggesting that discovering something is a single simple act unequivocally attributable, if only we knew enough, to an individual and an instant in time. When the discovery is unexpected, however, the latter attribution is always impossible and the former often is as well. Ignoring Scheele, we can, for example, safely say that oxygen had not been discovered before 1774; probably we would also insist that it had been discovered by 1774; probably we would also insist that it had been discovered by 1777 or shortly thereafter. But within those limits any attempt to date the discovery or to attribute it to an individual must inevitably be arbitrary. Furthermore, it must be arbitrary just because discovering a new sort of phenomenon is necessarily a complex process which involves recognizing both *that* something is and *what* it is. Observation and conceptualization, fact and the assimilation of fact to theory, are inseparably linked in the discovery of scientific novelty. Inevitably, that process extends over time and may often involve a number of people. Only for discoveries in my second category — those whose nature is known in advance — can discovering *that* and discovering *what* occur together and in an instant.

Two last, simpler, and far briefer examples will simultaneously show how typical the case of oxygen is and also prepare the way for a somewhat more precise conclusion. On the night of 13 March 1781, the astronomer William Herschel made the following entry in his journal: "In the quartile near Zeta Tauri . . . is a curious either nebulous star or perhaps a comet." That entry is generally said to record the discovery of the planet Uranus, but it cannot quite have done that. Between 1690 and Herschel's observation in 1781 the same object had been seen and recorded at least seventeen times by men who took it to be a star. Herschel differed from them only in supposing that, because in his telescope it appeared especially large, it might actually be a *comet!* Two additional observations on 17 and 19 March confirmed that suspicion by showing that the object he had observed moved among the stars. As a result, astronomers throughout Europe were informed of the discovery, and the mathematicians among them began to compute the new comet's orbit. Only several months later, after all those attempts had repeatedly failed to square with observation, did the astronomer Lexell suggest that the object observed by Herschel might be a planet. And only when additional computations, using a planet's rather than a comet's orbit, proved reconcilable with observation was that suggestion generally accepted. At what point during 1781 do we want to say that the planet Uranus was discovered? And are we entirely and unequivocally clear that it was Herschel rather than Lexell who discovered it?

Or consider still more briefly the story of the discovery of X rays, a story which opens on the day in 1895 when the physicist Roentgen interrupted a well-precedented investigation of cathode rays because he noticed that a barium platinocyanide screen far from his shielded apparatus glowed when the discharge was in process. Additional investigations — they required seven hectic weeks during which Roentgen rarely left the laboratory — indicated that the cause of the glow traveled in straight lines from the cathode ray tube, that the radiation cast shadows, that it could not be deflected by a magnet, and much else besides. Before announcing his discovery Roentgen had convinced himself that his effect was not due to cathode rays themselves but to a new form of radiation with at least some similarity to light. Once again the question suggests itself: When shall we say that X rays were actually discovered? Not, in any case, at the first instant, when all that had been noted was a glowing screen. At least one other investigator had seen that glow and, to his subsequent chagrin, discovered nothing at all. Nor, it is almost as clear, can the moment of discovery be pushed back to a point during the last week of investigation. By that time Roentgen was exploring the properties of the new radiation he had *already* discovered. We may have to settle for the remark that X rays emerged in Würzburg between 8 November and 28 December 1895.

The characteristics shared by these examples are, I think, common to all the episodes by which unanticipated novelties become subjects for scientific attention. I therefore conclude these brief remarks by discussing three such common characteristics, ones which may help to provide a framework for the further study of the extended episodes we customarily call "discoveries."

In the first place, notice that all three of our discoveries — oxygen, Uranus, and X rays — began with the experimental or observational isolation of an anomaly, that is, with nature's failure to conform entirely to expectation. Notice, further, that the process by which that anomaly was educed displays simultaneously the apparently incompatible characteristics of the inevitable and the accidental. In the case of X rays, the anomalous glow which provided Roentgen's first clue was clearly the result of an accidental disposition of his apparatus. But by 1895 cathode rays were a normal subject for research all over Europe; that research quite regularly juxtaposed cathode-ray tubes with sensitive screens and films; as a result, Roentgen's accident was almost certain to occur elsewhere, as in fact it had. Those remarks, however, should make Roentgen's case look very much like those of Herschel and Priestley. Herschel first observed his oversized and thus anomalous star in the course of a prolonged survey of the northern heavens. That survey was, except for the magnification provided by Herschel's instruments, precisely of the sort that had repeatedly been carried through before and that had occasionally resulted in prior observations of Uranus. And Priestley, too — when he isolated the gas that behaved almost but not quite like nitrous air and then almost but not quite like common air — was seeing something unintended and wrong in the outcome of a sort of experiment for which there was much European precedent and which had more than once before led to the production of the new gas.

These features suggest the existence of two normal requisites for the begin-   15
ning of an episode of discovery. The first, which throughout this paper I have largely taken for granted, is the individual skill, wit, or genius to recognize that something has gone wrong in ways that may prove consequential. Not any and every scientist would have noted that no recorded star should be so large, that the screen ought not to have glowed, that nitrous air should not have supported life. But that requisite presupposes another which is less frequently taken for granted. Whatever the level of genius available to observe them, anomalies do not emerge from the normal course of scientific research until both instruments and concepts have developed sufficiently to make their emergence likely and to make the anomaly which results recognizable as a violation of expectation. To say that an unexpected discovery begins only when something goes wrong is to say that it begins only when scientists know well both how their instruments and how nature should behave. What distinguished Priestley, who saw an anomaly, from Hales, who did not, is largely the considerable articulation of pneumatic techniques and expectations that had come into being during the four decades which separate their two isolations of oxygen. The very number of claimants indicates that after 1770 the discovery could not have been postponed for long.

The role of anomaly is the first of the characteristics shared by our three examples. A second can be considered more briefly, for it has provided the main theme for the body of my text. Though awareness of anomaly marks the beginning of a discovery, it marks only the beginning. What necessarily follows, if anything at all is to be discovered, is a more or less extended period during which the individual and often many members of his group struggle to make the anomaly lawlike. Invariably that period demands additional observation or experimentation as well as repeated cogitation. While it continues, scientists repeatedly revise their expectations, usually their instrumental standards, and sometimes their most fundamental theories as well. In this sense discoveries have a proper internal history as well as prehistory and a posthistory. Furthermore, within the rather vaguely delimited interval of internal history, there is no single moment or day which the historian, however complete his data, can identify as the point at which the discovery was made. Often, when several individuals are involved, it is even impossible unequivocally to identify any one of them as the discoverer.

Finally, turning to the third of these selected common characteristics, note briefly what happens as the period of discovery draws to a close. A full discussion of that question would require additional evidence and a separate paper, for I have had little to say about the aftermath of discovery in the body of my text. Nevertheless, the topic must not be entirely neglected, for it is in part a corollary of what has already been said.

Discoveries are often described as mere additions or increments to the growing stockpile of scientific knowledge, and that description has helped make the unit discovery seem a significant measure of progress. I suggest, however, that it is fully appropriate only to those discoveries which, like the elements that filled missing places in the periodic table, were anticipated and sought in advance and which therefore demanded no adjustment, adaptation, and assimilation from the profession. Though the sorts of discoveries we have here been examining are undoubtedly additions to scientific knowledge, they are also something more. In a sense that I can now develop only in part, they also react back upon what has previously been known, providing a new view of some previously familiar objects and simultaneously changing the way in which even some traditional parts of science are practiced. Those in whose area of special competence the new phenomenon falls often see both the world and their work differently as they emerge from the extended struggle with anomaly which constitutes the discovery of that phenomenon.

William Herschel, for example, when he increased by one the time-honored number of planetary bodies, taught astronomers to see new things when they looked at the familiar heavens even with instruments more traditional than his own. That change in the vision of astronomers must be a principal reason why, in the half century after the discovery of Uranus, twenty additional circumsolar bodies were added to the traditional seven. A similar transformation is even clearer in the aftermath of Roentgen's work. In the first place, established techniques for cathode-ray research had to be changed, for scientists found they had failed to control a relevant variable. Those changes included both the redesign of old apparatus and revised ways of asking old questions. In addition, those scientists most concerned experienced the same transformation of vision that we have just noted in the aftermath of the discovery of Uranus. X rays were the first new sort of radiation discovered since infrared and ultraviolet at the beginning of the century. But within less than a decade after Roentgen's work, four more were disclosed by the new scientific sensitivity (for example, to fogged photographic plates) and by some of the new instrumental techniques that had resulted from Roentgen's work and its assimilation.

Very often these transformations in the established techniques of scientific practice prove even more important than the incremental knowledge provided by the discovery itself. That could at least be argued in the cases of Uranus and of X rays; in the case of my third example, oxygen, it is categorically clear. Like the work of Herschel and Roentgen, that of Priestley and Lavoisier taught scientists to view old situations in new ways. Therefore, as we might anticipate, oxygen was not the only new chemical species to be identified in the aftermath of their work. But, in the case of oxygen, the readjustments demanded by assimilation were so profound that they played an integral and essential role — though they were not by themselves the cause — in the gigantic upheaval of chemical theory and practice which has since been known as the chemical revolution. I do not suggest that every unanticipated discovery has consequences for science so deep and so far-reaching as those which followed the discovery of oxygen. But I do suggest that every such discovery demands, from those most concerned, the sorts of readjustment that, when they are more obvious, we equate with scientific revolution. It is, I believe, just because they demand readjustments like these that the process of discovery is necessarily and inevitably one that shows structure and that therefore extends in time.

Edible Knowledge: The Chemical Transfer of Memory

HARRY COLLINS and TREVOR PINCH

INTRODUCTION

E VERYONE IS FASCINATED by memory and nearly everyone feels that they would prefer their memory to be a little better. Memorising lines in a play, or memorising multiplication tables, is the kind of hard work that people like to avoid. The slow growth of experience that counts as wisdom seems to be the gradual accumulation of memories over a lifetime. If only we could pass on our memories directly we could use our creative abilities from an early age without needing to spend years building the foundations first.

Between the late 1950s and the mid-1970s it began to look as though one day we might be able to build our memories without the usual effort. This was as a result of experiments done by James V. McConnell and, later, George Ungar, on the chemical transfer of memory in worms and rats. If memories are encoded in molecules then, in principle, it should be possible to transfer *The Complete Works of Shakespeare* to memory by ingesting a pill, to master the multiplication tables by injection into the bloodstream, or to become fluent in a foreign language by having it deposited under the skin; a whole new meaning would be given to the notion of "swallowing the dictionary." McConnell and Ungar believed they had shown that memories were stored in chemicals that could be transferred from animal to animal. They believed they had shown that substances corresponding to memories could be extracted from the brain of one creature and given to a second creature with beneficial effects. If the first creature had been trained in a task, such as turning left or right in an alley in order to reach food, the second creature would know how to reach the food without training — or, at least, with less than the usual amount of training. The second creature would have, as one might say, "a head start," compared with one which had not had the benefit of the substance corresponding to the memory.

WORMS

The first experiments were done by McConnell on planarian worms, a type of flatworm. McConnell trained them to scrunch up their bodies in response to light. He shone a bright light on the worms as they swam along the bottom of a trough, and then gave them a mild shock which caused their bodies to arch or "scrunch." Eventually the worms learned to associate light with shock and began to scrunch when a light was shone upon them whether or not the shock was delivered. Worms that scrunched in response to light alone counted as "trained" worms. This is how McConnell described the experiments:

> Imagine a trough gouged out of plastic, 12 inches in length, semi-circular in cross-section, and filled with pond water. At either end are brass electrodes attached to a power source. Above the trough are two electric light bulbs. Back and forth in the trough crawls a single flatworm, and in front of the apparatus sits the experimenter, his eye on the worm, his hands on two switches. When the worm is gliding smoothly in a straight line on the bottom of the trough, the experimenter turns on the lights for 3 seconds. After the light has been on for two of the three seconds, the experimenter adds one second of electric shock, which passes through the water and causes the worm to contract. The experimenter records the behaviour of the worm during the two-second period after the light has come on but before the shock has started. If the animal gives a noticeable turning movement or a contraction prior to the onset to the shock this is scored as a "correct" or "conditioned" response.

Now this sounds fairly straightforward but it is necessary to go into detail from the very beginning. Planarian worms scrunch their bodies and turn their heads from time to time even if they are left alone. They will also scrunch in response to many stimuli, including bright light. To train the worms, McConnell had first to discover the level of light that was bright enough for the worms to sense, but not so bright as to cause them to scrunch without the electric shock. Since worm behaviour varies from time to time and from worm to worm we are immediately into statistics rather than unambiguous yes's and no's. What is worse, the effectiveness of the shock training depends upon the worm not being scrunched when the shock is delivered. A worm that is already scrunched has no response left to make to light and shock, and therefore experiences no increment in its training regime when the stimulus is administered. It turns out, then, that to train worms well, it is necessary to watch them carefully and deliver the stimuli only when they are swimming calmly. All these aspects of worm training require skill — skill that McConnell and his assistants built up slowly over a period. When McConnell began his experiments in the 1950s he found that if he trained worms with 150 "pairings" of light followed by shock it resulted in a 45% scrunch response rate to light alone. In the 1960s, by which time he and his associates had become much more practised, the same number of pairings produced a 90% response rate.

In the mid-1950s McConnell tried cutting trained worms in half. The pla-   5
narian worms can regenerate into a whole worm from either half of a dissected specimen. McConnell was interested in whether worms that regenerated from the front half, containing the putative brain, would retain the training. They did, but the real surprise was that worms regenerated from the brain-less rear did at least as well if not better. This suggested that the training was somehow distributed throughout the worm, rather than being localised in the brain. The idea emerged that the training might be stored chemically.

McConnell tried to transfer training by grafting parts of trained worms to untrained specimens, but these experiments met with little success. Some planarian worms are cannibalistic. McConnell next tried feeding minced portions of trained worms to their naive brothers and sisters and found that those who had ingested trained meat were about one-and-a-half times more likely to respond to light alone than they otherwise would be. These experiments were being reported around 1962. By now, the notion that memory could be *transferred* by chemical means was the driving force of the experiments.

Arguments about the Worm Experiments

Transplantation versus chemical transfer   The notion that training or memory could be transferred by chemical means gave rise to substantial controversy. One counter argument was to agree that training was being transferred between worm and worm but to argue that it had no great significance. The planarian worm has a digestive system that is quite different from that of a mammal. The worm's digestive system does not break down its food into small chemical components but rather incorporates large components of ingested material into its body. To speak loosely, it might be that the naive worms were being given "implants" of trained worm — either bits of brain, or some other kind of distributed memory structure — rather than absorbing memory substance. This would be interesting but would not imply that memory was a chemical phenomenon and, in any case, would probably have no significance for our understanding of memory in mammals. McConnell's response to this was to concentrate on what he believed was the memory substance. Eventually he was injecting naive worms with RNA extracted from trained creatures, and claiming considerable success.

Sensitisation versus training   Another line of attack rested on the much more basic argument that planarian worms were too primitive to be trained. According to this line, McConnell had fooled himself into thinking that he had trained the worms to respond to light, whereas he had merely increased their general level of sensitivity to all stimuli. If anything was being transferred between worm and worm, it was a sensitising substance rather than something that carried a specific memory.

It is difficult to counter this argument because any kind of training regime is likely to increase sensitivity. Training is done by "pairing" exposure to light with electric shock. One way of countering the sensitisation hypothesis is to subject the worms to the same number of shocks and bursts of light, but in randomised order. If sensitisation is the main effect, then worms subjected to a randomised pattern of shocks and light bursts should be just as likely to scrunch in response to light alone as worms subjected to properly organised pairings of stimuli. If it is training rather than sensitisation that is important, the trained worms will do better.

Once more, this sounds simple. Indeed, McConnell and other "worm runners" did find a significant difference between *trained* and *sensitised* worms, but the effect is difficult to repeat because training is a matter of *skilled practice*. As explained above, to effect good training it is necessary to observe the worms closely and learn to understand when they are calm enough for a shock to produce a training increment. Different trainers may obtain widely differing outcomes from training regimes however much they try to repeat the experiments according to the specification.

To the critic, the claim that a poor result is the outcome of poor training technique — specifically, a failure to understand the worms — sounds like an *ad hoc* excuse. To say that only certain technicians understand the worms well enough to be able to get a result sounds like a most unscientific argument. Critics always think that the claim that only some people are able to get results — the "golden hands" argument, as one might call it — is *prima facie* evidence that something unsound is going on. And there are many cases in the history of science where a supposedly golden-handed experimenter has turned out to be a fraud. Nevertheless, the existence of specially skilful experimenters — the one person in a lab who can successfully manage an extraction or a delicate measurement — is also widely attested. In the field of pharmacology, for example, the "bioassay" is widely used. In a bioassay, the existence and quantity of a drug is determined by its effects on living matter or whole organisms. In a sense, the measurement of the effect of various brain extracts on worms and rats could be seen as itself a bioassay rather than a transfer experiment. Yet the bioassay is a technique that has the reputation of being potentially difficult to "transfer" from one group of scientists to another because it requires so much skill and practice. It is, then, very hard to separate golden hands from *ad hocery,* a problem that has a particular salience in this field. Certainly attributions of dishonesty are not always appropriate.

10

For this kind of reason the argument between McConnell and his critics was able to drag on, reaching its zenith in 1964 with the publication of a special supplement to the journal, *Animal Behaviour,* devoted to the controversy. At this point it would be hard to say who was winning, but it was clear that McConnell's claim that training worms required special skills was becoming a little more acceptable.

Confounding variables and replication   Sensitisation could be looked at as a confounding variable, and critics put forward a number of others. For example, planarian worms produce slime as they slither along. Nervous worms prefer swimming into slimed areas which have been frequented by other worms. A naive worm swimming in a two-branched alley will naturally prefer to follow the path marked out most strongly by the slime of worms that have gone before. If the alley has been used for training, the preferred route will be that which the trainee worms have used most often. Thus, naive worms might prefer to follow their trained counterparts not because of the transfer of any substance, but because of the slime trails left before. Even in an individual worm it might be that the development of a preference for, say, right turns, might be the build-up of a self-reinforcing slime trail rather than a trained response.

Once this has been pointed out there are a number of remedies. For example, the troughs might be scrubbed between sessions (though it is never quite clear when enough scrubbing has been done), or new troughs might be regularly employed. One critic found that in properly cleaned troughs no learning effect could be discovered, but McConnell, as a result of further research, claimed that worms could not be trained properly in a clean environment. He suggested that worms were unhappy in an environment made unfamiliar because it was free of slime; too much hygiene prevented the experiments working. One can readily imagine the nature of the argument between McConnell and his critics over the effects of sliming.

Eventually, this part of the argument was resolved, at least to McConnell's satisfaction, by pre-sliming training grounds with naive worms that were not part of the experiment. This made the troughs and alleys comfortable for the experimental subjects without reinforcing any particular behaviour. [15]

All these arguments take time, and it is not always clear to everyone exactly what has been established at any point. This is one of the reasons why controversies drag on for so long when the logic of the experiments seems clear and simple. Remember, too, that every experiment requires a large number of trials and a statistical analysis. The levels of the final effects are usually low so it is not always clear just what has been proved.

Whether or not McConnell's results could be replicated by others, or could be said to be replicable, depended on common agreement about what were the important variables in the experiment. We have already discussed the necessity — from McConnell's point of view — of understanding and of skilled handling of the worms. In his own laboratory, the training of "worm runners" by an experienced scientist was followed by weeks of practice. It was necessary to learn not to "push the worms too hard." In his own words:

> [it is necessary to] treat them tenderly, almost with love . . . it seems certain that the variability in success rate from one laboratory to another is due, at least in part, to differences in personality and past experience among the various investigators.

As explained, to look at it from the critics point of view, this was one of the *excuses* McConnell used in the face of the palpable nonrepeatability of his work. The effect of sliming was another variable cited by both proponents and critics in their different ways.

As a scientific controversy develops more variables that might affect the experiments come to the fore. For the proponents these are more reasons why the unpractised might have difficulty in making the experiments work; for the critics, they are more excuses that can be used when others fail to replicate the original findings.

In the case of the worm experiments up to 70 variables were cited at one time or another to account for discrepancies in experimental results. They included: the species and size of the worms; the way they were housed when not undergoing training — was it in the dark or the light?; the type of feeding; the frequency of training; the temperature and chemical composition of the water; the strength of the light, its colour and duration; the nature of the electric shock — its pulse shape, strength, polarity and so forth; the worm's feeding schedule; the season of the year; and the time of day when the worms were trained. Even the barometric pressure, the phase of the moon, and the orientation of the training trough with respect to the earth's magnetic field were cited at one time or another. This provided ample scope for accusation and counter-accusation — skill versus *ad hocery*. The greater the number of potential variables, the harder it is to decide whether one experiment really replicates the conditions of another.

The Worm Runner's Digest

McConnell was an unusual scientist. What people are prepared to believe is [20] not just a function of what a scientist discovers but of the image of the work that he or she presents. McConnell was no respecter of scientific convention and in this he did himself no favours. Among his unconventional acts was founding, in 1959, a journal called *The Worm Runner's Digest*. He claimed this was a way of coping with the huge amount of mail that he received as a result of the initial work on worms, but the *Digest* also published cartoons and scientific spoofs.

Ironically, one of the disadvantages of the worm experiments was that they seemed so easy. It meant that many experimenters, including high school students, could try the transfer tests for themselves. It was these high school students who swamped McConnell with requests for information and accounts of their results. The newsletter, which became *The Worm Runner's Digest,* was McConnell's response.

It is not necessarily a good thing to have high school students repeat one's experiments for it makes them appear to lack *gravitas.* What is worse, it makes it even more difficult than usual to separate serious and competent scientific work from the slapdash or incompetent. It is certainly not a good thing to found a "jokey" newsletter if you want your work to be taken seriously.

In 1967 the journal split into two halves, printed back to back, with the second half being re-titled *The Journal of Biological Psychology.* This journal was treated in a more conventional way, with articles being refereed. The idea was that the more serious work would appear in the refereed end of the journal while the jokey newsletter material would be reserved for the *Digest* half. (The analogy between the journal and the front and back halves of regenerating worms was not lost on McConnell and the contributors. Which end contained the brain?) *The Journal of Biological Psychology,* refereed though it was, never attained the full respectability of a conventional scientific outlet. How could it with *The Worm Runner's Digest* simultaneously showing its backside to scientific convention in every issue?

Because a number of McConnell's results were published in *The Worm Runner's Digest/The Journal of Biological Psychology* scientists did not know how to take them. To put it another way, any critic who was determined not to take McConnell's work seriously had a good excuse to ignore his claims if their only scientific outlet was in McConnell's own, less than fully attested, journal. In the competition between scientific claims, the manner of presentation is just as important as the content. The scientific community has its ceremonies and its peculiar heraldic traditions. The symbols may be different — Albert Einstein's unruly hair and Richard Feynman's Brooklyn accent in place of gilded lions and rampant unicorns — but the division between scientific propriety and eccentricity is firm if visible only to the enlightened. Much of what McConnell did fell on the wrong side of the line.

The Ending of the Worm Controversy

Around the mid-1960s, as McConnell was beginning to establish that   25
worms could be trained, if not that the transfer phenomenon could be demonstrated, the stakes were changed in such a way as to make some of the earlier arguments seem petty. This was the result of experiments suggesting that the transfer phenomenon could be found in mammals.

Some of McConnell's most trenchant critics had argued that planarian learning was impossible, others that it had not been fully proved. We may be sure that the strong attacks on learning were motivated by the importance of the transfer phenomenon. With the apparent demonstration of transfer in rats and mice, the objections to planarian learning dropped away. Rats and mice are familiar laboratory animals. There is no dispute that they can learn, and there is no dispute that in order to learn they have to be carefully handled. It is acknowledged that the technicians who handle the rats in a psychology or biology laboratory must be skilled at their job. Once the worm experiments were seen through the re-fracted light of the later experiments on rats it appeared entirely reasonable that worms should need special handling, and entirely reasonable that they could learn. The believers in McConnell's results stressed this, as in the following quo-tation from two experimenters:

> It seems paradoxical that when we run rats, we handle our subjects, we specify what breeding line the stock is from, we train them in sound-proof boxes, and we specify a large number of factors which when put together give us an output we call learning . . . Planarians on the other hand are popped into a trough, given a . . . [conditioned stimulus] and . . . [an unconditioned stimulus] and are ex-pected to perform like a learning rat.

But this kind of *cri de coeur* only came to seem reasonable to the majority at a later date. It only became acceptable when nobody cared very much because their attention had been turned to the much more exciting subject of transfer of behaviour among mammals. This was a much more important challenge to re-ceived wisdom about the nature of memory.

MAMMALS

Early Experiments

The first claims to have demonstrated memory transfer in mammals came from four independent groups working without knowledge of each other's re-search. The first four studies were associated with the names, in alphabetical or-der, of Fjerdingstad, Jacobson, Reinis, and Ungar. All these studies were being done around 1964, and were published in 1965.

Fjerdingstad placed rats in a training box with two alleyways, one was lit and one was darkened according to a random sequence. The rats were deprived of water for 24 hours, but received a few drops if they entered the illuminated alley. Injections of trained brain extract caused naive rats to prefer the box in which their trained colleagues had found relief from thirst.

Jacobson had hungry rats learn to associate the sound of a clicker with a food reward. The association of clicks with food could, so he claimed, be transferred to naive rats by injection.

Reinis taught rats to take food from a dispenser during the period of a con-ditioned stimulus — either a light or a buzzer. This expectation, it appeared, could also be transferred by injections.

McConnell's laboratory also began to work on rats in the mid-1960s but, in the long term, the most important mammal experimenter was Georges Ungar. Ungar began by showing that tolerance to morphine could be transferred. As an animal becomes accustomed to a drug it requires greater doses to produce the same effects on its behaviour. This is known as "tolerance" to the drug. Ungar ground up the brains of 50 tolerant rats and injected an extract into unexposed rats. The result, reported in 1965, seemed to be that the tolerance was trans-ferred. Whether this is to be counted as the transfer of *learning* is not clear. As explained earlier, Ungar might be thought of as doing a complicated bioassay rather than an experiment in the transfer of learning. The significance of this point will become more evident in due course.

Ungar moved on to attempt to transfer "habituation." He exposed rats to the sound of a loud bell until they became accustomed to it and ceased to exhibit the usual "startle reaction." Habituation too could be transferred, apparently, through injection of brain extract. Interestingly, Ungar transferred the habituation not to rats but from rats to mice.

Early Reactions

It is important to get some of the flavour of the early reaction of scientists to these strange and unorthodox results. The following reports of reactions are from 1966, just after the early mammal results had appeared. It is probable that part of the strength of the response was caused by association with the earlier worm experiments.

One scientist reported that after he had given his presentation he found that people "drifted away from him" in the bar. Other scientists told of similar reactions to the exposure of the transfer results at conferences:

[T]he nightly private gatherings brought to the surface all the deeply felt emotional objections which, for reasons I have difficulty to understand and analyse, some people have against the whole idea. This was particularly manifest after a few drinks.

I was stunned. People were really — vicious is maybe too strong a word — but certainly mean . . . It took me quite a while to realize I had trodden on sacred territory. It was "Why didn't you do this?," "Why didn't you do that?" . . . it was all accusations.

. . . [I]t was one of those times when you see the people who are at the absolute cutting edge of a science, all packed together . . . in a smoke-filled room, trying to decide what was right . . . I remember that meeting particularly, because at the end of the evening those people who had gotten positive results were telling the people who had gotten negative results that they were totally incompetent and didn't know how to run an experiment; and the people who had gotten negative results were telling those people who had gotten positive results that they were frauds. That they were faking the data.

Georges Ungar's Main Work

Ungar's best-known work began in 1967. In these experiments rats had to choose between entering a lighted or a darkened box. A rat's natural preference would be for the dark but on entering the darkened box they were locked in and given a five second electric shock delivered through the metal grid of the floor. The rats learned to avoid the dark box very quickly, but Ungar gave his rats five trials a day, for six to eight days, to make sure that a good supply of the "fear of the dark" chemical was produced in the rats' brains.

After training, the rats were killed and an extract was prepared from their

35

brains. This was injected into mice, who were tested in the same apparatus. By measuring the proportion of time spent in the light or dark box during a three minute trial it was possible to tell if mice which had been injected with brain extract from trained rats were more likely to avoid the dark than those which had been injected with a similar extract prepared from the brains of normal rats.

Replication in Mammals

As explained, all the work on mammals was violently contested and attempts were made both to support and disprove the findings. According to Ungar's rough (and contentious) analysis of published experimental reports between 1965 and 1975, there were 105 positive and 23 negative replications, following the pattern below:

Ungar's analysis of transfer experiments in mammals, 1965–75

	1965	1966	1967	1968	1969	1970	1971	1972	1973	1974	1975
Positive	13	13	13	16	23	17	27	13	23	17	8
Negative	1	6	4	5	1	3	1	1	—	—	1

This is a good point at which to note a feature of science that is often misunderstood. The sheer number and weight of experimental replications is not usually enough to persuade the scientific community to believe in some unorthodox finding. In this case, for example, a single one of the negative experiments, carried out by a number of influential scientists, outweighed the far larger number of positive results. Scientists have to have grounds for believing the result of an experiment — and this is quite reasonable given, as we demonstrate throughout the book, the skill involved. Scientists will demand better grounds where an experiment produces more unorthodox results; one might say that they start with grounds for not believing. Again, among the sorts of grounds people look for in deciding whether or not to believe a result are the scientist's reputation and the respectability of his or her institution. This, of course, militates still more strongly against the unorthodox. Ungar's figures show clearly that experimental replication is not a straightforward business and neither are the conclusions that scientists draw from replications.

Naturally, competing results were supported by competing arguments about the competence and skill of the experimenters. Let us give an example of the "flavour" of these problems with illustrations from the debate between Ungar and the group at Stanford University.

The Debate with Stanford

Stanford attempted to replicate Ungar's work as closely as possible. It was 40 felt that in Ungar's experiments:

[S]ome . . . peptide material has evidently been isolated . . . if this material — whatever its exact structure or state of purity — is truly capable of specifically transferring a learned behaviour to untrained recipient animals, the discovery ranks among the most fundamental in modern biology.

In the event they obtained negative results. Inevitably, this led Ungar to point to residual differences between the Stanford experiments and his own which could account for the failure. In what follows, then, we first see the two series of experiments looking more and more like each other as the Stanford group tried to replicate every detail of Ungar's work, and then the experiments are "prised apart" again when the unexpected Stanford outcome is reported.

The leader of the Stanford group, Avram Goldstein, first spent three days at Ungar's laboratory to make sure that he could follow the published procedures accurately. In a 1971 publication, the subsequent work of him and his collaborators was described as follows:

> In the next three months we carried out eighteen unsuccessful experiments with 125 donor rats and 383 recipient saline and control mice. We then did a blind test on our mice using control and trained donor extracts provided by Dr. Ungar. Next, we sent 100 of our mice to Houston, for testing as recipients concurrently with the local strain. Finally, we selected, from all our experiments, those mice (of both sexes) which seemed to avoid the black box more often after receiving extracts. These animals were bred and the offspring tested as recipients. We hoped to select for recipient capability that might be under genetic influence. The results of all these experiments were negative.

These various collaborations with Ungar's laboratories were meant to eliminate any residual differences between the Stanford procedures and those used by Ungar. Stanford, as was clear from the same publication, were trying their best in an open-minded spirit:

> We should not dismiss the possibility that acquired behaviour . . . can be transferred by brain extracts, merely because the proposed mechanisms . . . seem fanciful, especially since confirmatory results have been published by several laboratories.

After their failure the tone of the debate changed. The Stanford group suggested that their "rather exhaustive" attempts showed that the conditions for a successful transfer would have to be specified more exactly.

> Can the investigators state precisely the conditions for carrying out an assay, in such detail that competent scientists elsewhere can reproduce their results? Our own repeated failure . . . could be dismissed as the bungling work of incompetents were it not matched by published experiences of others.

The difference between the two experiments began to emerge. With reference to the interpretation of one aspect of the results, Goldstein and his team noted:

> Because we were unable to agree with Dr. Ungar on the interpretation of the results they are not included here but will presumably be published independently by him.

To this, Ungar replied:

> . . . [S]ome of the most important parameters were arbitrarily changed . . . This was certainly not done because he was unaware of our procedures.

Ungar also stated that the Stanford group had "eliminated one of the three boxes of our testing device, trained some of the donors only once instead of five times . . . and used a different strain of mice."

Ungar also objected to the measure of dark avoidance that the Stanford group had used. Rather than presenting the results in terms of the length of time the rats spent in the darkened box, they had measured "latency." This is the length of time the mouse is in the apparatus before it *first* enters the dark box. Goldstein stated that he had noted that Ungar also recorded latencies, but always published data in terms of dark box time.

> I thought this curious, because if dark avoidance behaviour were really induced by the injections, the latency would be increased. This is elementary logic. Indeed, latency is the common and accepted measure for such behavioural phenomena among experimental psychologists. Yet Ungar has never used latency . . .

Ungar replied:

> . . . [I]n his latest comments, he tries to justify one of these changes, the use of latency, as a criterion of dark avoidance, instead of the total time spent in the dark box. We have shown empirically, and showed it to him, that a number of mice run rapidly into the dark but come out immediately and spend the rest of the time in the light . . . latency would, therefore, give misleading results.

Goldstein felt:

> Dark box time . . . would probably be sensitive to other behavioural effects. A recipient mouse that wanders around more because it is hyperactive would naturally be more likely to leave the dark box than a passive animal.

As can be seen, Ungar and Goldstein disagreed about whether enough detail had been published, whether certain differences between the original and the replication were significant, and the appropriateness of different measures of fear of the dark. Ungar saw Goldstein's work as having departed clearly and significantly from his procedures.

Competing Strategies

In so far as the memory transfer technique was important to psychologists, it was important primarily because it seemed to offer a tool for "dissecting" memory. For many of the psychologists the main hope was that the technique would allow them to take apart some aspects of learning. The precise chemical nature of memory transfer substances was of secondary importance to this group. Thus, McConnell remarked, jokingly, that as far as he was concerned the active material might as well be boot polish.

45

McConnell and other behavioural psychologists worked to find out whether further memory-related behavioural tendencies could be chemically transferred from mammal to mammal. Fear of the dark might be seen as a general disposition rather than something specific that had been learned.

The *specificity* argument paralleled the sensitisation debate in the case of the worms but was even more salient in the case of mammals. The exciting thing would be if there were specific molecules related to specific memories or learned behaviours. For many, this claim was difficult to accept. Much more palatable was the notion that molecules would have a non-specific effect on behaviour that would vary in different circumstances. For example, suppose the effect of the memory molecule was to alter the overall emotional state of the animal rather than providing it with a particular memory. In such a case, placing an injected but untrained animal in the same circumstances that its dead colleague had experienced in training — say a choice between light and dark — should cause it to produce the response that had been induced during the training — choosing the light. In different circumstances, however, the effect might be quite different; for example, if the injected animal was given a choice between pink and blue boxes it might cause it to bite its tail. If this was what transfer was all about, there would never be a *Complete Works of Shakespeare* pill.

McConnell wanted to find out if what psychologists would count as "grade-A learning" could be transferred. One might say that proving that something like the works of Shakespeare could exist in chemical form was what drove McConnell on.

To show "grade-A learning" McConnell and other experimenters taught rats more complex tasks such as the choice of a left or a right turn in an alley in order to get food. These experiments were done in the late 1960s. "Discrimination" tasks such as these seemed to be transferable among rats as well as other creatures such as cats, goldfish, cockroaches and the praying mantis. A degree of cross-species transfer was also found.

Unlike McConnell, Ungar was a pharmacologist by training and was much more interested in a "biochemical strategy." That is, he wanted to isolate, analyse and synthesise active molecules. For Ungar the important thing was to find some reproducible transfer effect and study the chemical that was responsible for it, whether or not the transferred behaviour was grade-A learning. Concentrating on fear of the dark, Ungar set about extracting what became known as "Scotophobin." To obtain a measurable amount, he required the brains of 4,000 trained rats. This was certainly big, expensive, science as far as psychologists were concerned, and even other biochemists could not compete with him. Eventually Ungar believed he had isolated, analysed and then synthesised Scotophobin.

Ungar had hoped that the problems of repeating chemical transfer experiments would be solved by the availability of the synthetic material but, as so often in contested science, there is so much detail that is contestable that experiments can force no one to agree that anything significant has been found.

There were disputes over the purity of the synthetic material; its stability and the way it was kept by other laboratories before it was used; and the kind of behavioural changes (if any) it induced. In addition, Ungar announced several alterations to the precise chemical structure of Scotophobin. The upshot was continued controversy. A few of those who believed in the chemical transfer effect felt that there was a "family" of Scotophobin-like chemicals for different species, with similar but slightly different formulae. Our experiment showed that the synthetic version of Scotophobin had no effect on mice, but produced dark avoidance in goldfish!

It is difficult to be precise about the numbers of experiments on synthetic Scotophobin that were completed, since different synthetic versions were produced, many results were never published, and some of these were concerned only with testing exactly where the material ended up in the recipient's brain. Several dozens of experiments are known, but there is sufficient ambiguity for both believers and sceptics to draw comfort from the results.

THE END OF THE STORY

McConnell closed his laboratory in 1971. He was unable to obtain further funding for the work and, in any case, he could see that to prove the transfer effect it would be necessary to adopt an Ungar-like strategy of isolating and synthesising the active agents. Ungar, one might say, had won the competition over experimental strategy. The psychologists had lost out to the "big science" of biochemistry.

Ungar pressed ahead with his programme of research. Training thousands of rats was too large a project to be done frequently, and he turned his attention to goldfish. Goldfish are good at colour discrimination tasks and are relatively cheap. Nearly 17,000 trained goldfish gave their lives in the production of about 750 grams of colour discriminating brains but this was still insufficient for him to identify the chemical structure of the putative memory substances, "chromodiopsins."

Ungar, who was of normal retiring age when he began the work on transfer, died in 1977 at the age of 71 and the field died with him. It was Ungar's very dominance of the field, brought about by his ambitious approach, that had killed off competing laboratories. On the one hand there was never quite enough reliability in the transfer effect to make the experiments really attractive to a beginner or someone short of resources; on the other hand, Ungar had raised the stakes so much that the investment required to make a serious attempt at repeating his work was too high. Thus when Ungar died there was no one to take over the mantle.

Ungar left behind a number of formulae for behaviourally active molecules that were the result of his work on rats and goldfish. Some scientists tried to synthesise Scotophobin and test it on animals but, as noted above, tests on Scotophobin did not provide any clear answer to the question of whether it really was the chemical embodiment of "fear of the dark" or something more general such as fear. In any case, if Ungar's heroic efforts did have valuable implications, they were lost to view when the related field of brain-peptide chemistry exploded in the late 1970s. Scientists now had brain chemicals to work on which had clear effects, but effects unrelated to memory transfer.

Scotophobin thus lost its special salience and its historical relationship to the disreputable transfer phenomenon became a disadvantage. Most scientists, then, simply forgot about the area. Like many controversies, it ended with a whimper rather than a bang.

It is hard to say that any particular experiment or set of experiments demonstrated the non-existence of the transfer phenomenon, but three publications seemed decisive at the time. Their *historical* interest lies in the negative effect they had when they were published while one might say that their *sociological* interest lies in the reasons for that effect, especially given that in retrospect they appear much less decisive.

The first paper was published in 1964 and came from the laboratory of Nobel Laureate Melvin Calvin (Bennett and Calvin, 1964); it concerned planarian worms. The paper described a series of experiments — some employing McConnell's ex-students to perform the training — that seemed to show that learning had not taken place. This paper had a powerful effect, and for many years was quoted as undermining the early research on the chemical transfer of memory. Today, its cautious verdict that learning was "not yet proven" has been superseded and it is accepted that worms not only turn, but learn.

The second paper, by Byrne and 22 others, was published in 1966. It was a short piece in *Science* reporting the failure of the attempts by seven different laboratories to replicate one of the early chemical transfer experiments. Again, it is often cited as a "knockdown blow" to the field. Indeed, it was at the time. But for Ungar, and other proponents, all of the experiments mentioned in the paper — and the original experiment they attempted to replicate — are flawed because they assumed the transfer material to be RNA rather than a peptide. According to Ungar, the chemical techniques used by the replicators in treating the brain extract probably destroyed the active, peptide, material. On this account, the original experiment, fortuitously, used *poor* biochemical techniques and, failing to destroy the peptide, obtained the correct positive result!

The last paper is the best known. Ungar's five-page report of his analysis and synthesis of Scotophobin was published in *Nature*, perhaps the highest prestige journal for the biological sciences. Accompanying it, however, was a critical, fifteen-page, signed report by the referee. The detailed critical comments of the referee, and perhaps the mere fact of this exceptional form of publication significantly reduced the credibility of the memory transfer phenomenon. It is worth noting that *Nature* has used this unusual form of publication subsequently to the disadvantage of other pieces of fringe science and, perhaps, to the disadvantage of science as a whole.

In spite of the widespread demise of the credibility of the chemical transfer of memory, a determined upholder of the idea would find no published disproof that rests on decisive technical evidence. For such a person it would not be unreasonable or unscientific to start experimenting once more. Each negative result can be explained away while many of the positive ones have not been. In this, memory transfer is an exemplary case of controversial science. We no longer believe in memory transfer but this is because we tired of it, because more interesting problems came along, and because the principal experimenters lost their credibility. Memory transfer was never quite disproved; it just ceased to occupy the scientific imagination. The gaze of the golem turned elsewhere.

▩ ▩ TWO VIEWS OF ECONOMIC INEQUALITY

The economy is an elaborate system of causes and effects. Economists try to study these causal relationships in a systematic and scientific way. Because changes in the economy can affect everyone, the public takes a great interest in the issues discussed in the next two essays: economic inequality and poverty. Robert Reich, a former faculty member at the John F. Kennedy School of Government at Harvard University and a Clinton advisor, considers the causes and effects of current economic inequality in the United States. John Kenneth Galbraith, considered by some to be one of the most significant economists of the 20th century, surveys attitudes toward the poor throughout history. He examines the causes of these attitudes and the effects of government intervention on poverty. As you read these essays, consider the following questions:

1. What section of economic society do you and your family most resemble?
2. Do you accept Robert Reich's description of economic inequality in the United States? Do you feel this inequality is unjust?
3. What causes differences in economic status? What effects do these differences have?
4. How do you feel about the poor? What are the sources of these feelings?
5. What do you think we as a community should do about economic inequality and poverty?

The Global Elite

ROBERT REICH

T HE IDEA OF "COMMUNITY" has always held a special attraction for Americans. In a 1984 speech, President Ronald Reagan celebrated America's "bedrock" — "its communities where neighbors help one another, where families bring up kids together, where American values are born." Governor Mario M. Cuomo of New York, with a very different political leaning, has been almost as lyrical. "Community . . . is the reality on which our national life has been founded," he said in 1987.

There is only one problem with this picture. Most Americans no longer live in traditional communities. They live in suburban subdivisions bordered by highways and sprinkled with shopping malls, or in tony condominiums and residential clusters, or in ramshackle apartment buildings and housing projects. Most of them commute to work and socialize on some basis other than geographic proximity. And most people pick up and move to a different neighborhood every five years or so.

But Americans generally have one thing in common with their neighbors: They have similar incomes. And that simple fact lies at the heart of the new community. This means that their educational backgrounds are likely to be similar, that they pay roughly the same in taxes, and that they indulge in the same consumer impulses. "Tell me someone's ZIP code," the founder of a direct-mail company once bragged, "and I can predict what they eat, drink, drive — even think."

Americans who own their homes usually share one political cause with their neighbors: a near obsessive concern with maintaining or upgrading property values. And this common interest is responsible for much of what has brought neighbors together in recent years. Complete strangers, although they may live on the same street or in the same condominium complex, suddenly feel intense solidarity when it is rumored that low-income housing will be constructed in their midst or that a poorer school district will be consolidated with their own.

The renewed emphasis on "community" in American life has justified and legitimized these economic enclaves. If generosity and solidarity end at the border of similarly valued properties, then the most fortunate can be virtuous citizens at little cost. Since most people in one neighborhood or town are equally well off, there is no cause for a guilty conscience. If inhabitants of another area are poorer, let them look to one another. Why should *we* pay for *their* schools?

So the argument goes, without acknowledging that the critical assumption has already been made: "We" and "they" belong to fundamentally different communities. Through such reasoning, it has become possible to maintain a self-image of generosity toward, and solidarity with, one's "community" without bearing any responsibility to "them" — the other "community."

America's high earners — the fortunate top fifth — thus feel increasingly justified in paying only what is necessary to insure that everyone in their community is sufficiently well educated and has access to the public services they need to succeed.

Last year, the top fifth of working Americans took home more money than the other four-fifths put together — the highest portion in postwar history. These high earners will relinquish somewhat more of their income to the Federal Government this year than in 1990 as a result of last fall's tax changes, although considerably less than in the late 1970s, when the tax code was more progressive. But the continuing debate over whether the wealthy are paying their fair share of taxes obscures a larger issue, with more profound implications for America: The fortunate fifth is quietly seceding from the rest of the nation.

This is occurring gradually, without much awareness by members of the top group — or, for that matter, by anyone else. And the Government is speeding this process as Washington shifts responsibility for many public services to state and local governments.

The secession is taking several forms. In many cities and towns, the wealthy   10
have in effect withdrawn their dollars from the support of public spaces and institutions shared by all and dedicated the savings to their own private services. As
public parks and playgrounds deteriorate, there is a proliferation of private health
clubs, golf clubs, tennis clubs, skating clubs, and every other type of recreational
association in which costs are shared among members. Condominiums and the
omnipresent residential communities dun their members to undertake work that
financially strapped local governments can no longer afford to do well — maintaining roads, mending sidewalks, pruning trees, repairing street lights, cleaning
swimming pools, paying for lifeguards, and, notably, hiring security guards to
protect life and property. (The number of private security guards in the United
States now exceeds the number of public police officers.)

Of course, wealthier Americans have been withdrawing into their own
neighborhoods and clubs for generations. But the new secession is more dramatic because the highest earners now inhabit a different economy from other
Americans. The new elite is linked by jet, modem, fax, satellite, and fiber-optic
cable to the great commercial and recreational centers of the world, but it is not
particularly connected to the rest of the nation.

That is because the work this group does is becoming less tied to the activities of other Americans. Most of their jobs consist of analyzing and manipulating
symbols — words, numbers, or visual images. Among the most prominent of
these "symbolic analysts" are management consultants, lawyers, software and
design engineers, research scientists, corporate executives, financial advisers, strategic planners, advertising executives, television and movie producers, and other
workers whose job titles include terms like "strategy," "planning," "consultant," "policy," "resources," or "engineer."

These workers typically spend long hours in meetings or on the telephone
and even longer hours in planes or hotels — advising, making presentations, giving briefings, and making deals. Periodically, they issue reports, plans, designs,
drafts, briefs, blueprints, analyses, memorandums, layouts, renderings, scripts,
or projections. It contrast with people whose jobs tend to be tedious and repeti-
tive, symbolic analysts find their work varied and intellectually challenging. In
fact, the work is often enjoyable.

These symbolic analysts are in ever greater demand in a world market that
places an increasing value on identifying and solving problems. Requests for their
software designs, financial advice, or engineering blueprints come from all parts
of the globe. This largely explains why most (but by no means all) symbolic
analysts have become wealthier, even as the ever-growing worldwide supply of
unskilled labor continues to depress the wages of other Americans.

Successful Americans have not completely disengaged themselves from the   15
lives of their less fortunate compatriots. Some devote substantial resources and
energies to helping the rest of society, not through their tax payments, but
through voluntary efforts. "Generosity is a reflection of what one does with his
or her resources — and not what he or she advocates the government do with
everyone's money," Ronald Reagan said in 1984.

The argument is fair enough. Government is not the only device for redistributing wealth. In his speech accepting the Presidential nomination at the Republican National Convention in 1988, George Bush said that the real magnanimity of America was to be found in a "brilliant diversity" of private charities, "spread like stars, like a thousand points of light in a broad and peaceful sky."

No nation congratulates itself more enthusiastically on its charitable acts than America; none engages in a greater number of charity balls, bake sales, benefit auctions, and border-to-border hand holdings for good causes. Much of this is sincerely motivated and admirable.

But close examination reveals that many of these acts of benevolence do not help the needy. Particularly suspect is the private giving of those in the top income-tax bracket. Studies have revealed that their largess does not flow mainly to social services for the poor — to better schools, health clinics, or recreational centers. Instead, most voluntary contributions of wealthy Americans go to the places and institutions that entertain, inspire, cure, or educate wealthy Americans — art museums, opera houses, theaters, orchestras, ballet companies, private hospitals, and elite universities.

And even these charitable contributions are relatively skimpy. Last year, American households with incomes of less than $10,000 gave an average of 5.5 percent of their earnings to charity or to a religious organization; those making more than $100,000 a year gave only 2.9 percent. After the 1986 tax-code overhaul reduced the benefits of charitable giving, the very rich became even stingier. According to Internal Revenue Service data, taxpayers earning $500,000 or more slashed their average donations to $16,062 in 1988 from $47,432 in 1980.

Corporate philanthropy is following the same general pattern. In recent 20 years, the largest American corporations have been sounding the alarm about the nation's fast deteriorating primary and secondary schools. Few are more eloquent and impassioned about the need for better schools than American executives. "How well we educate all of our children will determine our competitiveness globally, and our economic health domestically, and our communities' character and vitality," said a report of The Business Roundtable, a New York-based association of top executives.

Accordingly, there are numerous "partnerships" between corporations and public schools: scholarships for poor children qualified to attend college, and programs in which businesses adopt individual schools by making conspicuous donations of computers, books, and, on occasion, even money. That such activities are loudly touted by corporate public relations staffs should not detract from the good they do.

Despite the hoopla, business donations to education and charitable causes actually tapered off markedly in the 1980s, even as the economy boomed. In the 1970s, corporate giving to education jumped an average of 15 percent a year. In 1990, however, giving was only 5 percent over that in 1989; in 1989 it was 3 percent over 1988. Moreover, most of this money goes to colleges and universities — in particular, to the alma maters of symbolic analysts, who expect their children and grandchildren to follow in their footsteps. Only 1.5 percent of corporate giving in the late 1980s was to public primary and secondary schools.

Notably, these contributions have been smaller than the amounts corporations are receiving from states and communities in the form of subsidies or tax breaks. Companies are quietly procuring such deals by threatening to move their operations — and jobs — to places around the world with a more congenial tax climate. The paradoxical result has been even less corporate revenue to spend on schools and other community services than before. The executives of General Motors, for example, who have been among the loudest to proclaim the need for better schools, have also been among the most relentless in pursuing local tax abatements and in challenging their tax assessments. G.M.'s successful efforts to reduce its taxes in North Tarrytown, N.Y., where the company has had a factory since 1914, cut local revenues by $1 million in 1990, part of a larger shortfall that forced the town to lay off scores of teachers.

The secession of the fortunate fifth has been most apparent in how and where they have chosen to work and live. In effect, most of America's large urban centers have splintered into two separate cities. One is composed of those whose symbolic and analytic services are linked to the world economy. The other consists of local service workers — custodians, security guards, taxi drivers, clerical aides, parking attendants, salespeople, restaurant employees — whose jobs are dependent on the symbolic analysts. Few blue-collar manufacturing workers remain in American cities. Between 1953 and 1984, for example, New York City lost about 600,000 factory jobs; in the same interval, it added about 700,000 jobs for symbolic analysts and service workers.

The separation of symbolic analysts from local service workers within cities has been reinforced in several ways. Most large cities now possess two school systems — a private one for the children of the top-earning group and a public one for the children of service workers, the remaining blue-collar workers, and the unemployed. Symbolic analysts spend considerable time and energy insuring that their children gain entrance to good private schools, and then small fortunes keeping them there — dollars that under a more progressive tax code might finance better public education.

People with high incomes live, shop, and work within areas of cities that, if not beautiful, are at least esthetically tolerable and reasonably safe, precincts not meeting these minimum standards of charm and security have been left to the less fortunate.

Here again, symbolic analysts have pooled their resources to the exclusive benefit of themselves. Public funds have been spent in earnest on downtown "revitalization" projects, entailing the construction of clusters of post-modern office buildings (complete with fiber-optic cables, private branch exchanges, satellite dishes, and other communications equipment linking them to the rest of the world), multilevel parking garages, hotels with glass-enclosed atriums, upscale shopping plazas and galleries, theaters, convention centers, and luxury condominiums.

Ideally, these complexes are entirely self-contained, with air-conditioned walkways linking residences, businesses, and recreational space. The lucky resident is able to shop, work, and attend the theater without risking direct contact with the outside world — that is, the other city.

When not living in urban enclaves, symbolic analysts are increasingly congregating in suburbs and exurbs where corporate headquarters have been relocated, research parks have been created, and where bucolic universities have spawned entrepreneurial ventures. Among the most desirable of such locations are Princeton, N.J.; northern Westchester and Putnam Counties in New York; Palo Alto, Calif.; Austin, Tex.; Bethesda, Md.; and Raleigh-Durham, N.C.

Engineers and strategists of American auto companies, for example, do not   30
live in Flint or Saginaw, Mich., where the blue-collar workers reside; they cluster in their own towns of Troy, Warren, and Auburn Hills. Likewise, the vast majority of the financial specialists, lawyers, and executives working for the insurance companies of Hartford would never consider living there; after all, Hartford is the nation's fourth-poorest city. Instead, they flock to Windsor, Middlebury, West Hartford, and other towns that are among the wealthiest in the country.

This trend, too, has been growing for decades. But technology has accelerated it. Today's symbolic analysts linked directly to the rest of the globe can choose to live and work in the most pastoral of settings.

The secession has been encouraged by the Federal Government. For the last decade, Washington has in effect shifted responsibility for many public services to local governments. At their peak, Federal grants made up 25 percent of state and local spending in the late 1970s. Today, the Federal share has dwindled to 17 percent. Direct aid to local governments, in the form of programs introduced in the Johnson and Nixon Administrations, has been the hardest hit by budget cuts. In the 1980s, Federal dollars for clean water, job training and transfers, low-income housing, sewage treatment, and garbage disposal shrank by some $50 billion a year, and Washington's share of spending on local transit declined by 50 percent. (The Bush Administration has proposed that states and localities take on even more of the costs of building and maintaining roads, and wants to cut Federal aid for mass transit.) In 1990, New York City received only 9.6 percent of all its revenue from the Federal Government, compared with 16 percent in 1981.

States have quickly transferred many of these new expenses to fiscally strapped cities and towns, with a result that by the start of the 1990s, localities were bearing more than half of the costs of water and sewage, roads, parks, welfare, and public schools. In New York State, the local communities' share has risen to about 75 percent of these costs.

Cities and towns with affluent inhabitants can bear these burdens relatively easily. Poorer ones, faced with the twin problems of lower incomes and greater demand for social services, have had far more difficulty. And as the gap between the richest and poorest communities has widened, the shift in responsibility for public services to cities and towns has functioned as another means of relieving wealthier Americans of the cost of aiding less fortunate citizens.

The result has been a growing inequality in basic social and community ser-   35 vices. While the city tax rate in Philadelphia, for example, is about triple that of communities around it, the suburbs enjoy far better schools, hospitals, recreation, and police protection. Eighty-five percent of the richest families in the greater Philadelphia area live outside the city limits, and 80 percent of the region's poorest live inside. The quality of a city's infrastructure — roads, bridges, sewage, water treatment — is likewise related to the average income of its inhabitants.

The growing inequality in government services has been most apparent in the public schools. The Federal Government's share of the costs of primary and secondary education has dwindled to about 6 percent. The bulk of the cost is divided about equally between the states and local school districts. States with a higher concentration of wealthy residents can afford to spend more on their schools than other states. In 1989, the average public-school teacher in Arkansas, for example, received $21,700; in Connecticut, $37,300.

Even among adjoining suburban towns in the same state the differences can be quite large. Consider three Boston-area communities located within minutes of one another. All are predominantly white, and most residents within each town earn about the same as their neighbors. But the disparity of incomes between towns is substantial.

Belmont, northwest of Boston, is inhabited mainly by symbolic analysts and their families. In 1988, the average teacher in its public schools earned $36,100. Only 3 percent of Belmont's eighteen-year-olds dropped out of high school, and more than 80 percent of graduating seniors chose to go on to a four-year college.

Just east of Belmont is Somerville, most of whose residents are low-wage service workers. In 1988, the average Somerville teacher earned $29,400. A third of the town's eighteen-year-olds did not finish high school, and fewer than a third planned to attend college.

Chelsea, across the Mystic River from Somerville, is the poorest of the three   40 towns. Most of its inhabitants are unskilled, and many are unemployed or only employed part time. The average teacher in Chelsea, facing tougher educational challenges than his or her counterparts in Belmont, earned $26,200 in 1988, almost a third less than the average teacher in the more affluent town just a few miles away. More than half of Chelsea's eighteen-year-olds did not graduate from high school, and only 10 percent planned to attend college.

Similar disparities can be found all over the nation. Students at Highland Park High School in a wealthy suburb of Dallas, for example, enjoy a campus with a planetarium, indoor swimming pool, closed-circuit television studio and state-of-the-art science laboratory. Highland Park spends about $6,000 a year to educate each student. This is almost twice that spent per pupil by the towns of Wilmer and Hutchins in southern Dallas County. According to Texas education officials, the richest school district in the state spends $19,300 a year per pupil; its poorest, $2,100 a year.

The courts have become involved in trying to repair such imbalances, but the issues are not open to easy judicial remedy.

The four-fifths of Americans left in the wake of the secession of the fortunate fifth include many poor blacks, but racial exclusion is neither the primary motive for the separation nor a necessary consequence. Lower-income whites are similarly excluded, and high-income black symbolic analysts are often welcomed. The segregation is economic rather than racial, although economically motivated separation often results in *de facto* racial segregation. Where courts have found a pattern of racially motivated segregation, it usually has involved lower-income white communities bordering on lower-income black neighborhoods.

In states where courts have ordered equalized state spending in school districts, the vast differences in a town's property values — and thus local tax revenues — continue to result in substantial inequities. Where courts or state governments have tried to impose limits on what affluent communities can pay their teachers, not a few parents in upscale towns have simply removed their children from the public schools and applied the money they might otherwise have willingly paid in higher taxes to private school tuitions instead. And, of course, even if statewide expenditures were better equalized, poorer states would continue to be at a substantial disadvantage.

In all these ways, the gap between America's symbolic analysts and everyone else is widening into a chasm. Their secession from the rest of the population raises fundamental questions about the future of American society. In the new global economy — in which money, technologies, and corporations cross borders effortlessly — a citizen's standard of living depends more and more on skills and insights, and on the infrastructure needed to link these abilities to the rest of the world. But the most skilled and insightful Americans, who are already positioned to thrive in the world market, are now able to slip the bonds of national allegiance, and by so doing disengage themselves from their less-favored fellows. The stark political challenge in the decades ahead will be to reaffirm that, even though America is no longer a separate and distinct economy, it is still a society whose members have abiding obligations to one another.

How to Get the Poor Off Our Conscience

JOHN KENNETH GALBRAITH

I WOULD LIKE to reflect on one of the oldest of human exercises, the process by which over the years, and indeed over the centuries, we have undertaken to get the poor off our conscience.

Rich and poor have lived together, always uncomfortably and sometimes perilously, since the beginning of time. Plutarch was led to say: "An imbalance between the rich and poor is the oldest and most fatal ailment of republics." And the problems that arise from the continuing coexistence of affluence and poverty — and particularly the process by which good fortune is justified in the presence of the ill fortune of others — have been an intellectual preoccupation for centuries. They continue to be so in our own time.

One begins with the solution proposed in the Bible: The poor suffer in this world but are wonderfully rewarded in the next. Their poverty is a temporary misfortune; if they are poor and also meek, they eventually will inherit the earth. This is, in some ways, an admirable solution. It allows the rich to enjoy their wealth while envying the poor their future fortune.

Much, much later, in the twenty or thirty years following the publication in 1776 of *The Wealth of Nations* — the late dawn of the Industrial Revolution in Britain — the problem and its solution began to take on their modern form. Jeremy Bentham, a near contemporary of Adam Smith, came up with the formula that for perhaps fifty years was extraordinarily influential in British and, to some degree, American thought. This was utilitarianism. "By the principle of utility," Bentham said in 1789, "is meant the principle which approves or disapproves of every action whatsoever according to the tendency which it appears to have to augment or diminish the happiness of the party whose interest is in question." Virtue is, indeed must be, self-centered. While there were people with great good fortune and many more with great ill fortune, the social problem was solved as long as, again in Bentham's words, there was "the greatest good for the greatest number." Society did its best for the largest possible number of people; one accepted that the result might be sadly unpleasant for the many whose happiness was not served.

In the 1830s a new formula, influential in no slight degree to this day, became available for getting the poor off the public conscience. This is associated with the names of David Ricardo, a stockbroker, and Thomas Robert Malthus, a divine. The essentials are familiar: the poverty of the poor was the fault of the poor. And it was so because it was a product of their excessive fecundity: their grievously uncontrolled lust caused them to breed up to the full limits of the available subsistence.

This was Malthusianism. Poverty being caused in the bed meant that the rich were not responsible for either its creation or its amelioration. However, Malthus was himself not without a certain feeling of responsibility: he urged that the marriage ceremony contain a warning against undue and irresponsible sexual intercourse — a warning, it is fair to say, that has not been accepted as a fully effective method of birth control. In more recent times, Ronald Reagan has said that the best form of population control emerges from the market. (Couples in love should repair to R. H. Macy's, not their bedrooms.) Malthus, it must be said, was at least as relevant.

By the middle of the nineteenth century, a new form of denial achieved great influence, especially in the United States. The new doctrine, associated with the name of Herbert Spencer, was Social Darwinism. In economic life, as in biological development, the overriding rule was survival of the fittest. That phrase — "survival of the fittest" — came, in fact, not from Charles Darwin but from Spencer, and expressed his view of economic life. The elimination of the poor is nature's way of improving the race. The weak and unfortunate being extruded, the quality of the human family is thus strengthened.

One of the most notable American spokespersons of Social Darwinism was

John D. Rockefeller — the first Rockefeller — who said in a famous speech: "The American Beauty rose can be produced in the splendor and fragrance which bring cheer to its beholder only by sacrificing the early buds which grow up around it. And so it is in economic life. It is merely the working out of a law of nature and a law of God."

In the course of the present century, however, Social Darwinism came to be considered a bit too cruel. It declined in popularity, and references to it acquired a condemnatory tone. We passed on to the more amorphous denial of poverty associated with Calvin Coolidge and Herbert Hoover. They held that public assistance to the poor interfered with the effective operation of the economic system — that such assistance was inconsistent with the economic design that had come to serve most people very well. The notion that there is something economically damaging about helping the poor remains with us to this day as one of the ways by which we get them off our conscience.

With the Roosevelt revolution (as previously with that of Lloyd George in Britain), a specific responsibility was assumed by the government for the least fortunate people in the republic. Roosevelt and the presidents who followed him accepted a substantial measure of responsibility for the old through Social Security, for the unemployed through unemployment insurance, for the unemployable and the handicapped through direct relief, and for the sick through Medicare and Medicaid. This was a truly great change, and for a time, the age-old tendency to avoid thinking about the poor gave way to the feeling that we didn't need to try — that we were, indeed, doing something about them.

In recent years, however, it has become clear that the search for a way of getting the poor off our conscience was not at an end; it was only suspended. And so we are now again engaged in this search in a highly energetic way. It has again become a major philosophical, literary, and rhetorical preoccupation, and an economically not unrewarding enterprise.

Of the four, maybe five, current designs we have to get the poor off our conscience, the first proceeds from the inescapable fact that most of the things that must be done on behalf of the poor must be done in one way or another by the government. It is then argued that the government is inherently incompetent, except as regards weapon design and procurement and the overall management of the Pentagon. Being incompetent and ineffective, it must not be asked to succor the poor; it will only louse things up or make things worse.

The allegation of government incompetence is associated in our time with the general condemnation of the bureaucrat — again excluding those concerned with national defense. The only form of discrimination that is still permissible — that is, still officially encouraged in the United States today — is discrimination against people who work for the federal government, especially on social welfare activities. We have great corporate bureaucracies replete with corporate bureaucrats, but they are good; only public bureaucracy and government servants are bad. In fact, we have in the United States an extraordinarily good public service — one made up of talented and dedicated people who are overwhelmingly honest and only rarely given to overpaying for monkey wrenches, flashlights,

10

coffee makers, and toilet seats. (When these aberrations have occurred, they have, oddly enough, all been in the Pentagon.) We have nearly abolished poverty among the old, greatly democratized health care, assured minorities of their civil rights, and vastly enhanced educational opportunity. All this would seem a considerable achievement for incompetent and otherwise ineffective people. We must recognize that the present condemnation of government and government administration is really part of the continuing design for avoiding responsibility for the poor.

The second design in this great centuries-old tradition is to argue that any form of public help to the poor only hurts the poor. It destroys morale. It seduces people away from gainful employment. It breaks up marriages, since women can seek welfare for themselves and their children once they are without their husbands.

There is no proof of this — none, certainly, that compares that damage with   15
the damage that would be inflicted by the loss of public assistance. Still, the case is made — and believed — that there is something gravely damaging about aid to the unfortunate. This is perhaps our most highly influential piece of fiction.

The third, and closely related, design for relieving ourselves of responsibility for the poor is the argument that public-assistance measures have an adverse effect on incentive. They transfer income from the diligent to the idle and feckless, thus reducing the effort of the diligent and encouraging the idleness of the idle. The modern manifestation of this is supply-side economics. Supply-side economics holds that the rich in the United States have not been working because they have too little income. So, by taking money from the poor and giving it to the rich, we increase effort and stimulate the economy. Can we really believe that any considerable number of the poor prefer welfare to a good job? Or that business people — corporate executives, the key figures in our time — are idling away their hours because of the insufficiency of their pay? This is a scandalous charge against the American businessperson, notably a hard worker. Belief can be the servant of truth — but even more of convenience.

The fourth design for getting the poor off our conscience is to point to the presumed adverse effect on freedom of taking responsibility for them. Freedom consists of the right to spend a maximum of one's money by one's own choice, and to see a minimum taken and spent by the government. (Again, expenditure on national defense is excepted.) In the enduring words of Professor Milton Friedman, people must be "free to choose."

This is probably the most transparent of all of the designs; no mention is ordinarily made of the relation of income to the freedom of the poor. (Professor Friedman is here an exception; through the negative income tax, he would assure everyone a basic income.) There is, we can surely agree, no form of oppression that is quite so great, no constriction on thought and effort quite so comprehensive, as that which comes from having no money at all. Though we hear much about the limitation on the freedom of the affluent when their income is reduced through taxes, we hear nothing of the extraordinary enhancement of the freedom of the poor from having some money of their own to spend. Yet the loss of freedom from taxation to the rich is a small thing as compared with the gain in freedom from providing some income to the impoverished. Freedom we rightly cherish. Cherishing it, we should not use it as a cover for denying freedom to those in need.

Finally, when all else fails, we resort to simple psychological denial. This is a psychic tendency that in various manifestations is common to us all. It causes us to avoid thinking about death. It causes a great many people to avoid thought of the arms race and the consequent rush toward a highly probable extinction. By the same process of psychological denial, we decline to think of the poor. Whether they be in Ethiopia, the South Bronx, or even in such an Elysium as Los Angeles, we resolve to keep them off our minds. Think, we are often advised, of something pleasant.

These are the modern designs by which we escape concern for the poor. All, 20 save perhaps the last, are in great inventive descent from Bentham, Malthus, and Spencer. Ronald Reagan and his colleagues are clearly in a notable tradition — at the end of a long history of effort to escape responsibility for one's fellow beings. So are the philosophers now celebrated in Washington: George Gilder, a greatly favored figure of the recent past, who tells to much applause that the poor must have the cruel spur of their own suffering to ensure effort; Charles Murray, who, to greater cheers, contemplates "scrapping the entire federal welfare and income-support structure for working and aged persons, including A.F.D.C., Medicaid, food stamps, unemployment insurance, Workers' Compensation, subsidized housing, disability insurance, and," he adds, "the rest. Cut the knot, for there is no way to untie it." By a triage, the worthy would be selected to survive; the loss of the rest is the penalty we should pay. Murray is the voice of Spencer in our time; he is enjoying, as indicated, unparalleled popularity in high Washington circles.

Compassion, along with the associated public effort, is the least comfortable, the least convenient, course of behavior and action in our time. But it remains the only one that is consistent with a totally civilized life. Also, it is, in the end, the most truly conservative course. There is no paradox here. Civil discontent and its consequences do not come from contented people — an obvious point. To the extent that we can make contentment as nearly universal as possible, we will preserve and enlarge the social and political tranquility for which conservatives, above all, should yearn.

Chapter 9

Arguing about Language

Our Differences about Language

The seventeenth-century English philosopher Francis Bacon listed language as one of the barriers to exact thinking. Paradoxically, it is also language that makes it possible for us to communicate our ideas at all. Language allows us to understand one another, but it is also through language that we misunderstand. The twentieth-century philosopher Kenneth Burke argued that language is like a screen or a filter on a camera: It lets some meanings in and excludes others. Many disagreements in a community are about language. What do words mean? How should we interpret language? What language is appropriate or proper for a particular occasion? In addition to differences about language itself, there are also differences or disagreements caused by language, by the inability to communicate ideas in terms that others will understand. Sometimes disagreements are not really disagreements at all; they only seem so because people misunderstand each other. We often misunderstand each other because we assume that the meanings of words are obvious or that everyone is working with the same definitions and the same meanings. The process of arguing about language can help us to use language more precisely and to focus our attention on our real disagreements rather than on seeming disagreements that are actually misunderstandings.

Arguing about Language

▓ ▓ DEFINITIONS OF TERMS

Many arguments depend on the precise definition of key terms, and many disagreements arise when those using key terms have not defined them for one another. For instance, the question "Is there more racism on college campuses today?" is about experience, but answering the question depends on how one defines "racism." "Is pornography immoral?" is a question relating to values, but answering it requires not only a definition of "pornography" but also a definition of what is "moral" and "immoral." Some may argue that abortion should be banned because it is murder. Is it really murder? It depends on one's definition. Some environmental activists argue that the clear cutting of timber should be banned because it is ecological rape. Can the definition of rape be extended, even in a figurative sense, to the cutting of timber? Here are examples of other questions about defining key terms:

What is terrorism?

What is democracy or freedom?

What is courage?

What is justice?

What is sexual harassment?

What is a liberal?

What is a conservative?

These are terms that are used all the time in debates about political issues, but their definitions can be somewhat difficult to pin down.

Denotation and Connotation   One way to settle a dispute about definitions is to appeal to an authority, such as a dictionary or an expert, that is acknowledged by everyone involved in the dispute. When my friends and I play Scrabble, we agree before the game even starts on a dictionary that will be used to settle any disputes about whether a word is legitimate or not. As a student, you should become familiar with dictionaries that are considered authoritative, such as *Webster's Third International Dictionary, Black's Law Dictionary,* the *Random House Unabridged Dictionary,* and the *Oxford English Dictionary.* The *Oxford English Dictionary,* known as the OED, is particularly valuable because it not only gives the current meaning of a word, but also traces the changes in a word's meaning since its earliest appearances in print.

A dictionary, no matter how authoritative, has its limitations. It can describe how a community uses a word in very general terms, but it may not describe the shades of meaning the word has within different contexts. A dictionary provides the "denotative" definition of a word, what the word literally means, but dictionaries seldom provide "connotative" meanings, the associations a word carries with it. For instance, the following words all have the same denotative meaning as the word *dead: deceased, departed, passed away, passed on, extinct, inanimate, late, lifeless, croaked, belly up, six feet under, pushing daisies, food for worms.* These words do not have the same connotation, however, and would not all be appropriate for the same contexts.

A word that has a particularly emotional connotation is often used in an argument to harm or injure. It is loaded language, language used as a weapon. Hate speech, the use of derogatory and demeaning terms to express anger or to attack others, provides a good example. In the academic community, as well as many others, this type of violence through language is not acceptable.

Euphemisms and Doublespeak   A word that is chosen for its positive connotations is called a "euphemism," from the Greek for "good meaning." When you use "departed" or "passed on" for "dead," you are using a euphemism, selecting a word for its positive connotations.

Sometimes euphemisms can be deceptive or misleading, giving an idea a more positive connotation than a straightforward statement will allow. Politicians have used the term "revenue enhancement" to hide the fact that they are imposing a "tax." Military leaders have used the phrase "engaging the enemy on all sides" to hide the fact that their troops have become surrounded; and the phrase "collateral damage to soft targets" was used during the Gulf War to hide the fact that U.S. bombs and missiles had harmed civilians. Governments refer to rebel groups they support as "freedom fighters" and rebel groups that they oppose as "terrorists," even when both groups use the same methods.

The use of language to obscure meaning in this way is called "doublespeak," a term that comes from George Orwell's novel *1984,* in which the government attempts to convince people that "war is peace" and "ignorance is knowledge," completely changing the denotative as well as connotative meanings of words.

Troublesome Terms   Simply looking a word up in a dictionary may not be enough when complex questions and concepts are concerned. For instance, most dictionaries define "life" as an organism's ability to carry out metabolic functions, grow, respond to stimuli, and reproduce. This definition is generally useful, but how helpful is it in determining when human life begins or ends? A human cell does all of the above, but is it alive in the same sense that a human being is? At what stage does a fertilized egg change from a human cell to a human being? Life support can keep the human cells alive, but is the body on life support still a human life? And how helpful is this definition in determining whether something like a virus is really "alive"? In such cases you may need to formulate your own definition of the term for the purposes of argument. Here are some techniques for defining troublesome terms.

SYNONYMS AND PARAPHRASES   If a word requires a simple definition, then you can define it by choosing synonyms, words that mean approximately the same thing. You should seek out synonyms that are more familiar to your audience than the word you are trying to define. When you recast an entire passage in terms that are more familiar to the audience, then you have written a paraphrase.

CRITERIA AND MATCH   This is really a type of classification. You define the criteria that determine the members of a class, and then you examine a particular event or object to determine whether it fits those criteria. Criteria-and-match definitions take the following form:

> If something possesses features A, B, and C, then it is a Y.
>
> X possesses features A, B, and C.
>
> Therefore, X is a Y.

In determining the criteria, you need to determine which criteria are necessary and which are optional. For instance, the chromosomal structure of a horse is a necessary criterion for determining whether an animal is a horse or not, but the color brown is optional: Some horses are brown and some are not.

Here is an example of defining and matching criteria using the argument that abortion is murder. To respond to this argument, you first determine the criteria for defining murder. The dictionary defines murder as the unlawful killing of a human being with malicious forethought. Using the criteria based on this definition, the act must

> kill a human being
>
> be unlawful
>
> be malicious
>
> be done with forethought

Do you accept these criteria? Are there others you would add? Are they all necessary, or are some optional? Certainly, the killing of a human being is necessary. But does murder only apply to human beings? Is it not possible to murder animals? If the killing is sanctioned by law is it, therefore, not murder? The systematic killing of Jews by the Nazis during World War II and the shooting of defectors by East German border guards were sanctioned by law, yet the individuals who committed these acts were tried as murderers. Must the act be premeditated and malicious? The American legal system recognizes different degrees of murder, some of which do not require premeditation but are still considered murder. Establishing the criteria for what counts as murder and what doesn't is not as simple as it may first seem.

Let's say that you and your audience agree on these four criteria. You must now decide whether abortion matches these criteria for murder. Does an abortion kill a human being? It terminates a pregnancy and stops the growth of a fetus, but some dispute the stage at which a fetus can be considered a human being. Is a fertilized egg a human being? What happens when twinning occurs after the egg is fertilized? Did one human being turn into two? Is the differentiated zygote a human being? Some abortions are sanctioned by law. Does that mean they cannot be defined as murders? Or can these acts be judged by some higher law just as the Nazis and East German border guards were? Is a doctor who performs an abortion performing a malicious act? Is the abortion always done with forethought, or could it be accidental or unintentional? If it is unintentional, is it still murder?

Of course, there are no easy answers to these questions: That is why there are disputes about definitions in the first place. But determining criteria and matching these to topics of debate can help to clarify complex issues.

FORMAL DEFINITION   A formal definition is similar to criteria-and-match definition, but there is an extra step. In a formal definition, after placing an object in a group, you go on to distinguish it from all other members of that group. It is usually stated in the following format: "An X is a Y that has features A, B, and C" (Y is the group, and A, B, C are the features that distinguish X from all other members of the group). Some formal definitions can be fairly simple: "Brigham Young University is a comprehensive four-year university sponsored by the Church of Jesus Christ of Latter Day Saints (L.D.S.), also known as the Mormon Church. There are other colleges sponsored by the L.D.S. church, but they are not comprehensive four-year universities. There are other comprehensive four-year universities that are not sponsored by the L.D.S. church. This definition places Brigham Young University in a class (comprehensive four-year university) and then distinguishes it from all other members of that class (sponsored by the L.D.S. church). Try writing a formal definition for the university or college that you attend. What class does it belong to? How is it different from all other members of that class?

ETYMOLOGY AND WORD HISTORY   Sometimes, when defining a word, it helps to know the etymology (origin) or history of the word. For instance, the word *obscene* comes from Greek and it refers to the story elements of a Greek tragedy that were shown "off stage," the literal meaning of the Greek word. In a Greek tragedy, no actual violence was shown on stage, only its results: A character murdering her children or gouging out her husband's eyes took place off stage; the violence was often reported by a messenger, and then the character might appear covered in blood, but direct violence was "obscene." The meaning of *obscene* has changed in the last two thousand years. Today it can indicate things that are repulsive, but it usually applies to something that is crude and sexually explicit.

The change in this word indicates a change in culture, a change in what we now consider repulsive or inappropriate. The fact the violence is no longer considered obscene in the same way that sex is may indicate our society has come to accept violence. At any rate, the etymology of this word provides an interesting perspective on its meaning, a perspective that could easily be incorporated into an argument about sex and violence.

OPERATIONAL DEFINITION   An operational definition is a precise or technical definition of a term developed for a specific purpose. An operational definition often quantifies something or describes it in precise terms. For instance, a sociologist studying the effects of television violence on young children needs a definition of "violence." The dictionary definition — "the use of force to harm or abuse" — is not adequate because it cannot help *measure* violence. For the purposes of the study, the sociologist might define violence as certain types of violent acts: punching, slapping, or kicking a stuffed toy, for instance. This operational definition would allow the researcher to measure the effects of watching violent programs by counting the number of violent acts a child commits afterwards.

EXAMPLES, COMPARISONS, AND ANALOGIES   An example or analogy is an attempt to use the familiar to explain the unfamiliar. These may be literal or figurative, real or imagined. Instructors often use examples to explain difficult concepts, as I have used examples throughout this book. In a passage earlier in this chapter, Kenneth Burke used the analogy of a filter on a camera, something many may be familiar with or can imagine, to describe the way that language allows some meanings and excludes others. Obviously this analogy can work only for those who are familiar with cameras; it would be ineffective for those who have never seen a camera, so one would have to find another. When you are addressing a complex audience, made up of individuals with different experiences and background knowledge, it may be necessary to use multiple examples or comparisons in order to find something that is familiar to each individual.

NEGATION   One way to understand something is to describe what it is *not*. Theologians often use this approach in trying to describe the attributes of God. Scientists may use this approach to limit the possibilities for classifying or describing an unknown event. Be careful, though, not to mistake negation for definition. Negation limits the possibilities for what something may mean, but it doesn't reveal that meaning.

Evaluating a Definition   After you have made a first attempt at constructing a definition, here are some questions that will help you evaluate that definition:

1. Is it inclusive?
2. Is it sufficiently exclusive?
3. Is the language clear?
4. Does it emphasize the relevant detail, excluding unnecessary detail?

These questions are particularly valuable when you evaluate another writer's attempt to redefine a term or to settle a dispute about the meaning of the term.

You might also ask: What is the effect of defining a term in this way (for example, making the meaning more or less inclusive)?

▪ ▪ ARGUING ABOUT HOW LANGUAGE SHOULD BE USED

Some disputes in a community may arise over the meaning of words. Other disputes may revolve around deciding what language is appropriate for the community. One recent such dispute in the United States is about the official language of the American community: The "English Only" movement has attempted to establish English as the only appropriate language for official, public use in the United States. Even so, English is made up of a number of varieties and dialects, some of which are considered more valuable or appropriate depending on the community.

Claims about how language should be used are closely related to claims about experience and claims about value and will usually be supported by reasons that are statements about experience or about values. For instance, an argument might state that using language in a particular way leads to harmful or beneficial effects. This argument about language includes an argument about experience (causality) and an argument about values (harmful and beneficial). Another argument might state that using language in a particular way violates some principle of correctness or morality. This argument also includes an argument about values (principles of correctness and morality).

Arguments about language use are not just about individual words; they are about metaphors as well. The metaphors that govern the way we think and act reveal themselves in the words we use. When we use them unconsciously they can do our thinking for us. George Lakoff and Mark Johnson, in the following excerpt from their book *Metaphors We Live By,* explain how metaphors work in arguments.

from *Metaphors We Live By*

GEORGE LAKOFF and MARK JOHNSON

M ETAPHOR IS for most people a device of the poetic imagination and the   1
rhetorical flourish — a matter of extraordinary rather than ordinary language. Moreover, metaphor is typically viewed as characteristic of language alone, a matter of words rather than thought or action. For this reason, most people think they can get along perfectly well without metaphor. We have found, on the contrary, that metaphor is pervasive in everyday life, not just in language but in thought and action. Our ordinary conceptual system, in terms of which we both think and act, is fundamentally metaphorical in nature.

The concepts that govern our thought are not just matters of the intellect. They also govern our everyday functioning, down to the most mundane details. Our concepts structure what we perceive, how we get around in the world, and how we relate to other people. Our conceptual system thus plays a central role in defining our everyday realities. If we are right in suggesting that our conceptual system is largely metaphorical, then the way we think, what we experience, and what we do every day is very much a matter of metaphor.

But our conceptual system is not something we are normally aware of. In most of the little things we do every day, we simply think and act more or less automatically along certain lines. Just what these lines are is by no means obvious. One way to find out is by looking at language. Since communication is based on the same conceptual system that we use in thinking and acting, language is an important source of evidence for what that system is like.

Primarily on the basis of linguistic evidence, we have found that most of our ordinary conceptual system is metaphorical in nature. And we have found a way to begin to identify in detail just what the metaphors are that structure how we perceive, how we think, and what we do.

To give some idea of what it could mean for a concept to be metaphorical   5 and for such a concept to structure an everyday activity, let us start with the concept ARGUMENT and the conceptual metaphor ARGUMENT IS WAR. This metaphor is reflected in our everyday language by a wide variety of expressions:

Argument Is War

Your claims are *indefensible.*

He *attacked every weak point* in my argument.

His criticisms were *right on target.*

I *demolished* his argument.

I've never *won* an argument with him.

You disagree? Okay, *shoot!*

If you use that *strategy,* he'll *wipe you out.*

He *shot down* all of my arguments.

It is important to see that we don't just *talk* about arguments in terms of war. We can actually win or lose arguments. We see the person we are arguing with as an opponent. We attack his positions and we defend our own. We gain and lose ground. We plan and use strategies. If we find a position indefensible, we can abandon it and take a new line of attack. Many of the things we *do* in arguing are partially structured by the concept of war. Though there is no physical battle, there is a verbal battle, and the structure of an argument — attack, defense, counterattack, etc. — reflects this. It is in this sense that the ARGUMENT IS WAR metaphor is one that we live by in this culture; it structures the actions we perform in arguing.

Try to imagine a culture where arguments are not viewed in terms of war, where no one wins or loses, where there is no sense of attacking or defending, gaining or losing ground. Imagine a culture where an argument is viewed as a dance, the participants are seen as performers, and the goal is to perform in a balanced and aesthetically pleasing way. In such a culture, people would view arguments differently, experience them differently, carry them out differently, and talk about them differently. But *we* would probably not view them as arguing at all: They would simply be doing something different. It would seem strange even to call what they were doing "arguing." Perhaps the most neutral way of describing this difference between their culture and ours would be to say that we have a discourse form structured in terms of battle and they have one structured in terms of dance.

This is an example of what it means for a metaphorical concept, namely, ARGUMENT IS WAR, to structure (at least in part) what we do and how we understand what we are doing when we argue. *The essence of metaphor is understanding and experiencing one kind of thing in terms of another.* It is not that arguments are a subspecies of war. Arguments and wars are different kinds of things — verbal discourse and armed conflict — and the actions performed are different kinds of actions. But ARGUMENT is partially structured, understood, performed, and talked about in terms of WAR. The concept is metaphorically structured, the activity is metaphorically structured, and, consequently, the language is metaphorically structured.

Moreover, this is the *ordinary* way of having an argument and talking about one. The normal way for us to talk about attacking a position is to use the words "attack a position." Our conventional ways of talking about arguments presuppose a metaphor we are hardly ever conscious of. The metaphor is not merely in the words we use — it is in our very concept of an argument. The language of argument is not poetic, fanciful, or rhetorical; it is literal. We talk about arguments that way because we conceive of them that way — and we act according to the way we conceive of things.

The most important claim we have made so far is that metaphor is not just a matter of language, that is, of mere words. We shall argue that, on the contrary, human *thought processes* are largely metaphorical. This is what we mean when we say that the human conceptual system is metaphorically structured and defined. Metaphors as linguistic expressions are possible precisely because there are metaphors in a person's conceptual system. Therefore, whenever in this book we speak of metaphors, such as ARGUMENT IS WAR, it should be understood that *metaphor* means *metaphorical concept.* . . .

. . . [The] metaphor [ARGUMENT IS WAR] allows us to conceptualize what a rational argument is in terms of something that we understand more readily, namely, physical conflict. Fighting is found everywhere in the animal kingdom and nowhere so much as among human animals. Animals fight to get what they want — food, sex, territory, control, etc. — because there are other animals who want the same thing or who want to stop them from getting it. The same is true of human animals, except that we have developed more sophisticated techniques for getting our way. Being "rational animals," we have institutionalized our fighting in a number of ways, one of them being war. Even though we have over the ages institutionalized physical conflict and have employed many of our finest minds to develop more effective means of carrying it out, its basic structure remains essentially unchanged. In fights between two brute animals, scientists have observed the practices of issuing challenges for the sake of intimidation, of establishing and defending territory, attacking, defending, counterattacking, retreating, and surrendering. Human fighting involves the same practices.

Part of being a rational animal, however, involves getting what you want without subjecting yourself to the dangers of actual physical conflict. As a result, we humans have evolved the social institution of verbal argument. We have arguments all the time in order to try to get what we want, and sometimes these "degenerate" into physical violence. Such verbal battles are comprehended in much the same terms as physical battles. Take a domestic quarrel, for instance. Husband and wife are both trying to get what each of them wants, such as getting the other to accept a certain viewpoint on some issue or at least to act according to that viewpoint. Each sees himself as having something to win and something to lose, territory to establish and territory to defend. In a no-holds-barred argument, you attack, defend, counterattack, etc., using whatever verbal means you have at your disposal — intimidation, threat, invoking authority, insult, belittling, challenging authority, evading issues, bargaining, flattering, and even trying to give "rational reasons." But all of these tactics can be, and often are, presented as *reasons;* for example:

> . . . because I'm bigger than you. *(intimidation)*
>
> . . . because if you don't, I'll . . . *(threat)*
>
> . . . because I'm the boss. *(authority)*
>
> . . . because you're stupid. *(insult)*
>
> . . . because you usually do it wrong. *(belittling)*
>
> . . . because I have as much right as you do. *(challenging authority)*
>
> . . . because I love you. *(evading the issue)*
>
> . . . because if you will. . . , I'll . . . *(bargaining)*
>
> . . . because you're so much better at it. *(flattery)*

Arguments that use tactics like these are the most common in our culture, and because they are so much a part of our daily lives, we sometimes don't notice them. However, there are important and powerful segments of our culture where such tactics are, at least in principle, frowned upon because they are considered to be "irrational" and "unfair." The academic world, the legal world, the diplomatic world, the ecclesiastical world, and the world of journalism claim to present an ideal, or "higher," form of RATIONAL ARGUMENT, in which all of these tactics are forbidden. The only permissible tactics in this RATIONAL ARGUMENT are supposedly the stating of premises, the citing of supporting evidence, and the drawing of logical conclusions. But even in the most ideal cases, where all of these conditions hold, RATIONAL ARGUMENT is still comprehended and carried out in terms of WAR. There is still a position to be established and defended, you can win or lose, you have an opponent whose position you attack and try to destroy and whose argument you try to shoot down. If you are completely successful, you can wipe him out.

The point here is that not only our conception of an argument but the way we carry it out is grounded in our knowledge and experience of physical combat. Even if you have never fought a fistfight in your life, much less a war, but have been arguing from the time you began to talk, you still conceive of arguments, and execute them, according to the ARGUMENT IS WAR metaphor because the metaphor is built into the conceptual system of the culture in which you live. Not only are all the "rational" arguments that are assumed to actually live up to the ideal of RATIONAL ARGUMENT conceived of in terms of WAR, but almost all of them contain, in hidden form, the "irrational" and "unfair" tactics that rational arguments in their ideal form are supposed to transcend. Here are some typical examples:

It is plausible to assume that . . . *(intimidation)*
Clearly, . . .
Obviously, . . .

It would be unscientific to fail to . . . *(threat)*
To say that would be to commit the Fallacy of . . .

As Descartes showed, . . . *(authority)*
Hume observed that . . .
Footnote 374: cf. Verschlungenheimer, 1954.

The work lacks the necessary rigor for . . . *(insult)*
Let us call such a theory "Narrow" Rationalism.
In a display of "scholarly objectivity," . . .

The work will not lead to a formalized theory. *(belittling)*
His results cannot be quantified.
Few people today seriously hold that view.

Lest we succumb to the error of positivist approaches, . . .
(challenging authority)
Behaviorism has led to . . .

He does not present any alternative theory. *(evading the issue)*
But that is a matter of . . .
The author does present some challenging facts, although . . .

Your position is right as far as it goes, . . . *(bargaining)*
If one takes a realist point of view, one can accept the claim that . . .

In his stimulating paper, . . . *(flattery)*
His paper raises some interesting issues.

Examples like these allow us to trace the lineage of our rational argument back through "irrational" argument (= *everyday arguing*) to its origins in physical combat. The tactics of intimidation, threat, appeal to authority, etc., though couched, perhaps, in more refined phrases, are just as present in rational argument as they are in everyday arguing and in war. Whether we are in a scientific, academic, or legal setting, aspiring to the ideal of rational argument, or whether we are just trying to get our way in our own household by haggling, the way we conceive of, carry out, and describe our arguments is grounded in the ARGUMENT IS WAR metaphor.

Applying the Principles

■ ■ ARGUING ABOUT DEFINITIONS: LANGUAGE AND IDENTITY

The following essays are attempts by two writers to define (or redefine) troublesome terms. As you read these essays, refer to the techniques outlined earlier. What techniques do these authors use? Do they use any techniques that are not described in this chapter? In addition, use the questions on page 324 to evaluate their definitions. What is the effect of accepting their definitions? How might you change their definitions?

Defining the "American Indian": A Case Study in the Language of Suppression

HAIG A. BOSMAJIAN

Thesis

ONE OF THE FIRST important acts of an oppressor is to redefine the oppressed victims he intends to jail or eradicate so that they will be looked upon as creatures warranting suppression and in some cases separation and annihilation. I say "creatures" because the redefinition usually implies a dehumanization of the individual. The Nazis redefined the Jews as "bacilli," "parasites," "disease," and "demon."[1] The language of white racism has for centuries attempted to "keep the nigger in his place."[2] Our sexist language has allowed men to define who and what a woman is.[3] The labels "traitors," "queers," "pinkos,"

---

[1] See Haig A. Bosmajian, "The Magic Word in Nazi Persuasion," *ETC.*, 23 (March 1966), 9–23; Werner Betz, "The National-Socialist Vocabulary," *The Third Reich* (London: Weidenfeld and Nicolson, 1955); Heinz Paechter, *Nazi-Deutsch* (New York: Frederick Ungar, 1944).

[2] See Simon Podair, "Language and Prejudice," *Phylon Review*, 17 (1956), 390–394; Haig A. Bosmajian, "The Language of White Racism," *College English*, 31 (December 1969), 263–272.

[3] See Haig A. Bosmajian, "The Language of Sexism," *ETC.*, 29 (September 1972), 305–313.

"saboteurs," and "obscene degenerates" have all been used to attack students protesting the war in Vietnam and the economic and political injustices in this country.[4] One obviously does not listen to, much less talk to, traitors and outlaws, sensualists and queers. One only punishes them or, as Spiro Agnew suggested in one of his 1970 campaign speeches, indicates that there are some dissenters who should be separated "from our society with no more regret than we should feel over discarding rotten apples from a barrel."[5]

Through the use of the language of suppression, the human animal can seemingly justify the unjustifiable, make palatable the unpalatable, and make decent the indecent. Just as our thoughts affect our language, so does our language affect our thoughts and eventually our action and behavior. As George Orwell observed in his famous essay "Politics and the English Language," our language becomes ugly and inaccurate because our thoughts are foolish and then "the slovenliness of our language makes it easier for us to have foolish thoughts." Orwell maintained that "the decadence of our language is probably curable" and that "silly words and expressions have often disappeared, not through any evolutionary process but owing to the conscious action of a minority."[6] This then is our task: to identify the decadence in our language, the silly words and expressions which have been used to justify oppression of varying degrees. . . .

A case study of this inhumane use of language and of the linguistic dehumanization process is provided in the manner in which the European invaders of the New World redefined the occupants of what is now called North America and the manner in which white Americans have perpetuated through language the suppression of the "Indians" into the twentieth century. This essay will focus on and examine (1) the natural-religious redefinition of the "Indians"; (2) the political-cultural redefinition of the "Indians"; and (3) the legal redefinition of the "Indians."

THE NATURAL-RELIGIOUS REDEFINITION

The "de-civilization," the dehumanization and redefinition of the Indian, began with the arrival of Columbus in the New World. The various peoples in the New World, even though the differences between them were as great as between Italians and Irish or Finns and Portuguese, were all dubbed "Indians," and then "American Indians."[7] Having renamed the inhabitants, the invaders then proceeded to enslave, torture, and kill them, justifying this inhumanity by defining these inhabitants as "savages" and "barbarians." The Europeans' plundering and killing of the Indians in the West Indies outraged a Spanish Domini-

---

[4] See Haig A. Bosmajian, "The Protest Generation and Its Critics," *Discourse: A Review of the Liberal Arts*, 9 (Autumn 1966), 464–469.

[5] *The New York Times*, October 31, 1969, p. 25.

[6] "Politics and the English Language," in C. Muscatine and M. Griffith, *The Borzoi College Reader*, 2nd ed. (New York: Alfred A. Knopf, 1971), p. 88.

[7] Peter Farb, *Man's Rise to Civilization as Shown by the Indians of North America from Primeval Times to the Coming of the Industrial State* (New York: E. P. Dutton and Company, 1968), p. xx.

can missionary, Bartolome de las Casas, who provided the following account of the conquest of the Arawaks and Caribs in his *Brief Relation of the Destruction of the Indies:*

brutal
inigvitos They [the Spaniards] came with their Horsemen well armed with Sword and
diabolical Launce, making most cruel havocks and slaughters. . . . Overruning Cities and
Villages, where they spared no sex nor age; neither would their cruelty pity
Women with childe, whose bellies they would rip up, taking out the Infant to
hew it in pieces. . . . The children they would take by the feet and dash their
innocent heads against the rocks, and when they were fallen into the water, with
a strange and cruel derision they would call on them to swim. . . . They erected
certain Gallowses . . . upon every one of which they would hang thirteen persons,
blasphemously affirming that they did it in honor of our Redeemer and his Apos-
tles, and then putting fire under them, they burnt the poor wretches alive. Those
whom their pity did think to spare, they would send away with their hands cut
off, and so hanging by the skin.[8]

After the arrival of the Spaniards, "whole Arawak villages disappeared through slavery, disease, and warfare, as well as by flight into the mountains. As a result, the native population of Haiti, for example, declined from an estimated 200,000 in 1492 to a mere 29,000 only twenty-two years later."[9]

The Spaniards were followed by the English who brought with them their ideas of their white supremacy. In his *The Indian Heritage in America*, Alvin M. Josephy, Jr., observes that "in the early years of the sixteenth century educated whites, steeped in the theological teaching of Europe, argued learnedly about whether or not Indians were humans with souls, whether they, too, derived from Adam and Eve (and were therefore sinful like the rest of mankind), or whether they were a previously subhuman species."[10] Uncivilized and satanic as the In-dian may have been, according to the European invaders, he could be saved; but if he could not be saved then he would be destroyed. As Roy H. Pearce has put it, "Convinced thus of his divine right to Indian lands, the Puritan discovered in the Indians themselves evidence of a Satanic opposition to the very principle of divinity."[11] However, continues Pearce, the Indian "also was a man who had to be brought to the civilized responsibilities of Christian manhood, a wild man to be improved along with wild lands, a creature who had to be made into a Puritan if he was to be saved. Save him, and you saved one of Satan's victims. Destroy him, and you destroy one of Satan's partisans."[12] Indians who resisted Puritan invasions of their lands were dubbed "heathens," the "heathen" definition and status in turn justifying mass killing of Indians who refused to give up their lands

[8] Alvin M. Josephy, Jr., *The Indian Heritage of America* (New York: Bantam Books, Inc., 1969), p. 286.
[9] Farb, p. 243.
[10] Josephy, p. 4.
[11] Roy H. Pearce, *The Savages of America* (Baltimore: The Johns Hopkins Press, 1965), p. 21.
[12] Pearce, pp. 21–22.

to the white invaders: "When the Pequots resisted the migration of settlers into the Connecticut Valley in 1637, a party of Puritans surrounded the Pequot village and set fire to it. . . . Cotton Mather was grateful to the Lord that 'on this day we have sent six hundred heathen souls to hell.'"[13]

The European invaders, having defined themselves as culturally superior to the inhabitants they found in the New World, proceeded to their "manifest destiny" and subsequently to the massive killing of the "savages." "This sense of superiority over the Indians," write L. L. Knowles and K. Prewitt in *Institutional Racism in America,* "which was fostered by the religious ideology they carried to the new land, found its expression in the self-proclaimed mission to civilize and Christianize — a mission which was to find its ultimate expression in ideas of a 'manifest destiny' and a 'white man's burden.'"[14] But the Christianizing and "civilizing" process did not succeed and "thus began an extended process of genocide, giving rise to such aphorisms as "The only good Indian is a dead Indian. . . . Since Indians were capable of reaching only the state of 'savage,' they should not be allowed to impede the forward (westward, to be exact) progress of white civilization. The Church quickly acquiesced in this redefinition of the situation."[15]

THE POLITICAL-CULTURAL REDEFINTION

If the Indians were not defined as outright "savages" or "barbarians," they were labeled "natives," and as Arnold Toynbee has observed in Volume One of *A Study of History,* "when we Westerners call people 'Natives' we implicitly take the cultural colour out of our perceptions of them. We see them as trees walking, or as wild animals infesting the country in which we happen to come across them. In fact, we see them as part of the local flora and fauna, and not as men of like passions with ourselves; and, seeing them thus as something infrahuman, we feel entitled to treat them as though they did not possess ordinary human rights."[16] Once the Indian was labeled "native" by the white invaders, the latter had in effect established the basis for domesticating or exterminating the former.

In 1787, at the Constitutional Convention, it had to be decided what inhabitants of the total population in the newly formed United States should be counted in determining how many representatives each state would have in Congress. The Founding Father decided: "Representatives and direct taxes shall be apportioned among the several states . . . according to their respective numbers, which shall be determined by adding to the whole number of free persons, including those bound to service for a term of years, and excluding Indians not

[13] Farb, p. 247.
[14] Louis L. Knowles and Kenneth Prewitt, eds., *Institutional Racism in America* (Englewood Cliffs, N.J.: Prentice-Hall, Inc., 1969), p. 7.
[15] Knowles and Prewitt, p. 8.
[16] *A Study of History* (London: Oxford University Press, 1935), I, p. 152. For further discussion of the connotation of "natives," see Volume II of *A Study of History,* pp. 574–580.

taxed, three fifths of all other persons." The enslaved black came out three fifths of a person and the Indian came out a nonentity.

When the Indians had been defined as "savages" with no future, the final result, as Pearce states, "was an image of the Indian out of society and out of history."[17] Once the Indians were successfully defined as governmental nonentities, no more justification was needed to drive them off their lands and to force them into migration and eventual death. In the nineteenth century, even the "civilized Indians" found themselves being systematically deprived of life and property. . . .

While the state and the church as institutions have defined the Indians into   10 subjugation, there has been in operation the use of a suppressive language by society at large which has perpetuated the dehumanization of the Indian. Our language includes various phrases and words which relegate the Indian to an inferior status: "The only good Indian is a dead Indian"; "Give it back to the Indians"; "drunken Indians," "dumb Indians," and "Redskins." Writings and speeches include references to the "Indian problem" in the same manner that references have been made by white Americans to the "Negro problem" and by the Nazis to the "Jewish problem." There was no "Jewish problem" in Germany until the Nazis created the myth; there was no "Negro problem" until white Americans created the myth; similarly, the "Indian problem" has been created in such a way that the oppressed, not the oppressor, evolve as "the problem."

THE LEGAL REDEFINITION

As the list of negative "racial characteristics" of the "Indian race" grew longer and longer over the years, the redefinition of the individual Indian became easier and easier. He was trapped by the racial definitions, stereotypes, and myths. No matter how intelligent, how "civilized" the Indian became, he or she was still an Indian. Even the one who managed to become a citizen (prior to 1924) could not discard his or her "Indian-ness" sufficiently to participate in white society. The language of the law was used to reinforce the redefinition of the oppressed into non-persons and this language of suppression, as law, became governmentally institutionalized, and in effect legitimatized. One of the most blatant examples of the use of the racial characteristic argument appears in an 1897 Minnesota Supreme Court decision dealing with the indictment of one Edward Wise for selling intoxicating liquors to an Indian who had severed all his relations with his tribe and had through the provision of the "Land in Severality Act" of February 8, 1887, become a citizen of the United States.[18] Wise was indicted for violating a statute which provided that "whosoever sells . . . any spiritous liquors or wines to any Indian in this state shall on conviction thereof be punished. . . ." In finding against Wise, the Minnesota Supreme Court em-

[17] Pearce, p. 135.
[18] *State v. Wise*, 72 N.W. 843 (1897).

phasized the weaknesses of the "Indian race" and the fact that as a race Indians were not as "civilized" as the whites:

> . . . [I]n view of the nature and manifest purpose of this statute and the well-known conditions which induce its enactment, there is no warrant for limiting it by excluding from its operation sales of intoxicating liquors to any person of Indian blood, even although he may have become a citizen of the United States, by compliance with the act of congress. The statute is a police regulation. It was enacted in view of the well-known social condition, habits, and tendencies of Indians as a race. While there are doubtless notable individual exceptions to the rule, yet it is a well-known fact that Indians as a race are not as highly civilized as the whites; that they are less subject to moral restraint, more liable to acquire an inordinate appetite for intoxicating liquors, and also more liable to be dangerous to themselves and others when intoxicated.[19]

The Minnesota statute, said the Court, applied to and included "all Indians as a race, without reference to their political status. . . . The difference in condition between Indians as a race and the white race constituted a sufficient basis of classification."[20] Under the Court's reasoning, the individual Indian could not control his or her identity. Like it or not, the individual Indian was defined by the Court's language, by the "well-known fact" that "Indians as a race are not as highly civilized as whites," that Indians are "less subject to moral restraint." Like it or not, the individual Indian was identified in terms of the "characteristics" of the "Indians as a race," whether he or she had those characteristics or not, whether he or she was a citizen of the United States or not.

Twenty years later, Minnesota denied voting rights to Indians on the basis of their not being "civilized." . . .[21]

The state of Arizona, the state with the largest Indian population, until 1948 did not allow Indians the right to vote. Article 7 of Arizona's Constitution concerning the qualification of voters placed the Indians in that state in the same category as traitors and felons, the same category as persons not of sound mind and the insane; Article 7 provided, in part: "No person under guardianship, *non compos mentis* or insane shall be qualified to vote in any election or shall any person convicted of treason or felony, be qualified to vote at any election unless restored to civil rights." In 1928, the Arizona Supreme Court decided in *Porter v. Hall* that Arizona Indians did not have the right to vote since they were within the specific provisions of Article 7 denying suffrage to "persons under guardianship";[22] the Arizona Supreme Court said that ". . . so long as the federal government insists that, notwithstanding their citizenship, their responsibility under our law differs from that of the ordinary citizen, and that they are, or may be, regulated by that government, by virtue of its guardianship, in any manner different from that which may be used in the regulation of white citizens, they are,

---

[19] *In re Liquor Election in Beltrami County,* 989.
[20] *In re Liquor Election in Beltrami County,* 989.
[21] *In re Liquor Election in Beltrami County,* 990.
[22] *Porter v. Hall,* 271 P. 411 (1928).

within the meaning of our constitutional provision, 'persons under guardian-ship,' and not entitled to vote."[23] In defining the Indians of Arizona as it did in the above decision, the Arizona Supreme Court denied suffrage rights to the Indians even though four years earlier, on June 2, 1924, all non-citizen Indians born within the territorial limits of the United States were made citizens thereof by an Act of Congress. After devoting a paragraph to defining "insanity" and "*non compos mentis,*" the Arizona Supreme Court followed with a definition and discussion of "persons under guardianship," the category into which the Indians were placed:

> Broadly speaking, persons under guardianship may be defined as those who, be-cause of some peculiarity of status, defect of age, understanding or self-control, are considered incapable of managing their own affairs, and who therefore have some other person lawfully invested with the power and charged with the duty of taking care of their persons or managing their property, or both. It will be seen from the foregoing definitions that there is one common quality found in each: The person falling within any one of the classes is to some extent and for some reason considered by the law as incapable of managing his own affairs as a normal person, and needing some special care from the state.[24]

In 1948, however, the Porter decision was overruled in the case of *Harrison v. Laveen,*[25] thus allowing Indians in Arizona the right to vote. In the 1948 de-cision, the Supreme Court of Arizona stated that the designation of "persons under guardianship" as it appeared in Article 7 did not apply to Indians. As to the argument that the Indians generally fell into that group of people "incapable of managing their own affairs," the Court said in 1948 that "to ascribe to all Indians residing on reservations the quality of being 'incapable of handling their own affairs in an ordinary manner' would be a grave injustice, for amongst them are educated persons as fully capable of handling their affairs as their white neighbors."[26] Finally, four and a half centuries after Columbus "discovered" "America," almost all the descendants of the original occupants of this land were allowed by the descendants of the invaders to participate, through the vote, in effecting some control (however small) over their destiny in their own land. Al-most all of the "red natives" of the land finally were recognized legally as being as fully capable of handling their affairs as "their white neighbors." . . .

---

[23] *Porter v. Hall,* 419.
[24] *Porter v. Hall,* 416.
[25] *Harrison v. Laveen,* 196 P. 2d 456 (1948).
[26] *Harrison v. Laveen,* 463.

AIDS: The Linguistic Battlefield

MICHAEL CALLEN

IDS IS THE moment-to-moment management of uncertainty. It's like standing in the middle of the New York Stock Exchange at midday, buzzers and lights flashing, everyone yelling, a million opinions. AIDS is about loss of control — of one's bowels, one's bladder, one's life. And so there is often a ferocious drive by those of us with AIDS to exert at least *some* control over it. When I was diagnosed in 1982, I decided that I'd have to pay close attention to the language of AIDS — to keep my wits about me in order to see beyond the obfuscating medical mumbo-jumbo meant to dazzle me into a deadly passivity.

AIDS is a sprawling topic. War is being waged on many fronts. From the beginning of this epidemic, there have been a number of important battles over how we speak about AIDS which have had subtle but profound effects on how we think about — and respond to — AIDS. These linguistic battles have also affected how those of us diagnosed as having AIDS experience our own illness.

In the early seventies, the gay liberation movement won a smashing victory when it forced the American Psychiatric Association to declassify homosexuality as an illness. But with the creation of a new disease called G.R.I.D., or gay-related immune deficiency, as AIDS was first termed, in an instant, those of us whose primary sexual and affectional attraction is to members of our own sex once again became medicalized and pathologized — only now we were considered literally, as opposed to merely morally, contagious.

Soon, gay-related immune deficiency was discovered in nongay people and a new name for this disease had to be found. All factions were poised for a political battle over the new name. Instinctively, those empowered to create and police the definition of AIDS (and those who would be profoundly affected by it) were aware that the new name would affect how the epidemic would be handled by the federal government and the "general" (meaning, generally, the non-homosexual, non-IV-drug-using, rest-of-you) public.

In the end, a neutral sounding, almost cheerful name was chosen: A.I.D.S. Words can resonate with other words and take on subtle, sympathetic vibrations. AIDS: as in "health and beauty aids" or, to retain some of the sexual connotations of the disease, "marital aids." Or AIDS: as in "aid to the Contras." Or, "now is the time for all good men to come to the aid of their country." "AIDS" sounded like something . . . well, helpful.

My highly trained eye can now spot the letters A-I-D on a page of newsprint at lightning speed. It's amazing how often those three letters appear in headlines: afrAID, mislAID, medicAID, pAID — even bridesmAIDS. Every time I would hear a newscaster say "The president's aide reported today . . . ," I'd be momentarily disoriented by the linkage of "president" and "AIDS."

It's interesting to speculate, by the way, what the public response to AIDS might have been had the name proposed by a group from Boston prevailed: *herpes virus reactivation syndrome*. Prior to AIDS, the American public — general or otherwise — had been barraged by *Time* magazine cover stories about another fearsome, sexually transmitted epidemic: herpes. If those with the power to name the current plague had linked its name to the herpes epidemic, getting the American public to take AIDS seriously might not have been quite so difficult. One important consequence (some would say cause) of the profound immune disturbance we now call *AIDS* is that latent herpes viruses are reactivated, leading to a vicious cycle of immune suppression. Had the name *herpes virus reactivation syndrome,* or *HVRS,* been selected instead of *AIDS,* it might not have taken so long to convince Americans to support research into a disease which, by name at least, everyone was theoretically at risk for. But perhaps because *HVRS,* as an acronym, does not roll tripplingly off the tongue, the more neutral sounding *AIDS,* was chosen.

WHAT THE "L" IS GOING ON HERE?

The most momentous semantic battle yet fought in the AIDS war concerned the naming of the so-called AIDS virus. The stakes were high; two nations — France and the United States — were at war over who first identified (and therefore had the right to name) the retrovirus presumed to cause AIDS. Hanging in the balance was a Nobel prize and millions of dollars in patent royalties.

U.S. researcher Dr. Robert Gallo had originally proposed that HTLV-I (human T-cell leukemia virus) was the cause of AIDS. Meanwhile, scientists at the Pasteur Institute isolated a novel retrovirus, which they named *LAV,* to stand for "Lymphadenopathy Associated Virus." The U.S. scoffed at French claims, arrogantly asserting that HTLV-I or HTLV-II must be the cause of AIDS. When it became obvious that neither HTLV-I nor II could possibly be the cause, if for no other reason than because Japan (where HTLV-I and II are endemic) was not in the midst of an AIDS epidemic, the U.S. had to find some way to steal both LAV itself as well as the credit for having discovered it first, while covering over the embarrassing fact that they had proposed the wrong virus as "the cause" of AIDS.[1]

What to do? In an election year (1984), it was simply unthinkable that the 10 French could so outshine U.S. medical research. The United States hit upon a brilliant solution. Gallo simply renamed LAV "HTLV-III" and Secretary of Health and Human Services Margaret Heckler staged a preemptive press strike. She declared that another achievement had been added to the long list of U.S. medical breakthroughs: "The probable cause of AIDS has been found — HTLV-III, a variant of a known, human cancer virus. . . ."

The ploy was certainly ballsy. And looking back, amazingly successful.

But what was going on here? The *L* in HTLV-I and II stands for leukemia, since it proposed that HTLV-I and II account for a particular form of leukemia. Unfortunately for the perpetrators of this massive fraud, it just so happens that leukemia is one of the few diseases which is *not* a complication of AIDS. So, in order to retain the symmetry of nomenclature, Gallo quietly proposed that the *L* in HTLV-III and HTLV-IV now stand for *lymphotropic* instead of *leukemia*.

It is now widely acknowledged that HIV is not a member of the HTLV family at all. It is a lentivirus. But the consequences of Gallo's bold attempt at semantic damage control are still with us. The *Index Medicus* listing for AIDS still refers to HTLV-III, not HIV. The legal dispute was eventually settled by the state department; the presidents of the U.S. and France signed an agreement whereby their nations would share credit and royalties, a settlement potentially worth billions. But what was the cost in human lives lost from research delays caused by the willful misclassification of HIV? . . .

WHO HAS THE POWER TO NAME?

The question of who has the power to name is an ongoing turf battle between people with AIDS and those who insist on defining us as victims. I was at the founding of the people with AIDS self-empowerment movement in Denver, Colorado, in 1983. When the California contingent insisted that we make part of our manifesto the demand that we be referred to as "people with AIDS" (or the inevitable acronym "PWAs") instead of "AIDS victims," I must confess that I rolled my eyes heavenward. How California, I thought.

But time has proven them right. Americans, whose ability to think has been dessicated by decades of television and its ten-second-sound-bite mentality, think in one-word descriptors. Someone on the TV screen must be labeled: a feminist, a communist, a homosexual, an AIDS victim. The difference between the descriptors *person with AIDS* and *AIDS victim* seems subtle until one watches oneself on reruns on TV. To see oneself on screen and have the words *AIDS victim* magically flash underneath has a very different feel about it than when the description *person with AIDS* appears. Its very cumbersomeness is startling and makes the viewer ask: "Person? Why person? Of course he's a person. . . ." In that moment, we achieve a small but important victory. Viewers are forced to be conscious, if only for a moment, that we *are* people first.

The founding statement of the PWA self-empowerment movement (known as the "Denver Principles") is quite eloquent on this point:

> We condemn attempts to label us as "victims," which implies defeat; and we are only occasionally "patients," which implies passivity, helplessness and dependence upon the care of others. We are "people with AIDS."[2]

This statement was further refined in the founding Mission Statement of the National Association of People with AIDS (NAPWA):

> We are people with AIDS and people with AIDS-Related Complex (ARC) who can speak for ourselves to advocate for our own causes and concerns. We are your sons and daughters, your brothers and sisters, your family, friends and lovers. As people now living with AIDS and ARC, we have a unique and essential contribution to make to the dialogue surrounding AIDS and we will actively participate with full and equal credibility to help shape the perception and reality surrounding this disease.

We do not see ourselves as victims. We will not be victimized. We have the right to be treated with respect, dignity, compassion and understanding. We have the right to lead fulfilling, productive lives — to live and die with dignity and compassion.

In a gratuitous aside in his best-selling AIDS epic, *And the Band Played On,* Randy Shilts attacked the right of people with AIDS to choose how they wished to be referred to. Completely twisting the empowering impulse of people with AIDS to wrest some control of our lives, Shilts accused us of attempting to minimize the tragedy of AIDS:

AIDSpeak, a new language forged by public health officials, anxious gay politicians, and the burgeoning ranks of "AIDS activists." The linguistic roots of AIDSpeak sprouted not so much from the truth as from what was politically facile and psychologically reassuring. Semantics was the major denominator of AIDSpeak jargon, because the language went to great lengths never to offend.

A new lexicon was evolving. Under the rules of AIDSpeak, for example, AIDS victims could not be called victims. Instead, they were to be called People with AIDS, or PWAs, as if contracting this uniquely brutal disease was not a victimizing experience. "Promiscuous" became "sexually active," because gay politicians declared "promiscuous" to be "judgmental," a major cuss word in AIDSpeak. The most-used circumlocution in AIDSpeak was "bodily fluids," an expression that avoided troublesome words like "semen."

. . . Thus, the verbiage tended toward the intransitive. AIDSpeak was rarely empowered to motivate action; rather, it was most articulately pronounced when justifying inertia. Nobody meant any harm by this; quite to the contrary, AIDSpeak was the tongue designed to make everyone content. AIDSpeak was the language of good intentions in the AIDS epidemic; AIDSpeak was a language of death.[3]

Shilts notwithstanding, there is now a movement to further emphasize hope. In some quarters PLWAs and PLWArcs have entered the language: Persons *Living* With AIDS and Persons *Living* with ARC, respectively. There is also a new movement to organize all individuals suffering from conditions related to immune deficiency. Acronym conscious, its leaders say they are "PISD" (pronounced "pissed"), which stands for "Persons with Immune System Disorders."

The *New York Times,* whose editorial policies influence other newspapers, has been drawn into the battle being waged by people with AIDS to reclaim some small amount of linguistic control over their lives — a battle similar to one being waged by gay people over the *Times*'s intransigent use of *homosexual* instead of *gay.* The following exchange concerns the *Times*'s obituary of the first president of the New York People with AIDS Coalition:

December 1986

We protest the New York Times' not listing Kenneth Meeks' surviving lifemate of over ten years, Mr. Jack Steinhebel. Upon calling your office, I spoke to "Fred," who told me that it was the policy of the Times "not to include lovers" as survivors. That policy is totally inappropriate in that it lacks sensitivity and basic respect. "Fred" also informed me that in his "six years at the Times and with hundreds of phone calls the policy had not changed" and that we should "not expect it to change in the future." How sad.

Finally, the labeling of People with AIDS as "victims" in Ken's obit was incorrect and more so in light of Ken's extensive work to end such practices. We are greatly disappointed by such journalism.

> Sincerely,
> Michael Hirsch
> Executive Director
> People with AIDS Coalition

The *New York Times* responded:

> No slurs were intended, but I can well understand your feelings about Kenneth Meeks's obituary. We are reviewing our obituary conventions regarding mention of intimates other than blood relatives and spouses. I cannot predict what we will decide to do, but think you have contributed to consciousness-raising.
>
> As for the word "victim," I cannot agree that it is pejorative. Along with most of society, we have long written about "stroke victims," "heart attack victims," and "cancer victims." The logic is equally applicable to AIDS, and I am uncomfortable about drying [*sic*] idiom for any cause, no matter how meritorious.
>
> Sincerely,
> Alan M. Siegel
> News Editor
> New York Times[4]

In the ensuing three years, there has been no change in the *Times*'s policy of refusing to acknowledge the status of "intimates other than blood relatives and spouses" (now, there's a mouthful) in the obituaries of lesbian and gay people. If a change of policy so obviously just and easy to accommodate cannot be made by the *Times,* one holds out little hope that they'll ever use a descriptor other than *victim* when referring to PWAs. . . .   20

Is there anyone who can talk about AIDS and emerge from the battle unscathed? Probably not. We all want to control AIDS somehow, and at times language seems to be our only weapon. But we must not try to master AIDS by crushing its complexities, mysteries, and terrors into convenient labels that roll trippingly and with false authority off the tongue. We must always speak fully and carefully about AIDS, even if that often requires a mouthful — cumbersome constructions full of words strung together by hyphens — to say precisely what we mean. The stakes are simply too high to do otherwise.

NOTES

1. The saga of the competition between U.S. and French AIDS researchers reads like a bad espionage novel. Gallo requested, and the French twice supplied, cultures of LAV. At the time, Gallo claimed that he was not able to grow LAV from these samples. A recent BBC documentary, however, produced evidence of altered docu-

ments, suggesting that in fact U.S. researchers had grown LAV from the French cultures. Embarrassingly for Gallo, when he first published on "HTLV-III," he mistakenly provided an electron micrograph photo of "LAV" taken for the French. More damning still, when a DNA-fingerprinting was done on Gallo's HTLV-III and the French's LAV, they were found to be essentially identical.

2. "The Denver Principles," quoted in *Surviving and Thriving with AIDS: Collected Wisdom*, vol. 2, ed. Michael Callen (New York, 1988).

3. Randy Shilts, *And the Band Played On: The Politics of AIDS* (New York, 1987), pp. 314–15.

4. Reprinted in *PWA Coalition Newsletter* 18 (December 1986). [The *New York Times* and many other newspapers now routinely list surviving companions in obituaries of lesbians and gay men. (Ed.)]

▪ ▪ ARGUING ABOUT USAGE: GENDER AND LANGUAGE

The following essays are attempts to influence how a community uses language. In the first Alleen Pace Nilson describes the inherent sexism of the English language and suggests some recent changes in the way Americans talk. The following guidelines from the National Council of Teachers of English (NCTE) suggest ways to avoid gender-biased language in your writing. As your read these selections, consider the following questions:

1. What claim is Alleen Pace Nilson making about language? What reasons does she give to support this claim? What assumptions does she make? To what extent do you accept Nilson's argument?
2. What assumptions are there behind the NCTE Guidelines? How explicitly are these assumptions stated?
3. Do you believe that gender bias in language exists in the communities you belong to? If so, how important is the problem of gender bias in language?
4. What effect can establishing guidelines have on the usage of a community?

Sexism in English: A 1990s Update

ALLEEN PACE NILSEN

T WENTY YEARS AGO I embarked on a study of the sexism inherent in   1
American English. I had just returned to Ann Arbor, Michigan, after living for two years (1967–1969) in Kabul, Afghanistan, where I had begun to look critically at the role society assigned to women. The Afghan version of the *chaderi* prescribed for Moslem women was particularly confining. Few women attended the American-built Kabul University where my husband was teaching linguistics because there were no women's dormitories, which meant that the only females who could attend were those whose families happened to live in the

capital city. Afghan jokes and folklore were blatantly sexist; for example, this proverb: "If you see an old man, sit down and take a lesson; if you see an old woman, throw a stone."

But it wasn't only the native culture that made question women's roles; it was also the American community. Nearly 600 Americans lived in Kabul, mostly supported by U.S. taxpayers. The single women were career secretaries, school teachers, or nurses. The three women who had jobs comparable to the American men's jobs were textbook editors with the assignment of developing reading books in Dari (Afghan Persian) for young children. They worked at the Ministry of Education, a large building in the center of the city. There were no women's restrooms so during their two-year assignment whenever they need to go to the bathroom they had to walk across the street and down the block to the Kabul Hotel.

The rest of the American women were like myself — wives and mothers whose husbands were either career diplomats, employees of USAID, or college professors teaching at Kabul University. These were the women who were most influential in changing my way of thinking because we were suddenly bereft of our traditional roles. Servants worked for $1.00 a day and our lives revolved around supervising these men (women were not allowed to work for foreigners). One woman's husband grew so tired of hearing her stories that he scheduled an hour a week for listening to complaints. The rest of the time he wanted to keep his mind clear to focus on working with his Afghan counterparts and with the president of the University and the Minister of Education. He was going to make a difference in this country, while in the great eternal scheme of things it mattered little that the servant stole the batteries out of the flashlight or put chili powder instead of paprika on the eggs.

I continued to ponder this dramatic contrast between men's and women's work, and when we finished our contract and returned in the fall of 1969 to the University of Michigan in Ann Arbor I was surprised to find that many other women were also questioning the expectations that they had grown up with. I attended a campus women's conference, but I returned home more troubled than ever. Now that I knew housework was worth only a dollar a day, I couldn't take it seriously, but I wasn't angry in the same way these women were. Their militancy frightened me. I wasn't ready for a revolution, so I decided I would have my own feminist movement. I would study the English language and see what it could tell me about sexism. I started reading a desk dictionary and making notecards on every entry that seemed to tell something about male and female. I soon had a dog-eared dictionary, along with a collection of notecards filling two shoe boxes.

Ironically, I started reading the dictionary because I wanted to avoid getting   5
involved in social issues, but what happened was that my notecards brought me right back to looking at society. Language and society are as intertwined as a chicken and an egg. The language that a culture uses is telltale evidence of the values and beliefs of that culture. And because there is a lag in how fast a language changes — new words can easily be introduced, but it takes a long time

for old words and usages to disappear — a careful look at English will reveal the attitudes that our ancestors held and that we as a culture are therefore predisposed to hold. My notecards revealed three main points. Friends have offered the opinion that I didn't need to read the dictionary to learn such obvious facts. Nevertheless, it was interesting to have linguistic evidence of sociological observations.

WOMEN ARE SEXY: MEN ARE SUCCESSFUL

First, in American culture a woman is valued for the attractiveness and sexiness of her body, while a man is valued for his physical strength and accomplishments. A woman is sexy. A man is successful.

A persuasive piece of evidence supporting this view are the eponyms — words that have come from someone's name — found in English. I had a two-and-a-half-inch stack of cards taken from men's names, but less than a half-inch stack from women's names, and most of those came from Greek mythology. In the words that came into American English since we separated from Britain, there are many eponyms based on the names of famous American men: bartlett pear, boysenberry, diesel engine, franklin stove, ferris wheel, gatling gun, mason jar, sideburns, sousaphone, schick test, and winchester rifle. The only common eponyms taken from American women's names are *Alice blue* (after Alice Roosevelt Longworth), bloomers (after Amelia Jenks Bloomer) and *Mae West jacket* (after the buxom actress). Two out of the three feminine eponyms relate closely to a woman's physical anatomy, while the masculine eponyms (except for *sideburns* after General Burnsides) have nothing to do with the namesake's body, but instead honor the man for an accomplishment of some kind.

Although in Greek mythology women played a bigger role than they did in the biblical stories of the Judeo-Christian cultures and so the names of goddesses are accepted parts of the language in such place names as Pomona from the goddess of fruit and Athens from Athena, and in such common words as *cereal* from Ceres, *psychology* from Psyche, and *arachnoid* from Arachne, the same tendency to think of women in relation to sexuality is seen in the eponyms *aphrodisiac* from Aphrodite, the Greek name for the goddess of love and beauty, and *venereal disease,* from Venus, the Roman name for Aphrodite.

Another interesting word from Greek mythology is *Amazon.* According to Greek folk etymology, the *a* means "without" as in *atypical* or *amoral* while *mazon* comes from *mazos* meaning *breast* as still seen in *mastectomy.* In the Greek legend, Amazon women cut off their right breasts so that they could better shoot their bows. Apparently, the storytellers had a feeling that for women to play the active "masculine" role that the Amazons adopted for themselves, they had to trade in part of their femininity.

This preoccupation with women's breasts is not limited to ancient stories. 10 As a volunteer for the University of Wisconsin's *Dictionary of American Regional English (DARE),* I read a western trapper's diary from the 1830s. I was to make notes of any unusual usages or language patterns. My most interesting finding was that he referred to a range of mountains as *The Teats,* a metaphor based on the similarity between the shapes of the mountains and women's breasts. Because today we use the French wording, *The Grand Tetons,* the metaphor isn't as obvious, but I wrote to mapmakers and found the following listings: *Nippletop* and *Little Nipple Top* near Mt. Marcy in the Adirondacks; *Nipple Mountain* in Archuleta County, Colorado; *Nipple Peak* in Coke County, Texas; *Nipple Butte* in Pennington, South Dakota; *Squaw Peak* in Placer County, California (and many other locations); *Maiden's Peak* and *Squaw Tit* (they're the same mountain) in the Cascade Range in Oregon; *Mary's Nipple* near Salt Lake City, Utah; and *Jane Russell Peaks* near Stark, New Hampshire.

Except for the movie star Jane Russell, the women being referred to are anonymous — it's only a sexual part of their body that is mentioned. When topographical features are named after men, it's probably not going to be to draw attention to a sexual part of their bodies but instead to honor individuals for an accomplishment. For example, no one thinks of a part of the male body when hearing a reference to Pike's Peak, Colorado, or Jackson Hole, Wyoming.

Going back to what I learned from my dictionary cards, I was surprised to realize how many pairs of words we have in which the feminine word has acquired sexual connotations while the masculine word retains a serious business-like aura. For example, a *callboy* is the person who calls actors when it is time for them to go on stage, but a *callgirl* is a prostitute. Compare *sir* and *madam. Sir* is a term of respect while *madam* has acquired the specialized meaning of a brothel manager. Something similar has happened to *master* and *mistress.* Would you rather have a painting by *an old master* or *an old mistress?*

It's because the word *woman* had sexual connotations as in "She's his woman," that people began avoiding its use, hence such terminology as *ladies room, lady of the house,* and *girls' school* or *school for young ladies.* Feminists, who ask that people use the term *woman* rather than *girl* or *lady,* are rejecting the idea that *woman* is primarily a sexual term. They have been at least partially successful in that today *woman* is commonly used to communicate gender without intending implications about sexuality.

I found 200 pairs of words with masculine and feminine forms, for example, *heir/heiress, hero/heroine, steward/stewardess, usher/usherette,* etc. In nearly all such pairs, the masculine word is considered the base with some kind of a feminine suffix being added. The masculine form is the one from which compounds are made; for example, from *king/queen* comes *kingdom* but not *queendom,* from *sportsman/sportslady* comes *sportsmanship* but not *sports/ladyship.* There is one — and only one — semantic area in which the masculine word is not the base or more powerful word. This is in the area dealing with sex and marriage. When someone refers to a *virgin,* a listener will probably think of a female unless the speaker specifies *male* or uses a masculine pronoun. The same is true for *prostitute.*

In relation to marriage, there is much linguistic evidence showing that weddings are more important to women than to men. A woman cherishes the wedding and is considered a bride for a whole year, but a man is referred to as a

15

groom only on the day of the wedding. The word *bride* appears in *bridal atten-dant, bridal gown, bridesmaid, bridal shower,* and even *bridegroom. Groom* comes from the Middle English *grom,* meaning "man," and in this sense is seldom used outside of a wedding. With most pairs of male/female words, people habitually put the masculine words first, *Mr. and Mrs., his and hers, boys and girls, men and women, kings and queens, brothers and sisters, guys and dolls,* and *host and hostess,* but it is the *bride and groom* who are talked about, not the *groom and bride.*

The importance of marriage to a woman is also shown by the fact that when a marriage ends in death, the woman gets the title of *widow.* A man gets the derived title of *widower.* This term is not used in other phrases or contexts, but *widow* is seen in *widowhood, widow's peak,* and *widow's walk.* A *widow* in a card game is an extra hand of cards, while in typesetting it is an extra line of type.

How changing cultural ideas bring changes to language is clearly visible in this semantic area. The feminist movement has caused the differences between the sexes to be downplayed, and since I did my dictionary study two decades ago the word *singles* has largely replaced such sex specific and value-laden terms as *bachelor, old maid, spinster, divorcee, widow,* and *widower.* And in 1970, I wrote that when a man is called *a professional* he is thought to be a doctor or a lawyer, but when people hear a woman referred to as *a professional* they are likely to think of a prostitute. That's not as true today because so many women have become doctors and lawyers that it's no longer incongruous to think of women in those professional roles.

Another change that has taken place is in wedding announcements. They used to be sent out from the bride's parents and did not even give the name of the groom's parents. Today, most couples choose to list either all or none of the parents' names. Also, it is now much more likely that both the bride and groom's picture will be in the newspaper, while a decade ago only the bride's picture was published on the "Women's" or the "Society" page. Even the traditional word-ing of the ceremony is being changed. Many officials now pronounce the couple "husband and wife" instead of the old "man and wife," and they ask the bride if she promises "to love, honor, and cherish," instead of "to love, honor, and obey."

WOMEN ARE PASSIVE; MEN ARE ACTIVE

The wording of the wedding ceremony also relates to the second point that my cards showed, which is that women are expected to play a passive or weak role while men play an active or strong role. In the traditional ceremony, the official asks "Who gives the bride away?" and the father answers "I do." Some fathers answer "Her mother and I do," but that doesn't solve the problem in-herent in the question. The idea that a bride is something to be handed over from one man to another bothers people because it goes back to the days when a man's servants, his children, and his wife were all considered to be his property. They were known by his name because they belonged to him and he was respon-sible for their actions and their debts.

The grammar used in talking or writing about weddings as well as other 20
sexual relationships shows the expectation of men playing the active role. Men
wed women while women *become* brides of men. A man *possesses* a woman; he
deflowers her; he *performs;* he *scores;* he *takes away* her virginity. Although a
woman can *seduce* a man, she cannot offer him her virginity. When talking about
virginity, the only way to make the woman the actor in the sentence is to say that
"She lost her virginity," but people lose things by accident rather than by purposeful actions and so she's only the grammatical, not the real-life, actor.

The reason that women tried to bring the term *Ms.* into the language to
replace *Miss* and *Mrs.* relates to this point. Married women resented being
identified only under their husband's names. For example, when Susan Glascoe
did something newsworthy she would be identified in the newspaper only as
Mrs. John Glascoe. The dictionary cards showed what appeared to be an attitude
on the part of editors that it was almost indecent to let a respectable woman's
name march unaccompanied across the pages of a dictionary. Women were listed
with male names whether or not the male contributed to the woman's reason
for being in the dictionary or in his own right was as famous as the woman.
For example, Charlotte Brontë was identified as Mrs. Arthur B. Nicholls, Amelia
Earhart as Mrs. George Palmer Putnam, Helen Hayes as Mrs. Charles MacArthur, Jenny Lind as Mme. Otto Goldschmit, Cornelia Otis Skinner as the daughter of Otis, Harriet Beecher Stowe as the sister of Henry Ward Beecher, and
Edith Sitwell as the sister of Osbert and Sacheverell. A very small number of
women got into the dictionary without the benefit of a masculine escort. They
were rebels and crusaders: temperance leaders Frances Elizabeth Caroline Wil-
lard and Carry Nation, women's rights leaders Carrie Chapman Catt and Elizabeth Cady Stanton, birth control educator Margaret Sanger, religious leader
Mary Baker Eddy, and slaves Harriet Tubman and Phillis Wheatley.

Etiquette books used to teach that if a woman had *Mrs.* in front of her name,
then the husband's name should follow because *Mrs.* is an abbreviated form of
Mistress and a woman couldn't be a mistress of herself. As with many arguments
about "correct" language usage, this isn't very logical because *Miss* is also an
abbreviation of *Mistress.* Feminists hoped to simplify matters by introducing *Ms.*
as an alternative to both *Mrs.* and *Miss,* but what happened is that *Ms.* largely
replaced *Miss* to become a catchall business title for women. Many married
women still prefer the title *Mrs.* and some resent being addressed with the term
Ms. As one frustrated newspaper reporter complained, "Before I can write about
a woman, I have to know not only her marital status but also her political philosophy." The result of such complications may contribute to the demise of titles
which are already being ignored by many computer programmers who find it
more efficient to simply use names, for example, in a business letter, "Dear Joan
Garcia," instead of "Dear Mrs. Joan Garcia," "Dear Ms. Garcia," or "Dear Mrs.
Louis Garcia."

The titles given to royalty provide an example of how males can be disadvantaged by the assumption that they are always to play the more powerful role. In
British royalty, when a male holds a title, his wife is automatically given the femi-

nine equivalent. But the reverse is not true. For example, a *count* is a high political officer with a *countess* being his wife. The same is true for a *duke* and a *duchess* and a *king* and a *queen*. But when the female holds the royal title, the man she marries does not automatically acquire the matching title. For example, Queen Elizabeth's husband has the title of *prince* rather than *king,* but if Prince Charles should become king while he is still married to Lady or Princess Diana, she will be known as the queen. The reasoning appears to be that since masculine words are stronger, they are reserved for true heirs and withheld from males coming into the royal family by marriage. If Prince Phillip were called *King Phillip,* it would be much easier for British subjects to forget where the true power lies.

The names that people give their children show the hopes and dreams they have for them, and when we look at the differences between male and female names in a culture we can see the cumulative expectations of that culture. In our culture girls often have names taken from small, aesthetically pleasing items, for example, *Ruby, Jewel,* and *Pearl. Esther* and *Stella* mean "star," *Ada* means "ornament," and *Vanessa* means "butterfly." Boys are more likely to be given names with meanings of power and strength; for example, *Neil* means "champion," *Martin* is from Mars, the God of War, *Raymond* means "wise protection," *Harold* means "chief of the army," *Ira* means "vigilant," *Rex* means "king," and *Richard* means "strong king."

We see similar differences in food metaphors. Food is a passive substance just 25 sitting there waiting to be eaten. Many people have recognized this and so no longer feel comfortable describing women as "delectable morsels." However, when I was a teenager, it was considered a compliment to refer to a girl (we didn't call anyone a *woman* until she was middle-aged) as a *cute tomato, a peach, a dish, a cookie, honey, sugar,* or *sweetie-pie.* When being affectionate, women will occasionally call a man *honey* or *sweetie,* but, in general, food metaphors are used much less often with men than with women. If a man is called a *fruit,* his masculinity is being questioned. But it's perfectly acceptable to use a food metaphor if the food is heavier and more substantive than that used for women. For example, pinup pictures of women have long been known as *cheesecake,* but when Burt Reynolds posed for a nude centerfold the picture was immediately dubbed *beefcake,* that is, *a hunk of meat.* That such sexual references to men have come into the general language is another reflection of how society is beginning to lessen the differences between their attitudes toward men and women.

Something similar to the *fruit* metaphor happens with references to plants. We insult a man by calling him a *pansy,* but it wasn't considered particularly insulting to talk about a girl being a *wallflower,* a *clinging vine,* or a *shrinking violet,* or to give girls such names as *Ivy, Rose, Lily, Iris, Daisy, Camellia, Heather,* or *Flora.* A plant metaphor can be used with a man if the plant is big and strong, for example, Andrew Jackson's nickname of *Old Hickory.* Also the phrases *blooming idiots* and *budding geniuses* can be used with either sex, but notice how they are based on the most active thing a plant can do, which is to bloom or bud.

Animal metaphors also illustrate the different expectations for males and females. Men are referred to as *studs, bucks,* and *wolves* while women are referred to with such metaphors as *kitten, bunny, beaver, bird, chick,* or *lamb.* In the 1950s, we said that boys went *tomcatting,* but today it's just *catting around* and both boys and girls do it. When the term *foxy,* meaning that someone was sexy, first became popular it was used only for girls, but now someone of either sex can be described as a *fox.* Some animal metaphors that are used predominantly with men have negative connotations based on the size and/or strength of the animals, for example, *beast, bullheaded, jackass, rat, loanshark,* and *vulture.* Negative metaphors used with women are based on smaller animals, for example, *social butterfly, mousy, catty,* and *vixen.* The feminine terms connote action, but not the same kind of large-scale action as with the masculine terms.

WOMEN ARE CONNECTED WITH NEGATIVE CONNOTATIONS, MEN WITH POSITIVE CONNOTATIONS

The final point that my notecards illustrated was how many positive connotations are associated with the concept of masculine, while there are either trivial or negative connotations connected with the corresponding feminine concept. An example from the animal metaphors makes a good illustration. The word *shrew* taken from the name of a small but especially vicious animal was defined in my dictionary as "an ill tempered scolding woman," but the word *shrewd* taken from the same root was defined as "marked by clever, discerning awareness" and was illustrated with the phrase "a shrewd businessman."

Early in life, children are conditioned to the superiority of the masculine role. As child psychologists point out, little girls have much more freedom to experiment with sex roles than do little boys. If a little girl acts like a *tomboy,* most parents have mixed feelings, being at least partially proud. But if their little boy acts like a *sissy* (derived from *sister*), they call a psychologist. It's perfectly acceptable for a little girl to sleep in the crib that was purchased for her brother, to wear his hand-me-down jeans and shirts, and to ride the bicycle that he has outgrown. But few parents would put a boy baby in a white and gold crib decorated with frills and lace, and virtually no parents would have their little boy wear his sister's hand-me-down dresses, nor would they have their son ride a girl's pink bicycle with a flower-bedecked basket. The proper names given to girls and boys show this same attitude. Girls can have "boy" names — *Chris, Craig, Jo, Kelly, Shawn, Teri, Toni,* and *Sam* — but it doesn't work the other way around. A couple of generations ago, *Beverley, Frances, Hazel, Marion,* and *Shirley* were common boys' names. As parents gave these names to more and more girls, they fell into disuse for males, and some older men who have these names prefer to go by their initials or by such abbreviated forms as *Haze* or *Shirl.*

When a little girl is told to *be a lady,* she is being told to sit with her knees together and to be quiet and dainty. But when a little boy is told to *be a man* he is being told to be noble, strong, and virtuous — to have all the qualities that the speaker looks on as desirable. The concept of manliness has such positive

30

connotations that it used to be a compliment to call someone a *he-man,* to say that he was doubly a man. Today, many people are more ambivalent about this term and respond to it much as they do to the word *macho.* But calling someone a *manly man* or a *virile man* is nearly always meant as a compliment. *Virile* comes from the Indo-European *vir* meaning "man," which is also the basis of *virtuous.* Contrast the positive connotations of both *virile* and *virtuous* with the negative connotations of *hysterical.* The Greeks took this latter word from their name for *uterus* (as still seen in *hysterectomy*). They thought that women were the only ones who experienced uncontrolled emotional outbursts and so the condition must have something to do with a part of the body that only women have.

Differences between positive male connotations and negative female connotations can be seen in several pairs of words which differ denotatively only in the matter of sex. *Bachelor* as compared to *spinster* or *old maid* has such positive connotations that women try to adopt them by using the term *bachelor-girl* or *bachelorette.* *Old maid* is so negative that it's the basis for metaphors: pretentious and fussy old men are called *old maids* as are the leftover kernels of unpopped popcorn and the last card in a popular children's game.

Patron and *matron* (Middle English for *father* and *mother*) have such different levels of prestige that women try to borrow the more positive masculine connotations with the word *patroness,* literally "female father." Such a peculiar term came about because of the high prestige attached to *patron* in such phrases as *a patron of the arts* or *patron saint. Matron* is more apt to be used in talking about a woman in charge of a jail or a public restroom.

When men are doing jobs that women often do, we apparently try to pay the men extra by giving them fancy titles; for example, a male cook is more likely to be called a *chef* while a male seamstress will get the title of *tailor.* The Armed Forces have a special problem in that they recruit under such slogans as "The Marine Corps builds men!" and "Join the Army! Become a Man." Once the recruits are enlisted, they find themselves doing much of the work that has been traditionally thought of as "women's work." The solution to getting the work done and not insulting anyone's masculinity was to change the titles as shown below:

waitress	orderly
nurse	medic or corpsman
secretary	clerk-typist
assistant	adjutant
dishwasher or kitchen helper	KP (kitchen police)

Compare *brave* and *squaw.* Early settlers in America truly admired Indian men and hence named them with a word that carried connotations of youth, vigor, and courage. But they used the Algonquin's name for "woman," and over the years it developed almost opposite connotations to those of *brave. Wizard* and *witch* contrast almost as much. The masculine *wizard* implies skill and wisdom combined with magic, while the feminine *witch* implies evil intentions combined with magic. Part of the unattractiveness of both *witch* and *squaw* is that they have been used so often to refer to old women, something with which our culture is particularly uncomfortable, just as the Afghans were. Imagine my surprise, when I ran across the phrases *grandfatherly advice* and *old wives' tales* and realized that the underlying implication is the same as the Afghan proverb about old men being worth listening to while old women talk only foolishness.

Other terms that show how negatively we view old women as compared to   35
young women are *old nag* as compared to *filly*, *old crow* or *old bat* as compared to *bird*, and being *catty* as compared to being *kittenish*. There is no matching set of metaphors for men. The chicken metaphor tells the whole story of a woman's life. In her youth she is a *chick*. Then she marries and begins *feathering her nest*. Soon she begins feeling *cooped up*, so she goes to *hen parties* where she *cackles* with her friends. Then she has her *brood*, begins to *henpeck* her husband, and finally turns into *an old biddy*.

I embarked on my study of the dictionary not with the intention of prescribing language change but simply to see what the language would tell me about sexism. Nevertheless, I have been both surprised and pleased as I've watched the changes that have occurred over the past two decades. I'm one of those linguists who believes that new language customs will cause a new generation of speakers to grow up with different expectations. This is why I'm happy about people's efforts to use inclusive language, to say *he or she* or *they* when speaking about individuals whose names they do not know. I'm glad that leading publishers have developed guidelines to help writers use language that is fair to both sexes and I'm glad that most newspapers and magazines list women by their own names instead of only by their husbands' names and that educated and thoughtful people no longer begin their business letters with "Dear Sir" or "Gentlemen" but instead use a memo form or begin with salutations as "Dear Colleagues," "Dear Reader," or "Dear Committee Members." I'm also glad that such words as *poetess, authoress, conductress,* and *aviatrix* now sound quaint and old fashioned and that *chairman* is giving way to *chair* or *head, mailman* to *mail carrier, clergyman* to *clergy,* and *stewardess* to *flight attendant.* I was also pleased when the National Oceanic and Atmospheric Administration bowed to feminist complaints and in the late seventies began to alternate men's and women's names for hurricanes. However, I wasn't so pleased to discover that the change did not immediately erase sexist thoughts from everyone's mind as shown by a headline about Hurricane David in a 1979 New York tabloid, "David Rapes Virgin Islands." More recently, a similar metaphor appeared in a headline in the *Arizona Republic* about Hurricane Charlie, "Charlie Quits Carolinas, Flirts with Virginia."

What these incidents show is that sexism is not something existing independently in American English or in the particular dictionary that I happened to read. Rather, it exists in people's minds. Language is like an x-ray in providing visible evidence of invisible thoughts. The best thing about people being interested in and discussing sexist language is that as they make conscious decisions about what pronouns they will use, what jokes they will tell or laugh at, how they will write their names, or how they will begin their letters, they are forced to think about the underlying issue of sexism. This is good because as a problem that begins in people's assumptions and expectations, it's a problem that will be solved only when a great many people have given it a great deal of thought.

Guidelines for Nonsexist Use of Language in NCTE Publications (Revised, 1985)

NATIONAL COUNCIL OF TEACHERS OF ENGLISH

INTRODUCTION

D URING THE 1971 Annual Convention of the National Council of Teach-   1
ers of English in Las Vegas, Nevada, the Executive Committee and the Board of Directors approved the formation of an NCTE Committee on the Role and Image of Women in the Council and the Profession. As the result of a resolution passed by the members of NCTE at the 1974 Annual Convention, one of the committee's responsibilities was to assist in setting guidelines for nonsexist [1] use of language in NCTE publications.

Suggestions were elicited from editors of Council journals and from professional staff members at NCTE, as well as from members of the Women's Committee. Copies of the guidelines also went to all members of the Board of Directors. At the 1975 Annual Convention, the Board of Directors adopted a formal policy statement that read in part: "The National Council of Teachers of English should encourage the use of nonsexist language, particularly through its publications and periodicals."

Ten years have passed since these guidelines were created, and although language usage has begun to change, the importance of the guidelines has not diminished. Because language plays a central role in the way human beings think and behave, we still need to promote language that opens rather than closes possibilities for women and men. Whether teaching in the classroom, assigning texts, determining curriculum, serving on national committees, or writing in professional publications, NCTE members directly and indirectly influence thought and behavior.

---

[1] Although *nonsexist* is the word traditionally used to describe such language, other terms have come into common use, namely, *gender-neutral, sex-fair, gender-free.*

As an educational publisher, NCTE is not alone in its concern for fair treatment of men and women. The role of education is to make choices available, not to limit opportunities. Censorship removes possibilities; these guidelines extend what is available by offering alternatives to traditional usages and to editorial choices that restrict meaning.

LANGUAGE

This section deals primarily with word choice. Many of the examples are matters of vocabulary; a few are matters of grammatical choice. The vocabulary items are relatively easy to deal with, since the English lexicon has a history of rapid change. Grammar is a more difficult area, and we have chosen to use alternatives that already exist in the language rather than to invent new constructions. In both cases, recommended alternatives have been determined by what is graceful and unobtrusive. The purpose of these changes is to suggest alternative styles.

Generic "Man"

1. Since the word *man* has come to refer almost exclusively to adult males, it is sometimes difficult to recognize its generic meaning.

Problems	*Alternatives*
mankind	humanity, human beings, people[2]
man's achievements	human achievements
the best man for the job	the best person for the job
the common man	the average person, ordinary people
cavemen	cave dwellers, prehistoric people

2. Sometimes the combining form -*woman* is used alongside -*man* in occupational terms and job titles, but we prefer using the same titles for men and women when naming jobs that could be held by both. Note, too, that using the same forms for men and women is a way to avoid using the combining form -*person* as a substitute for -*woman* only.

Problems	*Alternatives*
chairman/chairwoman	chair, coordinator (of a committee or department), moderator (of a meeting), presiding officer, head, chairperson
businessman/businesswoman	business executive, manager
congressman/congresswoman	congressional representative

---

[2] A one-word substitution for *mankind* isn't always possible, especially in set phrases like *the story of mankind*. Sometimes recasting the sentence altogether may be the best solution.

policeman/policewoman   police officer
salesman/saleswoman   sales clerk, sales representative,
                                        salesperson
fireman   fire fighter
mailman   letter carrier

Generic "He" and "His"

Because there is no one pronoun in English that can be effectively substituted for *he* or *his,* we offer several alternatives. The form *he or she* has been the NCTE house style over the last ten years, on the premise that it is less distracting then *she or he* or *he/she.* There are other choices, however. The one you make will depend on what you are writing.

1. Sometimes it is possible to drop the possessive form *his* altogether to substitute an article.

Problems	*Alternatives*
The average student is worried about his grades.	The average student is worried about grades.
When the student hands in his paper, read it immediately.	When the student hands in the paper, read it immediately.

2. Often, it makes sense to use the plural instead of the singular.

Problems	*Alternatives*
Give the student his grade right away.	Give the students their grades right away.
Ask the student to hand in his work as soon as he is finished.	Ask students to hand in their work as soon as they are finished.

3. The first or second person can sometimes be substituted for the third person.

Problems	*Alternatives*
As a teacher, he is faced daily with the problem of paperwork.	As teachers, we are faced daily with the problem of paperwork.
When a teacher asks his students for an evaluation, he is putting himself on the spot.	When you ask your students for an evaluation, you are putting yourself on the spot.

4. In some situations, the pronoun *one (one's)* can be substituted for *he (his),* but it should be used sparingly. Notice that the use of *one* — like the use of *we* or *you* — changes the tone of what you are writing.

Problem	*Alternative*
He might well wonder what his response should be.	One might well wonder what one's response should be.

5. A sentence with *he* or *his* can sometimes be recast in the passive voice or another impersonal construction.

Problems	Alternatives
Each student should hand in his paper promptly.	Papers should be handed in promptly.
He found such an idea intolerable.	Such an idea was intolerable.

6. When the subject is an indefinite pronoun, the plural form *their* can occasionally be used with it, especially when the referent for the pronoun is clearly understood to be plural.

Problem	Alternative
When everyone contributes his own ideas, the discussion will be a success.	When everyone contributes their own ideas, the discussion will be a success.

But since this usage is transitional, it is usually better to recast the sentence and avoid the indefinite pronoun.

Problem	Alternative
When everyone contributes his own ideas, the discussion will be a success.	When all the students contribute their own ideas, the discussion will be a success.

7. Finally, sparing use can be made of *he or she* and *his or her*. It is best to restrict this choice to contexts in which the pronouns are not repeated.

Problems	Alternatives
Each student will do better if he has a voice in the decision.	Each student will do better if he or she has a voice in the decision.
Each student can select his own topic.	Each student can select his or her own topic.

Sex-Role Stereotyping

Word choices sometimes reflect unfortunate and unconscious assumptions about sex roles — for example, that farmers are always men and elementary school teachers are always women; that men are valued for their accomplishments and women for their physical attributes; or that men are strong and brave while women are weak and timid. We need to examine the assumptions inherent in certain stock phrases and choose nonstereotyped alternatives.

1. Identify men and women in the same way. Diminutive or special forms to name women are usually unnecessary. In most cases, generic terms such as *doctor* or *actor* should be assumed to include both men and women. Only occasionally are alternate forms needed, and in these cases, the alternate form replaces both the masculine and the feminine titles.

Problems	*Alternatives*
stewardess	flight attendant (for both *steward* and *stewardess*)
authoress	author
waitress	server, food server
poetess	poet
coed	student
lady lawyer	lawyer . . . she
male nurse	nurse . . . he

2. Do not represent women as occupying only certain jobs or roles and men as occupying only certain others.

Problems	*Alternatives*
the kindergarten teacher . . . she	*occasionally use* the kindergarten teacher . . . he *or* kindergarten teachers . . . they
the principal . . . he	*occasionally use* the principal . . . she *or* principals . . . they
Have your mother send a snack for the party.	Have a parent send a snack for the party. *occasionally use* Have your father . . . *or* Have your parents. . . .
NCTE conventiongoers and their wives are invited.	NCTE conventiongoers and their spouses are invited.
Writers become so involved in their work that they neglect their wives and children.	Writers become so involved in their work that they neglect their families.

3. Treat men and women in a parallel manner.

Problems	*Alternatives*
The class interviewed Chief Justice Burger and Mrs. O'Connor.	The class interviewed Warren Burger and Sandra O'Connor. *or* . . . Mr. Burger and Ms. O'Connor. *or* . . . Chief Justice Burger and Justice O'Connor.
The reading list included Proust, Joyce, Gide, and Virginia Woolf	The reading list included Proust, Joyce, Gide, and Woolf. *or* . . . Marcel Proust, James Joyce, André Gide, and Virginia Woolf.

Both Bill Smith, a straight-A sophomore, and Kathy Ryan, a pert junior, won writing awards.	Both sophomore Bill Smith, a straight-A student, and junior Kathy Ryan, editor of the school paper, won writing awards.

4. Seek alternatives to language that patronizes or trivializes women, as well as to language that reinforces stereotyped images of both women and men.

Problems	*Alternatives*
The president of the company hired a gal Friday.	The president of the company hired an assistant.
I'll have my girl do it.	I'll ask my secretary to do it.
Stella is a career woman.	Stella is a professional. *or* Stella is a doctor (architect, etc.).
The ladies on the committee all supported the bill.	The women on the committee all supported the bill.
Pam had lunch with the girls from the office.	Pam had lunch with the women from the office.
This is a man-sized job.	This is a big (huge, enormous) job.
That's just an old wives' tale.	That's just a superstition (superstitious story).
Don't be such an old lady.	Don't be so fussy.

Sexist Language in a Direct Quotation

Quotations cannot be altered, but there are other ways of dealing with this problem.

1. Avoid the quotation altogether if it is not really necessary.
2. Paraphrase the quotation, giving the original author credit for the idea.
3. If the quotation is fairly short, recast it as an indirect quotation, substituting nonsexist words as necessary.

Problem	*Alternative*
Among the questions asked by the school representatives was the following: "Considering the ideal college graduate, what degree of knowledge would you prefer him to have in each of the curricular areas?"	Among the questions asked by the school representatives was one about what degree of knowledge the ideal college graduate should have in each of the curricular areas.

Sample Revised Passage

Substantial revisions or deletions are sometimes necessary when problems overlap or when stereotyped assumptions about men and women so pervade a passage that simple replacement of words is inadequate.

Problem

Each student who entered the classroom to find himself at the mercy of an elitist, Vassar-trained Miss Fidditch could tell right away that the semester would be a trial. The trend in composition pedagogy toward student-centered essays and away from hours of drill on grammatical correctness has meant, at least for him, that he can finally learn to write. But Macrorie, Elbow, and Janet Emig could drive the exasperated teacher of a cute and perky cheerleader type to embrace the impersonal truth of *whom* as direct object rather than fight his way against the undertow of a gush of personal experience. As Somerset Maugham remarked, "Good prose should resemble the conversation of a well-bred man," and both Miss Fidditch and the bearded guru who wants to "get inside your head" must realize it.

Alternative

The trend in composition pedagogy toward student-centered essays, represented by such writers as Ken Macrorie, Peter Elbow, and Janet Emig, has meant that some students are finally learning to write. Yet the movement away from hours of drill on grammatical correctness has brought with it a new problem: In the hands of the inexperienced teacher, student essays can remain little more than unedited piles of personal experiences and emotions.

REPRESENTATION OF MEN AND WOMEN

Important as language is, striving for nonsexist usage is to little purpose if   10
the underlying assumptions about men and women continue to restrict them to traditional roles. If women never enter an author's world, for example, it little avails a writer or editor to refer scrupulously to students as "they" and prehistoric people as "cave dwellers." Thus, teachers and other professionals must be alert to the possible sexist implications of the content as well as the language of educational materials.

It has been enheartening to note that in the last ten years, trade publishers, textbook publishers, and publishers of reference works have become acutely aware of sexist language, thus largely alleviating the problem of discriminatory reference. Still, vigilance must be exercised.

The following recommendations concerning educational materials are made to correct traditional omissions of women or perpetuations of stereotypes.

Booklists

1. Items for a booklist should be chosen to emphasize the equality of men and women and to show them in nontraditional as well as traditional roles. Many children's favorites and classics may contain sexist elements, but books that

are valuable for other reasons should not be excluded. The annotations, however, should be written in nonsexist language.

2. Picture books should be chosen showing males and females actively participating in a variety of situations at home, work, and play.
3. Booklists should be organized by subject headings that do not assume stereotyped male and female interests.

Problems	*Alternatives*
Books for Boys	Arts and Crafts
Books for Girls	Sports
	Travel

Teaching Units

1. The topic and organization of teaching units should be carefully considered to avoid sexist implications. Literature by and about women and men should be included wherever possible.
2. When materials are chosen that present stereotyped assumptions about men and women, they should be balanced by others that show nontraditional roles and assumptions. *Jemima Puddle-Duck* and *Peter Rabbit* read together, for instance, show foolishness is not a sex-linked characteristic. Vera Brittain's *A Testament of Youth* and Ernest Hemingway's *The Sun Also Rises* present the aftermath of World War I from provocative perspectives. Placing a book in the proper historical context and using discussion questions that reflect an awareness of the sexist elements are good strategies.
3. Activities suggested in teaching units should not be segregated by sex: Boys can make costumes and girls can build sets.

Reference Books and Research Materials

Reference books can be implicitly sexist in their titles, organizations, content, and language. Editors of such books should follow the suggestions in this publication to ensure nonsexist language in bibliographies, indexes, style manuals, and teacher's guides. In research works, if both males and females were studied, references to individual subjects should not assume that they are all one sex.

IMPLEMENTATION OF GUIDELINES

These guidelines for nonsexist language are suggestions for teachers, writers, and contributors to NCTE publications. For the editors of NCTE publications, however, they are a statement of editorial policy.

Traditionally, editors have set the style for the publications — deciding, for example, whether there should be a comma before the conjunction in a series or whether the first item in a list after a colon should begin with a capital letter. Style decisions have sometimes been made in response to public pressure. Writing *Negro* with a capital letter instead of a lowercase letter and, later, using *Black* instead of *Negro* were both style decisions of this sort for many publishing houses, newspapers, and magazines.

15

It is an editor's job to rewrite whenever necessary to eliminate awkward language, inconsistency, or inaccuracy. If a job title is inaccurately identified in an article as Director of Public Instruction but the title is actually Supervisor of Public Instruction, the editor changes the wording as a matter of course and without asking the author's approval. If the subject matter or tone of an article is totally inappropriate for the particular publication, it would also be the editor's prerogative to return the manuscript to the author. In the case of language inconsistent with the guidelines, it is the editor's duty to question the author's use of a particular term; on the other hand, the author has the right to insist on its use, but a footnote will be provided to reflect such insistence.

The choices suggested in these guidelines are intended as additions to the style sheets and manuals already in use.

■ ■ TWO VIEWS OF LANGUAGE AND CONSUMER ADVERTISING

Advertising is a particularly pervasive form of language use. Each day you probably encounter numerous messages advertising consumer products: billboards, television and radio commercials, magazine and newspaper ads, bumper stickers, t-shirts, even college classroom bulletin boards. With such a blur of messages, it is difficult to think critically about the arguments these messages contain. The following essays consider the persuasive potential of advertising. As you read them, consider the following questions:

1. How many different advertisements do you think you encounter every day? What kind of influence do you think advertising has?
2. What kind of persuasive strategies do you see in ads you encounter? What kind of claims, reasons, and assumptions do these ads contain? Are any of these strategies unfair or illegitimate?
3. To what extent do you accept the assumptions in ads?
4. Is advertising good or bad? Or is it both good and bad?

The Bribed Soul

LESLIE SAVAN

TELEVISION-WATCHING AMERICANS — that is, just about *all* Americans — see approximately 100 TV commercials a day. In that same 24 hours they also see a host of print ads, billboard signs, and other corporate messages slapped onto every available surface, from the fuselages of NASA rockets right down to the bottom of golf holes and the inside doors of restroom stalls. Studies estimate that, counting all the logos, labels, and announcements, some 16,000 ads flicker across an individual's consciousness daily.

Advertising now infects just about every organ of society, and wherever advertising gains a foothold it tends to slowly take over, like a vampire or a virus. When television broadcasting began about 50 years ago, the idea of a network that would air nothing but commercials was never seriously considered, not even when single-sponsor shows were produced straight out of the sponsor's ad agency. But today, by the grace of cable, we have several such channels, including MTV, stylistically the most advanced programming on the air, and FYI, a proposed new channel that would run only ads — infomercials, home-shopping shows, regular-length commercials, and, for a real treat, programs of "classic" ads. Similarly, product placement in the movies started small, with the occasional Tab showing up in a star's hand, but now it's grown big enough to eat the whole thing. In its 1993 futuristic thriller *Demolition Man,* Warner Bros. not only scattered the usual corporate logos throughout the sets but it also rewrote the script so that the only fast-food chain to survive the "franchise wars" of the 20th century was Taco Bell — which, in return, promoted the movie in all its outlets.

Even older, far statelier cultural institutions have had their original values hollowed out and replaced by ad values, leaving behind the merest fossil of their founders' purpose. Modernist masters enjoy art museum blockbusters only when they can be prominently underwritten by an oil company or a telecommunication giant; new magazines are conceived not on the basis of their editorial content but on their ability to identify potential advertisers and groom their copy to fit marketing needs. In the process, the function of sponsored institutions is almost comically betrayed. The exotic bug exhibit at the Smithsonian Museum's new O. Orkin Insect Zoo, for example, opens with the red diamond logo of Orkin Pest Control and displays various little beasties, ever so subtly planting the suggestion that if they were to escape their glass cages you'd know who to call. Though the Smithsonian would never be so crass as to actually recommend Orkin's services, it is crass enough to never once mention in its exhibits the dangers of pesticides.

As for all those television-watching Americans, hit on by those 16,000 paid (and tax-deductible) messages a day, they're even more vulnerable than their institutions. Most admakers understand that in order to sell to you they have to know your desires and dreams better than you may know them yourself, and they've tried to reduce that understanding to a science. Market research, in which psychologists, polling organizations, trends analysts, focus group leaders, "mall-intercept" interviewers, and the whole panoply of mass communications try to figure out what will make you buy, has become a $2.5 billion annual business growing at a healthy clip of about 4.2 percent a year (after adjustment for inflation). Yet even this sophisticated program for the study of the individual consumer is only a starter kit for the technological advances that will sweep through the advertising-industrial complex in the 1990s. Today, the most we can do when another TV commercial comes on — and we are repeatedly told that this is our great freedom — is to switch channels. But soon technology will take even that tiny tantrum of resistance and make it "interactive," providing advertisers with information on the exact moment we became bored — vital data that can be crunched, analyzed, and processed into the next set of ads, the better to zap-proof *them.*

Impressive as such research may be, the real masterwork of advertising is the   5
way it uses the techniques of art to seduce the human soul. Virtually all of modern experience now has a sponsor, or at least a sponsored accessory, and there is
no human emotion or concern — love, lust, war, childhood innocence, social re-
bellion, spiritual enlightenment, even disgust with advertising — that cannot be
reworked into a sales pitch. The transcendent look in a bride's eyes the moment
before she kisses her groom turns into a promo for Du Pont. The teeth-gnashing
humiliation of an office rival becomes an inducement to switch to AT&T.

In short, we're living the sponsored life. From Huggies to Maalox, the necessities and little luxuries of an American's passage through this world are provided and promoted by one advertiser or another. The sponsored life is born
when commercial culture sells our own experiences back to us. It grows as those
experiences are then reconstituted inside us, mixing the most intimate processes
of individual thought with commercial values, rhythms, and expectations. It has
often been said by television's critics that TV doesn't deliver products to viewers
but that viewers themselves are the *real* product, one that TV delivers to its advertisers. True, but the symbiotic relationship between advertising and audience
goes deeper than that. The viewer who lives the sponsored life — and that is
most of us to one degree or the other — is slowly re-created in the ad's image.

Inside each "consumer," advertising's all-you-can-eat, all-the-time, all-
dessert buffet produces a build-up of mass-produced stimuli, all hissing and sput-
tering to get out. Sometimes they burst out as sponsored speech, as when we
talk in the cadences of sitcom one-liners, imitate Letterman, laugh uproariously
at lines like "I've fallen and I can't get up," or mouth the words of familiar
commercials, like the entranced high school student I meet in a communication
class who moved his lips with the voiceover of a Toyota spot. Sometimes they slip
out as sponsored dress, as when white suburban kids don the baggy pants and
backward baseball caps they see on MTV rappers. Sometimes they simply come
out as sponsored equations, as when we attribute "purity" and "honesty" to
clear products like Crystal Pepsi or Ban's clear deodorant.

To lead the sponsored life you don't really have to do anything. You don't
need to have a corporate sponsor as the museums or the movies do. You don't
even have to buy anything — though it helps, and you will. You just have to live
in America and share with the nation, or at least with your mall-intercept co-
horts, certain paid-for expectations and values, rhythms and reflexes.

Those expectations and how they unfold through advertising is the subject
of this book. It's based on eight years of columns and articles I wrote about ads
and other pop culture phenomena for *The Village Voice*. Despite advertising's
enormous role in our lives, most of the media feel that, like hot dogs and military
budgets, advertising goes down most easily when it's unexamined. They react
this way, of course, because they're sponsored. Conveyors of commercial culture
are free to question nearly all of modern life except their own life-support system.
This conflict of interest means that unlike "official" cultural products — films,
TV shows, books, paintings, and so on — advertising finds few regular critics in
the mainstream press.

When the Center for the Study of Commercialism, a well-respected, Wash-   10 ington, D.C.-based nonprofit group, called a press conference in 1992 to announce the results of a study that showed the press repeatedly censoring itself under direct or anticipated advertiser pressure, not a single TV or radio reporter attended, and only a few papers even mentioned it. If journalism looks at ads at all, it usually settles for soft-shoe analysis, pieces that ask, essentially, "Does this ad work?" Most newspapers are pleased to do celebrity profiles of ad directors or agencies that have a few hits on their hands (possibly the agency will direct more ad dollars the paper's way, but more importantly over the long run, such stories prove that the publication offers a "positive environment" for advertisers). Ads are usually examined only when they make "news," through scandal, product failure, or superstar megadeals, like Madonna's or Michael Jackson's with Pepsi.

At the *Voice,* however, I could criticize ads in a fuller social and political context because, first of all, the paper is an alternative exception and does try to maintain a separation between advertising and editorial. And, as much to the point, I wasn't tearing into ads run by the futon shops, restaurants, and other local retailers that make up the bulk of *Voice* advertising.

That has allowed me to do the basic spadework of ad criticism — looking at the false claims ads occasionally make or the corporate misdeeds lurking behind the PR spin. But the real subject of my column, "Op Ad," has always been more *how* it works — how commercial values infiltrate our beliefs and desires, how we become more and more sponsored.

The chief expectation of the sponsored life is that there will and always should be regular blips of excitement and resolution, the frequency of which is determined by money. We begin to pulse to the beat, the one-two beat, that moves most ads: problem/solution, old/new Brand X/hero brand, desire/gratification. In order to dance to the rhythm, we adjust other expectations a little here, a little there: Our notions of what's desirable behavior, our lust for novelty, even our visions of the perfect love affair or thrilling adventure adapt to the mass consensus coaxed out by marketing. Cultural forms that don't fit these patterns tend to fade away, and eventually *everything* in commercial culture — not just the 30-second spot but the drama, news segment, stage performance, novel, magazine layout — comes to share the same insipid insistence on canned excitement and neat resolution.

What's all the excitement about? Anything and nothing. You know you've entered the commercial zone when the excitement building in you is idly incommensurate with the content dangled before you: Does a sip of Diet Coke really warrant an expensive production number celebrating the rebel prowess of "ministers who surf," "insurance agents who speed," and "people who live their life as an exclamation not an explanation"?!? Of course not. Yet through the sympathetic magic of materialism we learn how to respond to excitement: It's less important that we purchase any particular product than that we come to expect resolution *in the form of* something buyable.

The way ads have of jacking up false excitement in the name of ultimately unsatisfying purchases has given Western societies a bad case of commercial blue balls. You're hit on, say, by yet another guy on TV hawking fabric whitener, 15 but — wait a minute — he "can't be a man" because he packs a different brand of smokes. And maybe you moan, "I can't get no, no no no . . ."

Anyway, that's how the Rolling Stones put it in that seminal semiotic text "(I Can't Get No) Satisfaction" back in 1965. Commercials are the tinny jingles in our heads that remind us of all we've abandoned in exchange for our materially comfortable lives — real extended families, real human empathy, real rebel prowess. The result of stale promises endlessly repeated is massive frustration.

But Mick Jagger is younger than that now: Long after "Satisfaction" had dropped off the charts, the Rolling Stones became the first major band to tour for a corporate sponsor, Jovan perfumes, in 1981. By then Jagger had become a symbol of the most popular postmodern response to advertising's dominant role in our culture: the ironic reflex.

Irony has become a hallmark of the sponsored life because it provides a certain distance from the frustration inherent in commercial correctness. For some time now the people raised on television, the baby boomers and the "Generation Xers" that followed, have mentally adjusted the set, as it were, in order to convince themselves that watching is cool. They may be doing exactly what their parents do — but they do it *differently.* They take in TV with a Lettermanesque wink, and they like it when it winks back. In many cases (as Mark Crispin Miller has described so well in *Boxed In*), the winkers have enthusiastically embraced the artifice, even the manipulativeness, of advertising as an essential paradox of modern life, a paradox that is at the crux of their own identity.

The winkers believe that by rolling their collective eyes when they watch TV they can control *it,* rather than letting it control them. But unfortunately, as a defense against the power of advertising, irony is a leaky condom — in fact, it's the same old condom that advertising brings over every night. A lot of ads have learned that to break through to the all-important boomer and Xer markets they have to be as cool, hip, and ironic as the target audience likes to think of itself as being. That requires at least the pose of opposition to commercial values. The cool commercials — I'm thinking of Nike spots, some Reeboks, most 501s, certainly all MTV promos — flatter us by saying we're too cool to fall for commercial values, and therefore cool enough to want their product.

If irony is weak armor, how do we ward off the effect of billions of words 20 and images from our sponsors? No perfect wolfsbane exists, but I can suggest some tactics to keep in mind.

When watching, watch out. Literally. Watch as an outsider, from as far a distance as you can muster (farther even than irony) — *especially* when watching ads that flatter you for being an outsider, as more and more are doing.

Big lie, little lie. All advertising tells lies, but there are little lies and there are big lies. Little lie: This beer tastes great. Big lie: This beer makes *you* great. Not all ads tell little lies — they're more likely to be legally actionable (while big lies by definition aren't). And many products do live up to their modest material claims: This car runs. But all ads *must* tell big lies: This car will attract babes and make others slobber in envy. Don't be shocked that ads lie — that's their job. But do try to distinguish between the two kinds of lies.

Read the box. Look not just at whether an ad's claims are false or exaggerated, but try to figure out what portion of an ad is about the culture as opposed to the product. Read the contents as you would a cereal box's: Instead of how much sugar to wheat, consider how much style to information. Not that a high ratio of sugar to wheat is necessarily more malevolent than the other way around. But it's a sure sign that they're fattening you up for the shill.

Assume no relationship between a brand and its image. Marlboro was originally sold as a woman's cigarette, and its image was elegant, if not downright prissy. It wasn't until 1955 that the Marlboro Man was invented to ride herd on all that. The arbitrary relationship between a product and its ads becomes even clearer when you realize how much advertising is created to overcome "brand parity" — a plague more troubling to marketers than bodily odors. Brand parity means that there's little or no difference between competing brands and that the best a brand can do is hire a more appealing image. When advertising works at all, it's because the public more or less believes that something serious is going on between a product and its image, as if the latter reveals intrinsic qualities of the former. Peel image off item, and you too can have more of the freedom that ads are always promising. Likewise . . .

We don't buy products, we buy the world that presents them. Over the long run, whether you actually buy a particular product is less important than that you buy the world that makes the product seem desirable. Not so long ago a BMW or Mercedes was required if you seriously bought the worldview that their ads conveyed. Still, buying an attitude doesn't automatically translate into product purchase. If your income precluded a BMW, you might have bought instead a Ralph Lauren polo shirt or even a Dove bar (which is how yuppie snack foods positioned themselves — as achievable class). Sure, GE wants you to buy its bulbs, but even more it wants you to buy the paternalistic, everything's-under-control world that GE seems to rule. Buying *that* will result, GE is betting, not only in more appliance sales but also in more credibility when spokesmen insist that defrauding the Pentagon is not *really* what GE's all about. That is to say . . .

The promotional is the political. Each world that commercials use to sell things comes packed with biases: Entire classes, races, and genders may be excluded for the coddling of the sponsored one. Lee Jeans's world (circa 1989) is a place where young people are hip, sexual, and wear jeans, while old people are square, nonsexual, and wear uniforms. The class and age politics here is more powerful than the Young Republicans'. There is politics in all advertising (and, more obviously, advertising in all politics). It makes sense that these two professions call what they do "campaigns."

Advertising shepherds herds of individuals. When Monty Python's mistaken messiah in *The Life of Brian* exhorts the crowd of devotees to "Don't follow me! Don't follow anyone! Think for yourselves! . . . You are all individuals!" they reply in unison, "We are all individuals!" That is advertising in a nutshell.

Advertising's most basic paradox is to say: Join us and become unique. Advertisers learned long ago that individuality sells, like sex or patriotism. The urge toward individualism is a constant in America, with icons ranging from Thomas

25

Jefferson's yeoman farmer to the kooky girl bouncing to the jingle "I like the Sprite in you!" Commercial nonconformity always operates in the service of . . . conformity. Our system of laws and our one-man-one-vote politics may be based on individualism, but successful marketing depends on the exact opposite: By identifying (through research) the ways we are alike, it hopes to convince the largest number of people that they need the exact same product. Furthermore, in modern pop culture, we construct our individuality by the unique combination of mass-produced goods and services we buy. I sip Evian, you slug Bud Light; I drive a Geo, you gun a Ford pickup; I kick sidewalk in cowboy boots, you bop in Reeboks. Individuality is a good angle for all advertising, but it's crucial for TV commercials. There you are sitting at home, not doing anything for hours on end, but then the very box you're staring at tells you that you are different, that you are vibrantly alive, that your quest for freedom — freedom of speech, freedom of movement, freedom to do whatever you damn well choose — will not be impeded! And you can do all that, says the box, without leaving your couch.

It's the real ad. The one question I'm most often asked is, Does advertising shape who we are and what we want, or does it merely reflect back to us our own emotions and desires? As with most nature-or-nurture questions, the answer is both. The real ad in any campaign is controlled neither by admakers nor ad-watchers; it exists somewhere between the TV set and the viewer, like a huge hairball, collecting bits of material and meaning from both. The real ad isn't even activated until viewers hand it their frustrations from work, the mood of their love life, their idiosyncratic misinterpretations, and most of all, I think, their everyday politics. On which class rung do they see themselves teetering? Do they ever so subtly flinch when a different race comes on TV? In this way, we all coproduce the ads we see. Agency people are often aghast that anyone would find offensive meanings in their ads because "that's not what we intended." Intention has little to do with it. Whatever they meant, once an ad hits the air it becomes public property. That, I think, is where criticism should aim — at the fluctuating, multimeaning thing that floats over the country, reflecting us as we reflect it.

Follow the flattery. I use the word *flattery* a lot. When trying to understand what an ad's really up to, following the flattery is as useful as following the money. You'll find the ad's target market by asking who in any 30-second drama is being praised for qualities they probably don't possess. When a black teenager plays basketball with a white baby boomer for Canada Dry, it's not black youth that's being pandered to. It's white boomers — the flattery being that they're cool enough to be accepted by blacks. Ads don't even have to put people on stage to toady up to them. Ads can flatter by style alone, as do all the spots that turn on hyperquick cuts or obscure meanings, telling us — uh, *some* of us — that we're special enough to get it.

We participate in our own seduction. Once properly flattered, all that's left is to close the sale — and only we can do that. Not only do we coproduce ads, but we're our own best voiceover — that little inner voice that ultimately decides to buy or not. The best ads tell us we're cool *coolly* — in the other meaning of the word. McLuhan[1] used to say that a cool medium, like television, involves us more by not giving us everything; the very spaces between TV's flickering dots are filled in by our central nervous system. He refers to "the involvement of the viewer with the completion or 'closing' of the TV image." This is seduction: We're stirred to a state so that not only do we close the image but, given the right image at the right time, we open our wallet. All television is erotically engaged in this way, but commercials are TV's G-spot. The smart ads always hold back a little to get us to lean forward a little. Some ads have become caricatures of this tease, withholding the product's name until the last second to keep you wondering who could possibly be sponsoring such intrigue. The seduction may continue right to the cash register, where one last image is completed: you and product together at last. It'd be nice to say that now that you've consumed, you've climaxed, and everyone can relax. But sponsorship is a lifetime proposition that must be renewed every day.

The Language of Advertising

CHARLES A. O'NEILL

TOWARD THE END of her concert in a downtown park in Manchester, New   1
Hampshire — not far, as the wind blows, from the long-suffering nuclear power plant at Seabrook — Bonnie Raitt, the rock star, looked out over her audience and noticed the Marlboro and Dunkin' Donut signs in the distance. "If you think Marlboro country and donuts are where the flavor is, I've got news: it's not." She proceeded to tell the sympathetic, energized late-evening crowd that "where it is" was somewhere between a thing called love and a nonprofit group she supported, International Physicians for the Prevention of Nuclear War.

Ms. Raitt said nothing to indicate that she really had anything against Dunkin' Donuts — or, for that matter, cigarettes. And if she had anything against Miller beer, one of the sponsors of the event, she didn't say. Ms. Raitt's midconcert comments were, after all, not meant to start a debate. But she was, in her own way, commenting on one aspect of something we in America have long accepted as part of our culture; something pervasive, often taken for granted but often criticized: advertising.

If Marlboro is not truly "where the flavor is," it's not for lack of effort. Perhaps they have not convinced Ms. Raitt, but the architects of "Marlboro country" know how to reach into millions of smokers' heads and touch the desired motivational lever: the one labelled "buy!" The "real truth" doesn't matter, for

[1] Canadian philosopher Marshall McLuhan whose focus was often on changes brought about by the mass media.

advertising is not about truth, virtue, love or positive social values; it is about making money. When the writers of Marlboro's ads sat down in front of their word processors, they set in motion a sequence of events that changed the buying habits of millions of people. The final test of any advertising program (whether for donuts, cigarettes, nonprofit groups, detergents, cereals, life insurance, or pantyhose) is simply the degree to which it creates that impulse, the impulse to buy.

What creates the impulse? The strategy may call for billboards in a city in New Hampshire, full-page ads in Rolling Stone, 30-second spots on the CBS Evening News, T-shirts imprinted with a corporate logo, music videos — or, for that matter, Ms. Raitt at the microphone. Whatever the strategy, advertisements derive their power from a purposeful, directed combination of images. Images can take several forms: words — spoken or written — or visuals; or, most powerfully, a combination of the two. The precise formula is determined by the creative concept and the medium chosen. The combination is the language of advertising.

Everyone who grows up in the Western world soon learns that advertising 5 language is different from other languages. Most children would be unable to explain how such lines as "With Nice 'n Easy, it's color so natural, the closer he gets the better you look!" (the famous ad for Clairol's Nice 'n Easy hair coloring product) or Marlboro's "come to where the flavor is" differs from ordinary language, but they would be able to tell you, "It sounds like an ad." Whether printed on a page, blended with music on the radio or smoothly whispered on the sound track of a television commercial, advertising language is "different."

Over the years, the texture of advertising language has frequently changed. Styles and creative concepts come and go. But there are at least four distinct general characteristics of the language of advertising that make it different from other languages; characteristics that, taken together, lend advertising its persuasive power:

1. The language of advertising is edited and purposeful.
2. The language of advertising is rich and arresting; it is specifically intended to attract and hold our attention.
3. The language of advertising involves us; in effect, *we* complete the message.
4. The language of advertising holds no secrets from us; it is a simple language.

EDITED AND PURPOSEFUL

One easy way to develop a feeling for the basic difference between advertising language and other languages is to transcribe a television talk show. An examination of such a transcript will show the conversation skipping from one topic to another, even though the guest and the host may attempt to stick to a specific subject. The conversation also is rife with repetition. After all, informal, conversational language transactions are not ordinarily intended to meet specific objectives. Advertising language cannot afford to be so desultory. It *does* have a specific purpose — to sell us something.

In *Future Shock,* Alvin Toffler draws a distinction between normal "coded" messages and "engineered" messages. As an example of an uncoded message, Toffler writes about a random, unstructured experience:

> A man walks along a street and notices a leaf whipped along a sidewalk by the wind. He perceives this event through his sensory apparatus. He hears a rustling sound. He sees movement and greenness. He feels the wind. From these sensory perceptions he somehow forms a mental image. We can refer to these sensory signals as a message. But the message is not, in any ordinary sense of [the] term, man-made. It is not designed by anyone to communicate anything, and the man's understanding of it does not depend directly on a social code — a set of agreed-upon signs and definitions.[1]

The talk show conversation, however, is coded; the guests' ability to exchange information with their host, and our ability to understand it, depend, as Toffler puts it, upon social conventions.

Beyond coded and uncoded messages there is another kind — the engineered message — a variation of the coded message. The language of advertising is a language of finely engineered, ruthlessly purposeful messages. By Toffler's calculation,[2] the average adult American is assaulted by at least 560 advertising messages a day. Not one of these messages would reach us, to attract and hold our attention, if it were completely unstructured. Advertising messages have a clear purpose; they are intended to trigger a specific response.

RICH AND ARRESTING

Advertisements — no matter how carefully "engineered" and packed with information — cannot succeed unless they capture our attention in the first place. Of the hundreds of advertising messages in store for us each day, very few (Toffler estimates seventy-six) will actually obtain our conscious attention.[3] The rest are screened out. The people who design and write ads know about this screening process; they anticipate and accept it as a basic premise of their business. They expend a great deal of energy to guarantee that their ads will make it past the defenses and distractions that surround us. The classic, all-time favorite device used to penetrate the barrier is sex. The desire to be attractive to the opposite sex is an ages-old instinct, and few drives are more powerful. Whether it takes this approach or another, every successful advertisement contains a "hook." The hook can take the form of strong visuals (photos or illustrations with emotional value) or a disarming, unexpected — even incongruous — set of words:

"Reeboks let U B U."	(Reebok)
"My chickens eat better than you do."	(Perdue Chickens)
"Introducing the ultimate concept in air freight. Men that fly."	(Emery Air Freight)
"Look deep into our ryes."	(Wigler's bakery products)
"Me. 4 U."	(The State of Maine)
"If gas pains persist, try Volkswagen."	(Volkswagen)

Even if the text contains no incongruity and does not rely on a pun for its impact, every effective ad needs a creative strategy based on some striking concept or idea. In fact, the concept and execution are often so good that many successful ads entertain while they sell.

For example, consider the campaigns created by Ally and Gargano for Federal Express. A campaign was developed to position Federal Express as the company that would deliver packages, not just "overnight," but "by 10:30 A.M." the next day. The plight of the junior executive in "Presentation," one ad in the campaign, is stretched for dramatic purposes, but it is, nonetheless, all too real: The young executive, who is presumably trying to climb his way up the corporate ladder, is shown calling another parcel delivery service and all but begging for assurance that he will have his slides in hand by 10:30 the next morning. "No slides, no presentation," he pleads. Only a viewer with a heart of stone can watch without feeling sympathetic, as the next morning our junior executive struggles to make his presentation *sans* slides. He is so lost without them that he is reduced to using his hands to perform imitations of birds and animals in shadows on the movie screen. What does the junior executive *viewer* think when he or she sees the ad?

1. Federal Express guarantees to deliver packages "absolutely, positively overnight."
2. Federal Express packages arrive early in the day.
3. What happened to that fellow in the commercial will absolutely not happen to me, now that I know what package delivery service to call.

A sound creative strategy supporting a truly innovative service idea sold Federal Express. But the quality of execution and imagination doesn't really matter. An ad for Merit Ultra Lights (August 1990) made use of one slang word in its headline: "Yo!" Soft drink and fast food companies often take another approach. "Slice of life" ads (so-called because they purport to provide glimpses of people in "real life" situations), replete with beautiful babies frolicking at family picnics or Fourth of July parades, seduce us into thinking that if we drink the right beverage or eat the right hamburger, we'll fulfill our deep yearning for a world where old folks and young folks live together in perfect suburban bliss. Lifestyle — and the natural affiliation of a particular lifestyle with a product — has also been used effectively as an advertising strategy for other types of merchandise. This TV spot for Levi's Corduroys was produced by Foote, Cone & Belding (1985):

	Music up. (Open on quick shot of saxophone player. Cut to man at sink drying his face with a towel. Reflection seen in mirror.)
Male Singer:	Gotta be there at eight. Gotta luminate. (Cut to two women at a table in a 24-hour diner. A man tries to coax them.)
Male Singer:	Got to be lookin' much better than great. (Cut to man and woman walking down the street.)

Male Singer:	Grab a flash of color, add a little more style . . .
	(Cut to shot of two different women at a table. Man does a quick turn landing on a chair. He laughs. The women get up to leave.)
Male Singer:	. . . Looks like Levi's Corduroy night.
	(Cut to shot of large neon sign "Levi's Cords Tonight.")
Male Singer with Group Singers:	Levi's Corduroy night.
	(Cut back to last man on chair. He shrugs.)
Male Singer:	Lookin' good . . .
	(Quick cut to neon sign. Camera pulls back.
Male Singer with Group Singers:	It's a Levi's Corduroy night.
	(Cut to two women at phone booth. One is talking on phone, other waits impatiently.)
Male Singer:	Looks like it's gonna be another Levi's Corduroy night/ Levi's . . .
	(Cut back to first man at the mirror. He taps the mirror and walks away.)
Group Singers:	Corduroy night.
Super:	Levi's batwing. Quality never goes out of style.
	Music fade out.

Of course, the printed word cannot begin to capture the pace or ambiance of this ad; nonetheless, it is clear that this effort doesn't appeal to everyone, and that's just the point. It *will* appeal to the young people identified by Levi's marketing research as the prime target market for the product. The ad encourages the viewer to make a connection: "I'm a flexible, luminous, streetwise kind of guy, just like the man in the mirror. Levi's Corduroys are O.K. Better buy some soon."

The prominence of ads containing puns or cleverly constructed headlines would seem to suggest that ads emerge, like Botticelli's Venus from the sea, flawless and full grown. Usually they do not. The idea that becomes the platform for an effective creative strategy is most often developed only after exhaustive research. The product is examined for its potential, and the prospective buyers are examined for their habits, characteristics and preferences. 15

"Who will be interested in our product? How old are they? Where do they live? How much money do they earn? What problem will our product solve?" Answers to these questions provide the foundation on which the creative strategy is built.

The creative people in the advertising business are well aware that consumers do not watch television or read magazines in order to see ads. Ads have to earn the right to be seen, read, and heard.

INVOLVING

We have seen that the language of advertising is carefully engineered; we have seen that it uses various devices to get our attention. Frank Perdue has us looking at a photo of his chickens at a dinner table. Sneaker companies have us watching athletes at work, Marlboro has us looking at a cowboy on an outdoor billboard. Now that they have our attention, advertisers present information intended to show us that the product they are offering for sale fills a need and, in filling this need, differs from the competition. The process is called "product positioning." Once our attention has been captured, it is the copywriter's responsibility to express such product differences and to exploit and intensify them.

What happens when product differences do not exist? Then the writer must glamorize the superficial differences (for example, difference of color, packaging, or other qualities without direct bearing on the product's basic function) or else *create* differences. As long as the ad is trying to get our attention, the "action" is mostly in the ad itself, in the words and visual images. But as we read an ad or watch it on television, we become more deeply involved. The action starts to take place in *us.* Our imagination is set in motion, and our individual fears and aspirations, our little quirks and insecurities, superimpose themselves on that tightly engineered, attractively packaged message.

Consider, for example, the running battle among the low-calorie soft drinks.   20 The cola wars have spawned many "look-alike" advertisements, because the product features and consumer benefits are generic, applying to all products in the category. Substitute one product name for another, and the messages are often identical, right down to the way the cans are photographed in the closing sequence. This strategy relies upon mass saturation and exposure for impact. In contrast, consider the way sneaker companies have attempted to create a "sense" of product differentiation where few significant differences exist. Reebok said their sneakers were different — meriting their high price tag — because "Reeboks Let U B U" (presumably, other brands of footwear failed to deliver this benefit.) To further underscore the difference between their brands and those of competitors, some sneaker companies in 1990 offered such "significant" innovations as inflatable air bladders, possibly in order to bring the wearer to a new state of walking ecstasy heretofore unavailable to mortals . . . but more likely in an effort to differentiate the product in a crowded, competitive field. Interestingly, competitors "rebelled," against Reebok's "innovation" (thus making themselves appear to be different). As reported in the *Boston Globe* (August 13, 1990), a print ad for Keds is to show a Reebok shoe, adjacent to its $65 price tag, with the headline, "U Gotta B Kidding." Not to be outdone, Puma ran ads depicting a sneaker they described as "too much," replete with bells, a whistle, electric sockets, wings and an air pump! (Guess whose sneaker, in contrast, is depicted as offering "just enough?") Sneakers are shoes, but they are also, in effect, "lifestyle indicators," or symbols: If I think of myself as somewhat rebellious, with a clear sense of independent spirit, I'll go with the Reeboks, since, after all, they'll Let me B Me; if I'm the practical sort — unswayed by technical hype — perhaps I'll go with the "practical" Keds or Pumas.

Symbols have become important elements in the language of advertising in other ways, too; not so much because they carry meanings of their own but because we bring a meaning to them: we charge them with significance. Symbols are efficient, compact vehicles for the communication of an advertising message; they are pervasive and powerful.

One noteworthy example of symbolism at work is provided by the campaign begun in 1978 by Somerset Importers for Johnnie Walker Red Scotch. Sales of Johnnie Walker Red had been trailing sales of Johnnie Walker Black, and Somerset Importers needed to position Red as a fine product in its own right. The Smith/Greenland Agency produced ads which made heavy use of the color red. One ad, often printed as a two-page spread, is dominated by a close-up photo of red autumn leaves. At lower right, the copy reads, "When their work is done, even the leaves turn to red." Another ad — also suitably dominated by a photograph in the appropriate color — reads: "When it's time to quiet down at the end of the day, even a fire turns to Red." *Red*. Warm. Experienced. Seductive. A perfect symbol to use in a liquor advertisement; all the more for the fact that it offers great possibilities for graphic design and copywriting: more fuel for the advertiser's creative art.

From time to time, many people believe, a more disturbing form of symbolism is also used — the "hidden message" symbol. Take a close, hard look at liquor ads and occasionally you will see, reflected in the photograph of a glass of spirits, peculiar, demonlike shapes. Are these shapes merely the product of one consumer's imagination or an accident of photography? Were they deliberately superimposed onto the product photograph by the careful application of ink and airbrush?

The art of advertising contains many such ambiguities. Some are charged, like this one, with multiple shades of meaning. The demons may be taken to represent the problems and cares which one can presumably chase away through consumption of the advertised product. Or they can, just as easily, be taken as representations of the playful spirits which will be unleashed once the product has been consumed. The advertising creative director did not create the need to relax, or to get away from the stresses of daily life; he or she merely took advantage of these common human needs in developing a promotion strategy for the product.

Another human desire advertising writers did not invent (although they liberally exploit it) is the desire to associate with successful people. All of us tend to admire or in some way identify ourselves with famous or successful people. We are therefore already primed for the common advertising device of the testimonial or personality ad. Once we have seen a famous person in an advertisement, we associate the product with the person. "I like Mr. X. If Mr. X likes (endorses) this product, I would like it too." The logic is faulty, but we fall for it just the same. That is how Joe DiMaggio sold Mr. Coffee. The people who write testimonial ads did not create our trust in famous personalities. They merely recognize our inclinations and exploit them.

The language of advertising is different from other languages because we participate in it; in fact, we — not the words we read on the magazine page or the pictures flashing before us on the television screen — charge the ads with most of their power.

A SIMPLE LANGUAGE

Clip a typical story from the publication you read most frequently. Calculate the number of words in an average sentence. Count the number of words of three or more syllables in a typical 100-word passage, omitting words that are capitalized, combinations of two simple words, or verb forms made into three-syllable words by the addition of *-ed* or *-es*. Add the two figures (the average number of words per sentence and the number of three-syllable words per 100 words), then multiply the result by .4. According to Robert Gunning, if the resulting number is seven, there is a good chance that you are reading *True Confessions.*[4] He developed this formula, the "Fog Index," to determine the comparative ease with which any given piece of written communication can be read. Here is the complete text of a typical cigarette advertisement:

> I demand two things from my cigarette. I want a cigarette with low tar and nicotine. But, I also want taste. That's why I smoke Winston Lights. I get a lighter cigarette, but I still get a real taste. And real pleasure. Only one cigarette gives me that: Winston Lights.

The average sentence in this ad runs seven words. *Cigarette* and *nicotine* are three-syllable words, with *cigarette* appearing four times; *nicotine,* once. Considering *that's* as two words, the ad is exactly fifty words long, so the average number of three-syllable words per 100 is ten.

$$
\begin{array}{rl}
7 & \text{words per sentence} \\
+10 & \text{three-syllable words/100} \\
\hline
17 & \\
\times\,.4 & \\
\hline
6.8 & \text{Fog Index}
\end{array}
$$

According to Gunning's scale, this particular ad is written at about the seventh grade level, comparable to most of the ads found in mass circulation magazines.[5] It's about as sophisticated as *True Confessions;* harder to read than a comic book, but easier than *Ladies Home Journal.*

Of course, the Fog Index cannot evaluate the visual aspect of an ad. The headline, "I demand two things from my cigarette," works with the picture (that of an attractive woman) to arouse consumer interest. The text reinforces the image. It is unlikely that many consumers actually take the trouble to read the entire text, but it is not necessary for them to do so in order for the ad to work.

Since three-syllable words are harder to read than one- or two-syllable words, and since simple ideas are more easily transferred from one human to another than complex ideas, advertising copy tends to use even simpler language all the time. Toffler speculates:

> If the [English] language had the same number of words in Shakespeare's time as it does today, at least 200,000 words — perhaps several times that many — have dropped out and been replaced in the intervening four centuries. The high

30

turnover rate reflects changes in things, processes, and qualities in the environment from the world of consumer products and technology.[6]

It is no accident that the first terms Toffler uses to illustrate his point ("fastback," "wash-and-wear," and "flashcube") were invented not by engineers, or journalists, but by advertising copywriters.

Advertising language is simple language; in the engineering process, difficult words or images (which could be used in other forms of communication to lend color or fine shades of meaning) are edited out and replaced by simple words or images not open to misinterpretation.

WHO IS RESPONSIBLE?

Some critics view the entire advertising business as a cranky, unwelcomed child of the free enterprise system, a noisy, whining, brash kid who must somehow be kept in line, but can't just yet be thrown out of the house. Because advertising mirrors the fears, quirks, and aspirations of the society that creates it (and is, in turn, sold by it), it is wide open to parody and ridicule.

Perhaps the strongest, most authoritative critic of advertising language in recent years is journalist Edwin Newman. In his book *Strictly Speaking*, he poses the question, "Will America be the death of English?" Newman's "mature, well thought out judgement" is that it will. As evidence, he cites a number of examples of fuzzy thinking and careless use of the language, not just by advertisers, but by many people in public life, including politicians and journalists:

> The federal government has adopted the comic strip character Snoopy as a symbol and showed us Snoopy on top of his doghouse, flat on his back, with a balloon coming out of his mouth, containing the words, "I believe in conserving energy," while below there was this exhortation: savEnergy.
>
> savEnergy. An entire letter e at the end was savd. In addition, an entire space was savd. Perhaps the government should say onlYou can prevent forest fires. . . . Spelling has been assaulted by Duz, E-Z Off, Fantastik, Kool, Kleen . . . and by products that make you briter, so that you will not be left hi and dri at a parti, but made welkom. . . . Under this pressure, adjectives become adverbs; nouns become adjectives; prepositions disappear; compounds abound.[7]

In this passage, Newman presents three of the charges most often levied against advertising:

1. Advertising debases English.
2. Advertising downgrades the intelligence of the public.
3. Advertising warps our vision of reality, implanting in us groundless fears and insecurities. (He cites, as examples of these groundless fears, "tattle-tale grey," "denture breath," "morning mouth," "unsightly bulge," "ring around the collar.")

Other charges have been made from time to time. They include:

1. Advertising sells daydreams; distracting, purposeless visions of lifestyles beyond the reach of most of the people who are most exposed to advertising.

2. Advertising feeds on human weaknesses and exaggerates the importance of material things, encouraging "impure" emotions and vanities.
3. Advertising encourages bad, even unhealthy habits like smoking.
4. Advertising perpetuates racial and sexual stereotypes.

What can be said in advertising's defense? Advertising is only a reflection of society; slaying the messenger (and just one of the messengers, at that) would not alter the fact — if it is a fact — that "America will be the death of English." A case can be made for the concept that advertising language is an acceptable stimulus for the natural evolution of language. (At the very least, advertising may stimulate debate about what current trends in language are "good" and "bad.") Another point: Is "proper English" the language most Americans actually speak and write, or is it the language we are told we should speak and write, the language of *The Elements of Style* and *The Oxford English Dictionary*?

What about the charge that advertising debases the intelligence of the public? Those who support this particular criticism would do well to ask themselves another question: Exactly how intelligent is the public? How many people know the difference between adverbs and adjectives? How many people *want* to know? The fact is that advertisements are effective, not because agencies say they are effective, but because they sell products.

Advertising attempts to convince us to buy products; we are not forced to buy something because it is heavily advertised. Who, for example, is to be blamed for the success, in the mid-70s, of a nonsensical, nonfunctional product — "Pet Rocks"? The people who designed the packaging, those who created the idea of selling ordinary rocks as pets, or those who bought the product?

Perhaps much of the fault lies with the public, for accepting advertising so readily. S. I. Hayakawa finds "the uncritical response to the incantations of advertising . . . a serious symptom of a widespread evaluational disorder." He does not find it "beyond the bounds of possibility" that today's suckers for national advertising will be tomorrow's suckers for the master political propagandist who will, "by playing up the 'Jewish menace,' in the same way as national advertisers play up the 'pink toothbrush menace,' and by promising us national glory and prosperity, sell fascism in America."[8]

Fascism in America is fortunately a far cry from Pet Rocks, but the point is   40 well taken. In the end, advertising simply attempts to change behavior. It is a neutral tool, just as a gun is a neutral tool, but advertising at least has not been known to cause accidental deaths. Like any form of communication, it can be used for positive social purposes, neutral commercial purposes, or for the most pernicious kind of paranoid propaganda. Accepting, for the purpose of this discussion, that propaganda is, at heart, an extension of politics and therefore is materially different from commercial advertising as practiced in the United States of America, circa 1990, *do* advertisements sell distracting, purposeless visions? Occasionally. But perhaps such visions are necessary components of the process through which our society changes and improves.

And recognize this: advertising is a mirror. It is not perfect; sometimes it distorts. When we view ourselves in it, we're not always pleased with what we see. Perhaps all things considered, that's the way it should be.

NOTES

1. Alvin Toffler, *Future Shock* (New York: Random House, 1970), p. 146.
2. Ibid., p. 149.
3. Ibid.
4. Curtis D. MacDougall, *Interpretive Reporting* (New York: Macmillan, 1968), p. 94.
5. Ibid., p. 95.
6. Toffler, *Future Shock,* p. 151.
7. Edwin Newman, *Strictly Speaking* (Indianapolis: Bobbs-Merrill, 1974), p. 13.
8. S. I. Hayakawa, *Language in Action* (New York: Harcourt, Brace, 1941), p. 235.

Chapter 10

Arguing about Values

Our Disagreements about Values

Personal tastes are often informal and private. As the saying goes, "There is no accounting for taste." Some people like Chinese food; some don't. Some like one kind of music; some prefer another. It is difficult to argue about personal tastes. It is difficult to argue that someone else should like Chinese food just because you do or that Chinese food is somehow better than other kinds of food just because you think it is. One who disagrees can always respond, "You like what you like, and I'll like what I like."

To be meaningful, arguments about values must be based in the common values of a community, those things that we value collectively. It is one thing to say that you like or don't like Shakespeare. It is quite another to say that Shakespeare is the greatest English writer and then support that claim with community-based reasons. The first is a statement about personal taste; the second is a statement about community values. The fact that you personally like or don't like Shakespeare does nothing to change the community's value of Shakespeare as a writer.

If you find yourself at odds with the values of the community, then you can seek to change them through arguing. Or if you encounter members of the community who disagree with the community's values, you can seek to persuade them to accept those values. As with other aspects of living in a community, there is a tension here, between what individuals desire or value and what the community as a whole desires and values. Because individuals are so different and individual desires are so various, disputes about values are frequent in communities. In fact, nearly all disputes in communities are in some way related to values, to what we desire.

Values are often expressed as abstract ideas or principles about what is

379

"good" or "bad," "desirable" or "undesirable," "advantageous," or "disadvantageous," "moral" or "immoral," "good" or "evil," "righteous" or "wicked," "beautiful" or "ugly." These abstract terms carry the force of judgment. The philosopher Richard Weaver calls them "ultimate terms," terms that express the ultimate values of a society, around which other values are clustered. Something "good" is something we accept and desire. Something "bad" is something we reject.

But these abstractions have little meaning outside the context of a particular community. In other words, the key to understanding the values of a community is understanding how that community defines "good" and "bad," "beautiful" and "ugly." What do members of the community accept and reject, and why? That is to say, what do they value?

Here are some abstract terms commonly used to describe things people in the United States value:

> adventure, ambition, autonomy, collective responsibility, comfort, competition, cooperation, courage, creativity, equality of condition, equality of opportunity, excellence, flexibility, freedom of speech, generosity, harmony, honesty, justice, novelty, order, patriotism, peace, rationality, security, spontaneity, tolerance, tradition, wisdom

How do you define these terms? What examples would you give of each? For you, are these values good, bad, or mixed?

Think about the things you desire. Are there abstract terms to describe what you value? If you desire a college education, for example, ask yourself why. Will a college education bring you something else you desire: financial security, prestige, respect? Is education itself a value for you? If you desire a happy family life, then how would you describe that value? Consider the things you think your community values. How do your personal values compare with the community's values?

As you examine your personal values, you may notice some conflicts. For instance, you may value both adventure and security, even though the two don't always go together. You may value the freedom to do what you want but also the order that comes when everyone follows the same rules. You may value reliability and spontaneity, saving money and spending money, tradition and novelty, and so on. It is often the case in arguments about values that the dispute is not over accepting one value and rejecting another; rather the dispute is an attempt to find a balance between two conflicting values.

Arguments about values take two basic forms. The first, the argument about what a community should value, takes the form "X is good (or bad)." "Good" or "bad" in such claims can be replaced by any of the "ultimate terms" used by a community: "right" or "wrong," "moral" or "immoral," "beautiful" or "ugly," and so on. Here are some sample claims:

> Anyone who is involved in an abortion is evil.

> Giving tax breaks to the wealthy is unfair.

Pornography is immoral.

Plagiarism is wrong.

The right to freedom of speech is sacred.

It is unethical for politicians to mislead the public.

The second type of value argument is the argument about evaluating. In this argument the focus is not on what constitutes "goodness" or "badness" but rather on whether a particular object or event fits the criteria for determining what is "good" or "bad." This argument takes the form "X is a good (or bad) X," again with any of the ultimate terms possibly substituting for "good" or "bad." Comparative and superlative forms of the terms (*better, best, worse, worst*) can also be used to show the relation among the objects being evaluated. For instance, to say that an object is "best" in its class is to say that it is closest to the ideal of what is valuable or desirable for that class. To say that one object is "better than" another is to say that the better object is closer to the ideal than the other. Here are some sample claims:

William Faulkner is the greatest American writer.

Star Trek: The Next Generation is better than the original series.

That car is worth more than $6,000.

This place serves the worst Mexican food I've ever had.

Arguing about Values

▓ ▓ APPEAL TO AUTHORITY AND PRINCIPLES

How does a community negotiate the various personal tastes and preferences of its individual members in order to come up with a common set of values? One way is appeal to an acknowledged authority, such as an expert, judge, critic, or arbitrator. For instance, ethical questions related to the law are usually resolved by a judge, with the Supreme Court being the highest authority on legal questions in the United States. Aesthetic questions (questions about what is beautiful) may be decided by a critic, such as a movie or book reviewer or art critic. The authority may be a written statement of what the community believes and values: the Constitution, the Declaration of Independence, religious texts like the Bible or the Koran. Sometimes, the role of the expert is to interpret these foundational writings. The Supreme Court interprets the Constitution in deciding issues of legal "right" or "wrong." Religious leaders interpret sacred texts in deciding religious values. Art critics may examine what artists have written about their own work or what philosophers have said about what is valuable in art.

Once specific principles are laid down by authoritative members of the community or authoritative texts, the principles themselves may take on a certain authority. Principles are values that have been codified. The Ten Commandments are part of the legacy of Moses, an authoritative text for Jews and Christians, but many of the principles set forth in the Ten Commandments — "Thou shalt not kill," "Thou shalt not steal," and so forth — have taken on an authority of their own. The so-called Golden Rule — "Do unto others as you would have others do unto you" — is based on the teachings of Jesus in the New Testament, but it has also taken on an authority of its own in American culture. The Declaration of Independence, the Constitution, and the Bill of Rights provide good examples of authoritative texts for the community defined by the United States.

▩ ▩ CONSEQUENCES

Another way a community determines its values is by considering the consequences for the community of pursuing one or another value. What is in the best interest of the community as a whole? Most people value both airline safety and saving money, for example, but what are the consequences of pursuing one value over the other? How much would it cost to make flying absolutely risk free? Probably so much that no one could afford to fly — if it could be done at all. But what about cutting costs at the expense of safety? If the risk of flying became so great that no one was willing to fly, then the lower costs wouldn't matter. Most people value the efforts of the government to eliminate crime, but what would be the consequences of trying to capture and prosecute every criminal? Is there a point at which the costs outweigh the benefits? To eliminate crime entirely might require turning the country into a police state and foregoing many of our civil rights. Many of our values have what economists call a "point of diminishing returns," a point after which the consequences of pursuing what we desire outweighs any benefits we gain.

▩ ▩ PRINCIPLES VERSUS CONSEQUENCES

Neither authority and principles nor consequences are without problems for determining values. For instance, when authorities or principles conflict with one another, how does a community decide among these conflicting opinions? One way is to appeal to a higher authority. Another is to consider consequences along with principles, to consider the effects of following one principle rather than another. However, if a community only considers consequences, always making decisions based on what is popular or expedient at the moment, then its decisions will be arbitrary, and there will be no justice or integrity. Usually, a community combines these two approaches, deferring to principles or authorities while also considering the consequences for the community.

Consider ethical issues, for example. Ethical issues involve claims about values: "X is right (or wrong)." Because individuals in a community do not all share the same values or the same beliefs about what constitutes ethical behavior, there are bound to be disputes. One way to resolve such disputes is by appealing to authority or principle. When Gandhi and Martin Luther King argued that there are higher laws which supersede the unjust laws passed by particular governments, they were basing their arguments on principle. When the philosopher Immanuel Kant argued that no one should use another as a means to an end and that one should always act as if every action could become universal law, he was outlining a set of principles to govern human behavior. It would be difficult, however, to follow Kant's principle without ever considering consequences or weighing costs against benefits. For instance, when someone serves you lunch or helps you at a store, you are using that person as a means to an end. On the other hand, that person is also using you, the customer, as a means to an end. The interaction is mutually beneficial: You get served, while the person helping you get paid. At the same time, following Kant's principles can have beneficial effects. There are other times when using a person as a means to an end, such as extorting money from someone or becoming emotionally dependent on someone, has adverse consequences. Considering only consequences without being guided by principles at all would destroy the fabric of a community. Selfishness would guide every decision. Those who were most powerful would get their way.

Evaluation

As explained earlier, evaluation involves applying values to particular objects or events in order to judge their worth. In such arguments the values themselves may not be under dispute. The focus of the argument may rather be on the application of these values. The form of evaluation ("X is a good X") is similar to the form of the criteria and match definition outlined in Chapter 9. First, you develop the criteria for deciding what constitutes a "good X." Then you apply these criteria to a particular object or event to see how well it matches these criteria. The criteria are based on the values of the community, the "ultimate terms" used to characterized "good" and "bad" (and so on). Here are the steps to follow when conducting an evaluation.

First, determine the group to which the object belongs. You can't agree that "X is a good X" if it is not an "X" at all. For instance, you can't say that a horror movie is a bad romantic comedy. It's not a romantic comedy at all. Choose the group carefully. If you make it too large, then the grouping becomes meaningless. One problem with the awards for a year's "best movie," for example, is that movies are so different from one another that grouping them together as "movies" becomes almost meaningless for purposes of evaluation. Similarly, imagine trying to select the "best computer program." On the other hand, if the category is too small, then it can become a category of one, in which case evaluation becomes completely meaningless. Imagine giving an award for the "best full-length animated feature by a Disney studio for the year 1994."

Second, determine what the community values in the members of this group. What does the community value in a sports car or sports/utility vehicle? One way to determine the values of a community is to find a model or standard system of measurement by which all others of the group can be judged. For instance, one can make claims about the relative value of two objects by comparing their cost. Money is a symbol Americans use to mark the value of things. If one object from a group costs more than another, you can examine the features of each object to determine what makes one more expensive. These features will give you a clue about what the community values. For instance, by examining the features that make a home more valuable, you can determine what the community values in a home. By comparing two pieces of property, you can determine what the community values in land. Does the community value a coal mine more than a red rock desert? Which costs more?

Third, determine criteria based on these values. What does an object have to have to meet the values of the community? Which criteria are absolutely necessary and which are recommended or beneficial?

Fourth, weigh the criteria against one another. The word "critic" comes from a Greek word meaning "to weigh." A critic or evaluator must weigh the criteria against one another to decide which are essential or most important and which are optional or less important.

Fifth, determine the extent to which the object matches the criteria. This involves critical judgment when an object being evaluated meets some but not all of the criteria or when it meets some criteria more than others. Can the object still be considered good? Can there be a range of values (excellent, good, fair, poor)?

Applying the Principles

▨ ▨ EVALUATION

The following article from *Consumer Reports* evaluates fast food. The chart provides a detailed evaluation of eight types of food: basic burgers, burgers with the works, roast beef sandwiches, fish sandwiches, chicken sandwiches, chicken nuggets, chicken pieces, and french fries. Each item is evaluated against the other members of the group and against items in other groups using standard systems of measurement, such as price, weight, and nutritional measurements. There is also an assessment of overall quality and a description by the tasters of "taste and texture."

Can Fast Food Be Good Food?

CONSUMER REPORTS

E VERY DAY, America's biggest hamburger chains — McDonald's, Burger 1
King, and Wendy's — serve more than 40 million customers from more
than 25,000 restaurants around the world. KFC, the biggest chicken chain, fries
or roasts another 6.6 million meals at 9000 locations. That may sound like a lot,
but it's nothing compared with what's coming.

McDonald's, founded in 1955, took 13 years to open its first 1,000 restaurants. Now about 14,000 outlets strong, McDonald's plans to construct approximately 1,000 more golden arches this year alone. Subway, an even
faster-growing sandwich chain, sets up 25 new restaurants a week. PepsiCo,
which owns KFC, Taco Bell, and Pizza Hut, opens a restaurant somewhere in
the world every four hours.

Although much of the expansion is overseas, the domestic industry is growing so quickly that the National Restaurant Association predicts consumers will
spend $86 billion on fast food this year — more, for the first time, than they'll
spend at full-service restaurants. Fast-food restaurants are also becoming an extension of the family kitchen: Nearly two-thirds of all fast food (including pizza)
is takeout, and much of that goes home, according to CREST, a Chicago company
that tracks eating habits.

McDonald's, Burger King, and other chains are placing kiosks and mobile
units where no fast-food restaurant has fit before — in mass-merchandise stores
like Wal-Mart, in hospitals, in schools, and in gas stations. McDonald's now aims
to serve its products "wherever customers live, work, shop, or gather."

WHAT WE TESTED

With fast food such an integral part of the American diet, we decided to take 5
a close look at what so many Americans are eating. We zeroed in on 30 items —
burgers, roast-beef sandwiches, breaded- and rotisserie-chicken dishes, fish sandwiches, and french fries — from Arby's, Burger King, Hardee's, Jack in the Box,
KFC, McDonald's, Popeye's, and Wendy's. (There is some overlap between
Hardee's products and those at Roy Rogers, a division of Hardee's.)

We bought each item at 12 outlets and tested each for fat, saturated fat,
cholesterol, protein, and sodium. We determined calorie content. And we sent a
trained taster to outlets in six cities to note the firmness of the meat (or flakiness
of the fish), the freshness of the vegetables and buns, the crispness of the fries,
and the flavor of everything.

We rated the foods according to the percentage of calories that each gets
from fat. That measurement allows for easy comparison of foods that differed in
size and other nutritional measures. The Ratings also include comments regarding taste and texture.

We didn't test the meat for bacteria, but we did talk to Joseph Madden, strategic manager of microbiology in the U.S. Food and Drug Administration. He notes that since 1993, when four children died after eating Jack in the Box hamburgers contaminated with a rare strain of the bacteria *E. coli,* most fast-food chains have been paying closer attention to how burgers are cooked. At most stores, for instance, cooked burgers are checked several times an hour to make sure they're brown inside. (Bacteria are killed — and ground beef turns from pink to brown — when the meat is cooked at 155° for 15 seconds.)

Such procedures follow Federal recommendations and many state laws that specify minimum guidelines for keeping food safe.

WHERE'S THE FAT?

Although fast-food companies have promoted newer, low-fat offerings — 10 such as grilled-chicken sandwiches, lean-beef sandwiches, and assorted salads — most people still order the items we tested for this report. Those staples are heavy in fat, saturated fat, and other nutrients that should be limited in a prudent diet. Five of the sandwiches we tested each provide more than half the fat that a person on a 2,000-calorie diet should eat in an entire day, according to Government guidelines, and three provide half the saturated fat. The *Big Mac* and all the larger pieces of chicken have at least a third of the Government's recommended daily intake for cholesterol and sodium.

Best, nutritionally, were the basic burgers and roast-beef sandwiches. But before you celebrate with a *Whopper,* note that we're talking about the chains' *smaller* burgers: The big burgers, slathered with extras, are pretty much off limits to fat watchers. For instance, Hardee's *Frisco Burger* — topped with bacon, cheese, and sauce — had more than two-thirds of the fat, almost half the sodium, and almost all the saturated fat the Government recommends as a daily limit.

The chicken and fish sandwiches were nutritional runners-up to the basic burgers; they were fattened by their breading and mayonnaise-based sauce.

Who's the fattiest of them all? KFC's *Rotisserie Gold* chicken, in its dark-meat version. It may sound healthful because it's not fried; nevertheless, it gets 65 percent of its calories from fat. That's an even higher percentage than you'll find in a super-rich ice cream.

For the most part, an order of fries has at least as many calories and as much fat as a basic burger. And although the chains touted their change of frying oil from beef tallow to hydrogenated vegetable oil, that switch may not have helped much. The vegetable oil contains trans-fatty acids, which some studies have shown can raise blood cholesterol levels.

It is possible to include a traditional fast-food meal in a healthy diet; just eat 15 less-fatty food — fruit or salads, say — the rest of the day.

WHERE'S THE TASTE?

No restaurant had the tastiest food overall, according to our taster, who tried the foods as they're served, complete with the usual toppings. But our taster did find at least one good dish at each chain, and a total of 10 very good items. When we compared the taste scores with our nutritional data, we found, not surprisingly, that good taste and good nutrition in fast food are often mutually exclusive.

With a few exceptions, the overall flavor and quality of the food at each chain was similar from city to city — a help to travelers who want to know that the burger they get on the road bears a passing resemblance to the one they got back home.

Still, some chains were more consistent than others. Wendy's and Arby's sandwiches were always fresh and hot; McDonald's and Burger King came closest to getting french fries right every time.

Among the problems our taster occasionally encountered were cold or overcooked meat, dry chicken that had sat around too long, and soggy french fries.

The Ratings describe each food's taste. 20

Burgers. The basic burgers may not be too bad nutritionally — but most don't taste very good. An exception is the medium-sized, unadorned Wendy's *Plain Single*.

The bigger burgers generally tasted better than the small. Hardee's *Frisco Burger* was very good; Jack in the Box's *Jumbo Jack*, Burger King's *Whopper*, and McDonald's *Big Mac* were all good. But be warned: All the big burgers are quite high in calories and fat.

Sandwiches. The meat in Arby's roast-beef sandwich was more moist and tender than that in Hardee's. The McDonald's fish sandwich was not very flavorful; Burger King's was better. As for breaded-chicken sandwiches, Burger King's and Arby's had the moistest meat.

Chicken bits and pieces. Although none of the chicken nuggets were very good, most of the larger pieces of chicken were. The *Rotisserie Gold* from KFC was more plump and juicy than the other chicken dishes, though it was quite greasy and salty.

Fries. The thin-cut fries at Burger King and McDonald's were best; the 25 thickcut fries at Hardee's and Wendy's sometimes had unpleasant off-tastes.

RECOMMENDATIONS

Fast food can be good for you if you choose sensibly. Last year, for instance we found that Arby's *Light Roast Turkey* (and *Chicken*) *Deluxe,* Wendy's *Grilled Chicken,* McDonald's *McLean Deluxe,* and several salads, eaten without high-fat dressing, were especially low in fat.

If, like most Americans, you prefer the standard foods, you'll probably sacrifice nutrition to taste. Ordering chicken or fish won't always help; sauce and breading or skin add fat and calories. In fact, the skin and dark meat of KFC's *Rotisserie Gold* chicken helps make it the fattiest food we tested. The best way to improve the nutritional value of any fast food is to avoid fried or breaded items and to leave off cheese, dressing, and other trimmings.

If you east fast food as an occasional treat rather than a staple, enjoy it and try to eat prudently the rest of the day. Among the items that tasted best:

RATINGS Fast foods

	Excellent	Very Good	Good	Fair	Poor
	●	◐	○	◑	●

Notes on the table

Price is the estimated average, based on national and regional surveys. Weight and most nutrition information come from the manufacturers. Percent calories from fat is an index of nutritional quality. The Government recommends that people get no more than 30 percent of the calories in their overall diet from fat. If you eat a high-fat burger for lunch, you'll need to compensate by eating a lower-fat dinner. Many nutritionists say the goal should be even lower than 30 percent. The figures for total fat, saturated fat, cholesterol, and protein are rounded to the nearest gram or milligram. Taste and texture quality gives results of our consultant's evaluation of each item, sampled at six different restaurants. Basic burgers generally come with ketchup, mustard, and pickle; Wendy's Plain Single is, as advertised, plain, and slightly larger than the others. "The works" on the bigger burgers include such additions as lettuce, cheese, dressing, and tomato. Chicken sandwiches generally come with lettuce and mayonnaise; chicken nuggets, with assorted dipping sauces; fish sandwiches, with tartar sauce.

Within type, listed in order of the percentage of calories from fat

Menu item	Price	Weight	Calories from fat	Calories	Total fat	Saturated fat
BASIC BURGERS						
McDonald's	$.59	4 oz.	32%	255	9 g.	3 g.
Burger King	.78	4	35	260	10	4
Hardee's	.75	3	35	260	10	4
Jack in the Box	.79	3	37	267	11	4
Wendy's Plain Single	1.85	5	39	350	15	6
BURGERS WITH THE WORKS						
McDonald's Big Mac	1.99	8	47	500	26	9
Jack in the Box Jumbo Jack	1.99	8	52	584	34	11
Burger King Whopper	1.99	10	56	630	39	11
Hardee's Frisco Burger	2.49	8	58	730	47	17
ROAST BEEF SANDWICHES						
Hardee's	1.93	4	35	280	11	4
Arby's	1.99	5	42	383	18	7
FISH SANDWICHES						
McDonald's Filet-O-Fish	1.56	5	44	370	18	4
Burger King BK Big Fish	1.93	9	54	720	43	8
CHICKEN SANDWICHES						
Wendy's Breaded Chicken	2.68	7	40	450	20	4
Arby's Chicken Breast Fillet	2.55	7	47	445	23	3
McDonald's McChicken	2.09	7	48	470	25	5
KFC Colonel's Chicken	1.99	6	50	482	27	6
Burger King Chicken	2.49	8	55	700	43	9
CHICKEN NUGGETS (six pieces)						
Burger King Chicken Tenders	1.99	3	43	250	12	3
McDonald's Chicken McNuggets	1.79	4	50	270	15	4
KFC Kentucky Nuggets	1.83	3	57	284	18	4
CHICKEN PIECES (two pieces or ¼ rotisserie chicken)						
Hardee's Fried Chicken	2.49	6	49	492	27	10
KFC Original Recipe	2.30	7	50	490	27	7
KFC Rotisserie Gold (white meat)	2.88	6	51	335	19	5
Popeye's Chicken Dinner	3.22	5	53	390	23	10
KFC Rotisserie Gold (dark meat)	2.24	5	65	333	24	7
FRENCH FRIES (medium/regular)						
Hardee's	.89	3	43	230	11	2
Burger King	1.03	4	45	400	20	5
Wendy's	.89	5	45	340	17	4
McDonald's	1.02	3	48	320	17	4

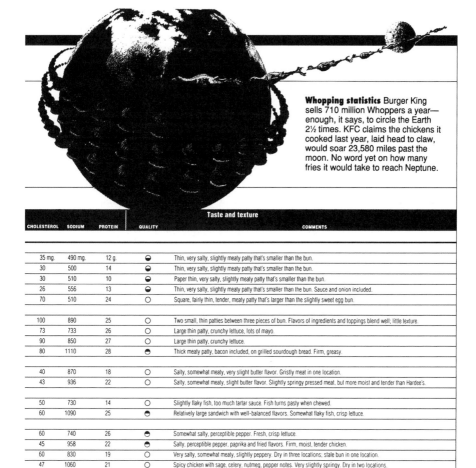

Whopping statistics Burger King sells 710 million Whoppers a year—enough, it says, to circle the Earth 2½ times. KFC claims the chickens it cooked last year, laid head to claw, would soar 23,580 miles past the moon. No word yet on how many fries it would take to reach Neptune.

CHOLESTEROL	SODIUM	PROTEIN	QUALITY	Taste and texture / COMMENTS
35 mg.	490 mg.	12 g.	◒	Thin, very salty, slightly meaty patty that's smaller than the bun.
30	500	14	◒	Thin, very salty, slightly meaty patty that's smaller than the bun.
30	510	10	◒	Paper thin, very salty, slightly meaty patty that's smaller than the bun.
26	556	13	◒	Thin, very salty, slightly meaty patty that's smaller than the bun. Sauce and onion included.
70	510	24	○	Square, fairly thin, tender, mealy patty that's larger than the slightly sweet egg bun.
100	890	25	○	Two small, thin patties between three pieces of bun. Flavors of ingredients and toppings blend well; little texture.
73	733	26	○	Large thin patty, crunchy lettuce, lots of mayo.
90	850	27	○	Large thin patty, crunchy lettuce.
80	1110	28	◐	Thick mealy patty, bacon included, on grilled sourdough bread. Firm, greasy.
40	870	18	○	Salty, somewhat mealy, very slight butter flavor. Gristly meat in one location.
43	936	22	○	Salty, somewhat mealy, slight butter flavor. Slightly springy pressed meat, but more moist and tender than Hardee's.
50	730	14	○	Slightly flaky fish, too much tartar sauce. Fish turns pasty when chewed.
60	1090	25	◐	Relatively large sandwich with well-balanced flavors. Somewhat flaky fish, crisp lettuce.
60	740	26	◐	Somewhat salty, perceptible pepper. Fresh, crisp lettuce.
45	958	22	◐	Salty, perceptible pepper, paprika and fried flavors. Firm, moist, tender chicken.
60	830	19	○	Very salty, somewhat mealy, slightly peppery. Dry in three locations; stale bun in one location.
47	1060	21	○	Spicy chicken with sage, celery, nutmeg, pepper notes. Very slightly springy. Dry in two locations.
60	1400	26	○	Moist, springy, peppery piece of oblong pressed chicken on hefty sesame bun.
35	530	16	○	Very salty, somewhat mealy, slightly peppery. Springy and mushy in parts.
55	580	20	◒	Very salty, slightly mealy, some pepper and nutmeg. Moist, springy, fatty, or mushy, depending on where one bites. Gristly in some locations.
66	865	16	◒	Salty, slightly mealy, perceptible pepper. Springy, mushy. Fat pieces, tough meat in some locations.
84	866	39	◐	Moist, tender, mealy. Crispy browned flour coating.
85	1080	46	○	Moist, tender, mealy. Coating partly crispy, partly soggy.
157	1104	40	◐	Plump, moist, tender, mealy, with marinated herbed coating. Very salty, greasy.
100	900	33	◐	Moist, tender, mealy. Crispy browned flour coating.
163	980	30	◐	Plump, moist, tender, mealy, with marinated herbed coating. Very salty, greasy. Overcooked in one location.
0	85	3	○	Tough, thick. Varied: some salty, some not; cold, bitter in one location; thinner, longer in another.
0	240	5	◐	Thin, crispy. Good balance of potato, oil, salt. Would be excellent, but not consistent: soggy in one location, tough in another.
0	210	5	○	Tough-skinned, thick. Varied: sometimes soggy or a bit dry. Thinner in one location, slightly soapy notes in another.
0	150	4	◐	Thin, crispy. Good balance of potato, oil, salt. Would be excellent, but not consistent: tough in two locations.

389

Hardee's *Frisco Burger,* Burger King's *BK Big Fish,* Wendy's and Arby's breaded-chicken sandwiches, Popeye's and Hardee's fried chicken pieces, KFC's rotisserie-chicken quarters, and Burger King's and McDonald's fries.

▨ ▨ DEVELOPING YOUR OWN EVALUATIONS

Select a group of consumer products with which you are familiar. Decide on criteria for evaluating these products, and develop a chart like the one used in the *Consumer Reports* article. If these products have been rated by *CR,* check your evaluation with theirs.

As an alternative, write an evaluation of your college in comparison with your ideal college. What do you value in a college? How might your evaluation be different if you consider what others may value in college (parents, alumni, business, government agencies, sports fans, and so on).

▨ ▨ ETHICAL DECISION IN BUSINESS AND LAW

In the following essays, Albert Z. Carr and Monroe H. Freedman address issues related to honesty and professional ethics in the practice of business and law. Carr asks whether it is acceptable to lie when conducting business as long as that lying is a form of bluffing. He argues that a different set of ethical values applies to business than, for example, to religion. Freedman focuses on the frequent dilemma faced by the criminal defense lawyer between betraying the confidence of the client/lawyer relationship and knowingly giving false information to the court. Freedman's views were so controversial when he first presented them to the American Bar Association that some of his colleagues tried to have him suspended or disbarred.

As you read each of these essays, identify the values of the writer: What claim is the writer making about values? Then identify the reasons and assumptions that the writer uses to support these claims. In particular, analyze the extent to which the writer relies upon authorities and principles or on consequences in trying to influence the values of the community.

Is Business Bluffing Ethical?

ALBERT Z. CARR

A RESPECTED BUSINESSMAN with whom I discussed the theme of this arti- 1
cle remarked with some heat, "You mean to say you're going to encourage
men to bluff? Why, bluffing is nothing more than a form of lying! You're advising
them to lie!"

I agreed that the basis of private morality is a respect for truth and that the
closer a businessman comes to the truth, the more he deserves respect. At the
same time, I suggested that most bluffing in business might be regarded simply
as game strategy — much like bluffing in poker, which does not reflect on the
morality of the bluffer.

I quoted Henry Taylor, the British statesman who pointed out that "falsehood ceases to be falsehood when it is understood on all sides that the truth is
not expected to be spoken" — an exact description of bluffing in poker, diplo-
macy, and business. I cited the analogy of the criminal court, where the criminal
is not expected to tell the truth when he pleads "not guilty." Everyone from the
judge down takes it for granted that the job of the defendant's attorney is to get
his client off, not to reveal the truth; and this is considered ethical practice. I
mentioned Representative Omar Burleson, the Democrat from Texas, who was
quoted as saying, in regard to the ethics of Congress, "Ethics is a barrel of
worms" — a pungent summing up of the problem of deciding who is ethical in
politics.

I reminded my friend that millions of businessmen feel constrained every day
to say *yes* to their bosses when they secretly believe *no* and that this is generally
accepted as permissible strategy when the alternative might be the loss of a job.
The essential point, I said, is that the ethics of business are game ethics, different
from the ethics of religion.

We can learn a good deal about the nature of business by comparing it with 5
poker. While both have a large element of chance, in the long run the winner is
the man who plays with steady skill. In both games ultimate victory requires
intimate knowledge of the rules, insight into the psychology of the other players,
a bold front, a considerable amount of self-discipline, and the ability to respond
swiftly and effectively to opportunities provided by chance.

No one expects poker to be played on the ethical principles preached in
churches. In poker it is right and proper to bluff a friend out of the rewards of
being dealt a good hand. A player feels no more than a slight twinge of sympathy,
if that, when — with nothing better than a single ace in his hand — he strips a
heavy loser, who holds a pair, of the rest of his chips. It was up to the other fellow
to protect himself. In the words of an excellent poker player, former President
Harry Truman, "If you can't stand the heat, stay out of the kitchen." If one
shows mercy to a loser in poker, it is a personal gesture, divorced from the rules
of the game.

Poker has its special ethics, and here I am not referring to rules against cheating. The man who keeps an ace up his sleeve or who marks the cards is more than unethical; he is a crook, and can be punished as such — kicked out of the game or, in the Old West, shot.

In contrast to the cheat, the unethical poker player is one who, while abiding by the letter of the rules, finds ways to put the other players at an unfair disadvantage. Perhaps he unnerves them with loud talk. Or he tries to get them drunk. Or he plays in cahoots with someone else at the table. Ethical poker players frown on such tactics.

Poker's own brand of ethics is different from the ethical ideals of civilized human relationships. The game calls for distrust of the other fellow. It ignores the claim of friendship. Cunning deception and concealment of one's strength and intentions, not kindness and openheartedness, are vital in poker. No one thinks any the worse of poker on that account. And no one should think any worse of the game of business because its standards of right and wrong differ from the prevailing traditions of morality in our society. That most businessmen are not indifferent to ethics in their private lives, everyone will agree. My point is that in their office lives they cease to be private citizens; they become game players who must be guided by a somewhat different set of ethical standards.

The point was forcefully made to me by a Midwestern executive who has given a good deal of thought to the question: "So long as a businessman complies with the laws of the land and avoids telling malicious lies, he's ethical. If the law as written gives a man a wide-open chance to make a killing, he'd be a fool not to take advantage of it. If he doesn't, somebody else will. There's no obligation on him to stop and consider who is going to get hurt. If the law says he can do it, that's all the justification he needs. There's nothing unethical about that. It's just plain business sense."

The illusion that business can afford to be guided by ethics as conceived in private life is often fostered by speeches and articles containing such phrases as, "It pays to be ethical," or "Sound ethics is good business." Actually this is not an ethical position at all; it is a self-serving calculation in disguise. The speaker is really saying that in the long run a company can make more money if it does not antagonize competitors, suppliers, employees, and customers by squeezing them too hard. He is saying that oversharp policies reduce ultimate gains. That is true, but it has nothing to do with ethics. The underlying attitude is much like that in the familiar story of the shopkeeper who finds an extra $20 bill in the cash register, debates with himself the ethical problem — should he tell his partner? — and finally decides to share the money because the gesture will give him an edge over the s.o.b. the next time they quarrel.

I think it is fair to sum up the prevailing attitude of businessmen on ethics as follows:

We live in what is probably the most competitive of the world's civilized societies. Our customs encourage a high degree of aggression in the individual's striving for success. Business is our main area of competition, and it has been ritualized into a game of strategy. The basic rules of the game have been set by the government, which attempts to detect and punish business frauds. But as long as a company does not transgress the rules of the game set by law, it has the legal right to shape its strategy without reference to anything but its profits. If it takes a long-term view of its profits, it will preserve amicable relations, so far as possible, with those with whom it deals. A wise businessman will not seek advantage to the point where he generates dangerous hostility among employees, competitors, customers, government, or the public at large. But decisions in this area are, in the final test, decisions of strategy, not of ethics.

If a man plans to take a seat in the business game, he owes it to himself to master the principles by which the game is played, including its special ethical outlook. He can then hardly fail to recognize that an occasional bluff may well be justified in terms of the game's ethics and warranted in terms of economic necessity. Once he clears his mind on this point, he is in a good position to match his strategy against that of the other players. He can then determine objectively whether a bluff in a given situation has a good chance of succeeding and can decide when and how to bluff, without a feeling of ethical transgression.

To be a winner, a man must play to win. This does not mean that he must be ruthless, cruel, harsh, or treacherous. On the contrary, the better his reputation for integrity, honesty, and decency, the better his chances of victory will be in the long run. But from time to time every businessman, like every poker player, is offered a choice between certain loss or bluffing within the legal rules of the games. If he is not resigned to losing, if he wants to rise in his company and industry, then in such a crisis he will bluff — and bluff hard.

Every now and then one meets a successful businessman who has conveniently forgotten the small or large deceptions that he practiced on his way to fortune. "God gave me my money," old John D. Rockefeller once piously told a Sunday school class. It would be a rare tycoon in our time who would risk the horse laugh with which such a remark would be greeted.

In the last third of the twentieth century even children are aware that if a man has become prosperous in business, he has sometimes departed from the strict truth in order to overcome obstacles or has practiced the more subtle deceptions of the half-truth or the misleading omission. Whatever the form of the bluff, it is an integral part of the game, and the executive who does not master its techniques is not likely to accumulate much money or power.

Professional Responsibility of the Criminal Defense Lawyer: The Three Hardest Questions

MONROE H. FREEDMAN

I N ALMOST ANY AREA of legal counseling and advocacy, the lawyer may be   1
faced with the dilemma of either betraying the confidential communications of his client or participating to some extent in the purposeful deception of the court. This problem is nowhere more acute than in the practice of criminal law, particularly in the representation of the indigent accused. The purpose of this article is to analyze and attempt to resolve three of the most difficult issues in this general area:

1. Is it proper to cross-examine for the purpose of discrediting the reliability or credibility of an adverse witness whom you know to be telling the truth?
2. Is it proper to put a witness on the stand when you know he will commit perjury?
3. Is it proper to give your client legal advice when you have reason to believe that the knowledge you give him will tempt him to commit perjury?

These questions present serious difficulties with respect to a lawyer's ethical responsibilities. Moreover, if one admits the possibility of an affirmative answer, it is difficult even to discuss them without appearing to some to be unethical.[1] It is not surprising, therefore, that reasonable, rational discussion of these has been uncommon and that the problems have for so long remained unresolved. In this regard it should be recognized that the Canons of Ethics, which were promulgated in 1908 "as a general guide," are both inadequate and self-contradictory.

I. THE ADVERSARY SYSTEM AND THE NECESSITY FOR CONFIDENTIALITY

At the outset, we should dispose of some common question-begging responses. The attorney is indeed an officer of the court, and he does participate in a search for truth. These two propositions, however, merely serve to state the problem in different words: As an officer of the court, participating in a search

---

[1] The substance of this paper was recently presented to a Criminal Trial Institute attended by forty-five members of the District of Columbia Bar. As a consequence, several judges (none of whom had either heard the lecture or read it) complained to the Committee on Admissions and Grievances of the District Court for the District of Columbia, urging the author's disbarment or suspension. Only after four months of proceedings, including a hearing, two meetings, and a *de novo* review by eleven federal district court judges, did the Committee announce its decision to "proceed no further in the matter." Professor Freedman has expanded and updated his analysis in his latest book, *Understanding Lawyers' Ethics* (Matthew Bender/Irwin, 1990).

for truth, what is the attorney's special responsibility, and how does that responsibility affect his resolution of the questions posed above?

The attorney functions in an adversary system based upon the presupposition that the most effective means of determining truth is to present to a judge and jury a clash between proponents of conflicting views. It is essential to the effective functioning of this system that each adversary have, in the words of Canon 15, "entire devotion to the interest of the client, warm zeal in the maintenance and defense of his rights and the exertion of his utmost learning and ability." It is also essential to maintain the fullest uninhibited communication between the client and his attorney, so that the attorney can most effectively counsel his client and advocate the latter's cause. This policy is safeguarded by the requirement that the lawyer must, in the words of Canon 37, "preserve his client's confidences." Canon 15 does, of course, qualify these obligations by stating that "the office of attorney does not permit, much less does it demand of him for any client, violations of law or any manner of fraud or chicane." In addition, Canon 22 requires candor toward the court.

The problem presented by these salutary generalities of the Canons in the context of particular litigation is illustrated by the personal experience of Samuel Williston, which was related in his autobiography. Because of his examination of a client's correspondence file, Williston learned of a fact extremely damaging to his client's case. When the judge announced his decision, it was apparent that a critical factor in the favorable judgment for Williston's client was the judge's ignorance of this fact. Williston remained silent and did not thereafter inform the judge of what he knew. He was convinced . . . that it was his duty to remain silent.

In an opinion by the American Bar Association Committee on Professional Ethics and Grievances, an eminent panel headed by Henry Drinker held that a lawyer should remain silent when his client lies to the judge by saying that he has no prior record, despite the attorney's knowledge to the contrary. The majority of the panel distinguished the situation in which the attorney has learned of the client's prior record from a source other than the client himself. William B. Jones, a distinguished trial lawyer and now a judge in the United States District Court for the District of Columbia, wrote a separate opinion in which he asserted that in neither event should the lawyer expose his client's lie. If these two cases do not constitute "fraud or chicane" or lack of candor within the meaning of the Canons (and I agree with the authorities cited that they do not), it is clear that the meaning of the Canons is ambiguous.

The adversary system has further ramifications in a criminal case. The defendant is presumed to be innocent. The burden is on the prosecution to prove beyond a reasonable doubt that the defendant is guilty. The plea of not guilty does not necessarily mean "not guilty in fact," for the defendant may mean "not legally guilty." Even the accused who knows that he committed the crime is entitled to put the government to its proof. Indeed, the accused who knows that he is guilty has an absolute constitutional right to remain silent. The moralist might quite reasonably understand this to mean that, under these circumstances, the defendant and his lawyer are privileged to "lie" to the court in pleading not guilty. In my judgment, the moralist is right. However, our adversary system and related notions of the proper administration of criminal justice sanction the lie.

Some derive solace from the sophistry of calling the lie a "legal fiction," but this is hardly an adequate answer to the moralist. Moreover, this answer has no particularly appeal for the practicing attorney, who knows that the plea of not guilty commits him to the most effective advocacy of which he is capable. Criminal defense lawyers do not win their cases by arguing reasonable doubt. Effective trial advocacy requires that the attorney's every word, action, and attitude be consistent with the conclusion that his client is innocent. As every trial lawyer knows, the jury is certain that the defense attorney knows whether his client is guilty. The jury is therefore alert to, and will be enormously affected by, any indication by the attorney that he believes the defendant to be guilty. Thus, the plea of not guilty commits the advocate to a trial, including a closing argument, in which he must argue that "not guilty" means "not guilty in fact." [2]

There is, of course, a simple way to evade the dilemma raised by the not guilty plea. Some attorneys rationalize the problem by insisting that a lawyer never knows for sure whether his client is guilty. The client who insists upon his guilt may in fact be protecting his wife, or may know that he pulled the trigger and the victim was killed, but not that his gun was loaded with blanks and that the fatal shot was fired from across the street. For anyone who finds this reasoning satisfactory, there is, of course, no need to think further about the issue.

It is also argued that a defense attorney can remain selectively ignorant. He ₁₀ can insist in his first interview with his client that, if his client is guilty, he simply does not want to know. It is inconceivable, however, that an attorney could give adequate counsel under such circumstances. How is the client to know, for example, precisely which relevant circumstances his lawyer does not want to be told? The lawyer might ask whether his client has a prior record. The client, assuming that this is the kind of knowledge that might present ethical problems for his lawyer, might respond that he has no record. The lawyer would then put the defendant on the stand and, on cross-examination, be appalled to learn that his client has two prior convictions for offenses identical to that for which he is being tried.

Of course, an attorney can guard against this specific problem by telling his client that he must know about the client's past record. However, a lawyer can never anticipate all of the innumerable and potentially critical factors that his client, once cautioned, may decide not to reveal. In one instance, for example,

---

[2] "The failure to argue the case before the jury, while ordinarily only a trial tactic not subject to review, manifestly enters the field of incompetency when the reason assigned is the attorney's conscience. It is as improper as though the attorney had told the jury that his client had uttered a falsehood in making the statement. The right to an attorney embraces effective representation throughout all stages of the trial, and where the representation is of such low caliber as to amount to no representation, the guarantee of due process has been violated," Johns v. Smyth, 176 E. Supp. 949, 953 E.D. Va. 1959); Schwartz, *Cases on Professional Responsibility and the Administration of Criminal Justice* 79 (1962).

the defendant assumed that his lawyer would prefer to be ignorant of the fact that the client had been having sexual relations with the chief defense witness. The client was innocent of the robbery with which he was charged, but was found guilty by the jury — probably because he was guilty of fornication, a far less serious offense for which he had not even been charged.

The problem is compounded by the practice of plea bargaining. It is considered improper for a defendant to plead guilty to a lesser offense unless he is in fact guilty. Nevertheless, it is common knowledge that plea bargaining frequently results in improper guilty pleas by innocent people. For example, a defendant falsely accused of robbery may plead guilty to simple assault, rather than risk a robbery conviction and a substantial prison term. If an attorney is to be scrupulous in bargaining pleas, however, he must know in advance that his client is guilty, since the guilty plea is improper if the defendant is innocent. Of course, if the attempt to bargain for a lesser offense should fail, the lawyer would know the truth and thereafter be unable to rationalize that he was uncertain of his client's guilt.

If one recognizes that professional responsibility requires that an advocate have full knowledge of every pertinent fact, it follows that he must seek the truth from his client, not shun it.[3] This means that he will have to dig and pry and cajole, and, even then, he will not be successful unless he can convince the client that full and confidential disclosure to his lawyer will never result in prejudice to the client by any word or action of the lawyer. This is, perhaps, particularly true in the case of the indigent defendant, who meets his lawyer for the first time in the cell block or the rotunda. He did not choose the lawyer, nor does he know him. The lawyer has been sent by the judge and is part of the system that is attempting to punish the defendant. It is no easy task to persuade this client that he can talk freely without fear of prejudice. However, the inclination to mislead one's lawyer is not restricted to the indigent or even to the criminal defendant. Randolph Paul has observed a similar phenomenon among the wealthier class in a far more congenial atmosphere:

> The tax advisor will sometimes have to dynamite the facts of his case out of the unwilling witnesses on his own side — witnesses who are nervous, witnesses who are confused about their own interest, witnesses who try to be too smart for their own good, and witnesses who subconsciously do not want to understand what has happened despite the fact that they must if they are to testify coherently.

Paul goes on to explain that the truth can be obtained only by persuading the client that it would be a violation of a sacred obligation for the lawyer ever to reveal a client's confidence. Beyond any question, once a lawyer has persuaded his client of the obligation of confidentiality, he must respect that obligation scrupulously.

---

[3] "Counsel cannot properly perform their duties without knowing the truth." Opinion 23, Committee on Professional Ethics and Grievances of the American Bar Association (1930).

II. THE SPECIFIC QUESTIONS

The first of the difficult problems posed above will now be considered: Is it proper to cross-examine for the purpose of discrediting the reliability or the credibility of a witness whom you know to be telling the truth? Assume the following situation. Your client has been falsely accused of a robbery committed at 16th and P Streets at 11:00 p.m. He tells you at first that at no time on the evening of the crime was he within six blocks of that location. However, you are able to persuade him that he must tell you the truth and that doing so will in no way prejudice him. He then reveals to you that he was at 15th and P Streets at 10:55 that evening, but that he was walking east, away from the scene of the crime, and that, by 11:00 p.m., he was six blocks away. At the trial, there are two prosecution witnesses. The first mistakenly, but with some degree of persuasion identifies your client as the criminal. At that point, the prosecution's case depends on this single witness, who might or might not be believed. Since your client has a prior record, you do not want to put him on the stand, but you feel that there is at least a chance for acquittal. The second prosecution witness is an elderly woman who is somewhat nervous and who wears glasses. She testifies truthfully and accurately that she saw your client at 15th and P Streets at 10:55 p.m. She has corroborated the erroneous testimony of the first witness and made conviction virtually certain. However, if you destroy her reliability through cross-examination designed to show that she is easily confused and has poor eyesight, you may not only eliminate the corroboration, but also cast doubt in the jury's mind on the prosecution's entire case. On the other hand, if you should refuse to cross-examine her because she is telling the truth, your client may well feel betrayed, since you knew of the witnesses' veracity only because your client confided in you, under your assurance that his truthfulness would not prejudice him.

The client would be right. Viewed strictly, the attorney's failure to cross-   15 examine would not be violative of the client's confidence because it would not constitute a disclosure. However, the same policy that supports the obligation of confidentiality precludes the attorney from prejudicing his client's interest in any other way because of knowledge gained in his professional capacity. When a lawyer fails to cross-examine only because his client, placing confidence in the lawyer, has been candid with him, the basis of such confidence and candor collapses. Our legal system cannot tolerate such a result.

> The purposes and necessities of the relation between a client and his attorney require, in many cases, on the part of the client, the fullest and freest disclosures to the attorney of the client's objects, motives and acts. . . . To permit the attorney to reveal to others what is so disclosed, would be not only a gross violation of a sacred trust upon his part, but it would utterly destroy and prevent the usefulness and benefits to be derived from professional assistance.

The client's confidences must "upon all occasions be inviolable," to avoid the "greater mischiefs" that would probably result if a client could not feel free "to repose [confidence] in the attorney to whom he resorts for legal advice and assistance." Destroy that confidence, and "a man would not venture to consult any skillful person, or would only dare to tell his counsellor half his case."

Therefore, one must conclude that the attorney is obligated to attack, if he can, the reliability or credibility of an opposing witness whom he knows to be truthful. The contrary result would inevitably impair the "perfect freedom of consultation by client with attorney," which is "essential to the administration of justice."

The second question is generally considered to be the hardest of all: Is it proper to put a witness on the stand when you know he will commit perjury? Assume, for example, that the witness in question is the accused himself, and that he has admitted to you, in response to your assurances of confidentiality, that he is guilty. However, he insists upon taking the stand to protect his innocence. There is a clear consensus among prosecutors and defense attorneys that the likelihood of conviction is increased enormously when the defendant does not take the stand. Consequently, the attorney who prevents his client from testifying only because the client has confided his guilt to him is violating that confidence by acting upon the information in a way that will seriously prejudice his client's interests.

Perhaps the most common method for avoiding the ethical problem just posed is for the lawyer to withdraw from the case, at least if there is sufficient time before trial for the client to retain another attorney.[4] The client will then go to the nearest law office, realizing that the obligation of confidentiality is not what it has been represented to be, and withhold incriminating information or the fact of his guilt from his new attorney. On ethical grounds, the practice of withdrawing from a case under such circumstances is indefensible, since the identical perjured testimony will ultimately be presented. More important, perhaps, is the practical consideration that the new attorney will be ignorant of the perjury and therefore will be in no position to attempt to discourage the client from presenting it. Only the original attorney, who knows the truth, has that opportunity, but he loses it in the very act of evading the ethical problem.

The problem is all the more difficult when the client is indigent. He cannot retain other counsel, and in many jurisdictions, including the District of Columbia, it is impossible for appointed counsel to withdraw from a case except for extraordinary reasons. Thus, appointed counsel, unless he lies to the judge, can successfully withdraw only by revealing to the judge that the attorney has received knowledge of his client's guilt. Such a revelation in itself would seem to be a sufficiently serious violation of the obligation of confidentiality to merit severe condemnation. In fact, however, the situation is far worse, since it is entirely possible that the same judge who permits the attorney to withdraw will subsequently hear the case and sentence the defendant. When he does so, of course, he will have had personal knowledge of the defendant's guilt before the

---

[4] Unless the lawyer has told the client at the outset that he will withdraw if he learns that the client is guilty, "it is plain enough as a matter of good morals and professional ethics" that the lawyer should not withdraw on this ground.

trial began.[5] Moreover, this will be knowledge of which the newly appointed counsel for the defendant will probably be ignorant.

The difficulty is further aggravated when the client informs the lawyer for the first time during trial that he intends to take the stand and commit perjury. The perjury in question may not necessarily be a protestation of innocence by a guilty man. Referring to the earlier hypothetical of the defendant wrongly accused of a robbery at 16th and P, the only perjury may be his denial of the truthful, but highly damaging, testimony of the corroborating witness who placed him one block away from the intersection five minutes prior to the crime. Of course, if he tells the truth and thus verifies the corroborating witness, the jury will be far more inclined to accept the inaccurate testimony of the principal witness, who specifically identified him as the criminal.[6]

If a lawyer has discovered his client's intent to perjure himself, one possible solution to this problem is for the lawyer to approach the bench, explain his ethical difficulty to the judge, and ask to be relieved, thereby causing a mistrial. This request is certain to be denied, if only because it would empower the defendant to cause a series of mistrials in the same fashion. At this point, some feel that the lawyer has avoided the ethical problem and can put the defendant on the stand. However, one objection to this solution, apart from the violation of confidentiality, is that the lawyer's ethical problem has not been solved, but has only been transferred to the judge. Moreover, the client in such a case might well have grounds for appeal on the basis of deprivation of due process and denial of the right to counsel, since he will have been tried before, and sentenced by, a judge who has been informed of the client's guilt by his own attorney.

A solution even less satisfactory than informing the judge of the defendant's guilt would be to let the client take the stand without the attorney's participation and to omit reference to the client's testimony in closing argument. The latter solution, of course, would be as damaging as to fail entirely to argue the case to the jury, and failing to argue the case is "as improper as though the attorney had told the jury that his client had uttered a falsehood in making the statement."

Therefore, the obligation of confidentiality, in the context of our adversary system, apparently allows the attorney no alternative to putting a perjurious witness on the stand without explicit or implicit disclosure of the attorney's knowledge to either the judge or the jury. Canon 37 does not proscribe this conclusion; the canon recognizes only two exceptions to the obligation of con-

20

---

[5] The judge may infer that the situation is worse than it is in fact. In the case related in note 8, the attorney's actual difficulty was that he did not want to permit a plea of guilty by a client who was maintaining his innocence. However, as is commonly done, he told the judge only that he had to withdraw because of "an ethical problem." The judge reasonably inferred that the defendant had admitted his guilt and wanted to offer a perjured alibi.

[6] One lawyer, who considers it clearly unethical for the attorney to present the alibi in this hypothetical case, found no ethical difficulty himself in the following case. His client was prosecuted for robbery. The prosecution witness testified that the robbery had taken place at 10:15, and identified the defendant as the criminal. However, the defendant had a convincing alibi for 10:00 to 10:30. The attorney presented the alibi, and the client was acquitted. The alibi was truthful, but the attorney knew that the prosecution witness had been confused about the time, and that his client had in fact committed the crime at 10:45.

fidentiality. The first relates to the lawyer who is accused by his client and may disclose the truth to defend himself. The other exemption relates to the "announced intention of a client to commit a crime." On the basis of the ethical and practical considerations discussed above, the Canon's exception to the obligation of confidentiality cannot logically be understood to include the crime of perjury committed during the specific case in which the lawyer is serving. Moreover, even when the intention is to commit a crime in the future, Canon 37 does not require disclosure, but only permits it. Furthermore, Canon 15, which does proscribe "violation of law" by the attorney for his client, does not apply to the lawyer who unwillingly puts a perjurious client on the stand after having made every effort to dissuade him from committing perjury. Such an act by the attorney cannot properly be found to be subornation — corrupt inducement — of perjury. Canon 29 requires counsel to inform the prosecuting authorities of perjury committed in a case in which he has been involved, but this can only refer to perjury by opposing witnesses. For an attorney to disclose his client's perjury "would involve a direct violation of Canon 37." Despite Canon 29, therefore, the attorney should not reveal his client's perjury "to the court or to the authorities."

Of course, before the client testifies perjuriously, the lawyer has a duty to attempt to dissuade him on grounds of both law and morality. In addition, the client should be impressed with the fact that his untruthful alibi is tactically dangerous. There is always a strong possibility that the prosecutor will expose the perjury on cross-examination. However, for the reasons already given, the final decision must necessarily be the client's. The lawyer's best course thereafter would be to avoid any further professional relationship with a client whom he knew to have perjured himself.

The third question is whether it is proper to give your client legal advice when you have reason to believe that the knowledge you give him will tempt him to commit perjury. This may indeed be the most difficult problem of all, because giving such advice creates the appearance that the attorney is encouraging and condoning perjury.

If the lawyer is not certain what the facts are when he gives the advice, the problem is substantially minimized, if not eliminated. It is not the lawyer's function to prejudge his client as a perjurer. He cannot presume that the client will make unlawful use of his advice. Apart from this, there is a natural predisposition in most people to recollect facts, entirely honestly, in a way most favorable to their own interest. As Randolph Paul has observed, some witnesses are nervous, some are confused about their own interests, some try to be too smart for their own good, and some subconsciously do not want to understand what has happened to them. Before he begins to remember essential facts, the client is entitled to know what his own interests are.

The above argument does not apply merely to factual questions such as whether a particular event occurred at 10:15 or at 10:45.[7] One of the most critical problems in a criminal case, as in many others, is intention. A German writer,

25

---

[7] Even this kind of "objective fact" is subject to honest error. See note 6.

considering the question of intention as a test of legal consequences, suggests the following situations. A young man and a young woman decide to get married. Each has a thousand dollars. They decide to begin a business with these funds, and the young lady gives her money to the young man for this purpose. Was the intention to form a joint venture or a partnership? Did they intend that the young man be an agent or a trustee? Was the transaction a gift or a loan? If the couple should subsequently visit a tax attorney and discover that it is in their interest that the transaction be viewed as a gift, it is submitted that they could, with complete honesty, so remember it. On the other hand, should their engagement be broken and the young woman consult an attorney for the purpose of recovering her money, she could with equal honesty remember that her intention was to make a loan.

Assume that your client, on trial for his life in a first-degree murder case, has killed another man with a penknife but insists that the killing was in self-defense. You ask him, "Do you customarily carry the penknife in your pocket, do you carry it frequently or infrequently, or did you take it with you only on this occasion?" He replies, "Why do you ask me a question like that?" It is entirely appropriate to inform him that his carrying the knife only on this occasion, or infrequently, supports an inference of premeditation, while if he carried the knife constantly, or frequently, the inference of premeditation would be negated. Thus, your client's life may depend upon his recollection as to whether he carried the knife frequently or infrequently. Despite the possibility that the client or a third party might infer that the lawyer was prompting the client to lie, the lawyer must apprise the defendant of the significance of his answer. There is no conceivable ethical requirement that the lawyer trap his client into a hasty and ill-considered answer before telling him the significance of the question.

A similar problem is created if the client has given the lawyer incriminating information before being fully aware of its significance. For example, assume that a man consults a tax lawyer and says, "I am fifty years old. Nobody in my immediate family has lived past fifty. Therefore, I would like to put my affairs in order. Specifically, I understand that I can avoid substantial estate taxes by setting up a trust. Can I do it?" The lawyer informs the client that he can successfully avoid the estate taxes only if he lives at least three years after establishing the trust or, should he die within three years, if the trust is found not to have been created in contemplation of death. The client then might ask who decides whether the trust is in contemplation of death. After learning that the determination is made by the court, the client might inquire about the factors on which such a decision would be based.

At this point, the lawyer can do one of two things. He can refuse to answer the question, or he can inform the client that the court will consider the wording of the trust instrument and will hear evidence about any conversations which he may have or any letters he may write expressing motives other than avoidance of estate taxes. It is likely that virtually every tax attorney in the country would answer the client's question, and that no one would consider the answer unethical. However, the lawyer might well appear to have prompted his client to de-

30

ceive the Internal Revenue Service and the courts, and this appearance would remain regardless of the lawyer's explicit disclaimer to the client of any intent so to prompt him. Nevertheless, it should not be unethical for the lawyer to give the advice.

In a criminal case, a lawyer may be representing a client who protests his innocence, and whom the lawyer believes to be innocent. Assume, for example, that the charge is assault with intent to kill, that the prosecution has erroneous but credible eyewitness testimony against the defendant, and that the defendant's truthful alibi witness is impeachable on the basis of several felony convictions. The prosecutor, perhaps having doubts about the case, offers to permit the defendant to plead guilty to simply assault. If the defendant should go to trial and be convicted, he might well be sent to jail for fifteen years; on a plea of simple assault, the maximum penalty would be one year, and sentence might well be suspended.

The common practice of conveying the prosecutor's offer to the defendant should not be considered unethical, even if the defense lawyer is convinced of his client's innocence. Yet the lawyer is clearly in the position of prompting his client to lie, since the defendant cannot make the plea without saying to the judge that he is pleading guilty because he is guilty. Furthermore, if the client does decide to plead guilty, it would be improper for the lawyer to inform the court that his client is innocent, thereby compelling the defendant to stand trial and take the substantial risk of fifteen years' imprisonment.[8]

Essentially no different from the problem discussed above, but apparently more difficult, is the so-called *Anatomy of a Murder* situation. The lawyer, who has received from his client an incriminating story of murder in the first degree, says, "If the facts are as you have stated them so far, you have no defense, and you will probably be electrocuted. On the other hand, if you acted in a blind rage, there is a possibility of saving your life. Think it over, and we will talk about it tomorrow." As in the tax case, and as in the case of the plea of guilty to a lesser offense, the lawyer has given his client a legal opinion that might induce the client to lie. This is information which the lawyer himself would have, without advice, were he in the client's position. It is submitted that the client is entitled

---

[8] In a recent case, the defendant was accused of unauthorized use of an automobile, for which the maximum penalty is five years. He told his court-appointed attorney that he had borrowed the car from a man known to him only as "Junior," that he had not known the car was stolen, and that he had an alibi for the time of the theft. The defendant had three prior convictions for larceny, and the alibi was weak. The prosecutor offered to accept a guilty plea to two misdemeanors (taking property without right and petty larceny) carrying a combined maximum sentence of eighteen months. The defendant was willing to plead guilty to the lesser offenses, but the attorney felt that, because of his client's alibi, he could not permit him to do so. The lawyer therefore informed the judge that he had an ethical problem and asked to be relieved. The attorney who was appointed in his place permitted the client to plead guilty to the two lesser offenses, and the defendant was sentenced to nine months. The alternative would have been five or six months in jail while the defendant waited for his jury trial, and a very substantial risk of conviction and a much heavier sentence. Neither the client nor justice would have been well served by compelling the defendant to go to trial against his will under these circumstances.

to have this information about the law and to make his own decision as to whether to act upon it. To decide otherwise would not only penalize the less well-educated defendant, but would also prejudice the client because of his initial truthfulness in telling his story in confidence to the attorney.

III. CONCLUSION

The lawyer is an officer of the court, participating in a search for truth. Yet no lawyer would consider that he had acted unethically in pleading the statute of frauds or the statute of limitations as a bar to a just claim. Similarly, no lawyer would consider it unethical to prevent the introduction of evidence such as a murder weapon seized in violation of the fourth amendment or a truthful but involuntary confession, or to defend a guilty man on grounds of denial of a speedy trial. Such actions are permissible because there are policy considerations that at times justify frustrating the search for truth and the prosecution of a just claim. Similarly, there are policies that justify an affirmative answer to the three questions that have been posed in this article. These policies include the maintenance of an adversary system, the presumption of innocence, the prosecution's burden to prove guilt beyond a reasonable doubt, the right to counsel, and the obligation of confidentiality between lawyer and client.

■ ■ TWO VIEWS OF THE VALUE OF ELECTRONIC COMMUNITIES

The expansion of the Internet, the computer network commonly called the "information superhighway," has had a noticeable impact on recent American culture. As more and more people across the world log on to the "net," many wonder what the value will be of this electronic "global village." The following two selections are adaptations from two books on Internet culture. They were reprinted together in *Harper's* magazine. In the first Sven Birkerts argues that we should refuse the electronic revolution because of the harmful effects it will have on the quality of human experience. Kevin Kelly, on the other hand, argues that computer networks, such as the Internet, enable us to express our humanity most fully. As you read these essays, consider the following questions:

1. How frequently do you use computers each day? How many of the things you own are run by computers or microprocessors?
2. How would your life be different without computers?
3. To what extent have you participated in the type of electronic community described by Birkerts and Kelly? If you have participated, have you found such communities to be valuable? If you have not, do you feel like you are missing out?
4. What influence have computer networks, such as the Internet, had on your college community? What effects have computers and computer networks had on your education?
5. Do you think that computers separate humans from one another?

from *The Gutenberg Elegies: The Fate of Reading in an Electronic Age*

SVEN BIRKERTS

T HE DIGITAL FUTURE is upon us. From our President on down, people are 1
smitten, more than they have been with anything in a very long time. I
can't open a newspaper without reading another story about the Internet, the
information highway. The dollar, not the poet, is the antenna of the race, and
right now the dollar is all about mergers and acquisitions: the fierce battles being
waged for control of the system that will allow us, soon enough, to cohabit in
the all but infinite information space. The dollar is smart. It is betting that the
trend will be a juggernaut, unstoppable; that we are collectively ready to round
the corner into a new age. We are not about to turn from this millennial remak-
ing of the world; indeed, we are all excited to see just how much power and
ingenuity we command. By degrees — it is happening year by year, appliance by
appliance — we are wiring ourselves into a gigantic hive.

When we look at the large-scale shift to an electronic culture, looking as if
at a time-lapse motion study, we can see not only how our situation has come
about but also how it is in our nature that it should have. At every step — this is
clear — we trade for ease. And ease is what quickly swallows up the initial
strangeness of a new medium or tool. Moreover, each accommodation paves the
way for the next. The telegraph must have seemed to its first users a surpassingly
strange device, but its newfangledness was overridden by its usefulness. Once we
had accepted the idea of mechanical transmission over distances, the path was
clear for the telephone. Again, a monumental transformation: Turn select digits
on a dial and hear the voice of another human being. And on it goes, the inventions coming gradually, one by one, allowing the society to adapt. We mastered
the telephone, the television with its few networks running black-and-white programs. And although no law required citizens to own or use either, these technologies did in a remarkably short time achieve near total saturation.

We are, then, accustomed to the process; we take the step that will enlarge
our reach, simplify our communication, and abbreviate our physical involvement
in some task or chore. The difference between the epoch of early modernity and
the present is — to simplify drastically — that formerly the body had time to
accept the graft, the new organ, whereas now we are hurtling forward willy-nilly,
assuming that if a technology is connected with communications or information processing it must be good, we must need it. I never cease to be astonished
at what a mere two decades have brought us. Consider the evidence. Since the
early 1970s we have seen the arrival of — we have accepted, deemed all but
indispensable — personal computers, laptops, telephone-answering machines,
calling cards, fax machines, cellular phones, VCRs, modems, Nintendo games,
E-mail, voice mail, camcorders, and CD players. Very quickly, with almost no
pause between increments, these circuit-driven tools and entertainments have

moved into our lives, and with a minimum rippling of the waters, really — which, of course, makes them seem natural, even inevitable. Which perhaps they are. Marshall McLuhan called improvements of this sort "extensions of man," and this is their secret. We embrace them because they seem a part of us, an enhancement. They don't seem to challenge our power so much as add to it.

I am startled, though, by how little we are debating the deeper philosophical ramifications. We talk up a storm when it comes to policy issues — who should have jurisdiction, what rates may be charged — and there is great fascination in some quarters with the practical minutiae of functioning, compatibility, and so on. But why do we hear so few people asking whether we might not *ourselves* be changing, and whether the changes are necessarily for the good?

In our technological obsession we may be forgetting that circuited intercon-   5
nectedness and individualism are, at a primary level, inimical notions, warring terms. Being "on line" and having the subjective experience of depth, of existential coherence, are mutually exclusive situations. Electricity and inwardness are fundamentally discordant. Electricity is, implicitly, of the moment — *now*. Depth, meaning, and the narrative structuring of subjectivity — these are *not* now; they flourish only in that order of time Henri Bergson called "duration." Duration is deep time, time experienced without the awareness of time passing. Until quite recently — I would not want to put a date to it — most people on the planet lived mainly in terms of duration: time not artificially broken, but shaped around natural rhythmic cycles; time bound to the integrated functioning of the senses.

We have destroyed that duration. We have created invisible elsewheres that are as immediate as our actual surroundings. We have fractured the flow of time, layered it into competing simultaneities. We learn to do five things at once or pay the price. Immersed in an environment of invisible signals and operations, we find it as unthinkable to walk five miles to visit a friend as it was once unthinkable to speak across that distance through a wire.

My explanation for our blithe indifference to the inward consequences of our becoming "wired" is simple. I believe that we are — biologically, neuro-psychologically — creatures of extraordinary adaptability. We fit ourselves to situations, be they ones of privation or beneficent surplus. And in many respects this is to the good. The species is fit because it knows how to fit.

But there are drawbacks as well. The late Walker Percy made it his work to explore the implications of our constant adaptation. Over and over, in his fiction as well as his speculative essays, he asks the same basic questions. As he writes in the opening of his essay "The Delta Factor": "Why does man feel so sad in the twentieth century? Why does man feel so bad in the very age when, more than in any other age, he has succeeded in satisfying his needs and making over the world for his own use?" One of his answers is that the price of adaptation is habit, and that habit — habit of perception as well as behavior — distances the self from the primary things that give meaning and purpose to life. We accept these gifts of technology, these labor-saving devices, these extensions of the senses, by adapting and adapting again. Each improvement provides a new level of abstraction to which we accommodate ourselves. Abstraction is, however, a movement away from the natural given — a step away from our fundamental selves rooted for millennia in an awe before the unknown, a fear and trembling in the face of the outer dark. We widen the gulf, and if at some level we fear the widening, we respond by investing more of our faith in the systems we have wrought.

We sacrifice the potential life of the solitary self by enlisting ourselves in the collective. For this is finally — even more than the saving of labor — what these systems are all about. They are not only extensions of the sense; they are extensions of the senses that put us in touch with the extended senses of others. The ultimate point of the ever-expanding electronic web is to bridge once and for all the individual solitude that has hitherto always set the terms of existence. Each appliance is a strand, another addition to the virtual place wherein we will all find ourselves together. Telephone, fax, computer networks, E-mail, interactive television — these are the components out of which the hive is being built. The end of it all, the *telos,* is a kind of amniotic environment of impulses, a condition of connectedness. And in time — I don't know how long it will take — it will feel as strange (and exhilarating) for a person to stand momentarily free of it as it feels now for a city dweller to look up at night and see a sky full of stars.

Whether this sounds dire or not depends upon your assumptions about the human condition — assumptions, that is, in the largest sense. For those who ask, with Gauguin, "Who are we? Why are we here? Where are we going?" — and who feel that the answering of those questions is the grand mission of the species — the prospect of a collective life in an electronic hive is bound to seem terrifying. But there are others, maybe even a majority, who have never except fleetingly posed those same questions, who have repressed them so that they might "get on," and who gravitate toward that life because they see it as a way of vanquishing once and for all the anxious gnawings they feel whenever any intimations of depth sneak through the inner barriers.

My core fear is that we are, as a culture, as a species, becoming shallower; that we have turned from depth — from the Judeo-Christian premise of unfathomable mystery — and are adapting ourselves to the ersatz security of a vast lateral connectedness. That we are giving up on wisdom, the struggle for which has for millennia been central to the very idea of culture, and that we are pledging instead to a faith in the web.

There is, finally, a tremendous difference between communication in the instrumental sense and communion in the affective, soul-oriented sense. Somewhere we have gotten hold of the idea that the more all-embracing we can make our communications networks, the closer we will be to that connection that we long for deep down. For change us as they will, our technologies have not yet eradicated that flame of a desire — not merely to be in touch, but to be, at least figuratively, embraced, known and valued not abstractly but in presence. We seem to believe that our instruments can get us there, but they can't. Their great power is all in the service of division and acceleration. They work in — and create — an unreal time that has nothing to do with the deep time in which we thrive: the time of history, tradition, ritual, art, and true communion.

The proselytizers have shown me in their vision, and in my more susceptible

10

moods I have felt myself almost persuaded. I have imagined what it could be like, our toil and misery replaced by a vivid, pleasant dream. Fingers tap keys, oceans of fact and sensation get downloaded, are dissolved through the nervous system. Bottomless wells of data are accessed and manipulated, everything flowing at circuit speed. Gone the rock in the field, the broken hoe, the grueling distances. "History," said Stephen Daedalus, "is a nightmare from which I am trying to awaken." This may be the awakening, but it feels curiously like the fantasies that circulate through our sleep. From deep in the heart I hear the voice that says, "Refuse it."

from *Out of Control: The Rise of Neo-Biological Civilization*

KEVIN KELLY

I F TWENTIETH-CENTURY SCIENCE can be said to have a single icon, it is   1
the Atom. As depicted in the popular mind, the symbol of the Atom is stark: a black dot encircled by the hairline orbits of several smaller dots. The Atom whirls alone, the epitome of singleness. It is the metaphor for individuality. At its center is the animus, the It, the life force, holding all to their appropriate whirling station. The Atom stands for power and knowledge and certainty. It conveys the naked power of simplicity.

The iconic reign of the Atom is now passing. The symbol of science for the next century is the dynamic Net. The icon of the Net, in contradistinction to the Atom, has no center. It is a bunch of dots connected to other dots, a cobweb of arrows pouring into one another, squirming together like a nest of snakes, the restless image fading at indeterminate edges. The Net is the archetype displayed to represent all circuits, all intelligence, all interdependence, all things economic and social and ecological, all communications, all democracy, all groups, all large systems. This icon is slippery, ensnaring the unwary in its paradox of no beginning, no end, no center.

The Net conveys the logic of both the computer and nature. In nature, the Nets finds form in, for example, the beehive. The hive is irredeemably social, unabashedly of many minds, but it decides as a whole when to swarm and where to move. A hive possesses an intelligence that none of its parts does. A single honeybee brain operates with a memory of six days; the hive as a whole operates with a memory of three months, twice as long as the average bee lives.

Although many philosophers in the past have suspected that one could abstract the laws of life and apply them to machines, it wasn't until computers and human-made systems became as complex as living things — as intricately composed as a beehive — that it was possible to prove this. Just as a beehive functions as if it were a single sentient organism, so does an electronic hive, made up of millions of buzzing, dim-witted personal computers, behave like a single organism. Out of networked parts — whether of insects, neurons, or chips — come learning, evolution, and life. Out of a planet-wide swarm of silicon calculators comes an emergent self-governing intelligence: the Net.

I live on computer networks. The network of networks — the Net, also 5 known as the Internet — links several million personal computers around the world. No one knows exactly how many millions are connected, or even how many intermediate nodes there are. The Internet Society made an educated guess last year that the Net was made up of 1.7 million host computers and 17 million users. Like the beehive, the Net is controlled by no one: No one is in charge. The Net is, as its users are proud to boast, the largest functioning anarchy in the world. Every day hundreds of millions of messages are passed between its members without the benefit of a central authority.

In addition to a vast flow of individual letters, there exists between its wires that disembodied cyberspace where messages interact, a shared space of written public conversations. Every day authors all over the world add millions of words to an uncountable number of overlapping conversations. They daily build an immense distributed document, one that is under eternal construction, in constant flux, and of fleeting permanence. The users of this media are creating an entirely new writing space, far different from that carved out by a printed book or even a chat around a table. Because of this impermanence, the type of thought encouraged by the Net tends toward the non-dogmatic — the experimental idea, the quip, the global perspective, the interdisciplinary synthesis, and the uninhibited, often emotional, response. Many participants prefer the quality of writing on the Net to book writing because Net writing is of a conversational, peer-to-peer style, frank and communicative, rather than precise and self-consciously literary. Instead of the rigid canonical thinking cultivated by the book, the Net stimulates another way of thinking: telegraphic, modular, non-linear, malleable, cooperative.

A person on the Internet sees the world in a different light. He or she views the world as decidedly decentralized, every far-flung member a producer as well as a consumer, all parts of it equidistant from all others, no matter how large it gets, and every participant responsible for manufacturing truth out of a noisy cacophony of ideas, opinions, and facts. There is no central meaning, no official canon, no manufactured consent rippling through the wires from which one can borrow a viewpoint. Instead, every idea has a backer, and every backer has an idea, while contradiction, paradox, irony, and multifaceted truth rise up in a flood.

A recurring vision swirls in the shared mind of the Net, a vision that nearly every member glimpses, if only momentarily: of wiring human and artificial minds into one planetary soul. This incipient techno-spiritualism is all the more remarkable because of how unexpected it has been. The Net, after all, is nothing more than a bunch of highly engineered pieces of rock braided together with strands of metal or glass. It is routine technology. Computers, which have been in our lives for twenty years, have made our life faster but not that much different. Nobody expected a new culture, a new thrill, or even a new politics to be born when we married calculating circuits with the ordinary telephone; but that's exactly what happened.

There are other machines, such as the automobile and the air conditioner, that have radically reshaped our lives and the landscape of our civilization. The Net (and its future progeny) is another one of those disrupting machines and may yet surpass the scope of all the others together in altering how we live.

The Net is an organism/machine whose exact size and boundaries are unknown. All we do know is that new portions and new uses are being added to it at such an accelerating rate that it may be more of an explosion than a thing. So vast is this embryonic Net, and so fast is it developing into something else, that no single human can fathom it deeply enough to claim expertise on the whole.

The tiny bees in a hive are more or less unaware of their colony, but their collective hive mind transcends their small bee minds. As we wire ourselves up into a hivish network, many things will emerge that we, as mere neurons in the network, don't expect, don't understand, can't control, or don't even perceive. That's the price for any emergent hive mind.

At the same time the very shape of this network space shapes us. It is no coincidence that the post-modernists arose as the networks formed. In the last half-century a uniform mass market has collapsed into a network of small niches — the result of the information tide. An aggregation of fragments is the only kind of whole we now have. The fragmentation of business markets, of social mores, of spiritual beliefs, of ethnicity, and of truth itself into tinier and tinier shards is the hallmark of this era. Our society is a working pandemonium of fragments — much like the Internet itself.

People in a highly connected yet deeply fragmented society can no longer rely on a central canon for guidance. They are forced into the modern existential blackness of creating their own cultures, beliefs, markets, and identities from a sticky mess of interdependent pieces. The industrial icon of a grand central or a hidden "I am" becomes hollow. Distributed, headless, emergent wholeness becomes the social ideal.

The critics of early computers capitalized on a common fear: that a Big Brother brain would watch over us and control us. What we know now of our own brains is that they too are only networks of mini-minds, a society of dumber minds linked together, and that when we peer into them deeply we find that there is no "I" in charge. Not only does a central-command economy not work: a central-command brain won't either. In its stead, we can make a nation of personal computers, a country of decentralized nodes of governance and thought. Almost every type of large-scale governance we can find, from the body of a giraffe, to the energy regulation in a tidal marsh, to the temperature regulation of a beehive, to the flow of traffic on the Internet, resolves into a swarmy distributed net of autonomous units and heterogeneous parts.

No one has been more wrong about computerization than George Orwell   15
in *1984*. So far, nearly everything about the actual possibility-space that computers have created indicates they are not the beginning of authority but its end. In
the process of connecting everything to everything, computers elevate the power
of the small player. They make room for the different, and they reward small
innovations. Instead of enforcing uniformity, they promote heterogeneity and
autonomy. Instead of sucking the soul from human bodies, turning computer
users into an army of dull clones, *networked* computers — by reflecting the networked nature of our own brains — encourage the humanism of their users.
Because they have taken on the flexibility, adaptability, and self-connecting governance of organic systems, we become more human, not less so, when we
use them.

Chapter 11

Arguing about Actions

Our Disagreements about Actions

One of the most important issues that people disagree about, and one of the most complex to negotiate, is how one should act. Questions about actions may refer to the past: How should we have acted in the past? Most legal systems and studies of human history turn on this question. These questions may refer to the present and the future: How should we be acting right now? Should we be doing what we are doing? How should we act in the future? Most political debates turn on these questions. But people also face questions about actions on a smaller scale each day. And within our individual communities, the decisions we make about actions can have far-reaching consequences.

Arguing about actions is a complex activity because it involves each of the subjects described in earlier chapters: arguing about existence, arguing about causality, arguing about language, and arguing about values. Disagreements about actions are often phrased as "should" questions:

Should the United States have sent troops to Bosnia early in that conflict?

Should the U.N. forces in the Persian Gulf have attempted to capture Baghdad?

Should Congress pass a comprehensive health care package?

Should you major in English?

Should society legally sanction homosexual relationships?

Should the U.S. legalize the use of peyote in Native American religious ceremonies?

Should the federal government regulate children's programming?

413

When members of a community have conflicting answers to questions such as these, then they may become the issues for debate.

The reasons offered to justify actions are usually one of the types of claims already discussed. For instance, one could argue that abortion should be banned because it is murder (a claim about language), because it is physically and psychologically harmful to the mother (a claim about causality), or because it violates the Judeo-Christian system of ethics (a claim about values). One could argue, on the other hand, that banning abortions would create a black market for abortions (a claim about causality) and would violate a woman's right to privacy (a claim about values). Claims about actions almost always involve claims about existence because the question of whether we *should* do something is related to the question of whether we *can* do it. Because the reasons used to justify actions take the form of claims themselves, they may require further reasons, leading to a chain of reasons and claims. For example, if you argue that abortion should be banned because it is murder, then you may need to defend the claim implicit in the reason (abortion is murder) with a further reason. Refer to Chapter 1 for a discussion of chains of reasons.

Arguing about Actions

▪ ▪ PROBLEMS AND SOLUTIONS

An argument about actions often takes the form of an argument about problems and solutions. Some members of a community feel that there is something wrong with the current state of the community (problem) and propose an action or actions to change that state (solution). The first step in an argument about problems and solutions is to analyze the problem. The following questions are useful for doing so:

What is the current situation? (existence)

Is it a "problem"? (language)

How did it get to be this way? (causality)

What happens if we don't do anything about it? (causality)

How desirable or undesirable are these effects? (values)

The next step is to analyze possible solutions:

What actions may possibly change the current state? (existence and causality)

What would be the effects of these changes? (causality)

How desirable or undesirable would these changes be? (values)

Once this analysis is complete, the next stage is to identify how the action or actions will be carried out:

Who should take the action? (existence)

What means should they use? (existence and causality)

Where and when should the action take place? (existence)

What purpose or motives are behind these actions? Who wants to make these changes and why? (causality)

Every action must have an agent, some person or group of people who will carry it out, although not every claim about action will reveal the proposed agent explicitly. (In some instances, such as advertising, the person who is supposed to do the action is the reader.) And, as I suggested in Chapter 1, action is purposeful. It is driven by human intention and motives. If I trip and fall down a flight of stairs, I may be moving, but I am not acting, unless I caused myself to trip. When I decide to go to the refrigerator for a snack, I am acting. My movement is purposeful and intentional. But the beating of my heart and the functioning of my digestive tract involve only motion; they are not actions because they are not purposeful.

Every action is also accomplished through some means. Like the agent, the means is frequently not stated in the claim, but it is useful to ask not only who will perform the action but also how it will be carried out.

Every action also has an "occasion," a time (when) and place (where) proper for the action. Often, the occasion is "here and now" or "as soon as possible." Sometimes the time and place must be determined precisely for the action to succeed. Whenever we make appointments or schedule events, we are determining the occasion for actions.

The final question about action relates to causality, to purpose or motive as cause. This question leads us to discover whether there are other purposes, besides solving the particular problem under consideration, that will be served by the action. What interests do particular parties in the community have in the proposed action or actions?

▧ ▧ INDIVIDUAL AND COLLECTIVE ACTION

The agent performing the action can be either an individual or a group. For instance, questions about actions may involve personal decisions: Should I buy a car? Should I major in English? Should I get married? Should I go skiing this weekend? Or they may involve deciding actions for a group: Should the English Department get a new computer lab? Should my friends and I go fishing this weekend? Should our family take a trip to Disneyland? Should the city put a new stop sign at the intersection near our house? Should the State of Utah spend money on a light rail transport system? Should the federal government regulate citizen militia groups?

A Model for Individual Decision-Making   The process of making a decision about individual action can take two forms. First of all, you might be facing a problem that has no clear solution. In this case, you have to brainstorm about possible solutions before you can decide among them. In the second case, you may not be trying to solve a problem as much as choose among possible actions: Should I do X or Y? As an example of the first model for decision-making, let's say you face a problem with one of your assignments: You've put off working on a paper. It's due in a couple of days, and you are just now realizing that it may require more time than you originally thought. You begin by defining the problem, its causes, and effects.

The problem is that you think you won't be able to do a good job on your assignment and complete it by the due date. This is a claim about existence, about what things may be like in the future. You may start by examining whether what you think is really the case. What evidence do you have that you will not be able to complete the essay on time? Your performance on past assignments? Your estimate of how much time will be required for each part of the task of writing? Is the problem really a problem?

You decide, based on past experience, that the problem really exists. The next step is to define what caused this problem. What brought this situation about? You go over your activities for the semester and realize that you had the assignment in plenty of time, but you put off working on it until the last minute. Perhaps you recognize that you have done this sort of thing before on assignments. You just had other things on your mind. You resolve to do better in the future, but what about the present?

What are the effects of the problem? What will happen if you don't turn this paper in or don't do very well on it? If the harmful effects are not great, you may want to turn in what you can finish in two days and hope for the best. You read through the syllabus and realize that you have to turn in the paper to get credit for the course and that it counts for a large portion of your final grade. Using the syllabus as evidence to predict your instructor's action, you reason that this problem will have a negative, or undesirable, effect on your grade. You can take your analysis of effects further: What will be the effect of not doing well in this class or not getting credit for it? Is it required for graduation? How badly will this affect your overall grade point average? And what effect might this have on your prospects for graduate study or employment?

Once you have defined the problem and its effects, you need to use brainstorming and research to determine solutions that will solve this problem. What are your possibilities? You could choose not to write the paper at all, a decision to let the problem stand. You could choose to do what you can in two days and hope for the best. You could try to adapt a paper that someone else has written. You could talk to the instructor and see whether you could arrange to turn in the paper a couple of days late.

Next you look at these solutions in terms of their causes and effects. First, what is the motivation behind each of these proposals? The decision to let the problem stand might be motivated by your conclusion that none of the other solutions will make much of a difference. It could also be motivated by laziness or irresponsibility. What about the decision to do what you can hope for the best? This might be motivated by a desire to make the best of a poor situation and to learn from your mistakes, as well as a fear of discussing this problem with the instructor. What would motivate the decision to use someone else's paper? Certainly not a desire to learn what you could from working on the paper. Perhaps, it is the desire to do well in the class no matter what it takes, without any regard for what is right. The decision to talk to the instructor might be motivated by a desire to admit your mistakes and to try to do your best on the assignment, taking the time to learn what you can in the process.

What are the effects of these proposed solutions? We've already examined the effects of letting the problem stand. If you do what you can in two days, you might not produce a very good paper, but you would probably get credit for the assignment and pass the course. This solution would require a lot of work, possibly pulling a couple of all-nighters, and it might have a negative effect on your work for other classes. Using someone else's paper would save you a lot of work, and you might even do well on the assignment if it were a good paper to begin with and you could adapt it successfully. But if you were to be caught, you could fail the class or even be kicked out of school. At the least you wouldn't learn what the assignment was intended to teach, which is one reason you came to school in the first place. Moreover, you might not be able to live with yourself knowing that you cheated. If you decide to talk to the instructor, you might get more time to work on the paper without penalty, which would allow you the advantage of completing the assignment without the disadvantage of it affecting your work for other classes. Of course, your instructor might not give you any more time and would also know in advance how little time you had to spend on the paper.

What would you decide to do? After going through this process, I think I would call the instructor right away, plead my case, and try to make some arrangement to turn the paper in a little late. If this didn't work, I would do what I could in the time I had and hope for the best. Borrowing a paper from someone else would violate my sense of right and wrong and could have very undesirable effects.

Of course, when I decide to include the teacher in my decision-making process, then my decision is no longer an individual decision; it becomes a group decision. The teacher and I must use language to negotiate a consensus about collective action.

You follow a similar process when you are presented with actions to choose among. Let's say that you apply to graduate school and are accepted at three different places. In this case, you are not really searching for a solution to a problem; you are trying to decide among competing possibilities. First, examine some questions of existence: Is it really possible for you to take each of these actions? Must you really choose among them? Does choosing one exclude choosing the others? You decide, in this case, that you can really only go to one graduate school.

Now you consider each of these actions in terms of its causes and effects.

What is motivating your decision to go to each school? What will happen if you choose one school over the others? What will happen if you decide not to go to any of them at all?

Once you have identified the possible causes and effects, you then consider the values attached to these causes and effects: What are the advantages and disadvantages of each choice? Which values are most important to you?

You make so many decisions about actions each day that you don't always have the time or the inclination to examine each decision in such detail. This kind of analysis is an action in itself that has positive and negative effects. You can't spend all day deciding what you will eat for breakfast. Sometimes you have to act on the knowledge you have and hope for the best.

A Model for Collective Decision-Making   Few decisions are truly individual. When you start considering who else might be affected by your decisions and try to involve them in the decision-making process, then what at first was an individual decision quickly becomes a group decision. But collective decision-making is tricky: The further you move away from what you control as an individual, the more difficult it is to have a full voice in the decisions that are made. When I was single, I could make many decisions on my own, but I still had to work things out with a boss or a roommate and occasionally my parents or siblings. When I got married, I started participating in a lot more group decisions. My wife and I had to work out how we were going to decide our collective actions: Who would decide what? What kind of input would others have? Who would carry out what kind of actions? Now that we have children, decision-making becomes even more complicated.

What my example shows is the effect on decision-making of membership in a community — in this case the community defined by my individual family. As you become more involved in any community, you will find that you participate in more group decisions and that you have more responsibility to consider others when contemplating your own actions. As a student passing through the English Department at Brigham Young University, I did not have a lot of say in what took place there: what classes were offered, who was hired and assigned to teach those classes, what books were ordered, how the money was spent. I was part of the English Department community, but I was not nearly as involved in that community as I am now as a faculty member. Because of my greater involvement in the English Department community, I find that my actions have greater impact within the community and that more of my actions are group actions. I serve on committees to decide who gets into our graduate program and who gets to teach our composition courses. As a teacher, my actions in the classroom have much more effect than my actions as a student did.

Collective decisions are complex and involve related claims about existence, causality, language, values, and actions. Here are some examples:

Only people who can pass a literacy test should be allowed to vote.

Health care reform should be administered by the states rather than the federal government.

Season ticket holders should be allowed to vote on a salary cap for major league baseball.

Unless there is an immediate threat to American interests, the President should seek Congressional approval before sending American troops into combat situations.

Churches have a right to speak out on political issues.

In order to have an effect on group decision-making, it is important to understand how the community considering the action is organized. (See Chapter 3.) The "journalistic questions" are helpful for identifying the organization of a community: who?, what?, where?, why?, how?

Who makes decisions?

What kind of decisions can they make?

When do they typically make decisions?

Where do they make decisions?

Why do they make decisions? (What is the mission or purpose of the community?)

How do they make decisions?

You can ask the same questions about how decisions are implemented and enforced.

Arguments about collective action are at the very heart of community life. Addressing such actions is really the purpose of this book: How can we use language to participate more fully in the collective decisions and actions of the communities we belong to?

When groups make decisions, they can follow much the same process described for making individual decisions: defining the nature of a problem, identifying solutions, and examining positive and negative causes and effects. Group decision-making involves the additional task of resolving differences and disagreements about existence, causality, language, and values.

Applying the Principles

■ ■ OPPOSING VIEWPOINTS ON SOCIAL ACTIONS

In each of the following sets of essays, two writers present opposing viewpoints on social actions. Molly Ivins and Wayne R. LaPierre take opposing positions on whether the U.S. government should limit the use and possession of guns. In part, their disagreement is one about how the second amendment should be interpreted. In part, it is about the consequences of such a ban. Coretta Scott King and H. L. Mencken take opposing sides on the rightness and effectiveness of the death penalty. Catholic theologian Daniel C. Maguire and medical school professors Raymond S. Duff and A.G.M. Campbell offer differing views on the decision to terminate life in certain cases. As you read each of these essays, consider the following questions:

1. What references does each writer make to actions? Which actions are individual actions and which are collective?
2. What claims does each writer make? What reasons are used to support these claims? What assumptions are implied by these reasons?
3. What further claims are implied in the reasons given to support these actions? What kinds of claims are they? What further support do these claims receive (what chain of reasoning does author use)?
4. To what extent do you accept the arguments presented by each of these writers? If you disagree, what is the crux of your disagreement?
5. If you were going to respond to each of these writers, what common assumptions or beliefs could you build on?
6. If you were going to resolve the dispute between each opposing set of writers, what common beliefs or assumptions could you find that both writers share?

"Ban the Things. Ban Them All."

MOLLY IVINS

G UNS. EVERYWHERE GUNS. 1
        Let me start this discussion by pointing out that I am not anti-gun. I'm pro-knife. Consider the merits of the knife.

In the first place, you have to catch up with someone to stab him. A general substitution of knives for guns would promote physical fitness. We'd turn into a whole nation of great runners. Plus, knives don't ricochet. And people are seldom killed while cleaning their knives.

As a civil libertarian, I of course support the Second Amendment. And I believe it means exactly what it says: "A well-regulated militia being necessary to the security of a free state, the right of the people to keep and bear arms shall not be infringed." Fourteen-year-old boys are not part of a well-regulated militia. Members of wacky religious cults are not part of a well-regulated militia. Permitting unregulated citizens to have guns is destroying the security of this free state.

I am intrigued by the arguments of those who claim to follow the judicial 5 doctrine of original intent. How do they know it was the dearest wish of Thomas Jefferson's heart that teenage drug dealers should cruise the cities of this nation perforating their fellow citizens with assault rifles? Channeling?

There is more hooey spread about the Second Amendment. It says quite clearly that guns are for those who form part of a well-regulated militia, i.e., the armed forces including the National Guard. The reasons for keeping them away from everyone else get clearer by the day.

The comparison most often used is that of the automobile, another lethal object that is regularly used to wreck great carnage. Obviously, this society is full of people who haven't got enough common sense to use an automobile properly. But we haven't outlawed cars yet.

We do, however, license them and their owners, restrict their use to presumably sane and sober adults and keep track of who sells them to whom. At a minimum, we should do the same with guns.

In truth, there is no rational argument for guns in this society. This is no longer a frontier nation in which people hunt their own food. It is a crowded, overwhelmingly urban country in which letting people have access to guns is a continuing disaster. Those who want guns — whether for target shooting, hunting or potting rattlesnakes (get a hoe) — should be subject to the same restrictions placed on gun owners in England — a nation in which liberty has survived nicely without an armed populace.

The argument that "guns don't kill people" is patent nonsense. Anyone who has ever worked in a cop shop knows how many family arguments end in murder because there was a gun in the house. Did the gun kill someone? No. But if there had been no gun, no one would have died. At least not without a good footrace first. Guns do kill. Unlike cars, that is all they do.

Michael Crichton makes an interesting argument about technology in his thriller *Jurassic Park*. He points out that power without discipline is making this society into a wreckage. By the time someone who studies the martial arts becomes a master — literally able to kill with bare hands — that person has also undergone years of training and discipline. But any fool can pick up a gun and kill with it.

"A well-regulated militia" surely implies both long training and long discipline. That is the least, the very least, that should be required of those who are permitted to have guns, because a gun is literally the power to kill. For years, I used to enjoy taunting my gun-nut friends about their psycho-sexual hangups — always in a spirit of good cheer, you understand. But letting the noisy minority in the National Rifle Association force us to allow this carnage to continue is just plain insane.

I do think gun nuts have a power hangup. I don't know what is missing in their psyches that they need to feel they have the power to kill. But no sane society would allow this to continue.

Ban the damn things. Ban them all.

You want protection? Get a dog.

The Second Amendment: "The Right of the People to Keep and Bear Arms"

WAYNE R. LAPIERRE

C OLUMNIST DON SHOEMAKER dismisses as "idiocy" the belief that the Sec-   1
ond Amendment prevents government from banning guns.

Leonard Larsen of Scripps-Howard News Service says "only gun nut simple-tons [and] NRA propagandists . . . defend against gun controls on constitutional grounds."

Such rhetoric, including the suggestion that the constitutional right to keep and bear arms applies only to the state militia and National Guard, is commonly heard in the media's anti-gun campaign.

Some columnists, however, are willing to concede that their views on the Second Amendment don't square with scholarship on the issue. In a column in the *Washington Post,* March 21, 1991, George Will wrote concerning Sanford Levinson's *Yale Law Journal* article, "The Embarrassing Second Amendment":

> The National Rifle Association is perhaps correct and certainly is plausible in its "strong" reading of the Second Amendment protection of private gun owner-ship. Therefore gun control advocates who want to square their policy prefer-ences with the Constitution should squarely face the need to deconstitutionalize the subject by repealing the embarrassing amendment.

Anti-gun lawyer-activist Michael Kinsley, co-host on CNN's *Crossfire* and   5
formerly editor-in-chief of the *New Republic,* regularly calls for gun control and proudly holds membership in Handgun Control, Inc. But in an op-ed article in the *Washington Post,* January 8, 1990, Kinsley wrote:

> Unfortunately, there is the Second Amendment to the Constitution.
>   The purpose of the first Amendment's free-speech guarantee was pretty clearly to protect political discourse. But liberals reject the notion that free speech is therefore limited to political topics, even broadly defined. True, that purpose is not inscribed in the amendment itself. But why leap to the conclusion that a broadly worded constitutional freedom ("the right of the people to keep and bear arms") is narrowly limited by its stated purpose, *unless you're trying to explain it away?* My *New Republic* colleague Mickey Kaus says that *if liberals interpreted the Second Amendment the way they interpret the rest of the Bill of Rights, there would be law professors arguing that gun ownership is mandatory.* [Emphasis added.]

Despite an occasional admission that the Second Amendment means what it says, many columnists, with little or no understanding of the roots of the Con-stitution, rush to embrace a view that finds virtually no support among high-ranking constitutional scholars.

According to an article in the *Encyclopedia of the American Constitution* summarizing Second Amendment literature in 1986, of the thirty-six law review articles published since 1980, only four support the anti-gun position, while thirty-two articles support the individual right position advocated by the National Rifle Association.

The individual rights authors include leading constitutional scholars who don't own guns and who "never expected or desired the evidence to crush the anti-gun position."

Professor Sanford Levinson of the University of Texas Law School, co-author of the standard law school text on the Constitution, *Processes of Constitutional Decision Making,* is an ACLU stalwart. In his 1989 *Yale Law Journal* article, cited by George Will, Professor Levinson admits his own embarrassment at having to conclude from his research that private gun ownership *cannot* be prohibited — he must have hoped to find the opposite.

Like Levinson, Yale Law Professor Akhil Amar, a visiting professor of con-   10
stitutional law at Columbia University, is held in high repute by liberal constitutional scholars. Yet Amar trounces the anti-gun states' right theory, emphasizing again and again that the Second Amendment guarantees the right to arms to "the people," not "the states":

> [W]hen the Constitution means "states" it says so . . . The ultimate right to keep and bear arms belongs to "the people," not the "states." . . . Thus the "people" at the core of the Second Amendment [a]re [the] Citizens — the same "We the People" who "ordain and establish" the Constitution and whose right to assemble . . . [is] at the core of the First Amendment. . . . Nowadays, it is quite common to speak loosely of the National Guard as "the state militia," but [when the Second Amendment was written] . . . "the militia" referred to all Citizens capable of bearing arms. [Thus] "the militia" is identical to "the people." . . .

Are these eminent constitutional scholars "gun nut simpletons, [and] NRA propagandists"? Activist Michael Kinsley doesn't think so.

After reviewing a *Michigan Law Review* article by Professor Don Kates, Kinsley wrote in an op-ed piece, February 8, 1990, in the *Washington Post:*

> If there is a reply, the [gun] controllers haven't made it. . . . Establishing that a flat ban on handguns would be [unconstitutional,] Kates builds a *distressingly* good case.

Kinsley is distressed because "a flat ban on handguns," preferably all guns, is precisely what he wants. His article concludes:

> Gun nuts are unconvincing (at least to me) in their attempts to argue that the individual right to bear arms is still as vital to freedom as it was in 1792. *But the right is still there.* [Emphasis added.]

Two major contributors to constitutional scholarship are neutral historians with no personal interest in the "gun control" debate. One is Professor Joyce Malcolm, a political historian whose work on the English and American origins of the right to arms has been underwritten by the American Bar Foundation, Harvard Law School, and the National Endowment for the Humanities. In *To*

Keep and Bear Arms: The Origins of an Anglo-American Right (Harvard University Press, 1994), Professor Malcolm writes:

> The Second Amendment was meant to accomplish two distinct goals. . . . First, it was meant to *guarantee the individual's right to have arms for self-defense and self-preservation, . . . These privately owned arms* [emphasis added] were meant to serve a larger purpose [militia service] as well . . . and it is the coupling of these two objectives that has caused the most confusion. The customary American militia necessitated an armed public . . . the militia [being] . . . the body of the people. . . . The argument that today's National Guardsmen, members of a select militia, would constitute the *only* [emphasis hers] persons entitled to keep and bear arms has no historical foundation.

Professor Robert Shalhope, a non-gun-owning intellectual historian, whose   15 interest is the philosophy of the Founding Fathers, agrees. In the 1982 edition of the *Journal of American History,* Professor Shalhope writes:

> When James Madison and his colleagues drafted the Bill of Rights they . . . firmly believed in two distinct principles: (1) *Individuals had the right to possess arms to defend themselves and their property;* and (2) states retained the right to maintain militias *composed of these individually armed citizens.* . . . Clearly, these men believed that the perpetuation of a republican spirit and character in their society depended upon *the freeman's possession of arms* as well as his ability and willingness to defend *both himself and his society.* [Emphasis added.]

As Professor Kates put it, "Historical research shows that our Founding Fathers out NRAed the NRA."

Thomas Paine believed it would be better for "all the world to lay [arms] aside . . . and settle matters by negotiation" — "but unless the whole will, the matter ends, and I take up my musket and thank Heaven He has put it in my power."

Paine clearly doubted that criminals could be disarmed and deemed it important that decent people be armed against them:

> The peaceable part of mankind will be continually overrun by the vile and abandoned while they neglect the means of self-defense. . . . [Weakness] allures the ruffian [but] arms like laws discourage and keep the invader and plunderer in awe and preserve order in the world. . . . Horrid mischief would ensue were [the good] deprived of the use of them . . . [and] the weak will become a prey to the strong.

Or, simply stated — criminals prefer unarmed victims. Consider the similar views of the great eighteenth-century Italian criminologist Cesare Beccaria, which could be described as an older rendition of today's slogan "when guns are outlawed only outlaws will have guns."

Thomas Jefferson translated the following from Beccaria's Italian and la-   20 boriously copied it in longhand into his own personal compilation of great quotations:

False is the idea of utility that sacrifices a thousand real advantages for one imaginary or trifling inconvenience; that would take fire from men because it burns, and water because one may drown in it; that has no remedy for evils, except destruction. The laws that forbid the carrying of arms are laws of such a nature. They disarm those only who are neither inclined nor determined to commit crimes. Can it be supposed that those who have the courage to violate the most sacred laws of humanity, the most important of the code, will respect the less important and arbitrary ones, which can be violated with ease and impunity, and which, if strictly obeyed, would put an end to personal liberty — so dear to men, so dear to the enlightened legislator — and subject innocent persons to all the vexations that the quality alone ought to suffer? Such laws make things worse for the assaulted and better for the assailants; they serve rather to encourage than to prevent homicides, for an unarmed man may be attacked with greater confidence than an armed man. They ought to be designated as laws not preventive but fearful of crimes, produced by the tumultuous impression of a few isolated facts, and not by thoughtful consideration of the inconveniences and advantages of a universal decree.

The Founders unanimously agreed. "The great object," thundered Anti-Federalist Patrick Henry, "is that every man be armed." James Madison, Federalist author of the Bill of Rights, reviled tyrants for being "afraid to trust the people with arms" and extolled "the advantage of being armed, which the Americans possess over the people of almost every other nation."

The Anti-Federalists endorsed Madison's Bill of Rights while claiming it was their own idea. They characterized the Second Amendment as a mere rewording of their Sam Adams' proposal "that the [federal] Constitution be never construed to prevent the people who are peaceable citizens from keeping *their own* arms." The Federalist analysis said the amendment confirmed to the people "their *private* arms."

LIMITATIONS ON THE RIGHT TO ARMS

Are there any limits on either kinds of arms the Second Amendment guarantees or the kinds of people it protects?

Neither felons nor children under eighteen, of course, have the right to own arms — any more than they have the right to vote. This restriction is based on solid historical reasons. The National Rifle Association, moreover, has for over seventy years supported laws to prohibit gun ownership by those who have been convicted of violent felonies.

By the same token, the NRA has for decades supported and helped pass tough penalties to keep those who misuse guns in prison where they belong. The NRA was among the earliest and strongest proponents of "Three Strikes and You're Out" laws which would put repeat violent offenders in jail *permanently.*

Yet the anti-individual rights crowd accuse the NRA of claiming the Second Amendment guarantees guns for all — including criminals — and all weapons — including weapons of war like bazookas and bombs. Such has never been the case, and there is no reason for anyone to believe otherwise — the facts have been available to all. Prominent constitutional scholar Professor Stephen Halbrook has summed it up: "[A]rtillery pieces, tanks, nuclear devices and other heavy ordinances," he said, "are not constitutionally protected" arms which civilians have a Second Amendment right to possess; neither are "grenades, bombs, bazookas and other devices . . . which have never been commonly possessed for self-defense. . . ."

But the right to arms *does* protect ordinary small arms — handguns, rifles, and shotguns — including "assault weapons." Indeed, "assault weapons" are just ordinary semiautomatic firearms like those that have existed in this country for over a century. They fire no faster than revolvers or pump action rifles and shotguns. As Rutgers law professor Robert Cottrol notes:

> It has been argued that "assault weapons" are far more deadly than 18th Century arms. Actually, modern medical technology makes them far less deadly than blunderbusses were in the 18th Century. (In fact, "assault weapons" are less deadly — and far less often used in crime — than ordinary shotguns or hunting rifles.)

Professors Cottrol and Don Kates agree that if the many changes in conditions since 1792 when the Second Amendment was enacted could justify ignoring it, other rights protected by the Bill of Rights would also be endangered: *"changing times affect many constitutional rights, not just the right to arms."*

Take, for instance, radio, TV, and the movies. These didn't exist when the Bill of Rights was written, yet all three are now embraced by its free speech and press clauses. The Supreme Court enforces that stand. The media's First Amendment rights are soundly defended even though it is widely accepted that they may exert far more influence than a book or newspaper — even prompting some suggestible people to commit violent acts.

By the same token, sensationalized national network coverage can spread new crimes. Car-jacking, first confined to Michigan, caught on nationwide as other criminals picked up on the idea. Freedom of the press in our modern era has many other drawbacks, but we continue to expand our constitutional free press protections to cover new forms of disseminating news and opinion. 30

To quote Professors Cottrol and Kates:

> If the Bill of Rights is to continue, we must apply its spirit even as conditions change. That is the nub of the Second Amendment controversy: Modern intellectuals who tend to feel self-defense is barbaric — that government should have a monopoly of arms with the people being dependent on it for protection — have difficulty accepting the Founders' diametrically opposite views.

The Warren Court had this to say when its decisions vindicating the privilege against self-incrimination were assailed as inconsistent with the government's need to detect modern criminals and subversives:

> If it be thought that the privilege is outmoded in the conditions of this modern age, then the thing to do is to [amend] it out of the Constitution, not to whittle it down by the subtle encroachments of judicial opinion.

CAN AN ARMED PEOPLE RESIST TYRANNY?

Those who claim that the *only* purpose of the right to arms is to enable citizens to resist a military takeover of our government sometimes argue that the Second Amendment is obsolete since a populace armed with only small arms cannot defeat a modern army. That is doubly wrong. Even if overthrowing tyranny were the amendment's only purpose, the claim that an armed populace cannot successfully resist assault stems from an unproved theory.

The twentieth century provides *no example* of a determined populace with access to small arms having been defeated by a modern army. The Russians lost in Afghanistan, the United States lost in Vietnam, and the French lost in Indo-China. In each case, it was the poorly armed populace that beat the "modern" army. In China, Cuba, and Nicaragua, the established leaders, Chiang Kai-shek, Battista, and Somoza lost. Modern nations like Algeria, Angola, Ireland, Israel, Mozambique, and Zimbabwe only exist because guerrilla warfare can triumph over modern armies. While we may not approve of all the resulting governments, each of these triumphs tells a simple truth: A determined people who have the means to maintain prolonged war against a modern army can battle it to a standstill, subverting major portions of the army or defeating it themselves or with major arms supplied by outside forces.

The Founders' purpose in guaranteeing the right to keep and bear arms was not merely to overthrow tyrants. They saw the right to arms as crucial to what they believed was a prime natural right — self-defense.   35

Those who claim that the right to arms is outmoded tend to think of armed personal self-defense as does former Attorney General Ramsey Clark, who described it as "anarchy, not order under law — a jungle where each relies on himself for survival."

Handgun Control, Inc. (HCI) chairperson Sarah Brady claims that "the only reason for guns in civilian hands is for sporting purposes," i.e., not self-defense. "Pete" Shields, Brady's predecessor as HCI head, in the book titled *Guns Don't Die*, advised victims *never* to resist rape or robbery: "give them what they want or run."

Not surprisingly, HCI has proposed a national licensing law confining gun ownership to sportsmen — self-defense not being considered proper grounds for ownership. In an October 22, 1993, editorial, the *Los Angeles Times* agreed.

But author Jeff Snyder points out in his essay "A Nation of Cowards," in *Public Interest* quarterly Fall 1993:

> As the Founding Fathers knew well, a government that does not trust its honest, law-abiding, taxpaying citizens with the means of self-defense is not itself worthy of trust. Laws disarming honest citizens proclaim that the government is the master, not the servant of the people. . . .
>
> The Bill of Rights does not *grant* rights to the people, such that its repeal would legitimately confer upon government the powers otherwise proscribed. The Bill of Rights is the list of the fundamental, inalienable rights, endowed in man by his Creator, that define what it means to be a free and independent people, the rights which must exist to ensure that government governs only with the consent of the people.

The Death Penalty Is a Step Back

CORETTA SCOTT KING

W HEN STEVEN JUDY was executed in Indiana [in 1981] America took an-   1
other step backwards towards legitimizing murder as a way of dealing with
evil in our society.

Although Judy was convicted of four of the most horrible and brutal murders imaginable, and his case is probably the worst in recent memory for opponents of the death penalty, we still have to face the real issue squarely: Can we
expect a decent society if the state is allowed to kill its own people?

In recent years, an increase of violence in America, both individual and political, has prompted a backlash of public opinion on capital punishment. But
however much we abhor violence, legally sanctioned executions are no deterrent
and are, in fact, immoral and unconstitutional.

Although I have suffered the loss of two family members by assassination, I
remain firmly and unequivocally opposed to the death penalty for those convicted of capital offenses.

An evil deed is not redeemed by an evil deed of retaliation. Justice is never   5
advanced in the taking of a human life.

Morality is never upheld by legalized murder. Morality apart, there are a
number of practical reasons which form a powerful argument against capital
punishment.

First, capital punishment makes irrevocable any possible miscarriage of justice. Time and again we have witnessed the specter of mistakenly convicted
people being put to death in the name of American criminal justice. To those
who say that, after all, this doesn't occur too often, I can only reply that if it
happens just once, that is too often. And it has occurred many times.

Second, the death penalty reflects an unwarranted assumption that the
wrongdoer is beyond rehabilitation. Perhaps some individuals cannot be reha-
bilitated; but who shall make that determination? Is any amount of academic
training sufficient to entitle one person to judge another incapable of rehabilitation?

Third, the death penalty is inequitable. Approximately half of the 711 persons now on death row are black. From 1930 through 1968, 53.5 percent of
those executed were black Americans, all too many of whom were represented
by court-appointed attorneys and convicted after hasty trials.

The argument that this may be an accurate reflection of guilt, and homicide   10
trends, instead of a racist application of laws lacks credibility in light of a recent
Florida survey which showed that persons convicted of killing whites were four
times more likely to receive a death sentence than those convicted of killing
blacks.

Proponents of capital punishment often cite a "deterrent effect" as the main
benefit of the death penalty. Not only is there no hard evidence that murdering

murderers will deter other potential killers, but even the "logic" of this argument defies comprehension.

Numerous studies show that the majority of homicides committed in this country are the acts of victim's relatives, friends and acquaintances in the "heat of passion."

What this strongly suggests is that rational consideration of future consequences are seldom a part of the killer's attitude at the time he commits a crime.

The only way to break the chain of violent reaction is to practice nonviolence as individuals and collectively through our laws and institutions.

The Penalty of Death

H. L. MENCKEN

OF THE ARGUMENTS against capital punishment that issue from uplifters, 1
two are commonly heard most often, to wit:

1. That hanging a man (or frying him or gassing him) is a dreadful business, degrading to those who have to do it and revolting to those who have to witness it.
2. That it is useless, for it does not deter others from the same crime.

The first of these arguments, it seems to me, is plainly too weak to need serious refutation. All it says, in brief, is that the work of the hangman is unpleasant. Granted. But suppose it is? It may be quite necessary to society for all that. There are, indeed, many other jobs that are unpleasant, and yet no one thinks of abolishing them — that of the plumber, that of the soldier, that of the garbageman, that of the priest hearing confessions, that of the sand-hog, and so on. Moreover, what evidence is there that any actual hangman complains of his work? I have heard none. On the contrary, I have known many who delighted in their ancient art, and practiced it proudly.

In the second argument of the abolitionists there is rather more force, but even here, I believe, the ground under them is shaky. Their fundamental error consists in assuming that the whole aim of punishing criminals is to deter other (potential) criminals — that we hang or electrocute A simply in order to so alarm B that he will not kill C. This, I believe, is an assumption which confuses a part with the whole. Deterrence, obviously, is *one* of the aims of punishment, but it is surely not the only one. On the contrary, there are at least a half dozen, and some are probably quite as important. At least one of them, practically considered, is *more* important. Commonly, it is described as revenge, but revenge is really not the word for it. I borrow a better term from the late Aristotle: *katharsis*. *Katharsis*, so used, means a salubrious discharge of emotions, a healthy letting off of steam. A school-boy, disliking his teacher, deposits a tack upon the pedagogical chair; the teacher jumps and the boy laughs. This is *katharsis*. What I contend is that one of the prime objects of all judicial punishments is to afford the same grateful relief (*a*) to the immediate victims of the criminal punished, and (*b*) to the general body of moral and timorous men.

These persons, and particularly the first group, are concerned only indirectly with deterring other criminals. The thing they crave primarily is the satisfaction of seeing the criminal actually before them suffer as he made them suffer. What they want is the peace of mind that goes with the feeling that accounts are squared. Until they get that satisfaction they are in a state of emotional tension, and hence unhappy. The instant they get it they are comfortable. I do not argue that this yearning is noble; I simply argue that it is almost universal among human beings. In the face of injuries that are unimportant and can be borne without damage it may yield to higher impulses; that is to say, it may yield to what is called Christian charity. But when the injury is serious Christianity is adjourned, and even saints reach for their sidearms. It is plainly asking too much of human nature to expect it to conquer so natural an impulse. A keeps a store and has a bookkeeper, B. B steals $700, employs it in playing at dice or bingo, and is cleaned out. What is A to do? Let B go? If he does so he will be unable to sleep at night. The sense of injury, of injustice, of frustration will haunt him like pruritus. So he turns B over to the police, and they hustle B to prison. Thereafter A can sleep. More, he has pleasant dreams. He pictures B chained to the wall of a dungeon a hundred feet underground, devoured by rats and scorpions. It is so agreeable that it makes him forget his $700. He has got his *katharsis*.

The same thing precisely takes place on a larger scale when there is a crime   5 which destroys a whole community's sense of security. Every law-abiding citizen feels menaced and frustrated until the criminals have been struck down — until the communal capacity to get even with them, and more than even, has been dramatically demonstrated. Here, manifestly, the business of deterring others is no more than an afterthought. The main thing is to destroy the concrete scoundrels whose act has alarmed everyone, and thus made everyone unhappy. Until they are brought to book that unhappiness continues; when the law has been executed upon them there is a sigh of relief. In other words, there is *katharsis*.

I know of no public demand for the death penalty for ordinary crimes, even for ordinary homicides. Its infliction would shock all men of normal decency of feeling. But for crimes involving the deliberate and inexcusable taking of human life, by men openly defiant of all civilized order — for such crimes it seems, to nine men out of ten, a just and proper punishment. Any lesser penalty leaves them feeling that the criminal has got the better of society — that he is free to add insult to injury by laughing. That feeling can be dissipated only by a recourse to *katharsis,* the invention of the aforesaid Aristotle. It is more effectively and economically achieved, as human nature now is, by wafting the criminal to realms of bliss.

The real objection to capital punishment doesn't lie against the actual extermination of the condemned, but against our brutal American habit of putting it off so long. After all, every one of us must die soon or late, and a murderer, it must be assumed, is one who makes that sad fact the cornerstone of his meta-physic. But it is one thing to die, and quite another thing to lie for long months and even years under the shadow of death. No sane man would choose such a finish. All of us, despite the Prayer Book, long for a swift and unexpected end. Unhappily, a murderer, under the irrational American system, is tortured for what, to him, must seem a whole series of eternities. For months on end he sits in prison while his lawyers carry on their idiotic buffoonery with writs, injunctions, mandamuses, and appeals. In order to get his money (or that of his friends) they have to feed him with hope. Now and then, by the imbecility of a judge or some trick of juridic science, they actually justify it. But let us say that, his money all gone, they finally throw up their hands. Their client is now ready for the rope or the chair. But he must still wait for months before it fetches him.

That wait, I believe, is horribly cruel. I have seen more than one man sitting in the death-house, and I don't want to see any more. Worse, it is wholly useless. Why should he wait at all? Why not hang him the day after the last court dissipates his last hope? Why torture him as not even cannibals would torture their victims? The common answer is that he must have time to make his peace with God. But how long does that take? It may be accomplished, I believe, in two hours quite as comfortably as in two years. There are, indeed, no temporal limitations upon God. He could forgive a whole herd of murderers in a millionth of a second. More, it has been done.

Death by Choice: Who Should Decide?

DANIEL C. MAGUIRE

WHO WOULD DARE arrogate to himself the decision to impose death on a child or unconscious person who is not in a position to assent or dissent to the action? What right does any person have to make decisions about life and death in a way that assumes absolute and ultimate authority over another human being? Could a doctor make such a decision? It would seem that he could not. His medical skills are one thing, the moral decision to end a life is another. How would a family feel who learned that a doctor had reached an independent decision to terminate their father's life?

Could the family make such a decision? It would seem not, for several good reasons. There might be a conflict of interest arising from avarice, spite, or impatience with the illness of the patient. And even if these things were not present, the family might be emotionally traumatized when their pain of loss is complicated by the recollection of their decision. Also, the family might constitute a split and therefore a hung jury. Then what?

Could a court-appointed committee of impartial persons make the decision? No, it would seem not. They would not only be impartial but also uninformed about the personal realities of the patient. The decision to terminate life requires a full and intimate knowledge of all the reality-constituting circumstances of the case. Strangers would not have this.

The conclusion, therefore, would seem inescapable that there is no moral way in which death could be imposed on a person who is incapable of consent because of youth or irreversible loss of consciousness.

This objection contains so much truth that my reply to it will contain much   5
agreement as well as disagreement. To begin with, it should be noted that we are discussing not the legality but the morality of terminating life without the consent of the patient. Terminating life by a deliberate act of commission in the kinds of cases here discussed is illegal in this country. By an ongoing fiction of American law it would be classified as murder in the first degree. Terminating by calculated omission is murky at best and perilous at worst under current law. Therefore, it can be presumed that any conclusion we reach here will probably be illegal. This is a morally relevant fact; it is not to be presumed morally decisive, however, since there may be good moral grounds to assume the risk or illegality. As we have stated, morality and legality are not identical.

With this said, then, let us face up to the objection. There are two parts to my response. First, holding the question of who should decide in abeyance for the moment, I would suggest that there are cases where, if that difficult question could be satisfactorily answered, it would seem to be a morally good option (among other morally good options) to terminate a life. In other words, there are cases where the termination of a life could be defended as a moral good if the proper authority for making the decision could be located. Of course, if the objections raised against all those who could decide are decisive, then this otherwise morally desirable act would be immoral by reason of improper agency.

There are cases where it would appear to be arguably moral to take the necessary action (or to make the necessary omission) to end a life. Dr. Ruth Russell tells this story:

> I used to annually take a class of senior students in abnormal psychology to visit the hospital ward in a training school for medical defectives. There was a little boy about 4 years old the first time we visited him in the hospital. He was a hydrocephalic with a head so immensely large that he had never been able to raise it off the pillow and he never would. He had a tiny little body with this huge head and it is very difficult to keep him from developing sores. The students asked, "Why do we keep a child like that alive?"
>
> The next year we went back with another class. This year the child's hands had been padded to keep him from hitting his head. Again the students asked, "Why do we do this?" The third year we went back and visited the same child. Now the nurses explained that he had been hitting his head so hard that in spite of the padding he was injuring it severely and they had tied his arms down to the sides of his crib.[1]

---

[1] See *Dilemmas of Euthanasia*, a pamphlet containing excerpts, papers and discussions from the Fourth Euthanasia Conference, held in New York on December 4, 1971; this is a publication of the Euthanasia Educational Council, Inc. [now called Concern for Dying], New York, p. 35.

What are the defensible moral options in this kind of case? One might be to keep the child alive in the way that was being done. This might show a great reverence for life and re-enforce society's commitment to weak and defective human life. It may indeed be the hallmark of advancing civilization that continuing care would be taken of this child. Termination of this child's life by omission or commission might set us on the slippery slope that has led other societies to the mass murder of physically and mentally defective persons.

All of this is possibly true but it is by no means self-evidently true to the point that other alternatives are apodictically excluded. This case is a singularly drastic one. Given its special qualities, action to end life here is not necessarily going to precipitate the killing of persons in distinguishably different circumstances.

Furthermore, keeping this child alive might exemplify the materialistic error 10 interpreting the sanctity of life in merely physical terms. This interpretation, of course, is a stark oversimplification. It is just as wrong as the other side of the simplistic coin, which would say that life has no value until it attains a capacity for distinctively personal acts such as intellectual knowledge, love, and imagination. A fetus, while not yet capable of intellectual and other distinctively personal activity, is on a trajectory toward personhood and already shares in the sanctity of human life. (This does not mean that it may never be terminated when other sacred values out-weigh its claim to life in a conflict situation.)

The sanctity of life is a generic notion that does not yield a precisely spelled-out code of ethics. Deciding what the sanctity of life requires in conflict situations such as the case of the hydrocephalic child described by Dr. Russell, may lead persons to contradictory judgments. To say that the sanctity of life requires keeping that child alive regardless of his condition and that all other alternatives impeach the perception of life as sacred, is both arrogant and epistemologically unsound. In this case, maintaining this child in this condition might be incompatible with its sacred human dignity. It might not meet the minimal needs of human physical existence. In different terms, the sanctity of death might here take precedence over a physicalist interpretation of the sanctity of life. There is a time when human death befits human life, when nothing is more germane to the person's current needs. This conclusion appears defensible in the case of the hydrocephalic boy.

Also, to keep this child alive to manifest and maintain society's respect for life appears to be an unacceptable reduction of this child to the status of means. Society should be able to admit the value of death in this case and still maintain its respect for life. Our reverence for life should not be dependent on this sort of martyrdom.

The decision, therefore, that it is morally desirable to bring on this boy's death is a defensible conclusion from the facts and prognosis of this case. (We are still holding in abeyance the question of who should make that decision.) There are two courses of action that could flow from that decision. The decision could be made to stop all special medication and treatment and limit care to nourishment, or the decision could be made in the light of all circumstances to take more direct action to induce death.

There is another case, a famous one . . . , where the life of a radically deformed child was ended. This is the tragic case of Corinne van de Put, who was a victim of thalidomide, a drug that interfered with the limb buds between the sixth and eighth weeks of pregnancy. Corinne was born on May 11, 1962, with no arms or shoulder structure and with deformed feet. It would not even be possible to fit the child with artificial limbs since there was no shoulder structure, but only cartilage. Some experts said the chances for survival were one in ten and Dr. Hoet, a professor of pathological embryology at the Catholic University of Louvain, was of the opinion that the child had only a year or two to live. Eight days after the baby was born, the mother Madame Suzanne van de Put, mixed barbiturates with water and honey in the baby's bottle and thus killed her daughter.

During the trial, Madame van de Put was asked why she had not followed 15 the gynecologist's advice to put the child in a home. "I did not want it," she replied. "Absolutely not. For me, as an egoist, I could have been rid of her. But it wouldn't have given her back her arms." The president of the court pointed out that the child appeared to be mentally normal. "That was only worse," said Madame van de Put. "If she had grown up to realize the state she was in, she would never have forgiven me for letting her live."[2]

Is Madame van de Put's decision to be seen as one of the several morally defensible options available in this case? I think that it is. Again, this does not say that other solutions have no moral probability. As Norman St. John-Stevas points out in his discussion of this case, there are individuals who, though terribly disadvantaged, live fruitful and apparently happy lives. He speaks of Arthur Kavanagh, who was born in 1831 without limbs. No mechanical mechanism could be devised to help him. According to St. John-Stevas, however, Kavanagh managed to achieve some mystifying successes.

> Yet throughout his life he rode and drove, traveled widely, shot and fished. From 1868 until 1880 he sat as member for Carlow and spoke in the Commons. In addition, he was a magistrate, a grand juror, a poor-law guardian, and he organized a body to defend the rights of landlords.[3]

St. John-Stevas, however, does admit that "Not everyone can be an Arthur Kavanagh. . . ." Neither could everyone be a Helen Keller. The problem is that no one knows this when these decisions are made. The option to let the person live and find out is not necessarily safe. The person may not have the resources of a Kavanagh or a Keller and may rue both the day of birth and the decision to let him live. As Madame van de Put said, Corinne may "never have forgiven me for letting her live." The decision to let live is not inherently safe. It may be a decision for a personal disaster. There are persons living who have found their

---

[2] For an account of this case and a negative judgment on Madame van de Put's action, see Norman St. John-Stevas, *The Right to Life* (New York: Holt, Rinehart & Winston, 1964), pp. 3–24.
[3] Ibid., p. 16.

lives a horror, who do not think they have the moral freedom to end their lives, and who ardently wish someone had ended life for them before they reached consciousness. It is little consolation to these people to be told that they were let live on the chance that they might have been a Beethoven. The presumption that the decision to let live will have a happy moral ending is gratuitous and is not a pat solution to the moral quandary presented by such cases.

Interestingly, in the van de Put case, the defense counsel told the jury that he did not think Madame van de Put's solution was the only one, but that it was not possible to condemn her for having chosen it.[4] It could have been moral also to muster all possible resources of imagination and affection and give Corinne the ability to transcend her considerable impairments and achieve fullness of life. In this very unclear situation, this could have been a defensible option. It was not, however, one without risks. It could have proved itself wrong.

The decision to end Corinne's life was also arguably moral, though, again, not without risks. It could not be called immoral on the grounds that it is better to live than not to live regardless of the meaning of that life. This is again a physicalist interpretation of the sanctity of life. It also could not be called immoral on the grounds that this kind of killing is likely to spill over and be used against unwanted children, etc., since this case has its own distinguishing characteristics which make it quite exceptional. It could not be called immoral because it is direct killing since . . . the issue is not directness or indirectness, but whether there is proportionate reason.

In this case, then, as in the case of the hydrocephalic boy, we have a situation where the imposition of death could seem a moral good, prescinding still from the question of who should decide. There could be other cases, too, where death could be seen as a good. Suppose someone suffers severe cerebral damage in an accident but due to continuing brainstem activity can be kept alive almost indefinitely through tubal nourishing and other supportive measures. Would it not seem a clear good if a decision could be made to withdraw support and allow death to have its final say? The spectacle of living with the breathing but depersonalized remains of a loved one could make death seem a needed blessing. In conclusion, then, there are cases where the imposition of death would seem a good. It was logically indicated to state that conclusion before going to the main thrust of the objection, the question of who could decide when the person in question can give no consent.

20

[4] Ibid., pp. 7–8.

Moral and Ethical Dilemmas in the Special-Care Nursery

RAYMOND S. DUFF and A.G.M. CAMPBELL

ABSTRACT. Of 299 consecutive deaths occurring in a special-care nursery, 43 (14 percent) were related to withholding treatment. In this group were 15 with multiple anomalies, eight with trisomy, eight with cardiopulmonary disease, seven with meningomyelocele, three with other central-nervous system disorders, and two with short-bowel syndrome. After careful consideration of each of these 43 infants, parents and physicians in a group decision concluded that prognosis for meaningful life was extremely poor or hopeless, and therefore rejected further treatment. The awesome finality of these decisions, combined with a potential for error in prognosis, made the choice agonizing for families and health professionals. Nevertheless, the issue has to be faced, for not to decide is an arbitrary and potentially devastating decision of default.

(N. ENGL. J. MED. 289: 890–894, 1973)

D ISCUSSION. That decisions are made not to treat severely defective infants   1
may be no surprise to those familiar with special-care facilities. All laymen
and professionals familiar with our nursery appeared to set some limits upon their
application of treatment to extend life or to investigate a pathologic process. For
example, an experienced nurse said about one child, "We lost him several weeks
ago. Isn't it time to quit?" In another case, a house officer said to a physician
investigating an aspect of a child's disease, "For this child, don't you think it's
time to turn off your curiosity so you can turn on your kindness?" Like many
others, these children eventually acquired the "right to die."

Arguments among staff members and families for and against such decisions
were based on varied notions of the rights and interests of defective infants, their
families professionals and society. They were also related to varying ideas about
prognosis. Regarding the infants, some contended that individuals should have
a right to die in some circumstances such as anencephaly, hydranencephaly, and
some severely deforming and incapacitating conditions. Such very defective individuals were considered to have little or no hope of achieving meaningful "humanhood."[1] For example, they have little or no capacity to love or be loved.
They are often cared for in facilities that have been characterized as "hardly more
than dying bins,"[2] an assessment with which, in our experience, knowledgeable
parents (those who visited chronic-care facilities for placement of their children)
agreed. With institutionalized well children, social participation may be essen-

---

[1] J. Fletcher, Indicators of humanhood: A tentative profile of man, *The Hastings Center Report*,
2, no. 5 (Hastings-on-Hudson, N.Y., Institute of Society, Ethics and the Life Sciences, November 1972), pp. 1–4.
[2] H. E. Freeman, O. G. Brim, Jr., G. Williams, *New dimensions of dying. The dying patient*,
edited by O. G. Brim, Jr. (New York: Russell Sage Foundation, 1970), pp. xii–xxvi.

tially nonexistent, and maternal deprivation severe; this is known to have an adverse, usually disastrous, effect upon the child.[3] The situation for the defective child is probably worse, for he is restricted socially both by his need for care and by his defects. To escape "wrongful life,"[4] a fate rated as worse than death, seemed right. In this regard, Lasagna[5] notes, "We may, as a society, scorn the civilizations that slaughtered their infants, but our present treatment of the retarded is in some ways more cruel."

Others considered allowing a child to die wrong for several reasons. The person most involved, the infant, had no voice in the decision. Prognosis was not always exact, and a few children with extensive care might live for months, and occasionally years. Some might survive and function satisfactorily. To a few persons, withholding treatment and accepting death was condemned as criminal.

Families had strong but mixed feelings about management decisions. Living with the handicapped is clearly a family affair, and families of deformed infants thought there were limits to what they could bear or should be expected to bear. Most of them wanted maximal efforts to sustain life and to rehabilitate the handicapped; in such cases, they were supported fully. However, some families, especially those having children with severe defects, feared that they and their other children would become socially enslaved, economically deprived, and permanently stigmatized, all perhaps for a lost cause. Such a state of "chronic sorrow" until death has been described by Olshansky.[6] In some cases, families considered the death of the child right both for the child and for the family. They asked if that choice could be theirs or their doctor's.

As Feifel has reported,[7] physicians on the whole are reluctant to deal with the issues. Some, particularly specialists based in the medical center, gave specific reasons for this disinclination. There was a feeling that to "give up" was disloyal to the cause of the profession. Since major research, teaching and patient-care efforts were being made, professionals were expected to discover, transmit and apply knowledge and skills; patients and families were supposed to co-operate fully even if they were not always grateful. Some physicians recognized that the wishes of families went against their own, but they were resolute. They commonly agreed that if they were the parents of very defective children, withholding treatment would be most desirable for them. However, they argued that aggressive management was indicated for others. Some believed that allowing death as a management option was euthanasia and must be stopped for fear of setting a "poor ethical example" or for fear of personal prosecution or damage to their clinical departments or to the medical center as a whole. Alexander's

5

[3] R. A. Spitz, Hospitalism: An inquiry into the gensis of psychiatric conditions in early childhood, *Psychoanal. Study Child,* I: 53–74, 1945.
[4] H. T. Engelhardt, Euthanasia and children: The injury of continued existence. *J. Pediatr.,* 83: 170–171, 1973.
[5] L. Lasagna, *Life, death, and the doctor* (New York: Alfred A. Knopf, 1968).
[6] S. Olshansky, Chronic sorrow: A response to having a mentally defective child, *Soc. Casework,* 43: 190–193, 1962.
[7] H. Feifel, Perception of death, *Ann. N.Y. Acad. Sci. 164:* 669–677, 1969.

report on Nazi Germany[8] was cited in some cases as providing justification for pressing the effort to combat disease. Some persons were concerned about the loss through death of "teaching material." They feared the training of professionals for the care of defective children in the future and the advancing of the state of the art would be compromised. Some parents who became aware of this concern thought their children should not become experimental subjects. . . .

Is it possible that some physicians and some families may join in a conspiracy to deny the right of a defective child to live or to die? Either could occur. Prolongation of the dying process by resident physicians having a vested interest in their careers has been described by Sudnow.[9] On the other hand, from the fatigue of working long and hard some physicians may give up too soon, assuming that their cause is lost. Families, similarly, may have mixed motives. They may demand death to obtain relief from the high costs and the tensions inherent in suffering, but their sense of guilt in this thought may produce the opposite demand, perhaps in violation of the sick person's rights. Thus, the challenge of deciding what course to take can be most tormenting for the family and the physician. Unquestionably, not facing the issue would appear to be the easier course, at least temporarily; no doubt many patients, families, and physicians decline to join in an effort to solve the problems. They can readily assume that what is being done is right and sufficient and ask no questions. But pretending there is no decision to be made is an arbitrary and potentially devastating decision of default. Since families and patients must live with the problems one way or another in any case, the physician's failure to face the issues may constitute a victimizing abandonment of patients and their families in times of greatest need. As Lasagna[10] pointed out, "There is no place for the physician to hide."

Can families in the shock resulting from the birth of a defective child understand what faces them? Can they give truly "informed consent" for treatment or withholding treatment? Some of our colleagues answer no to both questions. In our opinion, if families regardless of background are heard sympathetically and at length and are given information and answers to their questions in words they understand, the problems of their children as well as the expected benefits and limits of any proposed care can be understood clearly in practically all instances. Parents *are* able to understand the implications of such things as chronic dyspnea, oxygen dependency, incontinence, paralysis, contractures, sexual handicaps and mental retardation.

Another problem concerns who decides for a child. It may be acceptable for a person to reject treatment and bring about his own death. But it is quite a different situation when others are doing this for him. We do not know how often families and their physicians will make just decisions for severely handicapped children. Clearly, this issue is central in evaluation of the process of deci-

[8] L. Alexander, Medical science under dictatorship. *N. Engl. J. Med. 241:* 39–47, 1949.
[9] D. Sudnow, *Passing on* (Englewood Cliffs, N.J. Prentice-Hall, 1967).
[10] Lasagna, *Life, death, and the doctor.*

sion making that we have described. But we also ask, if these parties cannot make such decisions justly, who can?

We recognize great variability and often much uncertainty in prognoses and in family capacities to deal with defective newborn infants. We also acknowledge that there are limits of support that society can or will give to assist handicapped persons and their families. Severely deforming conditions that are associated with little or no hope of a functional existence pose painful dilemmas for the laymen and professionals who must decide how to cope with severe handicaps. We believe the burdens of decision making must be borne by families and their professional advisers because they are most familiar with the respective situations. Since families primarily must live with and are most affected by the decisions, it therefore appears that society and the health professions should provide only general guidelines for decision making. Moreover, since variations between situations are so great, and the situations themselves so complex, it follows that much latitude in decision making should be expected and tolerated. Otherwise, the rules of society or the policies most convenient for medical technologists may become cruel masters of human beings instead of their servants. Regarding any "allocation of death"[11] policy we readily acknowledge that the extreme excesses of Hegelian "rational utility" under dictatorships must be avoided. Perhaps it is less recognized that the uncontrolled application of medical technology may be detrimental to individuals and families. In this regard, our views are similar to those of Waitzkin and Stoekle.[12] Physicians may hold excessive power over decision making by limiting or controlling the information made available to patients or families. It seems appropriate that the profession be held accountable for presenting fully all management options and their expected consequences. Also, the public should be aware that professionals often face conflicts of interest that may result in decisions against individual preferences.

What are the legal implications of actions like those described in this paper? Some persons may argue that the law has been broken, and others would contend otherwise. Perhaps more than anything else, the public and professional silence on a major social taboo and some common practices has been broken further. That seems appropriate, for out of the ensuing dialogue perhaps better choices for patients and families can be made. If working out these dilemmas in ways such as those we suggest is in violation of the law, we believe the law should be changed.

[11] B. Manning, *Legal and policy issues in the allocation of death. The dying patient,* edited by O. G. Brim, Jr. (New York: Russell Sage Foundation, 1970), pp. 253–274.
[12] H. Waitzkin and J. D. Stoeckle. The communication of information about illness, *Adv. Psychosom. Med., 8:* 180–215, 1972.

Appendix A
Electronic Communities

▪ ▪ E-MAIL AND ELECTRONIC CONFERENCES

In an e-mail address, the first part is the person's name or password. This is followed by the "at" symbol "@." What follows "@" is the address or site of the host computer, the computer that your computer links up with to deliver the message. A "gov" ending is short for "government." University addresses end in "edu." Commercial Internet providers such as America On-line or Compuserve have addresses that end in "com." Some addresses use the ending "bitnet" to identify the type of network that address belongs to, but more and more systems are switching from the "bitnet" designation to one of the Internet forms.

To join an electronic discussion, you need to know two addresses. The first address is the server address, the address used to subscribe to the discussion list. It executes computer commands. You generally subscribe by sending the following message to the server address:

subscribe [list name] [your name]

Here is an example. ACTIV-L is a list for political activism on college campuses. Its server address is listserv@mizzou1.missouri.edu. To subscribe to ACTIV-L, you would send the following e-mail message to listserv@mizzou1.missouri.edu:

subscribe activ-l Jane Doe

The second address you need is the list address, the address used to send messages to the list. Anything sent to the list address is distributed to all the members of the list—so be careful what you send.

▩ ▩ A LIST OF ELECTRONIC CONFERENCES

The following are some discussion lists you may want to examine. There are thousands more, but I have chosen these because they provide good opportunities for observing debate and discussion of community issues. First, I provide the list address, with the server address following after a slash mark. I also give a brief description of the list. Information on these lists was current when this book went to press, but it has no doubt changed since then. For current information on Internet resources, check the most recent edition of *On Internet*, published by Meckler.

> 1996@webcom.com/1996-request@webcom.com
>   (candidates, issues, and electorate in the 1996 U.S. presidential election)
>
> activ-l@mizzoul.missouri.edu/listserv@mizzoul.missouri.edu
>   (political activism on college campuses)
>
> actnow-l@brownvm.brown.edu/listserv@brownvm.brown.edu
>   (college political activism)
>
> animal-rights@cs.odu.edu/listserv@cs.odu.edu
>   (animal rights activism)
>
> arms-l@buacca.bu.edu/listserv@buacca.bu.edu
>   (arms proliferation)
>
> biosph-l@ubvm.bitnet/listserv@ubvm.bitnet
>   (biosphere and environmental issues)
>
> campclim@uafsysb.bitnet/listserv@uafsysb.bitnet
>   (campus political environment)
>
> canada-l@mcgill1.bitnet/listserv@mcgill1.bitnet
>   (Canadian politics)
>
> centam-l@ubvm.bitnet/listserv@ubvm.bitnet
>   (Central America)
>
> conservative-action@world.std.com/majordomo@world.std.com
>   (conservative politics)
>
> current@netcom.com/listserv@netcom.com
>   (current events)
>
> dem-net-digest@webcom.com/dem-net-digest-request@webcom.com
>   (issues and personalities of the U.S. Democratic party)
>
> ecology@emuvml.bitnet/listserv@emuvml.bitnet
>   (politics and the environment)
>
> gaynet@athena.mit.edu/listserv@athena.mit.edu
>   (gay issues on campus)
>
> healthre@ukcc.bitnet/listserv@ukcc.bitnet
>   (health care reform)
>
> irl-pol@irlearn.bitnet/listserv@irlearn.bitnet
>   (Irish politics)

libernet-d-batch-list@dartmouth.edu/majordomo@dartmouth.edu
(Libertarian politics)

MN-Politics@mr.net/majordomo@mr.net
(Minnesota politics and public policy)

mopoly-l@mizzou1.missouri.edu/listserv@mizzou1.missouri.edu
(Missouri political issues)

rego-l@pandora.sf.ca.us/listserv@pandora.sf.ca.us
(reinventing government)

repub-l@vm.marist.edu/listserv@vm.marist.edu
(Republican politics)

rkba-alert@nra.org/rkba-alert-request@nra.org
(announcements from the National Rifle Association)

rushtalk@ohionet.org/rushtalk-request@ohionet.org
(conservative politics according to views of Rush Limbaugh)

statepol@umab.bitnet/listserv@umab.bitnet
(state politics)

worldgov@tomahawk.welch.jhu.edu/worldgov-
request@tomahawk.welch.jhu.edu
(world government)

▪ ▪ USENET NEWS GROUPS

Some universities provide students access to Usenet through library computer terminals or other computer systems. Usenet provides selections from Internet news groups arranged according to topic. (Check with your campus computer advisors for more information.) The following Usenet sites are concerned with public issues:

alt.politics.clinton
alt.politics.org.misc
alt.politics.reform
alt.politics.usa.misc
alt.new-media
alt.activism
talk.politics.misc
misc.activism.progressive

Appendix B

Samples of Citing and Documenting Sources

This appendix provides samples of how to document various kinds of sources, first according to the style recommended by the Modern Language Association (MLA), followed by a sample student paper, and then according to the style recommended by the American Psychological Association (APA), again followed by a sample student paper. (See pages 129–138 in Chapter 4 for general information about documenting sources and about MLA and APA style.)

In general, papers written for language and literature courses will be expected to conform to MLA style; those written for courses in the social sciences will be expected to conform to APA style. Other styles may be expected in the humanities and the biological/physical sciences. Check with your instructor to determine which style to use.

■ ■ SAMPLE ENTRIES FOR A WORKS CITED PAGE: MLA STYLE   MLA

For a more detailed discussion of MLA style, see the latest edition of the *MLA Handbook for Writers of Research Papers* or the *MLA Style Manual*.

Books

Single Author

> Bardwick, Judith M. The Plateauing Trap. New York: AMACOM,
>
> 1986.

Two or Three Authors

> Hecht, Michael L., Mary Jane Collier, and Sidney A.
>
> Ribeau. African-American Communication: Ethnic

> Identity and Cultural Interpretation. Newbury Park:
> Sage, 1993.

Names of authors after the first are not reversed.

Four or More Authors

You may cite the first author, last name first, followed by *et al.* for the remaining authors. (This Latin phrase means "and others.") You may also cite all names in the order they appear on the original work.

Editors

> Solomon, William, and Robert McChesney, eds. Ruthless
> Criticism: New Perspectives in U.S. Communication
> History. Minneapolis: U of Minnesota P, 1993.

Author with an Editor

> Austen, Jane. Mansfield Park. Ed. James Kinsley. Oxford:
> Oxford UP, 1992.

Translation

> Dinesen, Isak. On Modern Marriage and Other Observations.
> Trans. Anne Born. New York: St. Martin's, 1986.

Corporate Author

> Humane Farming Association. Bovine Growth Hormones. San
> Rafael: Humane Farming Association, 1994.

Unknown Author

> The Times Atlas of the World. 9th ed. New York: Times,
> 1992.

Two or More Works by the Same Author

> Conway, Jill Ker. The Road from Coorain. New York: Random,
> 1990.
>
> ---. True North. New York: Knopf, 1994.

List works alphabetically by title.

Edition Other Than the First

> Murray, Donald M. The Craft of Revision. 2nd ed. Fort
> Worth: Harcourt, 1995.

Multivolume Work

> Smith, Adam. The Glasgow Edition of the Works and
> Correspondence of Adam Smith. Ed. A. S. Skinner.
> 6 vols. Oxford: Oxford UP, 1983.

One Volume from a Multivolume Work

> Smith, Adam. Essays on Philosophical Subjects. Ed.
> W. P. D. Wightman. Vol. 3 of The Glasgow Edition of
> the Works and Correspondence of Adam Smith. A. S.
> Skinner, gen. ed. 6 vols. Oxford: Oxford UP, 1983.

Encyclopedia or Dictionary Entry

> "Value." Merriam-Webster's Collegiate Dictionary. 10th.
> ed. 1993.

> Dolling, W. R. "Bugs." The Encyclopedia of Insects. New
> York: Facts on File, 1986. 54-60.

Work in an Anthology

> Callen, Michael. "AIDS: The Linguistic Battlefield." The
> State of the Language. Ed. Leonard Michaels and
> Christopher Ricks. Berkeley: U of California P, 1990.
> 171-184.

Foreword, Introduction, Preface, or Afterword

> French, Marilyn. Introduction. The House of Mirth. By
> Edith Wharton. New York: Berkley, 1981. v-xxxv.

Periodicals

Article in a Monthly Magazine

> Loftus, Elizabeth. "Eyewitnesses: Essential but
> Unreliable." Psychology Today Feb. 1984: 22-27.

Article in a Weekly Magazine

> Shaheen, Jack. "The Media's Image of Arabs." Newsweek
> 29 Feb. 1988: 10.

Article in a Journal Paginated by Volume

> Madrian, Brigitte C. "Employment-Based Health Insurance
> and Job Mobility: Is There Evidence of Job-Lock?"
> Quarterly Journal of Economics 109 (1994): 27-54.

Article in a Journal Paginated by Issue

> Fotsch, Paul M. "Rap Music Resisting Resistance." Popular
> Culture Review 5.1 (1994): 57-74.

Article in a Daily Newspaper

> Ivins, Molly. "Ban the Things. Ban Them All." Fort Worth
> Star-Telegram 11 Mar. 1993: 17A.

Unsigned Article in a Magazine or Newspaper

> "Say It Ain't So, O.J." USA Today 14 June 1994: 1A.

Editorial in a Newspaper

> "Wilderness Bill Offers No Protection." Editorial. Deseret
> News 8 July 1995: A17.

Letter to the Editor

> Owens, Wayne. Letter. Deseret News 8 July 1995: A14.

CD-ROM and Online Sources

CD-ROM Issued in a Single Edition

> The Oxford English Dictionary. 1st ed. CD-ROM. Oxford:
> Oxford UP, 1987.

> "Australia." Compton's Interactive Encyclopedia. CD-ROM.
> Compton's, 1994.

Online Material from a Computer Service

> Ivins, Molly. "Ban the Things. Ban Them All." <u>Fort Worth
>   Star-Telegram</u> 11 Mar. 1993: 17A. Online. Lexis/Nexis.
>   25 Sept. 1995.

Online Material from a Computer Network

> "CBS News Coverage of Mission STS-73." Online. Internet.
>   25 Oct. 1995. Available uttm.com/space/missions/
>   current.html.

Electronic Mail (E-mail)

> Vawdrey, Steve. E-mail to the author. 25 Oct. 1995.

Legal References

If you are using a number of legal sources in your essay, consult the most recent edition of *A Uniform System of Citation* published by the Harvard Law Review Association.

> 15 US Code. Sec. 78j(b). 1964.

> US Const. Art. 1, sec. 1.

> Estes v. Texas. 381 USC 755. U.S. Supr. Ct. 1965.

Other Sources

Government Publication

> United States. Cong. Committee on Agriculture.
>   Subcommittee on Wheat, Soybeans, and Feed Grains.
>   <u>Formulation of the 1990 Farm Bill</u>. 101st Cong., 1st
>   sess. 8 vols. Washington: GPO, 1990.

Pamphlet

> <u>Shop Recycled!: A Consumer's Guide to Recycled Plastics</u>.
>   Washington: American Plastics Council, 1994.

Published Dissertation

> Schmitz, Robert M. <u>Hugh Blair</u>. Diss. Columbia U, 1936. New
>   York: King's Crown, 1936.

Unpublished Dissertation

> Thulin, Craig D. "Posttranslational Processing and Human
> Profilaggrin." Diss. U of Washington, 1995.

Abstract of a Dissertation

> Gaisford, John W. "Priorities in Health Care: A Resource
> Allocation Method and Empirical Investigation." Diss.
> U of Oregon, 1993. DAI 53 (1993): 2023A.

Published Proceedings of a Conference

> Gretel, Richard, ed. Water Quality in Boston Harbor. Conf.
> on Water Quality and Pollution, 1968, Boston.
> Washington: GPO, 1970.

Work of Art

> Hatcher, Brower. Seer. Brigham Young University Museum of
> Art, Provo.

Musical Composition

> Gershwin, George. Rhapsody in Blue.

> Beethoven, Ludwig van. Symphony no. 7 in A, op. 92.

Personal Letter

> Thulin, Craig. Letter to the author. 15 May 1995.

Lecture or Public Address

> Hallen, Cynthia. "Creating an Emily Dickinson Lexicon."
> Brigham Young University College of Humanities,
> Provo. 11 Nov. 1993.

Personal Interview

> Rifberg, Klaus. Personal interview. 12 Dec. 1995.

Published Interview

> Brooks, Gwendolyn. Interview. Literature and Belief 12
> (1992): 1-12.

Radio or Television Interview

> Welch, John W. Interview. Booktalk. KSL Radio. KSL, Salt
> Lake City. 5 June 1994.

Film or Videotape

> Tom Jones. Dir. Tony Richardson. Screenplay by John
> Osborne. Perf. Albert Finney, Susannah York, Hugh
> Griffith, Edith Evans, and Joan Greenwood. United
> Artists, 1963.

> Revising Prose. Narr. Richard Lanham. Videocassette.
> Macmillan, 1990.

Radio or Television Program

> Murphy Brown. KCBS, Los Angeles. 10 Nov. 1993.

> "Amelia Earhart." The American Experience. Narr. Kathy
> Bates. Writ./Dir. Nancy Porter. PBS. WEDU, Tampa.
> 3 Nov. 1995.

Live Performance of a Play

> The Comedy of Errors. By William Shakespeare. Dir. Marion
> Bentley. Perf. Richard Tullis, Harold Vance, Jan
> Nichols, and Phyllis Cundick. Brigham Young
> University Theatre, Provo. 10 Oct. 1995.

Sound Recording

> Handel, George. Handel's Messiah: A Soulful Celebration.
> Perf. Vanessa Bell Armstrong, Daryl Coley, Lizz Lee,
> Chris Willis, Mike E., Tramaine Hawkins, Howard
> Hewitt, Stevie Wonder, Al Jarreau, and Tevin
> Campbell. Reprise, 1992.

If recording is not a CD, the medium precedes the manufacturer's name: Audio-cassette. Reprise, 1992. Other personnel (conductor, orchestra) may be listed if pertinent.

Cartoon

> Yates, Bill. "The Small Society." Cartoon. Deseret News
>   8 July 1995: A14.

Map or Chart

> Madrid. Map. New York: Baedeker's-Prentice Hall, 1995.

Computer Software

> Myst. Computer software. Novato: Brøderbund, 1992. Windows
>   3.1, 486, CD-ROM.

Bryson 1

Will Bryson

Dr. Gideon Burton

English 312

27 November 1995

Free Press vs. Fair Trial:

The Right of a Defendant to Keep Pre-Trial Activities Private

The Constitution of the United States, along with the Bill

of Rights, provides the framework to establish the human rights

protected by the U.S. government for its citizens. Yet for all its

genius and brilliance, the Constitution is not without flaws. What

is to be done when two sections of the Constitution seemingly con-

tradict each other? This question keeps the American judicial sys-

tem busy in attempting to interpret the law fairly and accurately.

One major issue that has occupied the courts is the conflict

between the right of the accused to a fair trial and the right of

the mass media to report on the trial. Although the media has the

right to report on criminal trial proceedings, given the media's

current power it seems reasonable that a defendant should have

the right to initiate a motion to have pre-trial hearings closed

to the press and public, because doing so is the best way to ensure

that the defendant's constitutional right to an impartial jury is

protected.

The Sixth Amendment to the U.S. Constitution states, "In all

criminal prosecutions, the accused shall enjoy the right to a

speedy and public trial by an impartial jury." Some argue that

these guarantees do not include a "fair trial" because those exact

words are not explicitly mentioned in the Constitution (Donahue and

Stoner 52). Even though a "fair trial" is not specified, however,

the term is used more generally as a summary of the guarantees of

the Sixth Amendment, guarantees included for the purpose of ensur-

ing that the accused receives as fair a trial as possible. One way

the legal system helps ensure a fair trial is through pre-trial

Provide identify-
ing information in
the upper left cor-
ner of the first
page. If your in-
structor asks for
an outline, use a
separate title page
(see the sample
paper in APA style
on page 466).

Center the title.
Use a colon to
separate title and
subtitle.

Double-space
throughout. Set
top, bottom, and
side margins at
one inch. Indent
paragraphs one-
half inch, or five
spaces.

In the right-hand
corner of each
page, include
your name beside
the page number,
in case pages get
separated. Most
word processors
have a running
head feature
that can be set
up to do this
automatically.

When you quote,
paraphrase, or
summarize with-
out mentioning
the author name
in your text, in-
clude the last
name of the au-
thor (or authors)
and the page
number(s) in pa-
rentheses with no
comma in be-
tween. Note that
for a cite at the
end of a sentence,
the period fol-
lows the close
parenthesis.

453

Bryson 2

activities. Pre-trial hearings help determine whether there is just cause to criminally try one who stands accused. In these hearings, evidence against the defendant is presented and its legality is tested. If there is sufficient evidence and probable cause, the defendant is brought to trial.

Pre-trial activities occur prior to jury selection. Therefore, if pre-trial hearings are highly publicized, the ability of the court to assemble an impartial jury is endangered. Evidence obtained illegally or deemed inadmissible can become known and could bias potential jurors. Paul C. Reardon and Clifton Daniel, in their 1968 report of the American Bar Association Advisory Committee of Fair Trial and Free Press, suggest that if a defendant feels his or her Sixth Amendment rights may be violated by heavy media coverage during pre-trial hearings, he or she should be given the option of requesting that these hearings be held in the judge's chambers or in closed court (16). The judge would then rule to grant or deny this motion, depending on his or her judgment of the circumstances. If deemed appropriate, the proceedings would be held in private, and a record would be kept to be made available to the press after jury selection is completed or after the case is disposed of without a trial.

It could be argued that closing pre-trial proceedings to the public and press would constitute a dangerous breach of the First Amendment guarantee of freedom of the press. Indeed, the Supreme Court has held that the news-gathering abilities of the press must be protected in order for the rights of a free press to be guaranteed (Branzburg 681). However, the Court has also found that the Sixth Amendment right to a fair trial must be protected at almost all costs, including that of other constitutional rights. In Nebraska Press Association v. Stuart, Supreme Court Justice William Brennan said, "The right to a fair trial is essential to the preservation and enjoyment of all other rights, providing a necessary

When you mention the author's name, you need only include the page number(s) parenthetically.

The name of a court case is underlined in the body of the essay but not in parenthetical citations or on the "Works Cited" list. Underlining is preferred to italics, which may not be as clearly distinguishable.

Bryson 3

means of safeguarding personal liberties against government oppression" (586, emphasis added). According to the Sixth Amendment, the ability to face an impartial jury is essential to the right of a fair trial, and thus must be given consideration over the right of the press to have immediate access to pre-trial proceedings (586).

Perhaps one might think that keeping any information that comes from court proceedings private would violate the rights of a free press guaranteed in the First Amendment. However, if a transcript is recorded and later released to the press, then the media would still have access to the information. The argument then becomes one of the right of the press to instant information. In our contemporary world, our belief is that the faster the better, especially with such technological advances as the Internet and facsimiles to help speed news along the information superhighway.

However, when examined closely, the Constitution gives no provision to the press for immediate access to information. In Estes v. Texas, the Supreme Court found that the right to broadcast a court proceeding is not guaranteed to the press, especially when such broadcasting may interfere with the rights of the defendant. In writing the opinion of the court, Justice Clark noted that live coverage of a trial could have a negative impact on jurors, witnesses, judges (especially elected judges), and the defendant (535). Indeed, waiting to publish pre-trial information could lead to more press accuracy and reliability.

For example, in June of 1994 Nicole Brown Simpson and Ronald Goldman were murdered in Los Angeles. Immediately the media began publishing lists of evidence that would implicate Ms. Simpson's ex-husband, O.J. Simpson. Among the evidence mentioned in USA Today were a murder weapon and a bloody ski mask ("Say" 1A). Upon further investigation, no weapon or mask was found. Had USA Today waited to report on evidence until after a pre-trial hearing transcript was released, the news would have been more accurate and might have led

Underline for emphasis, but do so sparingly. If you add your own emphasis to a quotation, include the phrase "emphasis added" parenthetically at the end of the quotation.

For sources with anonymous authors, use a brief version of the title that provides clear identification of the full title on the "Works Cited" list.

to less prejudice in the minds of the public as to Simpson's guilt. This is not the first time this has happened.

In a similar case, Sheppard v. Maxwell, Dr. Sam Sheppard had been accused of the murder of his wife. The media was in a frenzy over the trial, and Dr. Sheppard was convicted in the local news- paper even before he was arraigned. The Cleveland Press ran front page editorials with such headlines as "Why Isn't Sam Sheppard in Jail?" and "Quit Stalling; Bring Him In" (Kane 10). Media coverage of the event was constant, and every bit of potential evidence was printed by the Press. In addition, names and addresses of all prospective jurors were printed, and free copies of the Press were delivered to their homes (11). Sam Sheppard was convicted of murder and spent ten years in jail before being released on a writ of habeas corpus. His case was reviewed by the U.S. Supreme Court, which found that his Sixth Amendment rights had been violated, and Sheppard was granted a new trial, in which he was acquitted. Had the pre-trial proceedings in the original action been held in the judge's chambers or in a closed courtroom, and information withheld until the selection of the jurors was complete, perhaps the first trial would have resulted in a more just decision. This could have saved ten years of Sam Sheppard's life and weeks of the court's time.

Another case in which a defendant's Sixth Amendment rights were highlighted is Gannett Co. v. DePasquale. In this case, a trial judge closed off a preliminary hearing dealing with suppression of evidence. The Supreme Court upheld the right of the judge to do so. The Court found that a trial judge could bar access to pre-trial hearings if a "reasonable probability of prejudice" would occur from allowing the public to attend (Gannett 392-3). One could argue that this reasonable probability standard was later overturned by the Supreme Court in Richmond Newspapers v. Virginia. However, in this case the court only altered its previous decision, abandoning

---

When citing additional material from a source just cited, you need only include the page number parenthetically.

Show where a summary begins by referring to the source. Show where it ends by providing parenthetical documentation.

Bryson 5

the "reasonable probability" standard in favor of a "substantial

probability of prejudice" standard. Under this new standard, it has

been held that a criminal hearing should be closed "only if spe-

cific findings are made demonstrating that . . . there is a sub-

stantial probability that the defendant's right to a fair trial

will be prejudiced by publicity that closure would prevent. . . ."

(Press Enterprise 14). Thus, the ruling remains that "the defen-

dant's right to a fair trial outweigh[s] the interests of the press

and public" (Gannett 376). It may also be argued that the Court

has upheld the right of the public to attend criminal trials and

that the right to a public trial is not the exclusive right of the

defendant. However, the Court has found in and since <u>DePasquale</u>

that the right to an open courtroom is not an absolute right, and

that pre-trial proceedings may be closed in "the interest of the

fair administration of justice" (Richmond 563). Pre-trial hearings

are separate from the actual trial, and neither the Constitution

nor any Court ruling guarantees the right of the public to attend

pre-trial activities. As long as the trial is accessible to the

public, and transcripts of pre-trial proceedings are eventually

made available, it is prudent to close pre-trial activities when

the circumstances are deemed appropriate by the presiding judge.

    Another example of a case in which the judge found it best to

close pre-trial hearings is <u>Federated Publications v. Swedberg</u>. In

this case, the judge found that the inclusion of the press would

endanger the right of the defendant to a fair trial and excluded

the press from the courtroom. The press appealed the decision to

the Supreme Court of Washington State, which upheld the judge's de-

cision. In giving the opinion of the court, Justice Rosellini said,

        While this court has found a right of the public to attend

        a pre-trial hearing . . . that right is qualified by the

        court's right and duty to see that the defendant has a

        fair trial. The court may order closure, if the objectors

---

Use ellipsis points (three spaced periods) to show where part of a quotation has been omitted. If the omission comes at the end of a sentence, use a period followed by ellipsis points.

Quotations of more than four typed lines are set off from the text and indented one inch from the left margin (or ten spaces using a typewriter). Do *not* indent the first line further to indicate that it begins a new paragraph in the original, but if a new paragraph begins later in the quotation, indent it an additional quarter inch (or three spaces).

Bryson 6

The parenthetical
citation *follows* the
final period in a
block quotation.
It is not followed
by a period.

fail to demonstrate the availability of some practical

alternative. (634)

The U.S. Supreme Court supported this decision by refusing to grant
certioari, and even though this case is law only in the State of
Washington, it sets a precedent which provides a judge the option
to order closure to protect the Sixth Amendment rights of those who
stand accused.

Returning to the O.J. Simpson murder trial, it is clear that
this case could have benefited from closed pre-trial proceedings.
The media coverage of the case was unparalleled in history. When
Mr. Simpson was arrested for the crime, his picture was on the
front page of nearly every newspaper in the country, and the coverage did not stop there. All the preliminary hearings and pre-
trial motions were broadcast live on national television. Newsweek
printed a list of thirty-four pieces of evidence that defense
attorneys wished to suppress because they were illegally obtained
(Turque et al. 23). All this publicity occurred before jury selection ever began. Even if Mr. Simpson had been convicted of the
murders, he would have had grounds for appeal based on the argument
that an impartial jury was practically impossible to find due to
the media circus that surrounded his case. Perhaps, if the pre-
trial proceedings had been closed, even more outrageous rumors and
stories about evidence would have surfaced. Unethical journalists
might have gone to unknown lengths to get a scoop. However, such
practices would probably have been limited to sensational tabloids,
and stories in such publications would have had less effect on potential jurors than a list of possible illegal evidence published
in such a respected news magazine as Newsweek. Surely, if the pre-
trial hearings and motions to suppress evidence had been held behind closed doors, the interest of justice would have been better
served.

It could be argued that despite heavy media coverage, impartial

Bryson 7

jurors have been found in many cases, including the Mike Tyson and William Kennedy Smith rape trials, the Manuel Noriega drug case, and the trial of Los Angeles police officers in connection with the beating of Rodney King, among others (Litt 380). However, the jury selection process tends to produce uneducated jurors, resulting in easily persuaded juries and other problems. Mark Twain, in a criticism of the judicial process, told a story of jury selection in which anyone who had read or heard about the trial was automatically disqualified for jury duty. The jury ended up consisting of "two desperadoes, two low beer-house politicians, three barkeepers, two [illiterate] ranchmen and three dull, stupid, human donkeys. It actually came out afterwards that one of these latter thought that incest and arson were the same thing" (qtd. in Gillmour 485). Although the jurors selected for modern trials may not be ignorant to this extent, the problems addressed by Twain still exist. In the O.J. Simpson trial, over half of the jurors were not high school graduates, and Judge Lance Ito had problems keeping jurors; five were dismissed and only four alternates ultimately remained. Experts worried that the jury pool would run out and a mistrial would result (O.J. Simpson). In any case, if the jury had returned a guilty verdict, the problems experienced with jury members would probably have provided grounds for an appeal of the verdict. If the press were to be controlled until a jury was selected, perhaps there would be fewer problems finding and maintaining an impartial jury.

Of course, one could also argue that unless the press has access to pre-trial activities, secrecy and cover-ups could occur that might endanger the very rights a closed pre-trial is designed to protect. However, it should be remembered that the merits of a motion to close pre-trial activities would be left to the discretion of the judge, and a record of all proceedings would be kept for release to the press after jury selection. Many trials that

Use brackets to indicate any changes or additions you make in a quotation and to insert brief explanatory comments, if necessary.

Note that no period is necessary immediately following an in-text quotation; the period follows the parenthetical citation.

A brief title may be used to refer to a television program.

have been surrounded in controversy over the question of the right to a fair trial could have been much less so had pre-trial activities occurred in private.

    The conflict between the rights of a free press and the right to a fair trial is not a new one. The problem has been the subject of debate and court cases from the time the Constitution was written. A solution may be impossible to find. However, by limiting access to pre-trial hearings in appropriate situations, the interest of justice can be better served than it is under the present system of mass media hype which has led to "trial by newspaper" rather than "trial by jury" in so many instances.

Bryson 9

Works Cited

Branzburg v. Hayes. 404 USC 665. U.S. Supr. Ct. 1972.

Donahue, Hugh Carter, and Kevin R. Stoner. "Publication Delayed Is Justice Denied." Editor and Publsher 22 Dec. 1990: 52.

Estes v. Texas. 381 USC 532. U.S. Supr. Ct. 1965.

Federated Publications v. Swedberg. 7 Media Law Reporter 1865. WA St. Supr. Ct. 1981.

Gannett Co. v. DePasquale. 443 USC 368. U.S. Supr. Ct. 1979.

Gillmour, Donald M., and Jerome A. Barron. Mass Communication Law: Cases and Comment. St. Paul: West, 1984.

Kane, Peter E. Murder, Courts, and the Press: Issues in Free Press/ Fair Trial. Carbondale: Southern Illinois UP, 1982.

Litt, Marc O. "'Citizen Soldiers' if Anonymous Justice: Reconciling the Sixth Amendment Right of the Accused, the First Amendment Right of the Media and the Privacy Right of Jurors." Columbia Journal of Law and Social Problems 25.3 (1992): 371-421.

Nebraska Press Association v. Stuart. 427 USC 539. U.S. Supr. Ct. 1976.

O.J. Simpson on Trial. Cable News Network. 13 Apr. 1995.

Press-Enterprise v. Superior Court. 478 USC 1. U.S. Supr. Ct. 1986.

Reardon, Paul C., and Clifton Daniel. Fair Trial and Free Press. Washington: American Institute for Public Policy Research, 1968.

Richmond Newspapers, Inc. v. Virginia. 448 USC 555. U.S. Supr. Ct. 1980.

"Say It Ain't So, O.J." USA Today 14 June 1994: 1A.

Sheppard v. Maxwell. 384 USC 333. U.S. Supr. Ct. 1966.

Turque, Bill, Mark Miller, Andrew Murr, Jim Crogan, and Tim Pryor. "Body of Evidence." Newsweek 11 July 1994: 20-4.

Full bibliographic information for each source cited is included on a separate "Works Cited" page, which, like the rest of the paper, is double-spaced throughout. Entries are listed alphabetically by authors' last names (or the first main word in titles, for entries with no author). The first line of each entry is flush with the right margin; subsequent lines for the entry indent one-half inch, or five spaces. See pages 445–452 for MLA guidelines regarding the information required and the format for specific types of sources.

▪ ▪ **SAMPLE ENTRIES FOR A REFERENCES PAGE: APA STYLE**

For a more detailed discussion of APA style, see the most recent edition of the *Publication Manual of the American Psychological Association.* (Note that the student format recommended by the APA differs somewhat from that required for papers being submitted for publication.)

Books

Single Author

> Bardwick, J. M. (1986). The plateauing trap. New York: AMACOM.

Note that initials are used for the author's first and second names and that the date follows before the title.

Two or More Authors

> Hecht, M. L., Collier, M. J., & Ribeau, S. A. (1993). African-American communication: Ethnic identity and cultural interpretation. Newbury Park, CA: Sage.

In titles and subtitles, only initial words and proper nouns are capitalized.

Editors

> Solomon, W., & McChesney, R. (Eds.). (1993). Ruthless criticism: New perspectives in U.S. communication history. Minneapolis: University of Minnesota Press.

Corporate Author

> Humane Farming Association. (1993). Bovine growth hormones. San Rafael, CA: Author.

An Article or Chapter in an Edited Book

> Callen, Michael. (1990). AIDS: The linguistic battlefield. In L. Michaels & C. Ricks (Eds.), The state of the language (pp. 171-184). Berkeley: University of California Press.

Unknown Author

> The Times atlas of the world (9th ed.). (1992). New York: Times Books.

Two or More Works by the Same Author

> Conway, J. K. (1990). The road from Coorain. New York: Random House.

> Conway, J. K. (1994). True north. New York: A. A. Knopf.

List works by date of publication, earlier date first. For two or more works by the same author in the same year, add lowercase letters following the year, beginning with *a:* (1990a), (1990b), and so on; works by the same author in the same year are listed alphabetically by title.

Edition Other Than the First

> Murray, D. M. (1995). The craft of revision (2nd ed.). Fort Worth, TX: Harcourt Brace.

Translation

> Dinesen, I. (1985). On modern marriage and other observations (Anne Born, Trans.). New York: St. Martin's. (Original work published in 1981)

Encyclopedia Entry

> Dolling, W. R. (1986). Bugs. In The encyclopedia of insects (Vol. 2, pp. 54-60). New York: Facts on File.

Periodicals

Article in a Magazine

> Lopez, B. (1995, October). On the wings of commerce. Harpers, 291, 39-54.

> Gordimer, N. (1995, October 5). Adam's rib. The New York Review of Books, XLII, 28-29.

Include volume number, where available.

Article in a Journal Paginated by Volume

> Madrian, B. C. (1994). Employment-based health insurance and job mobility: Is there evidence of job-lock? Quarterly Journal of Economics, 109, 27-54.

Article in a Journal Paginated by Issue

> Fotsch, P. M. (1994). Rap music resisting resistance. Popular Culture Review, 5(1), 57-74.

Article in a Daily Newspaper

> Ivins, M. (1993, March 11). Ban the things. Ban them all. Fort Worth Star-Telegram, p. 17A.

Unsigned Article in a Magazine or Newspaper

> Say it ain't so, O.J. (1994, June 14). USA Today, p. 1A.

Letter to the Editor

> Owens, W. (1995, July 8). Wilderness bill offers no protection [Letter to the editor]. Deseret News, p. A14.

Other Sources

Government Publication

> U.S. Congress. House Committee on Agriculture, Subcommittee on Wheat, Soybeans, and Feed Grains. (August 1990). Formulation of the 1990 farm bill (101st Cong., 1st sess.) Washington, DC: U.S. Government Printing Office.

Pamphlet

> American Plastics Council. (1994). Shop recycled!: A consumer's guide to recycled plastics [Brochure]. Washington, DC: Author.

Unpublished Dissertation

> Thulin, C. D. (1995). Posttranslational processing and human profilaggrin. Unpublished doctoral dissertation, University of Washington, Seattle.

Lectures, Speeches, and Addresses

> Bizzell, P. (1985, March). Separation and resistance in academic discourse. Paper presented at the annual

meeting of the Conference on College Composition and Communication, Minneapolis, MN.

Unpublished Paper

Jones, R. L. (1989). Treating long-term depression. Unpublished manuscript.

ERIC Microfilm Document

Hansen, K. (1987). Relationships between expert and novice performance in disciplinary writing and reading. (Report No. 2). East Lansing, MI: National Center for Research on Teacher Learning. (ERIC Document Reproduction Service No. ED 283 220)

Computer Software

Myst [Computer software]. (1992). Novato, CA: Brøderbund.

Videotape

National Geographic Society (Producer). (1987). In the shadow of Vesuvius [Videotape]. Washington, DC: National Geographic Society.

Television Broadcast

Porter, N. (1993). Amelia Earhart (N. Porter, Director). In J. Crichton (Producer), The American experience. Boston: WGBH.

For individual episodes of a series, list by writer's name; otherwise, list by the series producer's name: Crichton, J. (Producer). If pertinent, cite complete date of broadcast; otherwise, cite year of production.

Provide identify-
ing information
on a separate title
page. Note that
the running head
(in the upper left
corner through-
out) includes a
short title along
with the page
number. Most
word processors
include a feature
for setting up
such heads.

Children Testifying in Sexual Abuse Trials:
Right to Emotional Safety vs. Right to Confrontation

Jessica Miskin

English 315

April 13, 1993

Abstract

As the incidence of child sexual abuse increases, so do concerns about having child victims testify in court against the alleged perpetrators of their abuse. The Sixth Amendment guarantees that the accused shall have the right to face the accuser; but when the accuser is a child, the trauma of facing the perpetrator may seriously impair the child's ability to give complete and credible testimony and may further hinder the child's recovery from the abuse. Because of these stresses, courts should seriously consider allowing children to use alternate methods of testimony, such as videotaped interviews and interviews using closed-circuit television or one-way screens. Although most courts have been reluctant to allow these methods, and although in some cases their use has been disallowed on appeal, the Supreme Court held in Maryland vs. Craig that "the Confrontation Clause does not prohibit the use of a procedure that, despite the absense of face-to-face confrontation, ensures the reliability of the evidence" (cited in Goodman, et al., 1991, p. 15). Therefore, when all the issues are weighed, society's responsibility to protect children from harm should have priority over protecting the accused's rights to confront the accuser.

APA style requires an abstract, or brief summary of the main ideas of the paper, on a separate page following the title page. It should be accurate, self-contained, and specific. Some instructors may not require an abstract.

Children Testifying in Sexual Abuse Trials:

Right to Emotional Safety vs. Right to Confrontation

    Child sexual abuse has existed at least since Biblical times, but in recent years reports of such abuse have grown dramatically, with the number of reported cases increasing by 593% over the last 10 years (S. Norton, personal communication, January 15, 1993). It is impossible to know whether this is because the number of incidents is actually increasing or because people are just more willing than before to talk about the abuse. Experts in the field of social work vote both ways. But whatever the reason, caseworkers are swamped. Just four years ago in Utah County, workers only had fifteen cases each. Now the number is up to twenty-five per worker (B. Peterson, personal communication, February 5, 1993), and the number of workers has doubled from six to twelve (D. Crowley, personal communication, February 12, 1993).

    With the increased number of reported cases also comes an increased number of trials, and hence an increased number of children who must testify. In the past, children had no options but to testify in person. The Sixth Amendment mandates that the accused has the right to face the accuser, and in sexual abuse cases the accuser is the child. However, there has been much controversy in the past ten years about such children testifying in court. The court systems have historically been adult-oriented and were not prepared for the large number of children who have entered them. Recently it has been suggested that adjustments are necessary to accommodate these young witnesses.

    While quite a few children are capable of testifying live without serious trauma, some children will experience great emotional harm if they aren't protected (Goodman, Levine, Melton, & Ogdens, 1991). The court may not arrive at the truth because of this harm. If children fear testifying, they may refuse to do so altogether.

Margin notes (left column):

Leave margins of at least one inch at top, sides, and bottom.

Center title at top of first text page. Indent paragraphs five spaces.

Note that personal communication citations include the full date of the interview or letter. These are not included on the "References" list.

For the first reference to a source by up to five authors, include the last name of each in the parenthetical citation. Use an ampersand (&) before the last author's name. (If you name the authors in your text, however, rather than in a parenthetical citation, spell out *and*.) For a source by six or more authors, include only the first author's last name followed by "et al." The date of publication follows the author name(s), separated by a comma.

Children Testifying 4

or they may withhold information. Neither trauma to the children nor incomplete evidence is in the best interest of the state. For this reason, court systems should seriously consider using alternate methods of testimony.

In this paper I will explain the stresses of live testimony on children; the benefits and detriments of live testimony; alternate methods for child testimony; and the legal system's reaction to these alternate methods. I believe that despite the controversy surrounding alternate methods of testimony, we must find ways to protect from unnecessary trauma these young accusers who are forced to enter our court systems.

Stress Associated With Testifying

Vulnerability

Whenever someone testifies in court, that person is bound to feel some anxiety. Goodman et al. (1991) note that this is true for adults, not just children: "As court dates approach, fear of testifying is one of adult rape victims' strongest fears" (p. 20). However, children are likely to feel more distress than adults for several reasons. First, children are at a very vulnerable period of life. They are still developing emotionally and mentally. Stress from court proceedings can interrupt this development, causing periods of stagnation and regression, occurrences which will affect them for the rest of their lives (Goodman et al., 1991).

Confusion About Proceedings

A second reason for increased distress in children is that they have less understanding of court proceedings than adults do. Goodman et al. (1991) state that by the latter part of elementary school, children have a fairly good understanding of legal processes. However, children who are still in preschool or lower grades have little, if any, understanding of the court system. Many people fear what they do not understand, and children are not

In subsequent references to a source by three or more authors, include only the first author's last name, followed by "et al." Note that for direct quotations, page numbers follow the date (preceded by "p." or "pp."). Page numbers are included only for quotations, not for summaries.

Children Testifying 5

exempt from this. Because they do not completely understand what is
going to happen, they have higher levels of distress than adults
do when testifying (Goodman et al., 1991).

Effects of Testifying Live

Beneficial Effects

High levels of stress do not have to create serious trauma to
the child, however. If handled with a good deal of support, it can
actually be a beneficial experience for children to testify, note
Goodman et al. (1991). Appelbaum (1989) states that this is because
it allows them "to participate in a process designed to redress the
wrongs done to them" (p. 14). D. Crowley, (personal communication,
February 12, 1993) says that testifying can be helpful in the
child's healing process. In order to heal, one must talk about what
has happened and deal with the emotions and the pain. While talking
about one's experiences in front of strangers may not be helpful in
every case, participating in the process of righting a wrong
against oneself can be therapeutic.

Detrimental Effects

    Increased Distress. However, in addition to possible benefits,
there are potential detriments. Some children will be adversely
affected by testifying live. Goodman et al. (1991) have found that
children who participate in court proceedings experience more
stress than children who do not have to testify. Some of the main
reasons for this stress are having to testify more than once, facing the defendant, answering embarrassing questions, being harassed
during cross-examination, and speaking in front of so many adults
(Appelbaum, 1989; Goodman et al., 1991). Research indicates that
testifying in front of the defendant is the most traumatic part of
the court process (Appelbaum, 1989; Goodman et al., 1991; Naylor,
1989): "Indeed, research shows that the most frequent fear expressed by children awaiting testimony is a fear of facing the
defendant" (Goodman et al., 1991, p. 21). When Goodman asked par-

---

Margin notes:

A first-level head is centered. A second-level head is flush left and underlined.

When you refer to the author in your text, indicate the date of the source's publication immediately following his or her last name. If you also include direct quotation, the page number(s) should follow immediately in parentheses.

A third-level head is indented and underlined.

If a reference is to more than one source, separate the authors' names with colons in the parenthetical citation.

Children Testifying 6

ents and children how some of the stress of testifying could have been alleviated, the most frequent response was "the use of closed circuit television or videotaped testimony" (Goodman et al., 1991, p. 21).

Note that end punctuation follows the parenthetical cite, not the quotation.

Obstructed Justice. Increased distress in child witnesses is not the only harmful effect of having the defendant in the courtroom or having to testify numerous times. The whole purpose of our legal system--arriving at the truth--can be obstructed. Goodman et al. (1991) note that some children will refuse to testify or may leave out important information if they are forced to testify with the defendant in the room; consequently, criminals sometimes go free due to lack of clear evidence. If alternate methods of testimony were used, this problem could be minimized. According to Goodman et al. (1991), "It is true that protective measures may be necessary in many cases to ensure that a child victim will be able to tell 'the whole truth and nothing but the truth'" (p. 18).

Alternate Methods of Testifying

Explanation

Certain innovations have been developed in the past several years to try to protect children from the harms of giving live testimony and to ensure that justice is served. Some of these are the use of videotaped interviews and interviews using closed-circuit television or one-way screens.

Videotaped interviews used as evidence are usually ones made by a social worker or psychologist. In recent decades social workers started taping their interviews with children reporting abuse in order to minimize the number of times the children would have to give statements, thereby decreasing confusion and trauma. In addition to social workers, children used to have to be interviewed by police, the prosecuting attorney, and the defense attorney. Now all those other people can just look at the tape. Pre-taped interviews were not admissible as evidence, however, until the mid-1980s, when a judge in a Dade County, Florida, child sexual abuse case allowed such tapes to be used, along with a mixture of live testimony and closed-circuit television testimony (B. Peterson, personal communication, February 5, 1993).

Closed-circuit television testimony is broadcast to the courtroom from another room in the court house, often the judge's chambers. The child, the attorneys, and the judge leave the courtroom while the defendant, jury, and spectators remain. (In some countries it is the defendant who leaves [Naylor, 1989, p. 400.]) The accuser and the defendant can still see each other via television, but the child is spared the physical presence of the accused. Since that is considered by researchers to be the most traumatic aspect of testifying, closed-circuit television testimony is an effective method for protecting the child from trauma.

If a citation occurs within a parenthetical discussion, it is enclosed in brackets. Brackets are also used to indicate changes or additions to a quotation and for explanatory comments within a quotation, if necessary.

Another method that has been used to decrease the trauma associated with the presence of the defendant is a one-way screen or mirror (Naylor, 1989, p. 401), which is set up in the courtroom between the witness stand and the defendant. Neither the accused nor the accuser leaves the room. The child's view of the defendant is blocked, but the defendant can still see the child (Appelbaum, 1989, p. 13). This is to allow the child to concentrate more fully on testifying and to worry less about the defendant; while the defendant more or less retains the right to confront his or her accuser--and the jury can watch the defendant's reactions to the child and the child's testimony. In addition to decreasing the child's trauma associated with testifying, this method can also contribute to the search for truth because the child is more willing and able to testify completely.

History

Use underlining or italics for court cases.

In Coy vs. Ohio the defense appealed the decision of the presiding judge to allow the use of a one-way screen so that the accused could see the accuser, but not vice versa. The appeal went

Children Testifying 8

through several higher courts until it finally reached the U.S. Supreme Court. The Court overturned the judge's decision, declaring that the screen violated the accused's Sixth Amendment rights. The Justices qualified their decision with the statement that it may be too early in the history of child sexual abuse trials to be certain that rights are violated (Appelbaum, 1989).

Indeed, that statement turned out to be confirmed. In a more recent case, <u>Maryland vs. Craig</u> (cited in Goodman et al., 1991), the Supreme Court reached a similar decision, but clarified the use of protective measures. In <u>Craig</u>, the presiding judge ordered that the children testify outside of the courtroom, via closed-circuit television, in keeping with a state law allowing such a procedure. The defendant, a day-care operator, appealed her conviction on the basis that her Sixth Amendment right to face her accusers had been violated. The Court reversed her conviction, but it did not entirely rule out the usefulness of such protective measures, stating:

> Where necessary to protect a child witness from trauma that would be caused by testifying in the physical presence of the defendant . . . the Confrontation Clause does not prohibit the use of a procedure that, despite the absence of face-to-face confrontation, ensures the reliability of the evidence. (Goodman et al., 1991, p. 15)

In order to use these protective measures, the court must show the necessity of using them for each case. If it is shown, however, that the child will suffer great trauma from testifying in the same room as the defendant, that child's protection supersedes the defendant's right to confrontation (Goodman et al., 1991).

<u>Controversy</u>

<u>Obstructed Truth.</u> In the case of <u>Coy vs. Ohio</u>, one of the arguments against using the protective measures was that doing so could prevent finding the truth. Justice Scalia said, "It is always more

Quotations of forty words or more are set off in a free-standing block of text indented five spaces, without quotation marks. The parenthetical citation for a block quotation *follows* the final period. No punctuation follows the close parenthesis.

Children Testifying 9

difficult to tell a lie about a person 'to his face' than 'behind his back'" (cited in Appelbaum, 1989, p. 13). It was thought at the time of Coy that justice would be obstructed if the child did not have to see the accused face-to-face. The truth would be more elusive. Maryland vs. Craig addressed this idea two years later when the Supreme Court overturned that concept. Many experts believe that using protective measures can actually improve the quality of testimony given by a child. Children will generally feel more free to speak about what happened to them because they will have less fear (Goodman et al., 1991; Koszuth, 1991; Nurcombe, 1986).

Violated Rights. It is also argued that the defendant's Sixth Amendment rights are violated by using protective measures. One basic right is the right to face the accuser. If the child gives testimony from another room or by way of a pre-taped interview, then the defendant can't face the accuser (Appelbaum, 1989). Once again, this idea was addressed by Craig. The right of the child to be protected against trauma supersedes the right of the defendant to face-to-face confrontation. Thus, if the court can show sufficient evidence that serious harm will come to the child, protective measures can justifiably be used (Goodman et al., 1991).

In the face of the new definitions that Maryland vs. Craig established, definitions that are now two years old, one would think that people would understand the importance of protecting the interests of the child. Even today, however, judges are afraid to test these measures. Some states allow the use of one-way screens, video-taped evidence, and/or closed circuit television. Many, however, still consider these measures unconstitutional (Naylor, 1989; D. Crowley, personal communication, February 12, 1993).

Juries' Views on Alternate Methods of Testifying
Decreased Credibility

Aside from being seen as unconstitutional in most states, alternate methods of testimony are also viewed as less credible. There is nothing so convincing as giving live testimony, even when

Use semicolons between multiple source citations.

faced with the threat of the accused in such close proximity
(D. Crowley, personal communication, February 12, 1993). Justice
Scalia's comment about lying seems to be a commonly held opinion.
If children need to be out of the room to testify, it is because
they aren't telling the truth. If they were telling the truth, they
would be able to testify in front of the defendant easily, without
feeling guilt or tripping up. If the jury can see them face-to-
face, they are much more convinced of the truth of their testimo-
nies (D. Crowley, personal communication, February 12, 1993).

This is only true if the child testifies confidently, however.
Often, due to the pressure of being in the same room as the defendant, a child will give quiet, faltering testimony. Such children
may thus be viewed as less credible because they are less confident. Research has indicated, though, that confidence and truthfulness are not related (Naylor, 1989). And so victimized children are
in a double bind.

Declaration of Defendant's Guilt

However, juries can be led to believe the defendant is guilty
through the use of alternate methods of testimony. If a child testifies out of the room or her pre-taped interview is used as testimony, the jury realizes that this is because the child is afraid
of the defendant. If the child is so afraid that she can't testify
live, the jury may assume that the defendant must be guilty. Their
impartiality to "just the facts, ma'am" is already tainted (Naylor,
1989).

Discussion

While it is evident that constitutionality and credibility issues must still be resolved, it should also be evident that child-
protective measures in the courtroom are vital to the emotional
safety of children who must testify. While the measures still have
limitations, they also have an impact on the lives of the children
who testify, an impact that can be beneficial or detrimental, depending on whether and how the courts decide to use them. It is

APA papers
end with a
"Discussion"
of the author's
conclusions.

Children Testifying 11

interesting to me that people seem unwilling to test the system. Crowley (personal communication, February 12, 1993) states that these methods are not used at all in Utah; in Texas they are unconstitutional (Naylor, 1989). This is surprising because the Maryland vs. Craig decision allowed their use. I realize that evidence must be shown that indicates that the trauma to the child will be severe enough to warrant these protective measures. I understand that proving this could take a long time, but children are worth the time.

I also realize that, although these measures address two of the largest sources of stress for child witnesses (facing the defendant and testifying numerous times), they don't address all sources of stress. There will still be the stress of answering embarrassing questions in front of many adults, being cross-examined, and reliving their horrible experiences of abuse. But if we can alleviate some of the stress, we should. Perhaps we can't make the court system perfect, but we could at least make it bearable for children and protect them from as much harm as we can.

Protecting our children from harm is the most important issue. We understand that people are innocent until proven guilty. We know that the prosecution has the burden of proof. It's horrible when an innocent person is convicted. But it's just as horrible when a perpetrator goes free. Children should not be treated as though they are on trial, yet sometimes they are. We should give them every chance to speak. If the only way for them to speak is through closed-circuit television or pretaped interviews, they should be allowed these avenues of speech. Their rights to emotional safety are more important than the defendant's right to face-to-face confrontation.

The children are the ones who have been harmed already. In our zeal to protect those who are "innocent until proven guilty," let's not forget to protect those who are truly innocent--our children.

Children Testifying 12

References

Appelbaum, P. S. (1989). Protecting child witnesses in sexual abuse cases. Hospital and Community Psychiatry, 40, 13-14.

Corder, B. F., & Whiteside, R. (1988). A survey of jurors' perception of issues related to child sexual abuse. American Journal of Forensic Psychology, 6, 37-43.

Goodman, G. S., Levine, M., Melton, G. B., & Ogdens, D. W. (1991). Child witnesses and the confrontation clause. Law and Human Behavior, 15, 13-29.

Koszuth, A. M. (1991). Sexually abused child syndrome. Law and Psychology Review, 15, 13-29.

Naylor, B. (1989). Dealing with child sexual assault: Recent developments. British Journal of Criminology, 29, 395-407.

Nurcombe, B. (1986). The child as witness: Competency and credibility. Journal of the American Academy of Child Psychiatry, 25, 473-480.

Full bibliographic information for each source cited is included on a separate page titled "References," which, like the rest of the paper, is double-spaced throughout. Entries are listed alphabetically by authors' last names (or the first main word in titles, for entries with no author). For papers that are not going to be typeset for publication, the first line of each entry is flush with the right margin; subsequent lines for the entry indent one-half inch, or five spaces. See pages 462–465 for APA guidelines regarding the information required and the format for specific types of sources.

Glossary

Ad populum A logical fallacy wherein a statement is assumed to be true because of the number of people who believe in it. (The Latin phrase means "to the people.") This fallacy depends on the assumption that just because an idea is popular or commonly held, it is true or right.

Agency The means by which an agent brings about a change.

Agent An individual who takes purposeful action to bring about a change.

Analogy A comparison between two objects or events wherein a familiar idea is used to explain an unfamiliar one.

Appeal to force A logical fallacy that takes the form of a threat, diverting attention from the real issue to the negative consequences of not accepting the argument. Extortion, blackmail, intimidation, and sexual harassment are all examples of the appeal to force.

Appeal to ignorance A logical fallacy wherein the burden of proof is refused and a statement is claimed to be true because no one has ever proved it otherwise.

Appeal to reward A logical fallacy that takes the form of a reward or bribe, diverting attention from the real issue to the positive consequences of accepting the argument. Buying votes, trading favors, and bribery are all examples of the appeal to reward.

Arguing, argument A form of rational persuasion. The word *argument* comes from the Latin word for "silver" and literally refers to making an idea clear. An argument consists of three parts: claims, reasons, and assumptions.

Assumptions The information necessary to move logically from the reasons to the claim in an argument. Assumptions "fill in the gaps" in arguments, answering the question, If I accept the reasons, what else do I have to believe to accept the claim? They are often left unstated. Stephen Toulmin refers to assumptions as "warrants."

Begging the question A logical fallacy wherein a reason offered to support a conclusion or claim is really just a restatement of that conclusion or claim.

Brainstorming A group activity to generate ideas. In brainstorming, a group generally focuses on a problem and determines a specified amount of time for discussing it. Members of the group all suggest ideas without any being evaluated or rejected until the brainstorming session has ended.

Causality A relationship between events such that (1) an earlier event in someway causes or influences a later event or (2) a later event in someway explains an earlier one. A number of elements may be components in analyzing causality: sufficient cause, necessary cause, contributing cause, logical cause, constraint, correlation, agent, instrument or agency, and purpose.

Claims Along with reasons and assumptions, one of the three parts of an argument. A claim is a statement under dispute that takes a stand on a controversial issue about which at least some people disagree. It is the focus of the argument. In academic writing, the claim is often the *thesis*. Claims may be made about existence, causality, language, values, or actions.

Classical argument An argument that takes the following form: introduction, thesis, supporting reasons and assumptions, answers to possible objections, and conclusion.

Clustering A type of mapping to discover ideas that involves writing down and circling a topic or issue in the center of a sheet of paper, jotting down and circling related words and ideas around this central topic, and then joining or "clustering" these ideas by drawing lines among those that are related.

Communication The process of sharing or achieving a common understanding through language. The word *communication* comes from the same Latin root as the word *community* does.

Community A group of people who have something in common. The word *community* comes from a Latin word meaning "common" or "shared." For instance, a community may be defined by shared interests, common ancestors, or shared language or geographic location.

Community-based reasons Reasons that are grounded in the beliefs shared by a community.

Complex question A logical fallacy wherein two different questions are phrased as if they were one, so that the same answer must be given for both. This is also called a "loaded question."

Conciliatory argument An argument that focuses on common assumptions, values, or definitions but does not assert the specific claim. The goal of this kind of argument is to move a hostile audience from a position of unconditional opposition to a more moderate position, even one of conditional support for the unstated claim.

Connotation   The associations a word carries, what it suggests in addition to its literal meaning.

Constraint   A necessary element that, when removed, allows an event or phenomenon to occur.

Contributing cause   A cause that may enable or influence a second event or phenomenon but that is not necessary or sufficient to cause the second.

Correlation   A relationship between two events or phenomena occurring together that is not necessarily causal; both may actually be caused by something else. Mistaking correlation for cause results in the post hoc fallacy.

Criteria and match   A type of classification and definition wherein the criteria that determine the members of a class are first defined and then a particular event or object is examined to determine whether it fits those criteria.

Delayed thesis   An argument that is similar to classical argument except that the thesis is not stated until the conclusion.

Denotation   The dictionary definition of a word, what the word means literally.

Dicto simpliciter   A logical fallacy wherein statements that are true in simple cases are applied to more complex cases without qualification. This Latin phrase literally means "simple speech."

Discourse community   A community defined by a common language and body of knowledge.

Doublespeak   The use of language to obscure meaning.

Ethos   Along with pathos and logos, one of the three means of persuasion described by Aristotle. Related to the English word *ethics*, ethos refers to the trustworthiness or credibility of a speaker or writer, based on how others perceive his or her character. Ethos or credibility depends to a certain degree on an individual's standing or status in the community and to a degree on how he or she uses language.

Etymology   The history of a word.

Euphemism   A word chosen for its positive connotations. The Greek root for this word means "good meaning."

Fact   A statement or belief that is commonly accepted as true within a community.

False analogy   An analogy that is fallacious because the differences between the two things being compared are greater than their similarities.

False dilemma   A logical fallacy wherein the audience is misleadingly presented with only two options, one of which is clearly more desirable than the other. This is also called the "either/or fallacy."

Formal definition A definition wherein a term is placed in a group and then distinguished from other members of the group: *X is an A (group) that B (distinguishing characteristics).*

Freewriting A method for discovering ideas by writing down everything that comes into one's mind, without stopping, for a set period of time.

Guilt by association A logical fallacy wherein all members of a group are stereotyped based on how only some members of the group behave. This is another name for "stereotyping."

Hasty generalization A logical fallacy wherein a conclusion is formed based on inadequate evidence. This is another name for "jumping to conclusions."

In-group In audience analysis, a group whose opinions on a controversial issue are most similar to the writer's or speaker's.

Instrument See *agency.*

Internet A network of computers across the world that makes possible e-mail, discussion lists, bulletin boards, gopher space, and the World Wide Web.

Loaded question See *complex question.*

Logical cause A justification or explanation. A "reason" that justifies the claim in an argument is a logical cause.

Logos Along with ethos and pathos, one of the three persuasive appeals described by Aristotle. Logos involves an appeal to reason. It is rational persuasion, the structure of the argument.

Mapping A visual representation for planning the relationships among ideas in an essay. A map may be a formal outline, a branching tree diagram, a series of pictures, or a set of circled words joined by lines ("cluster").

Middle-group In audience analysis, a group that is uninformed or uncommitted or whose position on a controversial issue lies between the writer's or speaker's and that of those who hold the opposite opinion.

Monroe's motivational sequence A motivational argument that begins with a description of a need or problem, followed by a description of the consequences of not meeting that need or solving that problem. The argument then offers a solution to the problem, followed by a "vision" of how the situation would be improved by the adoption of this solution. This sequence ends by suggesting specific actions the audience can take to achieve the solution.

Motivational arguments An argument that aims to motivate those who already accept the claim. Monroe's motivated sequence is an example of a motivational argument.

Necessary cause An event or phenomenon that must exist for a second to occur but that is not sufficient in itself to cause the second.

Negation Defining something by describing what it is not.

Non sequitur A reason or chain of reasons that cannot be connected logically to the claim. This Latin phrase literally means "does not follow" and refers to an argument in which the claim does not clearly follow from the reasons.

Operational definition A precise or technical definition of a term developed for a specific purpose or task.

Opinion A statement or belief about which at least some people disagree, that is controversial or under dispute in a community.

Option three An argument that appeals to a moderate position between two extreme positions.

Out-group In audience analysis, a group whose opinions on a controversial issue are furthest opposed to the writer's or speaker's.

Oversimplified cause A logical fallacy wherein a complex event or phenomenon is reduced to one simple cause.

Paraphrase A method of recording and reporting information from sources. In a paraphrase the original passage is rewritten using different words and sentence structure but preserving as much of the meaning of the original as possible.

Pathos Along with ethos and logos, one of the three persuasive appeals described by Aristotle. Pathos involves creating an emotional response in others by using emotionally charged language and description. Trying to generate a greater emotional response than is warranted by the situation is considered a fallacious appeal to the emotions.

Personal attack A logical fallacy wherein an attack on a person's character is used to distract the audience from a serious evaluation of the argument.

Persuasion Urging, influencing, or enticing through language in a manner that is not constraining or threatening. The word *persuasion* originally comes from a Latin word that means "sweet" and is related to the Greek word for "pleasure" or "sweetness." According to the ancient Greek philosopher Zeno, persuasion is represented by an open hand rather than a closed fist. Persuasion involves three appeals: ethos, pathos, and logos.

Plagiarism Knowingly presenting the ideas or language of others as one's own. Plagiarism is considered a kind of academic fraud.

Point of view The relationship that a writer establishes with his or her audience and subject. Use of "I" or "we" indicates a first-person point of view. Use of "you" is second-person. Use of "they," "he," "she," "it," or "one" establishes a third-person point of view.

Poisoning the well A logical fallacy wherein an argument is presented in such an emotionally biased way that it is difficult for a critic to respond without seeming dishonest or immoral. This strategy is intended as a distraction from the real issue and may involve personal attacks or fallacious appeals to emotion.

Post hoc, ergo propter hoc   A logical fallacy wherein it is assumed that just because one event follows another, the first caused the second. This Latin phrase means "after this, therefore because of this."

Purpose   A cause that follows what it causes, with the later event or phenomenon serving as the reason for the earlier one.

Quotation   A word-for-word transcription of what someone else said or wrote.

Rational   Relating to the ability to think and reason, but also to the ability to offer reasons as justification.

Reasons   Statements offered to justify, explain, or increase adherence to a claim. The reasons answer the question, What do I need to believe in order to accept the claim the author is making? Along with claims and assumptions, one of the three parts of an argument.

Red herring   A logical fallacy wherein an attempt is made to draw attention away from the issue at hand by raising irrelevant issues.

Rogerian argument   A type of negotiation based on the theories of psychologist Carl Rogers. In this kind of argument, the opposing views are described as objectively as possible and common values and goals are identified in order to bring opposing parties to a consensus.

Site of communication   A point of contact, place, or channel where communication happens, where members interact to discuss, debate, and decide the affairs of a community. These sites may be actual physical locations such as legislatures, courtrooms, or meeting houses, or they may be more abstract sites such as magazines, e-mail discussion lists, or library shelves.

Stacking the deck   A logical fallacy wherein any evidence or arguments that do not support the claim are ignored.

Sufficient cause   An event or phenomenon which, under normal conditions, can by itself cause a second.

Summary   A method of recording and reporting information from sources. In a summary the main ideas of a larger piece of writing are reported in a much briefer form in the summarizer's own words.

Synonyms   Words with similar meanings.

Troping   A means of drawing attention to an argument by deviating intentionally from conventions, presenting ideas in a surprising or unexpected way.

Virtual space   The site of communication created electronically through computer networks. The Internet's World Wide Web is the largest virtual site.

Acknowledgments

Page 17 CHRISTOPHER LASCH, "The Lost Art of Political Argument." Copyright © 1990 by *Harper's Magazine*. All rights reserved. Reproduced from the September issue by special permission.

Page 24 WALTER LIPPMANN, "The Indispensable Opposition," from *The Atlantic Monthly,* August 1939: 186–190. Used with permission of the President and Fellows of Harvard College.

Page 52 GRETCHEN LETTERMAN, "Tiny Fighters Are Victims of Mothers' Smoke." From *St. Petersburg Times,* City Edition, Sunday, April 16, 1995: 6D.

Page 59 URSULA K. LE GUIN, "The Ones Who Walk Away from Omelas." Copyright © 1973 by Ursula K. Le Guin; first appeared in *New Dimensions 3*; reprinted by permission of the author and the author's agent, Virginia Kidd.

Page 69 DAVID RUSSELL, "Writing in the Academic Disciplines." Copyright © 1991 by the Board of Trustees, Southern Illinois University. Reprinted by permission of the publisher.

Page 82 THEODORE R. SIZER, "What High School Is," from *Horace's Compromise: The Dilemma of the American High School,* by Theodore R. Sizer. Copyright © 1984 by Theodore R. Sizer. Reprinted by permission of Houghton Mifflin Co. All rights reserved.

Page 92 A. L. MINKES, "What Is Management All About?" from *The Entrepreneurial Manager: Decisions, Goals, and Business Ideas,* by A. L. Minkes. Copyright © 1987 by A. L. Minkes. Used by permission of Viking Penguin, a division of Penguin Books USA Inc.

Page 103 PHIL PATTON, "Life on the Net," *Esquire,* December 1994: 131–138. Reprinted by permission of the author and *Esquire* magazine.

Page 111 J. B. PRIESTLEY, "Wrong Ism," from *Essays of Five Decades.* Reprinted by permission of Sterling Lord Literistic, Inc. Copyright © 1968 by J. B. Priestley.

Page 121 Figure 4-1 Research Strategy Model. Reprinted by permission of Burgess International Group, Inc.

Page 139 "Background Study Guide," from English 115 Supplement, 11th edition. Reprinted by permission of Burgess International Group, Inc.

Page 143 J. C. HERZ, "Lurking," from *Surfing on the Internet,* by J. C. Herz. Copyright © 1995 by J. C. Herz. By permission of Little, Brown & Company.

Page 144 WILLIAM A. WILSON, "Documenting Folklore," from *Folk Groups and Folk Genres: An Introduction,* ed. Elliott Oring. Copyright © 1986 by Utah State University Press. Reprinted by permission of the author.

Page 179 STEPHEN BUDIANSKY, "The Numbers Racket: How Polls and Statistics Lie," from *U.S. News and World Report*, July 11, 1988.

Page 186 WILLIAM LUTZ, "Beware of the Polls," from *Doublespeak*, by William Lutz. Copyright © 1989 by Blonde Bear, Inc. Reprinted by permission of HarperCollins Publishers, Inc.

Page 192 STEPHEN JAY GOULD, "Racist Arguments and IQ," from *Ever Since Darwin: Reflections in Natural History*, by Stephen Jay Gould. Copyright © 1977 by Stephen Jay Gould. Copyright © 1974 by The American Museum of Natural History. Reprinted by permission of W. W. Norton & Company, Inc.

Page 195 RICHARD J. HERRNSTEIN and CHARLES MURRAY, from "The Bell Curve," reprinted with the permission of The Free Press, an imprint of Simon & Schuster from *The Bell Curve: Intelligence and Class Structure in American Life*, by Richard J. Herrnstein and Charles Murray. Copyright © 1994 by Richard J. Herrnstein and Charles Murray.

Page 219 BILL WODRASKA, "The Gentle Art of Hunkering," from *Mother Earth News* 100 (July/August 1986). Copyright © 1986 Sussex Publishers, Inc. Reprinted with permission from Mother Earth News.

Page 222 ROBERTA MAYNARD, "Help Newcomers Learn the Ropes." Reprinted by permission, *Nation's Business*, August 1991. Copyright 1991, U.S. Chamber of Commerce.

Page 225 J. C. HERZ, "The Newbies Are Coming! The Newbies Are Coming!" from *Surfing on the Internet*, by J. C. Herz. Copyright © 1995 by J. C. Herz. By permission of Little, Brown & Company.

Page 229 HORACE MINER, "Body Ritual among the Nacirema." Reproduced by permission of the American Anthropological Association from *American Anthropologist* 58:3, June 1956. Not for further reproduction.

Page 248 ELIZABETH F. LOFTUS, "Eyewitnesses: Essential but Unreliable." Copyright © 1984 Sussex Publishers, Inc. Reprinted with permission from *Psychology Today Magazine*.

Page 253 BARRY WINSTON, "Stranger Than True: Why I Defend Guilty Clients." Copyright © 1986 by *Harper's Magazine*. All rights reserved. Reproduced from the December issue by special permission.

Page 256 P. J. WINGATE, "The Philosophy of H. L. Mencken" from *Menckeniana: A Quarterly Review* 87 (1983): 14–16. Courtesy Enoch Pratt Free Library.

Page 260 BARRY O'NEILL, "The History of a Hoax," from *The New York Times Magazine*, 3/6/94. Copyright © 1994 by The New York Times Company. Reprinted by permission.

Page 267 NEIL POSTMAN and STEVE POWERS, "What Is News?" from *How to Watch TV News*, by Neil Postman and Steve Powers. Copyright © 1992 by Neil Postman and Steve Powers. Used by permission of Viking Penguin, a division of Penguin Books USA Inc.

Page 273 MORGAN STRONG, "Portions of the Gulf War Were Brought to You by . . . the Folks at Hill and Knowlton," *TV Guide*, Feb. 22, 1992. Reprinted by permission of the author.

Page 275 JACK G. SHAHEEN, "The Media's Image of Arabs," *Newsweek*, Feb. 29, 1988. Reprinted by permission of the author.

Page 285 THOMAS KUHN, "The Historical Structure of Scientific Discovery," from *Science* 136 (1962).

Page 292 HARRY COLLINS and TREVOR PINCH, "Edible Knowledge: The Chemical Transfer of Memory," from *The Golem: What Everyone Should Know about Science*. Copyright © 1993 by Harry Collins and Trevor Pinch. Reprinted with the permission of Cambridge University Press.

Page 307 ROBERT REICH, "The Gobal Elite," *New York Times Magazine*, January 1991. Copyright © 1991 The New York Times. Reprinted with permission.

Page 314 JOHN KENNETH GALBRAITH, "How to Get the Poor Off Our Conscience." Copyright © 1985 by *Harper's Magazine*. All rights reserved. Reproduced by special permission.

Page 325 GEORGE LAKOFF and MARK JOHNSON, "Concepts We Live By," excerpted from *Metaphors We Live By*. Copyright © 1980 by George Lakoff and Mark Johnson. Reprinted by permission of University of Chicago Press.

Page 330 HAIG A. BOSMAJIAN, "Defining the 'American Indian': A Case Study in the Language of Suppression," from *The Speech Teacher*, March 1973: 89–99. Used by permission of the Speech Communication Association.

Page 337 MICHAEL CALLEN, "AIDS: The Linguistic Battlefield," from *The State of the Language,* eds. Christopher Ricks and Leonard Michaels. Copyright © 1989 The Regents of the University of California. Reprinted with permission.

Page 342 ALLEEN PACE NILSEN, "Sexism in English: A 1990s Update." Copyright © 1990 by Alleen Pace Nilsen. Reprinted by permission of the author.

Page 352 NATIONAL COUNCIL OF TEACHERS OF ENGLISH, *Guidelines for Nonsexist Use of Language in NCTE Publications* (Revised, 1985). Copyright 1985 by National Council of Teachers of English. Reprinted with permission.

Page 360 LESLIE SAVAN, extract from *The Bribed Soul.* Reprinted by permission of Don Congdon Associates, Inc. Copyright © 1994 by Leslie Savan.

Page 367 CHARLES A. O'NEILL "The Language of Advertising," from *Exploring Language,* ed. Gary Goshgarian, 5th ed. Scott, Foresman, 1989. Reprinted by permission of the author.

Page 385 CONSUMER REPORTS, "Can Fast Food Be Good Food?" Copyright 1994 by Consumers Union of U.S., Inc., Yonkers, NY 10703-1057. Reprinted by permission from CONSUMER REPORTS, August 1994.

Page 391 ALBERT Z. CARR, "Is Business Bluffing Ethical?" from *Harvard Business Review,* January/February 1968. Copyright © 1968 by the President and Fellows of Harvard College. Reprinted by permission of *Harvard Business Review.* All rights reserved.

Page 394 MONROE H. FREEDMAN, "Professional Responsibility of the Criminal Defense Lawyer: The Three Hardest Questions," reprinted from *Michigan Law Review,* June 1956, Vol. 64, No 8. Reprinted by permission of the Michigan Law Review and the author.

Page 405 SVEN BIRKERTS, excerpt from *The Gutenberg Elegies: The Fate of Reading in an Electronic Age.* Copyright © 1994 by *Harper's Magazine.* All rights reserved. Reproduced from the May issue by special permission.

Page 408 KEVIN KELLY, excerpt from *Out of Control: The Rise of Neo-Biological Civilization.* Copyright © 1994 by *Harper's Magazine.* All rights reserved. Reproduced from the May issue by special permission.

Page 420 MOLLY IVINS, " 'Ban the Things. Ban Them All,' " *Fort Worth Star-Telegram,* March 11, 1993. Reprinted courtesy of the Fort Worth Star-Telegram.

Page 422 WAYNE R. LAPIERRE, "The Second Amendment: 'The Right of the People to Keep and Bear Arms,' " from *Guns, Crime and Freedom,* by Wayne LaPierre. Copyright © 1995 by Regnery Publishing, Inc. All rights reserved. Reprinted by special permission of Regnery Publishing Inc., Washington, D.C.

Page 428 CORETTA SCOTT KING, "The Death Penalty Is a Step Back." Reprinted by arrangement with The Heirs to the Estate of Martin Luther King, Jr., % Writers House, Inc. as agent for the proprietor. Copyright 1985 Coretta Scott King.

Page 429 H. L. MENCKEN, "The Penalty of Death," from *A Mencken Chrestomathy,* by H. L. Mencken. Copyright 1926 by Alfred A. Knopf Inc. and renewed 1954 by H. L. Mencken. Reprinted by permission of the publisher.

Page 431 DANIEL C. MAGUIRE, "Death by Choice: Who Should Decide?" from *Death by Choice,* by Daniel Maguire. Copyright © 1973, 1974 by Daniel C. Maguire. Used by permission of Doubleday, a division of Bantam Doubleday Dell Publishing Group, Inc.

Page 436 RAYMOND S. DUFF and A. G. M. CAMPBELL, "Moral and Ethical Dilemmas in the Special-Care Nursery," from *The New England Journal of Medicine,* Vol. 289: 893–94, 1973. Copyright 1973 by Massachusetts Medical Society. All rights reserved.

Index